102

D1274893

The Fragmentation of Afghanistan

Yale University Press New Haven and London

Barnett R. Rubin

The Fragmentation
of Afghanistan

State Formation
and Collapse in
the International
System
Second Edition

Second edition first published by Yale University Press in 2002.

First edition published by Yale University Press in 1995.

Preface to second edition copyright © 2002 by Yale University.

Copyright © 1995 by Yale University.

Printed in the United States of America

Library of Congress Control Number: 2001098990

ISBN 0-300-09520-1 (cloth : alk. paper)
ISBN 0-300-09519-8 (pbk. : alk. paper)

A catalogue record for this book is available from the British Library.

10 9 8 7 6 5 4 3 2 1

To Susan.

Without the rose, there is no mirror for spring.

You have painted a very ugly picture of the situation in Afghanistan, but I must admit that what you say is true. My father used to quote an old Persian poem, "If you do not like the image in the mirror, do not break the mirror, break your face."

Letter from Nejat Khalili, February 12, 1992.

The people of one of the poorest countries in the world successfully resisted a super-power. They had to fight for their lives in a world system imposed on them by others. If the situation in Afghanistan is ugly today, it is not because the people of Afghanistan are ugly. Afghanistan is not only the mirror of the Afghans; it is the mirror of the world.

From my reply, March 26, 1992.

Contents

Preface to the

Second Edition

No one I knew personally died in the World Trade Center, the Pentagon, or the plane crash in Pennsylvania on September 11, 2001, though friends and colleagues suffered great loss. In the next days and weeks I saw my city become a shrine, with photocopied notices of the missing everywhere, and firehouses, above all, turned into memorials to—what else can we call them?—the martyrs of September 11. But unlike most New Yorkers, I had witnessed similar scenes before, and certain images and phrases came back to me, like the quotation from the Quran I once read at the bottom of a list of hundreds of civilians slaughtered in Kunduz province, Afghanistan, in the winter of 1986: "We come from God, and to him we return."

I remembered the posters and photo-book memorials of the martyrs everywhere in Peshawar, the grief of the widows who gathered in Haripur refugee camp, and the bent, gray-bearded man whose shaking hand passed me a crumpled slip of paper bearing the names of his martyred sons through the half-open window of my car as it slowly jounced over the rocky ground. I remembered riding for hours in the winter of 1996 from Taluqan to Pul-i Khumri in northern Afghanistan, past ruined villages one after another, with no sign of life but the long-unpruned fruit trees poking over shattered walls. Above all I recalled my tour of Kabul in June 1998, as my embittered driver showed me one ruin after another—the pockmarked and burned-out palace of Darulaman, the pulverized main street of Jada-yi Maiwand—exploded, flattened, burned, as completely as the World Trade Center, and with munitions partly supplied by the U.S. government. Far more innocent civilians died in Kabul than in the United States on September 11. Although it took longer than one day to kill them, the agony of those burned, mutilated, and shattered, and the endless grief of their survivors, is just as real.

The transition from shock to analysis took some time, but one evening, after the journalists had stopped calling, I opened the earlier edition of this book, published in 1995, to its concluding paragraph. In the book I had demonstrated that Afghanistan, far from being an unchanged "traditional" society living in a different time, had been thoroughly shaped by its interactions with the modern state system. Today's state of Afghanistan developed as a buffer state between competing empires (Russian and British) and then competing alliance systems (Soviet and American). Its rulers sought to mobilize resources from both the peoples of Afghanistan and from international sources, including both states and markets. These rulers created new elites through a foreign-funded educational system in the hope that these new elites would help them control, penetrate, and transform the society. The limits of such a strategy revealed themselves when regional instability and escalating tensions between the Cold War antagonists tore that state apart. The obvious story of the 1980s was that of the Soviet invasion and the Afghan resistance. The underlying story was about the breakdown, indeed the fragmentation, of social control and social power in Afghanistan. The painstakingly constructed state shattered when a Soviet-supported Communist elite tried to use that fragile apparatus as an instrument of massive, coercive social change. The coherence of the society that tried to resist that onslaught and the invasion that followed was shattered not only by the Soviet counterinsurgency strategy but also by the way that Pakistan used U.S. and Saudi aid to the Afghan resistance. Seeking to ensure that Afghanistan would never again be able to pursue hostile policies toward its eastern neighbor, Pakistan distributed the aid through seven religious parties, weakening and undermining secular nationalist leadership, and fragmenting power in every locality into as many as seven competing armies. Iran's policy of arming various Shi'a groups intensified the divisions.

Hence, when the Soviet Union withdrew and then dissolved, and the United States disengaged, Afghanistan was left with no legitimate state, no national leadership, multiple armed groups in every locality, a devastated economy, and a people dispersed throughout the region, indeed the world. This was the situation that led me to conclude, in the book's last sentence, that "if the international community does not find a way to rebuild Afghanistan, a floodtide of weapons, cash, and contraband will escape that state's porous boundaries and make the world less secure for all."

Afghanistan became, in the lingo of the time, a "failed state," where Afghans suffered from a "humanitarian emergency." For the United States and other major powers, Afghanistan became an object of charity and neglect, not necessarily in that order. Regional powers, especially Pakistan, but also private networks—smugglers, drug dealers, and terrorists—treated it as an open field for manipulation and exploitation. The failure of major powers to come to the aid of Afghanistan provided ample time and opportunity for malign forces to exploit this situation in ways I could never have envisaged. Not until a month after the atrocities of September 11 did President George W. Bush announce that the United States would "work for a stable Afghanistan."[1] Whether the Afghan people will finally have a chance to live lives of relatively peaceful deprivation or, instead, fall back into an abyss of violence depends on incalculable factors. This updated version of my earlier analysis will, I hope, help some understand the genesis of a catastrophe that now bridges the eras of the Cold War, the post–Cold War, and the war against terrorism.

Enter the Taliban: From Failed State to Rogue State

By September 11, 2001, Afghanistan was already arguably the world's worst humanitarian emergency, as well as a state in a crisis of governance. More than a million people had died in a country whose population was estimated at 26 million, and the proportion of disabled in the population from both landmines and polio may have been the world's highest. Afghanistan ranked at the bottom of all measures of human welfare (table 1), and illicit activities had become key elements of its people's survival strategies.

Table 1 Measures of Humanitarian Emergency in Afghanistan

Indicators	Afghanistan	South Asia	Developing countries	Industrial countries
Human development index rank (out of 174)[a]	169	N/A	N/A	N/A
Population % with access to				
Health care (1985–93)[a]	29	65	79	100
Safe water (1990–95)[b]	12 (rural 5, urban 39)	77	69	100
Daily calorie supply per capita (1992)[b]	1,523	2,356	2,546	3,108
Infant mortality per 1,000 live births (1993)[b]	165	85	70	N/A
Under five mortality per 1,000 live births (1993)[c]	257	122	101	N/A
Maternal mortality per 100,000 live births (1993)	1,700[d] or 640[e]	469	351	10
Life expectancy at birth in years (1993)[a]	44	60	62	76
Adult literacy rate (%, 1993)[a,b]	28 (men 45, women 14)	48	68	98

Sources: All comparative data from other regions are from United Nations Office of the Coordinator of Humanitarian Affairs for Afghanistan (UNOCHA), *Afghanistan Consolidated Appeal for Assistance, 1997* (Islamabad: UNOCHA, 1996). One indicator of humanitarian emergency in Afghanistan is the collapse of institutions able to produce such statistics. Hence, unlike such presumably better governed countries as Sierra Leone and Burundi, Afghanistan has not been listed in the standard source for such data, the United Nations Development Program's (UNDP) Human Development Report, since 1996.

[a]UNOCHA, *Afghanistan Appeal, 1997,* p. 4, citing UNDP, Human Development Report, 1996.

[b]UNOCHA, *1998 Afghanistan Appeal,* p. 4, citing UNDP, Human Development Report, 1997.

[c]UNOCHA, *1998 Afghanistan Appeal,* citing UNICEF, State of the World's Children Report, 1996.

[d]Ibid., citing Study by UNICEF/World Health Organization, 1996.

[e]UNDP, Human Development Report, 1997.

Anarchic violence and criminality spread through much of Afghanistan after 1992 as a result of the destruction of most institutions of governance. As I describe in chapter 12, mujahidin and some former government militias coalesced into several ethno-regional political-military coalitions. The dissolution of the Pashtun-dominated central state, combined with the vast, uncontrolled supplies of weapons from both sides in the Cold War, provided an opportunity to assert either autonomy from the center (as did elites of the Hazara and Uzbek ethnic groups, as well as Persian-speakers around Herat in western Afghanistan) or greater control over it (as did Tajik elites from northeast Afghanistan and the Kabul area). Although relatively homogeneous elites led these coalitions, they did not engage in mass mobilization around an explicit ethnic discourse or project (Hazaras excepted to some extent).

Pashtuns were fragmented. Pakistan, which after 1979 increasingly sought a kind of indirect hegemony over the Pashtun areas, was determined to prevent reestablishment of a Pashtun nationalist force that would ally with India or other hostile powers to challenge Pakistani control over Pashtun populations and territories in Pakistan. Pakistan had for years worked to undermine and fragment Pashtun tribal power and nationalist leadership, supporting Islamist leaders instead. With the failure to secure power of its chosen Afghan surrogate, the Hizb-i Islami of Gulbuddin Hikmatyar, Pakistan saw a new opportunity in the Taliban, a group that appeared in southern Afghanistan in the fall of 1994. Pakistan ultimately sought to create a corridor to Central Asia by bringing the fragmented Pashtuns under the control of the Taliban, a purely religious leadership that did not support nationalist demands, that would not ally with non-Muslim powers, and that depended on Pakistan through a variety of networks that had developed over twenty years of war and dispersion. Pakistani support for a Pashtun group, combined with that group's extensive intertwining with networks within Pakistan, changed the meaning of the Pashtun question for Pakistan and led to a violent rebalancing of ethnic power in Afghanistan in favor of Pashtuns, who had temporarily lost power to the newly armed non-Pashtun groups.

While various militias fought over and destroyed large swaths of the national capital, mujahidin commanders in parts of the countryside had become virtual warlords. In Qandahar, in particular, internecine fighting led to chronic anarchy, manifested in rape and abduction of women, and omnipresent checkpoints where armed men extorted tribute from traders and travelers. This was the context in which, according to the unverifiable founding legend, a group of madrasa teachers and students led by Mullah Muhammad Umar formed the Taliban movement to end the power of these warlords and establish a pure Islamic regime. They succeeded largely because of the military aid they received from Pakistan. This aid enabled them initially to seize control of Qandahar city and province in October–November 1994 and to expand until they took control of virtually the entire country by August 1998.[2]

The Taliban did not represent a totally new phenomenon in Afghanistan. The network of teachers and students from private, rural-based madrasas in Afghanistan and the neighboring Pashtun-populated areas of Pakistan (previously India) has played an important part in the history of the country for centuries. As I show in chapter 9, during the anti-Soviet jihad, ulama and students from these madrasas constituted one of the important sources of recruitment for mujahidin in the tribal areas.

This group had become marginalized as a result of years of state building by the royal regime, which created a new elite (including Islamic scholars and judicial officials) trained in modern schools and universities. The royal regime, the Communists, and the Islamists recruited primarily from different sectors of this new elite (chapter 4). The internecine battles of the past twenty years, in which one faction after another of that intelligentsia succeeded to power, each decimating its rivals, eventually led to the eclipse of this modernizing group. At the same time, as millions of Afghans became refugees, and the country's educational system collapsed, rural madrasas provided almost the only education available to a generation of Pashtun boys reaching school age since 1978. The West did little to provide refugees with any other education, leaving the madrasas supported by Middle Eastern donors with a virtual monopoly. The rise of the Taliban occurred as the first of these students were completing this new educational process, just as the Communist coup d'état (and Islamist resistance) occurred about twenty years after the massive expansion of the state educational system (chapter 5). The collapse of the state administration and community leadership in many places also increased the importance of the mosques and the mullahs and taliban (students) who staffed them.

The madrasa networks created ties among a potential new elite while other institutions were being destroyed. But the mullahs lost the ties to the landlord-dominated local economy and society that had circumscribed their power. As described in particular in my discussions of Qandahar (chapter 11), both the state and the rural economy that had sustained tribal leaders collapsed. The ulama became more autonomous in exile and in warlord-dominated Afghanistan, and as a result they became more extremist and deracinated. In exile they also became linked to international networks, both political and economic, including Pakistani political parties and intelligence agencies and the Arab Islamists who aided the jihad. The Taliban attitude toward the state and reforms are not the continuation of some unchanging "tradition" but the result of their own uprooting and trauma of the past twenty years, during much of which period a central state dominated by a foreign ideology destroyed the country in the name of progressive reform. Foreign aid, commercial agriculture (opium), and long-distance contraband provided this newly armed elite with the opportunity to mobilize resources for a direct exercise of power, which had been out of its reach before. The mosque network enabled it to penetrate society as well.

The Taliban movement initially responded to some needs felt by Afghan people and received some popular support in Pashtun-dominated areas during its initial advances in 1994–95. By establishing a common authority, collecting weapons, and establishing order through strict enforcement of sharia, the Taliban presented themselves as an Islamic solution to the problems of a failed state. Had they stopped after bringing order to the Pashtun areas of southern Afghanistan, they might have joined about five other ethnoregional coalitions that existed at that time in negotiating a decentralized form of Afghan statehood. Besides the numerous other obstacles, however, such a state did not meet the needs of Pakistan, which wanted a centralized state that would reliably control the territory in its interests. At that time interest by several international corporations in oil and gas pipelines through Afghanistan also increased incentives for a centralized force to impose order. The United States regarded the Taliban as a force that might make Afghanistan more secure and enable U.S. companies to export gas and oil from Central Asia while maintaining sanctions on Iran.[3] Hence Pakistan, initially with U.S. acceptance, supported the Taliban's growing aspirations to reconstruct a centralized state.

The domination of the country by this previously marginalized group reversed the pattern of social, political, and economic bifurcation developed under the royal regime and intensified under the Communists (parts I and II of this book). Under these regimes, foreign financial and military aid enabled an urbanized elite to insulate itself from the countryside and create a sort of parallel society of at least superficially modernized institutions. Under the Taliban, however, foreign aid empowered a network based in Afghan rural areas and refugee settlements in Pakistan to control the capital city, reversing the reforms of past decades. The annihilation of the state and the development and reformist agenda it had pursued under several governments spelled the end of the halting emancipation of urban women that decrees by modernizing male leaders had effected.

Although the leadership of such a state by ulama was unprecedented, the underlying structure reproduced a historic pattern (chapter 2): the state was dominated by a small solidarity group of Pashtuns, in this case Qandahari mullahs (rather than Muhammadzais), dependent for its resources on foreign aid and taxing commercial agriculture, now mostly illegal drugs rather than karakul lamb and cotton, and foreign trade, now mostly smuggling rather than exports of natural gas.

The social network of the elite at the core of the coalition was formed from Qandahari mullahs who studied in the same set of madrasas in Pakistan and participated in the jihad. Mullah Umar and all but one member of the Supreme Shura were Qandahari Pashtuns.[4] All the members of the military shura whose ethnic and regional origins I know were Qandahari Pashtuns. The Kabul shura was also predominantly Qandahari but included more eastern Pashtuns, a few Persian speakers, and at least one Uzbek. All without a single exception were Sunni mullahs trained in private madrasas. Hence the movement had a strong ethnic and regional characteristic, without its leaders having any intention to form such a movement, and it therefore attracted support from some who sought a Pashtun ethnic movement capable of ruling Afghanistan.

These core leaders belonged to the Deobandi movement in Afghanistan and Pakistan. The Deobandi movement, which owes its name to the Indian town where a famous madrasa was established in the nineteenth century, developed from conservative reform movements among Indian Muslims. Deobandis reject all forms of

ijtihad—the use of reason to create innovations in sharia in response to new conditions—the revival of which is a key plank in the platform of the Islamic modernists.
They oppose all forms of hierarchy within the Muslim community, including tribalism or royalty, they strive to exclude Shi'a from participation in the polity, and they
take a very restrictive view of the social role of women. All of these characteristics of
the Indian and Pakistani Deobandis were found in exaggerated forms among the
Afghan Taliban.[5]

Mullah Muhammad Umar, the head of state, was elected as amir al-mu'minin
(commander of the believers, a title of the caliph) by an assembly of about 1,200
invited ulama in Qandahar from March 20 to April 4, 1996. With this decision, the
Taliban transformed their movement into a state structure, the Islamic Emirate of
Afghanistan (IEA) in whose name they captured Kabul in September 1996. Mullah
Umar had the final say on all matters and increasingly centralized control. He originally acted in consultation with a number of shuras, though their importance diminished over time as that of the Arabs in al-Qa'ida increased. The Kabul shura,
effectively a cabinet of ministers, was the Taliban's main interlocutor with the mainstream international community, which established its agencies in Kabul. Mullah
Umar also consulted a shura of ulama and a military shura.

The IEA appointed provincial governors and administrators of districts, cities,
towns, and precincts from the center, following the administrative divisions of former
Afghan governments. As in most such governments, the administrators were invariably natives of areas other than the ones they governed and were regularly shuffled
between areas. The Taliban established a nationwide judiciary with sharia courts at all
levels, culminating in the Supreme Court of Sharia in Kabul. The Taliban also established a new security service, the Ministry of Enforcement of Virtue and Suppression
of Vice (al-Amr bi al-Ma'ruf wa al-Nahi 'an al-Munkir), named after a similar organization in Saudi Arabia. This ministry has been responsible for the enforcement of all
decrees regarding moral behavior, including the decrees restricting women's employment and dress, enforcing men's beard length and mosque attendance, regulating
activities of U.N. agencies and nongovernmental organizations, commanding destruction of "graven images," and requiring the labeling of religious minorities.
Through the networks of local mullahs, the Taliban also penetrated into the village
structure, perhaps more than previous Afghan governments, enabling the IEA to carry
out such policies as the eradication of opium growing in 2000–2001.

The Qa'ida organization became increasingly integrated into the IEA structure,
through both the personal relationship that developed between Usama Bin Ladin and
Mullah Umar and the military services that the former provided. Al-Qa'ida provided
most of the manpower of Brigade 055, originally a military unit based in Khairkhana,
in northern Kabul. Service in this unit constituted part of the training of militants who
came to Afghanistan, and, as Afghans became increasingly reluctant to fight for the
Taliban in an inter-Afghan war, the unit also supplied the most committed and effective part of the Taliban military. These networks constituted in effect an alternative

international community to the official one. The deterioration of relations with one was mirrored in the improvement of relations with the other.

The Taliban were effectively a transnational organization, reflecting the multi-faceted links between Afghan Pashtuns and many parts of Pakistani society, links that became even denser after 1978. At least until the change in Pakistan's policy after September 11, 2001, the Taliban's military advisory structure included Pakistani officers. Their decision-making process included routine consultation with Pakistani Deobandi religious leaders. Their foreign relations depended on access to the outside world through Pakistan and on Pakistani advice and logistical assistance. Their military force recruited fighters from Pakistani madrasas, whose students were estimated to form as much as 20–30 percent of the total. Extremist Pakistani Deobandi organizations (Sipah-i Sahaba, Lashkar-i Jhangvi, Harakat-ul-Mujahidin) had bases in areas under their control. A U.S. bomb killed twenty-two Harakat-ul-Mujahidin fighters in a residence in Kabul on October 23, 2001.

The Taliban's economic resources derive from networks linked to the Pashtun diaspora in Karachi and Dubai, and to the Pakistani administration in the Northwest Frontier Province and Baluchistan. The Pakistani rupee was so widely used as currency in areas under Taliban control that the Pakistan banking authorities launched an investigation of the impact of that practice on their economy. The integration of Pakistani elements into the Taliban and IEA at all levels was not simply a result of a policy of the Pakistani government or military. Rather, the Pakistani state used and responded to pressures from these transnational links, which reflected changes in the social and political structures of the region.

The Taliban also became increasingly linked to the transnational fringe of global Islamist politics, including Usama Bin Ladin, especially as their isolation from the global mainstream grew. They provided a haven to the Islamic Movement of Uzbekistan, some Chechens and Uyghurs, and assorted militants from other countries. Although these links began opportunistically, as they persisted, they were complemented by various forms of structural integration, as through Brigade 055.

In the west the Taliban were best known for their repressive policies, especially against women, but they boasted in particular of their policies to restore security. Taliban officials told visitors, "You can drive from one end of the country to the other even at night with a car full of gold, and no one will disturb you." This expression was hardly a metaphor. Driving across southern Afghanistan from Qandahar to Farah and back in June 1998, I saw many trucks doing just that, though their cargoes comprised not gold but consumer goods for smugglers' markets in Pakistan. In two days' drive I encountered only three unobtrusive checkpoints. The greater security provided by Taliban also improved the conditions for the trade in opium, even after the government officially proscribed poppy cultivation and opium trafficking in 2000–2001.[6] The Taliban also vaunted their efforts to collect weapons and combat crime, including rape and murder.

For the Taliban these efforts at restoring order were of a piece with the decrees on women and religious behavior that seem bizarre and repressive to many in the West, as well as to many Afghans, especially the urban and educated part of the population. These policies were all justified as the enforcement of sharia. The way that the Taliban interpreted sharia, however, as well as the violent way they enforced it, betrayed a concern with Pashtun conceptions of honor and control, as well as a desire to subordinate and even punish the population of Kabul, seen as the source of Afghanistan's ills.

Increased freedom for women, including voluntary unveiling, secular education, and professional employment, had been largely urban phenomena dependent on the state sector. They were decreed by the highest (male) leadership of the state in order to implement a (lightly) imposed vision of modernization. The collapse and loss of legitimacy of the weakly modernizing state also meant the weakening of the institutional support for women's public roles.[7] During the Soviet occupation, the Kabul regime expanded women's roles, as men were largely enrolled in the security organs. In refugee settlements and rural areas of Afghanistan, however, patriarchal strictures on women were retained or reinforced. These restrictions resulted from male reaction to both the insecurities of life in exile and reforms associated with the disaster that had overtaken the country.[8] The Taliban codified and extended many of these practices, and as a result women were excluded from public life to an unprecedented degree. They were forbidden from going to school (though exceptions were later made for religious education up to the age of nine or training in health care), from going out in public without a male guardian (though casual observation indicated that this rule was weakly enforced), and from employment outside the home (with later exceptions for employment in health care).

Although the Taliban justified some of these rules under Islamic strictures on sexual mixing, they also frequently referred to the need for security and the prevention of the rapes that had occurred under warlord rule. These restrictions thus constituted a reassertion of male honor through control over women, just as the Taliban's attempted conquest of the rest of the country constituted an attempt to reassert honor by controlling the homeland. The use of Islamic discourse to legitimate protection of honor through control (see the discussion of *namus* in chapter 2) thus asserted the unity of the values often cited by Pashtuns as motivation for participating in jihad: for Islam, for homeland, and for honor *(da islam da para, da watan da para, da namus da para).*[9]

These policies often brought the Taliban into conflict with the international aid community, led by the United Nations. A dialectic of confrontation and concession developed, and especially after the imposition of the first round of U.N. sanctions against the Taliban at the end of 1999, the core leadership seemed to conclude that it was unlikely to win the favor of the official international community and drew closer to Bin Ladin and his allies. The July 2000 decree of Mullah Umar banning the cultivation of opium poppy, a ban which, to the surprise of most, was effectively enforced despite the hardship of a three-year drought, constituted for the Taliban a final test of the goodwill of the international community. The Taliban had identified one demand they could meet without violating their religious principles, but the response seemed to them inadequate. International actors reacted not only to the opium ban but to new restrictions on aid workers and the continued harboring of terrorists, as well as the Taliban's violations of human rights—not only the decrees limiting women's rights but also the massacres of Hazaras. The destruction of the Bamiyan Buddhas in March 2001 symbolized the Taliban's new direction: by destroying a key symbol of Afghanistan's pre-Islamic glory, they showed they were not nationalists but pan-Islamists, and under "Wahhabi" influence to boot. This decision alienated many within their own ranks and solidified relations between the Arabs and Mullah Umar.

Opposition to the Taliban

The rise of the Taliban depended on Pakistani support but also on the failure of the mujahidin groups to establish a stable government. Under constant attack by Pakistan through its agent Hikmatyar, who was aided by Arab radicals, the post-Najibullah regime in Kabul, the Islamic State of Afghanistan (ISA), became increasingly narrow in its base and riven by infighting. When the Taliban captured Kabul on September 27, 1996, the ISA gave up almost without a fight, and the people of Kabul were not sorry to see it go.

As described in chapter 12, and in more detail in my book *The Search for Peace in Afghanistan,* The ISA was formally set up under an agreement among the Pakistan-based parties of the jihad. In practice it was dominated by the major military groups that took control of the capital, in particular Ahmad Shah Massoud's Supervisory Council of the North (chapter 12) and the party to which it adhered, the Jamiat-i Islami. Originally this group's main partners in capturing the city were the ex-Communist militias led by Abdul Rashid Dostum and the Shiʿa Hizb-i Wahdat, who formed the Northern Alliance (Ittilaf-i Shamali) with Iranian assistance and encouragement. The capital was thus effectively under the control of non-Pashtun militias. Pashtun portions of the former military either disbanded or joined Hikmatyar in attacks on the city from the south. Other mujahidin parties were allotted ministries, which they treated more as patronage for their leaders than as administrative units of governance.

Hikmatyar's rockets devastated the city after mid-1992, and Massoud battled both Dostum's militia and the Hazaras for control of various neighborhoods. Interethnic atrocities mounted, including rape, which took on an intense importance as a symbol of the violation of honor by the ex-mujahidin. So embittered did relations become among the former allies that in January 1994 Dostum and Wahdat joined with Hikmatyar in an attack on Massoud, leading to a new round of devastation in the city. In the opening of *The Search for Peace in Afghanistan* I describe the scene I witnessed outside Jalalabad at that time, as displaced people from Kabul shouted how they had been looted and attacked by all groups, especially Massoud's Shura-yi Nazar (Supervisory Council).

The Taliban's destruction of Hikmatyar's bases in early 1995 and the death of Wahdat leader Abdul Ali Mazari in Taliban custody in March 1995 paradoxically helped Massoud regain control of Kabul. But as the Taliban captured Herat in September 1995 and advanced once again on Kabul a year later, Massoud's increasing isolation counted against him. Not only had he lost much Afghan popular support, he had also antagonized Pakistan without obtaining a firm alternative source of foreign assistance.

When the Taliban captured Kabul on September 27, 1996, Massoud evacuated his associates to the Panjsher Valley. By October 1996 the quarreling groups that had all lost to the Taliban met again in northern Afghanistan to form an alliance originally called the Supreme Council for the Defense of the Motherland. The northern areas had four main administrative and political centers: Mazar-i Sharif, which some aspired to turn into a temporary capital for a government in exile of the ISA, but which instead became a locus for conflict among Abdul Rashid Dostum's Junbish, Wahdat, and Jamiat, as well as for factional warfare within Junbish itself; Taluqan, in Takhar, the headquarters of Massoud's SCN; Shiberghan, in Samangan, Dostum's headquarters; and Bamiyan, headquarters of the Hizb-i Wahdat administration of Hazarajat. Ismail Khan, former governor and mujahid commander of Herat, was exiled in Iran at the time that Kabul fell. Some elements of the former state administration survived in each region, but political power resided in the various armed groups rather than in a unitary structure. There was no effective counterpart even to the administrative structure of the IEA, nor could the opposition mobilize fighters from beyond Afghanistan, as could the Taliban.

The country remained divided between the north, controlled by the elements of the former Northern Alliance, and the south (including Kabul and Herat), controlled by the Taliban, until the end of May 1997, when a dispute within Junbish created an opening for Taliban advance. In early May, one of Dostum's top commanders, Ghulam Rasul Pahlawan, another Uzbek militia leader, was assassinated in Mazar-i Sharif. Illustrating the principle that blood is stronger than politics or ethnicity, Ghulam Rasul's brother, Abdul Malik, who blamed Dostum for the killing, made a deal with the Taliban. He promised to expel Dostum from the north in return for Taliban support. He also agreed to hand over Ismail Khan, who had returned from Iran and was fighting on a front northeast of Herat. On May 20 he started an uprising, leading to the arrest of Ismail Khan and to Dostum's flight, first to Uzbekistan and then to Turkey, where he took up residence in Ankara. The change of power in the north also persuaded pockets of Pashtun commanders, in particular in Baghlan and Kunduz, to join the Taliban, who thus secured air bases in the north. Kunduz, in particular, gave the Taliban a staging area close to Massoud's headquarters in Taluqan. A Pakistani delegation led by then–Foreign Minister Gohar Ayub air-dashed to Mazar, proclaimed that the war was over, and recognized the Islamic Emirate.

The handover of power did not go smoothly in Mazar, however, and the Pakistani delegation barely escaped ahead of the mounting revolt. Malik had not consulted with Junbish's Hazara allies in Hizb-i Wahdat. He also apparently expected the Taliban to recognize him, rather than Dostum, as the warlord or amir of the north, but there was only one amir in the Islamic Emirate, and instead, Taliban troops poured into the airport, started disarming people, and proclaimed the application of the laws of the IEA. The result was a revolt started by Hazaras and then joined by Malik himself against his erstwhile allies. They expelled the Taliban from the city and executed an estimated 1,500 Taliban prisoners, whose bodies were left to rot in the desert or dumped in wells. In spite of requests by the Taliban for an investigation, the United Nations failed to document responsibility for these atrocities, reinforcing the Taliban's conviction that the international community was hypocritical and biased against them.

Soon after, in June 1997, the Supreme Defense Council was reshaped into the National Islamic United Front for the Salvation of Afghanistan (U.F.). This political grouping, commonly known as the Northern Alliance, supported the Islamic State of Afghanistan (ISA), which continued to hold Afghanistan's U.N. seat. The alliance included Jamiat, Dostum's Junbish-i Milli, the main faction of Hizb-i Wahdat (one of whose leaders joined the Taliban), the Shi'a Harakat-i Islami, Sayyaf's Ittihad-i Islami, and the remnants of the ousted Jalalabad shura, under the name Shura-yi Mashriqi (Eastern Council), led by Haji Abdul Qadir. Ittihad-i Islami and Shura-yi Mashriqi enabled the United Front to claim it was not exclusively composed of non-Pashtuns. Hikmatyar did not join the United Front, but neither did he support the Taliban until the U.S. attacks that started on October 7, 2001, after which he appealed from his home in Tehran for united resistance to the United States. In this book I describe the history and origin of all these groups.

The United Front was intended to act as the political support mechanism for a new government in Mazar-i Sharif, but that attempt suffered a major setback when a plane carrying forty U.F. leaders, including Abdul Rahim Ghaffurzai, the prime minister–designate, crashed, killing all passengers, in August 1997.[10] Ghaffurzai, a Muhammadzai Pashtun with extensive foreign affairs experience, would have given this alliance a more national image and a better international presence. Thereafter, the United Front was unable to agree on a prime minister.

In August 1998, in another attack, the Taliban captured not only Mazar but Bamiyan and most of Hazarajat as well. In Mazar they gave their troops license to take revenge for several days, and the estimates of those murdered, mostly Hazaras, reach into the thousands. Many were killed in Bamiyan as well, where the local Tajiks sided with their fellow Sunnis in the Taliban against the Shi'a Hazaras, who had previously burned their houses in another change of power. As parts of Hazarajat changed hands several times, the Taliban exacted reprisals, including the well-documented torture and massacre in May 2000 in Yakawlang of at least thirty-one Hazaras, of whom twenty-six have been identified as civilians.[11] The Taliban further extended their control by capturing Taluqan in September 2000, driving Massoud from his headquarters and pushing him closer to Tajikistan.

Massoud responded to these reverses by analyzing the sources of his defeat and formulating a plan to overcome them. As a result of his attempt to mobilize international support through campaigns against the Taliban, he was invited to address the European Parliament in Strasbourg in April 2001. Within Afghanistan, he tried both to reunite and remobilize the defeated United Front and to reach out to Pashtuns, in particular by signaling a new willingness to collaborate with the former king, Zahir Shah, in his plan for a Loya Jirga. He sought to establish a unified military command by reaching agreement with his Iranian and Russian suppliers that future military aid would go entirely through him, as defense minister of the ISA, rather than directly to various commanders. Through a series of meetings in Uzbekistan and Iran, he reached agreements with Dostum and Ismail Khan and brought both back to Afghanistan in the spring of 2001. Ismail Khan had escaped from a Taliban prison in Qandahar to Iran in 2000. Before September 11, both were in the field, though only Ismail Khan had made modest advances. Massoud also met with such key Pashtun former mujahidin leaders as Abdul Haq of Nangarhar and Hamid Karzai of Qandahar. He met as well with representatives of the former king. These actions laid the base for Massoud's posthumous victories in November–December 2001. No doubt these efforts intensified the determination of the Taliban to defeat him, and of the al-Qaʿida network to eliminate him before Western attention would turn to Afghanistan after September 11, 2001. Massoud died at the hands of suspected al-Qaʿida assassins on September 9, 2001. Abdul Haq was executed by the Taliban on October 26, 2001, after being captured inside Afghanistan, where he had gone to organize support for the former king's initiative. With U.S. assistance, Hamid Karzai entered Uruzgan, north of Qandahar, in October 2001 and was chosen as chairman of the interim administration of Afghanistan in The Bonn Accords of December 5, 2001.

Development of a Regional War Economy

This war, with its transnational linkages, was supported by the growth of a regional war economy, including smuggling of consumer goods, the drug trade, and the gem trade. These economic activities provided resources for the warring parties and cemented their ties to the social groups that profited from these activities. As elsewhere, the war economy entrenched interests in maintaining the social linkages that supported the conflict.

The "security" enforced by the Taliban corresponded to an economic need. Before the ascent of the Taliban, predation by commanders imposed heavy costs on commerce, blocked Pakistan's access to Central Asia, and prevented consolidation of Islamic order, or any other kind. Hence a coalition of Pakistani authorities, Afghan and Pakistani traders, and ultraconservative Afghan and Pakistan religious leaders created the Taliban. The Taliban's control by 1998 over nearly all the country's roads, cities, airports, and customs posts drastically lowered the cost and risk of transport and consolidated Afghanistan's position at the center of a regional war economy.

This war economy built on structures that developed during the anti-Soviet war and even before (chapter 9). The infrastructure of support for the resistance had poured cash into several social networks. Before reaching its intended beneficiaries, both military and humanitarian aid passed through many international, Pakistani, and Afghan intermediaries, some of whom skimmed off cash and resold arms and commodities. These resources provided capital to expand smuggling and other businesses. While the Pakistani military delivered arms to mujahidin parties in its own trucks, private teamsters moved the supplies to the border region and into Afghanistan. Many of these trucks were already active in Pakistani-Afghan smuggling that exploited the Afghan Transit Trade Agreement (ATTA). Under this agreement, listed goods can be imported duty-free in sealed containers into Pakistan for onward shipment to land-locked Afghanistan. Many if not most of the goods were instead sold in smugglers' markets (*bara* bazaars) in Pakistan. During the war the trucks used in this lucrative trade were also leased for arms transport, income from which expanded the capital available for investment in smuggling linked to the ATTA, as well as the growing drug trade.

The breakup of the Soviet Union raised the economic stakes in Afghanistan and pitted Iran and Pakistan against each other in competition for access to the oil and gas-rich Central Asian states. Pakistan saw commercial and political connections to Central Asia via Afghanistan as key to the development of "strategic depth" in its confrontation with India. The United States defined an interest in the independence and economic diversification of the Central Asian states, without relaxing sanctions on Iran, which would have provided an economically feasible pipeline route. Pipe-lines through Afghanistan would reconcile those often contradictory goals. Various companies, including the U.S.-based UNOCAL in alliance with the Saudi company Delta (whose consortium received U.S. government encouragement), and its Argentine rival Bridas, began negotiations with the Rabbani government and de facto power holders. Traders chafed at the growing insecurity along the major routes crossing the country.

The Taliban, in their first major operation, in October 1994, freed a Pakistani trade convoy. Led by a Pakistani intelligence officer who had played a leading role in supporting the mujahidin, Colonel Imam, this convoy was headed for Turkmenistan via Qandahar and Herat, along the projected pipeline route.[12] When it encountered a checkpoint set up by Achakzai tribal militia demanding exorbitant tolls, waves of newly armed Taliban flooded across the border to break the blockade. The convoy rolled on to Turkmenistan as the Taliban marched into Qandahar.[13] This event was emblematic of Taliban "security" and provided both a model and an economic basis for their nearly nationwide consolidation.

The projected oil and gas pipelines have been stymied by the continuing war and Taliban's harboring of Bin Ladin. The war economy in Afghanistan has consisted of the transit trade, the drug trade, the gem trade, service industries stimulated by the growth of the former three, and the emission of currency. Foreign exchange earned by exports financed Afghanistan's imports of war matériel as well as food and other necessities.[14] The Taliban controlled the transit trade, which seemed to be the largest of these sectors. Massoud and his successors have controlled the gem trade. Until 2000, opium production and trade expanded in regions controlled by both sides, but in 1999 areas controlled by the Taliban produced 97 percent of Afghanistan's poppy.[15] In 2000–2001, however, with the Taliban's ban on poppy in effect, the U.F.-controlled areas appeared to have a higher production. Sales of opium and its derivatives continued, drawing on the stocks of two consecutive bumper crops. Traders sold off these stocks in the aftermath of September 11, causing raw opium prices to fall by about two-thirds.

Control by the Taliban of most of the main road system cleared a corridor for the smuggling of duty-free consumer goods from Dubai to Pakistan. Until a ban on international flights from Taliban territory imposed under U.N. Security Council sanctions on November 14, 1999, some goods were flown directly to Afghanistan from Dubai. Most goods crossed the Persian Gulf by ship to Iran, where truckers hauled them to Afghanistan and then into Pakistan.[16] This trade complemented smuggling into Pakistan under cover of the ATTA. In June 1998 I observed that many of the trucks appeared to be carrying automotive vehicle tires and spare parts rather than the electronic appliances I had heard so much about. I later learned that because automotive parts had recently been eliminated from the list of goods eligible for import under the ATTA, they were being imported to Pakistan by this alternate route.[17]

A World Bank study estimated the value of unofficial re-exports to Pakistan at $2.1 billion in 1997 (out of a total of $2.5 billion in exports), the first year after the Taliban had captured Kabul. The total re-exports amounted to nearly half of Afghanistan's estimated GDP, and those to Pakistan constituted around 12–13 percent of Pakistan's total trade.[18] A follow-up study found that unofficial re-exports had decreased to about $1.1 billion by 2000, of which $885 million went to Pakistan, probably due both to a liberalization in Pakistan's trade regulations that reduced the incentive for smuggling and to tighter controls. The earlier World Bank study estimated that the Taliban derived at least $75 million in 1997 from taxing Afghanistan-Pakistan transit trade. The effective tax rates (taking into account the difference between valuations at official and market exchange rates) were less than 10 percent for all commodities in 2000.[19] Although this is a significant income in the context of Afghanistan, it is far less than the amount of Pakistani duties that would be owed on these goods, so the more indirect contraband route was still profitable.

Before the appearance of the Taliban, Afghanistan was already a major opium producer (table 2). About 56 percent of the poppy crop was grown in the areas of southern Afghanistan that the Taliban captured in the fall of 1994, and 39 percent was grown in eastern Afghanistan, which the Taliban took two years later. These remained the principal opium growing areas, though poppy also spread to new regions.[20]

Table 2 Estimated Opium Poppy Cultivation in Afghanistan, 1994–99

Year	Hectares-cultivated	Opium harvested (metric tons)	Average yield (kg/ha)	Districts with reported poppy cultivation	Hectares cultivated in Taliban areas (percentage of total)[a]
1994	71,470	3,416	48	55	(56)[b]
1995	53,759	2,335	43	60	65
1996	56,824	2,248	40	63	65
1997	58,416	2,804	48	60	93
1998	63,674	2,692	42	73	94
1999	90,983	4,581	50	104	97

Sources: United Nations International Drug Control Programme (UNDCP), Afghanistan Programme, *Annual Opium Poppy Survey, 1998* (Islamabad: UNDCP, 1998); UNDCP, Afghanistan Programme, *Annual Opium Poppy Survey, 1999* (Islamabad: UNDCP, 1999).

[a]Taliban control at time of planting.

[b]There was no Taliban control at time of planting in 1994. This figure is the percentage planted in provinces controlled by the Taliban in 1995.

Afghans, including the Taliban, earned relatively little from this crop. Superprofits in the global drug market derive from the risk premium of marketing an illegal commodity in wealthy societies. Producers and marketers of the raw material share in these profits only if they develop vertical integration through to the retail markets, as the Colombian cocaine cartels did in the 1980s.[21] Afghan opium traders, however, generally sell only to the border. A few are involved as far as the Persian Gulf, but not in the lucrative retail markets.[22]

Within Afghanistan, although opium growing and trading involved economic risk, neither the Taliban nor their opponents originally treated these as criminal activities, and there was consequently neither a high risk premium nor violent competition for markets. After the ban on opium cultivation, the Taliban continued to permit opium trade, leading some to speculate that the ban was an attempt to increase profits by raising prices. The opium trade in Afghanistan has been by and large peaceful and competitive.[23]

It is difficult to estimate how much revenue the Taliban derived from this trade. Growers paid the Islamic tithe *(ushr)* at the farmgate on opium and other produce, mostly in kind. Less consistent reports indicate that the Taliban also levied *zakat* of 20 percent on traders in opium and opium derivatives. Some evidence indicates that this *zakat* was collected only in the south, not in the east, where Taliban control was less stable.[24]

The transit and drug trades were complemented by service industries, such as fuel stations, shops, and tea houses. Much of the fuel was smuggled from Iran, where its subsidized price is approximately nine cents per liter, less than a soft drink. The official budget in Kabul (which does not include military expenses) seems to have been paid for by direct foreign aid from Pakistan (Rs. 500 million, or about $10 million in 1998) and a few taxes from Kabul itself. Until the summer of 1998 the Taliban also received direct financial assistance from Saudi Arabia, which provided subsidized fuel, as well as cash grants. These were ended in protest over the Taliban's failure to expel or curb Bin Ladin. Bin Ladin himself is reputed to have put some of his wealth at the Taliban's service, paying, reportedly, for the capture of Kabul in September 1996.

Although the Taliban controlled all major branches of the central bank, Da Afghanistan Bank, they did not print their own money. The Taliban continued to recognize the notes delivered to the Massoud-Rabbani forces, despite their protest against this funding of their enemies and the resulting devaluation of their currency. Taliban banking officials said they recognized the Rabbani currency because they did not wish to undermine national unity by circulating two currencies.[25] In practice, the Taliban would probably have had difficulty obtaining professionally printed notes.[26]

Northeast Afghanistan, controlled by Massoud until his assassination on September 9, 2001, produced only 3 percent of Afghanistan's opium before the Taliban's ban. Commanders levied *ushr* on opium farmers, and at least some local authorities taxed opium traders as well.[27] There were a number of heroin refineries, though authorities destroyed some. Besides the aid it received, mainly from Iran, and the continued delivery of new Afghan currency, the United Front's main income (actually scn's) came from the gem trade. Massoud taxed trade in lapis lazuli and emeralds, collecting *ushr* from mine owners and *zakat* from traders. In 1997, however, Massoud established a monopoly in purchase of the gems, and in 1999 he signed an agreement with a Polish firm, Inter Commerce, to market them. His aides estimated that the trade had previously brought in $40–60 million per year and that the new joint venture might make as much as $200 million in annual income.[28]

From Civil War to Regional Conflict

This regional war economy constituted only one aspect of the spread of the effects of the continuing disaster in Afghanistan. It became the core of what scholars have come to call a regional conflict formation or complex, in which several different conflicts become linked through flows of people, arms, ideology, and resources. Such networks crisscrossed Afghanistan, reaching into all the surrounding countries, the Persian Gulf, and, eventually, the United States. These links originated in the foreign policies of states and in the responses of populations to threats to their survival and opportunities to seek power and security.

Pakistan's policy in Afghanistan derived from its quest for security from India. It sought to assure strategic depth through a friendly government on its western border, and its intelligence services came to use Afghan territory to train fighters for Kashmir. The Soviet war in Afghanistan introduced massive quantities of small arms into Pakistan and provided capital for investment in smuggling. The spread of an Afghan and Pashtun diaspora reaching into the Persian Gulf—Dubai, for example, includes the third-largest urban Pashtun population, after Peshawar and Karachi—facilitated trade and smuggling throughout the region. The drug and transborder trades are linked to organized-crime groups operating throughout the Indian Ocean periphery, the former Soviet Union, and Europe. The transborder trade has undermined Pakistan's fiscal integrity and funded corruption, thereby contributing to the crisis of legitimacy of Pakistani institutions, of which the 1999 coup was only a symptom. That crisis could be intensified by the return of tens of thousands of Pakistani Taliban from Afghanistan. The crisis of September 11 provided President Musharraf with additional leverage to isolate and limit the power of pro-Taliban, so-called jihadi elements in the military and the society, and the United States has promised to reward Pakistan handsomely for this choice.

Iran's policy, conversely, derived from its quest to break out of the isolation imposed by U.S. sanctions and a similar quest for strategic depth on its eastern border. It sought to link up with Central Asia by supporting groups in western, central, and northern Afghanistan against what it saw as attempted encirclement by a U.S.-led group including Saudi Arabia and Pakistan. The competition between Pakistan and Iran, which also took on a Sunni-Shi'a sectarian dimension, became a cultural confrontation between an Arab-Pashtun alliance and Persian and Turki speakers. It fueled escalation in Afghanistan and helped spread the conflict beyond Afghanistan's borders.

Afghanistan provided sources of weapons and refuge (facilitated by cross-border links among Tajiks) that helped intensify the war in Tajikistan, set off by the Soviet collapse. The drug trade also penetrated Tajikistan and its neighbors, drawing in the Russian mafia and corrupting the Russian border guards, as well as all Central Asian governments. Pakistan and Iran each became home to hundreds of thousands if not millions of opium and heroin addicts, and HIV and AIDS started to spread rapidly in Central Asia, as a result of both intravenous drug use and an increase in prostitution.

Members of a repressed Islamist group in Uzbekistan's Ferghana Valley fled to Afghanistan and Tajikistan in 1992. Some of the Uzbek fighters, reorganized as the Islamic Movement of Uzbekistan, established bases in opposition-controlled areas of Tajikistan as well as in Afghanistan, where they developed links to Usama Bin Ladin's al-Qa'ida organization. Since the implementation of the Tajikistan peace accord, members of this group have sought to fight their way back to Uzbekistan directly from Tajikistan and across southern Kyrgyzstan, taking hostages and setting off international crises. Some of their fighters received training in the same Pakistani madrasas that gave birth to the Taliban.

Uzbekistan also supported a militia from Tajikistan (led by Mahmud Khudaiberdiyev, an ethnic Uzbek from that country) that trained in Uzbek areas of north

Afghanistan and staged an uprising in northern Tajikistan in November 1998, in which Afghan Uzbeks participated. Sectarian killings in Pakistan (reflecting the regionwide politicization of Sunni-Shiʿa relations) and the insurgency in Kashmir are also linked to Afghanistan, where Pakistani Sunni extremists have had bases and had participated in fighting along with the Taliban against Afghanistan's Shiʿa, among others. Drug traders from Afghanistan threaten order in several Iranian provinces through which they have established smuggling routes.

Even before September 11, 2001, massive displacements caused by both war and drought had placed all the neighboring countries under pressure once again, but unlike in the 1980s, Afghan refugees were not welcome anywhere. Pakistan, Tajikistan, and Iran—all in different ways and for different reasons—rejected them, refusing to register them or forcing them to return.

Since the bombings of the U.S. embassies in Africa in August 1998, terrorism increasingly dominated the international agenda on Afghanistan. U.N. Security Council resolutions passed in 1999 and 2000 imposed increasingly stringent sanctions against the Taliban on the grounds that they were harboring Usama Bin Ladin, al-Qaʿida, and other terrorist groups and training centers.[29] In chapter 9 of this book I documented the role played by Arab organizations and fighters in the resistance to the Soviet Union.[30] Their role increased after the Soviet withdrawal, as many Afghans felt that jihad was over and put down their weapons. U.S. and Pakistani plans calling for the overthrow of the "Communist" regime increasingly relied on the foreign militants. They stayed on after the fall of Najibullah, fighting for Hikmatyar against Massoud, freely moving through Pakistan.

The links to Afghanistan and Pakistan of the first would-be destroyers of the World Trade Center in 1993 drew attention at least temporarily to the continuing activities of the Arab networks based in Afghanistan, but it was not until the return to Afghanistan of Usama Bin Ladin in May 1996 that the country turned into the focal point of the network which by then was known as al-Qaʿida. Bin Ladin, one of the first Arabs to join the mujahidin's struggle against the Soviet Union, stayed throughout the war. He helped fund the participation of Arab and other international volunteers. In March 1989, on a visit to Saudi Arabia, an Arab journalist first showed me a photograph of Usama Bin Ladin in eastern Afghanistan, and it was clear that others looked to him as a leader. Throughout that time he worked in collaboration with the Saudi intelligence agency and its Pakistani and U.S. counterparts. He turned against his erstwhile sponsors at the time of the Gulf War, when he opposed the invitation of U.S. troops to Saudi Arabia. He left Saudi Arabia for Sudan in 1992, and Saudi Arabia deprived him of his citizenship in 1994. Under pressure from Egypt, which held al-Qaʿida responsible for an assassination attempt on President Mubarak in Addis Ababa, Sudan expelled Bin Ladin in 1996, and in May he returned to Afghanistan, chartering a plane from Ariana Afghan Airlines, supposedly for a cargo flight from Khartoum to Jalalabad. Bin Ladin, together with a group of his followers, lived under the protection of Mawlawi Yunus Khelis until the Taliban captured the area in

September 1996. He reportedly funded the Taliban's efforts to capture eastern Afghanistan and Kabul. He shifted his main base to Qandahar in 1997.

Neither the United States nor Pakistan, over whose territory Bin Ladin's plane flew, seem to have objected to his taking up residence in Afghanistan. Although he had gathered a group of followers from throughout the Arab world in Sudan, and, with the support of Sudanese Islamist leaders, had tried to form a worldwide front of radical Islamists, at that time he was considered a threat mainly within the Middle East. The Taliban at first promised Riyadh that bin Laden would not use his refuge to support any acts of violence abroad, but by mid-1998 the Saudis seem to have become skeptical whether this agreement was being observed, and as a result Riyadh reduced its aid to the Taliban in the summer of 1998. After the bombings of the U.S. embassies in Kenya and Tanzania in August 1998 and U.S. reprisals, Mullah Umar reneged on what Saudi authorities thought was a commitment to hand over Bin Ladin, and Saudi Arabia withdrew assistance and froze diplomatic relations. Until then, Saudi Arabia had been one of three countries, along with Pakistan and the United Arab Emirates, that maintained diplomatic relations with the Islamic Emirate.

The embassy bombings awakened the Clinton administration to the dangers posed by Bin Ladin's organization and, together with subsequent intelligence, prompted both the immediate military riposte and the series of escalating sanctions imposed on the Taliban. Thus, even before September 11, the conflict in Afghanistan had already taken on not only regional but global dimensions.

International Organizations and the Search For Peace

Since a General Assembly resolution of December 1993, the United Nations has had a mandate to promote dialogue among Afghans with the goal of facilitating a comprehensive political settlement. In addition, it has provided humanitarian assistance. Until September 11, however, the United Nations was acting without adequate support from member states. Indeed, many states verbally supported the U.N. goals while actively undermining them.

It is only a slight exaggeration to say that the United Nations was for years pursuing at least three (maybe four) mutually conflicting policies in Afghanistan. The U.N. Security Council, led by Russia and the United States, focusing nearly entirely on Usama Bin Ladin, imposed sanctions on the Taliban only, including a ban on military assistance, financial transactions, foreign travel by high officials, international flights, and the import of materials for refining heroin. The only condition for lifting the sanctions was that Usama Bin Ladin be handed over for trial and the terrorist training facilities closed. This policy treated the Taliban's policies as a threat to international peace and security and implicitly favored the United Front, which one of the resolution's supporters (Russia) was arming.

The U.N. Special Mission to Afghanistan (UNSMA) was primarily charged with mediating between the Taliban and the United Front to promote a cease-fire and formation of a broad-based government, as well as other measures related to "peace-making." UNSMA's mission was largely defined by General Assembly resolutions and statements of the "six plus two" group of countries (Afghanistan's neighbors, plus the United States and Russia).[31] These resolutions originated at a time when Afghanistan was divided among various groups and warlords, rather than dominated by one organization increasingly at odds with the official international community. Unlike the Security Council resolution of 2000, which imposed an arms embargo on only the Taliban, the General Assembly Resolutions and six-plus-two declarations called for an end of military supplies to all warring parties. Nearly all of the external military support, of course, came from members of the group issuing the declaration, which effectively called on its issuers to reverse their own policies. UNSMA's mission required impartiality or neutrality among the warring parties and defined the threat to peace and security as the war, rather than the Taliban.

The U.N. Office of the Coordinator of Humanitarian Affairs in Afghanistan (UNOCHA) has had as its mission to deliver "rights-based" humanitarian assistance to the Afghan people through principled common programming (PCP) of all U.N. agencies under the strategic framework.[32] This mission required negotiated access to the Afghan population through the de facto authorities, mainly the Taliban. Because it operated on the ground, UNOCHA benefited from Taliban security (the lack of which made operations in some U.F. areas impossible) and the lower level of corruption, especially compared with Junbish and Wahdat. Hence despite its many and increasing conflicts with the Taliban, primarily over issues of women's employment, education, and access to assistance, UNOCHA was often perceived as more "pro-Taliban" by other parts of the U.N. system. The negotiation in May 1998 of a "memorandum of understanding" signed by the Taliban and a U.N. relief official heightened this impression; according to the memorandum, "women's access to health and education will need to be gradual."

The U.N. Human Rights Commission, through the special rapporteur on Afghanistan, reported on "violations of human rights" in Afghanistan, a legal category that has covered most political and military activities in that country. Under current human rights standards, many Afghan leaders should be arrested and tried as war criminals, a measure that would probably be quite popular with most Afghans.

A number of Afghans in exile also launched their own peace processes, with the help and support of foreign governments, including the "Rome process" focused on the former king, Zahir Shah (funded by Italy and indirectly supported by the United States) and the "Cyprus process" supported by some factions in Iran. The previous "Bonn process," which had received some support from companies interested in the pipeline, merged with the effort in Rome. The United States, Germany, Italy, Iran, and the United Nations formed the Geneva Group to support coordination among these processes.

The Rome process has attracted the most attention. As I described in *The Search for Peace in Afghanistan,* since 1983 Zahir Shah had periodically articulated the idea of resolving the Afghan conflict through the "traditional" means of convening Loya Jirga. The Loya Jirga ("great council" in Pashto) was a traditionalist institution of the Afghan state (one that reflected a state-constructed "tradition") by which the regime might claim a tribal legitimation. Afghan nationalist intellectuals retrospectively construed gatherings that called the tribes to jihad when there was no functioning legitimate state (as during the two British occupations) as "emergency" Loya Jirgas. But plans for such a convocation languished, because Zahir Shah and his advisers had no resources to implement these plans nor any leverage over either the groups that exercised power in Afghanistan or the foreign supporters of these groups. They finally obtained at least some token assistance when the United States turned against Pakistani policy in Afghanistan after 1998 and encouraged the government of Italy to provide support.

Afghans living in Afghanistan appear to retain a sentimental attachment to Zahir Shah as a symbol of national unity and of better, peaceful days. The concept of legitimating a new government through a Loya Jirga also appeals to many. Many hoped that under some new conditions, Zahir Shah might now be able to preside, at least symbolically, over a transitional authority that would summon a Loya Jirga. The Bonn Accords contain provisions that largely meet these expectations: the former king is to open the Loya Jirga scheduled for June 2002.

Before September 11, competing definitions of the problem confused international action on Afghanistan. The idea of a "peace process" among warring groups did 0not fit well a country where one group (the Taliban) enjoyed a vast preponderance of control. Had their ideology been minimally acceptable, any group with the degree of control that the Taliban had would have been accepted as the peacemakers of Afghanistan, and international efforts would have been directed to enabling other groups to join them. The Taliban's ideology, violations of human rights and strictures on women, and the growing closeness of the core leadership to al-Qaʻida, assured that the Taliban would not be accepted. Increasingly, the major problem that Afghanistan posed to international actors was not the persistence of a civil war in some corners of the country but the behavior of the force that was consolidating power. Yet no major power regarded the threat posed by the humanitarian emergency in Afghanistan, or even the terrorist presence there, as requiring the expenditure of billions of dollars or the attention of high-level officials, let alone the dispatch of the world's most powerful war machine.

Afghanistan After September 11

Once it became clear that the atrocities of September 11 in the United States had been carried out by affiliates of the al-Qaʻida network, international attention finally, if belatedly, returned to Afghanistan. The United States publicly announced what it had told the Taliban since January 1999: that it would hold them co-responsible for attacks traced to Bin Ladin, and would treat them accordingly.

President Bush soon stated that if the Taliban did not hand over the wanted leaders of al-Qaʿida and destroy the terrorist infrastructure, the United States, with whatever allies it could command, would remove the Taliban from power. But what did that mean? Bush had come to power opposed to U.S. involvement in "nation building" and skeptical, if not hostile, to multilateral initiatives and international organizations. The logic of the situation, however, seemed to dictate otherwise. Simply destroying the Taliban, who controlled the only governmental structure in most of Afghanistan, would leave the country and the region in a state of anarchy and war, the very conditions that had generated the Taliban and provided al-Qaʿida with the opportunity to use the country as its base. After some bitter internal debates, the government defined its goal, as President Bush said on October 11, as a "stable Afghanistan," including support for a political transition and a commitment to reconstruction. President Bush also noted that the United Nations could provide the framework for this process. This goal partly relieved the government of President Pervez Musharraf in Pakistan. Under tremendous pressure (the choice of being either a partner of the United States or a target of the war on terrorism), Musharraf had broken with Pakistan's official support for the Taliban, but his government did not want to be left once again with either a maelstrom of violence or an anti-Pakistan regime on Pakistan's long Afghan frontier.

The administration may initially have underestimated the obstacles to the success of such a program, however. It relied primarily on an agreement between Zahir Shah and the United Front to appoint members of a Supreme Council as a transitional authority to be legitimated by a Loya Jirga. Each would appoint fifty members, leaving twenty or more for others. Apparently some in Washington hoped that Zahir Shah's call, combined with bombing that weakened the Taliban and al-Qaʿida military structures, would lead to the defection of Pashtuns and quickly create the conditions for a viable successor government. The United States also counted on work by the ISI, which reluctantly dropped its objections to the ex-monarch and agreed at least verbally to recruit Pashtun leaders and Taliban defectors to the cause. The United Front agreed not to enter Kabul unilaterally (though always with an escape clause), despite resistance from some of its commanders and from Rabbani himself, urged on by elements in Iran who opposed any role for Zahir Shah. Both Zahir Shah and the United Front called for the demilitarization of Kabul by a neutral security force, whether international or Afghan. For several weeks, as a result, the United States appeared to hold back from trying to destroy Taliban front lines north of Kabul and south of Mazar-i Sharif, hoping that a political alternative would materialize.

Instead, regional competition re-emerged, both Zahir Shah's entourage and the United Front became increasingly factionalized, and Abdul Haq, the first well-known Pashtun commander to enter Afghanistan in support of the Loya Jirga initiative, was quickly captured, tortured, and summarily executed by the Taliban on October 26. President Musharraf repeated his demand for Pashtun predominance in a successor government and for the presence of "moderate Taliban" (though neither he nor anyone else defined either *moderate* or *Taliban,* leaving it unclear whether this excluded any official of the IEA or only certain leaders). Russia and Iran responded by demanding to name their own candidates. On his way back from the Asia-Pacific Economic Cooperation summit in Shanghai, Russian President Vladimir Putin ostentatiously met with Rabbani in Dushanbe, Tajikistan, and promised support to his "government."

Meanwhile, the United Nations had started to become involved once more. On October 2, U.N. Secretary-General Kofi Annan reappointed Lakhdar Brahimi, the former foreign minister of Algeria, as his special representative for Afghanistan. Brahimi had previous served as special representative of the secretary general (SRSG) during 1997–99. He suspended his mission in July 1999 when it became too obvious that member states—notably, but not solely, Pakistan—were articulating commitments they had no intention of keeping. In 2000, however, Brahimi had chaired an influential panel that reported on the sources of failure and conditions for success of U.N. operations. In New York and Washington in mid-October, he made clear that although the United Nations would do all it could, it would not be rushed into an ill-conceived mission without adequate support. Thinking through the interconnections of military, security, humanitarian, political, and economic action, and marshaling the needed personnel, political support, and funding would take some time.

The United States began its bombing campaign on October 7. At first, Washington seemed to hold back from bombing the Taliban front lines in the hope that the UF–Zahir Shah negotiations would produce a successor government. By the end of October, however, the United States decided to proceed with the military track without waiting for the rhythms of Afghan politics. It won this high-stakes gamble quickly: Mazar-i Sharif fell on November 9 and Kabul on November 13. The Taliban finally abandoned Qandahar on December 6, in a deal that took shape only one day after the selection of Hamid Karzai, a Qandahari, as chairman of the Interim Administration of Afghanistan established under the Bonn Accords.

Those accords, resulting from ten days of U.N.-sponsored talks, reflected the distribution of power that resulted from the U.S strategy. The SCN, whose military, despite earlier promises, had occupied Kabul when the U.S. bombing opened the way, kept control of the most powerful ministries. Resurgent warlords controlled most of the provinces, and some benefited from continued U.S. aid as they helped hunt down Mullah Umar, Usama bin Ladin, and the remnants of their followers. But the accords also contained provisions to make the Afghan government more representative and to disarm warlords. Working in the accords' favor was a wave of Afghan popular sentiment that demanded an end to war and the establishment of national governance and development, combined with an international commitment to aid in those goals. Whether international actors sustained their commitment would largely determine the outcome.

The ultimate test of our globalized world will not be on the streets outside a meeting of the World Trade Organization but in the mountains of Afghanistan.

Among the many memories these events stirred was a chain of images of a trip I took in January 1996 to Tajikistan and northern Afghanistan. Riding into the city of Dushanbe from the airport, I passed under a bridge decorated in faded and peeling Cyrillic characters with a couplet from the twelfth-century Persian poet Sa'adi. It took a moment to decipher the classical Persian hidden beneath the pentimento of the Russian script, but after spelling out a few words, I recognized the famous lines:

> The children of Adam are limbs of one another, created from a single substance.
> When one limb suffers misfortune, the others cannot be at rest.
> You who do not suffer the pain of others do not deserve to be called human.

A few days later, driving across the plain of Archi north of Kunduz, seeing the road crumbling into dust, I saw a family crouched by the side of the road. Wrapped in rags, a man and his daughters unearthed a treasure that glowed in the dusk—bright orange carrots, buried for a winter meal. Surprised by our white U.N. vehicle, they stared as we jounced past them, and I wondered, just how far out of the circle of human solidarity can people fall?

The devastation of Afghanistan enabled outlaws to establish a base for a global network that preys on the suffering of millions. September 11 showed that the words of Sa'adi, their predecessors in the Bible and Quran, and their less eloquent versions in the Charter of the United Nations and countless other documents are not just slogans or pious wishes. The interdependence of all human beings has become a fact that we ignore at our peril. More than I ever imagined when I pled for such a recognition in this book, our common fate depends on whether we can learn that lesson.

Notes

Parts of this preface appeared in different forms in: "Afghanistan Under the Taliban," *Current History* 98 (February 1999): 79–91; "The Political Economy of War and Peace in Afghanistan," *World Development* 28 (2000): 1789–1803; and "Afghanistan: Reconstruction and Peacebuilding in a Regional Framework," KOFF Peacebuilding Reports 1/2001, Swiss Peace Foundation, Berne, 2001. Excerpts appear with permission. I thank the publishers for their permission and Andrea Armstrong for her help in preparing this preface.

1. Bush, news conference, October 11, 2001. Office of the Press Secretary, "President Holds Prime Time News Conference." Accessed online: www.whitehouse.gov/news/releases/2001/10/20011011-7.html

2. Anthony Davis, "How the Taliban Became a Military Force," in William Maley, ed., *Fundamentalism Reborn? Afghanistan and the Taliban* (New York: St. Martin's, 1998), 43–71; and Ahmed Rashid, *Taliban: Militant Islam, Oil, and Fundamentalism in Central Asia* (New Haven: Yale University Press, 2000).

3. Despite numerous attempts by journalists and others to find evidence of material support for the Taliban by either the United States or the Unocal oil company, which had an interest in the pipeline project, no such evidence has materialized. See Rashid, *Taliban,* for a treatment of the available evidence.

4. "Qandahari" here denotes the broad region with Qandahar at its center, including several provinces in addition to the modern province of Qandahar.

5. Rashid, *Taliban;* Barbara Daly Metcalf, *Islamic Revival in British India: Deoband, 1860–1900* (Princeton: Princeton University Press, 1982).

6. United Nations International Drug Control Programme, Afghanistan Programme (UNDCP). Strategic study 2: *The Dynamics of the Farmgate Opium Trade and the Coping Strategies of Opium Traders,* final report. (Islamabad: UNDCP, 1998).

7. Nancy Dupree, "Afghan Women Under the Taliban" in Maley, *Fundamentalism Reborn?* 145–66.

8. For a literary treatment of this process, see Sayd Bahauddin Majrooh, "End of a Sojourn in the Abode of Refugees: Gul andam [body like a flower], or the Story of Laughing Lovers," trans. Ashraf Ghani, in *Izhda-yi Khudi (The Ego Monster),* book 1, vol. 5. (Peshawar: Unpublished, 1984).

9. This was analyzed well years before the Taliban in Hakim Taniwal, "The Impact of Pashtunwali on Afghan Jehad," *Quarterly Journal of Writers Union of Free Afghanistan* 2 (January–March 1987):1–24.

10. Agence France-Presse [Jabul Seraj], Emmanuel Dunand, "Anti-Taliban Figure's Death in Plane Crash a Massive Loss: Official," 22 August 1997.

11. Human Rights Watch, "Massacres of Hazaras in Afghanistan," February 2001. http://www.hrw.org.

12. After September 11, reports claimed that Colonel Imam and several like-minded ISI officers had returned to Qandahar to assist the Taliban despite the policy announced by President Musharraf of supporting the United States. These reports were soon followed by the resignation of the director of the ISI, as well two other senior corps commanders with Islamist sympathies.

13. Rubin, *The Search for Peace in Afghanistan;* Maley, *Fundamentalism Reborn;* Rashid, *Taliban.*

14. Z. F. Naqvi, "Afghanistan-Pakistan Trade Relations" (Islamabad: World Bank, 1999).

15. United Nations International Drug Control Programme (UNDCP), *Afghanistan Programme: Annual Opium Poppy Survey 1999.* (Islamabad: UNDCP, 1999); UNDCP, Strategic study 5: *An Analysis of the Process of Expansion of Opium Poppy to New Districts in Afghanistan,* second report (Islamabad: UNDCP, 1999).

16. In protest against the murder of Iranian diplomats and a journalist by Taliban troops in Mazar-i Sharif, Iran closed the border between August 1998 and November 1999. During that period the goods took a detour via Turkmenistan.

17. Z. F. Naqvi, *Afghanistan-Pakistan Trade Relations.* (Islamabad: World Bank, 1999).

18. Ibid.

19. Mohammad Zubair Khan, "Afghanistan's Trade Relations with Neighbouring Countries" (Islamabad: World Bank/UNDCP, 2001).

20. UNDCP, Strategic study 5: *Opium Poppy.*

21. Manuel Castells, "End of Millennium," *The Information Age: Economy, Society, and Culture,* vol. 3 (Oxford: Blackwell, 1998), 166–205.

22. UNDCP, Strategic study 2: *Dynamics of the Farmgate Opium Trade.*

23. Ibid.

24. Bizhan Torabi, "Entretien avec Mollah Mohammad Omar," *Politique internationale,* 74 (1996–97): 141–42; UNDCP, Strategic study 2: *Dynamics of the Farmgate Opium Trade,* p. 13; Rashid, *Taliban.* According to sharia, *zakat* is a tax on wealth levied at 2.5 percent, or one fortieth. It is unclear on what legal basis the Taliban imposed this tax at a much higher rate and on a flow of commerce rather than a stock of wealth. It is also unclear whether the *zakat* was assessed on gross income or on profit.

25. Interviews with director of Bank-i Milli Afghanistan, Qandahar, and deputy director of Da Afghanistan Bank, Kabul, June 1998. Both of these officials were graduates of Pakistani madrasas, with no economic, commercial, or financial background or experience.

26. The international legal regime for currency printing is complex and decentralized. In controversial cases the few companies that do "security printing" (of currency, passports and other official documents) look to their host governments (usually their major customers) for guidance. These governments generally use political criteria in giving opinions about such contracts. The major security printers are in the United States, the United Kingdom, Germany, and France, none of which looked favorably on the Taliban. I thank R. Scott Horton for clarifying these points for me.

27. Bernard Frahi, Tony Davis, personal communications.

28. Françoise. Chipaux, "Des mines d' émeraude pour financer la résistance du commandant Massoud," *Le Monde,* July 17, 1999.

29. United Nations Security Council, Resolution 1363 (July 2001); Resolution 1333 (December 2000); Resolution 1267 (October 1999).

30. For a fuller treatment, see Barnett R. Rubin, "Arab Islamists in Afghanistan," in John L. Esposito, ed., *Political Islam: Revolution, Radicalism, or Reform?* (Boulder, Colo.: Lynne Reinner, 1997), 179–206.

31. For original mission of UNSMA see United Nations General Assembly, A/RES/48/208; 86th plenary meeting; December 21, 1993. Also see the Tashkent Declaration of July 19, 1999, by the "six plus two" group and the Regional Action Plan of September 13, 2000, by the six-plus-two group (http://www.undcp.org/uzbekistan/actionplan.html).

32. On the strategic framework see www.pcpafg.org.

Acknowledgments

In the decade-long itinerary that led to this book, I benefited from generosity motivated by more than willingness to help a researcher. From the headquarters of the United Nations to the Ghaziabad State Farm in Nangarhar Province, Afghanistan; from the Institute of Oriental Studies in Moscow to the Haripur refugee camp in the Northwest Frontier Province of Pakistan; from the office of Médécins sans Frontières in Paris to the office of UNHCR in Dusti, Tajikistan, I was welcomed into the transnational community of those who, often in spite of ourselves, came to live the tragedy of Afghanistan. Our common concern for that land and for its people transcended even our sometimes bitter differences.

As for the people of Afghanistan, I can never thank all those who aided me, if only because I do not know or remember the names of the twelve-year-old girl in the refugee camp who told me how her father was shot on the long route of exile from Kunduz to Peshawar, of the elder who shoved through my car window a list of his martyred family members, of the interpreter who explained how his beard turned white in a night when his fourteen-year-old son was killed in battle, or of so many others. I have recorded below the names that I can.

I could never have completed this work without aid from a variety of sources. The Yale Junior Faculty Research Fund enabled me to hire research assistants, including Jay Chandrasekhar, Loc Vo, Alexandra Vo, and Konrad Stenzel. Konrad, whose tragic and premature death in 1990 deprived all who knew him of a staunch and sympathetic friend, helped me survey the German sociological literature on Afghanistan. The Yale Center for International Relations provided funds for travel to Pakistan in 1986 and to the USSR in 1988.

The United States Institute of Peace granted me a fellowship during 1989–90. During that period I benefited immensely from the assistance of Paula Smith, who tracked down obscure data and publications. I owe a continuing debt to Dan Snodderley of the USIP publications department, who read the manuscript as it grew and who offered continual encouragement.

I could hardly have started my work without the help of Rosanne Klass, then of Freedom House. The Committee for a Free Afghanistan also provided me with an entrée to policy circles in Washington.

Jeri Laber's invitation in 1984 to collaborate with her on a Helsinki Watch report on Afghanistan gave me my first opportunity to meet the refugees and mujahidin in Peshawar and Quetta. We relied in these early efforts on guidance from the late Louis Dupree and Nancy Hatch Dupree. After Asia Watch was founded in 1985, I returned to Pakistan and Afghanistan for that organization in 1985 and 1989. I was also invited to Saudi Arabia in 1989 as a guest of the United States Information Agency. In October 1990 the National Democratic Institute for International Affairs invited me to Pakistan as an election monitor. In October 1992 UNESCO invited me to participate in a conference in Almaty, Kazakhstan, on Promoting Free and Independent Media in Asia. In May–June 1993 I visited Tajikistan on behalf of Helsinki Watch and traveled to Uzbekistan as part of a grant from USIP and a conference organized by Jerry Hough of Duke University. On each of these trips, while the principal purpose was something else, I learned something that made its way into this book, and I thank all the people and organizations involved.

In the course of my early research I met Olivier Roy in November 1983. Since then, over convivial tables on various continents, I have learned more from him than can be acknowledged in footnotes. In France I also received the unstinting help of Médécins sans Frontières (Claude Malhuret and Juliette Fournot), Aide Médicale Internationale (Laurence Laumonier), Médécins du Monde (Michael Barry), and the members of Amitié Franco-Afghane (AFRANE).

During repeated trips to Pakistan, the Western expatriates, the Pakistani hosts, and the Afghan refugees provided hospitality, insight, and aid. Anders Fänge of the Swedish Committee for Afghanistan gave me the privilege of studying SCA files. He and Hanneke Kouwenberg welcomed me into their home. John Dixon of USIA, Peshawar, and his successor, Richard Hoagland, provided not only their indispensable contact lists but also their unique insights—and, of course, hospitality in a dry area. Both were also extraordinarily helpful back in Washington during 1989–90. Farshad Rastegar generously shared the Fulbright house with me in 1986 and later provided material I could not have obtained otherwise. Jan Goodwin, besides all that she had done for me in New York when she was working for *Ladies Home Journal,* also provided a home away from home in Peshawar after she moved there to work for Save the Children (USA). Reporters Edward Girardet and Donatella Lorch (who accompanied me into Afghanistan) provided information and anecdotes that inform this work even if they do not appear. Steve Holtzman, whom I first met in the UNHCR office in Peshawar, reappeared as my student at Columbia in 1990. The UNHCR background reports he obtained for me proved indispensable.

A sad aspect of this project is that some of the Afghans from whom I learned so much became victims of the war. I can, alas, never adequately thank Sayd Bahauddin Majrooh, a peaceful and brilliant intellectual, whose rickety manual typewriter frightened someone enough to order him riddled with bullets on February 11, 1988. I first met him in New York in 1983 at the apartment of Rosanne Klass, and I later had the privilege of welcoming him into my home in New Haven, as I was welcomed into his house of exile in Peshawar. I miss his insights—and his incomparable humor—now more then ever. Shah Bazgar, who left his comfortable post as a cancer researcher in Orléans to return to his homeland, risked all and lost it. He opened closed doors for me until he fell to an assassin's bullet near Qandahar in 1989.

The first time Jeri Laber and I met Jamiat political officer Muhammad Es'haq in Peshawar in 1984, he gave us the title of our book, A Nation Is Dying. From then to our most recent meeting in Tashkent in May 1993, no one has given me more help than he. When I needed data on the early militants of the Islamic movement, Es'haq told me to fax him the names. I received a database by return mail. When a reviewer of a manuscript insisted that I must read the mujahidin party programs before analyzing their ideology, I faxed Es'haq and received the programs by return mail. He has published articles of mine that he disagreed with and responded with closely argued and well-written commentary. This book would not be what it is without him.

Wakil Akbarzai, responsible for logistics and refugee affairs for NIFA and subsequently the IIGA, welcomed me into his network of friends, family, and coworkers. He took me into Afghanistan and shared his opinions, his knowledge, and his thoughts. Dr. Muhammad Azam Dadfar, Farhat Saeed, Fatima Gailani, Daoud Mir, Sher Muhammad Ittibari, Nawab Salim, Abdul Rahim, and many others guided and helped me.

I also learned much from conversations with members of the PDPA-Watan Party in New York, Tashkent, and Almaty. I would like to thank Sarwar Yurish, Sulaiman Laiq, Sayyid Ikram Paigir, Muhammad Nabi Azimi, and Daud Kawian. I could not have completed my database on the PDPA without the generous help of Miagol, Kabul's chargé d'affaires in Washington during 1989–90.

Equally vital to this work were unselfish offers by Anthony Arnold and David J. Katz to share with me their biographical databases on the PDPA and the DRA and by Tom Johnson and his colleagues at the Orkand Corporation for assuring me access to their reports. Every table on the composition of these groups is in effect co-authored by them.

The friendship of Lawrence Lifschultz and Rabia Ali sustained me throughout. Larry, together with Selig Harrison of the Carnegie Endowment for International Peace, made a key contribution to my work in the mid-1980s. He and Selig argued that I should concern myself not only with the problems of Afghanistan but also with a solution. They introduced me to Diego Cordovez, then under secretary–general of the United Nations, conversations with whom became part of my itinerary beginning in November 1985. Since then I learned much from contact with other U.N. officials as well, including Giandomenico Picco, Raymond Sommereyns, Charles Santos, Vassily Safronchuk, Benon Sevan, Sadruddin Aga Khan, and Alfredo Witschi-Cestari. I also owe thanks to Selig Harrison for many talks and for invitations to participate in various events at the Carnegie Endowment.

Several Pakistanis also provided assistance. I benefited much from conversations with Arif Ayub, member of the U.N. mission in the mid-1980s. Riaz Muhammad Khan of the Foreign Ministry provided me with his unique insights in both Islamabad and New York. Ambassador Jamshed Marker, my colleague at USIP during 1989–90, helped me understand the professional diplomat's point of view. Mushahid Hussain, in his various journalistic positions from 1985 to the present, was always a provocative interlocutor. Sitting in his office in *The Muslim* in 1985 and 1986, I met quite a spectrum of people, from an arms dealer in the tribal territories to the press attaché of the Soviet embassy. Ahmed Rashid, of the *Far Eastern Economic Review,* the *Nation* (Lahore), and *Independent* (London), deserves special thanks and recognition for his resourceful reporting and his efforts to keep me abreast of his discoveries.

In Moscow and elsewhere I learned much from Soviet and Russian colleagues. I will always be grateful for the encouragement—and invaluable information—I received from Yuri Gankovsky of the Institute of Oriental Studies, Moscow. Vladimir Plastun, also of the Institute, shared with me his unequaled on-the-ground experience from two tours in Afghanistan. Artem Borovik introduced me to the world of the Soviet soldier in Afghanistan and to the debates on Soviet involvement that were shaking the establishment in 1988. Nodari Simoniya, who courageously opposed the Soviet intervention before it was popular—or safe—to do so, earned my respect for his knowledge and his desire for peace.

I hope that human rights organizations benefited from my work as much as I did from theirs. Amnesty International provided me with information and press clippings over the years; I owe special gratitude to Abbas Faiz. In Washington, D.C., Patricia Gossman of Asia Watch, who took over the Afghanistan file along with her myriad other duties, repeatedly alerted me to things I had missed. Her own travels to Kabul, Herat, Mazar-i Sharif, and Peshawar enabled her to bring me data I lacked. Steve Galster of the National Security Archive provided access to an immense database and guidance on Freedom of Information Act requests; he and Joachim Hippler also brought me documents from Kabul. Anita Bhatia of the World Bank sent me data I would otherwise have been unable to obtain.

Ashraf Ghani, of Johns Hopkins University and the World Bank, from whose writings I had already learned so much, offered even sharper insights and additional information in person. Peter Hauslohner provided invaluable assistance on two trips to Moscow and in Washington. In the State Department, Ed McWilliams, Charles Dunbar, Zalmay Khalilzad, Peter Tomsen, and Robert Oakley offered assistance of various kinds. It saddens me that another friend, Robert Peck, former deputy assistant secretary of state for the Near East and South Asia, will be unable to see the book to which he contributed in so many on- and off-the-record meetings and private conversations. I know he would want me to record that he died of a plague that is killing far more people than even the war in Afghanistan: AIDS.

In Congress, I must thank former Rep. Steve Solarz for several opportunities to testify before him. I owe particular thanks to Eric Schwartz for arranging these events and keeping me abreast of legislative developments.

Journalists in Washington who provided information include Richard Mackenzie of *Insight, National Geographic,* and CNN, James Rupert of the *Washington Post,* and David Rogers of the *Wall Street Journal.* Tariq Fatemi of the Pakistani embassy and Shyam Mehra of the Indian U.N. mission provided information and insights over years of good lunches and dinners.

Afghan exile communities offered various forms of assistance. General Abdul Wali and the former king, Muhammad Zahir Shah, received me graciously in Rome. In Washington, I could not have done without the knowledge of Hafizullah Karzai. Sultan Ghazi facilitated all sorts of contacts and provided documents I would otherwise have lacked. Qadir Amiryar, Shah Mahmud, Naim Majrooh (both in the United States and earlier in Peshawar), Abdul Jabbar Sabet, Spozhmai Maiwandi, and many others provided information that otherwise would have been missing. Among Afghans in New York, I received help from Nangialai Tarzi of the OIC U.N. mission, Amin Tarzi of the Afghan U.N. mission (after April 1992), and Helena Malikyar. In California I appreciated the hospitality of Dr. Rawan Farhadi, the Afghan Center of Oakland, and the Beyond War organization.

A special word of thanks must go to Hasan Kakar, Afghanistan's leading historian, now in exile in San Diego. His peaceful resistance at Kabul University landed him in Pul-i Charkhi prison for five years, where he earned recognition as an Amnesty International Prisoner of the Month. For his hospitality in Peshawar after his release and for the sometimes bitter clarity of his thoughts, I owe him much. Rasul Amin and other exiled faculty from Kabul University provided a collegial and stimulating environment at the office of the Writers Union of Free Afghanistan.

Nazif Shahrani's close reading and incisive comments contributed significantly to improving parts of this book. Houchang Chehabi helped me sharpen some arguments and avoid some errors. Myron Weiner of MIT and Ali Banuazizi of Boston University asked me to write a paper for a seminar at MIT in the fall of 1988. Their comments and encouragement helped me formulate the arguments in Chapter 5. Shirin Akiner of the School of Oriental and African Studies of the University of London enabled me to present an early version of some of my arguments to a conference on Afghanistan in London in December 1988. At that conference I first met Anthony Hyman, whose ideas and research I still seek out. Lloyd I. Rudolph and Susanne Hoeber Rudolph invited me to present portions of this research to the University of Chicago seminar on the Political Economy of the Middle East and South Asia in February 1990 and again in March 1993. Ashutosh Varshney invited me to present some of my findings at the Seminar on South Asia of Harvard's Center for International Studies in December 1990. Atul Kohli invited me to speak together with William Maley and Amin Saikal at Princeton University in the fall of 1991. I benefited from responses I received to each of these presentations.

Abigail Spangler arranged for the Center for Social Sciences at Columbia, headed by Harrison White, to hold a seminar to discuss this manuscript in the winter of 1993. Both Harrison White and Lisa Anderson read an earlier version which was even longer than the present book. Both offered helpful comments and encouragement. Said Arjomand's enthusiasm helped me get through the last months of writing and editing. Henri Barkey, Phil Oldenburg, Shahrbanou Tadjbakhsh, and Shyama Venkateswar read selections and offered comments. At various times I also benefited from the comments of Robert Canfield, William Maley, Amin Saikal, Pierre Centlivres, and Micheline Centlivres-Demont. The support I received from James Scott of Yale greatly assisted me in getting the manuscript published.

In the final preparation of this manuscript, I enjoyed the help of Erika Weinthal and Sumantra Bose. Without them, I might still be chasing footnotes. Portions of Chapters 2 and 5 appeared as "Afghanistan: The Red Revolution Turns Green," in *The State and Social Transformation in Afghanistan, Iran, and Pakistan,* edited by Ali Banuazizi and Myron Weiner (Syracuse: Syracuse University Press, 1994). An earlier version of part of Chapter 3 appeared as "Lineages of the State in Afghanistan," *Asian Survey* 28 (November 1988): 1188–1209. An earlier version of other parts of Chapter 3 appeared as "The Old Regime in Afghanistan: Recruitment and Training of a State Elite," *Central Asian Survey* 10 (1991): 73–100. An earlier version of Chapter 4 appeared as "Political Elites in Afghanistan: Rentier State Building, Rentier State Wrecking," *International Journal of Middle East Studies* 24 (1992): 77–99. Portions of Chapter 12 appeared as "Post–Cold War State Disintegration: The Failure of International Conflict Resolution in Afghanistan," *Journal of International Affairs* 46 (Winter 1993): 469–92.

All excerpts appear with permission. Despite all the help I received, I know this book contains errors of fact, analysis, and judgment. I alone am responsible for these.

Finally, there is only one person who has lived with this project for as long as I have, enduring both my absences and the times when, though present, I was hardly there. Although she knows as little about Afghanistan as I do about gene transcription, I cannot imagine this book apart from my life with Susan. "Without the rose," wrote Ghalib, "there is no mirror for spring."

Abbreviations

AGSA	Da Afghanistan da Gato da Satalo Idara (Organization for the Defense of the Interests of Afghanistan)
AICMB	*Afghan Information Centre Monthly Bulletin*
ANLF	Afghanistan National Liberation Front
BBC	British Broadcasting Corporation
C.C.	Central Committee
CMEA	Council for Mutual Economic Assistance
CPSU	Communist Party of the Soviet Union
DCAR	Data Collection for Afghan Repatriation
DRA	Democratic Republic of Afghanistan
DWOA	Democratic Women's Organization of Afghanistan
DYOA	Democratic Youth Organization of Afghanistan
FBIS/MENA:SA	*Federal Broadcast Information Service, Middle East and North Africa: South Asia*
FBIS/NES	*Federal Broadcast Information Service, Near East and South Asia*
FBIS/SA	*Federal Broadcast Information Service, South Asia*
HAR	Harakat-i Inqilab-i Islami-yi Afghanistan (Movement of the Islamic Revolution/Uprising of Afghanistan)
HIH	Hizb-i Islami-yi Afghanistan (Islamic Party of Afghanistan), Hikmatyar group
HIK	Hizb-i Islami-yi Afghanistan (Islamic Party of Afghanistan), Khalis group

ICRC	International Committee of the Red Cross
IIGA	Interim Islamic Government of Afghanistan
ISA	Islamic State of Afghanistan
ISI	Directorate of Inter-Services Intelligence (Pakistan)
ITT	Ittihad-i Islami bara-yi Azadi-yi Afghanistan (Islamic Union for the Freedom of Afghanistan)
JIA	Jam'iyyat [Jamiat]-i Islami-yi Afghanistan (Islamic Society of Afghanistan)
KAM	Da Kargaro Istakhbarati Muassisa (Workers' Intelligence Agency)
KDS	Kabul Domestic Service
KhAD	Khidamat-i Ittila'at-i Dawlati (State Information Services)
KRAN	Kabul Radio Afghanistan Network
NCS	National Commanders Shura
NFF	National Fatherland Front
NGO	Non-governmental organization
NIFA	National Islamic Front of Afghanistan
NPP	National Progressive Party
NSA	National Security Archive
NSD	National Security Directive
NSS	National Salvation Society
NWFP	Northwest Frontier Province
OIC	Organization of the Islamic Conference
OIR	Organization of the Islamic Revolution (Iran)
PDPA	People's Democratic Party of Afghanistan
R.A.	Republic of Afghanistan
R.C.	Revolutionary Council
SAMA	Sazman-i Azadbakhsh-i Mardum-i Afghanistan (Liberation Organization of the People of Afghanistan)
SAZA	Sazman-i Inqilabi-yi Zahmatkishanan-i Afghanistan (Revolutionary Organization of the Toilers of Afghanistan)
SCA	Swedish Committee for Afghanistan
SCN	Supervisory Council of the North
SWB/FE	*Summary of World Broadcasts, Far East*
SYB	*Statistical Year Book of Afghanistan*
SZA	Sazman-i Zahmatkishanan-i Afghanistan (Organization of the Toilers of Afghanistan)
UBR	*UNHCR Background Report*
UNHCR	United Nations High Commissioner for Refugees
USAID	United States Agency for International Development
USIA	United States Information Agency
WAD	Wizarat-i Amaniyyat-i Dawlati (Ministry of State Security)

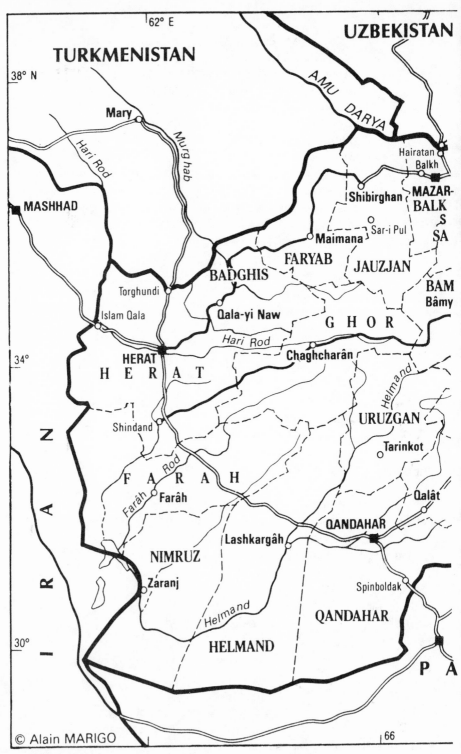

Political Map of Afghanistan and Surrounding Countries, January 1992
Note: Before 1992 the republics north of Afghanistan were part of the USSR.

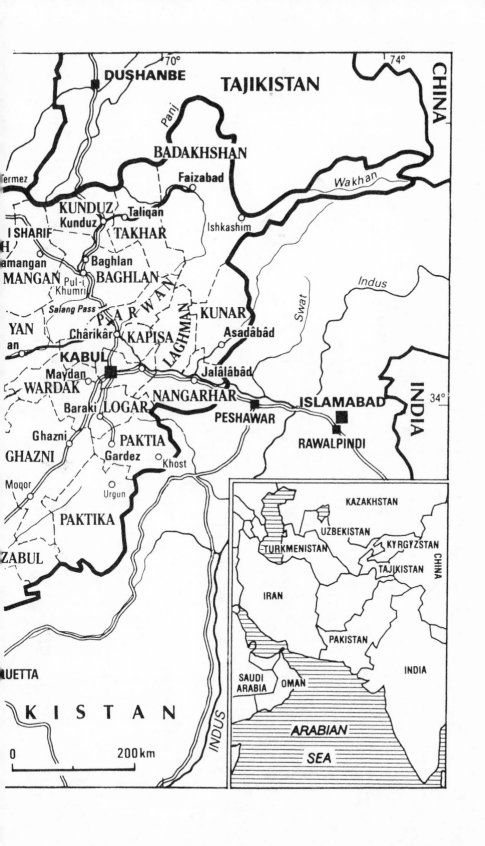

1

Afghanistan,
Mirror of
the World

On December 25, 1991, twelve years almost to the day after his predecessors had dispatched troops to Afghanistan, Soviet President Mikhail Gorbachev appeared on worldwide television to announce the dissolution of the Union of Soviet Socialist Republics. Within a week, at the start of 1992, an agreement took effect between the United States and the USSR (or the latter's successors) to end both deliveries of weapons and aid for the purchase of weapons to all parties in Afghanistan. The conflict fueled by those weapons had killed nearly a million of that country's fifteen to seventeen million people, driven over five million refugees to neighboring countries, and displaced two to three million more within Afghanistan's increasingly porous borders.[1]

Eleven weeks later, President Najibullah of Afghanistan also appeared on television, to announce his resignation. Once the United Nations had established an "interim government," Najibullah said, he would transfer to it all "powers and executive authority."[2] The loss of Soviet aid and collapse of the Soviet model, however, soon deprived Najibullah of any powers and executive authority to transfer. Less than a month later, as Najibullah tried to leave the country, mutinous armed forces blocked him from the airport, and he sought refuge in the U.N. offices in Kabul.

Even before the establishment of an interim government by a shaky coalition of *mujahidin* (Islamic resistance fighters), an iconic post–Cold War scene began to play itself out on the streets of the Afghan capital. As had already happened in Mogadishu and was soon to happen in Sarajevo, ethnic and factional battles killed thousands, devastated the city, blocked food and medical supplies, and increasingly threatened to split the country. These battles called into question not only the composition of the government but the nature—and existence—of the state.

As the world satellite communications networks momentarily focused on Kabul, I appeared on CNN, BBC, CBC, Deutsche Welle, and National Public Radio to answer the questions of the educated, prosperous, literate, peaceful, and (briefly) concerned Western world. Why were these people fighting? Were they "Islamic fundamental-

Figure 1.1 Cartoon by Tony Auth, *Philadelphia Inquirer*

Source: AUTH copyright 1992 The Philadelphia Inquirer. Reprinted with permission of UNI-
VERSAL PRESS SYNDICATE. All rights reserved.

ists" or "ethnic nationalists"? Now that the Soviet-imposed government had fallen,
were the Afghans reverting to their "tribal" traditions? Had American policy "succeeded" or "failed"?

The "freedom fighters" of the Reagan doctrine now appeared enigmatic and
atavistic. Afghanistan gained enough brief celebrity to merit a mention on NBC's
comedy program *Saturday Night Live,* where Kevin Nealon's Weekend Update news-
caster tried, and failed, to wrap his tongue around a series of increasingly unpro-
nounceable names. The cartoonist Tony Auth of the *Philadelphia Inquirer* showed a
bearded, turbaned man lofting a flintlock rifle and shouting, "Allah be praised!
Afghanistan is rid of Communism, that 20th century anachronism . . . and free," he
continues in the next frame, as a mob of his brothers slash each other with scimitars,
"to return to the 11th century" (Figure 1.1).

The basic weapon of the Afghan mujahidin, of course, was neither the Lee-
Enfield flintlock rifle, so popular with the Afghan tribes during the Anglo-Afghan
wars, nor the scimitar of Saladin, but the AK-47 (Kalashnikov) rifle. Indeed, as
Najibullah was confronting the revolts that forced him from power, Mikhail T. Kalashnikov, seventy-two years old and very much a man of the twentieth century, spoke
to the *New York Times* from Izhevsk, in the Russian Urals. Kalashnikov opposed plans
to turn the factory that produced his famous rifles there into a commercial arms-
exporting venture and spoke of establishing a foundation to treat the victims of rifle
wounds. Two years later, on April 14, 1994, Boris Yeltsin awarded Kalashnikov a

pension of 145,000 rubles (eighty dollars) per month for "special services to the Motherland."[3]

All of these people—Kalashnikov, the Afghans who used the rifles he had designed, the Americans whose tax dollars (together with Saudi petrodollars) bought so many of those rifles for delivery to the mujahidin (from factories in Egypt and China, from stocks captured in Lebanon by Israel), and the Soviet and Afghan officers and conscripts fighting against the mujahidin with rifles made in Izhevsk—all inhabited the same century. The security of some and the insecurity of others, our "modernity" and their "tradition," are parts of a simultaneous, linked, fragmented world. The agony of the citizens of Kabul and the fury of those who have subjected them to their agony represent at least as much of this century's experience as does the security that we and the Soviets tried to guarantee by sending Mr. Kalashnikov's rifle around the world in millions of mass-produced copies.

From Europe's first encounters with Afghan tribes and states, these Muslim men of the mountains have represented to the West the firmest resistance to its power and domination. The Afghans' resistance made them totally other, yet also stamped them as emblematic of a Western male romantic ideal, as in Kipling's ballad of the encounter between a Pashtun tribesman and a Scottish colonel's son:

Oh, East is East, and West is West, and never the twain shall meet,
Till Earth and Sky stand presently at God's great Judgment Seat;
But there is neither East nor West, Border, nor Breed, nor Birth,
When two strong men stand face to face, though they come from the ends of
the earth![4]

The women, too, became icons of ferocity for Kipling and his readers:

When you're wounded and left on Afghanistan's plains,
And the women come out to cut up what remains,
Jest roll to your rifle and blow out your brains
An' go to your Gawd like a soldier.[5]

Similar if less frankly expressed tropes dominated both Western and Soviet images of the Afghan-Soviet war. For the Soviets and their Afghan allies, the culture and society of Afghanistan were "tribal" or "feudal."[6] For the more "progressive" Soviet social scientists and scholars, as for many of their Western counterparts, Afghanistan was "traditional."

Americans and other supporters of the mujahidin admired the Afghans' resistance to an "evil" version of modernity, while still sharing, by and large, the view that the resistance represented ancient ways—perhaps admirable, if doomed—resisting the modern, centralized state. Soviets and Americans alike assumed that the inhabitants of powerful states with large armies and weapons factories knew the present and the future, while the Afghans knew only the past. The question was merely how quickly and how violently, and under whose sponsorship, to force or invite them into our modernity.

The political form of modernity is the territorial nation-state. During the Cold War, the two blocs represented opposed versions of the modern regime but a common model of the state. With the defeat of fascism and then communism, the discourse of the victor now claims capitalist democracy—the market and the election—as the end of modernity, if not, as Francis Fukuyama would have it, of History itself. The end of the great ideological struggles would lead to the normalization or Common Market-ization of world politics.[7]

In accordance with these ideas, the State Department where Fukuyama had served turned increasingly after the collapse of communism to "free and fair elections" as the means to resolve "regional conflicts" left from the Cold War. The confident winners and repentant losers of the Cold War agreed on a plan to replace Najibullah with an interim government that would hold "free and fair elections, in accord with Afghan traditions," to choose a "broad-based government."[8]

Did the failure of this plan represent a rejection by the Afghans of Western modernity's model of a democratic nation-state in favor of Islamic fundamentalism, ethnic identity, and tribalism? Such an argument attributes political outcomes directly to ideas without considering the objective circumstances, and to culture without considering the human actors who make choices using complex and often contradictory cultural resources.

Take the example of democracy. Democracy, in the liberal tradition, consists of procedures for making the government accountable to society so that society can govern itself by means of the state. Both "state" and "society," however, are historically contingent. Unless a state exercises effective control within borders, there is no means by which a government, however chosen, can govern. Without effective boundaries, not only on the ground but between citizens and noncitizens (granting to the former and denying to the latter certain political rights), there is no bounded society to be the subject of democracy.

Democratic theorists often assume rather than analyze the state. One influential account has identified two dimensions of political life that together define a democratic regime: inclusion of citizens in the polity's institutions, and opportunities to contest state power.[9] But only a relatively strong state can create institutions broad and effective enough to include all or most of a large population, and only populations much of whose daily life depends upon state power and functions are likely to demand an institutionalized right to contest state power. A government confident of the stability and strength of its basic institutions is likely to see the right of contestation as less of a threat. The balance between the cost and benefits of repression thus depends on both the instruments of control available to the state and the degree of interdependence between state and society.

Our understanding of such phenomena as "Islamic fundamentalism," ethnic conflict, and even tribalism in its contemporary manifestations also suffers when we ignore their dependence upon the vagaries of state formation and decay. Far from a manifestation of the persistence of "traditional" or precapitalist society, contemporary Islamic militancy is largely a response by young Muslims with modern educations to their encounter with the state and the international system in which it is embedded. Ethnic conflict results from the integration of populations into a common territorial state, creating incentives to compete for control of the internationally recognized center. And tribalism in the modern world is more often a strategy of state control or social resistance than the culture of an autarchic, kinship-based world that no longer exists, if it ever did.

The modern or postmodern world is not absent or weak in places like Afghanistan, but it exerts itself in ugly ways we prefer to deny. The fragmentation of postcolonial and post-Cold War states is the other side of the postmodern. The decline of border controls in a consolidating Europe has eased the way for Turkish syndicates to smuggle Afghan heroin from Pakistan in Panamanian-registered ships. The developed country does not, as Marx thought, show the backward country its future; the fragmenting countries show the integrating ones the dark side of their common present. The violence and decay of Afghanistan is the reflection in the mirror of that society of the violence that created and maintains our security. "If you do not like the image in the mirror," says an old Persian poem, "do not break the mirror, break your face."[10]

States, State Formation, and the Modern International System

Afghanistan confronted modernity through its forced integration into the Eurocentric state system as a buffer between the Russian and British empires. The formation and transformation of that state system created the contending forces of the conflict.

States of some sort have existed throughout history, if only because recorded "history" starts with the invention of writing by states that needed a way to record tribute. Charles Tilly defines states in general as "coercion-wielding organizations that are distinct from households and kinship groups and exercise clear priority in some respects over all other organizations within substantial territories."[11]

Such a definition includes what Anthony Giddens calls the *traditional state* and what others refer to as *empires,* as well as city-states and federations of towns.[12] These states included a core organization that fought and taxed. Rarely did such empires directly administer areas outside of cities and towns. They dealt with most of the rural or nomadic population as corporate groups. Control faded out toward ill-defined frontiers rather than shifting suddenly at monitored borders.

Today's state—called the *national state* by Tilly and more commonly called the *nation-state* or *modern state*—differs from such previous ones in a number of ways. Tilly defines national states as those "governing multiple contiguous regions and their cities by means of centralized, differentiated, and autonomous structures."[13] Thus the modern state not only wields coercion in a territory but actually "governs" it, making and enforcing uniform rules, and it does so through particular structures: bureaucracies, armies, police, courts.

These structures are what Max Weber focused on in his characterization (not definition) of the modern state:

> It possesses an administrative and legal order subject to change by legislation, to which the organized corporate activity of the administrative staff, which is also regulated by legislation, is oriented. This system of order claims binding authority, not only over the members of the state, the citizens, most of whom have obtained membership by birth, but also to a very large extent, over all action taking place in the area of its jurisdiction. It is thus a compulsory association with a territorial basis. Furthermore, today, the use of force is regarded as legitimate only so far as it is either permitted by the state or prescribed by it. . . . The claim of the modern state to monopolize the use of force is as essential to it as its character of compulsory jurisdiction and of continuous organization.[14]

All national states have citizens who share at least a juridical nationality. Juridical nationality may correspond more or less to ethnicity, but all states try to promote some "nationalism" based on the common history and fate of the territorial community, sometimes identified with a core ethnic group.[15] I shall use the terms *nation-state* or *modern state* interchangeably to refer to the entities composing the contemporary international state system, including Afghanistan, but the use of this term does not presuppose that the unit in question fully or even greatly shares the characteristics of a Weberian ideal type. Nor does it assume any commitment to nationalism on the part of the juridical citizens of the state.

The nation-state developed in the cities and on the battlefields of early modern Europe. Feudal Europe contained both multiple centers of military power—states or would-be states—and a dense network of cities, the loci of capital accumulation. Because no state grew large enough to subordinate the others in an empire, continual military competition led rulers to seek to strengthen their armies. The accumulation and mobility of capital, together with the development of industry and its application to warmaking, changed the relation of states to the economy. Unlike traditional empires, where expansion of the resource base of the state depended mainly on the conquest of trade routes or agricultural regions, states now relied on the accumulation of productive capital and technology in cities. Relative success in these ventures determined which states prevailed, survived, and founded the state system.

Promoting capitalist development required a legal system, a stable currency, and public order. Hence effective administration, including police forces and mechanisms for surveillance of the population, contributed to success as well. Surveillance required the storage of information, which typically is more important than the direct application of coercion to the "infrastructural power" of the modern state.[16]

Intense interactions between the nation-state and those under its rule, especially over taxation, gave rise to conflicts over legitimacy articulated in terms such as *rights* and *citizenship*. State formation thus created demands for incorporation or participation by citizens in the functioning of the state. Such demands could be satisfied through pluralist democracy, or they could be controlled through corporatist representation, totalitarian mobilization, or the coercive exclusion of some groups from politics. All of these, however, differed from the weak engagement between ruler and ruled in the premodern state. Administering such a system required not only capital and weapons but trained officials and a doctrine of legitimacy. How states trained their officials and citizens affected their relations to both the international system and the society they ruled or served.

In premodern states and empires the low level of interaction of most of the population with the state corresponded to the low level of literacy. In such states, reading and writing were the province of relatively small groups of specialists employed by either the state or a religious hierarchy. Subjecting the population of a territory to more centralized surveillance or control, however, required that laws, state decisions, and ideologies be disseminated and legitimated more widely.

The growth of the state apparatus itself required the expansion of the educated stratum that staffs it. State building also required standardization of language, both in order to regulate the use of language in government documents and to assure communication with the citizenry. The vernacular education systems that developed as a result frequently become centers for the development of nationalism.[17]

Nation-states did not develop one by one and form a system by juxtaposition; modern states grew out of conflict and other interactions within a system of such states. This competition forced rulers to encourage capitalists, whose capital and technology might give the developing state an edge over its competitors.[18]

As the state system expanded to cover more of the globe, wars and negotiations among previously existing states increasingly determined the establishment of later states.[19] The colonial expansion encouraged by the competitive state system and the expanding capitalist market of Europe ultimately spread this local process around the globe until it became a universal, self-monitoring system.

The rulers of later nation-states encountered different challenges and opportunities from those faced by state builders in the original core of the system. Rulers could no longer establish colonial empires to enrich themselves. A state's boundaries and identity were determined not only by its own struggles, but by institutions or dominant powers of the international system. Late state builders confronted an established global economy and found themselves in an international diplomatic and legal system that dictated certain uniform characteristics of states and enunciated laws and norms for their behavior. The dominant states had already developed military and administrative technologies dependent on industrial production. They subsequently formed alliance systems that used their oligopolistic control of these technologies to offer incentives and threats to rulers on the European periphery and the postcolonial states that during the Cold War came to be called the Third World.

This change in the international context transformed the process of state building. The "resource structure available to the would-be elite bent on creating or dominating a state" came to include new alternatives and to exclude some previously available. This formulation applies not only to rulers but also to such would-be rulers as insurgents or revolutionaries.[20]

The resource structure available to European state builders included different mixes of capital owned by merchants living in cities under their control; "coercive resources"—soldiers, horse, weapons; and cultural resources that they employed with varying success to elaborate doctrines of legitimacy and to train loyal officials and citizens. Institutions developed endogenously, creating a state integrated with society both structurally and culturally.

Later state builders often set about building and wielding state institutions consciously modeled on those developed elsewhere. They could tap external sources for access to capital, the means of coercion and administration, or professional training. Just as the importation of established production processes could create disarticulated economies, the importation of techniques of rule also exacted a cost in social and political integration.

Depending on their mode of integration into the world state system and market, states outside the European core, like states in different regions of Europe, exhibited different mixtures of capital and coercion. Some colonies—especially those with European settlers—attracted investment and consequently developed infrastructure that promoted capitalist development. At the other extreme, some peripheral countries or territories interested the imperialist powers only for their location, as a means of protecting another rich holding or blocking a competitor. In such countries the needs of the imperial power were met not by capital, but by military forces to maintain control. Afghanistan's role in the colonial world system was to block Russian advance toward British India; hence the British supported the construction of a state with a preponderance of coercive resources.

Capital can be obtained from any number of sources: sales of a scarce natural resource belonging to the state, such as oil; returns to investments on international markets financed by such sales; taxes on the export of primary commodities produced in an enclave, whether foreign or locally owned; remittances from citizens working abroad in richer countries; direct investment by transnational corporations; loans from foreign commercial banks; loans from public multilateral institutions; loans or grants from foreign governments or intergovernmental organizations; and loans or grants from foreign private foundations or voluntary organizations. Various foreign or international organizations also provide training and consulting services in the technical skills involved in the mobilization and use of capital.

Similarly, coercive resources are available in the form of military or police assistance packages, including the supply or coproduction of weapons and the training of personnel in their use. Postcolonial states (or insurgents) do not need to develop their own capacities to produce weapons as long as others are willing to sell or give them. Equipment for organizing, monitoring, and controlling populations (censuses, surveys, audits, policing) is also available from more developed states or international agencies.

Finally, states, international organizations, and private groups offer aid in legitimating governments, whether through conducting democratic elections or building Marxist-Leninist vanguard parties.

In some cases particular organizations, such as commercial banks, transnational corporations, or weapons manufacturers (public or private) may supply these resources in search of profit. In other cases resources, such as oil rents or labor remittances, accrue to the state through the market from more diffuse sources.[21]

Under colonialism, resources flowed to and from the colonial areas as imperial powers sought both profit and military advantage. During the half-century before the end of the Cold War, decolonization increased the bargaining leverage of some postcolonial rulers. Juridical sovereignty enabled these rulers to exert greater control over the resources that became available as a by-product of competition between the two blocs. Such locational rents largely financed the expansion of the state apparatus in Afghanistan after 1955.

Similarly, *human* capital became available to Third World states without their having to develop the technical or cultural means to produce and reproduce it domestically. At the limit, bureaucracies were largely supervised by foreign advisers, as in some of former French West Africa or Soviet-occupied Afghanistan. More commonly, many of the state elites received training from elsewhere in the international system. Administrators and teachers have received scholarships to study at universities in Europe, America, or the USSR. Military officers have undergone training in the same places. Islamic legal officials have been educated at al-Azhar University of Cairo if they are Sunni or in Najaf or Qom if they are Shi'a. Many United Nations specialized agencies have provided various sorts of training for Third World officials. The international training of state elites in peripheral countries has markedly different effects on national integration than has the training through national educational systems in core countries.

Tribe and State

Tilly argued that the absence of extensive kinship or tribal organizations favored the development of the national state in Western Europe. As Bertrand Badie and Pierre Birnbaum note, in parts of the Third World, states face societies that maintain "the persistence of tribal structures, the crucial importance of kinship, and the limited individualization of property rights in land." Research on the Middle East and South Asia points to the continuing interaction of tribe and caste with states. The study of state formation in the Middle East, in particular, has revived interest in the theories of Abd al-Rahman Ibn Khaldun on the relation of tribes, states, and Islam.[22]

Both Ibn Khaldun and traditional anthropology have seen tribe as prior to state or as a lower form of development. More recent research, however, shows that tribe, at least in its Middle East and Central Asian versions, always exists in interaction with state. Tribe is one of several models of social organization available to tribespeople. Which model people act on depends upon how tribe interacts in a particular situation with another model, that of state. Hence tribespeople may choose not to act on a tribal basis, while nonetheless holding the tribal model in reserve:

> [T]ribe and state are best thought of as two opposed modes of thought or models of organization that form a single system. As a basis for identity, political allegiance, and behavior, tribe gives primacy to ties of kinship and patrilineal descent, whereas state insists on the loyalty of all persons to a central authority, whatever their relation to each other. Tribe stresses personal, moral, and ascriptive factors in status; state is impersonal and recognizes contract, transaction, and achievement. The tribal mode is socially homogeneous, egalitarian, and segmentary; the state is heterogeneous, stratified, and hierarchical. Tribe is within the individual; state is external.[23]

This view grants to tribespeople the power to choose between tribal and nontribal modes of interaction, allowing for the possibility of a political transformation in which they act, rather than only being acted upon. Tribal people might join nontribal or antitribal political movements; conversely, even after the apparent destruction of tribalism by a state, tribalism might reemerge during a period of state weakness or collapse.[24]

The tribal model depicts tribes as largely self-governing groups of people united by a "group feeling" (Ibn Khaldun's *asabiyya*) based on a belief in common kinship. While a state claims authority over society within a *territory,* a tribe claims jurisdiction over a set of *persons* bound by kinship relations.[25]

Kinship-based political institutions, like territorial ones, have different political structures or regime types. Tribes of the type studied by Ibn Khaldun are egalitarian and structured according to a segmentary lineage system. This tribal type, found all across the Middle East, includes Berbers, Arabs, Kurds, and Pashtuns. According to Ernest Gellner, "A vital aspect of segmentary society is *nesting.* Groups contain subgroups, which in turn contain other subgroups, whose relationship to each other is once again similar. There is no preeminent or crucial level of social organization."[26]

As there is no central authority, feuds among these groups and subgroups are "the most characteristic institution of such a society." In the absence of a state or legal system, the blood feud is the main institution for the enforcement of justice. These feuds are pursued in a population where "in practice all adult males take part in organized violence and share the risks involved."[27] Leadership is weak and there is no unambiguous rule of succession.

Another type of tribe, the Turco-Mongolian type, is much more hierarchical. This type formed the basis of the military power of such great Turkic and Mongolian dynasties as the Mongol, Timurid, Ottoman, Mughal, and Safavid empires.[28] Egalitarian tribes, however, torn by feuds and rivalries, tend to have difficulties generating large-scale political leadership. Religion (in this region, Islam) provides an important means of conciliating feuding groups or forging broader political coalitions for raid or conquest.[29] Holy lineages, including "saints," often claiming descent from the Prophet and presiding over shrines, provide neutral arbiters respected by all parties. The mainly urban and orthodox Islamic scholars (*ulama*) also provide cultural resources, both legal and scriptural, needed for consolidating larger coalitions.

In Ibn Khaldun's formulation, the military prowess of the tribes enabled them to conquer the towns and settled areas whenever they were united, especially by a religious passion. Tribes could establish a state based on the military power of the unified tribal group and the legal and administrative skills of the townsmen, especially the ulama. But tribal organization broke down in the luxurious conditions of settled rule, leading to the decline of the dynasty in three or four generations.

In a passage of extraordinary relevance to Afghanistan, Gellner describes the dilemma of tribally based would-be state builders:

> Tribal chieftains proper did not possess the resource base for creating professional armies and bureaucracies. Their armed forces were the tribe, activated by conflict or prospect of loot or by inspired leadership. This characteristic was both their strength and their weakness. The tribal military unit was a preexisting social group, endowed with cohesion by its shared experience and concerns and habituated by the normal conditions of its life to mobility, violence, and frugality. The continuity between the social and military existences of the tribal armed forces often made them formidable; they did not need, like ordinary recruits, to be specially trained and endowed with an artificial esprit de corps. They arrived, fully trained and *encadré,* with recognized leaders and a familiarity with the terrain in which they were to be deployed.
>
> Their weakness lay in the very same attributes. Their social organization predisposed them to fissiparousness as well as cohesion. The lack of a separation between their civil and military roles made them exceedingly responsive to pressures other than the long-term plans of the supreme command. Notoriously, they went home when it suited them, oblivious to strategic considerations. Seasonal obligations and customs meant at least as much to them as long-term strategy. Hence any tribal chief whose domain came to exceed a purely tribal base naturally attempted to supplement and balance his tribal following by a professional, individually recruited armed force composed of mercenaries and slaves.[30]

Gellner thus argues that the *mamluk* option was one way a dynasty of tribal origin could transform itself into a longer-lived empire.[31] In this system the tribal rulers created a military and bureaucratic corps whose members were slaves of the ruler. The mamluks or janissaries were raised from childhood away from tribe and kin in order to inculcate in them loyalty only to the ruler. Different mixtures of tribalism, slave bureaucracy, and religious authority (saintly or clerical) characterized different state forms in the region.

Effects on State-Society Relations

Both the international system and the largely or partly tribal structure of society have far-reaching effects on the relation of the state to the society. The availability to the state of internationally supplied money, weapons, and training enables it to become stronger, "overdeveloped," or "autonomous" with respect to the society under its rule.[32] Arms may be had without industrialization, revenue without capital accumulation, growth of the state without bargaining between rulers and ruled.

Although these resources may promote autonomy from the society under the state's rule, they may also promote dependence on the state or organization that provides the resources. Such direct political dependence (as opposed to a more generalized economic dependence on the international capitalist market) is more likely when the resources come from a single, identifiable transnational actor rather than, say, from the oil market. Nonetheless, the legal reality of international sovereignty as well as the difficulty donors have in monitoring recipient governments often enables apparently dependent governments to exercise some autonomy from international patrons.[33]

Autonomy can describe a range of possibilities. A state autonomous from domestic society might be capable of restructuring that society for redistributive or developmental goals; or it might exercise unrestrained predatory powers over the population without fear of opposition or overthrow. Autonomy specifically from dominant or partial interests (rather than from all domestic groups outside of the state) may be quite consistent with links to society through political institutions. Such institutions as political parties may enable the state to take and implement collective decisions as the agent of an otherwise weak majority in society. This ability requires not only autonomy, but also the capacity to implement and monitor policy. State autonomy combined with a high level of state capacity, but without mechanisms of accountability, may enable a unified state elite to carry out social transformations, even some so radical as to qualify as a "revolution from above."[34]

The former type of autonomy in particular illustrates that the state is not external to society but rather a part of it, and that relations between state and society need not be zero-sum. The strength of an accountable state with a high capacity to manage policy can augment the strength of its society by enlarging the scope of collective actions it can take. In other cases, however, despite the overdevelopment of its apparatus, the state may lack the capacity to act as a coherent agent of collective interests. Rather than coordinating or transforming society, the state is merely "one organization among many" engaged in a struggle for social control. Its autonomy may amount to little more than the pursuit of the interest—ideological or material—of the stratum that staffs it.[35]

Indeed, the external resources that enable the state to become autonomous from society may ultimately inhibit it from developing the capacity to carry out its policies. Michael Mann has suggested a distinction between "despotic" and "infrastructural" power of the state. Despotic power enables the state to undertake actions "without routine, institutionalized negotiation with civil society groups." The typical example of despotic power is arbitrary coercion. External resources can strengthen the state's ability to exercise despotic power. Infrastructural power, on the other hand, is "the capacity of the state actually to penetrate civil society, and to implement logistically political decisions throughout the realm." Infrastructural power requires apparatuses of monitoring and surveillance more than of coercion.[36] Although external resources can give the state certain technical capabilities in these areas, successful development of these capacities has generally arisen out of the core state-society struggles over extraction and compliance, in which organized groups in civil society allow the state access to resources (including information) in return for citizenship rights and social services. Such bargains are the heart of the legitimacy of the modern state.

Availability of external resources reduces (although it never removes) the need to struggle with social groups over state policies. State building with external resources can also occur before domestic capitalist development. The most extreme such cases are the "rentier states," those that depend on oil revenues or foreign aid rather than on production of goods and services by their citizens. Hence the state may be well equipped, but not accountable; it may lack a sophisticated, differentiated apparatus capable of penetrating civil society; and a noncapitalist or nonmonetized society may pose costly obstacles to monitoring and information gathering.[37] Alfred Stepan expresses the paradox of an autonomous state with little infrastructural power in his discussion of military regimes that wish to institutionalize an "organic-statist" social order after taking power in a coup d'état: "While autonomy may be a source of strength in the installation phase, in the institutionalization phase relative autonomy may be a source of weakness because a state elite is not sustained by constituencies in civil society and therefore is almost exclusively dependent upon its own internal unity and coercive powers. The other side of the coin of autonomy is thus isolation and fragility."[38] Though written for a book on Peru, this passage captures well the situation of the Afghan Communists after they took power.

Furthermore, the expansion of the state apparatus itself has effects on society. As noted above, expansion of the state apparatus requires training a stratum of people to work for it. While these people work for an institution called the "state," they themselves are part of society. Their personal interests may become identified with the expansion of the power of the state at the expense of other groups in society. An ideology of progress or modernization, whether through socialist revolution or capitalist accumulation, may legitimate the power of these groups. Particularly when the state does not depend for its resources on domestic production organized by property-owning classes under its rule, the stratum of state officials may seek autonomy in their own interests. In some cases, such autonomy may be simply predatory, with each official engaging in "rent-seeking activities" for personal enrichment. At times, however, officials may organize collectively, with the support of army officers, to seize power and attempt a "revolution from above," restructuring the society in the image of the state's modernity. The ideology of progress that legitimates their actions may be in fact "the ideology of their own social advancement."[39]

This isolation from domestic social constituencies as a result of dependent state formation may also explain the brutality of some such autonomous states. Badie and Birnbaum, for instance, attribute the prevalence of authoritarian or despotic forms of state power in the Third World partly to conflict between the values and goals inherent to the imported state and the societies it rules. Similarly, in his analysis of the origins of bureaucratic authoritarian regimes in South America, Guillermo O'Donnell linked the imposition of bureaucratic-authoritarian regimes to the attempt by military officers and economic technocrats to apply to their own countries doctrines they learned during training in more developed societies.[40]

State-society relations, of course, depend not only on the structure of the state but on that of society outside the state. In Joel Migdal's words, "The ineffectiveness of state leaders who have faced impenetrable barriers to state predominance has stemmed from the nature of the societies they have confronted—from the resistance posed by chiefs, landlords, bosses, rich peasants, clan leaders, *za'im, effendis, aghas, caciques, kulaks* (for convenience 'strongmen') through their various social organizations."[41]

Third World societies have been shaped both by such forms of social organization as tribe and by varying encounters with colonialism and postcolonial states. In the developed world the state achieved predominance by defeating rivals for power. States in the Third World, because of their relation to the international system described above, could grow on the basis of external resources without defeating rivals who controlled resources within their territories. People in search of strategies of survival—"blueprints for action or belief"—in such states may be offered alternatives to the state by other institutions, such as strongmen or tribes.[42]

According to Ibn Khaldun, "A dynasty rarely establishes itself firmly in lands with many different tribes and groups." Migdal similarly notes that the mixture of groups in many Asian and African states complicates the states' tasks: "First, the groups exercising social control in a society may be heterogeneous both in their form (for example, a small family and a sprawling tribal organization) and in the rules they apply. . . . Second, the distribution of social control in society may be among numerous, fairly autonomous groups rather than concentrated largely in the state. . . . In this mélange, the state has been one organization among many."[43] Migdal calls such fragmented societies weblike. The state can snip away a part, but the rest persists. There are no centers of power to conquer like the forts of the feudal lords of France.

Where the population is fragmented and not integrated into a single national society, the state cannot represent a common interest. The state is instead another particular interest. In a society where tribal allegiances persist, the nation-state's apparatus may be captured by a particular solidarity group, like the Alawite clans in Syria or the Takritis in Iraq. Even political parties that take power in the name of universalist ideologies often are in fact disguised forms of such solidarities.[44]

These identities, however, do not represent "traditional" forces overpowering the "modern." As noted above, tribes or local strongmen were often created or mobilized as agents of control by colonial or postcolonial states. The struggle by states for control over tribal territories required the transformation of free tribes into taxpaying peasants. In more capital-rich areas of Europe, social processes had created individuals available for proletarianization or state control. On the periphery of these areas, however, the state tried to create strong landlords who in turn depended on it rather than on local society for their power, just as the state itself may have depended on international patrons. The imposed state engendered the imposed chief.[45]

Despite its isolation from the international capitalist market and its successful resistance to direct colonial rule, Afghanistan, too, was part of this system. Its rulers' attempts to consolidate a strong, independent, central state all failed. The resources needed for strength came at the price of independence; complete independence of action led to weakness and instability. To compensate for the state's weakness, its leaders encouraged further fragmentation of Afghanistan's society. The "traditionalism" and "localism" of Afghanistan are not survivals of ancient traditions but rather the results of the country's forced integration into the contemporary state system.

Part One

The Old Regime:

State, Society,

and Politics

In 1789, on the eve of the French Revolution, 85 percent of that country's population were peasants, and agriculture accounted for 60 percent of production. Most of the agricultural land was divided into small holdings.[1] In 1978, on the eve of the "Sawr [April] Revolution" in Afghanistan, 85 percent of the population were peasants or nomads, and agriculture accounted for 60 percent of production. Most of the agricultural land was divided into small holdings. But in France in 1789, the tax burden imposed by the absolutist state fell mainly on the peasants, whereas in Afghanistan in 1978, the peasants paid virtually no taxes. The government relied instead on links to an international state system and market that had hardly existed two centuries earlier. The state paid its soldiers and bureaucrats with revenue from foreign aid, sales of natural gas, and taxes on a few export commodities. Despite their common antifeudal discourse, these two revolutions and the reactions to them differed as much as the states they overthrew.

Through most of history, the region now included within the boundaries of Afghanistan was a borderland between empires that ruled from India, Iran, or Tartary (Central Asia). Its people lived off duties levied on the long-distance traders who crossed their lands by such roads as the famous Silk Route; they also grazed animals and cultivated crops on areas that enjoyed an adequate water supply. Conquest by Genghis Khan in the thirteenth century and the opening of the sea route between Europe and Asia in the fifteenth century sent the region into decline. In the sixteenth century the "gunpowder empires" founded by various Turco-Mongol conquerors— Ottomans, Safavids, Shaybanid Uzbeks, Mughals—dominated the west Asian land mass. The latter three fought over the territory of today's Afghanistan and divided it among themselves.

When these Turco-Mongol dynasties declined in the eighteenth century, a group of Pashtun tribes—their military organization strengthened by service to the Safavids—founded their own empire. That state drew its resources from conquests in the surrounding richer areas, especially India. Like other tribal conquest empires it proved unstable.

In the nineteenth century Afghanistan encountered the Europe-centered state system when Russia and Britain advanced through Central Asia and India. Afghan rulers tried to maintain their independence by copying military and other models from these empires. After two Anglo-Afghan wars, Afghanistan formally entered the state system under British suzerainty, as a buffer against Russia. To strengthen this state and stabilize the northwest frontier of India, the British lavished weapons and cash on Amir Abdul Rahman Khan (reigned 1881–1901). Abdul Rahman Khan used these coercive resources to establish the basic state structure that endured until the fall of Najibullah in 1992: a Pashtun ruler using external resources to reign over an ethnically heterogeneous society while manipulating that social segmentation to weaken society's resistance.

Abdul Rahman Khan's grandson, King Amanullah Khan, won independence for his country in the brief Third Anglo-Afghan War (1919). Without steady foreign aid, however, he could not implement his plan to transform Afghanistan into a modern autocracy like Ataturk's Turkey and Reza Shah's Iran. He was toppled by tribal and religious revolts in 1929.

His successors of the Musahiban dynasty (Nadir Shah, Zahir Shah, and Daoud Khan) encapsulated rather than confronted social resistance, imposing an external administration laid over the existing society. The Musahiban rulers tried to create an export enclave based on such primary products as fruit and karakul lambskins, for example, but these were too few to support a major state-building effort. During the Cold War, however, when Afghanistan regained its historical strategic significance, the Soviet Union and the United States poured aid into the Afghan state. This aid enabled the rulers to build an army, schools, roads, and bureaucracy without directly confronting resistance from rural power-holders. The Soviet Union became the major aid giver, sponsoring in particular the recruitment and equipping of a one hundred thousand-man army. From 1955 to 1978 the Soviet Union provided Afghanistan with $1.27 billion in economic aid and roughly $1.25 billion in military aid, while the United States furnished $533 million in economic aid.[2]

Aid enabled the state to expand its organization and influence without attempting an economic or social transformation of the countryside, but Afghan society was changed nonetheless by the introduction of new social actors: the "intelligentsia" trained for state service, including military service, in the foreign aid–supported state schools and in foreign countries. Although the state succeeded in insulating itself from the tribal forces that had threatened past dynasties, it increasingly depended on this new stratum, members of which increasingly adopted radical political ideologies, from communism to Islamism.

Rather than try to penetrate the countryside and govern it, the Afghan state continued to pursue a strategy of encapsulating traditional local institutions.[3] The political elite did not rule the people of Afghanistan by representing them and managing conflicts. Nor did it mobilize networks of clienteles into a national organization for a political struggle against colonialism (as in India, Tunisia, and elsewhere). The Anglo-Afghan wars, fought by tribal coalitions, left no organizational legacy. Rather than incorporating the various sectors of the population into a common national political system, the political elite acted as an ethnically stratified hierarchy of intermediaries between the foreign powers providing the resources and the groups receiving the largess of patronage.

Most of the population related to the government by using kinship to obtain patronage. Each solidarity group (qawm) remained isolated, linked to the nation-state only through personal ties to individuals in the government; the qawm did not need to form nationwide alliances to capture and exercise power. Indeed, the government had for decades pursued a policy of breaking larger tribes into smaller groups and recognizing only the village-level qawm. There were no longer any politically significant broad tribal coalitions. Nor were there national institutions like the Congress in India, the Neo-Destour in Tunisia, or any number of lesser organizations elsewhere, which might have created an institutional link between patronage networks in the country-side and either the state or the national elite.[4]

The consequent political fragmentation of the population meant that the elite of the old regime had no political or organizational base from which to resist those who deposed them. This elite had become a westernized, patrimonial patronage network in Kabul; their ties to society were mediated by the largess distributed by a state they no longer controlled.

2

Social Structure under the Old Regime

The territory of today's Afghanistan consists of a major mountain range, the Hindu Kush, with its fertile but isolated valleys, and the deserts and river valleys that flank it. This territory spreads over many geographical and ecological zones, and its peoples and societies are correspondingly distinct. Only their incorporation into a state has made them into a single society.

The elements of this society are the products of thousands of years of interaction with empires and states. Rulers of the territory that constitutes today's Afghanistan could draw on the wealth of well-irrigated river basins and on the long-distance trade routes—notably the Silk Route—that traversed its mountain passes. Genghis Khan destroyed many towns and much of the irrigation network in the thirteenth century; as a result much of the remaining population reverted to nomadism.[1] The Timurid Dynasty, based in the oasis of Herat, reconsolidated an empire in the area, only to fall in the sixteenth century to simultaneous pressure from new dynasties: the Safavids to the west, the Mughals to the east, and the Shaybanid Uzbeks to the north. Interaction with these empires affected the social structure and capacity for collective action of the peoples of Afghanistan in the seventeenth and eighteenth centuries. Indeed, the names of several ethnic groups (Hazaras, Aimaqs) were originally political designations deriving from their roles in tribal empires of the Turco-Mongolian type.

Kinship, Qawm, Tribe, Ethnicity

For all peoples of Afghanistan, kinship has been an essential means to mobilize political or economic resources. For instance, here is a description of a Pashtun landowning family near Girishk, Helmand Province, encountered by Swiss economist Gilbert Etienne in the late 1960s:

> In the same region, we visit Haji Gul Mohammed. . . . With his three brothers and their families, they constitute a group of 70 people, economically active in

the city and the countryside. They have 7 hectares [about 17 acres] of land and 3 shops in the bazaar (clothes, haberdashery, purchased at Kandahar). . . .

For three years now they have used the new varieties [of seeds] on all of their wheat fields (4 ha.) [ten acres]. They use chemical fertilizer and manure. The overly aggressive sparrows are chased away by five young boys of the family. Haji Gul Mohammed also cultivates a little cotton and maize.

He employs four *bozgars* [sharecroppers] who provide only their labor. They drive the four bulls of the landowners ("Brown Swiss" variety), which are remarkably stronger than the local types. Six well-cared-for cows furnish the milk consumed by this large, undivided family.[2]

In this extended patrilineal family, the sons inherited their father's property and continued to work it in common. Such large undivided families represent the ideal of most cultural groups, although in fact the nuclear family is the most typical.[3]

Afghanistan remains a patrilineal society, in which membership in both family and lineage, as well as property, is inherited only by agnatic kin. Clusters of agnatic kin form close alliances to defend or expand the patrimony but also risk splitting into antagonistic factions over its management or division. Indeed, the Pashto word for intense hatred, *tarburghanay,* appears to be derived from the word for agnatic cousin, *tarbur.* Affinal kinship relations are, on the other hand, important mechanisms for mobilizing allies. Especially in a society where polygamy is practiced, marriage can create networks of startling complexity.[4]

According to Islam, a man may have up to four wives if he can maintain them and treat them equally, and polygamy allows men of greater wealth to enlarge their power by increasing the size of their families.[5] Family members, male and female, contribute labor to the family enterprise. Sons and grandsons can earn money in other employment and provide a reserve of physical force. Educated women in Kabul can also bring home wages. Daughters, too, are an important political and economic resource because marriage agreements symbolize and cement alliances, and because daughters' marriages bring considerable brideprices. Marriage thus affects the economic well-being and political and social standing of an entire family and can hardly be left to the individual choice of the prospective mates. As elsewhere in Asia and the Middle East, marriage is a public decision of two families, not a private decision of two individuals.[6]

Marriage is an exchange between families in which one gives a bride in return for a substantial brideprice. According to Islam, the bride must receive a gift, usually of precious metal, called *mahr,* which is her personal property and security in case of divorce. But the brideprice is a separate tradition with no formal sanction in Islam. It may be the single largest expense of a man's lifetime, frequently amounting to the equivalent of several years' income. It is often a source of significant debt.[7]

One ideal form of marriage is between cousins; in this model, two brothers or agnatic cousins marry their children to each other, keeping both the daughters and the bridewealth within the lineage and strengthening their solidarity. Another form of marriage, which emphasizes the equality of the males, is exchange of sisters; this, too, economizes on bridewealth and strengthens relations between the families. By contrast, hypergamy is a form of marriage in which a man receives a bride from a socially inferior family, formalizing patron-client relations between two families.[8]

The traditional view of sex roles in Afghanistan has developed within this structure of marriage and family. The most important duty of a man is to support and protect his family. His honor requires him to defend and control those things collectively known as *namus: zan, zar, zamin* (woman, gold, land). Zamin includes both land owned by the family and the homeland of a broader kinship group—tribe or lineage. In some contexts, zamin can mean the territory of Afghanistan.[9]

Men thus see women as the repository of their honor, and any sign of sexual misconduct—especially, but not exclusively, adultery—is a political threat to the honor and strength of a family. The punishment for such misconduct, should knowledge of it become public, is therefore swift and harsh: death among some groups, ostracism among others. At the same time, women are, within a sexual division of labor, economically productive—indeed, indispensable—members of the household. Although it generally takes place in the home, women's work extends far beyond child care and cooking. It includes elements of food processing performed by industries in more developed countries, as well as vital crafts such as carpet weaving and felt making. In poorer agricultural families, women may also work in the fields. Among pastoralists, women perform most of the tasks involved in transforming animal products (mainly milk and wool) into items of use, and among some nomads they do much of the work required by the process of annual migration.

The social customs through which male control of women is sometimes expressed are *pardah* (segregation and seclusion of women) and *chadri* (veiling; *hijab* in Arabic). The extent of each varies according to ethnic group, social class, and location. Since Montstuart Elphinstone recorded his observations in the early nineteenth century, outside observers have agreed with him that in the country "the women . . . go unveiled, and there is less restraint in the intercourse between the sexes."[10] Those who practice veiling and seclusion claim they are required by Islam; others disagree. Some educated women, especially those in the Islamic movement, contest the reading of these customs as signs of male domination and reinterpret them as signs of female self-determination within Islam.

Veiling is prevalent among urban groups that preserve tradition. Peasant women coming to urban areas, where they will encounter many strangers, may also veil themselves more thoroughly than usual. The same is true of refugee camps. The government made veiling voluntary in 1959 and firmly suppressed all protests against the liberalized policy. Veiling thereafter tended to disappear among the urban educated classes in Kabul.

Women's role was not limited to solitary hard work. Although they could not participate in the public life of the mosque and village council, women had other ways of participating in both religion and politics. Among Pashtuns women would encourage and, if necessary, shame men into defending namus. This capacity emerges at important historic junctures. The most famous such heroine is Malalai, who prevented a tribal army from retreating before the British at Maiwand in 1880 and urged them on to victory by bearing her veil aloft as a banner and shouting the famous Pashto couplet:

My beloved, if you do not fall a martyr in battle at Maiwand,
By God, someone must be saving you for a life of shame.

The Afghan-Soviet war produced its own Malalai, the sixteen-year-old schoolgirl Nahid, who is supposed to have been shot by a Soviet helicopter gunship while leading a student demonstration in Kabul in February 1980.[11]

The "family" in Afghanistan shades off into larger groupings based on kinship and other components of identity. It is common to describe this phenomenon by calling Afghanistan a tribal society. The old regime in Afghanistan firmly adhered to this analysis and used certain state-recognized tribal institutions and leaders as means of control. In rural areas (*atraf*) the district administration interacted with the population indirectly, through officially appointed representatives (called *malik* or *arbab*) of units called *qawm*. *Qawm* is sometimes translated as *tribe,* but is in reality a more protean term, referring to any form of solidarity or asabiyya. Qawm identity might be based on kinship, residence, or occupation.

For those who carried identity cards under the old regime (primarily city dwellers), the line marked *qawm* contained an ethnolinguistic designation (Pashtun, Tajik, Uzbek), like the nationality designation on Soviet internal passports. In common use *qawm* may denote various forms of identity: any level of tribal organization; an area of residence such as a village, valley, or town; a linguistically based ethnic group or "nationality"; or an occupational group similar to a caste.[12] Qawm identity can be somewhat fluid, depending on what level or form of identity is relevant to a particular setting. The royal government, however, recognized membership by rural Afghans in specific, rather small units of qawm. Such a system facilitated limited control of the population by a weak state and aimed at preventing the formation of broader tribal coalitions. It is misleading to say that the government either opposed or supported "tribalism" per se. Among tribal peoples it tried to break large units into smaller ones; among nontribal peoples it tried to reinforce limited kinship- or residence-based political identities. Such a pattern is typical of a weak state attempting to retain its power by weakening society through fragmentation.

Observers (including the state itself) have used language, religion, and descent to define several major ethnic groups in Afghanistan. Table 2.1 and Map 2.1 give the approximate numerical and geographical distribution of these somewhat artificial categories. Ethnic maps are deceptive, since no single dimension of identity—language, tribe, region—always dominates and no areas of Afghanistan are eth-

Table 2.1 Population of Main Ethnic Groups, 1979

Group	Approximate number	Location
Pashtuns	7,000,000	Concentrated in South and Southeast, but settled in most regions
Tajiks	3,500,000	North, Northeast, and Kabul region
Hazaras	1,500,000	Center (Hazarajat) and Kabul
Uzbeks	1,300,000	North
Aimaq	800,000	West
Farsiwan, Heratis	600,000	West and South
Turkmen	300,000	North
Brahui	100,000	Southwest
Baluch	100,000	West and Northwest
Nuristanis	100,000	East

Source: Hyman, *Afghanistan under Soviet Domination,* 11.

nically uniform. Rather, regional social systems have various patterns of identity and stratification.[13]

The state's structure, however, created a recognizable pattern of tribal-ethnic stratification within the national political arena, an arena that became increasingly important with the expansion of the state after the mid-1950s. The head of state (king until 1973, president from 1973 to 1978) was a member of the Muhammadzai clan of the Barakzai tribe of the Durrani confederation, one of the three major groups of Pashtun tribes; the official religion of the state was Sunni Islam of the Hanafi school of jurisprudence (*fiqh*); and the state's capital was Kabul, where Persian is the primary language.[14] The Muhammadzais were at the top of the social hierarchy. Below them came the other Durranis, then the rest of the Pashtuns. After the Pashtuns came the other predominantly Sunni ethnic groups, the largest being Persian-speakers (primarily but not exclusively Tajiks) and Uzbeks. Persian-speakers played a far more important role than Uzbeks and others in the state, especially because Persian was prevalent in the cities of Kabul and Herat. Shi'a, most of them belonging to the Hazara ethnic group, were at the bottom.[15]

Some of the criteria used to define identity may conflict. Groups of Pashtun or Uzbek descent may speak Persian; some 'Tajiks' speak Pashto. A portion of one tribe may have been forcibly settled in an area associated with others, or may have voluntarily settled there. Some studies have found a contemporary tendency away from kinship and toward language or place of birth or residence as determinants of political action.[16] The following summary begins with the "official" accounts, which reify the

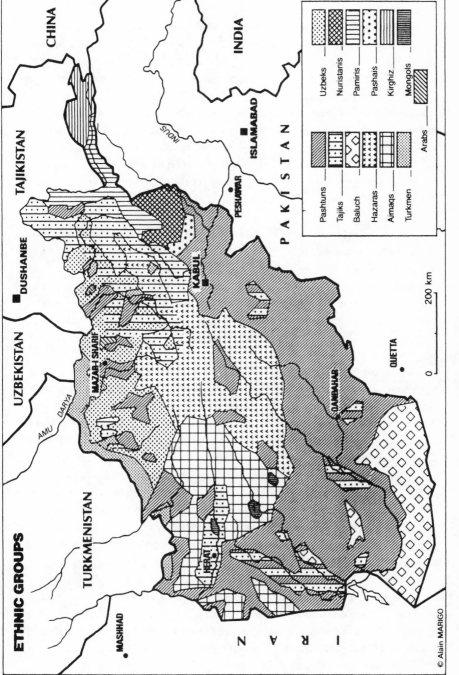

Map 2.1 Approximate Geographical Distribution of Ethnic Groups in Afghanistan

identities, and then tries to indicate some of the ways in which identities change with the political and social context.

The Pashtuns (Afghans) were the largest ethnic group in the country before 1978, although they do not seem to have constituted a majority even then. Most of these tribes speak Pashto, an eastern Iranian language, though some Pashtuns (both individuals and entire qawms) speak Persian, and some Pashto-speakers are not of Pashtun tribal descent. The Pashtuns' social construction of *tribe* is based on an idealized egalitarian model of segmentary lineages, although the actual structures are far more various. Every tribe member belongs to several such nested segments of greater or lesser inclusiveness. Although there is no universally accepted set of terms, I shall use *tribal confederation* for the two largest named units (Durranis and Ghilzais, which founded states in the eighteenth century), *tribe* for the next-most-inclusive units and those outside the two confederations, and *clan* and *lineage* for lower-level segments.[17]

Pashtuns include nomads, peasants, and city dwellers. Peasant Pashtuns conceive of the physical space inhabited by the tribes as mirroring the genealogical space, so that geographical proximity is proportional to proximity of (agnatic) kinship. Each segment thus has its own "homeland," *watan,* a term that in patriotic contexts also refers to the entire territory of the country.[18] (*Watani* means nationalist.) In practice I have found that contemporary Pashtuns are more likely to use residential designations (Nangarhari, Paktiawal, Qandahari) than genealogical ones to denote groupings of Pashtun tribes.

Like other tribal peoples, Pashtuns distinguish between areas of greater government control (*hukumat* in Afghanistan, *makhzen* in the Maghreb) and those areas where tribes are relatively free (*yaghistan* in Afghanistan, *siba* in the Maghreb). Although Afghanistan includes some deserts, most free tribal areas are in the mountains, and the distinction between mountain and plains tribes is central to the Pashtun self-conception. A Pashtun proverb says: "Honor (*nang*) ate up the mountains; taxes (*qalang*) ate up the plains." Nang and qalang—which includes rent as well as taxes— define two different models of Pashtun society. The qalang Pashtun are subjects or rulers of states; they pay or collect land rent and taxes. Among them tribalism takes the form of patronage networks dominated by landlords. The nang Pashtun, however, are free of domination by others (at least the adult males are), either within the tribal society or from outside. They embrace, much more fully than can the qalang Pashtun, the ideal type of egalitarian tribalism expressed in the Pashtun code, *Pashtunwali.*[19]

In the tribal model, conformity to Pashtunwali defines what it means to be "really" Pashtun. As in the codes of other egalitarian tribal peoples, the blood-feud is a major institution. Any family whose namus has been violated must take vengeance (*badal*) against the offender or his qawm. "Honor eats up the mountains" alludes mainly to the prevalence of feuds among nang Pashtun.

Elphinstone observed the corresponding positive form of reciprocity when he noted that "one of the most remarkable characteristics of the Afghauns is their hospitality [*melmastia*]."[20] This is of course a typical tribal virtue, for which the Bedouin are also famous. An extension of hospitality is the obligation to provide asylum (*nanawati*) to a fugitive. Feeding guests imposes reciprocal obligations on the recipient and is thus a way of building alliances or followings.

The major groupings of the Pashtun tribes reflect the way the Pashtuns were divided between the Safavid and Mughal empires. The Safavids and the empire of Nadir Shah Afshari, who deposed them, ruled Persia with armies mainly composed of hierarchically organized Turkic tribes. They also incorporated Pashtun tribal forces into their military, especially as cavalry. In order to make these egalitarian tribes into a more effective military force, the Safavid Shahs imposed elements of the Turco-Mongolian tribal structure onto those Pashtuns living in their territories. It was due to their efforts that Abdali (later Durrani) and Ghilzai Pashtuns developed Turkic-style confederations. The Safavids recognized (or created) the ruling lineages of these Pashtuns—Saddozais and Muhammadzais among the Abdalis, Hotakis among the Ghilzai—and appointed a chief (*khan,* a Turkish word) to head each confederation and each constituent tribe. Under the Durrani rulers of post-1747 Afghanistan, no khans were appointed for the Ghilzais, and today the Ghilzai identity is weak. Observers since Elphinstone have noted that the leadership of khans is much weaker among the Ghilzai than among the Durrani; this probably owes more to their different relation to the state than to autonomous social traditions.[21]

The Safavids and Mughals treated their Pashtun subjects quite differently, and under the Mughals the eastern Pashtuns never developed a broad confederation. The eastern Pashtuns include both the nang tribes of the ranges and passes straddling the frontier between Afghanistan and Pakistan and the qalang tribes of the valleys and plains to the east, between the mountains and the Indus River. Much of the peasantry in the plains is non-Pashtun, and the Mughals and their British successors treated the plains Pashtun as they did such dominant Indian groups as Rajputs in the Gangetic plain: they recognized Pashtun tribes as landlords and tax farmers ruling over other "castes."[22] At times the Mughals employed some of the mountain tribes as border militia or customs collectors, but the nang Pashtuns revolted when the emperor Aurangzeb attempted to standardize tax collection under Islamic law, and they have since posed intermittent problems to all rulers of both the Punjab plains and Kabul.

These models of tribalism fail to reflect the actual social structures in which many Pashtuns lived. Over the past century many Pashtun families have migrated from their tribal homelands either to new agricultural lands opened by irrigation or to cities. Some have been exiled to border areas by rulers. Some nomads have been settled in areas irrigated by major dam projects. Individual families who have moved to newly irrigated areas or to the capital may have retained their identity as Pashtuns or their memory of tribal descent, but they do not live among fellow tribesmen or participate in tribal political institutions. In urban areas of northern or western Afghanistan they may also adopt the Persian language.[23] Such Pashtuns are often referred to as *detribalized*.

The second-largest ethnolinguistic group, the Tajik, is more difficult to define. Elphinstone noted that "the name of Taujik is rather loosely used," and the succeeding centuries have not clarified matters. Following the Soviet usage, the term now refers to all settled, Persian-speaking, nontribal populations, although there are Pashto-speaking "Tajiks" in Pashtun areas and Persian-speaking Pashtuns, Uzbeks, and others in "Tajik" areas. The Persian speakers in and around Herat along the Iranian border to the west include a higher proportion of Shi'a Muslims (though still a minority) and are often known simply as Farsiwan—Persian speakers—rather than Tajiks. Tajiks and Farsiwan, when asked to give their qawm, generally give a place of residence or birth. Although they may have loose lineage structures, they do not have any tribal institutions or codes.[24]

In western Afghanistan there lives a group of Persian-speaking seminomadic peoples, probably of Turkic origin, known as the Aimaqs. Although *Aimaq* is sometimes treated as an ethnic designation, the term *uymaq* originally denoted a type of Turkic chieftancy that exercised indirect rule under the Safavids.[25] Aimaqs give various tribal identities (Jamshidi, Firuzkuhi) as their qawm, and these were probably the names of Safavid uymaqs in this area.

After the Pashtuns and the Persian-speakers, the speakers of Turkic languages are the next-largest linguistic group in Afghanistan; the most important groups of Turkic-speakers are Uzbeks and Turkmen. The term *Uzbek,* following the Soviet model, came to apply to those who speak variants of Chaghatai Turki, although unlike the Soviet government the Afghan state never made an official ethnic classification of Turki-speaking groups. Turkmen are members of Central Asian Turkic tribes who emigrated to northwest Afghanistan in the 1920s and 1930s. According to Barfield, "Turkmen . . . appears to be a residual category for a type of Turco-Mongolian frontier tribe that lived independently just beyond the control of state power—as much a political category as an ethnic label."[26] The Turkmen had a largely pastoral economy, which produced Afghanistan's most valued traditional exports, karakul pelts and fine carpets. Tajiks, Turkmen, and Uzbeks all had fellow ethnics in the Soviet Union's Central Asian republics. Because tens of thousands of both Turkmen and Uzbeks came to Afghanistan as refugees from the Bolshevik suppression of the *basmachi* revolt in Central Asia, anti-Communism was particularly strong among them even before the 1978 coup or the subsequent Soviet invasion. They continue to identify themselves by their place of origin in Central Asia.[27]

The massif of central Afghanistan is the home of the Hazaras, who speak a type of Persian called Hazaragi and are the only major group in Afghanistan that is predominantly Shi'a. Racially distinct, they seem to be of eastern Turkic descent. The Hazaras are probably the descendants of Mongol or Turkic hordes organized in units of thousands (*hazara*) settled in the area by the Timurids. The Safavids exercised sovereignty over their territory, the Hazarajat, and the population largely adopted Twelver Shi'ism, although there are groups of both Sunni and Ismaili Hazaras.[28]

Until their conquest by the Afghans, the Hazaras seem to have had a typically hierarchical Mongol tribal structure presided over by chiefs called *mirs* or *sultans,* who exercised absolute power. Inequality of land ownership and social status has remained greater among the Hazaras than among most other groups in the country. Their conquest by the Afghan state in the nineteenth century was the bloodiest of the land's civil wars before 1978. In what became a brutal Sunni-Shi'a sectarian war, Amir Abdul Rahman Khan destroyed the Hazaras' tribal institutions, gave a large part of their land to Pashtuns, and sold much of the population into slavery.[29] The Hazaras had the lowest status of any group in Afghanistan and furnished Kabul with much of its casual labor.

The other mainly Shi'a group in Afghanistan is the Qizilbash, Persian-speaking descendants of the Turkmen tribes who formed the basis of the military power of the Safavids.[30] The Qizilbash came to Afghanistan to administer the Safavid-controlled areas. They also served the Durrani empire and have largely continued to be members of the educated urban elite.

The Nuristanis of the Northeast inhabit isolated valleys, each with a separate language and somewhat different culture. They maintained their ancient polytheism until 1896, when Amir Abdul Rahman converted them to Sunni Islam and renamed their country Nuristan (Land of Light) from Kafiristan (Land of the Pagans—the related *kafirs,* or "unbelievers," of neighboring Chitral in Pakistan are polytheist to this day). As the Nuristanis became devout Muslims and firm allies of the ruling dynasties, they were permitted to retain their tribal institutions. With its equality of land ownership and traditions of blood feud and hospitality, Nuristani society resembles the egalitarian tribal or nang Pashtun models. Before 1978 the royal family sometimes extended to Nuristanis special protection against encroachment on their mountain homeland by their lowland neighbors. Their immediate identification has been with their valley, often identical with a linguistic region; they generally identify themselves as Nuristanis only in a national, not local, context. Some who have migrated to Kabul to work for the government, especially the military, have taken Nuristani as a family name, and they developed separate institutions in the resistance. Near neighbors to the Nuristanis are the Pashai, another mainly highland group. In the North and around Jalalabad are a few clans of Arabs who no longer speak Arabic.[31]

Two other tribal groups, largely nomadic, inhabit the desert areas of the Southwest: the Baluch and the Brahui, who overlap with their more numerous fellow ethnics in Pakistan and Iran. In the Wakhan corridor of the Northeast are settled peasants known as the Wakhi, who practice the Ismaili sect of Shi'a Islam, and a small group of Turkic-speaking Kirghiz nomads, originally refugees from the Soviet Union and China. The Kirghiz are now largely resettled in Turkey, having fled Afghanistan in 1978.[32]

Scattered among most of these groups and sharing such apparent ethnic characteristics as language with them are the *sayyids* (Arabic plural *sadat*), who claim descent from the Prophet Muhammad, and other groups claiming religious descent. Among Pashtun tribes, members of these groups play the typical role of "saints" outside the tribal structure. Sayyids are prominent among religious figures and intellectuals. Despite their adaptation of Pashtun, Hazara, or Tajik languages and ways of life, sayyids are considered descendants of Arabs rather than members of the groups among whom they live.

Material Production and Class

The major economic activities in Afghanistan before 1978 were agriculture and pastoralism, which accounted for nearly 60 percent of domestic production and employed about two-thirds of the labor force. If we include rural handicrafts and trade, as much as 85 percent of the population depended on the rural economy for its livelihood. About 2.5 million people (slightly less than one-sixth of a population estimated at 15.5 million in 1979) lived primarily by nomadic pastoralism. The distinction between nomads and peasants is not always clear, for groups employ economic strategies that apply varying mixes of pastoralism and agriculture.[33]

Almost 90 percent of the cultivated land was used for food grains to be consumed by the cultivators or sold on the domestic market. More than two-thirds of the area sown in grain was devoted to wheat. Agriculture also produced raw materials, mostly cotton, for industry. Dried and fresh fruit was another major product, for both domestic consumption and export. The scarcest agricultural resource was not land but water. Only about 12 percent of the surface area of Afghanistan is arable, but because water is scarce only half of that was cultivated in any given year, mainly for lack of water. About 30 percent of the arable land was irrigated each year. In some areas farmers irrigated with open canals fed by rivers or dams. Another widespread system was the underground channel (*karez* in Pashto, *qanat* in Persian) that brings water down from nearby hills to bottomland. In the 1960s the Afghan government introduced Green Revolution seed varieties, chemical fertilizers, an extension service, and tractors. By the mid-1970s, 30 percent of the cultivated land was sown with improved wheat seeds, and 12 percent was chemically fertilized.[34]

Only the techniques of nomadic pastoralism allow for the full exploitation of Afghanistan's potential livestock resources. Permanent pastures and meadows cover 84 percent of the country. In 1967–68 (a typical year) pastoralists, both settled and nomadic, herded about 21.5 million sheep, including 6.5 million karakuls. They had 3.2 million goats, 3.6 million cattle, 1.3 million donkeys, 300,000 camels, and 400,000 horses—a total of about 30 million herd animals, more than two head per person in the country.[35] These animals, besides providing meat, dairy products, fiber, and power for local use, also produced raw materials for chief exports: carpets and karakul lambskins.

All major ethnic groups and tribes were represented among the peasantry. Nomads, however, were overwhelmingly Ghilzai and Durrani Pashtun, with some Baluch and Arabs. Nomads and peasants both need and compete with each other. In some parts of Afghanistan, Pashtun nomads favored by the state often clashed with non-Pashtun (especially Hazara) peasants. Much of their pasture was granted to them by the state after being expropriated from conquered non-Pashtun communities. The nomads appear to have lost these pastures as the Hazaras gained autonomy in the recent war.

Nomads depend on peasants for their staple food, grain, while peasants rely on nomads for animal products, trade goods, credit, and information. Nomads were more fully integrated into the cash economy than many peasants, partly because nomads were more specialized in their production and partly because animals, unlike land, are a fecund form of capital. Combined with their greater mobility, which also made them carriers of information, nomads' access to cash made them a major source of credit and enabled them to buy goods in the winter and resell them to the more isolated highland peasantry in the summer. Nomads are also ideally situated for smuggling. For some Baluch and Pashtun nomads, as well as settled tribes in border areas, smuggling has been a source of more income than agriculture or pastoralism. Seasonal migration patterns of nomads have been disrupted by war and state formation throughout history, and the Afghan-Soviet war was no exception.[36]

Agriculture requires five major means of production: land, water, seed, labor, and draft animals (or tractors). Unirrigated land relies on rain; on irrigated land, water rights and land rights are generally conjoined. Each village has an official, the *mirab*, who is chosen by the elders or the village council to regulate the sharing of water among landowners. Because the landowner also usually provides the seed, the major variables of production are land, labor, and draft animals.

The most common forms of agricultural exploitation have been the family farm, where the family provided labor and animals to cultivate its own land; sharecropping, where the tenant received a portion of the crop; and commercial farming—common only on the peripheries of the cities—where the owner paid cash wages for labor. There were two main forms of sharecropping. Where the tenant owned his own draft animals, he received half the crop. Where the tenant used animals provided by the landlord, he received as little as one-fifth of the crop. Owner-operators and sharecroppers alike might employ hired labor by the day during peak seasons.[37]

Nomadic pastoralism requires flocks, labor, and pasture. Pasture formerly belonged to entire tribes or clans, but the Afghan government introduced private property in both summer and winter pasture in the 1920s. Shepherds without flocks traditionally received a portion of the flock that they brought to maturity in a type of sharecropping arrangement with large flock owners, and this could provide the start of a private flock. With improved transport in the 1970s, livestock from north of the Hindu Kush could be brought to market in Kabul; when sheep prices rose as a result, some flock owners began paying shepherds cash wages.[38]

Land ownership is a favored way of converting temporary income into secure wealth. More liquid forms of wealth are animals (which multiply, but which also sicken and die), precious metals (including jewelry), and cash. Debt is ubiquitous in rural Afghanistan because at certain points—marriage, a family crisis, a major investment—families need capital. Landowners, shopkeepers, and some nomads may make loans, sometimes at interest rates as high as 50 percent, despite an explicit prohibition in the Qur'an against usury. Peasants can also place their land in a type of mortgage, *geraw*, in which the lender receives a portion of the crop in lieu of interest and takes over the land if the principal is not repaid after a certain number of years.[39]

The distribution of ownership of the means of production and other assets, along with the relation between the owners of these assets and laborers in the production process, defines the distribution of the population into social classes. A 1970 agricultural survey of selected villages in seven provinces (Table 2.2) showed a wide disparity in landlessness: 13 percent of households in Parwan were landless, but the figure was 49 percent in Qandahar; the median was 34 percent in Kunduz. These findings are roughly consistent with other estimates, that about a third of rural households were landless in the mid-1970s. In none of the provinces surveyed did the proportion of agricultural wage laborers—those without guaranteed yearlong access to land—exceed 15 percent, and the median was only 8 percent. In every province but Qandahar more than half of the families were owner-operators. A 1972–73 survey of thirty-three villages in Kunduz and Baghlan, the richest agricultural area in the country, found that 1,789 of 2,291 families (78 percent) were owner-operators.[40]

Other research shows that small landholdings were the rule in 1978. Two-thirds of holdings were smaller than two hectares (five acres), and almost 40 percent of the landowning households had the equivalent of less than one hectare of good irrigated land. (Compare this, however, with the 60 percent of Indian landowners with plots smaller than one hectare, regardless of quality.) Extremely large holdings were unusual. According to Mukherjee, only 370 of 1.2 million landholdings were larger than one hundred hectares. By way of comparison, in Iran in 1960 (before the Shah's land reform), 4,086 of 1.9 million holdings were larger than one hundred hectares. Mukherjee also notes that properties that were large by Afghan standards were smaller than the *zamindari* feudal landholdings in India.[41]

A more systematic comparison shows that the distribution of landholdings in Afghanistan was more egalitarian than in either Iran or India (Figure 2.1). Note that landholding in prerevolutionary Afghanistan was more egalitarian than in India *after* the abolition of the zamindari.

Another way of looking at class structure is to examine the distribution of land tenure systems. Owner-operated farms predominated. In 1963, for example, 60.5 percent of the land was owner operated, 5.5 percent mortgaged but presumably still cultivated by the owner, 13.8 percent sharecropped, and 20.2 percent "other," perhaps state land.[42] Thus Elphinstone's characterization remained valid: "The estates of the proprietors are, of course, various in their extent; but, on the whole, the land is more equally divided in Afghaunistan than in most other countries. There are a great number of small proprietors who cultivate their lands themselves, assisted by their families, and sometimes by hired labourers and Buzgurs [sharecroppers]."[43] Since

Table 2.2 Village Class Structure in Seven Provinces, 1970 (percentage)

	Province						
Class	Baghlan	Qandahar	Parwan	Ghazni	Kunduz	Nangarhar	Laghman
Landlord	10	15	1	10	6	23	20
Owner-operator	55	37	86	53	60	54	63
Landless	35	49	13	37	34	23	17
Renter	3	2	2	1	2	3	—
Sharecropper	22	36	2	36	16	20	17
Agricultural laborers	10	12	8	—	15	—	—
Households surveyed	796	121	87	173	125	111	41

Source: Democratic Republic of Afghanistan, *Afghan Agriculture in Figures*, citing *Survey of Progress 1970–1971*, 32–58.

Note: The source does not explain how the categories were defined.

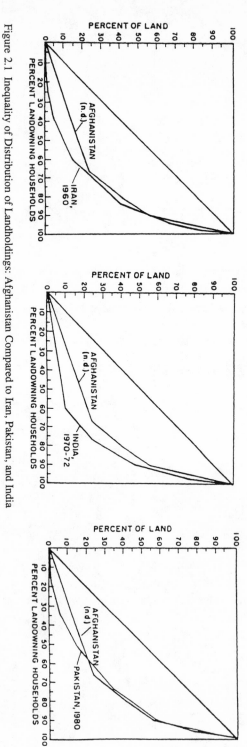

Figure 2.1 Inequality of Distribution of Landholdings: Afghanistan Compared to Iran, Pakistan, and India

Sources: Mukherjee, *From Tragedy to Triumph*; Iran Ministry of Interior, *First National Census of Agriculture: Mehr 1339*; Government of Pakistan, *Economic Survey, 1980*; Kohli, *State and Poverty in India.*

Note: The diagrams are Lorenz curves. The diagonal denotes equality. The farther a curve is from the diagonal, the more unequal the distribution.

Elphinstone's time, population pressure on the land has grown, and the extent of landlessness has probably increased. But rural Afghanistan has remained a poor, predominantly small-peasant society without a polarized class structure.

The distribution of land has differed greatly by region. In the mountainous areas of the East and Northeast, 90 percent of families owned land in the 1960s and 1970s. The fertile plains of the North and around Qandahar presented the opposite extreme. These areas had more large landlords and more landless sharecroppers and laborers. Etienne found that about 50 percent of the households around Qandahar were *baz-gars,* or sharecroppers, and Centlivres observed that large holdings constituted about half the land around Tashqurghan, in Balkh. In the Qandahar area both landlords and tenants were mostly Durrani, although the Pashtun tribes also have client groups, *hamsayas,* who are generally either non-Pashtuns or members of other tribes who sought refuge in the area. In this qalang Pashtun society tribes cohere around khans who were also landlords. In the plains of the North, by contrast, Pashtun landlords who benefited from government patronage often had non-Pashtun tenants and laborers, and landlordism constituted a form of ethnic rule over conquered non-Pashtun populations. Most areas of Afghanistan lay between these two extremes; in Logar and Maidan, for example, Etienne found that no one had more than ten hectares of land but that sharecropping was common.[44]

The distribution of assets in turn determines the standard of living. One study found that in 1976 the available calories per day per capita in Afghanistan was 2,025, compared with 2,005 in India and 2,260 in Pakistan. But the diet of the average Afghan included 62.5 grams of protein per day, 25 percent more than the mean of 50.0 in India. In Pakistan the figure was 61.7. The greater equality of land ownership in Afghanistan seemed to translate into a broader sharing of the limited goods available. Elphinstone calculated that the standard of living of agricultural laborers in Afghanistan "must be very superior to that of the same class in India, even if the difference of climate be allowed for." Etienne, who has considerable experience in rural India and Pakistan as well as in Afghanistan, echoed this finding a century and a half later: "Travelling through the countryside, speaking with different types of peasants, one does not encounter poverty in its most acute form. Of course, the diet [of poor and landless peasant families] is too monotonous to be well balanced, and there is no lack of quantitative deficiencies. Nevertheless, we do not find the exterior forms of deprivation which characterize certain regions of India and Pakistan. The landless peasant . . . does not have that self-effacing attitude, as if he were mentally and physically crushed by poverty to the point of merely surviving."[45] In spite of this slight but significant advantage, the margin of security of the poor peasantry was small enough that bad harvests in the early 1970s caused thousands of starvation deaths, which the government did little to prevent. This disaster had serious political repercussions.

Religion

"From their conversation," wrote Elphinstone of the Afghans, "one would think the whole people, from the King to the lowest peasant, was always occupied in holy reflections." In the 1970s Michael Barry still found much the same situation:

> Coming into [Afghanistan], the traveller entered into a sort of temple. At the hour of prayer, the buses stopped to let the passengers lay down their shawls by the side of the highway and prostrate themselves with a fierce joy. When the vehicles started up, the passengers turned their palms toward heaven as a form of benediction. Waiting for customers, the shopkeepers counted their prayer beads with half-closed eyes, whispering the attributes of God. The dervishes, their headdresses tied with the Arab-style cord, held out their begging bowls to pious passers-by in the bazaars. Friends greeted each other with hand on the heart, heads bowed, praising the Lord for his gift of good health. The peasants did not ride a horse, an ass, a camel, or a taxi without murmuring the name of God. The meals began with a divine invocation, the right hand silently kneading the grains of rice or the piece of bread, because thus had the Prophet done, and they ended with the saying of Grace. . . . Every gesture of life was dictated by ritual and impregnated with the sacred.[46]

Aside from a few tens of thousands of Hindus and Sikhs, plus small numbers of Armenian Christians and Jews in the major cities, all the people of Afghanistan are Muslims, more than 99 percent. About 85 percent of the Muslims are Sunnis of the Hanafi school. Most of the rest, including most Hazaras, the Qizilbash, and some Farsiwan, are Imami (twelver) Shiʿa, like the dominant Shiʿa sect in Iran. Some Hazaras are Ismaili (sevener) Shiʿa, as are the Wakhis of the Wakhan Corridor.[47]

Islam, of course, includes beliefs and practices that are "religious" as understood in secular societies. Muslims believe in the one God who created and rules heaven and earth and revealed his message to humanity through such prophets as Adam, Noah, Abraham, Moses, Jesus, and, the last and greatest, Muhammad, who received the final, perfect revelation of the Holy Qurʾan; they believe that God's revelation, the practice (*sunna*) and sayings (*hadith*) of his messenger Muhammad, the deeds of the early Islamic community, and the interpretations of the jurists define the law (*sharia*); they practice the five obligations: profession of the faith, prayer, taxes (*zakat*) for the upkeep of poor people and religious scholars, fasting during the month of Ramadan (when the angel Gabriel revealed the Qurʾan to Muhammad), and, if possible, the pilgrimage (*hajj*) to the Holy City of Mecca. But Islam involves more than a creed and a code of behavior.

The Islam of Afghanistan is part of an entire civilization. Besides the classical heritage of the Qurʾan that civilization encompasses the poetry of Persia, the military feats of the Timurids, Uzbeks, and Mughals, the reinterpreted philosophy of the Greeks, whose heritage the Muslims kept alive when it was forgotten in Western

Europe, and all the arts—miniature painting, carpet weaving, architecture, jewelry, calligraphy—of the Indo-Turco-Persian Islamic world.

Finally, Islam is the source of universal values and ethics that give life a transcendent meaning. It is through debate about religious principles that the peasant tries to understand the foreign visitor, and this same peasant knows that membership in the community of Islam (the *umma*) makes him or her a member of a supranational fellowship and a participant in world history.[48]

Many villagers express this allegiance through orthodox forms of piety: daily prayer alone or in the neighborhood mosque and communal Friday prayer in the central mosque. The religious leader of this popular piety is the mullah. Unlike the Shi'a mullahs of Iran, who since the Qajar period have adopted specific higher clergymen (*mujtahidin*) as "models for imitation" (*marja'-i taqlid*), the mullah of an Afghan village belongs to that village, not to any nationwide body of clergy. He is an occupational specialist, like the carpenter, barber, or blacksmith. Depending on the local social structure, he may be supported by all families in the village, perhaps receiving a portion of the harvest, or he may be kept on retainer by a wealthy khan.[49]

Views of mullahs have differed widely, and their status has been lower in the tribal regions than in northern Afghanistan. Among Pashtuns, especially the eastern Pashtuns, the mullah is a member not of the tribe but of an occupational qawm and might be the object of mockery. While the tribespeople respect his role in leading prayer and teaching children (generally boys) the fundamentals of piety and Islamic knowledge, they might shunt him aside if he attempts to intervene in public affairs in the name of Islam. Islam does not recognize priestly specialists as mediators between the individual and God, and the tribespeople consider themselves full Muslims even without the special services of the mullah.[50]

The village mullah is the lowest member in the hierarchy of orthodox Islamic leaders whose authority derives from their mastery of the law's texts and traditions. Islamic law requires a corps of scholars to interpret, apply, and transmit it. These scholars constitute the *ulama* (singular *alim*), known in Afghanistan colloquially as *mawlawis*.[51] When they act as judges they are known as *qazis*. Among Muslim tribes, the conflict between Islamic and tribal codes is manifest in conflict over whether disputes should be settled by a qazi or by a tribal council or chief.

Some ulama had advanced degrees and held government or academic positions. Despite efforts by the state to extend the reach of its judicial and educational system, some ulama, especially those trained in private *madrasas* (Islamic schools), continued to teach and judge in the villages without state authorization.

Beyond law, prayer, fasting, and pilgrimage, Islam includes a range of devotional activities, many of them lumped together under the rubric of Sufism. These forms of devotion include veneration of men of holy descent and of saints endowed with charisma (*karamat*) or blessing (*barakat*). The largest descent group is the *sayyids*, supposed descendants of Muhammad through his daughter Fatima and his son-in-law (and nephew) Ali. Many fewer are the *hazrats*, descendants of the Caliph Omar, and the *mians,* who claim other types of Arab descent. These descent groups, which are independent of tribal structure, are common to egalitarian tribal societies.[52]

Sufism is more widespread among Muslims than any such mystical movement among Christians or Jews. It most resembles Hasidic Judaism. Both Islam and Orthodox Judaism are legalistic religions in which study of the holy texts and laws is a prestigious devotional activity. Sufism, like Hasidism, provides a path of devotion for those who are not scholars.

In orthodox Sufism the basic relationship is between the spiritual guide (*pir* or *ruhani* in Persian, *shaikh* in Arabic) and the follower or student (*murid* or *mukhlis*). The pir is likely to be a religious scholar as well. The pir-murid relationship can be intense and intimate, much more so than the relationship of scholar and student in a madrasa. Because a pir may have several murids, each is at the center of a potential network of confidential contacts. Furthermore, each pir has been the murid of someone else, and chains (*silsila*) of pirs trace their affiliation back over generations.

The lesser emphasis on the text and the law in Sufism makes possible a slide toward heterodoxy, antinomianism, and superstition. Pirs may become an elite like the legal scholars, the ulama. Devotees may substitute mystical devotion or pir worship for observance of the religious law; some even attribute magical powers to pirs and ask them for tokens or amulets. An entire tribal group may follow a particular pir or family of pirs, usually members of a religious descent group.

Various methods and doctrines of spiritual exercise are spread by particular Sufi orders (*tariqas*). These orders (or brotherhoods) have their own schools and devotional centers. Both of the principal Sunni orders, the Qadiriyya and the Naqshbandiyya, have devotees in Afghanistan. There is also an outpost of the Chishti order in western Afghanistan. The leader of the Qadiriyya order, Sayyid Ahmad Gailani, is descended from its founder, Abdul Qadir al-Jilani of Baghdad. This prominent sayyid family is venerated by all Sunni Muslims. Many Pashtun tribes are followers of Pir Gailani, whose family is linked by marriage to several of the most aristocratic Muhammadzai lineages.

The traditional leader of the main branch of the Naqshbandiyya order has been the Hazrat of Shor Bazaar, chief of the madrasa in Shor Bazaar of Kabul. He came from the Mujaddidi family, who are descended from the seventeenth-century Indian Islamic reformer Shaikh Ahmad Sirhind—Mujaddid-i Alf-i Sani, or Renewer of the Second Millennium (of Islam). The Mujaddidi family tell of being invited to Afghanistan by the first king of the Afghans, Ahmad Shah Durrani, in the eighteenth century. The leader of the Naqshbandiyya order officially pronounced on the Islamic legitimacy of the rulers of Afghanistan. The last Hazrat of Shor Bazaar, along with most other male members of the Mujaddidi family, was executed in February 1979. Some of his followers have joined the organization led by his nephew, Sibghatullah Mujaddidi, an Egyptian-trained scholar who is not considered a pir.

The Qadiriyya order has been associated with a relatively liberal interpretation of Islam. The Naqshbandiyya order gained strength among South Asian Muslims as a reaction against the liberal, syncretist practices of the Mughal emperor Akbar and has continued to be more conservative. Nonetheless, Naqshbandi leaders, including the Hazrat of Shor Bazaar, have also been venerated by tribes.[53]

Social Control and Collective Action

The social relations established by kinship, production, and religion define and distribute such resources as ownership of land, flocks, and cash; seniority; family connections; relations with outside forces (political and economic); and Islamic knowledge, piety, and charisma. These are the resources out of which people fashion their strategies for living. Leaders deploy the same resources for social control or collective action.

The most successfully enforced form of social control, as well as the basic institution of production and consumption, has been the patriarchal family. It is almost impossible for women to escape male domination in Afghan society, but not all women passively accept it. Women contest male domination through "ordinary forms of resistance." They claim, for example, that, despite appearances, they actually wield much power; they create a distinct women's culture, such as that expressed in the *landai* form of poetry in Pashto; they have frequent discussions of the suffering that is the lot of woman; and, according to one woman anthropologist who worked among Uzbeks, some commit sexual indiscretions, which others help conceal. One element of women's self-image in Afghanistan, at least among Pashtuns, is the belief that men, for all their posturing, are weaker than women, and that women could defend namus at least as well if they had the chance—and the guns.[54]

Men's control of women, together with seniors' control over juniors and cooperation among male peers, organizes the Afghan people into families. These families are in turn organized into larger networks either by an extension of kinship and property relations or by religious leaders. Leaders who rely on religion for their influence and those who rely on kinship and property have often competed.

The most prevalent form of village politics in peaceful times is competition between leaders (khans) who use wealth and kinship ties to create political followings. A khan of this type, as opposed to a state-appointed tribal chief, has no officially recognized or hereditary office. A khan is not a feudal lord. Power in villages or tribes does not reside in any one person or structure but in fluidly structured networks of influence. These networks are not based on any single principle: neither wealth nor kinship ties alone can assure a man of influence, only the skill with which he deploys both against his rivals.[55] The main object of politics as practiced by khans is to be recognized as "bigger" than other khans by both villagers and the state.

Hospitality is an important form of the redistribution of resources necessary for recognition as a khan. Jon W. Anderson reports that a most common saying among Ghilzai Pashtuns is that khans "feed the people." Patronage establishes networks of reciprocal obligation that, as Ghilzai say, "tie the knot of the tribe." The khan's guest house (*hojra* in Pashto, *mihman-khana* in Persian) is the place where he recruits followers by feeding them, mediating disputes, arranging marriages, and discussing current affairs. These activities may require intercession with the state as well. The ability to obtain and distribute resources from the state or market, through patronage, trade, or smuggling, is an important asset for a khan.[56]

Local self-government can be based on either common residential location or kinship (tribe). Within each village there are distinct wards or neighborhoods that are often also the homes of different qawms. Each such ward has its own mosque and elders. Most villages also have a council of elders, consisting of the leaders of various lineages or wards in the village, and some have a large mosque where the men of the entire village pray on Friday. Such councils may settle disputes or organize economic cooperation in, for instance, the sharing of water. The government may designate one elder as arbab or malik, the official representative of a village, ward, or qawm, but the arbab is not necessarily or even usually the most powerful person.

In Pashtun tribal areas, where the villagers belong mainly or wholly to a single tribe or clan, the village council may be equivalent to a tribal council, or *jirga* (literally "circle," denoting the equality of the participants). The jirga includes all adult males and rules by consensus. In theory, a jirga can be convened at any level of tribal organization, from the smallest lineage to an entire confederation. Jirgas are most commonly held at the lineage level, but there are larger tribal or even intertribal jirgas as well, at least among the eastern Pashtuns. Since at least the 1920s, the Afghan state has defined an institutionalized, partly nontribal body, the Loya Jirga (Great Council), as the highest representative body of the Afghan state. The composition of the Loya Jirga has changed over time in accord with state interests.[57] The old regime also kept alive the tradition of the emergency Loya Jirga, an informal meeting of the leaders of different groups summoned to address a national emergency, such as the two British invasions of Afghanistan.

Whenever the state's monopoly of armed force weakens, or where it has not been established, the jirga can call its members to battle. The military institution of the Pashtuns is the *lashkar,* the armed tribe. Each family contributes its male members and weapons to the lashkar, which is further enriched by whatever booty it can take. As Gellner says of tribal peoples generally, a tribal army is not a differentiated body but simply the society in arms, from which arise both its strengths and failings.[58]

Both the jirga and the village council may be the scene of the political maneuverings among khans that also occur constantly in less formal settings. Khans compete with each other for clienteles and state patronage. Especially in the eastern Pashtun areas the competition can be extremely intense and can be expressed in vendettas that continue for generations between families, clans, and tribes. In such vendettas the khans may bring all possible resources to bear, including the support of political parties, the government, or foreign powers. The pattern of state formation in Afghanistan, based on redistribution of externally supplied resources rather than extraction from the countryside, encouraged the development of redistributive patronage in the rural areas.

Khans may exploit others, provide public goods, or do both. Some obtain help from the state to enlarge their wealth and power even at the cost of alienating the local population. Others build clienteles, and hence networks of power, by providing goods and shielding the local population from the state and its depredations. Although the exploitative khan is an ally of the state, the khan as public servant can be the state's strongest competitor for social control.[59]

Khans make loans and employ tenants on their lands, using their resources to build up a dependent clientele within the qawm. Depending on how the khan uses the resources he accumulates, villagers may not see such relationships solely or mainly as exploitation, but as what Latif Tabibi calls asymmetrical reciprocity. To Ghilzai, Anderson notes, "a khan is a self-financed public servant, expending his own wealth for the aggregate good of a community," and "khans emerge as social creditors and not as lords." Another study found that the Sheikhanzai Durrani Pashtuns wished to have bigger khans in order to have stronger collective organization, in particular to protect themselves from the state. These studies confirm that Elphinstone had it right, at least for the Pashtun tribes, when he wrote, "In their notion of their Khaun, the idea of a magistrate set up for the public good is certainly mixed with that of a patriarchal and natural superior, yet the former impression will always be found to be strongest."[60]

Poorer villagers engage in everyday forms of resistance against those in power. Landlords employing sharecroppers who do not own their own draft animals and who therefore receive as little as one-fifth of the crop, for example, have to devote much energy to supervising them, for these low-paid workers may be inefficient and may commit petty theft or encroach on the land. Nevertheless, villagers do not necessarily see wealth in land as a source of oppression. Since some khans redistribute wealth through patronage and use it to create public goods (irrigation, influence with or protection from outside powers), this perception is not merely the result of domination and false consciousness. The pattern of patronage based on qawm, strengthened by the pattern of state formation, explains why there are no known cases of peasant movements against landlords in the Afghan countryside; the Khalqi minister of agriculture during the early land reform, said in 1979 that the aim of the land reform was to introduce class struggle to a society with no such tradition.[61]

Khans, whose power depends in part on exploiting segmentation to mobilize kin groups, at times compete with religious leaders, who emphasize the unity of all Muslims. Islam and Islamic leaders play different roles during what used to be considered "normal"—that is, peaceful—times and times of crisis. Saints, sayyids, and pirs act as mediators in normal times, when politics in the village is dominated by the competition of the khans and recurrent disputes involving women, money, and land.

In some areas, sectarian affiliation may provide an element of difference in group identity. This is especially true around the borders of the Hazarajat, where Shiʿa Hazaras are intermixed with Sunnis belonging to various ethnic groups.[62]

One form of local political organization that is prevalent among the nontribal populations is the Islamic coalition, often based on pir-murid networks.[63] A local pir may have followers in several districts who, along with their kin, may support each other in disputes within local society or against the state. In this way a pir can translate his barakat into a position of leadership analogous to that of a khan. The pir, like the khan, must feed his followers, but, unlike the khan, his barakat entitles him to receive gifts, sometimes substantial ones. Islamic coalitions may encompass a few dozen people in a village or thousands of people across the country. When religious leaders believe that Islam is in danger, from either a foreign power or the government, Islamic coalitions come into play. Two of the traditionalist parties of the Afghan resistance, the National Islamic Front of Afghanistan and the Afghanistan National Liberation Front, were essentially such countrywide Islamic coalitions. Their leaders were the heads of the Gailani and Mujaddidi families.

It is only at times of crisis that mullahs and ulama mobilize people for protest or revolt. Tribal coalitions led by charismatic ulama correspond to Gellner's model of "tribal puritans." In a crisis, tribes may be mobilized by an orthodox Islamic leader who preaches reform. As interpreters of the law, the ulama are empowered to issue *fatwas* (legal rulings) that call on the believers to undertake jihad or that establish (or deny) the legitimacy of a ruler. Because the ulama are not as involved as the khans in intratribal or intravillage competition, they and the pirs are better able to achieve unity across tribes and qawms for jihad, as they did in the wars against the British. Among the eastern Pashtun tribes, in particular, charismatic ulama have repeatedly mobilized the tribes in protest.[64]

In some parts of the Islamic world, movements based on Sufi brotherhoods have founded states. In this category are the Wali of Swat in what is today Pakistan, the Safavid empire of Persia, and the Sanussiyya brotherhood that founded the Libyan monarchy. Neither ulama nor pirs, however, ruled Afghanistan before 1978; although religious leaders could (and several times did) declare a jihad, a tribal leader always assumed military leadership and took state power. Once head of the state, however, the ruler faced powerful competition from both khans and religious leaders. In the search for autonomous power such a ruler inevitably looked outward, whether for conquest or foreign aid. That external search for resources to buttress state power determined the troubled career of the Afghan state.

3

State, Tribe, and the
International System:
From Gunpowder
Empires to the Cold War

Various states or empires dominated the territories of present-day Afghanistan until the eighteenth century, but none of them constituted an Afghan state, that is, one ruled by Pashtuns. When Safavid rulers structured the Abdalis and Ghilzais into confederations, these Pashtun tribes attained large-scale military organization for the first time; the foundering of both the Safavid and Mughal dynasties in the mid-seventeenth century gave the Abdalis and Ghilzais an opportunity for conquest.

When a Safavid governor of Qandahar attempted to force Shi'ism on the Pashtuns, the Ghilzais revolted under the leadership of Mirwais, khan of the Hotakis. Mirwais's lashkar ousted the weakened Safavid shah from Isfahan in 1722. Mirwais ruled briefly, but his kingdom soon disintegrated in bloody battles of succession and ultimately succumbed to the cavalry of a new Turkic conqueror, Nadir Shah Afshar.

The Abdalis helped Nadir Shah defeat the Ghilzais, and they, along with some Ghilzai units, amassed wealth and military experience in Nadir Shah's army, which ranged far enough to sack Delhi and carry the Peacock Throne of the Mughals to Isfahan. Ahmad Khan Abdali was a young khan of the Popolzai tribe's Saddozai clan, recognized by the Safavids as the chiefly clan of the Abdalis. Ahmad Khan, who had been a commander in Nadir Shah's cavalry, was among the Afghans who returned to Qandahar in the wake of Nadir Shah's assassination in 1747. A jirga that met to choose a leader of the Abdali tribes deadlocked between Ahmad Khan and a candidate from the Muhammadzai lineage of the Barakzai, the largest Abdali tribe. The tribes called on a saintly mediator, a pir of the Chishti order, who supported Ahmad Khan. The new leader, to his great good fortune, soon captured a caravan transporting Nadir Shah's taxes back to Persia, and this windfall financed Ahmad Khan's initial alliances and military efforts. As his power grew, he acquired the Persian title of shah, or king, and became known as Ahmad Shah.[1] One of his honorifics was Durr-i Durran (pearl of pearls): the Abdalis consequently became known as Durranis.[2] From 1747 to 1978, except for nine months in 1929, all rulers of Afghanistan came from the rival chiefly clans of the Abdalis-Durranis, the Saddozais and Muhammadzais.

Ahmad Shah led the Durrani confederation and ultimately the united Pashtun tribes in the conquest of non-Pashtun lands. This empire at first conformed closely to the Ibn Khaldun model of tribal conquest; the tribes, their group-feeling cemented by a charismatic leader and the sharing of loot, ruled over towns and villages. Over three-fourths of the state's income came from conquests in India, mainly Punjab and Kashmir.[3] Because he extracted wealth from external sources, Ahmad Shah did not face the problem of how to extract resources from tribes on whom he depended for military power.

Tribal leaders commanded most of the military, leaving the state only indirect control. Half of the revenue was assigned to *jagirdars* or *toyuldars* (feudal chiefs, most of them Durrani khans). These chiefs furnished Ahmad Shah with the most effective part of his army and cavalry, the lashkar. To create a military power base independent of the tribes, the king also established non-Pashtun professional units under his direct command. Composed mainly of Qizilbash and Kohistani Tajiks, these units were never as large or effective as the tribal lashkar.[4]

The state restructured the tribes to suit its interest. For instance, to weaken the Barakzais, Ahmad Shah appointed a separate khan for the Achakzais, making the clan into a separate tribe, a status that they retain today. The employment of non-Pashtuns increased after 1775, when Timur Shah moved the capital from the Durrani center of Qandahar to the Persian-speaking city of Kabul.[5] This move was also designed to make the state more autonomous from the Pashtun khans.

The Durrani shahs also used Islam to legitimate central power. Ahmad Shah portrayed his rule as Islamic both through symbolic acts and by establishing sharia courts, although the latter seemed to function only in larger towns.[6] The Pashtun tribes settled their disputes among themselves. They considered themselves the ruling group, not subjects or citizens of the state.

As in Ibn Khaldun's model, the empire of Ahmad Shah began to dissolve within two generations of the founder's death. But the decline was due not so much to the decay of tribal asabiyya as to a change in the international system. Ahmad Shah had captured Punjab and Kashmir during a period of turmoil in India. By the end of the eighteenth century, however, the Sikh empire of Ranjit Singh was consolidating its hold on Punjab; the Sikhs took Peshawar in 1826. More important in the long term, the British were advancing toward northwest India from their base in Calcutta.

The loss of the Indian territories deprived the Saddozai rulers of the wealth with which they had cemented their tribal coalitions. Tribal warfare split the kingdom into several smaller states. This pattern has recurred: the loss of revenue from outside the territory of Afghanistan has led to a loss of state control and the emergence of regional power centers. The overthrow of Najibullah in 1992 after his loss of Soviet aid is the most recent example.

In the early nineteenth century, Iran, resurgent under the Qajars, reclaimed some territory in the West, and an Uzbek chief, Murad Beg, conquered territory claimed by

Bukhara in Afghan Turkestan. The last of the independent Saddozai monarchs lost the throne in 1818. Amir Dost Muhammad Khan, a Muhammadzai, took the throne in 1835 after years of civil war.[7] He reclaimed it after the first Anglo-Afghan war (1839–42), when the tribes expelled the British and their Saddozai puppet, Shah Shuja-ul-mulk. Virtually all rulers of Afghanistan from then until 1978 were Muhammadzais.

The First Anglo-Afghan War and the Reigns of Dost Muhammad and Sher Ali

The Anglo-Afghan wars incorporated Afghanistan into the new international state system. This system was approaching Afghanistan not only from India, but also from the north, where the Russians were subduing the peoples of Central Asia. In fact, both wars arose from British concerns about Russian advances.

The first Anglo-Afghan war (1839–42) ended in a disastrous defeat for the British. They permitted Dost Muhammad to resume his rule, which he maintained until his death in 1863. Dost Muhammad and his Muhammadzai successors faced a different set of opportunities than had Ahmad Shah.[8] The consolidation of British imperial control in India meant that tribes could not be unified as a ruling group through distribution of the fruits of conquest. Afghan rulers could consolidate their power only by playing groups against each other or by receiving aid from more powerful states. This foreign aid enabled them at times to subdue the peoples of Afghanistan and extract taxes from them, but state control remained precarious.[9] During both British invasions, tribalism reemerged as a potent force that weakened the state in its battle with the khans for social control. The balance of power between state and tribes—in contemporary terms, the degree of autonomy of the state from social forces—repeatedly shifted, often because of changes in the relations between the state and the international system.

Dost Muhammad, who had spent several years as an exile in British India, became the first Afghan ruler to see the power of modern state institutions firsthand. As with other colonial and postcolonial travelers after him, international experience increased his determination to "modernize" his state so that it could defend its independence and identity.[10]

Dost Muhammad sought and received military assistance from both Qajar Iran and British India. The Qajars had copied European forms of military organization, and Dost Muhammad sought to learn from them.[11] The British provided weapons in appreciation of his neutrality during the Indian revolt of 1857–59.

The relationship between the ruler and his staff was patrimonial, with some bureaucratic elements; although the military was increasingly detribalized, Dost Muhammad granted command over the major provinces only to his sons, whose rivalries cast the country again into civil war upon his death. One of them, Sher Ali, reconsolidated control in 1868 and further distanced the state from strict patrimony: he continued to build a professional army and delegated administration not to his sons but to ministers of diverse social origin.[12]

The Second Anglo-Afghan War and the Buffer State of Amir Abdul Rahman Khan

The second Anglo-Afghan War (1878–80) temporarily undid many of the state-building achievements of Dost Muhammad and Sher Ali.[13] The tribes, summoned to jihad by influential ulama, mobilized to fight the invader. The war ended with a partial victory of the Afghans, who maintained their internal sovereignty but ceded control of their foreign relations to the British. Amir Abdul Rahman Khan, a nephew of Sher Ali who seized the throne after the departure of the British troops, also agreed not to extend his administration across the frontier that came to be known as the Durand Line, for Sir Mortimer Durand, the British official who established it.[14] The British retained control of those Pashtun territories conquered by the Sikhs, including Peshawar.

Having failed to bring Afghanistan under their direct rule, the British sought to stabilize their northwest frontier and keep Russia at bay by supporting a ruler dependent on them for resources to subdue the peoples of Afghanistan and defeat rivals. True to Tilly's observation that late state formation largely depended on war and negotiations among more powerful states, the British and Russians together demarcated the territory of Afghanistan in order to make it an effective buffer state. At times they did so without prior consultation with the Afghan government.[15]

The British did not provide enough resources to enable the amir to rule by redistribution as in pure rentier states, although the lack of any formal state budget makes it difficult to estimate the importance of the foreign subsidy. A significant portion of the aid came as weapons rather than cash. These weapons enabled Abdul Rahman, known by the appropriately Prussian sobriquet the Iron Amir, to pursue a coercion-intensive path to state formation:

> 'Abd-al-Rahman acquired his means of destruction through British grants as well as purchases on the open market. Between 1880 and 1895, he was presented with 80 guns [cannon], 17,342 shots and shells, 33,302 rifles, 3,200 carbines and 21,308,000 cartridges (India Office, European mss., F III/287, viceroy to ruler, 1899, p. 5). In 1899, purchases of the Afghan government going through India were so large that they became the subject of a special correspondence between the viceroy and the secretary of state for India. In that year, 'Abd-al-Rahman had bought "2,000,000 cordite 33 bore cartridges, 2 ¾ tons Nordenfeldt and 9 tons Hotchkiss cases, besides several hundred thousand Lee-Metford and Mauser ball cartridges" (ibid., 11 May 1899, p. 1).[16]

In 1882 the British granted the amir a yearly subsidy of 1.2 million Indian rupees. They raised the amount to 1.8 million after the formal demarcation of the Durand Line in 1893 and to 1.85 million in 1897, when the British and Russians forced the amir to accept the addition to his realm of the Wakhan corridor—a mountainous strip of territory with little value, except to ensure that British India and Russia would have no border, and hence no border incidents. According to one estimate, the British subsidy amounted to about one-fifth of the amir's expenditures on the military and police. Adding the cash value of weapons might bring the total closer to the 40 percent benchmark that Luciani suggests for the definition of a rentier state, but it appears that foreign aid to Afghanistan at that time was not sufficient for the state to dispense with domestic extraction.[17]

The cash enabled the amir to employ conscripts as troops. He used a system of indirect conscription (called the *hasht nafari*, or "eight-person" system) under which village or clan elders chose one of each group of eight 20- to 40-year-old men to serve in the army while the seven other households were taxed to provide for his support. This expanded and well-equipped army enabled the amir to increase direct tax revenues from landowners, which provided the bulk of his domestic revenue.[18] He insisted on collecting more taxes in cash than had previous rulers. Given the lack of money, capital, and opportunities for trade, however, this measure did not lead mainly to commodification of land and labor but to an extensive emigration from some areas. Most taxes still had to be collected in kind, resulting in great expense and waste.

These policies thus brought the people of Afghanistan two of the major transformations identified by Migdal as key to the breakdown and reconstitution of social control in the nineteenth-century colonial world: changes in taxes and in land tenure.[19] Without these coercive resources, and in the absence of any opportunities for conquest, the only alternative would have been a more capital-intensive state-building strategy. Such a strategy would have required introducing to Afghanistan the third transformative force, modern transportation, in order to create a national market and link the country to the capitalist world market. The British in India were actively pursuing such a policy, extending their railroads throughout the Indian subcontinent, almost to the Afghan frontier. The Russians were also building railways into Central Asia, where they began to cultivate cotton for the factories of European Russia.

The amir, however, considered modern means of transportation and communication inimical to Afghan security, which depended on the impenetrability of its mountains. If traders or the amir's forces could use roads and telegraph lines, so, too, could foreign armies, and contact with foreign societies and foreign ideas might undermine the amir's power and the resolve of the Afghans to sacrifice themselves against any foreign enemy. Placing Afghan independence and military security above all other goals, the amir determined to maintain the country's isolation regardless of the economic cost.[20]

But if the amir pursued a coercion-intensive path, the availability of coercive resources from the international system made Afghanistan's version of that path to state formation different from that of Prussia or Russia. Those states extracted resources from rich agricultural areas by incorporating landed nobles as civil and military officials. The availability of a significant supply of weapons and cash from the British partly freed the amir from having to rule in alliance with local power holders. Still, the British grants were finite, and the amir of Afghanistan could never depend solely on an autonomous bureaucratic apparatus under his command. Abdul Rahman also continued to rely on the manipulation of tribal and ethnic rivalries.

The amir was confronted by tribes who had armed and mobilized themselves for the anti-British resistance. To impose his rule he strove both to defeat his main rivals on the battlefield and to fragment the tribes, as well as other social organizations that formed the base of their power. He faced many forms of opposition: challenges from other Muhammadzai contenders; resistance by peoples within his territory—Hazaras, Aimaqs, Nuristanis—who had never accepted the authority of the Afghan ruler; and revolts by various Pashtun tribal coalitions. The consolidation of the amir's rule gave rise to forty disturbances, including ten major rebellions, four of which he called civil wars.[21] In addition to direct military responses to these uprisings, the amir also used exile to undermine the tribes' power. He moved rebellious Pashtun tribes to non-Pashtun areas of the North and Northwest, where they became his allies in ruling over non-Pashtuns. He exiled both Muhammadzai rivals and Ghilzai elders to India, where the British kept watch over them.

Despite all his efforts, however, the amir failed to destroy tribal power. Like all Afghan rulers, he simultaneously opposed and manipulated social segmentation. He called out the Durranis, who had opposed his conquest of Qandahar from a Muhammadzai rival, to help suppress a Ghilzai revolt. He then reconciled with the Ghilzais by summoning them to jihad against the Shi'a (therefore heretic) Hazaras, whom they plundered, displaced, and sold into slavery.

The amir legitimated his centralized rule with a new doctrine of sovereignty, in which the Islamic concept of divine sanction played a role similar to that of the European absolutist notion of divine right. He signed formal agreements with many sections of his society in which they recognized him as *imam,* leader of the Islamic community. He institutionalized the claim of Islamic sovereignty by establishing in all the provinces official sharia courts operating by procedures laid down by the state.[22] The amir claimed that because he was waging jihad by strengthening the defenses of Afghanistan against non-Muslim powers, it was the duty of all Muslims in the territory of Afghanistan to support and pay taxes to him.

Making Islam rather than tribe the basis of the relationship of subject to ruler legitimated the amir's attack on institutions of indirect rule through such intermediaries as khans. He established direct rule based on territorial divisions headed by officials answerable to him—in contrast to the policy of previous Afghan rulers, who had recognized indirect rule and levied different levels of tax on various tribes, ethnic groups, and provinces.

Formerly Afghanistan had consisted of a few large provinces (Kabul, Qandahar,

Herat, Turkestan, Badakhshan) ruled (at least until the time of Sher Ali) in a feudal-federal fashion by the king's sons or brothers, who acted as tax farmers. The governors passed fixed amounts of taxes to the center and kept whatever else they took. Abdul Rahman, by contrast, appointed governors who were supposed to transmit all taxes to the center. He split the provinces into smaller territorial units, districts (*uluswalis*), and subdistricts (*alaqdaris*), that did not correspond to tribal or ethnic divisions. He personally appointed administrators over each area, and these officials were generally neither members of his family (whom he kept at court, the better to watch them) nor natives of the region they governed.

To support this administration the amir established a ruthless police force that spied on, arrested, tortured, and killed disobedient officials or suspected opponents. Like other absolutist state builders, he tried to establish that crimes were offenses against the state—a foreign notion in a tribal society accustomed to regulating itself through the mechanisms of the blood feud. He built new prisons and succeeded in reducing the rate of murder, though at the cost of an unprecedented level of state brutality.

The attempt by the amir to transform the ruler's relationship with the tribes was symbolized by the establishment of institutions of representation that were differentiated from those of administration. For as long as the ruler relied on the tribes for his armies, the jirga of the tribes was simultaneously a representative institution, a sort of electoral college for the shah, and a military force. Just such a jirga had chosen Ahmad Shah as leader of the Abdalis. The amir, however, modified this tradition of tribal representation by establishing the Loya Jirga. Afghans referred to previous large jirgas, such as the one that elected Ahmad Shah, as Loya Jirgas, but the term had never before been given a legally codified meaning. Membership in the council was not the result of the autonomous power of tribal leaders. Instead the amir appointed its members from among three estates: Muhammadzai *sardars* (tribal commanders), important khans from different parts of the country, and religious leaders. Although nominally representative, the Loya Jirga's actual role was limited to approving the measures that the amir submitted to it.[23] The required presence of tribal leaders at court also kept them isolated from their power base, a tactic known as well to European absolutism. The Loya Jirga thus co-opted a tribal tradition into a state institution.

The designation of the Muhammadzai sardars as one of three estates advising the amir symbolized the transformation of the clan from a warrior nobility like France's *noblesse d'épée* to a rentier class dependent on the ruler. This transformation was part of Abdul Rahman's effort to recruit a new elite for the state, distinct from the tribes and loyal to him. In doing so, he adopted the alternative to the tribal system that was familiar to him: a version of the Turkish Mamluk system. The Afghan intellectual class, like the Mamluks, originated as slaves of the ruler, and, like the latter (or the Young Turks), ultimately rebelled to become masters of the state. As Gellner put it, in such a system "political cohesion at the top was attained by the artificial creation of a new elite, technically 'slaves,' ideally free of kin links to distract them from their duty, and formed, not by the shared hardships of tribal life, but by systematic training and education for wars and administration. . . . In other words, the novel form of elite-recruitment enabled the state to dispense with each of the two key elements in the Ibn Khaldunian state (i.e. the tribal army and the urban clerics)."[24]

Amir Abdul Rahman Khan tried to create such an elite. The core of the elite was recruited from the royal family. Previous rulers had appointed their sons as provincial governors and military commanders, but Abdul Rahman kept his sons at court. According to Hasan Kawun Kakar, they regarded themselves as slaves of the amir. The next circle consisted of the Muhammadzais, whom the amir also brought to Kabul. The Muhammadzai clan had previously ruled under the king's leadership, in an arrangement that was not a genuine monarchy but what Kakar calls a despotic republic. Political power and responsibilities had been shared by the Muhammadzai sardars, who had an independent base of power in their provincial tribal forces. Consequently they had also contended for ultimate power at—or before—the death of the king. Amir Abdul Rahman, however, after much fighting and negotiation, agreed to pay the sardars cash stipends; in return they surrendered their military power and agreed not to contest his line in the succession to the throne. He signed a formal agreement with the Muhammadzais, naming them Sharik al-Dawlat, partners in the state. They thus became "identified more with the ruling dynasty in Kabul than with their tribe in Kandahar."[25]

Amir Abdul Rahman Khan also began to recruit a group of *ghulam bachas,* literally "slave boys," to his court. Some were slaves from areas conquered by the amir, such as Badakhshan or Kafiristan (Nuristan), while others were from mainly non-Pashtun bureaucratic lineages of Kabul or Herat. This form of recruitment was similar to that of the Ottoman Janissaries, who were originally slaves given as tribute by Balkan Christians.[26] Also brought to court were the *pishkhidmats,* or attendants, sons of influential families. Hostages for their fathers' good behavior, they were raised in the court milieu and trained to serve the state. This regimen produced servants whose loyalties to the state were ultimately supposed to infiltrate the tribes, although the reverse happened as well. Both ghulam bachas and pishkhidmats were often married to Muhammadzai women, creating closer ties among the ethnically heterogeneous elite. They could be raised to high office, but their status depended entirely on the goodwill of the amir; they could be imprisoned or executed for the slightest infringement of discipline.

The amir left a consolidated if terrorized state to his eldest son, Habibullah, who succeeded to the throne upon his father's natural death in 1901. Habibullah's peaceful succession was an event with no precedent and, thus far, no sequel, in the history of Afghanistan. The reign of Amir Habibullah Khan (1901–19) was "a period of the steady expansion of the policies instituted by his father."[27]

Creation of the Intelligentsia and Modern Political Movements

In one respect, Amir Habibullah's policies differed from those of his father: he began to open the country to modern education, which created a class of intellectuals separate from the clergy for the first time. These intellectuals were trained for state service in new state schools or abroad.

As noted by Gellner, "systematic training for wars and administration" was the source of elite cohesion in the Mamluk system, but Abdul Rahman Khan had established no institutions to train the state elite. The predominant form of education was privately financed schooling by mullahs and ulama, either at home or in an elementary *maktab* or higher-level madrasa. The traditional curriculum was not exclusively religious—it included Persian literature and the traditional mathematical, medical, and other sciences of the Islamic world—but it was controlled by a religiously trained occupational group and did not develop the skills necessary for modern state building: engineering, accounting, modern medicine, military sciences, and Western languages.[28]

Indeed, no one in Afghanistan could teach these subjects, which had not been developed indigenously. But Afghans had to learn them because their state was now compelled to find its place in the state system imposed on the world by colonial powers. The coercive path that Afghanistan took into that system is evident from the first course in a Western language offered in Kabul: English for Afghans who were to work with British experts employed by Amir Abdul Rahman to establish factories for the manufacture of arms. This purely instrumental approach to modern education established a cultural break between the country's traditional forms of education and culture and the new ones imported as part of coercive state building.[29]

Abdul Rahman's refusal to establish modern schools had stemmed from his policy of isolating Afghanistan. To expand the modern education of his subjects, he would have had either to import foreign teachers or to send his subjects abroad. He chose to do neither. Habibullah maintained strict limits on the entry of foreign experts into Afghanistan and on foreign travel, including study. He did, however, found the Habibia "College," or lycée, the first modern secondary school in Afghanistan (1904), and the Royal Military College (1904–1906). The teachers at Habibia were mainly Muslims from India, while the Military College was placed under the supervision of a Turkish colonel.[30]

Habibullah also permitted the return of the Muhammadzais exiled by his father, some of whom had studied in India or the Ottoman empire. Among them were two families who subsequently played vital roles in national politics: the Tarzis and the Yahya Khel, later known as the Musahiban. The Tarzis had lived in Damascus, then under Ottoman rule, and the Musahiban in British India. Ghulam Muhammad Tarzi, a prominent poet, and his son, Mahmud Beg Tarzi, also traveled to France and Egypt. The Musahiban included Nadir Khan, who became king in 1929, and his four brothers. Both the Tarzis and the Musahiban helped introduce Afghanistan to the ideology of modernization that they had imbibed during their years abroad.[31]

The returning exiles, the graduates of the new schools, and some of the ghulam bachas formed the nucleus of the state elite and the first reformist movements.[32] These movements were the first whose programs derived from comparisons of Afghanistan to other members of the nation-state system, for this tiny elite was the first group able to make such comparisons.

The most important vehicle for the program of modernization was the newspaper *Seraj al-Akhbar,* founded by Mahmud Tarzi. Tarzi, who had become acquainted while in exile with the works of thinkers like Muhammad Abduh and Jamaluddin al-Afghani, introduced the ideology of Islamic modernism to Afghanistan. The group around Tarzi, which included his son-in-law, Habibullah's son Amanullah, was known as the Young Afghans, after the Young Turks, whom it emulated.[33]

King Amanullah and the Revolts That Deposed Him

After World War I as in 1747, the vulnerability of neighboring empires gave Afghans the opportunity to act. With Britain weakened and Russia convulsed by revolution, two important court factions, the anti-British Islamic conservatives and the Young Afghans, decided that the time was right to declare Afghan independence. Habibullah, however, maintained the policy, inherited from his father, of cooperation with Britain. He was assassinated on February 20, 1919, while sleeping in his tent during a hunting expedition near Jalalabad.

Amanullah seized the throne and imprisoned the leader of the conservatives, his uncle Nasrullah, whom he charged with responsibility for the assassination.[34] Amanullah declared Afghanistan's independence, which the new Soviet government immediately recognized. When the British refused to recognize the state's independence, Amanullah launched a brief jihad into the tribal areas across the Durand Line. Although the regular army was ineffective, tribal forces led by the future king, Gen. Nadir Khan, forced the British, exhausted by the recent world war and beset by the freedom movement in India, to accede to Amanullah's demand. Afghanistan became a sovereign member of the state system, the only Muslim member of the League of Nations. Amanullah spent the next decade trying to transform the social and political structure of the country into that of a modern nation-state.

Independence cost Amanullah the British subsidy. He received some military and technical aid from many countries, including the Soviet Union, Turkey, Germany, France, Italy, and Britain, but none of these sources proved regular or generous enough to constitute a reliable basis for state power. Afghanistan had to pay for technical assistance, and Amanullah thus had to develop a domestic resource base. This imperative forced him to reverse Abdul Rahman Khan's isolationism. He sought to open the country to trade and to promote state-led capital accumulation. He also tried to create a disciplined professional army but refused to divert the necessary funds from other projects.[35]

Amanullah's reforms resembled those that had transformed other absolutist states to nation-states. They included radical new measures in all three areas identified by Migdal as necessary to the reconstitution of social control: taxes, land tenure, and transportation.[36] If carried through, these changes would have transformed the peasant-tribal rural society into an open, commercial society linked to both the state and the market.

Amanullah regularized the system of taxation, abolishing tax farming and requiring that all taxes be paid in cash. He abolished many arbitrary taxes. Because the capitalist development he wanted to promote had not yet begun, he continued to rely on the main revenue source of coercion-intensive state builders—direct taxes on agriculture. He raised the rates of direct tax on land and livestock, which together accounted for five-eighths of his domestic revenues in 1926.[37] This tax increase inevitably brought him into conflict with the landowning khans. He also simplified customs duties and actually tried to collect them, which in turn brought him into conflict with border tribes who lived by smuggling.

These measures depended on expansion of capitalist agriculture and accumulation of capital for trade, so Amanullah took measures to make both land and labor into commodities. He instituted full private property in arable land and pasture.[38] He sold off state land, thus creating a new class of peasant proprietors, and he abolished slavery and forced labor. He established a new currency, the afghani, which enjoyed a favorable exchange rate with the rupee, although he could not yet persuade the Afghans to accept paper money.

To encourage trade he planned a new transportation network. He opened and improved roads and tried to prevent border tribes from exacting duties from caravans. He also planned to build a railroad, something Afghanistan does not have to this day. To accumulate trading capital and wrest control of foreign trade from British, Indian, and Russian companies, he established the first joint-stock companies in Afghanistan; at the time of his overthrow he was planning to establish a central bank. He also introduced the first consumer (nonmilitary) industries into Afghanistan to initiate a moderate program of import substitution. Capital remained scarce, however, and at the end of his reign he undertook a lengthy international tour in search of foreign support. Whereas his grandfather had sought weapons and cash, Amanullah sought investment and technology.

From the beginning of his reign Amanullah took measures to strengthen the legality and accountability of the state. His grandfather had made many new laws and established regular administrative departments and ministries; Amanullah went beyond these measures to establish a complete legal basis for state power. He gave Afghanistan its first constitution (1921), according to which even the king's actions were, in principle, subordinated to law, and he promulgated written administrative regulations for all operations of government. The constitution introduced the notion of universal citizenship (defining as Afghans all citizens of Afghanistan, rather than only Pashtuns, a change not always reflected in popular usage even today) and for the first time declared that these citizens had rights. The constitution established the Loya Jirga as the highest representative organ of the state, and Amanullah convened it three times. He even attempted to require Afghans to carry identity cards, but this measure aroused such opposition, especially because of its relation to conscription, that it seems never to have been enforced.

Just as Amanullah ceased to run the Afghan state on the basis of payments from imperial powers, he also tried to eliminate the domestic elements of redistributive politics and indirect rule. He ended the allowances paid to tribal and other local leaders and tried to eliminate their role in tax collection and conscription. He also proposed the establishment of government licensing requirements for mullahs and qazis, which would have increased government supervision of the judiciary and of religious teaching. Amanullah undertook controversial social reforms to broaden effective civil rights and citizenship. He expanded state schools and encouraged public participation of women (whose confinement to the home is another form of indirect rule).

Amanullah not only expanded the Afghan educational system but opened it to foreign influences. He established three elite high schools that, together with Habibia, dominated secondary education in Kabul through the 1970s. Each was established with aid from a different foreign country and taught the corresponding foreign language. Amaniyya, the French lycée later renamed Istiqlal, opened in 1922; Amani, the German school later renamed Nijat, opened in 1924; and Ghazi, another Indian-staffed English school, opened in 1927. Amanullah also founded the French Malalai lycée, which opened in 1921 as the first high school for girls. He established primary schools in every district and experimented with dispatching teachers to accompany nomads on their migrations. He also began the policy of sending elite students abroad for higher education. He even shocked many Afghans by sending girls to study in Turkey and Switzerland.[39]

Although Amanullah tried to reform the army, he did not make the army's strength and loyalty his top priority, as had Abdul Rahman. Many of the reforms in the army were proposed by Turkish advisers. At their suggestion Amanullah eliminated the role of village elders in conscription and replaced them with a lottery among holders of the identity cards he had imposed. This scheme was apparently a major factor in setting off the 1924 rebellion by the Mangal tribe in Khost. Suppression of the rebellion (less by the army than by lashkars raised among the Mangals' tribal rivals) consumed two years' revenues and halted the state-building program for several years.

The army performed poorly in Khost (and later during the 1928 rebellions) in part because Amanullah's attempts to restructure it had left it in disarray. In line with a proposal by his Turkish military advisers, he drastically reduced cash pay. As compensation soldiers were to receive such noncash benefits as shelter and food, a strategy designed to make them more directly dependent on and loyal to the army. These measures apparently worked well in Turkey, but not in Afghanistan, where soldiers found themselves without cash, food, or shelter.[40]

In a pattern repeated in 1978–79, the demoralized army failed to respond to the 1928 rebellions; several important garrisons surrendered, and this demonstration of the government's weakness emboldened other rebels. The revolts erupted in November 1928 after Amanullah's return in July from a seven-month trip abroad. During this trip Amanullah had sought technical and financial aid in India, Egypt, Italy, Germany, England, the Soviet Union, Turkey, and Iran. Like Dost Muhammad, Mahmud Tarzi, and others to follow, Amanullah's encounter with more developed societies fired his determination to "modernize" Afghanistan. Shortly after his return, he announced a new set of reforms.

Some of his proposed measures, especially those that struck at the power of the religious establishment, aroused protests from leading ulama, depriving Amanullah of Islamic legitimacy in the eyes of much of the public. He also rejected the recommendations of a Loya Jirga he had convened, which effectively alienated any tribal base of power he might have mobilized. His government's attempts to curb smuggling and toll collection coincidentally led to what under normal circumstances might have been a routine confrontation with a border tribe. In this context, however, the army did not strike back, and the mullahs gave the tribal revolt Islamic sanction. Amanullah had ordered the collection of tax arrears before his departure for Europe, and the hardships occasioned by both tax collection and the effects of capitalist development had alienated Tajik peasants just north of Kabul, who were most exposed to these changes. When they also rose with the support of Sufis and ulama, the garrison of Charikar peaceably surrendered to them.

The revolts conformed in part to Ibn Khaldun's model of dynastic decay. Whereas Abdul Rahman had taken the throne himself, his grandson Amanullah was born and raised in Kabul city and had virtually no contact with tribal Afghanistan. The early revolts among Pashtuns were by tribes who were summoned to rise against the decaying dynasty by charismatic mullahs. Other aspects of the revolts, however, showed how the increasing integration of Afghanistan into the international state system was changing the pattern of state formation and resistance. The rebels from north of Kabul were led by a social bandit named Habibullah, commonly called Bacha-yi Saqao (son of the water carrier). Habibullah claimed to be a former army officer in Amanullah's Turkish-led model battalion who had turned to banditry after being unjustly imprisoned by a corrupt official. He had also been involved in a movement in support of the anti-Soviet basmachi rebels in Central Asia. He was not a traditional tribal or religious leader but a disaffected former state recruit involved in national and even international politics. Bacha-yi Saqao thus foreshadowed the modern Afghan resistance.[41]

His troops were the first to reach Kabul, where a Kohistani Sufi leader (the pir of Tagao) proclaimed him Amir Habibullah, Khadim-i Din-i Rasul Allah (servant of the religion of the Messenger of God). Amanullah's discontinuance of tribal allowances, his abolition of the role of tribal khans in administration, and his abuse of the Loya Jirga had alienated the tribal leadership, and the Durranis of Qandahar, where the deposed king fled from the Bacha in January, refused his appeal for aid. The Hazaras, to whom Amanullah had granted full citizenship and the right to celebrate Shiʿa rituals in public, continued to support him, and the Soviets sent a small contingent into northern Afghanistan, but without Pashtun support even against a Tajik amir, Amanullah had to flee the country. He retired into Italian exile, where he died in 1960.

As during the first two Anglo-Afghan wars, the defeat of the ruler led to a weakening of state power, a loss of social control, and the reemergence of tribalism. Pashtun tribal power soon deposed the Tajik amir. The nang tribes east of Kabul had set off the revolt against Amanullah, but true to their heritage of egalitarian tribalism, they were unable to unite to advance on the capital until the arrival of an outside leader. In this case the leader was Gen. Nadir Khan, eldest of the Musahiban brothers, who had been exiled as ambassador to France after a dispute with Amanullah. The British, happy over the departure of Amanullah but concerned over spreading anarchy in Afghanistan, allowed Nadir passage through India and ordered political agents in the tribal areas not to prevent the tribes from crossing the Durand Line into Afghanistan. After the harvest in October, Nadir and two of his four brothers assembled a tribal army that captured Kabul from the Bacha, whom they hanged. Once in Kabul, a jirga of Nadir's lashkar proclaimed him Nadir Shah, King of Afghanistan. Because Nadir had no money to pay the fighters, they methodically pillaged the city of Kabul. The victors returned home loaded with loot, leaving Nadir Shah at the head of a state with neither army nor treasury.

Afghanistan under Nadir Shah and His Brothers

Members of the Musahiban family ruled Afghanistan from 1929 to 1978. Nadir Shah was assassinated in 1933, and his nineteen-year-old son Muhammad Zahir succeeded him, reigning until 1973. For the first two decades of Zahir Shah's reign, his uncles effectively controlled the government as prime ministers. Muhammad Hashim ruled autocratically until 1946, when his brother, Shah Mahmud, replaced him. Shah Mahmud eventually held elections to the "Liberal Parliament," which sat from 1949 to 1952. In 1953 Zahir's cousin, Muhammad Daoud Khan, seized control and became prime minister. Zahir Shah asserted his own rule from 1963 to 1973 and tried to develop a constitutional monarchy. In 1973 Daoud ousted him, abolished the monarchy, and ruled as president of the Republic of Afghanistan until he and most of his immediate family met their deaths at the hands of the PDPA in 1978. Zahir Shah remained in exile in Rome with his nephew and son-in-law, Gen. Abdul Wali Khan.

The conditions under which Nadir Shah took power shaped the approach that all Musahiban rulers took toward social control. Changes in the international system, however—the British withdrawal from and partition of India and the beginning of Cold War competition between the United States and the USSR in the postcolonial states—transformed the structure of opportunities available to the Musahiban.

Nadir Shah, who had grown up in British India and spent much of the 1920s in southern France, shared with Amanullah the goal of modernizing Afghanistan. At least on paper he retained some of Amanullah's reforms, such as the structure of administration and the collection of all taxes in cash. But tribal society was now too strong, and the state too weak, for the latter to impose its plans on the former by coercion. Instead, Nadir and his successors turned to the international system for resources that would enable them gradually to enlarge a state-dominated modern sector centered in Kabul without confronting the rural power holders.[42]

Like Dost Muhammad and Abdul Rahman, Nadir Shah assumed the throne after a breakdown of state control and the reemergence of tribal power. Unlike them, he took power at a time when the external threat to Afghanistan was minimal. He did not need an army to defend the country against foreign enemies (in any case, no regular army had ever done so successfully). He sent Pashtun lashkars to reassert control over the rebellious Tajiks, who had supported Bacha-yi Saqao. In the 1930s the British gave the government a grant to help reestablish the army; Germany, France, and Italy also offered aid, but in relatively small amounts.[43]

The circumstances of their accession to power forced the Musahiban to compromise with rural power holders. Throughout their rule the proportion of revenue derived from direct taxes on agriculture and pastoralism declined. Whereas Amanullah had tried to initiate state-led industrialization to replace imports, the main focus of the state's effort to develop a resource base during the early Musahiban period (1929–53) was the cultivation of primary-product exports in alliance with the merchant class. These exports (karakul skins, fresh and dried fruit, cotton and some textiles) were an easy target of indirect taxes, requiring little direct coercion or monitoring. The taxes were collected from joint-stock companies operating under the aegis of the Bank-i Milli (National Bank), chartered in 1932 under the direction of Abdul Majid Zabuli, the leading Afghan capitalist. The private bank was granted far-reaching powers over the currency and economy. By 1931 land taxes were already less than a third of the total revenue, about half their share under Amanullah.[44] By 1952 only 18 percent of domestic revenue came from land and livestock taxes, but 40 percent came from taxes on foreign trade, 13 percent from corporate taxes, and 10 percent from government monopolies in imported commodities (petroleum and tobacco). Domestic revenue covered 74 percent of all government expenditure; foreign aid was still relatively small, supporting 18 percent of total expenditure (Appendix C and Table 3.1).

Under the early Musahiban, the state relied mainly on the merchant class, rather than on landowners. The merchants were not yet capitalists: most of their investments were in trade, not production. Bank-i Milli and the joint-stock companies were designed to make merchant capital more productive. The weak comprador bourgeoisie

Table 3.1 Composition of Government Domestic Revenue, 1952–1972

| Year | Domestic Revenue (millions of afghanis) | Direct Taxes | | | Indirect Taxes | | | Sales | | Other Revenues (%) |
		Total (%)	Land and Livestock (%)	Other (%)	Total (%)	Foreign Trade (%)	Other (%)	Total (%)	Natural Gas (%)	
1952	614	31	18	13	47	40	7	10	0	12
1953	775	27	14	13	44	39	5	10	0	19
1954	964	22	12	10	53	48	5	12	0	12
1955	1,283	17	9	8	37	33	4	19	0	28
1956	1,149	20	6	13	53	47	6	5	0	23
1957a	836	19	6	13	38	35	2	3	0	41
1957b	1,348	21	7	14	59	58	1	7	0	13
1958b	1,533	17	7	11	57	56	2	7	0	19
1959b	1,601	15	7	8	48	46	2	25	0	12
1960b	2,099	14	5	9	53	47	6	16	0	16
1961c	721	11	5	6	44	39	5	29	0	16
1962	2,123	15	6	9	53	50	3	24	0	8

1963	2,677	14	5	9	64	61	3	27	0	−5
1964	3,061	15	4	10	63	56	7	18	0	5
1965	3,976	15	4	10	55	52	2	26	0	5
1966	4,285	14	2	12	62	60	2	15	0	9
1967	4,211	13	2	11	59	58	2	20	1	8
1968	4,465	8	2	6	47	46	1	37	10	8
1969	5,085	8	2	6	50	48	3	34	9	8
1970	5,702	8	2	7	49	47	2	34	13	9
1971	5,823	7	1	6	51	49	2	32	10	10
1972	6,172	9	1	6	48	46	2	32	12	11
1973[d]	7,037	9	1	7	46	43	3	36	12	9

Source: Data from Fry, *Afghan Economy,* 170–71.

Note: Except as noted, years are Afghan (Islamic solar) years beginning in the given Common Era year. Because of rounding errors, sum of direct taxes, indirect taxes, sales, and other revenue does not always equal 100 percent.

[a]First half of 1336.

[b]Common Era years.

[c]Second half of 1340.

[d]Estimate; final figures not available.

that developed was dependent on the state, in particular on the royal lineage, to which it developed links of patronage, more colloquially known as corruption.

Because the state did not depend directly on the khans, it needed neither to confront them (as Abdul Rahman or Amanullah had) nor to mobilize them for conquest (as Ahmad Shah Durrani had). Instead both khans and ulama were given symbolic roles without real power and allowed considerable autonomy in their local affairs, a strategy called encapsulation. Nadir Shah's 1931 constitution gave the ulama an institutional role in reviewing legislation and provided for representation of ulama and khans in the Loya Jirga. Nadir Shah also gave a number of privileges, such as exemption from taxes and conscription, to four eastern tribes who had helped him to the throne.

The development of an enclave economy was extremely slow and the transport links to export markets difficult. Even with the aid of the merchant class, the state had limited autonomy from the tribes and religious establishment. As shown in Table 3.2, during World War II the already tiny proportion of GNP extracted by the state declined, along with the rest of Afghanistan's export-led cash economy. By the end of the 1940s domestic revenues and state expenditures were both less than 3 percent of GNP.

Development of a Weak Rentier State

The changes in the international system after 1947 gave the state more autonomy not only from tribes and the religious establishment but increasingly from the merchants as well. The autonomy was limited to the ability to pursue projects financed by foreign aid and, later, by sales of natural gas; these projects were significant compared with the previous level of government expenditure but still small with respect even to Afghanistan's weak economy. Although government expenditure, financed by foreign aid, could expand more quickly than domestic revenue, it still peaked at 11 percent of the economy, or 24 percent of its cash sector.

The circumstances that allowed the rulers to pursue this strategy of state expansion derived from Afghanistan's place in the postwar international system. Britain withdrew from India, leaving the new nation of Pakistan on one border of Afghanistan, while the Soviet Union, across another border, became one pole of the global alliance system. Afghanistan opposed Pakistan over the status of the Pashtuns there but depended on it for a link to the international market through the port of Karachi. When British India became independent as India and Pakistan, Afghanistan argued that the tribal areas, too, should have had the option of declaring independence as the nation of Pashtunistan, which presumably would have been integrated into Afghanistan, making the Pashtuns a clear majority there. Instead the colonial authorities allowed the tribes to choose only between India and Pakistan, and they opted for the latter. The resentments and fears that the Pashtunistan issue aroused in the

Table 3.2 Indicators of State Economic Capacity, 1935–1972

| Year | GNP (millions of afghanis) | Percentage of GNP | | |
		Cash Economy	Domestic Revenue	Government Expenditure
1935	2,493	40	6	6
1936	2,558	42	7	7
1937	2,740	42	7	7
1938	2,909	42	7	7
1939	3,084	43	8	8
1940	3,399	42	7	10
1941	3,726	41	7	8
1942	4,683	39	6	7
1943	6,038	39	5	5
1944	7,659	37	4	3
1945	9,596	35	3	3
1946	12,135	33	3	3
1947	13,432	33	2	3
1948	13,963	33	2	3
1949	16,040	29	2	3
1950	17,306	28	3	4
1951	18,015	30	3	4
1952	19,053	32	3	4
1953	19,449	33	4	4
1954	21,778	31	4	5
1955	24,491	34	5	5
1956	31,320	36	4	4
1957	34,262	38	4	4
1958	34,856	37	4	4

(*continued*)

Table 3.2 (*continued*)

Year	GNP (millions of afghanis)	Percentage of GNP		
		Cash Economy	Domestic Revenue	Government Expenditure
1959	30,999	39	5	6
1960	29,211	43	7	9
1961	31,120	43	7	10
1962	37,151	41	6	9
1963	40,121	46	7	11
1964	50,789	46	6	8
1965	62,652	46	6	7
1966	68,814	48	6	8
1967	69,877	48	6	8
1968	69,151	47	7	9
1969	72,391	46	7	9
1970	84,363	45	7	8
1971	91,146	47	6	8
1972	93,554	48	7	8

Source: Data from Fry, *Afghan Economy,* 37, 152.

Note: Years are Afghan (Islamic solar) years beginning in indicated Common Era years. For 1957–61 government revenue and expenditure are estimated using averages of partial years overlapping the given year.

predominantly Punjabi rulers of Pakistan, especially the military, continue to affect Pakistani perceptions of interests in Afghanistan.

The conflict inevitably made the Royal Government of Afghanistan seek ways to circumvent its dependence on Pakistan for access to the international market, on which its fragile cash economy and meager government revenue depended. Transportation through eastern Iran was extremely poor, so the only alternative outlet was Soviet Central Asia. Afghanistan's relations with the USSR warmed when the Soviets helped the Afghans evade a Pakistani slowdown of transit trade in 1950 in reprisal for the Pashtunistan campaign.

In the immediate postwar period the Musahiban had sought assistance from the United States, which was still uninvolved in the regional power struggle. By the time

Daoud took over in 1953, however, it was clear that U.S. economic aid was inadequate and that military aid would be precluded by the growing engagement of the United States with Pakistan. In February 1954, President Eisenhower approved the first U.S. arms assistance to Pakistan, and in December Secretary of State John Foster Dulles refused an Afghan request for military aid. One month later Daoud accepted a Soviet offer of assistance. This sequence of events fostered international realignments in southern Asia: India and Afghanistan received military equipment from the Soviet Union, which supported their positions on regional issues, while Pakistan received similar supplies and support from the United States and, later, China.[45]

The Soviets also offered a $100 million line of credit for development and soon tendered other aid. After 1956 the United States competed with the Soviet Union in offering development aid. From then until 1973, foreign grants and loans accounted for 80 percent of Afghan investment and development expenditure. The government of Afghanistan had chronic difficulties in paying for even the 20 percent of projects earmarked for local financing and in paying the operating costs incurred after projects were in place.[46]

Foreign aid enabled the Daoud regime to expand government expenditure in the late 1950s with a very modest increase in domestic revenue. The importance of taxes on land and livestock continued to decline; neither Daoud nor any of his successors used the new military power acquired from the USSR to pursue a coercive state-building strategy based on taxing agriculture. Land and livestock taxes, which accounted for only 18 percent of domestic revenue in the year ending in March 1953, fell to about a 7 percent share by 1958; in the 1970s they provided less than 2 percent (Table 3.1). Foreign trade continued to be the main source of taxes, supplying about 80 percent of all taxes by the 1960s. Tax revenue, however, diminished in importance relative to the income from government sales and enterprises, including natural gas after 1968. Indeed, of fifty developing countries surveyed in the early 1970s only Nepal had a lower tax effort—the ratio of actual tax revenues to estimated taxable capacity—than Afghanistan.[47]

Afghanistan became a weak rentier or allocation state. From 1958 to 1968 and again in the 1970s the state financed over 40 percent of its expenditures from "revenue accruing directly from abroad," including both foreign aid and sales of natural gas to the USSR.[48] Unlike oil states, however, which can control their sales volume (though not price), Afghanistan had no control over foreign aid, which declined sharply after 1966, causing a state fiscal crisis.

The most important effect of foreign aid was to provide both cash and weapons for the accumulation and concentration of the means of violence in a modern army and national police force. Nadir Shah originally had to reinstate the indirect hasht nafari form of conscription, but by 1978 Daoud's Republic was implementing universal conscription with reasonable success.[49] Otherwise, foreign aid generally financed the types of expenditure classified as developmental: education, health, transportation and communication (mostly the construction of roads and airports), agriculture (including Green Revolution technology), and industry and mines. As Table 3.3 shows, from 1958 to 1964, more than half of the expenditure went for transportation, primarily the construction of a nationwide paved system of roads and airports. The United States built the Kabul-Qandahar section of the main highway, with spurs leading to Pakistan, and the Qandahar airport. The USSR built the Qandahar-Herat highway, with spurs leading west to Iran and north to the USSR. The Soviets also built the key road linking Kabul to the Soviet Union via the Salang Tunnel, the opening of which in 1964 marked the high point of the construction effort; the highway was the first all-weather modern road connecting the areas south and north of the Hindu Kush. All the roads and bridges built by the Soviets were wide and heavy enough to withstand Soviet military traffic; as Abdul Rahman had feared, these roads and airports made the Soviet invasion of December 1979 possible.

The new road system created a national market, equalizing prices of wheat, rice, and meat north and south of the Hindu Kush. At the same time, it permitted the penetration of the countryside by manufactured imports, which a number of writers claim ruined the livelihood of many artisans. The road system also facilitated labor migration, both within the country and to oil-rich Iran.[50]

In the later 1960s agriculture, especially Green Revolution wheat technology, came to predominate in development spending. Foreign aid also permitted the opening of some state industries (and the nationalization of others, such as the Spinzar Cotton Mill) and the steady expansion of education. As a result, the state became less dependent on the merchant class for capital accumulation.

An analysis of who paid for these programs and who benefited from them shows that the government taxed the producers of such traditional agricultural exports as cotton, karakul skins, and wool while subsidizing wheat production and transportation. The subsidy of wheat production took the form of large (and often wasteful) investments in dam and irrigation projects, such as the Helmand-Arghandab Valley Authority. The transportation subsidy benefited the private sector by providing large investments in road construction with no user fees. The government also spent foreign aid on the education and employment of the new middle class.

These expenditures showed the domestic consequences of becoming an allocation state; they represented the distribution of foreign aid as patronage to favored groups. The beneficiaries of most of the irrigation projects were tribal Pashtuns. Eastern Pashtuns dominated the trucking industry, especially because much of the profit derived from smuggling across the nearby Pakistani border. Many of those recruited into the new middle class were also tribal Pashtuns; indeed, the Musahiban made a concerted though ultimately unsuccessful effort to Pashtunize the predominantly Persian-speaking civil service. Most producers of traditional exports, however, were non-Pashtuns. The Musahiban rulers used the resources obtained from their international connections to create a patronage network calculated to strengthen Pashtun nationalism, which they hoped would in turn prove an ideological buttress for their rule.

Table 3.3 Components of Government Expenditure, 1952–1972

Year	Ordinary Expenditure				Development Expenditure						
	Total (millions of afghanis)	Defense and Security (%)	Debt Service (%)	Other (%)	Total (millions of afghanis)	Education (%)	Health (%)	Transportation and Communication (%)	Agriculture (%)	Industry and Mines (%)	Other (%)
1952	660	38	0	62	170	15	0	0	0	0	85
1953	666	42	0	58	172	16	0	0	0	0	84
1954	825	26	0	74	205	9	3	24	5	0	59
1955	933	32	0	69	327	7	2	22	2	5	62
1956	910	29	0	72	381	7	2	35	4	3	49
1957[a]	526	34	0	66	214	9	3	38	4	2	44
1957[b]	1,007	42	14	44	374	12	3	45	27	12	3
1958[b]	1,251	41	14	45	421	8	1	55	20	11	4
1959[b]	1,394	37	13	50	705	7	3	62	13	16	0
1960[b]	1,558	41	12	47	1,550	10	4	61	7	12	5
1961[c]	878	34	15	51	520	7	4	59	10	19	2

(*continued*)

Table 3.3 (continued)

Year	Ordinary Expenditure				Development Expenditure						
	Total (millions of afghanis)	Defense and Security (%)	Debt Service (%)	Other (%)	Total (millions of afghanis)	Education (%)	Health (%)	Transportation and Communication (%)	Agriculture (%)	Industry and Mines (%)	Other (%)
1962	1,850	38	14	49	1,446	6	1	58	8	25	1
1963	2,416	31	23	46	1,830	6	1	51	10	24	8
1964	2,558	36	15	49	1,622	3	1	54	8	27	6
1965	2,902	36	9	55	1,720	5	1	23	25	38	8
1966	3,403	38	14	48	1,728	7	1	21	27	34	10
1967	3,613	38	18	44	1,707	7	1	18	40	25	9
1968	4,254	35	14	51	1,820	7	2	19	37	20	15
1969	4,732	33	18	48	1,920	7	2	20	44	17	11
1970	5,158	32	20	48	1,731	6	3	24	41	19	8
1971	5,504	30	21	50	1,916	3	3	20	48	17	8
1972	5,689	29	19	52	2,100	4	4	15	45	16	16

Source: Data from Fry, Afghan Economy, 194–95.

Note: Except where noted, years are Afghan (Islamic solar) years beginning in the given Common Era year. Because of rounding errors, sums do not always equal 100 percent.

aFirst half of 1336.
bCommon Era years.
cSecond half of 1340.

Table 3.4 Determinants of Government Expenditure, 1953–1971
(Standard Errors in Parentheses)

Type of Expenditure	Estimated Elasticity with Respect to					Durbin-Watson Statistic
	Previous Year's Expenditure		Domestic Revenue		Foreign Aid	
Ordinary	0.76[a]	(0.15)	0.30	(0.15)	−0.03 (0.02)	2.13
Development	0.35[a]	(0.07)	0.20[a]	(0.07)	0.49[a] (0.05)	1.36

Source: Data from Fry, *Afghan Economy,* 158–59.

Note: Both regressions were carried out on natural logarithms of all variables. Both regressions were significant at the .0001 level. Degrees of freedom: 3 for the regression, 15 for the residuals.

[a]Significant at the .05 level.

Government expenditures did not conform to any development plan. As is typical of the pattern of state expansion in rentier states, the apparatus of distribution (which is what the "development" projects were) expanded according to the availability of rentier income.[51] As Table 3.4 shows, ordinary expenditure remained relatively steady, as reflected in its strong relationship (elasticity of 0.76) to the previous year's expenditure. A 10 percent change in domestic revenue led to an immediate shift of only 3 percent in ordinary expenditure, although over time ordinary expenditure would adjust to a permanent shift in revenue; foreign aid did not affect it at all. Development expenditure, however, was much more variable. It was much less related to the previous year's expenditure and quickly expanded or contracted with changes in the level of foreign aid. During the Cold War the government's ability to pursue autonomous policies of "development," and to maintain the support of the new constituencies that it created with such programs, depended on the level of foreign aid.

Among the most important constituencies were the newly educated, loosely known as intellectuals. After the mid-1950s the school system expanded with foreign, largely American, aid.[52] The government established primary schools in some villages and district centers, secondary schools in many provincial centers, and secondary boarding schools in Kabul for some graduates of provincial primary schools. Several of the secondary boarding schools were Pashto-medium schools that recruited students from the sons of rural khans. Ibn Sina, a teacher's training high school, drew students from all over Afghanistan, while the Rahman Baba and Khushhal Khan schools enrolled students from the eastern tribes, along the Afghan and Pakistani sides of the Durand Line, respectively. Prime Minister Daoud's government also established a military boarding school that trained mainly eastern and Ghilzai Pashtuns for careers in the officer corps. These boarding schools again followed the model of the Janissaries, the Ottoman infantry, who were separated early from their families and trained in special boarding schools in Istanbul. Hafizullah Amin was for a time principal of Ibn Sina, which became a major recruiting ground for his Khalq faction of the People's Democratic Party of Afghanistan (PDPA).[53]

The establishment of an Afghan system of higher education, meanwhile, began with the founding of the Faculty of Medicine in 1932 under French sponsorship, reflecting the French-exile background of the Musahiban family. Other faculties followed, and they united to form Kabul University in 1947. Nearly every faculty had a foreign sponsor, which provided financial support, professors, and scholarships for the training of Afghan professors. The two most prestigious faculties, of Medicine and of Law and Political Science, had French affiliations. The United States sponsored those on Agriculture, Engineering, and Education; the Federal Republic of Germany sponsored the Faculties of Science and Economics and the Department of Anthropology in the Faculty of Letters; al-Azhar University in Egypt sponsored the Faculty of Sharia; and the Soviet Union sponsored the Polytechnic Institute.[54]

Other training establishments also had foreign patrons: West Germany sponsored the Police Academy, while Turkey, and later the Soviet Union, supported the Military Academy. In conjunction with the founding of these faculties, increasing numbers of Afghans received scholarships to study in France, Egypt, the United States, Germany, India, and the Soviet Union. In the early 1970s half of the teachers in the Sharia Faculty had degrees from al-Azhar, and two-thirds of those in the Faculty of Law and Political Science held degrees from French universities. As with other development projects, the various faculties grew according to the amount of foreign aid available to them, rather than according to any educational program or employment plan.[55]

Until the 1950s, access to secondary education, Kabul University, foreign study, and the officer corps was restricted to a small group, mainly residents of Kabul. As late as 1959 Kabul city, with 1.8 percent of the country's population, contained 73.7 percent of the secondary school students. In 1950 the number of students in all postsecondary institutions in Afghanistan was less than 500, and by 1955 there were still only 758 such students (Table 3.5). During the late 1940s and early 1950s 20 to 30 students went abroad to study each year.[56]

The foreign aid–funded growth of the education system, however, quickly multiplied the number of educated or semieducated Afghan youth of village backgrounds, although these remained an isolated minority in a country where less than 10 percent of the population and 2 percent of the women could read and write. During the last eight years of Daoud's premiership (1955–63), when foreign aid began to flow in large quantities, the number of students in primary and secondary schools nearly tripled, while the number of postsecondary students (mainly at Kabul University) increased more than fourfold (Table 3.5). By 1965 the number of students in higher education had grown to the still minuscule figure of 3,451, but that small group had disproportionate power: student demonstrations led by Babrak Karmal, for example, forced the resignation of Prime Minister Muhammad Yousof.

Table 3.5 Growth of State Schooling, Selected Years

	Primary and Secondary School Students			University and Other
Year	Primary	Secondary	Total	Third-Level Students[a]
1932	—	—	1,350	—
1936	—	—	9,275	—
1941	—	—	64,000	—
1946	—	—	93,545	—
1950–51	91,414[b]	4,908[c]	96,322	461[b]
1955	111,658	9,300	120,958	758
1961	213,676	20,133	233,809	1,987
1965	358,037	45,248	403,285	3,451
1970	540,685	116,174	656,859	7,732
1974	654,209	172,797	827,006	10,956
1975	784,568[d]	93,497[d]	878,065	12,256
1976	841,046	93,510	934,556	14,214
1977	889,134	98,420	987,554	16,147
1978	942,787	106,544	1,049,331	21,118
1979	929,822	133,433	1,063,255	22,974
1980	1,115,993	136,898	1,252,891	—
1981	1,198,286	159,390	1,357,676	—
1982	449,948	93,933	543,881	19,652
1984	545,959	99,729	645,688	—
1985	580,499	105,032	685,531	—

Source: Data from UNESCO, *Statistical Yearbook,* various years.

[a]May exclude military training.

[b]Data are for 1950.

[c]Data are for 1951.

[d]In 1975 grades seven and eight were shifted from the secondary to the primary school category, accounting for the abrupt change from 1974.

Under New Democracy (1963–73) the growth continued. The number of primary school students doubled, and secondary school enrollment increased more than six-fold, growing by an average of one-fifth per year. University enrollment grew slightly less rapidly than during the previous eight years, but it was 3.5 times as large at the end of the decade as at the beginning, nearly 11,000 students by 1974. By then about 1,500 students per year were also being sent abroad.[57] At the same time, the expansion of the army had led to the growth of training for a new officer corps. Between 1956 and 1978, an estimated 3,725 Afghan military officers—concentrated in the elite air force and armored corps—had been trained in the Soviet Union, some for as long as six years, while Afghan officers had taken a total of 487 courses in the United States.[58] Smaller numbers of officers had been trained in Egypt and India.

This state-building strategy made the government more independent of the tribes, peasants, and ulama. In 1959, after Daoud felt that his new army and police were strong enough, he confronted both the tribes and the religious establishment, using women as symbols. The women of Daoud's family and of senior army officers appeared unveiled at independence day celebrations and made it known through word of mouth that any woman who so wished was free to do likewise. Protests by religious figures were suppressed firmly but without violence and were also answered by the government's own religious authorities, in particular Musa Shafiq, the royal family's imam, who had degrees from both al-Azhar and Columbia University. At about the same time Daoud ordered the arrest of Sibghatullah Mujaddidi, who had preached against the government's relations with the Soviet Union. He also ordered the arrest and confinement in Kabul of several important tribal khans.[59]

Generally, however, the government countered tribal power with gradual encapsulation and fragmentation rather than confrontation. Its command over foreign aid, state enterprises, education, and state employment enabled it to compete with the khans for the allegiance of their tribes and even sons. The state also turned some khans into dependent allies; through the Ministry of Tribes, the government continued subsidies to some tribal leaders, especially those whose tribes had helped Nadir Shah to power.[60]

At the level of the uluswali or alaqdari the administration recognized (or reinforced) qawm as an institution and appointed maliks or arbabs to represent the qawm before the local administration. The level of segmentation that the local government recognized, however, was invariably a low one, generally no larger than a village or one of its wards. Because the government did not collect taxes from the villages, its influence there was limited. Indeed, in parts of the countryside state enterprises like the Spinzar Cotton Mill were more important conduits of government policies and presence than the administration. Local self-rule was a defense against the state, not a part of it. Because the state generally had little to offer, the villagers and tribespeople protected their interests by constructing parallel power networks, always at a local level, involving face-to-face interaction.[61] Qawm remained an active force locally, but was powerless regionally or nationally. Daoud called a Loya Jirga on a number of occasions, but the body of appointed representatives (arbabs and maliks) approved whatever was set before it, such as the proposal to accept Soviet military aid in 1955. The Loya Jirga showed the encapsulation of the tribes, not their continuing power.

As the state increasingly relied on the graduates of the state education system, the loyalties of that stratum grew in importance. The intellectuals had an ambivalent relationship with the Musahiban. Many bitterly opposed compromises the Musahiban had made with the traditional forces and with Britain, as well as their exclusion of intellectuals from power in favor of members of the ruling lineage. At the same time, the Musahiban, especially Daoud, invested heavily in the expansion of this class and widened the opportunities for teachers, bureaucrats, and army officers.[62]

During the Liberal Parliament of 1949–52 and the New Democracy of 1964–73, intellectuals were permitted limited freedoms; between those two periods their representatives suffered imprisonment and exile. Their intermittently banned publications, in which some of the intellectuals castigated both the government and the people (for their "ignorance"), became the focus of future political movements. At no time, however, did the rulers grant the intellectuals access to real power, and fear of radical challenge led the rulers to limit or repress the intellectuals' activities even when they themselves were cautiously and autocratically advancing some of the intellectuals' goals.

Zahir Shah's 1963 decision to introduce a more representative form of government was a recognition that, as the activities and size of the nation-state enclave expanded, it needed new forms of legitimation among both intellectuals and the traditional forces. To promulgate this representative system, in 1964 he summoned a Loya Jirga, probably the freest and most effective such body ever convened by the state. Rather than simply ratify the draft constitution, the representatives engaged in serious debate and rewrote several provisions.[63] The constitution provided for elected upper and lower houses of a consultative parliament, which—together with some appointed representatives of social groups—constituted the Loya Jirga. Districts were gerrymandered to assure Pashtun predominance, and each parliament was over 60 percent Pashtun.[64] Members of the royal family were prohibited from standing for election or serving as ministers, and the ministerial posts were filled from the upper stratum of the intellectuals. Still, the king, acting together with a few of his close relatives, retained control over the government, which was not responsible to or elected from the parliament. Nor did Zahir Shah ever sign the legislation legalizing political parties. Political parties would have both given the intellectuals a recognized mechanism for seeking state power and allowed the rural power holders and the ulama to develop national networks. In other countries, weakened or decaying tribes became the basis of patronage networks that sustained political parties, but the royal regime did not accommodate this process in Afghanistan.[65]

Hence the landowners who dominated the parliament did not see themselves as coming to Kabul to govern the country collectively. They saw their position as an opportunity to use their influence to reduce unwanted state intrusion and to ensure that foreign aid would be spent in their districts under their supervision. But foreign aid declined steadily after 1965, thus limiting the government's ability to employ new graduates and dispense other patronage goods that might have alleviated public discontent (Appendix C).[66]

Afghanistan in the Age of Petrodollars

Daoud was excluded from politics by the 1964 constitution, along with all other members of the royal family, but he became increasingly discontented with his distance from power and with the deteriorating economic situation. In 1973 he staged a coup d'état when his cousin was in Italy and proclaimed Afghanistan a republic with himself as president.

The coup cast doubts on the state's legitimacy, which, together with a crisis in

Afghanistan's relation to the international alliance system, led to the next coup five years later, the Soviet invasion, and the war. Previously, armed tribes had been the arbiters of power, and when a member of the royal family took power in the 1970s, many Afghans and foreign observers viewed the event as just another episode of agnatic rivalry in the royal family. But Daoud seized power not as his uncle had, at the head of a tribal army, but as the leader of a group of Soviet-trained military officers. Some whom Daoud initially appointed to several key posts were affiliated with the Parcham faction of the PDPA. The coup signaled the entry of the intellectuals into the struggle for state power.

These domestic political changes occurred within a changing global and regional context. Some analysts have emphasized actions by the Shah of Iran; others point to conduct of the Soviet Union.[67] In fact, several international developments coincided, affecting the regions that had largely determined Afghan destiny throughout history: Iran, the Indus Valley (Pakistan), and Turkestan, now controlled by the USSR. These developments included the massive flow of capital into the countries around the Persian Gulf as a result of the OPEC price increases that followed the October War of 1973, less than three months after Daoud's coup; the breakup of Pakistan in 1971; and a shift in the Soviet Union's perception of its interests and opportunities in the Third World due to events in Vietnam, Egypt, Portuguese Africa, the Horn of Africa, and South Yemen. Iran under the Shah, supported by the United States, used oil money to become a regional power. Pakistan recognized its vulnerability to separatist or irredentist movements and reoriented its foreign relations toward the Islamic world; it increasingly saw itself as a complementary partner of Saudi Arabia. The USSR developed a more ideological and activist view of its own interests and capabilities in the Third World as it became more skeptical about non-Communist Third World nationalists and more optimistic about the prospects of Third World Marxist-Leninist parties.

During his brief rule as president, Daoud benefited from the oil boom both directly and indirectly. The state's fiscal position was strengthened by higher revenues from natural gas and from foreign exchange derived from remittances sent back by Afghans working in the Persian Gulf. Daoud also began to receive aid from the Shah of Iran. Soon after the 1973 coup the Shah opened negotiations for extensive development assistance as part of his grandiose scheme to reconstitute a Persian empire. The United States endorsed the Shah's attempt to become a regional hegemon under the 1969 Nixon doctrine. Daoud eagerly seized this opportunity, which fit his own long-standing policy of enhancing Afghanistan's independence by playing off foreign donors against each other.[68]

By October 1974 agreement had been reached in principle that Iran would furnish Afghanistan with $2 billion in aid over ten years, a sum almost equal to the total received from all sources during the Cold War. Not only the amount, however, but also the purpose of the aid signified a shift in the alignment of the Afghan state. Most of the money ($1.7 billion) was allocated to build Afghanistan's first railroad, linking Kabul, Ghazni, Qandahar, and Herat to the Iranian port of Bandar Abbas. Providing Afghanistan with a secure and relatively low-cost outlet to the sea via Iran would have removed the leverage that the Soviets had as the only alternative route to Pakistan for Afghanistan's overland trade.[69] It would also have allowed Afghanistan to receive military assistance from sources other than the USSR without the cooperation of Pakistan. Saudi Arabia, Iraq, and Kuwait also promised or delivered assistance.

In addition to providing money, the Shah of Iran arranged for his secret police, SAVAK, to assist Daoud in setting up a similar organization in Kabul. Daoud also sought military training agreements with Egypt and India, where Afghan officers could learn to use Soviet-supplied equipment without direct exposure to the Soviets themselves. Daoud also planned to visit Washington, the first such visit by an Afghan head of state.

In 1977, Daoud's last year, rentier income (foreign aid and revenue from sales of natural gas) had once again financed approximately 40 percent of government expenditure for several years (Appendix C). For the first time since 1967 development expenditure exceeded 50 percent of the total. Tax revenues, however, covered only 37 percent of expenditure, and more than three-fourths of those were indirect taxes, mostly on foreign trade. Direct taxes financed less than 10 percent of expenditure, and those on agriculture were negligible (about 1 percent of government expenditure). State enterprises and sales of products other than natural gas (mostly tobacco and petroleum products) provided about twice the revenue that direct taxes did.[70] The state was financially less dependent than ever on administrative control or penetration of society. Its fiscal and administrative operations provided it with hardly any information on or leverage over the population.

Renewed external revenues relieved Daoud of whatever incentives he might have had to make his government accountable. He did little to transform the mode of governing to match the means by which he had taken power. In traditional tribal fashion, he relied almost exclusively on his family; his brother Naim, for example, although without formal office, outranked all government officials. Daoud removed all representatives of Parcham from higher offices and did not permit representative institutions. At a controlled Loya Jirga in 1977 he promulgated a new constitution, which included provisions for a single party, designed to function as a tool of national integration, like the Shah of Iran's Rastakhiz. Before Daoud could establish this system, leftist military officers, including some who had helped him to power, overthrew and killed him on April 27, 1978.

Breakdown of Social Control

However unplanned that coup might have been, it was anything but "accidental."[71] Foreign aid–funded state building had begun to undermine old patterns of social control.

The state educational process led to weakened traditional social controls over those who went through it. Schooling separated village youth from their kin groups and from most of the population, in which the literacy rate remained under 10 percent. It provided a small minority with both ideological perspectives and career opportunities external to the rural community. The late philosopher and poet Sayd Bahauddin Majrooh characterized the tensions that education created by describing one who passed through these institutions as "neither a complete Westerner nor a genuine Easterner. He became a stranger: a stranger to his own society and even worse, a stranger to himself." Indicative of the division of self created by the system is the observation of a Swiss anthropologist in northern Afghanistan, who saw primary school students changing out of their traditional clothes into their Western-style school uniforms while on the way to school.[72]

Especially in tribal Pashtun areas, the rural elite recognized that modern education was a challenge to their control. Initially, the khans treated modern education like conscription, paying poor families to replace their sons in the schools. They changed their views after seeing that an educated kinsman placed in the bureaucracy could influence government actions.[73] Thus the khans attempted to co-opt modern education and make the influence derived from it part of the package of benefits they could offer their constituents. But education estranged fathers from sons; a 1967 survey of graduates of Kabul University showed that 62 percent had fathers with minimal or no formal education, and the emotional and social distance between the generations was widening.[74]

More sons and even some daughters of provincial families found their way to boarding schools and Kabul University. There, adolescent students of isolated rural backgrounds, in the city for the first time, mixed with their peers from all over the country—male and female alike, for the university became coeducational in 1960. Foreign professors, too—bearers of all sorts of strange knowledge and ideas— awaited the students in a heady atmosphere of freedom from parental and family supervision. Other young Afghans were thrust onto foreign campuses or military bases. One can imagine few transitions more abrupt and destabilizing than that experienced by an adolescent moving from an extended family or clan compound in an isolated mountain village in Afghanistan to a Western or Soviet city, or even a dormitory on the coeducational campus of Kabul University. It can hardly be surprising that a variety of radical ideologies and organizations providing collective identities and social contacts flourished in such an environment. One observer characterized the Kabul University dormitory, where 1,200 students without family in Kabul lived in 1967, as a "center of insurgents."[75]

Indeed, the generation that crowded into secondary schools during the New Democracy period provided the core leadership for all sides in the war, although a few of the top leaders were older. In the broadest sense, this cohort includes the group bounded by those who entered seventh grade in 1973 and those who graduated from twelfth grade in 1964. Those in this group, born between 1945 and 1961, were seventeen to thirty-three years old at the time of the coup in 1978 and twenty-eight to forty-four years old when the Soviets completed their troop withdrawal in 1989. They confronted the initial decision about whether and for whom to fight, and much or all of their young adulthood was spent in the war. Najibullah, Gulbuddin Hikmatyar, and Ahmad Shah Massoud all belong to this group. They also belong to the more restricted group that subsequently enrolled in institutions of higher education, where they joined radical political groups. The resulting prison terms and exile meant that Najibullah took ten years to graduate from the Faculty of Medicine, while neither Hikmatyar nor Massoud finished his studies at, respectively, the U.S.-sponsored Faculty of Engineering or the Soviet-sponsored Polytechnic.

The ostensible aim of education was to train the youth for state-guided modernization, but the state failed to provide acceptable career paths or survival strategies for many graduates. Once a student was out of school, whether through graduation or dropping out, virtually the only source of employment was the government bureaucracy. The investment in a centralized state infrastructure had not led to any increase in private employment. As in other Third World countries, the government increased public employment partly in order to employ graduates: the number of state employees tripled in the late 1960s, even as the foreign aid financing the projects where they were supposed to work was declining. In 1974 there were 56,099 men and 6,323 women employed by the government; 35 percent of the men and 69 percent of the women worked as teachers. Nonetheless, by the early 1970s unemployment among university graduates was becoming visible.[76]

Even for those successful in finding work, a career in government service was likely to add to the frustration of those without the right family connections. Promotion was determined by seniority or personal and family connections, not by merit or achievement. There was neither on-the-job training nor skill-based assignment. Salaries were low, providing ample incentive for corruption. Under New Democracy rising inflation further reduced the real wages of government employees. The number of employees increased dramatically without a corresponding investment in offices and other facilities, so working conditions deteriorated markedly. And bureaucrats felt threatened by the arbitrary power of their superiors, who generally belonged to the less-educated older generation. Although there were few clear rules, there were disciplinary actions pending against about 20 percent of the employees in agencies studied by one team of sociologists.[77]

A variety of other conditions led to the breakdown of social control. The newly educated observed and analyzed the pervasive corruption and the neglect of the agricultural regions, trends that one of this generation, Shahrani, ascribes to "improved communications and increased penetration of world market forces."[78] These conditions encouraged a weakening of social control in the rural areas as had happened in other colonial states in the nineteenth century.

Innovations in transportation and communication increased the circulation of men (less so of women) and money. Fundamental was the effect of the network of paved roads connecting the major urban centers of Afghanistan to each other (the Kabul-Qandahar-Herat highway) and to surrounding countries. Between 1951 and 1972 Afghanistan built 1,500 miles of paved roads. These roads, as well as airfields, created new opportunities for trade, labor migration, and tourism. For the first time there were signs of the establishment of a national market, rather than regional ones linked to the surrounding countries. The expansion of trade was good for many of the bazaaris in the major urban centers, but the development of a national market bypassed many of the local or regional market centers, because the road system had inadequate feeders off the main routes. Furthermore, just as the introduction of British mill cloth led to the disappearance of the Indian weavers in the early nineteenth century, the introduction of cheap manufactured imports to Afghanistan in the 1960s led to the loss of livelihood for many traditional artisans.[79]

After 1973 the oil boom in neighboring areas of the Middle East, especially Iran, expanded opportunities for the Afghan state and for the Afghan population. Labor migration increased still further and provided a major new source of cash in the form of remittances. Since many of those who went to work in Iran were Shi'a Hazaras and Farsiwan, the money enriched previously marginal social groups, creating resentment among Pashtun government officials whose relative well-being was deteriorating. Many Pashtuns from eastern Afghanistan, meanwhile, went to India, Pakistan, or the Arab countries of the Persian Gulf.[80]

Labor migration both removed rural Aghans from the control of the tribal or family setting and exposed them to an urban society, Iran, in which both leftist and Islamic movements were far more visible and militant than in Afghanistan. Foreign education and the presence of significant numbers of foreign tourists, advisers, and publications, as well as the spread of radios that could pick up foreign broadcasts, all provided channels for the diffusion of new ideas.[81]

Labor migration was due not only to the pull of new opportunities abroad but also to the push of shrinking opportunities at home. Just as the government failed to provide adequate employment for the newly educated, it failed to create jobs for the growing rural population. Industrialization was negligible; there were only thirty thousand industrial workers in 1970, or about 1 percent of the economically active population. By 1978 this number had increased to forty thousand, a substantial percentage change, but barely perceptible in most of the country: most of these workers were peasants who commuted from their villages or made seasonal migrations to Kabul.[82]

The influx of foreign aid and the progressive nationalization of much of the banking system (culminating in the nationalization of Bank-i Milli under Daoud's Republic) increased the available liquidity. The establishment of military bases in the provinces, which often followed road building, also introduced greater supplies of cash into the countryside. Under New Democracy, the government compensated for the shortfall in foreign aid by inflationary expansion of the money supply (Appendix C), even as foreign loans contracted in the 1950s started to come due. The state also liberalized import regulations as a concession to urban consumers, thus creating an inflationary gap in the balance of payments.[83]

The cash economy increased from about a third of the GNP in the mid-1950s to nearly half in the early 1970s (Table 3.2). The increased need for cash led to a number of interrelated developments. Brideprices went up, and private indebtedness increased sharply. The interest rate on rural loans doubled during the 1960s, with rates for loans to pay for weddings reaching 50 percent. The demand for cash was also fueled by the penetration of such addictive products as opium, tea, and tobacco into previously isolated areas, another result of road building.[84]

Commercialization and the introduction of new agricultural technologies, as well as other effects of state building, affected social relations in the villages. Political stability had led to the settlement of nomad groups, which increased population pressure on the land. Underemployment in the rural sector became more evident as ever larger numbers of agricultural workers wandered from place to place with the seasons in search of work. The introduction of tractors and the increased accessibility of markets pushed some landowners toward outward-looking exploitation rather than inward-looking patronage. Spurred by the possibility of selling sheep for high prices in Kabul, nomad herd owners began to pay their shepherds in cash rather than shares of the flock.[85]

All of these trends were accelerated by the famine of 1971–72, a disaster of the sort that often shake structures of social control and precede political upheavals.[86] Reduced snowfall over much of the Hindu Kush led to food shortages that took thousands of lives. The government was slow to react, especially because some of the worst affected areas were Hazara. Once international aid began to pour in, it became a source of corruption. Many who survived did so only by mortgaging or even surrendering their land to landlords or merchants. Both khans and government failed to feed the people.

In the midst of these forces, the role of women in social change should not be neglected, regardless of their seeming invisibility at times. The rise of paid urban employment for both men and women (the latter especially as teachers of girls) created for the first time a widespread economic activity independent of the kinship unit. A man who earns a salary in a government office does not need his wife and children to help with his work, nor does he need tribal or kinship alliances cemented through marriages to guard his land, assure his supply of water, or fight his rivals. He may need other kinds of networks to assure his promotion or evade bureaucratic troubles, but tribe and kinship are less likely to help him in this context. An educated woman who teaches in a school or works in an office has a productive function that is separate from her reproductive one and a survival strategy not entirely dependent on male kin. In a sample of women in Kabul in the early 1970s, 42 percent had formal educations and 41 percent worked outside the house; 71 percent of those were teachers or students. This relative emancipation was limited to the younger generation of the upper and middle class in Kabul. These changes were reflected symbolically in

Kabul (and only in Kabul) by the decline in veiling after Daoud made it voluntary in 1959. In the provinces few people even knew of the changes of women's status in the capital.[87]

Traditions of family life and marriage did not alter to reflect the changes even in Kabul. As Erika Knabe has commented, "Opinions and attitudes about stereotype roles of women lag far behind reality." In one sample of educated women in Kabul in the early 1970s, only 24 percent had any say in their choice of husband. In another sample, of mostly male Kabul University graduates, 53 percent were married to relatives. The changes in women's social role paralleled the more general cleavage in the urban elite. Among the westernized upper elite, educated women were integrated into the upper-class lifestyle as proof of a family's modernity. Educated women from provincial backgrounds or lower strata, on the other hand, experienced severe internal conflicts over their roles, as well as conflicts with their families, whose traditional authority patterns had no place for such beings as they had become.[88]

Although it would be wrong to speak of radicalization of the countryside or even rural disaffection from the state before 1978, there was a growing malaise in the provinces, a feeling that something needed to change. The beginnings of national political activity under New Democracy created an outlet for this feeling. Pierre Centlivres and Micheline Centlivres-Demont observed a reformist movement led by ulama and some local figures around Tashqurghan (Khulm) in the early 1970s. Whereas the old Kabuli state elites were largely unaware of these developments, the newly educated, with their fresh provincial ties, were acutely sensitive to them. Henning Sawitzki, who studied academic elites in Kabul, wrote in 1972, "Everything indicates that conflicts will be inevitable, and that Afghanistan will not be spared sudden and violent change."[89]

4

Rentier State
and Rentier
Revolutionaries

The foreign aid–funded expansion of the state created new political elites. During such periods of liberalization as the Liberal Parliament and New Democracy, these elites began to form a rudimentary civil society, "that arena where manifold social movements . . . and civic organizations . . . attempt to constitute themselves in an ensemble of arrangements so that they can express themselves and advance their interests." The elites organized clubs, discussion groups, newspapers, and informal groupings in the consultative parliaments. During neither period, however, were they able to establish political society, "that arena in which the polity specifically arranges itself for political contestation to gain control over public power and the state apparatus."[1] The government never legalized political parties, nor did it allow elections to determine who held power. Representative bodies allowed society to express but not to govern itself. Hence none of the elite groups could create a national network that would empower society to control the state. Political groups tried either to influence the government through personal ties or to overthrow it through conspiracies.

Some of these groups adopted revolutionary ideologies and sought to seize control of the state in order to transform society. The would-be revolutionaries of Afghanistan, as much as those of France, Russia, and China, came from "the ranks of relatively highly educated groups oriented to state activities or employments . . . [a]nd from among those who were somewhat marginal to the established classes and governing elites under the Old Regimes."[2] Many Afghan revolutionaries, like those elsewhere, had studied abroad, an experience that provided a firsthand encounter with foreign models of modernity and a perspective from which to criticize the society of Afghanistan. Unlike the revolutionaries of France, Russia, or China, however, their structure of opportunities—like that of the rulers—permitted them to seek support from sources in the international system, not only from the discontented in their own society. A rentier state produced rentier revolutionaries.

Most studies of revolutionary "counterelites" during the Cold War equated revolutionaries with communists or leftists, foreign education with Western education, and cosmopolitanism or modernization with westernization. In Afghanistan, however, as in the rest of the Islamic world, Islamic revolutionary doctrine—Islamism—competed with Marxism for the allegiance of the disaffected.

Organizations and Resources

The coherence of the old elite did not depend on political parties or any formal organization beyond the patronage networks of the state itself. Although under New Democracy some leaders among or allied to the old-regime elite published newspapers or founded groups, few of these associations attained a high level of organization. The most significant were the National Progressive Party, led by Muhammad Hashim Maiwandwal, who became the second prime minister under New Democracy; and Afghan Millat (Afghan Nation) led by Muhammad Amin Wakman, a former mayor of Kabul. The ideology of the NPP was center-left, similar to the Pakistan People's Party of Zulfiqar Ali Bhutto; Afghan Millat called itself social democratic but was, above all, Pashtun nationalist.

The principal communist organization in Afghanistan was the People's Democratic Party of Afghanistan (PDPA), which was founded at its First Congress on January 1, 1965, at the home of Nur Muhammad Taraki. Taraki was elected secretary-general and Babrak Karmal his deputy. This group descended from the left wing of the nationalist and reformist Wish Zalmayan (Awakened Youth) of the Liberal Parliament period. Both Karmal and Taraki had been jailed or exiled as activists in that movement. In 1967 the party split into two factions: PDPA-Khalq was led by Taraki and Hafizullah Amin, who was in the United States when the PDPA was founded; PDPA-Parcham was led by Karmal.[3] Parcham and Khalq remained separate until 1977, when the Soviets, through communists in India and Pakistan, pressured them into reunion.

The PDPA had no monopoly on Marxism in Kabul. The alignment of the PDPA with Moscow was consistent with Pashtun nationalism, for the Soviet Union had consistently supported Afghanistan's position on Pashtunistan. The pro-Soviet position, however, was unpopular with some non-Pashtun leftist revolutionaries, who formed a number of what were called Maoist groups, at least one of which explicitly favored separatism for the non-Pashtun nationalities.[4]

The Soviet Union provided PDPA leaders some protection, if not total immunity, from government repression. The Parcham leaders in particular were frequent guests at Soviet embassy social events, a clear signal to the Afghan government that any move against them would be ill received. The PDPA also probably received financial assistance from the Soviet Union, aided by some Parchamis whose state positions gave them access to Soviet aid and trade.[5] Once Parcham and Khalq began to recruit Soviet-trained army officers, the military, with its close Soviet contacts, became their important institutional base in the state. Penetration of the military ultimately enabled the PDPA to seize power.

As Khalq and Parcham fought for leadership of the left, a new Islamic movement was gaining influence among students at Kabul University under the name of the Muslim Youth Organization (Sazman-i Javanan-i Musulman).[6] The Islamic movement in Kabul had roots in the 1950s at the Sharia Faculty of Kabul University. A group of students and teachers, some of whom had been introduced to the Muslim Brotherhood while studying in Egypt, began meeting to discuss how to refute the arguments of campus Marxists. Just as the PDPA had links to the pro-Soviet wing of the elite, so the Islamists were allied at times with conservatives on the fringes of the Kabul establishment and with traditional ulama. These groups could join Islamists for specific action, as they did later in the resistance, but the Islamicizing wing of the old regime remained politically and organizationally distinct from the revolutionary Islamists.

Around the beginning of 1973, the movement registered its members and formed a leadership *shura* (council). The first meeting of the shura took place in the home of Burhanuddin Rabbani, then a junior professor of the Sharia Faculty, who was elected leader and chairman of the leadership council. Ghulam Rasul Sayyaf, also a lecturer of the Sharia Faculty, was elected deputy leader. The leading figure in the movement, Ghulam Muhammad Niyazi, dean of the Sharia Faculty, did not attend the meeting or accept any official position in the movement because of the sensitivity of his position. Gulbuddin Hikmatyar, a former student of the Engineering Faculty, was in jail on charges of murdering a Maoist student and was not present at the meeting, but he was placed in charge of political activities, together with another jailed activist, Habib al-Rahman, who was killed in prison in 1979. The council later named the movement Jamiat-i Islami (Islamic Society).[7]

After Daoud's coup, the movement encountered greater repression and initiated conspiratorial activities. Its main activists fled to Pakistan, where they took up residence in Peshawar. Rifts had been evident in the movement since at least the early 1970s, and in 1975 it split into the Jamiat-i Islami, still led by Rabbani, and the Hizb-i Islami (Islamic Party), led by Hikmatyar. After the 1978 coup, another group, led by Mawlawi Yunus Khalis, broke with Hikmatyar and formed a second Hizb-i Islami. (The two are commonly referred to as Hizb-Hikmatyar and Hizb-Khalis.)

The Islamists had been in contact with the Muslim Brotherhood in Egypt and communicated regularly with the Pakistani Jama'at-i Islami, but no available evidence indicates that they received significant outside financial support while they remained in Afghanistan. While in Kabul the Islamists could use the resources of the Sharia Faculty, the part of the state where they were strongest, for meetings and publications.

In Pakistani exile after Daoud's coup, the Islamists sought foreign aid. In 1974 Rabbani spent six months in Saudi Arabia. The Saudis provided assistance for the first year of exile, but when Daoud shifted the state's alignment toward Iran and Saudi Arabia after 1975, Saudi aid to Rabbani stopped.[8] The Pakistani government of Zulfiqar Ali Bhutto, which saw the Islamists as a way of countering Daoud's pressure on the Pashtunistan issue, provided military and financial assistance. Perhaps because of Pakistan's focus on the Pashtun border areas, Bhutto's government made Hikmatyar, the leading Pashtun among the exiled Islamists (Rabbani was a Tajik, while Niyazi and Sayyaf were in jail in Kabul), the "contact person" for Afghan Islamists seeking assistance. The Pakistanis thus elevated Hikmatyar to a de facto leadership position; his leadership became official when he broke away from Jamiat and founded Hizb-i Islami.[9]

Ideologies

The intelligentsia was the social group most dependent on the Afghan state and most integrated into the international system, and it was thus uniquely able to view the nation both as a whole and as a part—a "backward" part—of that international system. The perception of Afghanistan's backwardness, limited to a tiny elite group at the beginning of the century, spread with modern education, especially education abroad. The earliest reform movements of the elite, those influenced by Mahmud Beg Tarzi, adopted the outlook of Islamic modernism, an ideology inspired by the gap in wealth and power between the world of Islam and the modern state system. Modernism attributed the relative decline of Islam to deviation from *true* Islam. Muslims would advance when they understood that genuine Islam was rational and consistent with science, technical progress, and human freedom—inheritances that the West had in fact developed on the basis of achievements of classical and medieval Islam.[10]

Despite the early efforts of Tarzi, however, the old regime in Afghanistan never developed a coherent ideology. Like other authoritarian regimes, it relied on unelaborated "mentalities," or general political orientations.[11] The regime stressed the need to modernize the country by importing technology and some Western models of social organization, but it acknowledged the necessity of doing so gradually to avoid provoking a reaction from the masses. Many members of the old regime were pious; others were lax in religious practice but adopted no secular ideology. The government could employ the idiom of Islamic modernism when necessary to counter resistance from traditionalist elements to such reforms as permitting the unveiling of women. But Islam was never a guide to policy or the central legitimating formula of the regime, which was also capable of using the idiom of Pashtun nationalism. The old regime was proud of Afghanistan's resistance to the British and the Russians and confident of its ability to maintain national independence by balancing competing foreign patrons.

Marxism-Leninism and the new revolutionary Islamism were in bitter opposition, but they had in common a rejection of the corruption and stagnation of the old regime and a belief in what one Afghan philosopher called the myth of revolution.[12] Both groups believed that revolution would transform society through the agency of a strong state, yet neither had a program for structuring that state and financing its activities. Like the state they opposed, both groups ultimately relied on foreign aid in the struggle for power.

Although the PDPA was the main Marxist organization, party leaders had a skimpy knowledge of Marxist theory, limited for the most part to what could be gleaned from Persian translations of a few classics published by the Iranian Tudeh Party. Marxism as a vehicle of social change was only a theory; more important from a practical standpoint was the role played by the neighboring USSR, which supported the Afghan state and offered to export the Soviet version of modernization.[13]

The assessment of Afghanistan set forth in the PDPA platform was essentially a canned Soviet critique that could have applied just as well (or ill) to any of dozens of postcolonial countries.[14] The PDPA claimed that Afghanistan had a "feudal economic and social system" in which the "basic contradiction[s]" were between "farmers and feudal lords, between the people of our country and the imperialists." It acknowledged its source by noting that "the most outstanding subject of contemporary history is . . . class struggle and war between international socialism and world imperialism which began with the Great Socialist Revolution of October."

This platform, amazingly enough, contained not a single reference, positive or negative, to Islam. The sole mention of tribalism was a promise to remove it by settling nomads and by "bring[ing] advantages to the oppressed factions" as part of the "fight of all sections of the population against national oppression." The platform included the standard Soviet policy regarding nationalities, which encouraged the use of indigenous languages but never mentioned tribal autonomy.

The PDPA's model of a better future for Afghanistan was the noncapitalist path of development that Soviet theorists then favored for the Third World. This model relied on Soviet-aided, state-led development, which would have made the newly educated—especially those with Soviet training—into the leading political and economic force in Afghanistan. The PDPA advocated economic development fostered by state investment in heavy industry, together with the protection of handicrafts and the manufacture of consumer goods. Rather than supporting allocation of major state resources to agriculture, through investment in major irrigation works or new productive technology, the PDPA advocated redistributive land reform, calculated to enhance production, as well as the development of state farms on unused land. The PDPA also advocated the social rights of labor, women, and linguistic groups and called for the expansion of education, health services, civil liberties, and democracy. The only political model it had was the Soviet one, which it tried to import.

The public platform did not advocate socialism or communism for Afghanistan, but in the secret party constitution the PDPA described itself as the Marxist-Leninist Party of the working class of Afghanistan and made clear that its ultimate goal was Soviet-style socialism.[15] The constitution revealed its derivative origin, containing prohibitions against all the usual deviations but failing to mention the particularly acute Afghan problem of qawm loyalties, except insofar as they might be subsumed under "factionalism."

There was little evidence of doctrinal disagreement between the Parcham and Khalq factions. Initially they differed mainly on strategy and tactics, Parcham favoring cooperation with the "progressive" wing of the ruling elite, and Khalq an ill-defined "uprising." After the PDPA seized power, however, some Khalqis under Amin advocated a stage-skipping forced march to socialism, rather than the "National Democratic" transition advocated by the Soviets and Parcham.

When the PDPA seized power in 1978, it had not organized any class-based mass organizations, such as trade unions or peasant associations. This reflected both the weakness of class formation in the society and the social character of the PDPA itself, a movement developed by members of the state bureaucracy who desired faster, state-directed Western-style modernization.

Just as the PDPA belonged to both its society and the international communist movement, so the Islamists belonged to both their own society and the international Islamist movement. The organizations with whom they felt the closest kinship were the Muslim Brotherhood of Egypt and the Jama'at-i Islami of Pakistan, but at first they had no formal links with either. The writer who seems to have influenced the Islamists the most was Sayyid Qutb; both Rabbani and Khalis translated his work in the 1960s.[16]

In the West revolutionary Islam is generally known by the vague term "fundamentalism," which obscures important differences between modern revolutionaries and those reformers and purifiers who have emerged, often among tribal peoples, throughout the history of Islam.[17] Islamism, like Islamic modernism, is a reaction by Muslims to the challenge of the Western models of state and development. A modern political movement, it seeks to take or influence state power in order to enact an ideologically defined program.

During the life of Muhammad and the four rightly guided caliphs (*al-khulafa al-rashidun*), the Muslims were united in a single community under a single imam, who was both religious and political leader. After the early caliphate, however, most Sunni ulama taught obedience to any ruler who was a Muslim and who allowed Muslims to live by their religion. The ulama recognized that an effective separation of politics and religion was necessary and even taught that a pious man should not involve himself deeply in the corrupting affairs of state. The cardinal virtue in politics was the avoidance of chaos and civil strife (*intiqa' al-fitna*). Abu Bakr al-Turtushi (1059–1126) taught that "sixty years of tyranny was preferable to an hour of revolt [*fitna*]."[18]

Islamic revolutionaries reject these traditions. They argue that in Islam there should be no separation between religion and politics, that Islam has its own system of politics and economics, and that Muslims must strive to return to the unity that existed under the early caliphate.

The ulama, too, have often pointed out corruption in the prevailing way of life.

They have argued for moral reform based on religious preaching or *dawa,* the call to Islam. At times dawa could take the form of a summons to jihad—in Afghanistan, for example, against Amanullah or the British. The Islamists argued, however, that the ulama lacked the means to defend Islam in the modern political arena. As one activist of Jamiat wrote, "The traditional clergy was not equipped with the right type of weapons to defend Islam, and the spiritual leadership [the major Sufi families] was also facing similar problems. Attempts by some individuals and small groups could [not] gather enough strength due to the wrong approach or to their connection [to] the traditional establishment."[19]

Islamists argue that the way to fight injustice is not through appeals for moral reform but through organized political activity aimed at taking state power. As Hizb-i Islami of Afghanistan wrote in its program, "Without a complete reform of the system of government, no individual reform is possible."[20]

The Islamists see both capitalism and communism as unjust systems based on *jahiliyya,* pre-Islamic ignorance or barbarism, a term first used in this way by Abu'l Ala Maududi of the Jama'at-i Islami and subsequently adopted by Sayyid Qutb, a leading thinker of the Muslim Brotherhood. To Islamists it is not merely lawful but obligatory for Muslims to wage jihad against governments promoting either Western models of society or communism. Depending on circumstances, this jihad might be military, or it might take a peaceful form, like electoral campaigning.

Since most nominal Muslims are living in non-Islamic societies and not waging jihad against them, Islamists question whether they are still Muslims. The same issue arose in the early Islamic community when a group called the Kharijites claimed that those who violated precepts of Islam were no longer Muslims but unbelievers or, worse, apostates. Such charges raise the issue of excommunication, or *takfir*— literally, proclaiming someone a kafir, or unbeliever. Sayyid Qutb introduced this term into modern political discourse when he branded nominally Muslim leaders and members of modern societies as unbelievers. The militant group that split from the mainstream Ikhwan in the mid-1960s, some of whose supporters later assassinated Anwar Sadat, did so over the belief that the leadership of the Muslim Brotherhood was not implementing Qutb's views on takfir. The amir of the Brothers, Umar Tilimasani, argued that it was not up to human beings to condemn as kafir a Muslim who still publicly professed a belief in God.[21]

All Islamists agree, however, that the aim of the struggle is to establish a state that will remake society according to the laws of Islam. For them Islam itself can render the state autonomous from society and be an engine of its transformation. The Islamists prescribe the forms of both state and economy according to Islam, rather than merely requiring that laws not contradict the sharia, as most ulama have done.

The programs of Jamiat-i Islami and Hizb-i Islami, the two main Islamist organizations in Afghanistan, bear out this ideological orientation and also reveal certain differences. Both exhibit adherence to the principles of Qutb and Maududi in their insistence that Islam is a complete system with its own prescriptions for economics and politics and in their depiction of modern capitalist and communist societies as examples of jahiliyya.[22] The Jamiat program is clearly an Afghan document, replete with references to the history of the country, while the Hizb program, somewhat like that of the PDPA, is much more a local adaptation of an international movement.

In their general attitude toward the old regime the Islamists had more in common with the communists than with the elite. They characterized the regime as corrupt (*fasid*) and tyrannical (*zalimanah*). They decried both economic injustice (accumulation of land and other kinds of property through impermissible means) and the penetration of non-Islamic culture and customs, leading to moral corruption. The main root of these abuses, the Islamists argued, was the failure of previous rulers to apply Islam in all its aspects. Both parties attributed this failure to the moral character of the old regime and to its alignment with non-Islamic foreign powers. Both parties agreed that Afghanistan remained an Islamic country (*kishvar*) and society (*jamiyyat*), but Hizb took a much more critical attitude toward that society and came close to condemning it as un-Islamic: "The way of life of the people is not established on the basis of its beliefs [in Islam]." The economic system of Afghanistan, it said, "is a summary of all the corruptions, tyrannical practices, and injustices of all the un-Islamic orders and systems."[23]

Jamiat-i Islami and Hizb-i Islami agreed that the problems of Afghanistan could be solved only if the state adhered strictly to Islamic principles. The longer Hizb program contained sections on law, religion and morals, education and training, administration, the economy (including agriculture, trade and industry, workers' and bureaucrats' rights, and general economic reforms), and foreign policy. Besides demanding that the state encourage Islamic training and values, both groups called on the schools to teach "technology." The Islamists attacked economic inequality and oppression as strongly as the communists did, but they proposed just and cooperative relations among social classes—a sort of Islamic corporatism—rather than class struggle. Their economic plan consisted of a set of ethically motivated reforms and prescriptions for national and international Islamic self-reliance, but it was not an integrated development strategy. Hizb's economic program, like that of the communists, supported investment in heavy industry but said nothing about how to accumulate the capital. The Islamists also advocated that Islamic countries should create their own arms industries to free themselves from external dependence.[24]

The Islamists' view of the international arena, of course, differed from that of the communists. Their foreign policy called for equal opposition to "imperialism of the East and West" and for solidarity with the Islamic world. The Islamists opposed the creation of Pashtunistan, but neither Hizb nor Jamiat mentioned this in its program.

Like the communists, the Islamists condemned divisions of language and ethnicity, but they gave little attention to the causes of these divisions. Except for a brief plea by Hizb that education should be available for all students in their native tongues, neither Islamic party proposed any institutional measures beyond the spread of Islamic ideas to overcome tribal and ethnic divisions.

Most strikingly, while both Islamist parties had much to say about how state power should be exercised, neither suggested how it should be constituted or financed. Hizb mentioned the rightly guided caliphs as a model, but because each of those leaders came to power in a different way, their reigns can offer models only for how to govern, not for how to constitute a government. Both Hizb and Jamiat advocated a legal system based solely on the sharia. Hizb also commented on the organization of the administration, emphasizing measures to prevent corruption and other abuses. Hizb called on the state to enforce Islamic taxes, but neither the Islamists nor the communists confronted the problem of establishing and maintaining a fiscal base to pay for the numerous projects they wanted the state to undertake.

According to Olivier Roy, the schism between Jamiat and Hizb arose not only from ethnic, personal, and organizational differences, it also reflected the split in the international Islamist movement over takfir. Roy claims that Hizb-i Islami took the more extreme position, and the evidence of its programs and other documents partly supports this claim. Hizb took a more revolutionary approach toward Afghan society but did not condemn it as wholly un-Islamic. On the other hand, Hizb's English-language magazine, which is aimed at international Islamic supporters rather than Westerners, published a laudatory obituary of Tilimasani, whose criticisms of the extreme position on takfir are well known.[25]

Since 1988 a group whose practice and theory conform to the strictest construction of the takfir doctrine has emerged in eastern Afghanistan. This group, led by a former Hizb field commander, is called Jama'at al-Da'wa ila al-Qur'an wa Ahl al-Hadith; most Afghans call it Wahhabi.[26] Aided and joined by Arab sympathizers, Jama'at al-Da'wa reportedly treated Afghans living in government-controlled areas as unbelievers to whom Muslims should apply the laws of *futuhat* (conquest), including execution of adult males who resisted and enslavement of women and children. The organization also rejected aid from non-Muslims; its mujahidin have attacked Western journalists and relief workers, including some traveling under protection of Hizb-i Islami.[27]

The differences between Hizb and Jamiat were thus more political and strategic than theological. As Roy notes, Hizb claimed to be the only vehicle for Islamic struggle and advocated a more thoroughgoing Islamic revolution; Jamiat favored a coalition of all Islamic forces in Afghanistan.[28] Jamiat, for example, took a conciliatory stance toward both traditional ulama and orthodox Sufi orders. Jamiat emphasized that an Islamic movement needed to be guided by ulama who could interpret the sharia systematically, and party leadership reflected this. The top leaders of Hizb, however, all had secular educations; as in the old regime, the ulama were in charge only of the administration of justice.

Contending Political Elites

Old regime, PDPA, Islamists—each group had a different relation to the state and society of Afghanistan. A statistical analysis of the ethnic origins and educational background of the leadership of each group will show how recruitment of the groups developed out of the relation of the expanding state to society.[29]

For purposes of statistical analysis, I define the elite of the old regime as all those who served as heads of state, cabinet ministers, governors, and members of the supreme court during the rule of the Musahiban family.[30] The core elite consisted of the head of state, the prime minister, and the ministers of foreign affairs, defense, and interior. Because both the communists and the Islamists first organized during New Democracy, I analyze the elite of that period separately.

Even when the PDPA was unified, Parcham and Khalq constituted distinct political and social groups, although other tiny factions existed as well, and the loyalties of some individuals were fluid. For purposes of statistical analysis, I define the leadership of Parcham and Khalq as those who served as members of the party's Central Committee before January 1980. The core leadership includes those members of the Central Committee who also served on the Politburo.

The organizational structure of the Islamist movement had no direct parallel in either the PDPA or the old regime. The core leaders were the members of the original Jamiat shura, plus Prof. Niyazi. A broader leadership included the members of the council plus all members in the following overlapping categories: those who were arrested during Daoud's repression of the movement; those who joined the movement before 1978 and subsequently rose to become heads of Jamiat or Hizb administrative departments; those who participated in the 1975 uprising; and those among the Islamist exiles in Pakistan before 1978 who subsequently became major resistance field commanders.[31] The data exclude some individuals belonging to these categories, partly because Jamiat sources were more readily available than Hizb sources. For this reason the members of the two parties are analyzed separately. Many of those in the sample, however, were either killed during the 1975 uprising or remained in prison until their mass execution in 1979 and hence did not participate in the Jamiat-Hizb split in Peshawar.

Information is incomplete for some members of all of the groups, hence the total number given for the groups differs in the tables here, for each includes only those on whom the information relevant for that table was available.

Under the old regime in Afghanistan, the national structure of tribal-ethnic affiliation strongly affected an individual's chances for promotion. Table 4.1 presents the tribal-ethnic affiliations of the various political elites.

The ethnic composition of the elite of the old regime was remarkably similar to that of the court circles originally recruited by Amir Abdul Rahman. The most salient characteristic of that elite was that it included more than ten times the concentration of Muhammadzais and Kabulis than in the population as a whole. Other Pashtuns were

Table 4.1 Tribal and Ethnic Origin of Political Elites

Tribes and Ethnic Groups

Elite	Pashtun				Tajik/Farsiwan	Sayyid	Other Sunni	Shi'a	Total	Kabuli
	Muhammadzai	Other Durrani	Other	Total						
Old Regime										
All	42	10	47	99	50	11	8	3	171	81
Core	17	0	11	28	6	2	2	0	38	18
New Democracy	17	6	28	51	30	3	5	2	91	51
Core	4	0	8	12	3	0	1	0	16	7
Parcham										
Central Committee	0	5	9	14	8	0	0	2	24	12
Politburo	0	2	0	2	1	0	0	1	4	3

(*continued*)

Table 4.1 (*continued*)

Tribes and Ethnic Groups

| | Pashtun | | | | Tajik/ Farsiwan | Sayyid | Other Sunni | Shi'a | Total | Kabuli |
Elite	Muhammadzai	Other Durrani	Other	Total						
Khalq										
Central Committee	1	4	19	24	4	0	1	2	31	2
Politburo	0	1	7	8	1	0	1	1	11	1
Islamists										
Early leaders	0	0	26	26	27	2	3	0	58	0
Shura	0	0	6	6	9	0	1	0	16	0
Jamiat	0	0	5	5	16	0	1	0	22	0
Hizb	0	0	8	8	2	1	1	0	12	0

Sources: See Appendix A.

also overrepresented, and the overrepresentation of Pashtuns and Muhammadzais was greater among the core power holders than it was in the elite as a whole. Tajiks (mostly Kabulis) were also quite prominent, but mainly in the legal, financial, and social ministries; Pashtuns held the core of power. In all the revolutionary elites, in contrast, there was only one Muhammadzai. The Parchamis alone of all the revolutionary groups included a significant number of Kabulis, about the same percentage as the old regime. The Islamic militants were entirely of provincial background, without a single Kabuli.

The social differences between PDPA factions also emerged in the differing roles of qawm, especially in marriage patterns.[32] Parcham, like the royal court, included individuals of different ethnic and tribal origins who generated a network of clientelism through marriage. Thus Politburo member Anahita Ratibzad, the sometime lover of Babrak Karmal, married her two daughters to Babrak's brother Mahmud Baryalai and to Politburo member Nur Ahmad Nur. Politburo member Sulaiman Laiq married his sister to Mir Akbar Khaibar. Parcham was also related to the establishment through marriage: Sulaiman Laiq's sister was married to Sibghatullah Mujaddidi and Najibullah to a Muhammadzai. Khalq, on the other hand, was more traditionally tribal: there were networks of tribes and clans within the party, and Khalqis (who were all male) married women from their own villages in accord with traditional tribal principles.

Parcham and especially Khalq resembled the old regime in being dominated by Pashtuns at the top.[33] Non-Pashtuns, however, played important roles in the cadres of Parcham, and many of the "Pashtuns" were urbanized and Persian-speaking. The Islamists were the only group in which the proportion of Pashtuns was no greater than their proportion in the population (less than half); Pashtun representation in their top leadership (the shura) was even less. The Turki-speaking groups were largely absent from all three elites, although both the PDPA and the Islamists developed some Uzbek support after 1978.

These data portray a hierarchy of social distance from the old-regime elite among the revolutionary groups. The Parchamis were the closest: indeed, they had direct links to Daoud and supported his coup in 1973. They came from the non-Muhammadzai lower ranks of groups whose upper echelons supplied the old regime elite. The Khalqis were outsiders, but shared a heavy Pashtun concentration with the elite. The Islamists were the most distant from the old-regime elite.

Distance from the elite does not mean that either the Khalqis or the Islamists came from the most deprived and impoverished sectors of the population. Most seem to have come from middle or upper-middle social levels in the countryside; otherwise they would have been unlikely to complete their education, as nearly all of them did.[34]

None of these factions was ethnically homogeneous, and all denied that ethnicity played any role in their politics. Nonetheless, Pashto was the main language within Hizb and Khalq, whereas Persian was the main language within Parcham and Jamiat. The Pashtuns in Parcham were largely urban and Persian-speaking. The Pashtuns who

Table 4.2 Secondary Education of Political Elites

Elite	State Secular Schools			State Madrasa	Private/ None	Total
	Elite	Military	Other			
	Old Regime					
All	94	8	5	2	29	138
Core	25	1	0	1	8	35
New Democracy	62	5	3	2	2	74
Core	12	0	0	1	0	13
	Parcham					
Central Committee	11	2	6	0	2	21
Politburo	4	0	0	0	0	4
	Khalq					
Central Committee	1	3	19	0	1	24
Politburo	0	0	7	0	1	8
	Islamists					
Early Leaders	3	2	22	22	3	52
Shura	0	1	4	11	0	16
Jamiat	2	0	9	9	0	20
Hizb	1	1	7	3	0	12

Sources: See Appendix A.

remained in Jamiat were primarily those who had attended either the top state madrasa or al-Azhar.

The difference in social status of the political elites is also reflected in the type of secondary school the leaders attended (Table 4.2). Both old regime and top Parcham leaders came overwhelmingly from the elite Kabul schools. Had entry to the elite schools depended solely on achievement, this concentration might have represented the creation of a system of *carrières ouvertes aux talents* on the Napoleonic model. Only a narrow segment of society, however, had access to the elementary education and social connections needed for admission to these schools, and even then entry depended largely on patronage.[35] Nearly all New Democracy leaders had lived in a westernized Kabuli milieu at least since early adolescence.

The Parchamis had a similar but slightly less elite background. Of the Central

Committee members over half—including all Politburo members—had attended the elite schools. About two-thirds of all Parchami Central Committee members attended high school in Kabul, including both elite schools and tribal boarding schools. Among Khalqis, by contrast, only one person in a position of marginal leadership attended an elite school.[36] Khalqis at all levels predominantly attended the nonelite, secular state schools. Among these, however, many attended either the military high school or the tribal boarding schools. Over half of the Khalqi Central Committee members attended high school in Kabul.

Nearly half of the Islamists and more than half of the members of the shura attended high school in Kabul, but the institutions they attended were very different from those where the old-regime elite or the PDPA members were educated. Only a few individuals attended elite schools or the military high school, and none attended the tribal boarding schools. Of those Islamist leaders and shura members who attended high school in Kabul, a large majority attended the Abu Hanifa Madrasa or its predecessor, Dar al-'Ulum-i 'Arabiyya. They came from an Islamic enclave in a westernizing educational system and capital city. Most of those with secular state educations attended provincial high schools, away from the Kabul milieu.

Most members of the original shura received state religious educations. On the lower levels of the Islamic movement before it split, a higher proportion received state secular educations. After the schism, religious education was more prevalent among Jamiat leaders than in Hizb. Although some of the early Islamists, including Pashtuns, who attended Abu Hanifa Madrasa later joined Jamiat, none joined Hizb. Jamiat's main leadership included graduates of both state madrasas and state secular schools, but the equivalent offices in Hizb were all filled by graduates of state secular schools. In the Hizb leadership only two men who headed the judicial committee graduated from madrasas.[37]

The data on secondary education thus present a similar picture of the social makeup of the parties as do the ethnic data. But although the Islamists came from the parts of the state educational system that had the lowest status and was the least westernized and most Islamic, they did come from that system rather than from a traditional background. This pattern is typical of revolutionary counterelites, not of traditionalist conservatives. The Islamists included virtually no representatives of traditional Afghan ulama, who were educated in private madrasas.

The various elites differed not only in their origins in the social hierarchy but in their links to the international community as well (Tables 4.3 and 4.4). Nearly all members of all of the elites had some formal higher education, which set them apart from most of the population of Afghanistan, a country with a single-digit literacy rate. Higher education in a Western country was important to entry into the top ranks of the old-regime elite.

Two characteristics distinguished the education of the old regime from that of the revolutionaries: a plurality of those who studied in Afghanistan attended the Faculty of Law and Political Science, the French-sponsored faculty of secular law that trained

Table 4.3 Higher Education of Political Elites and Place of Study

Elites with Higher Education Who Studied in[a]

Elite	Total	Afghanistan	West	Soviet Bloc	Foreign Islamic Institutions	Other Asian and/or Muslim Countries	Total
Old Regime							
All	172	56	96	6	4	18	125
Core	38	6	18	1	1	4	20
New Democracy	91	40	71	1	3	10	81
Core	16	5	13	0	1	1	14
Parcham							
Central Committee	25	20	2	8	0	0	22
Politburo	4	4	1	0	0	0	4
Khalq							
Central Committee	32	23	6	11	1	2	27
Politburo	12	8	3	3	1	2	10
Islamists							
Early Leaders	63	44	1	0	9	0	47
Shura	16	15	0	0	4	0	16
Jamiat	24	18	1	0	3	0	18
Hizb	13	12	0	0	1	0	12

Sources: See Appendix A.

Note: The West includes capitalist Europe, the United States, and Australia. Other institutions in Asian or Muslim countries includes Turkey and the American University in Beirut, both of which might be said to belong to Western culure.

[a]The numbers who studied in various places may add up to more than the total with higher education, because some individuals studied in more than one place and are counted more than once.

administrators and managers for the government (Table 4.4); and by the New Democracy period, almost all of its members studied in the West (Table 4.3). Exposure to Western-style modernity was part of the preparation for high posts in the foreign aid–funded government service.

Unlike the ruling leadership, both communists and Islamists were recruited primarily from the campus of Kabul University and hence were much more likely to have studied in Afghanistan. Those PDPA leaders who studied in Afghanistan were

Table 4.4 Political Elites Educated in Afghanistan: Institutions or Faculties Attended

Elite	Law and Political Science	Medicine	Economics	Science/Technology[a]	Humanities/Education	Sharia	Military Academy	Total
Old Regime								
All	23	5	5	9	2	2	6	52
Core	1	0	0	2	1	0	2	6
New Democracy	16	3	3	8	2	1	4	37
Core	1	0	0	2	1	0	1	5
Parcham								
Central Committee	3	3	3	3	1	1	6	20
Politburo	2	1	1	0	0	0	0	4
Khalq								
Central Committee	1	2	0	9	4	1	5	22
Politburo	1	2	0	3	1	1	0	8
Islamists								
Early leaders	1	6	0	15	7	20	1	50
Shura	0	1	0	3	1	10	0	15
Jamiat	0	3	0	7	0	8	0	18
Hizb	0	1	0	6	2	3	0	12

Sources: See Appendix A.

[a]Includes the Polytechnic Institute and the Faculties of Sciences, Engineering, and Agriculture.

enrolled in faculties and institutions different from those in which the old regime leaders had studied. About a quarter of both Parcham and Khalq had attended the Soviet-aided Kabul Military Academy, which drew on the graduates of the military high school, mainly tribal Pashtuns. Many Khalqis also came from the scientific and technical faculties, which prepared specialists for middle-level bureaucratic jobs.

Both Khalqis and Parchamis were less likely than the leaders of the old regime to have studied in the West and far likelier to have studied in the Soviet Union, about half of them in the military.

Higher education among Islamists shows a completely different pattern. Two-thirds of the shura members and about two-fifths of all the early leaders had advanced Islamic educations. The top three leaders and the official in charge of cultural affairs had all studied at al-Azhar. The cadres largely came from graduates of the provincial state high schools or madrasas who then attended nonelite faculties of Kabul University. As elsewhere in the Islamic world, the technical faculties provided the bulk of the student cadres.[38]

Differences between the religiously educated lecturers in the leadership and the radical Islamist students in the technical faculties figured in the split between Hizb and Jamiat. Several Jamiat leaders had taught at the Faculty of Sharia; no Hizb leaders had. Three Jamiat leaders had studied at al-Azhar; no Hizb leaders had. The Jamiat leaders from secular faculties were all from scientific, medical, or technical fields.

Finally, the education of the Islamists reflected one of their slogans: "Neither East nor West." No Islamist had been educated in the Soviet bloc or in a non-Islamic Third World institution like the American University of Beirut or a university in India; one individual of secondary importance had a master's degree in engineering from the United States, reflecting the American sponsorship of Kabul's Faculty of Engineering. The Islamists' only significant international ties were with the Islamic umma.

International Support for Revolutionary Elites

The new political organizations quickly benefited from foreign support. The Soviets —contrary to their practice in most nonsocialist countries on their borders—had never actively supported efforts to undermine the government of Afghanistan. As early as 1924 Stalin had written, "The struggle of the Amir of Afghanistan for the independence of Afghanistan is an objectively revolutionary struggle, despite the monarchist base of the ideas of the Amir and his partisans, for it weakens, breaks up, and undermines imperialism." In 1921 the People's Commissar for Foreign Affairs of Soviet Russia, Georgi Chicherin, instructed the first Soviet ambassador to Kabul: "You should by all means avoid the fatal mistake of trying to plant Communism in the country." British troops based in Iran had occupied areas of Central Asia just northwest of the Afghan border during the Soviet Civil War, so the independent or even anti-British stance of the Afghan government had contributed to Soviet security. Even at the height of Comintern activity, Soviet leaders refrained from establishing a Communist Party in Afghanistan, whereas all other countries bordering on the USSR had Communist parties by the 1920s.[39]

During the Cold War, Afghanistan's continued neutrality again protected the security interests of the USSR. Party theorists under Khrushchev favored support for Third World nationalists who pursued the "noncapitalist" (protectionist and statist) path of development and took an anti-Western stance, even if they were non- or anticommunist. This view provided a theoretical rationale for giving military and economic assistance to such countries as India under Nehru and Egypt under Nasser. Afghanistan under Premier Daoud was the first test case of a new policy.

Soviet policy toward the Third World changed in the 1970s, for both opportunistic and ideological reasons. Events like the overthrow of Sukarno in Indonesia and the expulsion of Soviet advisers from Egypt by Sadat were taken as signs of the instability of Soviet alliances with noncommunist nationalists. Victories by Soviet-supported Marxist-Leninists in Vietnam, Angola, Mozambique, South Yemen, and Ethiopia, on the other hand, gave credence to those who held that regimes led by Marxist-Leninist vanguard parties were the most reliable Soviet partners in the Third World. After the 1962 debacle in Cuba, the Soviets steadily expanded their military power and the ability to project that power around the world. By the 1970s they were ready to take a more activist role outside their traditional sphere of influence. The American defeat in Vietnam also reinforced the view that the socialist countries were gradually becoming stronger than the capitalist world.[40] All of these developments led to diminished support for President Daoud and growing sentiment in favor of both the PDPA and the use of Soviet military power in Afghanistan.

Nonetheless, these factors by themselves did not transform policy. Like U.S. foreign policy, Soviet policy reflected the relative weights of different considerations and bureaucracies, and the force of inertia was heavy. Support for the more ideological, leftist approach was strongest in the International Department of the Central Committee of the Communist Party of the Soviet Union (CPSU). Both the KGB and GRU (military intelligence) also seem to have had institutional interests in the PDPA members they had helped recruit and train.[41] Many in the Institute of Oriental Studies opposed the new ideological turn and remained skeptical about the prospects of revolutionary democratic regimes, and the Ministry of Foreign Affairs had spent decades developing good relations with the Afghan state. The likeliest scenario is that concern for l'après-Daoud and anxiety over the gradual reorientation of Afghanistan's foreign ties toward the Shah of Iran made it easier for the proponents of support for Marxist-Leninist vanguard parties to advance their approach as a second track of Soviet policy toward Afghanistan.

It appears that in 1975 or early 1976, about the time that Daoud expelled Parchamis from his government, Moscow decided to broaden its options. The public appearance of friendly state-to-state relations continued as before, but visits by Daoud to Moscow in 1975 and 1977 were tense.[42] For the first time the CPSU Central

Committee International Department adopted a role in making policy toward Afghanistan. Previously neither the CPSU nor any of the other Communist parties in the region had acknowledged either Parcham or Khalq as fraternal parties or publicly shown an interest in the PDPA. In 1976, however, the Soviet-led international communist movement suddenly took an interest in the PDPA. Articles about the party appeared nearly simultaneously in journals of the Communist parties of Iraq, Iran, Australia, and India. Most important was an article on May 22 by a Communist Party of India secretary and Politburo member lamenting the Parcham-Khalq split of 1967. After the CPSU suggested mediation by the CPI, Khalq and Parcham reunited in July 1977.[43]

There is no indication that the CPSU wanted the PDPA to take power as soon as it did or even that the Ministry of Foreign Affairs had fully assimilated the shift in policy coming from the International Department of the party. The immediate goal of the Soviet leadership "was the gradual development of a political force inside the country that would have to be taken into account in the making of policy, a source of leverage on Daoud."[44] In the medium term, Moscow wanted a united, pro-Soviet contender in position when Daoud died or fell from power. In a few years, they might have viewed the PDPA as a candidate to seize power on its own from an aging or weakened Daoud and construct a revolutionary democratic regime.

Pakistan under Premier Zulfiqar Ali Bhutto also began to support contenders for power in Afghanistan. Pakistan and Afghanistan had always harassed each other across the Durand Line. When Daoud returned to power in 1973, he revived Afghanistan's campaign for Pashtunistan and gave sanctuary to Baluch separatists. Bhutto, who had come to power in the wake of Pakistan's loss of its eastern wing, was particularly sensitive to these provocations and was eager to support any source of counterpressure against Daoud. Thus Bhutto's government welcomed Islamist exiles and consistently favored the Pashtuns among them. In 1970–71, during Pakistan's internal crisis, civil war, and war with India, the Islamists almost alone in Afghanistan had protested against the government's pro-Indian policy. The influx of Islamist refugees from Daoud after 1974 was a welcome opportunity, especially if the Pashtuns among them could be used to counter Daoud's nationalist propaganda among the tribes.[45] Pakistan covertly organized and supported the attempted uprising by the Islamists in 1975, which, together with pressure from the shah, had the desired effect of bringing Daoud to the bargaining table over his support for Pashtun and Baluch separatism in Pakistan and other regional issues.

Furthermore, Bhutto and his adviser on Afghan affairs, Gen. Nasrullah Babar (who later played the same role for Bhutto's daughter), foresaw the possibility of upheaval after Daoud's death and wanted Pakistan to have some leverage in the struggle. They not only trained and armed the Islamists to exert short-term pressure but also began a more long-term program that included building roads to the Afghan border—roads that later allowed Pakistani military trucks to supply the mujahidin.[46]

Thus were woven the powerful ties that have bound the Islamists to the Pakistani directorate of Inter-Services Intelligence. American military and intelligence agencies, with their long-standing commitment to Pakistan, especially its military, also were connected with the Afghan insurgents through the ISI. Saudi Arabia also provided some aid, at least in 1974 and 1975.[47] Thus by the mid-1970s, although the USSR, the United States, and Iran continued to compete in giving aid to the Afghan state and the elite that controlled it, the prospect of that state's instability and that elite's weakness had already led some of them to experiment with an alternative: covert support for alternative political elites plotting to seize state power.

Strategy and Actions

Under New Democracy both communists and Islamists were too preoccupied with organization and recruitment to develop a strategy to take power. Their main public activities consisted of publishing newspapers and holding demonstrations.[48] The PDPA also participated in elections; the party was organized in response to the calling of the first election of New Democracy. Because the king had never legalized political parties, the PDPA did not participate formally, but four of its members were elected in 1965. Of these only Babrak Karmal and Anahita Ratibzad, both elected from Kabul city, were widely known to be connected to the PDPA. In the 1969 elections the divided party won only two seats: Babrak Karmal again won from Kabul, while Hafizullah Amin was elected as a favorite-son candidate from his hometown of Paghman.

The Islamic revolutionaries, who formally organized after the 1969 election, had no representation in parliament, although the latter did include a conservative Islamic bloc. The Islamists at Kabul University demonstrated on campus against the royal regime and the communists.[49] By 1970 they had gained enough influence to defeat the leftists in the elections to the student council of Kabul University. Members who became teachers or government employees in the provinces also spread the movement to high schools in some areas.

The Khalqis spoke loosely about seizing power through a mass working-class uprising but seem to have made few concrete plans. As is typical of rentier states, a fall in foreign resources (Appendix C), which prompted the government to reduce spending and hiring, provoked student and worker protests in 1968. The Khalqis were involved, particularly in the teachers-training schools and at Kabul University, but the working class of Kabul, such as it was, was mainly Tajik and Hazara; consequently the Maoists seem to have been most successful in organizing leftist support among this group. Despite their class rhetoric, the Khalqis concentrated recruiting efforts among schoolteachers, writers, and others likely to have long-term effects on the ideology of educated Afghans.[50]

The Parchamis, after their poor showing in the electoral arena in 1969, resumed their alliance with the increasingly disaffected "progressive" wing of the ruling elite, including Daoud and a number of army officers. The Khalqis regarded their close ties with the ruling elites as opportunistic collaboration with the ruling class.[51]

Like the founders of the PDPA, Daoud belonged to the first generation of foreign-educated students in Afghanistan. His links to some of them reached back to the late 1940s, when as a young member of the royal family he had sympathized with Wish Zalmayan. Daoud was also the patron of the army officers: before becoming prime minister he had been commander-in-chief and minister of war, and he had also sponsored the Soviet training that had enabled the military to become the most technologically advanced sector of society in Afghanistan.

As New Democracy disintegrated, Daoud organized meetings with disaffected bureaucrats and army officers, including some Parchamis. He sought support not in the tribes themselves but in individuals of tribal origin whom his government had recruited into the expanded state apparatus. The success of his coup demonstrated that the support of the newly educated in the state apparatus could now be key to seizing state power.

After Daoud's coup, several other groups tried to profit from its apparent lesson. As Es'haq put it, "Daud's coup showed a short way to power. Since the coup was almost bloodless it seemed the easiest way of achieving revolutionary aims. Since the communists were sharing power with Daud, the people who tried this method belonged to the Islamic movement or to the nationalist groups."[52]

Only Parcham, however, initially shared power with Daoud. Khalq, which was frozen out of power, drew the same lesson as the other groups. According to an official biography of Khalq leader Taraki:

> Comrade Taraki . . . had intimated [to] the party since the 1973 coup that it was possible in Afghanistan to wrest . . . political power through a shortcut[, inasmuch] as the classical way in which the productive forces undergo different stages to build a society based on scientific socialism would take a long time. This shortcut could be utilized by working extensively in the armed forces. Previously the army was considered as the tool of dictatorship and despotism of the ruling class and it was not imaginable to use it before toppling its employer. However, Comrade Taraki suggested that this too should be wrested [away] in order to topple the ruling class.[53]

The intellectuals were ready to make what Majrooh called the myth of revolution a reality.

Within a few months after Daoud seized power, he arrested another group of alleged coup plotters, this one led by Muhammad Hashim Maiwandwal, the second prime minister under New Democracy and leader of the National Progressive Party. Maiwandwal died of torture in prison in October 1973, at a time when Parchamis controlled the Ministry of the Interior.

The Islamists turned to armed struggle partly in emulation of Daoud, but also out of fear of repression. Daoud was suppressing what liberty the Islamists had enjoyed and giving free rein to the PDPA. As Es'haq wrote, "The Islamic movement lost hope in a peaceful way of struggle and resorted to secret means of opposing Daud and his communist colleagues."[54]

Sayyed Musa Tawana remembers the decision to turn toward the armed struggle:

One day [in late 1973 or early 1974] in a meeting in a gathering room of the Faculty of Shariat, Prof. Rabbani . . . said, "Some of our brothers deem armed struggle necessary to topple this criminal government." Prof. Sayyaf said . . . that the Islamic Movement would be eliminated [in such a struggle because] the ranks of the Movement were not solid enough to face the Daud government. I asked Prof. Rabbani how those brothers wanted to overthrow the Government. He said they had contacts in the army which could bring units in some provinces to our side. I said that was not sufficient for victory in an armed struggle. Some brothers said, "How long should we avoid using force?" We had a long discussion on the issue. Finally we agreed to begin efforts to procure arms and to begin training youth in using weapons. We also agreed that it was more important how we obtained and distributed arms than the quantity.[55]

Rabbani thus proposed a coup, but of a different sort from the 1973 and 1978 coups: rather than an immediate seizure of the state offices in Kabul, he would build support for the Islamists among provincial army units. The Islamist guerrillas who were to be armed and trained might then stage an uprising in conjunction with sympathetic military units. This may have been the plan in 1974, when followers of the Islamic movement in the army planned a coup. Their plan was discovered and the leaders imprisoned. Others had planned to support the coup with an insurrection; a group of activists led by Muhammad Omar tried to start an uprising in Badakhshan but were easily thwarted.[56]

These earlier events also led to the arrest of several leaders of the Islamist movement. Rabbani escaped from the Sharia Faculty with the help of some students when the police came for him in the summer of 1974.[57] He made his way to Peshawar, as did Hikmatyar and some others.

While Rabbani was seeking support in Saudi Arabia, Hikmatyar, who was beginning to organize his own followers separately, agreed to a Pakistani proposal to launch an insurrection. Bhutto, who doubted that the Islamists could win any significant victories, aimed merely to pressure Daoud to negotiate with Pakistan on bilateral issues. In letters from Saudi Arabia, Rabbani argued that an insurrection was premature. Nonetheless, in July 1975 some Islamists staged an uprising, later known as the Panjsher Valley incident, after the only area where it had any significant impact. Thirty-six Islamist activists in Panjsher, led by the polytechnic student Ahmad Shah Massoud, captured one district and two subdistrict headquarters but had to retreat within twenty-four hours in the face of the army and a hostile population.[58] In other parts of the country, where groups as small or smaller incited revolts, the Islamists met with even less success. Ninety-three Islamists were arrested; Massoud and others who escaped capture returned to Pakistan.

For the Islamists, especially the students (as opposed to the Sharia Faculty professors), this uprising represented an attempt at Che Guevara–style *foco* insurgency. In this model, "a guerrilla band enters a rural area where it has never operated before with the hope of serving as the 'insurrectional focus' [*foco* in Spanish] for a larger rebellion through its 'exemplary revolutionary actions.'" A state whose repressive apparatus is relatively stable, however, as was that of Afghanistan in 1975, can easily wipe out isolated focos. The effectiveness of repression can be key: Es'haq recalls, for instance, that in 1975 when the people of Panjsher heard from Kabul that the government was sending the army, they turned against Massoud and the insurgents.[59]

The failure of the 1975 insurgency created tensions that contributed to the Jamiat-Hizb split. The Pakistanis continued to maintain the Islamists, mainly through Hikmatyar, but as long as Daoud was in office and kept moving away from both Soviet influence and irredentism, the Pakistanis kept both Hizb and Jamiat in cold storage. In 1976 other followers of the Islamic movement in the army, led by Gen. Mir Ahmad Shah, planned another coup, but this, too, was discovered.[60] The conflict over strategy did not erupt again until 1978, when the PDPA's coup and the beginning of spontaneous antigovernment revolts made such debates more than theoretical.

The Sawr Revolution

The PDPA was the group among the intelligentsia that first succeeded in taking power in Kabul not because it had public support or superior organization but because the military was the portion of the state apparatus where the Soviet model of modernization was most influential. Daoud's coup had both destroyed the monarchical symbolism that had concealed the gradual decay of the tribal state, and mobilized those who would attempt to replace it. How the final blow came was accidental; that it came was not.

In 1977, two years after the expulsion of the Parchamis from Daoud's government and the subsequent reunification of Parcham and Khalq, PDPA army officers began planning a coup. Although Daoud forced them to strike before they were ready, they succeeded in toppling him.

Parcham had been the first of the revolutionary groups actually to enter the government, but it had found that its dependence on a segment of the old-regime elite kept it from carrying out the program of the party. Furthermore, the party's position under Daoud was no more institutionalized than that of previous Afghan ministers and bureaucrats. Its members in the government depended on the personal favor of Daoud, who could elevate them to high office or dismiss them with equal ease. The same went for the party itself: Daoud allowed Parcham to operate openly at first, then banned it, along with all others except his own (projected) National Revolutionary

Party. Thus while Parcham continued to advocate a coup d'état by progressive elements of the armed forces, it came to believe that such a coup could succeed in carrying out revolutionary goals only if it was independent of the ruling class.

At the same time, Taraki and Amin had seen the possibilities for taking power through a coup. The social composition of the middle- and lower-ranking officer corps—Pashtuns of provincial, tribal origin—gave Khalq a recruiting advantage over Parcham. Despite a late start, Khalq seems to have overtaken Parcham by 1978. During 1975 and 1976, as Soviet interest in the PDPA increased, Parcham and Khalq competed for recognition by the international communist movement as the genuine Marxist-Leninist party of Afghanistan. Instead they encountered pressure— presumably unwelcome—to unite. At least unity reduced the possibility that Khalqi and Parchami military officers would sabotage each other's coup plans (though that did eventually happen in August 1978, March 1990, and April 1992). As Halliday put it in Leninist jargon, "It was when *Khalq* learnt the need to work in the army, and *Parcham* understood the perils of frontism, that a new genuinely revolutionary conjuncture developed."[61]

The assassination of Mir Akbar Khaibar set in motion the events that led to the coup. Khaibar, an officer of the Royal Afghan Police, was the liaison between Nur Ahmad Nur, the Politburo member responsible for Parcham's military network, and Gen. Muhammad Rafi, the military man who commanded it. At the time, the PDPA charged (and many others believed) that Khaibar was killed on the orders of Daoud's interior minister, who had a reputation as an anticommunist influenced by SAVAK.[62]

The assassination led to massive demonstrations in Kabul against both Daoud and the CIA, which Parcham claimed was behind the killing. Interpreting the demonstrations as an alarming indication of the extent of PDPA organization, Daoud and his closest associates decided to arrest the leadership of the party.[63] In response to these arrests, army and air force officers in the PDPA, including those who had helped Daoud to power in 1973, launched a coup on April 27, 1978, in the Afghan lunar month of Sawr (Taurus). In the Sawr Revolution, as the PDPA called it, President Muhammad Daoud was deposed and killed, ending Muhammadzai rule. On April 30 military officers handed over power to a Revolutionary Council headed by Nur Muhammad Taraki, who promptly signed Decree No. 1, which proclaimed the establishment of the Democratic Republic of Afghanistan.

Part Two

The PDPA in Power:

From the Second

Cold War to the

Collapse of the USSR

The PDPA regime went through several stages, each defined by the type and amount of foreign support the regime received. Changes in foreign support were driven not only by international changes but also by the impression that the Afghan resistance movement made on foreign decision makers (mainly in Moscow).

In the twenty months following the Sawr Revolution, until December 27, 1979, the Soviet Union increased aid of all sorts, including military advisers. Western and Islamic states, meanwhile, slashed their aid programs, particularly after U.S. Ambassador Adolph Dubs was killed in February 1979. Aid from these sources increasingly flowed instead to various resistance groups, while the Afghan state developed a unilateral dependence on the Soviet Union. Moscow, however, had only indirect leverage over the Afghan government, whose radical policies were destabilizing a state that played an important role in Soviet regional security calculations. The Soviets sent troops to install a more pliable government and assert more direct control.

From the Soviet intervention until the February 1986 Congress of the Communist Party of the Soviet Union, the Afghan government under Babrak Karmal received open-ended economic and military aid from the Soviets, including more than one hundred thousand Soviet troops. The intervention cost the Soviet Union about $5 billion per year.[1] The troops and the many Soviet advisers who followed them guaranteed more direct Soviet control over the party and government, which gained at least military strength from this support.

After the February 1986 Congress, CPSU Secretary-General Mikhail Gorbachev, convinced that the war could not be won at a price he was willing to pay, prepared to withdraw Soviet troops. In addition to diplomatic efforts aimed at ending aid to the resistance in return for Soviet troop withdrawal, Gorbachev urged an initiative within Afghanistan to prepare a political compromise under which the PDPA could coexist with other political forces. Moscow replaced Karmal with Najibullah, whose main task was to carry out this program. In November 1987 a Loya Jirga adopted a new constitution that changed the state's name back to the Republic of Afghanistan and provided for elections to a parliament.

On February 15, 1989, the last Soviet troops left Afghanistan. From then until the August 1991 coup in Moscow, no Soviet troops fought alongside the Afghan army, but the Soviet government maintained a high level of financial and material aid to Kabul. Western sources estimated the cost at $3–4 billion per year. Even by more conservative estimates, Soviet military aid made Afghanistan the world's fifth-largest importer of weapons during 1986–90, trailing only India, Japan, Saudi Arabia, and Iraq.[2] This aid enabled the government to buy support, or at least compliance, from many groups, at the price of abandoning virtually all of its original program. An unsuccessful coup attempt by the Khalqi defense minister in March 1990 left Najibullah increasingly dependent on non-Pashtun militias in northern Afghanistan. In June 1990 the PDPA held its Second Congress, where it changed its name to the Watan (Homeland) Party; renounced Marxism, one-party rule, and socialism; and proclaimed support for Islam, democracy, and market economics.

Nonetheless, as the state experienced an intensifying fiscal crisis, factional and ethnic conflict grew within the party and within the regime. In the absence of any mobilizing ideology or social base, only Soviet aid redistributed by Najibullah could hold together the various apparatuses that constituted the regime.

5

Failure of Revolution from Above

The army officers who carried out the April coup handed over power to a formally united PDPA, led by General Secretary Taraki, who also assumed the offices of president of the Revolutionary Council and prime minister. Babrak Karmal and Hafizullah Amin, who loathed each other, were also Politburo secretaries, members of the R.C. Presidium, and deputy prime ministers. The Soviet Union announced massive backing for the new regime.

Conflict soon broke out again within the PDPA. In July Taraki sent Karmal and five other Parchami leaders close to him into exile as ambassadors. In August the Khalqis arrested others for plotting a coup, and in November they expelled all Parchami leaders from the party and government. The government, under the sole control of Khalq—itself increasingly dominated by Hafizullah Amin—tried to carry out a revolutionary transformation of Afghan society by decree and terror.

This program provoked local rebellions, accelerating the disintegration of the ill-prepared state apparatus; the government's dwindling control in turn encouraged larger segments of the population to revolt. The refusal of Amin to moderate his policies or seek coalition partners alienated his Soviet backers, who felt their security threatened by the decay of the army and state that they had funded. A Soviet-sponsored plan to replace Amin with a Taraki-Karmal coalition failed in September 1979. Amin had Taraki killed and made overtures to the United States and Pakistan. Alarmed by growing disorder and fearful of an attempt by Washington to recoup in Afghanistan what it had lost in the February 1979 revolution in Iran, Leonid Brezhnev and his closest associates sent the Red Army across the Afghan border in December 1979. When a plan to force Amin to hand power over peacefully to a Soviet-approved leadership once again failed, a special KGB unit assaulted his palace and killed him.[1]

The State under Khalq

The victorious "revolutionaries" placed executive authority in the hands of a Revolutionary Council named by the PDPA leadership. Because they took power through a small coup in Kabul, rather than after a nationwide upheaval, they inherited the state institutions of the old regime more or less intact. The coup had no immediate impact on provincial administration, tax collection—such as it was—or the myriad other everyday activities of the government. The PDPA found these institutions too fragile, however, to support social revolution and mass repression. The construction of new institutions began only after Soviet intervention.

The PDPA had inherited an undisturbed rentier fiscal system (Table 5.1). But the party introduced changes in the sources of foreign aid and the direction of foreign trade, which was the main object of taxation. The PDPA transformed the international orientation of the Afghan state from balanced nonalignment, with some advantages to the USSR, to total alignment with the USSR. The alignment was manifest in security commitments, foreign policy, international trade (at least legal trade), development aid, and educational programs.[2]

Exports from Afghanistan to the countries of the Commission for Mutual Economic Assistance (CMEA) increased from about 40 percent in the 1970s to more than 60 percent by 1980. Imports from that area also increased from about a quarter to over half of the total. The Soviet share of foreign aid, which had been about one-half of the total from 1955 to the end of New Democracy, rose to almost 80 percent, with members of the Warsaw Pact accounting for most of the remainder. The number of students sent abroad for training increased, and the proportion going to the Soviet Union or Warsaw Pact countries approached 90 percent by the mid-1980s, compared with about one-fifth previously. Most Western advisory and aid personnel left the country—the United States suspended aid altogether—after the kidnapping and killing of Ambassador Dubs in February 1979. The number of Soviet advisers is not known exactly, but the U.S. Embassy estimated a jump from 350 to 3,000. The number increased further after August 1979, as the Soviets laid the groundwork for the invasion.[3]

Taraki and Amin apparently believed that the strength of the Soviet-supported state, along with policies that they claimed would benefit the vast majority of the Afghan population, made other political alliances unnecessary, even with Parcham. In the government announced directly after the coup, Khalq had received about 60 percent of the ministerial positions and Parcham the rest (Table 5.2), as good an indicator as any of the relative size of the two factions at that time.[4] No nonparty members held any positions. After July 1978 Khalqis virtually monopolized government and party positions. They treated all dissent as treason and repressed it ruthlessly, if ineffectively.

The coup that brought the regime to power was a mutiny of junior army officers in alliance with a political party; the high command, already damaged by Daoud's coup,

Table 5.1 Financing of Government Expenditure, 1975–1988

| | Expenditure | | | Revenue as Percentage of Expenditure | | | | | | | | |
| | Total (millions of afghanis) | Ordinary (%) | Development (%) | Domestic | Taxes | | | Natural Gas Sales | Other Nontax | Foreign Aid | Rentier Income | Residual Domestic Debt (%) |
Year					Total	Indirect	Direct					
1975	16,187	60	40	74	42	35	7	12	21	27	38	−1
1976	19,594	57	43	71	40	31	9	10	21	29	39	−1
1977	24,326	49	51	61	37	28	9	8	16	34	42	4
1978	26,397	47	53	62	36	26	10	9	18	34	42	4
1979	30,173	56	44	52	30	22	8	13	10	36	48	12
1980	31,692	62	38	83	34	27	8	33	16	28	61	−11
1981	40,751	66	34	74	22	14	8	34	18	26	59	1
1982	42,112	69	31	71	24	17	7	34	14	28	62	0
1986	88,700	74	26	48	—	—	—	17	—	29	46	23
1988	129,900	84	16	30	—	—	—	6	—	26	32	44

Sources: Data from DRA, *Statistical Information of Afghanistan, 1975–1978;* DRA, *SYB 1358;* DRA, *SYB 1359;* DRA, *SYB 1360;* DRA, *SYB 1361;* RA, "Afghanistan 1990."

Note: Residual domestic debt equals expenditures minus the sum of domestic revenue and foreign aid. Domestic revenue equals the sum of taxes, natural gas sales, and other nontax revenues. Rentier income equals foreign aid plus natural gas sales. Foreign aid includes both commodity and project aid.

Table 5.2 Political Composition of Governments, 1978–1989

Period	Positions	Parcham	Khalq	Non-PDPA	Total
May 1978	All	9	13	0	22
	Core[a]	3	4	0	7
July 1978–Dec. 1979	All	1[b]	23	0	24
	Core	0	10	0	10
Jan. 1980–Nov. 1985	All	29	7	3	39
	Core	7	2	0	9
Dec. 1986–Dec. 1989	All	25	9	30[c]	64
	Core	4	4	2	10

Sources: See Appendix A.

[a]Core includes the president, prime minister, and the ministers of defense, internal affairs, foreign affairs, and state security (director general of KhAD before January 1986).

[b]Muhammad Hasan Baraq-Shafi.

[c]Includes SZA and SAZA.

was destroyed. Some units that resisted suffered heavy casualties and were dissolved. Sixty of sixty-two serving generals were arrested, killed, or forced to retire and were replaced by PDPA members promoted from the ranks of colonel or major.[5] Many Parchamis among the new generals were in turn arrested in August 1978 and charged with planning another coup. The extent to which the command structure had been disrupted, however, was not clear until local revolts placed the army under stress. The number of effective forces remained about 120,000, and DRA leadership, unlike Nadir Shah, Abdul Rahman Khan, or Dost Muhammad, did not immediately perceive a need to concentrate efforts on building an army.

To carry out repression the Khalqis used not only the regular army and police but also a new intelligence organization, whose name, AGSA, is a Pashto acronym for Organization for the Defense of the Interests of Afghanistan. After his takeover Amin renamed it KAM, the Workers' Intelligence Agency. Although AGSA was technically attached to the Ministry of the Interior, Amin ran that agency—and later KAM—virtually independently, through relatives and close associates whom he appointed. These intelligence agencies received direct assistance from East Germany and the USSR but never developed the degree of sophistication shown by Khidamat-i Ittila'at-i Dawlati (KhAD), their successor after the Soviet invasion.[6]

Revolution from Above through Coercion

The goal of the Khalqis under Amin was to use the state apparatus to destroy all competition for social control in all sectors of Afghan society. Both repression and "reforms" were intended to achieve that goal. Repression would eliminate or neutralize both competitors for national power—the tribal aristocracy and rival intelligentsia—and the leaders of local society. The masses, liberated from domination, would then be enlightened through a mass literacy program and would gratefully support the Khalqis. The large group of schoolteachers in Khalq immediately changed the content of primary and secondary instruction to reflect party ideology. These changes were symbolized in the country's flag, redesigned in October 1978; the new banner dropped the traditional Islamic green stripe and was all red, like the flag of a Soviet republic. From the summer of 1978 to the fall of 1979, the government also omitted the traditional Islamic invocation, "In the name of God, the Merciful, the Compassionate," at the beginning of its decrees.[7]

The Khalqis' monopoly of power also symbolized an ethnic shift. The core of the old regime was a coalition of Muhammadzais: Persian-speaking bureaucrats and professionals mostly from Kabul, and educated sons of the leading Pashtun tribal families. The Khalqi regime was dominated by Ghilzai and Paktia Pashtuns of tribal origin. It was the most-Pashtun and the least-Durrani government Afghanistan had ever had.

In pursuit of a plan to eliminate opposition, Khalq used mass arrests, torture, and secret executions on a scale Afghanistan had not seen since the time of Abdul Rahman Khan, and probably not even then. Daoud and his immediate family perished in the coup. The rest of the Musahiban still in Afghanistan were arrested, deprived of their citizenship and property by decree of the Revolutionary Council, and subsequently allowed to emigrate through the efforts of the International Committee of the Red Cross. Nearly a quarter of the surviving former ministers of the old regime were killed or arrested. Political activists were also targeted—Islamists, Parchamis, Maoists, members of Afghan Millat. So was any social group likely to pose a threat or obstacle: students and teachers, army officers, bureaucrats, and members of ethnic groups who had revolted against the government, such as Nuristanis and Hazaras. The most influential national religious leadership was destroyed in February 1979, when the government killed all male members of the Mujaddidi family (about seventy people), whom it had arrested in the summer of 1978. All members of the Islamist movement jailed by Daoud were killed in one night. The government later published a list that named twelve thousand people purportedly killed in Kabul prisons during this period. In response to rural uprisings the government also engaged in such collective reprisals as the killing of an estimated 1,170 unarmed villagers in Kerala, Kunar, on April 20, 1979.[8]

In the countryside the battle for social control was first waged mainly around a set of reforms the regime began to introduce three months after the coup, following the dismissal of the Parchamis. These reforms, if implemented, would have allowed the Khalqis to supplant the traditional leadership as rulers and arbiters of rural society. The reforms were introduced by decree of the Revolutionary Council without any prior public discussion. Except for those party members involved in drafting the decrees, no one in Afghanistan knew of them until they were read over the radio and published in the official gazette, whereupon they took immediate effect.

The decrees containing the measures affecting the rural sector were Decree No. 6 (July 12, 1978), which regulated rural mortgages and debts; Decree No. 7 (October 17, 1978), which dealt with marriage and brideprice; Decree No. 8 (November 28, 1978), which prescribed land reform; and a statute governing agricultural cooperatives, issued on September 21, 1978.[9] If implemented, these decrees would have transformed Afghan rural society; the asymmetrical reciprocity dominated by khans or jirgas would be replaced by a system of economically comparable nuclear families linked through market relations and tied directly to the Khalqi state. These decrees would have destroyed the economic and social basis of the exchanges—marriage prestations, loans, mortgages, tenancy, hospitality—that enabled khans to "tie the knot of the tribe." The network of clientelism that held extended families together and knitted them into a qawm would have been replaced by direct dependence of nuclear families on the party and government bureaucracy. Where collective efforts were needed, they would be organized by state-sponsored cooperatives rather than khan-sponsored patronage.

Decree No. 6 provided relief for a broad category of debts. Sharecroppers and agricultural laborers (*bazgar* and *mazdur*) were freed of all debts (principal and interest) owed to the landlords for whom they worked or to moneylenders.[10] Many types of debts of small peasants were also canceled or rescheduled.

Enforcement of the decree depended on the claimant's ability to produce legal documents attesting to the loan. To administer the decree the government published a regulation providing for district (uluswali) and provincial committees to resolve the problems of the peasants. The district committee, presided over by the *uluswal*, was composed of bureaucrats from five government ministries plus two "representatives of the peasants," generally village schoolteachers who were members of Khalq.[11] The provincial committee, headed by the *wali* (governor), was to include six government bureaucrats and three "peasant representatives."

Decree No. 7 established minimum ages for marriage and specified that marriage required the free consent of both parties. It outlawed all marriage prestations except the Islamic mahr. The decree also forbade the groom's family to demand expenditures for the wedding ceremonies. Even though earlier Afghan governments had failed to implement similar reforms of marriage practices, the regime presented the decree as revolutionary, promising an end to "oppressive patriarchal and feudal conditions."[12] If implemented, Decree No. 7 would have transformed marriage from a social and economic transaction between two extended families (sometimes within one extended family) to a private decision of two individuals.

The statute for the organization of cooperatives opened them to peasants owning up to ten acres of first-quality land or the equivalent. The cooperative's elected officers were to deal with the collective affairs of the peasants and act as mediators with the administration as khans and maliks had done. The true significance of the cooperatives becomes apparent only when they are viewed in conjunction with the subsequently announced land reform measures. These measures would have created a rural society of small landholdings, many of which would be uneconomical and none of which would be adequate as an economic base for the provision of collective goods. The cooperatives would provide an alternative to the traditional role of the khan as a public servant and that of the malik as an intermediary with the government. They also might have been a first step toward collectivization, as they were in China.

Decree No. 8 aimed at eliminating "feudal and prefeudal conditions" by establishing a land ceiling of about fifteen acres for first-quality land or the equivalent for each "family." The family, defined as husband, wife, and unmarried children less than eighteen years of age, was to be the basic unit of land ownership. This definition was consistent with the intention of the marriage reform. The reform would thus have eliminated the joint family and larger kinship units (prefeudal relations) as economic entities.

Landholdings greater than the ceiling, as well as state land and the lands of the former royal family, were to be confiscated by the state and distributed to landless laborers and tenants, small peasants (those owning less than 2.5 acres), and landless nomads. Land ceilings combined with redistribution would have virtually eliminated tenancy (feudal relations).

The decree would also have given government an altogether new, intrusive role in agriculture. The state was to expropriate the surplus lands and place them under the authority of the Land Reform Department. The department would decide who was to receive the land and would ensure that all new landowners registered their deeds with the state, which Afghan peasants had not traditionally done. New owners were required to cultivate the land within three months, participate in a cadastral survey, and pay land tax. To prevent the emergence of new inequalities, the state forbade new owners to sell or mortgage the newly received land and imposed strict limits on tenancy. A later regulation (June 6, 1979) provided for "Special Popular Committees" to resolve legal disputes arising from land reform. Committees at both district and provincial levels were to be composed of four bureaucrats and three peasant representatives each; the peasants would be elected "under the control [or supervision]" of the Committee to Resolve the Problems of the Peasants, which was, of course, dominated by the government administration.

The implementation of the land reform began in the warm provinces in January 1979, then spread through other areas. At the same time, the growing revolt removed more and more of the country's territory from state control. Nonetheless, by July the government announced that land reform had been completed. In an address to the October 1987 party conference, Prime Minister Kishtmand denounced the effort retroactively. He claimed that land had not been distributed to 340,000 families who had "received" it. The government had claimed in April 1986 that 329,767 peasant families had received land, so Kishtmand's claim placed the whole land reform program in question. Kishtmand also excoriated the Khalqi-dominated Ministries of Land Reform and Irrigation for paying salaries to thousands of officials who did no work. As the Soviet army prepared to withdraw, a general with extensive experience in Afghanistan commented on the slow pace at which land and water reform was being carried out, estimating that only 30 to 35 percent of the program had been completed. The Soviet journalist interviewing him, who also had spent much time in Afghanistan, observed that even most of that progress was pro forma: "Approximately one third of the land the peasants have received has returned to the hands of its former owners, and almost half of the land in the peasants' hands is not being tilled." If both estimates are approximately accurate, by 1989 peasants in Afghanistan were cultivating only one-ninth of the land they had supposedly been allotted nine years before. My brief and unsystematic observation of one area of Nangarhar Province, which was controlled by the government until November 1988, indicates that much of the land actually received and cultivated by peasants was state land rather than property expropriated from larger private holdings.[13]

These reforms have usually been depicted primarily as an attempt, perhaps cynical or misguided, to redistribute wealth and power from the rural rich to the rural poor. But given not only the nature of the reforms but also the proposed means of implementation, these measures would never have empowered the poor peasants. Instead, they would have substituted the Khalqi party-state for the khan, jirga, or elders as the main authority in the rural community. The method of implementation communicated this message clearly: groups of armed Khalqi activists were dispatched to the villages, most of them schoolteachers and army officers with no connection to the community. The reforms were aimed at winning once and for all the battle for social control between the state and the rural strongmen. As it happened, the state disintegrated, lacking the capacity to win this battle; but neither could the rural strongmen, undermined by tribal and factional fragmentation, provide an alternative.

Why did the Khalqi regime lead to the breakdown of much of the state and the spread of popular resistance? Most observers, including even the later leaders of the PDPA, came to discard the explanation that the resistance represented a conservative, tribal society rejecting state intrusion. Analysts have generally agreed that Khalqi reforms were badly formulated and poorly implemented and that the state lacked the capacity to formulate and carry out better ones. Others have emphasized that the regime's ideological radicalism, in particular its attack on Islam and its ties to the Soviet Union, undermined the diffuse legitimacy of the state.[14] These assessments are accurate enough but not adequate to explain what happened.

The reforms were indeed poorly formulated; many of them worsened rather than improved the lives of the peasants. Afghanistan had a low level of state capacities of a very conventional (not revolutionary) sort—the ability to determine ownership of land, for example, or to extend credit to peasants. The state was so external to the society of rural Afghanistan that local traditions rather than state law played the primary role in defining property relations. Water, not land, was the major constraint on Afghan agriculture, but the reforms distributed land without providing for adequate irrigation. Because large landholdings in Afghanistan were rare, there was not nearly enough surplus land to distribute to all of the intended beneficiaries. Abolishing debts to landlords and moneylenders without providing alternative sources of credit deprived small peasants of the ability to obtain loans. Most landlords supplied seed, and some furnished draft animals, so landless tenants and laborers who received land from the state had no alternative source for these essentials of production. In one case in Laghman, in eastern Afghanistan, the musallis, an impoverished qawm of grain cleaners, were allotted land in far-off Helmand, in the Southwest. Thousands of musallis moved there, only to find that there were no tents or houses, no one to demarcate the plots, no water, and no tools. After subsisting for a few months on World Food Program handouts, they returned home "more disillusioned than ever."[15]

Most important, the choice the peasants were given was not between domination and exploitation on the one hand and freedom and equality on the other. Their choice was between leaders whom they knew, with whom they shared much, and leaders whom they did not know, who believed in an alien ideology and who showed by their actions that they could not be trusted. Long experience had taught the peasants that, pernicious as some khans could be, others were useful in protecting the village from the state administration, even when the state administration was Muslim. The ignorance underlying the formulation of the reforms and the incompetence and brutality of their implementation served only to further convince the peasantry that the proposed changes would not be in their interest. Indeed, they turned out not to be.[16]

But if poorly formulated and implemented redistributive policies could explain state breakdown, most postcolonial states would look like Afghanistan. As Migdal shows, it is much more common for the "web-like" societies of these countries to frustrate attempts at implementing policies and to co-opt lower levels of the bureaucracy. The willingness and ability of the Khalqis to use brutal but inadequate coercion prevented this more common script from being played out. Soviet and anti-Khalqi PDPA commentators cite the party's use of "impermissible" or "criminal" methods.[17] According to Farid Abolfathi, Leninist doctrine held that before attempting revolutionary social changes, a party must develop a base of political cadres backed up by adequate coercion to protect them. The Khalqis, however, took power with a very small organizational base but firm foreign (Soviet) support. In April 1978 PDPA membership was small—3,000–5,000 according to most Western observers, 15,000 according to a post-glasnost Soviet source.[18] Regardless of size, the discipline of the party organization and Soviet support prevented a retreat. The Soviets protested against some of Amin's policies and blamed him for atrocities committed, but firm Soviet support for the Afghan state was key to the Khalqis' ability to endure.

The role of Afghanistan in the international security system also enhanced the role of violence in relations between state and society. Having largely developed on the basis of funding by foreign powers interested in the potential of Aghanistan as a political and military buffer, the state had created hardly any institutions for interacting with society. There was no state legal framework for the operation of the collective networks of most of the society (qawm, tariqa, jirga). There was little police presence except in the towns. There were no nationwide political parties, civic associations, or formally organized interest groups.[19] There was, in other words, no civil or political society mediating between state and citizens. The autonomy of the state made it easy for a small, relatively well organized, highly ideological group to seize the state and hold it for a time. But autonomy also meant that the party in power had virtually no resources other than violence for implementing its program, and society had few other means of resistance.[20]

Breakdown of Portions of the State Apparatus

In the end, the persistence of revolt and the concomitant breakdown of the state resulted from its own internal weaknesses, aggravated by the Khalqi takeover. Scholars of revolts and revolutions have concluded that such events depend less on severe grievances—which are far more frequent than revolution—than on the availability of the resources needed for collective action and on a prior weakening of the state, typically (but not necessarily) through defeat in war.[21]

In Afghanistan during 1978 and 1979, the main reason the revolt spread so widely was that the army disintegrated in a series of insurrections, from unrecorded defections of small posts to mutinies in nearly all the major garrisons. The mutinies began at Herat in March 1979 and later struck Jalalabad, Asmar, Ghazni, Nahrin, and the Bala Hissar (Upper Fortress) of Kabul itself (August 1979). Although all of these revolts were ultimately suppressed—some allegedly with direct Soviet assistance—each brought a loss of troops and officers, and some of the mutiny leaders (Capt. Ismail Khan of Herat, Brig. Abdul Rauf of Asmar) escaped and joined the resistance. (After the change of power in April 1992, Ismail Khan became amir of the shura of Herat, and Abdul Rauf, promoted to general, became commander of the Central Forces of the Ministry of Defense.) It was the disintegration of the army rather than the initial military strength of the insurgents that allowed the resistance to spread in 1979.

These events could have occurred only in a country with a state that lacked a strong degree of internal coherence. The 1978 coup was led by dissident middle-level officers and deposed not only the government but also the high command. Successful coups d'état in more developed states—Pakistan, Indonesia, the southern cone of South America—have been organized by the entire military institution, often with the support of major elements of the bureaucracy; in such cases, the military is typically protecting its own institutional prerogatives and coherence. A low-level coup, in contrast, is often a revolt by a faction. Such a mutiny is likely only in a state with very weak internal control mechanisms, where the army is largely a network of clients and where the chain of command is weak.[22]

The Khalqi purges of the officer corps further weakened the state and the army. The attempt to use the state apparatus of the old regime to enforce a small faction's program was the final blow: the first and most important loss of legitimacy was within the state itself. Especially when the state is a largely external force in society, it may not require popular legitimacy, but it does require internal legitimacy.[23]

It was the internal disintegration of the state and party, more than the military force of the resistance, that prompted Soviet intervention. And so the new regime's efforts concentrated on rebuilding those institutions.

6

Under Soviet Occupation:
Party, State, and
Society, 1980-1985

The Red Army returned Babrak Karmal to Kabul and installed him as president of the Revolutionary Council, general secretary of the PDPA, and prime minister of the government. (He relinquished the premiership to Sultan Ali Kishtmand a year later.) The Soviets made Parcham the dominant force in all of these bodies, although Khalqis who had not been too closely associated with Amin continued to play a subordinate role. The new government terminated or significantly moderated the revolutionary programs whose coercive implementation had pushed the society into revolt. The installation of a government by foreign troops, however, helped turn the revolts into a nationwide uprising.

The Soviet army and air force took the lead in suppressing the rural insurgency, which received increasing support from Western and Islamic powers, in particular, the United States and Pakistan. KhAD, the KGB-organized secret police led by Najibullah, imposed pervasive terror on urban areas, as the government tried to impose a totalitarian system on those areas under its control. Despite massive and indiscriminate violence that ultimately killed nearly a million people, a military stalemate developed. The government controlled Kabul and other major towns, while the insurgents (mujahidin) operated freely in most of the countryside.

The regime installed by the Soviets at the beginning of 1980 faced a completely different situation from that encountered by the original revolutionary regime. In 1978 the would-be revolutionaries had seized control of a weak but growing state in fragile equilibrium with a fragmented society. In 1980, the new government confronted a disintegrating state and a society that was organizing itself for revolt. The guerrillas did not yet pose a military or economic threat to the existence of the government; U.S. diplomats in Afghanistan acknowledged that there was no such threat. Although the ability of the resistance to cut roads hindered the rebuilding of the territorial administration (including conscription), it did not much affect the state's income. The main problem caused by control of the roads by the resistance was that the government could not deliver pay packets to its provincial employees, not that it could not collect the tiny tax revenues.[1] The legacy of the distributive (rather than extractive) state made the central state apparatus less vulnerable to a massive rebellion.

What prompted Soviet intervention and posed the first challenge to the new regime was less the onslaught of the resistance than the disintegration of the army, the dissolution of provincial administration, and the atrophy of the party's institutions under Amin's charismatic-coercive style of rule. When institutions of the old regime had proved inadequate for their purposes, the Khalqis had disposed of the institutions in favor of generalized violence; the Soviets now made building new institutions their first priority.

The party itself was in disarray. Khalq had exiled leading Parchamis in July 1978 and had expelled them in November. Other Parchamis had been arrested, tortured, and even executed. Khalq itself had been badly damaged when Amin undermined Taraki's authority and later had him killed; in September 1979 major Khalqi military and police figures sought refuge with the Soviets.[2] Amin never even announced the composition of his Politburo. He ruled mainly through his family members and personal clients rather than through any formal institutions.

A reorganized party, dominated by Parcham under Soviet tutelage, was to function as the supreme power within the state, which the Soviets tried to remodel along the lines of their own institutions. This process required security for the state apparatus's core institutions while the regime strove to meet its longer-term challenge: the lack of trained and loyal cadres.

The Soviets and their Afghan clients tried to use these new institutions against the insurgency, but the strategy changed somewhat over time. The Soviets originally planned to withdraw their troops after six months. They thought that once Amin was removed and the new regime had taken a series of measures to allay antigovernment suspicions, most Afghans would accept the regime, and the remaining "reactionaries" could be eliminated. Thus the new regime released thousands of prisoners, declared its allegiance to Islam, restored the Islamic green stripe to the country's flag, announced that literacy classes would be segregated by sex and would be strictly voluntary for women, proclaimed an amnesty for refugees and "deceived compatriots," and appointed several nonparty individuals to posts as advisers.[3]

Nonetheless, the new leaders could hardly divide power between Khalq and Parcham, let alone share it with other factions, and hardliners in Moscow backed the maintenance of a political monopoly. All reforms took place under Soviet guns, within the framework of a national democratic regime led by the PDPA, which remained the only legal political organization.

In mid-1980 Moscow and Kabul began to devise a counterinsurgency and state-building strategy based on a long-term Soviet commitment to the regime. The state relied primarily on military techniques of coercion in the countryside and police techniques of coercion in the cities. Means of offering incentives were also different in city and country. In the countryside the state offered incentives to the qawm, which retained its identity; in the city rewards were offered to individuals recruited to the party-state apparatus. Because the regime had inherited market structures by which the state had dealt with much of the population—as a supplier of food and fuel and a purchaser of wheat, cotton, and sugar beets—it could also offer benefits to those who continued to deal with it commercially.

The regime's inheritance of an apparatus derived from late dependent state formation went far to explain why the Soviet intervention in Afghanistan proceeded so differently from that in Czechoslovakia, which Brezhnev and his advisers apparently had in mind as a model. Czechoslovakia had been a developed socialist society, and although some people were arrested, most of the postinvasion *Gleichshaltung* was carried out in the workplace, where everyone encountered the government every day as his or her employer.[4] The state seems to have had extensive dossiers on nearly everyone, reaching back to school days and extending throughout their employment history. Arrest and imprisonment were a rare last resort. In Afghanistan this form of coercion was available to a limited extent in Kabul and not at all anywhere else. Crude violence substituted for subtle blackmail based on control of information and economic benefits. Over time, however, the Soviets attempted to make the Afghan state more like that in Czechoslovakia, leading to corresponding changes in the mechanisms of control.

In regarding city dwellers (mostly Kabulis) mainly as individual citizens and rural people mainly as members of a qawm, the state reverted to the practice of the old regime. This geographical division, too, was the inheritance of the pattern of state formation. The weak rentier state had used foreign resources to build up a state apparatus and a society dependent on that apparatus without confronting or transforming the power holders in the countryside. In more extractive paths to state formation, capitalist development and tax collection weakened the rural corporate groups, opening them to direct rule and economic exploitation by state and market.

Abdul Rahman Khan had attempted to break up the corporate groups that resisted him, but mainly through coercion rather than economic penetration. No matter how much Abdul Rahman's military suppressed the tribes and other groups, he could not control the reproduction of the economic and kinship relations that generated those groups. Amanullah's attempt at centralized state building without foreign aid was overthrown by these reemerging networks. The Musahiban did not attack these networks militarily but tried to encapsulate and divide them, using resources from the international system to build up both a domestic market and a national state centered in Kabul. Like Abdul Rahman, the Khalqis again tried to use internationally supported coercion to destroy rural rivals for power. Learning from the Khalqis' failure, the Soviet-Parcham regime reverted to a policy of encapsulation and co-optation of rural society while accelerating efforts to construct the parallel power of the internationally supported state apparatus. This apparatus was to be structured as a Soviet-style Leninist party-state.

Loss of Sovereignty

During the Karmal period and the early part of Najibullah's rule, Soviet personnel were the final decision makers for the Afghan state, especially when the PDPA was paralyzed by factional conflict. The Soviet military contingent from the Fortieth Army headquartered in Termez, Uzbekistan, quickly grew to 105,000, with perhaps 20,000 more soldiers who were stationed in Central Asia operating occasionally in Afghanistan. They far outnumbered the desertion-ridden Afghan armed forces, which may have dwindled to 30,000 or fewer by 1983.

The Afghan leadership depended on Soviet forces for survival, at least during the Karmal period, and the PDPA and DRA depended completely on Soviet finances; this dependence provided the Soviets with the leverage they needed for control in other areas. All major policies were approved if not initiated by Soviet advisers, who supposedly wrote Karmal's speeches and kept him under Soviet guard in the Arg (the Presidential Palace) to prevent him from taking the impulsive actions to which he was prone, especially when drunk.[5]

All major offices of the PDPA and the Afghan government were staffed with Soviet advisers. According to Roy, most of these advisers reported directly to Moscow, but cultural affairs were run out of Tashkent, the capital of Uzbekistan. Defectors from the Ministry of Justice claimed that it, too, was under the supervision of the chairman of the Supreme Court of Tajikistan, Rajabov—at least until he was arrested for smuggling gold from Afghanistan during CPSU General Secretary Yuri Andropov's crackdown on corruption.[6] In the essential areas, however, Russians reporting to Moscow seemed to dominate the advisers, although Central Asians played important roles as interpreters and subordinate officials.

The largest contingents of advisers appear to have come from the International Department of the Central Committee of the CPSU (which was in charge of relations with other Communist parties), the KGB, and the Ministry of Defense. But every ministry and department had its own set of advisers from its Soviet counterpart; the degree of penetration varied according to the strategic importance of the ministry. There were also a few advisers from East Germany and Bulgaria, especially in KhAD.[7]

Soviet penetration of the Afghan state apparatus did not enable Moscow simply to issue orders that would be followed. The experience of Soviet advisers in Afghanistan seems to have been at least as frustrating as that of American advisers in Vietnam. Not only did PDPA leaders involve Soviet advisers in their factional conflicts, but the growing divisions within the Soviet party and state reinforced Afghan factionalism. Every major PDPA figure had one or more Soviet advisers, who in turn belonged to factions of the CPSU. According to a Soviet specialist who spent much of this period in Kabul, members of the PDPA Politburo had specific patrons in the CPSU Politburo to whom they would appeal if they were overruled in Kabul: "The KGB, Ministry of Defense, Ministry of Foreign Affairs, Ministry of Internal Affairs, the Central

Committee—they all told Babrak something different. It all depended on how many conservative members there were in each institution. We didn't work out one proper decision, one proper way to help the PDPA. It all depended on personal relations, like between the chief of KhAD and the KGB."[8]

Building the Party-State

Despite these obstacles, Soviet advisers set about building or rebuilding institutions of political leadership (the party), coercion (army and police), economy (state industries and state distribution systems), and cadre formation (education).

The Party

Of primary importance for the Soviets was rebuilding the party organization and linking it closely to the CPSU. Their public statements rehabilitated Taraki and blamed all the problems of the Afghan Revolution on Hafizullah Amin, even calling him a CIA agent. The KGB and the International Department of the Central Committee seem to have preferred Parcham, while the GRU and military favored Khalq. But in view of the small base of each faction—especially Parcham—and the particular importance of Khalqis to the officer corps, it was vital to maintain the allegiance of both. Karmal, however, seems to have defined party unity as obedience to him, and he was cordially detested by the rank and file of the Khalqis.[9]

The Soviets hoped to solve the problem by imposing Parchami domination on a formally reunified party. The closest associates of Amin were imprisoned in the more comfortable block 1 of Pul-i Charkhi prison; some individuals implicated in the killing of Taraki and perhaps Mir Akbar Khaibar were executed in June 1980. (No one was punished for killing non-PDPA members.) Some Khalqi leaders were incorporated into the Central Committee and Politburo, but Parcham received about two-thirds of the seats on the Central Committee (Table 6.1), the Politburo, the Secretariat, and the Revolutionary Council. Parcham (or Karmal) had some say over which Khalqis were appointed. As the senior Khalqi Politburo member, Salih Muhammad Ziari might have been expected to be recognized as leader of the faction, but Ziari was too friendly with Karmal for most of the rank and file of Khalq, who recognized Gulabzoy as their leader.[10] Gulabzoy, however, was not admitted to the Politburo until 1987, when Najibullah was balancing Khalqis against pro-Karmal Parchamis.

The return of Parcham signaled a changing ethnic balance as well. Karmal himself was a Persian-speaking Kabuli of Kashmiri descent, although he sometimes claimed some Pashtun ancestry. After 1981 the prime minister, Sultan Ali Kishtmand, was a Hazara. All officials in charge of security forces, however, were Pashtun, regardless

Table 6.1 Factional Composition of PDPA Central Committee

General Secretary	Parcham	Khalq	Total
Taraki[a]	15	15	30[b]
Amin	0	50	50[c]
Karmal	37	19	56
Najibullah	55	16	71

Source: See Appendix A.

Note: Each row includes those newly appointed under the given general secretary, not counting holdovers from the previous leader.

[a] 1977 Unity Central Committee.

[b] Approximate.

[c] Amin never announced the names of members of the Central Committee or Politburo. Anwar, *Tragedy of Afghanistan*, 182, gives this figure and lists eight Politburo members, all Khalqis. The Politburo normally reflected the political composition of the Central Committee.

of faction. In 1982 Karmal briefly appointed a non-Pashtun minister of defense, but he soon had to backtrack.

Within the government, three-fourths of the people appointed as ministers under Babrak Karmal were Parchamis. Parchamis filled the offices of president of the Revolutionary Council, prime minister, minister of foreign affairs, and chief of KhAD. At the cabinet level, the only core security position occupied by a Khalqi was minister of the interior (Gulabzoy). This ministry controlled the police (Sarandoy), which grew to include a heavily armed paramilitary militia; it also oversaw paramilitary groups often referred to by the Russian term *operatifi*. The minister of communications (Watanjar), a key post for a would-be Leninist regime, was also a Khalqi.

Najibullah's KhAD was staffed by ethnically mixed Karmal supporters; Gulabzoy's Sarandoy militia was composed almost entirely of Khalqi Pashtuns. The two security forces often feuded. Another center of factional and ethnic conflict was the officer corps. Originally the minister and the chief of army staff were Parchamis, both Pashtuns, although Khalqis dominated the officer corps. During the interregnum between Andropov's illness and Gorbachev's ascent, however, one Khalqi was appointed chief of staff in January 1984 and minister in December 1984.

As the party's tasks became more coercive, its membership changed accordingly. According to one source, party members before 1978 were 95 percent "intellectuals" —students from Kabul University, teachers, and disgruntled bureaucrats. Later recruits came largely from the security services, so that by 1985 official sources claimed that 65 percent of party members were working in the army, Sarandoy, militia, or

KhAD. Many low-level government employees were also pressured into taking out party cards; as a result, membership figures were inflated and, for the first time, included a small number of members classified as workers and peasants. Karmal, however, still had to warn the party against contempt for the worker and peasant members.[11]

The militarization of the party was reflected in leadership changes. In June 1981 three military or KhAD leaders (Rafi, Watanjar, Najibullah) joined the Politburo; a July 1983 expansion of the Central Committee added major air force commanders to that body. The promotion of KhAD chief Najibullah to the Secretariat in November 1985 was accompanied by the elevation of the new chief of KhAD (Yaaqubi) and the Sarandoy commander of Kabul city (Saifullah) to full Central Committee membership.[12] Najibullah acknowledged the militarization in July 1986 when he appointed an expanded Central Committee; 42 percent of the members had backgrounds in the military or KhAD, compared with 32 percent under Karmal. The party also established such organizations for the recruitment of new members as the Democratic Youth Organization of Afghanistan and trade unions, while encouraging groups like the Democratic Women's Organization of Afghanistan, which had existed before, under the leadership of Anahita Ratibzad.

On paper, at least, party membership increased dramatically. By 1985 the party claimed 140,000 members. Although many of these were students or government employees without any genuine commitment who had been pressured into joining, the party did manage to establish a significant presence in various sectors of society in Kabul and at various levels of the government. Recruitment continued to lag in the provinces, where counterinsurgency was based on qawm, not party ideology or organization. According to Najibullah himself, by mid-1986, only two provincial party secretaries actually lived outside Kabul.[13]

The State

The basic principle of leadership in the Soviet state, emulated by the governments of Taraki and Amin, was that party leadership and state leadership were fused. Under Babrak Karmal as well, two-thirds of the ministers were PDPA Central Committee members, and nearly all of the rest were party members (Table 6.2). Seven of eight members of the government core leadership were members of the Central Committee. Similarly, over four-fifths of the members of the Revolutionary Council were members of the Central Committee, and only three of sixty-six members came from outside the ranks of the party. Leaving aside the Soviet role, the PDPA leadership monopolized state power in both reality and appearance.

As elsewhere, this fused party-state elite became a law unto itself and engaged in nepotism and corruption, neither of which was novel in Afghanistan. The influx of large amounts of aid, however, in Kabul as in Peshawar, increased opportunities for

Table 6.2 PDPA Representation in DRA Institutions

Institution	Period	PDPA Members			Non-PDPA	Total
		Central Committee	Other	Total		
	Karmal					
Council of	All	26	10	36	3	39
Ministers	Core	7	1	8	0	8
	Najibullah					
	All	22	12	34	29	63
	Core	8	0	8	2	10
Revolutionary	Karmal	54	9	63	3	66
Council	Najibullah	16	12	28	53	81

Source: See Appendix A.

abuse, as did the presence of thousands of Soviet advisers and increased traffic across the Afghan-Soviet border. A former Soviet adviser claimed that the wife of one Soviet ambassador directed a large black market operation. The same adviser reported that four hundred trucks of Soviet relief supplies were once diverted to markets in the Pakistani tribal territories under cover of claims that they had been attacked by "counterrevolutionaries"; the proceeds, he said, were divided among members of the PDPA Politburo. Although such accounts are impossible to verify, they are strikingly similar to those from the other side of the war.

PDPA leadership presided over a state whose finances became ever more dependent on external support and whose activities increasingly concentrated on maintaining its own security. Development spending continued to decrease as a proportion of total expenditure (Table 5.1) while spending on the military and police increased. Even more than before, the government was able to finance these expenditures without taxing the population. Taxes financed less than a quarter of government expenditure, and, as previously, these were mostly indirect taxes, levied on a few items of foreign trade. Agriculture remained the major productive activity in Afghanistan, but except for the cultivation of export goods and raw materials for government industries, it contributed virtually nothing to the fiscal base of the state. Loss of control over the countryside meant that the government could hardly collect land taxes at all. In a 1983 speech, Prime Minister Kishtmand stated that whereas the government had collected Af 280 million in land tax in the Afghan year spanning 1978–79, it collected only Af 16 million three years later, in the Afghan year spanning 1981–82. This was about $350,000 at the official rate of exchange, amounting to 0.04

percent of government expenditure. Regardless of the low level of tax collection, however, the government repeatedly announced cancellation of both back taxes and fines for their nonpayment. And in spite of occasional exhortations to increase the efficiency of state enterprises, their profitability also apparently declined, although there was some improvement over the disastrous performance of 1979.[14]

Instead, rentier income—foreign aid and sales of natural gas—paid for increasing proportions of expenditure. These income sources, which had financed 40 percent of government expenditure before the 1978 coup, accounted for half of the total by 1979 and exceeded 60 percent of total expenditure after the Soviet invasion. The foreign aid came almost entirely from the Soviet Union and its allies.[15]

Revenues labeled as foreign assistance in official publications are mostly loans for development expenditure, and as the share of public expenditure devoted to development declined, so did the share of officially labeled foreign aid. The expenses spent by Moscow on the Soviet contingent—for advisers, military aid, and training—are not included, so official foreign aid figures underestimate the Afghan state's unilateral external economic dependence. Furthermore, unlike the oil or gas income of most exporters, who sell these materials on the international market to the highest bidder, Afghanistan's gas income was derived solely from a bilateral agreement with the USSR. The natural gas fields were developed with Soviet aid by Soviet experts; the gas was piped directly across the border into the Soviet Union (Uzbekistan and Turkmenia, now Turkmenistan), and it was metered on the Soviet side of the border. Revenue increased from sales of natural gas to the Soviet Union beginning in 1980 only because the Soviets were paying more for the same amount of gas. This pattern continued during periods for which comprehensive statistics are available. In January 1984, for instance, an official spokesman said that gas prices had multiplied in recent years, reaching the level of Western European prices; gas sales to the USSR, he said, provided nearly half of the state budget income. In 1985 Kabul Radio said that export of gas produced 40 percent of the annual income of Afghanistan.[16] After 1985, however, income from natural gas began to decline.

The effort to increase the Afghan state's capacities for coercion and surveillance was concentrated on two institutions, the armed forces and the secret police (KhAD). The army's functions were largely performed directly by Soviet troops, while KhAD had KGB advisers but few KGB personnel. As many as five thousand Soviet advisers may have been attached to the Afghan army down to the battalion level.[17]

The armed forces were threatened by factional and ethnic conflict throughout the officer corps. In 1980 Gen. Muhammad Rafi, head of the Parchami military network, became defense minister, and Gen. Baba Jan, another Parchami, became chief of army staff. Both were Ghilzai Pashtuns. Because the army continued to perform poorly and factional conflict increased, Rafi was replaced (probably a Soviet decision) with Gen. Abdul Qadir, a Herati, in January 1982. Abdul Qadir, though aligned with Parcham, had organized his own network among the officers. As vice chairman of the Revolutionary Council he had had the presumably thankless job of coordinating the activities of the Khalqi interior minister and the Parchami defense minister.[18] He, too, failed to improve army performance and quell factional conflict. In fact, this first—and, until the overthrow of Najibullah, only—non-Pashtun defense minister in the history of Afghanistan had differences with the Pashtun-dominated officer corps and exacerbated ethnic conflicts by attempting to extend conscription to certain exempt tribes.

In 1984, as the Afghan government came under heavy pressure from the Chernenko regime to advance militarily against the resistance, there was constant turmoil in the Defense Ministry, and it was unclear who, if anyone, was acting as minister. (In fact the Soviet army was in charge.) In January the top three generals under the minister were replaced. One appointment suggested that the Khalqis may have convinced Soviet hardliners under Chernenko that they stood a better chance than the Parchamis of defeating the mujahidin: Parchami Chief of Staff Baba Jan was replaced by Khalqi Air Force Commander Nazar Muhammad, who was finally appointed minister of defense on December 4, 1984.[19]

Soviet aid might have assured the Afghan army of more than sufficient supplies of weapons and ammunition, but reports from deserters and defectors indicated that Afghan troops were treated as stepchildren, at least in the early years, while modern supplies were reserved for the Soviets themselves. The Afghan army continued to lack food, fuel, clothing, and medicine. To improve and expand the army's officer corps, the highest-ranking officers and the newly promoted ones frequently went to the Soviet Union on training missions. But frequent promotions led to a top-heavy officer corps. According to one defector, a single logistical unit in Kabul in 1983 had twenty brigadiers among its four hundred men; such a unit would normally be commanded by one officer of that rank.[20]

Along with factional conflict in the command structure, the army faced a persistent problem of maintaining its size through conscription. Conscripts also served in the Ministry of the Interior and KhAD. Western observers estimated that from a prewar strength of more than 110,000, the Afghan armed forces had shrunk as a result of mutinies and desertions to between 20,000 and 40,000 by 1983. The estimate of 30,000 was common for years afterward, but the government appears to have gradually rebuilt army strength after 1985, when the top leadership became more stable. The regular army, however, increasingly drew conscripts only from Kabul city.[21]

The presence of Soviet forces ended mutinies at the largest garrisons, although smaller uprisings persisted. Desertion and evasion of conscription, meanwhile, became mass movements. Interviews with refugees in Pakistan and reports of travelers with the mujahidin testified to a constant escape of potential troops from the grasp of the Afghan state. Draft evasion became one of the principal reasons for young men to flee Kabul city.

To solve this problem the regime continually tightened conscription laws, and the army joined Soviet troops in press-ganging young men, some reportedly as young as fifteen. Under the system inherited from the old regime, men became liable for the draft at age twenty-two and served in the reserves—which had never been called up—until age forty-six. Conscript service lasted two years, during which the draftees were paid Af 2,000 per month.

The government announced new regulations on January 8, 1981, and tightened them over the next four years. The draft age was lowered to twenty and then to eighteen. The length of conscript service was raised to three and then four years, and all reservists were called to active duty. Student deferments were tightened and then virtually eliminated. On several occasions the extension of conscript terms led to mutinies and desertions that required Soviet intervention. The government did provide some compensation for increased military service. Pay was increased to Af 3,000 and then to 4,000, and draftees who finished their military service—apparently a small minority—were promised admission to institutes of higher education or grants to study abroad without entrance examinations. Students drafted out of school were permitted to count time in military service toward graduation. Party members could evade service for two years through alternative service in party and government institutions.

In October 1982, Minister of Defense Abdul Qadir revoked the exemption from conscription of the Shinwari, Momand, and Jaji tribes. In response, the tribes halted transportation of goods—which they largely controlled—in Kabul. Despite his repeated efforts, this order was never successfully enforced. By 1985 the government had stopped making conscription regulations more stringent and had begun to encourage volunteers by allowing them to serve only two years and by granting them various educational and economic privileges.[22]

Universal conscription requires a high state capacity for domestic surveillance, and the government set about establishing that capacity, at least on paper. Men were required to carry documentation of their military status at all times; those without proper documents were liable to be seized on the spot and inducted into the service. The state also enacted penalties for carrying forged documents, which "enemies of the revolution" were apparently manufacturing. Conscription committees were formed at the provincial and district levels, their members drawn from the administration, the Youth Organization, the party, the Ministry of the Interior, and KhAD. These committees were to compile lists of draft-eligible men, who were then supposed to present themselves to the administration. At least in Kabul, men could be drafted directly from schools and offices, where the government had records on them. Even more intrusive was indiscriminate press-ganging by Afghan troops, who would periodically blockade the Kabul bazaar or engage in house-to-house searches for men who at least appeared to be of the appropriate age. Such sweeps were also carried out elsewhere, often as part of cordon-and-search military operations by Afghan or Soviet units.

Although efforts to build Afghanistan's military encountered resistance, the Soviets had greater success in building up a new Afghan intelligence organization, the State Information Services, or KhAD. The government announced on January 11,

1980, that KhAD would replace Amin's security agency, KAM. The new organization was removed from the Khalqi-dominated Interior Ministry and made a department of the Office of the Prime Minister. Its director general, Najibullah (then known primarily as Dr. Najib), reported directly to the Soviet KGB. Najibullah's previous background as a medical student and party organizer did not seem to prepare him for a career in intelligence, but one source claims that while exiled by the Khalqis he had attended a Bulgarian intelligence school.[23] KhAD became the most important and successful institution of the new regime. In January 1986, after Najibullah had replaced Karmal as head of state, KhAD was elevated in status, becoming the Ministry of State Security (Wizarat-i Amaniyyat-i Dawlati, or WAD).

KhAD was divided into several directorates (*riyasat*), each with its own specialized focus, including Kabul city, educational institutions, the provinces, the military, interrogation and investigation, and counterinsurgency. The counterinsurgency directorate had branches for both domestic and foreign operations.[24]

According to one estimate, by 1987 WAD employed 15,000 to 30,000 professionals and about 100,000 paid informers.[25] The numbers may seem high, but government statistics indicate that they may be in the right order of magnitude. Official figures for 1980–81 show that the Office of the Prime Minister (which included KhAD) employed 5,802 people, of whom 2,301 (40 percent) were in the provinces; by the next year, although the total number of government employees (not including the Ministry of Defense) actually decreased slightly, the number of employees in the Prime Ministry increased over 130 percent, to 13,596, of whom 9,042 (67 percent) were in the provinces.[26] It is quite probable that most of the nearly 14,000 employees of the Prime Minister's Office in 1981–82 were working for KhAD, and the number of employees continued to grow.

Each KhAD official had one or more KGB advisers. These advisers were so numerous that they had their own headquarters in the Dar-ul-Aman area of Kabul. Former prisoners have reported that advisers had offices in interrogation centers and that they sometimes intervened directly in interrogations.

KhAD also wielded de facto judicial authority via the Special Revolutionary Court. In 1978 the DRA had set up military tribunals subordinate to the Revolutionary Council, but in practice people were often arrested, tortured, and killed with no legal proceedings whatever. In 1980 the new government established the Special Revolutionary Court. Like the military tribunals, the court was subordinate to the Revolutionary Council, but it was supervised by Soviet advisers and to all intents and purposes functioned as a branch of KhAD. As Babrak Karmal put it, KhAD, the Revolutionary Prosecution Department, and the Special Revolutionary Court "form one chain and one organism in the struggle." In all political or security matters these courts replaced the regular ones, which atrophied. The accused had no right of defense, and no one was ever acquitted. Babrak Karmal inveighed against "the imposing of light punishments for grave crimes" and demanded acquittals "only in the event of total and clear innocence of the accused." Obviously, the purpose of these courts was not to provide fair trials but to impose predictability upon the repressive apparatus as part of "socialist" or "revolutionary" legality.[27]

KhAD was assisted in counterinsurgency by other ministries with which it worked closely, particularly the Ministry of Nationalities and Tribes, and the Department (subsequently Ministry) of Islamic Affairs. In 1949 the Afghan state had established a Department (later Ministry) of Frontier and Tribal Affairs to handle relations with the tribes along the Durand Line, including those in the Pakistani tribal areas. This organization, whose first head was Daoud, organized the Pashtunistan Militia, which harassed Pakistani authorities and otherwise pressed Afghan claims to the Pashtun tribal areas both openly and covertly. The ministry was also the instrument through which the state co-opted tribal leaders, paying them subsidies, appointing them to token positions of tribal authority in the ministry, and recruiting their sons to Kabul boarding schools.

Karmal's first minister of tribal affairs, Faiz Muhammad, was assassinated by Jadran tribesmen in August 1980 while he was attending a jirga in hopes of winning their allegiance to the government. In May of the following year the ministry was reorganized as the Ministry of Nationalities (aqwam) and Tribes (qabail). In late October 1987 the PDPA split this ministry into two: a Ministry of Nationalities and— to more fully exploit opportunities to co-opt the border tribes—a Ministry of Tribal and Border Affairs.[28]

The regime officially recognized eight nationalities: Pashtun, Tajik, Uzbek, Hazara, Turkmen, Baluch, Nuristani, and Pashai.[29] The ministry's directorate of nationalities, however, dealt only with the smaller ethnolinguistic minorities. Both Pashtuns and Tajiks were dealt with primarily as members of small qawms. For instance, the directorate of nationalities organized "supreme councils" of the Hazara, Turkmen, Baluch, and Uzbek "nationalities," but does not seem to have done so for Pashtuns or Tajiks. The tribal directorate, which Roy claims operated under the direction of KhAD, continued to deal with the border tribes but was also responsible for all policies pursued throughout the country at the level of the local qawm. These policies were an essential part of the regime's counterinsurgency strategy.

Because the major challenge to the regime's legitimacy was being mounted in the name of Islam, the state also worked to establish institutions that would showcase the government's support for Islam. The Afghan state had previously dealt with Islamic figures mainly through the Ministry of Justice. The Karmal government, however, established a General Department of Islamic Affairs within the Council of Ministers. This department, which defectors claimed was supervised by a special directorate of KhAD, assumed responsibility for paying mullahs and imams of mosques, thus giving the government more power over public Islamic discourse. Under changes enacted in the land reform program, religious endowments (awqaf) were supposed to be returned to their owners, and the Department of Islamic Affairs also administered those endowments. In March 1985 the department was upgraded, becoming the Ministry of Islamic Affairs and Endowment (Wizarat-i Shu'un-i Islami wa Awqaf).[30]

State-Society Relations

For the regime and its Soviet sponsors, the various departments and ministries were tools to help legitimate the regime and to eradicate, co-opt, or neutralize the opposition. The counterinsurgency strategy adopted radically different approaches toward the urban society controlled by the state and the tribal-peasant society outside its purview.

Political Regime and Legitimation

In the first two months after the invasion, the new leaders of the DRA repeatedly spoke of the need for a broad national front. They seemed to be calling for a coalition government, apparently on the advice of a group of Afghan specialists convened in the Soviet Ministry of Foreign Affairs by Vassily Safronchuk, a former ambassador to Kabul. Government leaders even briefly reached out to some mujahidin, whom they described as "a patriotic and anti-imperialist part of the anti-government forces."[31] These appeals, which anticipated the policy of national reconciliation after 1987, ended after the uprising in Kabul of February 22, 1980, known as the Night of Allahu Akbar. This massive, largely spontaneous rejection of the regime and its Soviet sponsors threw the government into disarray and placed it on the defensive. The guidance of Safronchuk and his comrades was soon shoved aside by Soviet security agencies whose views were more to the liking of most of the PDPA leadership. As one Soviet specialist put it, "From 1980 to 1987 all of our writings went straight to the wastebasket. They [the Soviets and Parcham] should have started national reconciliation the day they arrived in Kabul."

Discarding the notion of a genuine coalition, the Soviets and PDPA decided to establish a National Fatherland Front (Jabha-yi Milli-yi Padarwatan) under PDPA leadership. This organization, founded as part of the development of a counterinsurgency strategy in late 1980 and 1981, was to organize nonparty support for the government. After several delays, apparently owing to the difficulty of finding enough people willing to join, the NFF was founded at a one-day congress on June 15, 1981. In reality the NFF was just a union of PDPA-led mass organizations. Its chairman was Salih Muhammad Ziari, the senior Khalqi on the Politburo, and virtually all of its leaders were PDPA activists. Little was heard of the NFF for several years; it took on a higher public profile during the Andropov period, when the state gave more attention to pacification and co-optation. In May 1985, hardly a month after the accession of Gorbachev, Abdul Rahim Hatif, a merchant close to Ziari who was not a party member, became NFF leader, signaling a heightened role for the front in the early stages of national reconciliation.[32]

The Democratic Youth Organization of Afghanistan, modeled on the Soviet Komsomol, held its first Congress on September 11, 1980. Like the Soviet model, it included an organization for younger children, the Pishahangan (Pioneers). These organizations recruited mainly from the schools of Kabul. Members engaged in political surveillance within the schools, although there were also KhAD informants who may have been outside the DYOA.[33] The organization was also supposed to assist the government in conscription. DYOA members themselves—and even some Pioneers—were recruited directly into the security forces. Many of them were sent to the Soviet Union for either summer visits or longer training programs. The Soviets seemed to hope that the DYOA would provide a new generation of PDPA members who were contaminated with neither the values of the old society nor—possibly worse— the conflict between Parcham and Khalq. DYOA leader Farid Mazdak, a Kabuli Tajik, emerged as one of the most outspoken advocates of reform after the Soviet withdrawal.

An overriding symbolic issue relevant to all sectors of the society was the attempt by the regime to demonstrate its Islamic bona fides. State leaders were photographed attending the mosque; government decrees prominently featured the invocation of the name of Allah; and representatives of Islam appeared at state gatherings. The government also publicized money that it spent on devotional activities. From 1980 to 1986 the government claimed to have spent more than Af 3.3 billion in support of Islam, including 310 million on building and maintaining mosques, 280 million on assistance to ulama and clergy, 726 million on subsidy for the hajj, and 2 billion on religious education.[34]

These efforts met with little success. The dependence of the government on Soviet troops, known in Afghanistan as soldiers of an avowedly atheistic regime, contradicted official claims of fidelity to Islam. Nor did Babrak Karmal and other government leaders of the time speak like believing Muslims, for all their professions of "deep respect" for the "holy religion of Islam." The mark of a true Muslim is not that he speaks respectfully of Islam but that he speaks Islamically of everything. Unlike Najibullah, Babrak never learned that rhetorical art. If all the policies had failed as fully as the attempt to portray Babrak Karmal as the defender of Islam, however, the regime would not have survived a week. Other policies were more successful.

Surveillance, Repression, and Recruitment

Within Kabul the regime's primary strategic goal was to build and strengthen the institutions of the party-state. As this apparatus became stronger and more consolidated, it would gradually absorb and outweigh the fragmented rural society without ever having fully to conquer it. Building up this apparatus required, first, the external and internal security of Kabul city. External security, mainly the responsibility of the Soviet and Afghan armies, included safety from external attack and protection of communication lines with the USSR, regional centers, and sources of hydroelectric power. Internal security, mainly the responsibility of KhAD, required the eradication of opposition networks from urban society and from the state itself. Once security was in place, other programs could begin to integrate the population into state-controlled institutions and to recruit future cadres. To increase economic resources available to the state, the Soviet-Karmal regime concentrated development efforts on industries run by the state. These industries, established with aid from the USSR, East Germany, or Czechoslovakia, were closely linked to those countries through bilateral agreements. Many used raw materials from agriculture, and the government offered incentives to suppliers of these resources, trying to make market-oriented farmers dependent on the state as well.

To secure Kabul from external infiltration and attack, the Soviet and Afghan armies established a defensive zone made of multiple rings of posts extending into rural areas. (A similar strategy was pursued on a smaller scale around Herat, Qandahar, Jalalabad, and Mazar-i Sharif.) Areas abutting the communication and transportation links of Kabul had to be secured, as did those necessary to its power supply, much of which came from hydroelectric stations connected to the city by power lines suspended from pylons in contested territory. The armies also protected the plains north of the Hindu Kush, where key commercial crops grew and many state industries were located; relatively easy overland links to the USSR eased the security problem for this region. In these areas the government applied a rural counterinsurgency strategy that involved both punitive measures carried out by the military and pacification measures carried out by KhAD.

For maintaining the internal security of Kabul city and other areas under government control, the main tool was terror imposed by KhAD. A representative of the Kabul government estimated in a 1990 interview that KhAD had arrested 150,000 people, mostly from Kabul city. In 1987–90 the government claimed to have released 19,514 prisoners in amnesties. Several thousand prisoners remained, while tens of thousands of other prisoners had been released after interrogation or after finishing their terms. According to a former examining magistrate interviewed by Amnesty International, 8,006 people were executed by sentence of the Special Revolutionary Court between 1980 and 1988.[35]

Although KhAD was indeed an organ of repression, it was above all an intelligence organization, operating, as its name implied, on the basis of *information* about the population. Acquisition and storage of information can in part substitute for the application of physical coercion by rendering smaller quantities of coercion more effective, and unlike its predecessors, AGSA and KAM, KhAD did not indiscriminately torture and murder suspected opponents. Torture was one of a variety of methods for extracting information, playing a role (which diminished over time, if it never disappeared) in an increasingly routinized system of surveillance and control.

The first challenge KhAD faced, beginning on February 22, 1980, was a series of mass demonstrations and strikes organized by shopkeepers and students. Girls from the Kabul high schools played a particularly militant role in the demonstrations, which continued for several months. The regime's initial approach was to attack the crowds with Soviet and Afghan armed forces, including tanks and helicopters, and to make mass arrests. Some of those arrested seem to have been subjected to group lectures by officials about the conciliatory policies of the new government. When speeches failed to convince the demonstrators, KhAD interrogators, many of whom presumably had simply been transferred from KAM, reportedly began to torture everyone arrested, using electric cattle prods and bluntly demanding to know who the leaders of the demonstrations were. Several thousand people were apparently arrested and tortured at that time, but most were released without trial after a few months. Those labeled leaders were given prison terms. Some may have been executed, but no such executions were announced.

In response to these demonstrations, KhAD began to develop its strategy for repression and surveillance in Kabul. KhAD interrogators were still unsophisticated —there were no "mind games" or trick questions—but even at this stage torture was primarily a means of extracting information, not of punishment. KhAD at that time possessed few if any informers within the opposition networks; with torture it could not only identify leaders, it could also cultivate informers: some who "broke" could then be "turned."

From this time on, under KGB tutelage, KhAD developed a vast network of informers. Informers were effective in Kabul because much of the population attended schools or worked in offices. People were also subject to bureaucratized surveillance by teachers and supervisors in those settings; indeed, Giddens, following Michel Foucault, regards the concentration of the working population in such institutions as a major component of the concentration of the means of surveillance in the hands of the state. Increasingly information from both bureaucratic supervisors and undercover informers complemented information obtained through torture, although throughout the Karmal period (when Najibullah was director general of KhAD), torture remained a standard administrative practice.[36]

Repression created a minimal level of security in Kabul. But more effective control of a population demands the integration of that population into bureaucratic institutions that continually collect information and offer incentives to cooperation as by-products of their daily operation. The economic and educational policies of the Karmal regime aimed at constructing such institutions. These institutions were mainly financed by Soviet aid and planned by Soviet advisers: project aid accounted for 62 percent of development expenditure in 1982–83, and total foreign aid accounted for 92 percent. Considerable effort consequently went into strengthening transport and communication links between Afghanistan and the USSR.

Economically, the DRA—or, more precisely, north Afghanistan plus Kabul— became, in effect, a Soviet republic. Moscow covered the government's deficits and provided financing and technical assistance for state investment. The proportion of investment going to agriculture declined from one-third before the war to about 10 percent. Most of the investment projects were concentrated in the corridor between

Kabul and the Soviet border, and three acres in the center of Mazar-i Sharif were set aside for new offices for Soviet economic consultants and trade representatives. The Soviets extended a railhead to the Afghan border, improved roads, expanded the Kabul airport, delivered an initial shipment of 1,500 trucks to a new state motor transport organization, and built new hydroelectric power stations. East Germany provided assistance in power generation as well as in telecommunications, and Czech experts aided the Ministry of Public Works and assisted on other projects. The improved transportation links were vital for the military effort as well as for trade, and contributed to the growing Soviet share of the DRA's foreign trade. Soviet-style state-to-state barter agreements soon came to dominate foreign trade. Afghanistan traded gas, fertilizer, wool, cotton, raisins, and carpets for industrial equipment and consumer goods. Most of Afghanistan's own industrial products went to local consumers. The Soviet Union also developed copper and other mines, and imported most of the minerals extracted.[37]

Concentration of investment in state industry was consistent with Soviet doctrine. It was also a practical necessity for an Afghan government that had little influence in the rural areas. Employment of workers in new enterprises bound growing numbers of families, including peasant families in and around Kabul, to the government. Government employment in factories, the bureaucracy, and the army, as well as membership in state-sanctioned organizations, also provided Afghans access to free or subsidized distribution of commodities supplied by the USSR.

Among the consequences of the Soviet intervention and the widening of the war were shortages of basic foods and fuel in Kabul. The government's attempt to buy the loyalty of employees and conscripts with frequent pay increases added to the inflation that these shortages created. War and emigration meant that less land was cultivated, and turmoil stirred by land reform decreased food production even further. And while commerce between Kabul and the countryside continued—largely through the efforts of gray-bearded men who were unmistakably beyond conscript age—these exchanges now encountered such obstacles as military operations and blocked roads. The arrival of the Soviet Fortieth Army and the continual military operations put a severe strain on the supply of motor fuel, which had to be transported by tanker truck from the USSR across the Hindu Kush.

By February 1980 the Soviets were already addressing the capital's food needs. The government announced that the USSR had donated one hundred thousand tons of wheat, which would be distributed by the Department of Foodstuffs and Cooperatives of the Ministry of Agriculture and Land Reform at a price one-third below the market rate. Cooking oil, tea, soap, and other commodities would be supplied under similar conditions. In future years the Soviet Union provided one hundred thousand tons of wheat annually as grants and an equal amount in exchange for goods. This amounted to nearly 7.5 percent of the estimated production of wheat in Afghanistan during the Afghan year spanning 1977–78. The country was also dependent on the USSR for petroleum products, which became exceedingly expensive. Kerosene, the main fuel in Kabul for cooking and heating, was distributed by the government, which subsidized its price through a rationing system.[38]

The government distributed other goods through a system of subsidized consumption for its employees and supporters. It established special stores, similar to those under the Soviet *propusk* system, for various categories of employees.[39]

All of these measures moved Kabul toward the "developed socialist" model of social control, although the proximity of areas controlled by the resistance and the internationally supported refugee communities in Pakistan gave citizens of the DRA easier options of exit than existed for most people in the USSR or eastern Europe. Still, the degree of social control attained by the state was sufficient to enable the Soviet-Karmal regime to pursue its other major strategic goal: ideological formation of the new generation and recruitment to the party-state through the schools, Pioneers, and DYOA.

Educational policy had two tracks. On the first track, the Karmal regime and its Soviet advisers transformed the existing system into a mechanism of political indoctrination and recruitment. On the second track, they set up a parallel system that targeted vulnerable groups—orphans, for example—for intensive training and indoctrination, including programs for long-term study in the Soviet Union.

The regime transformed the schools not only by changing the curriculum, but also by changing the faculty: especially at Kabul University, Afghan professors were replaced by Soviets and other Eastern bloc specialists. Teachers and students were also subject to arrest and political surveillance.

Changes in the curriculum included the introduction of new subjects and new textbooks for old subjects. Many of the textbooks seem to have been translations of ones used in Central Asia. Textbooks in all subjects had a preface lauding the regime and proclaiming that the goal of the educational system was to "help to train the 'new man.'" At all levels Russian became virtually the only foreign language taught. In high schools the regime downgraded religious instruction and introduced a new course in political science, in which students learned about Marxism-Leninism, the history of the Communist movement, and Afghan-Soviet friendship. These curriculum changes were reinforced by constant political pressures exerted on faculty and students by the party, DYOA, and KhAD, which recruited students as informers.[40]

In the university these pressures were even stronger. Rather than simply one class on politics, the regime established a whole set of classes that were required in each faculty: historical materialism, history of the USSR, and so on. The Faculties of Sharia and Engineering—the latter American-advised and both hotbeds of recruitment for the Islamists—were eliminated. An Afghan-Soviet Friendship Room was set up in every faculty. Political surveillance was intense at the university, which was a center of political activism and of urban resistance to the regime and the Soviets. Forty-two percent of the 750 full-time tenure-track faculty members who had served at the university in 1978 had emigrated or had been killed or jailed by 1986. Others had stopped teaching. So many Eastern bloc professors filled the vacancies that by 1983 the regime claimed that 60 percent of the faculty were from socialist countries.[41]

Thousands of students were also arrested, but the regime emphasized ex ante control by surveillance over ex post control by punishment. The state introduced the Soviet system of "satisfaction," a classic tool of "developed socialist" social control. The authorities compiled dossiers on students' political views; those with "satisfactory" views qualified for examinations, and those who twice failed "satisfaction" were inducted into the army.[42] These measures muted the outspoken opposition that Kabul University students had shown initially. Students were also appeased by conscription legislation that extended special privileges to those who had completed their military service.

The direct integration of the Afghan educational system into the Soviet one involved more than guest faculty at Kabul University. The USSR established numerous exchange programs that sent students to study in the Soviet Union for elementary, secondary, vocational, and higher education. In 1986 a U.S. State Department analyst estimated that about two thousand "military trainees" and thousands of younger Afghans were being sent to the USSR annually.[43] Some of these were elementary school children attending summer camp or helping with the harvest. Others were older students sent for lengthy programs of doctoral study.

The program that aroused the most anxiety in Kabul placed young children, especially orphans, in special schools and sent them for long-term study in the Soviet Union.[44] In Kabul the regime established the Homeland Nursery (Parvarishgah-i Watan), headed by Karmal's wife, Mahbuba. This institution was supposedly for children of "martyrs of the revolution," but in 1984–86 many refugees reported pressure on vulnerable families to send their young children there. Children at the nursery, including some orphaned by Soviet-Afghan bombing, were isolated from their extended families and from Afghan cultural influences and were raised in an environment that was totally supportive of the regime.

The Homeland Nursery was also a conduit for a program of long-term education of children in the USSR. In November 1984 the regime announced that "a number of children of the martyrs of the path of the revolution have left for the the Soviet Union to study different subjects for 10 years. . . . 870 boys and girls between the ages of 7 and 9 and 35 male and female teachers have been sent to the Soviet Asian Republics on several flights. . . . This process will be continued in the coming years too."[45]

According to a former director general of the Cultural Department of the Ministry of Foreign Affairs, an Afghan-Soviet agreement provided for ten thousand children a year to be sent on this program.[46] As with the Homeland Nursery, the official beneficiaries were orphans of martyrs of the revolution, but many others were recruited as well: children of the poor, those orphaned by Soviet bombings, and some who were more or less rounded up from poor neighborhoods or from schools in Kabul and sent without the knowledge or consent of their parents.[47] During 1984–86, this program created considerable resentment and fear in Kabul; many refugees said they had fled

Kabul for fear that their children might be sent to the USSR. Better than any other, this program indicated the long-term strategic perspective of the Soviets during the Chernenko period: the children who would return after 1994 were to be the core personnel of the future DRA.

The Soviet-Parcham Regime and Rural Society

The strategic goal of the Soviet military in rural Afghanistan was to reconquer selected strategic areas of the countryside. During 1985 the Soviets also tried without success to seal the Pakistani and Iranian borders. The Soviets never committed the forces needed for a purely military conquest of the mujahidin: the military defeat of a guerrilla force by a conventional army requires overwhelming numerical superiority. The combined Soviet and Afghan forces would have had to reach a level of 400,000–500,000 to attain even a theoretical chance of conventional victory.[48] During 1984–86, Soviet commanders tried to overcome these well-known odds through the use of helicopter-borne assaults and massive, indiscriminate air strikes. They managed to occupy some areas temporarily (Panjsher in April 1984) and to pulverize others (the area between Herat and the Iranian border, for example), but they never committed the manpower necessary to take and hold ground. The Red Army used its military might primarily to secure urban centers of power and their lines of communication; a second goal was to provide the threat of reprisals to complement incentives of the pacification strategy. The aim was to neutralize the countryside's threat to state power, not to reconquer it, certainly not to transform it. For these purposes the regime returned to a traditional tool of statecraft throughout the region, manipulation of social segmentation.

The 1981 amendment to the land reform decree was the cornerstone of the new approach.[49] Whereas the original decree mentioned the abolition of "feudal and prefeudal" relations, the amendment alludes to "observing the principle of legal property, respecting the religious and tribal traditions and customs and enhancing the living standards of the people."

Religious figures, khans who supported the government, military officers, and commercial farmers who sold produce to the state were exempted from land ceilings.[50] Refugee landowners would receive back any land expropriated from them or its equivalent, up to the legal ceiling. The state promised to pay cash compensation to any member of the specified categories whose land had already been distributed. The decree also gave priority in the distribution of land to peasants with sons in the armed forces.

This decree effectively transformed land reform into a counterinsurgency measure. Ownership of land became a privilege that the state would protect in return for allegiance. Islamic leaders had to have their exemptions approved by the Department of Islamic Affairs. Tribal (*qawmi*) leaders' exemptions required the approval of the

Ministry of Nationalities and Tribes and the Supreme Council of the Tribes. Service in the security apparatus brought direct economic benefits, and production of cash crops sold to the state—rather than food crops that could feed the insurgents—also exempted a landowner from limitations prescribed by the original reform.

The amendment provided a legal basis for incentives, but in practice the particular mix of punishment and inducement, as well as the intensity of the effort, depended on the strength, activity, and unity of the resistance in an area and on that area's relative geographic or economic importance. This strategic approach explained the most notorious element of Soviet counterinsurgency strategy, the bombardment of villages, sometimes randomly and sometimes in reprisal for an attack by the resistance. Bombing conveyed to a village and its neighbors *as collectivities* the message that supporting the resistance had a cost. (The Khalqi approach, which involved class struggle, had required selecting particular individuals for punishment, an impossible task for air power.) According to a Belgian nurse working with Médécins sans Frontières, villagers in southern Balkh province in 1985 knew that they could prevent their villages from being bombed by joining the National Fatherland Front. In some cases the regime negotiated accords with village elders in which it was explicit that bombing would stop once villagers cut their ties to the resistance. The policy of reprisals against civilians for resistance attacks was part of the same approach.[51]

Bombing also played a more conventional military role in cordon-and-search military operations, usually conducted near the main roads in order to eliminate active resistance from strategically located areas. Destroying or damaging fields, irrigation systems, and, especially, grain and livestock reduced the resource base of the mujahidin. In some strategic zones—several areas along the borders with Pakistan and Iran, for example, and such strongholds of the mujahidin as the Panjsher Valley— bombing and assault by ground troops not only destroyed supplies but also made the land uninhabitable and turned the surviving population into refugees. In contrast to the situation in Kabul and other areas under government control, there was no indication through the Karmal period that the use of violence had become more discriminating as a result of intelligence. Most of the nearly one million deaths resulted from the indiscriminate violence of the Soviet forces against the rural communities of Afghanistan.[52]

The pacification strategy also exploited conflicts within and between qawms to win some traditional leaders to the government side. The dominance of the Islamic discourse of jihad in the resistance and the links between the mujahidin and the parties in Peshawar promoted rivalries within the qawm: khans clashed with khans and with other classes of leaders, such as religious figures or Islamist intellectuals. The vast new military and financial resources available as a result of the war also destabilized relations among the qawms. According to traditional rules of competition, khans sought these resources where they could find them; sometimes that meant joining resistance parties in conflict with those that their rivals joined, and sometimes it meant supporting the government. Some qawms, especially Pashtun clans in eastern Afghanistan, supported the government out of allegiance to a group member in the PDPA leadership.

The militias retained the same qawm-based organization whether serving as mujahidin fronts or as one of the regime militias known as *operatifi*. Operatifi resembled the irregular forces that the Afghan state had largely relied upon to suppress revolts in the days before Daoud built a modern army. The militia leader and members generally did not join the PDPA, although they adhered to the NFF through the Council of Tribes. They were exempted from any government programs they found objectionable, including conscription into the regular armed forces.[53] These militia were responsible for keeping their areas clear of mujahidin and for keeping any major roads used by the government open. (Pakistani authorities have a similar arrangement with the militia in tribal territories.) As long as Soviet troops remained in the country, the operatifi played relatively minor military roles.

Whereas local qawm played an essential role in the government's rural counterinsurgency strategy, nationality played a much less important one. Because the major "nationalities" of northern Afghanistan—Tajiks, Uzbeks, Turkmen—were also recognized Soviet nationalities with their own republics and Communist parties, rumors persisted that the USSR would impose the Cyrillic script of the Soviet Central Asian Republics, reorganize northern Afghanistan into ethnically based provinces, or even partition it and annex the parts to its adjacent republics. Most of the economic and security infrastructure of the Afghan regime was located in these areas, which were increasingly integrated economically into the Central Asian Republics. Karmal was also most popular in the state-controlled areas of northern Afghanistan, for he had displaced the hated Pashtun-chauvinist Khalqis. But the Soviets did not use nationality to reorganize the administrative structure of the state. Any policy based on nationality in Afghanistan foundered on the PDPA itself: it could pursue neither a Pashtun nationalist nor a pro-minorities strategy without being torn apart by factional conflict.

Any strategy of extraction from the rural areas would have conflicted with the state's attempt to gain support through distribution. Land taxes virtually disappeared, and the regime actually encouraged limited capitalism in an attempt to bind commercial farmers to the state rather than to extract profits from dealings with them. This policy reflected the Soviet belief that state-guided capitalist development was a necessary part of the "national democratic"—as opposed to socialist—revolution. The government both raised procurement prices and placed increased emphasis on the technical requirements of such farming by promoting mechanization and attending to the need for water, credit, and fertilizer.[54]

Immediately after coming to power Karmal announced increases of 20 and 30 percent in the procurement price for cotton and sugar beets, and the government repeatedly raised the prices of commercial crops over the years.[55] Control over inputs also gave the government more effective power over farmers. Soviet authorities in the large military base at Kilagai, Baghlan Province, told local farmers that they would not receive any irrigation water unless they produced cotton. The mujahidin, meanwhile, were pressuring the farmers to plant rice. Production of food crops not only furnished the mujahidin with needed supplies, but also made the peasantry more independent of the government and of the national market. Reports from Laghman and Kunduz provinces also tell of peasants being pressured to produce cash crops by the government and subsistence crops by the resistance.[56]

The government established Soviet-style tractor stations to provide farmers with affordable machinery. According to Karmal (or his Soviet speechwriters), these stations were to become the "rally point of peasants." Indeed, tractor use by Afghan peasants increased significantly during the war, but that was partly because of a reduction of at least 40 percent in the livestock herd. Some of the tractors were leased from the government stations, but others were brought in from Pakistan or captured in resistance attacks on state farms.[57]

For all their efforts, the Soviets and the Afghan government made remarkably little progress toward reestablishing state control—or even state presence—in most of the countryside. It was not until 1984 (again, during the Chernenko period, when the Soviets were pursuing an uncompromising long-term strategy) that the regime proposed an institutional framework for consolidating gains made in the pacification program. In January of that year the PDPA Central Committee met to consider a draft law on "local organs of state power." The law provided that all local organs of state power be run by "democratic centralism," and it limited participation in elections to the PDPA and its front groups. According to official accounts cited by Anthony Arnold, however, although "local elections were scheduled for late 1985 and the first nine months of 1986, . . . by September 1986 they had been held in only 180 of the 628 villages in Kabul province, the area under tightest government control."[58]

By the time Gorbachev came to power in the Soviet Union in March 1985, it was becoming clear that consolidation of control by the PDPA-controlled party-state was at best a long-term and costly goal. Gorbachev let both the Afghan leadership and his own military know that they had one year to make decisive progress. When they failed to do so, Gorbachev changed course.

7

Soviet Withdrawal,
Political Retreat: State
and Society, 1986–1991

When Mikhail Gorbachev came to power as general secretary of the Communist Party of the Soviet Union in March 1985, he imposed a one-year deadline for making the old strategy work. As a result, the year after Gorbachev took power was the bloodiest of the war. By the time of the Soviet Party Congress of February 1986, Afghanistan had become, in Gorbachev's words, a bleeding wound. Confronted by limited resources at home and continuing resistance in Afghanistan, the congress authorized Gorbachev to promote a political compromise—"national reconciliation"—in Afghanistan and to negotiate the withdrawal of Soviet troops. At a Politburo meeting on November 13, 1986, the Soviet leaders decided to withdraw troops from Afghanistan by the end of 1988, in the meantime working to establish a friendly, neutral government.[1] After the withdrawal, the Soviet government continued to send arms, commodities, and cash to the hard-pressed government in Kabul, which used this aid to forestall defeat at the hands of the divided mujahidin.

Babrak Karmal, symbol of the Soviet intervention, attended the February 1986 Moscow Party Congress but failed to appear in Kabul for the subdued celebrations of the eighth anniversary of the Sawr Revolution on April 27. On May 4, as Soviet tanks guarded key intersections and military installations, a plenary meeting of the Central Committee of the PDPA "elected" Najibullah as general secretary. In November Karmal also lost the position of president of the Revolutionary Council and went into exile in the USSR.[2] His displacement spawned a new conflict in the PDPA, between largely non-Pashtun Parchamis who were allied with Karmal and largely Pashtun Parchamis who were allied with Najibullah.

After the Soviet Politburo's decision to withdraw, Najibullah and most PDPA leaders were summoned to Moscow, where they were told that they had two years to prepare to defend their government without Soviet troops. In January 1987 Najibullah announced the Soviet-formulated policy of national reconciliation, which included a

cease-fire, power sharing in the national government with other political parties or personalities, amnesty for thousands of political prisoners, and official recognition of the local control exercised by field commanders of the resistance.

In a speech on January 3, 1987, to the founding session of the Extraordinary Supreme Commission for National Reconciliation in Afghanistan, Comrade Najib, General Secretary of the PDPA Central Committee—as he then called himself—placated his listeners by asserting that the "REVOLUTIONARY PROCESS IS IRREVERS-IBLE" (printed in boldface capital letters in the English transcription). Over the next four years, however, President Sayyid Muhammad Najibullah—as he styled himself before a group of ulama in July 1990—presided over the reversal of virtually every aspect of the revolutionary process.[3]

In November 1987 a Loya Jirga convened by Najibullah ratified a new constitution, which had been drafted by Soviet advisers.[4] Under this constitution the Democratic Republic of Afghanistan reverted to its former name, the Republic of Afghanistan. The new constitution ostensibly provided for a multiparty system, a popularly elected parliament that would choose the prime minister, and a president elected by the Loya Jirga. (The Loya Jirga, modeled on that created by the 1964 constitution, was to include the elected parliament; the upper house, a chamber of tribes, nationalities, and religious and spiritual leaders; and some other government officials.) Najibullah became president of the Republic of Afghanistan, an office that concentrated all executive power. Elections were held in April 1988—confined to areas under government control—and in June, just before the start of the Soviet withdrawal, a new government led by Prime Minister Hasan Sharq took office. Sharq, technically a nonparty figure, had been Daoud's intermediary with Parcham.

The Soviets had agreed to withdraw their troops under accords signed at Geneva on April 14, 1988, by Afghanistan, Pakistan, the United States, and the USSR. The withdrawal began on May 15, 1988, and ended on February 15, 1989. The Soviets continued to supply Najibullah with aid and weapons, valued by Western sources at $3–4 billion per year, until the end of 1991, when the United States and the now defunct Soviet Union agreed to end aid.

As the direct Soviet presence diminished, political and economic means by which the state could pacify and control the people grew in importance, and military means diminished. Najibullah used Soviet aid to play off his antagonists against one another. Partly by cultivating divisions between various factions in the party and various parties and qawms in the countryside, he survived more than three years without Soviet troops.

Still, the loss of coercive resources—the Soviet army—deprived the state of its autonomy from society; forced to bargain with segments of the population, the state abandoned programs of Leninist state building in the cities and counterinsurgency in the countryside. Najibullah retreated even from the royal regime's attempt to disarm, fragment, and encapsulate the qawms, choosing instead to arm them and try to make them allies. This program of regime transformation had different consequences for different sectors of the society, depending on the degree to which they were subject to state control. In the cities national reconciliation meant a relaxed grip by a regime that had controlled much of daily life. The government actively encouraged capitalists and permitted some associations and demonstrations independent of party control. The government also gave up the effort to indoctrinate the youth with the discredited ideology of Marxism-Leninism; instead it returned to manipulating the discourses of Islam and nationalism, discourses that it found easier to interpret in its favor after the departure of Soviet troops. For the first time people could be arrested for articles they had written in legally published private newspapers, rather than for covertly distributing underground leaflets.

With respect to political society, the government wrote support for "political pluralism" into the constitution adopted in May 1990. Najibullah appointed even more nonparty figures to a new government in May 1990, headed by Prime Minister Fazl Haq Khaliqyar, a dignitary from Herat without Sharq's longtime association with the PDPA. In June 1990 the party convened its Second Congress, at which it renamed itself the Homeland Party (Hizb-i Watan) and renounced Marxism-Leninism, the monopoly of power, and socialism in favor of Islam, democracy, and a market economy.

The state apparatus, however, was far too weak to support genuine liberalization, to say nothing of democratization. Real power was increasingly concentrated in Najibullah and in the presidential apparatus, which monopolized the distribution of both Soviet aid and newly minted banknotes. Unable to create an effective, modern military, the government moved away from a bureaucratic chain of command toward a system based on brokerage, in which the state pays powerful leaders to supply troops from among their followings.[5] Najibullah relied increasingly on heavily armed qawm-based militias rather than on the regular armed forces. These militias evolved into powerful forces for regional and ethnic demands.

The regime recognized that matching coercive resources with rural society amounted to a stalemate at best. The field commanders of the mujahidin—the leaders who largely armed and organized the qawms—were members of these collectivities themselves. The regime offered the local commanders both a cease-fire and political incorporation. The mujahidin and their organizations could be recognized as part of the government, which now proclaimed loyalty to Islam and was free of the taint of foreign troops. This model of state-society relations, with its formal recognition of decentralization, was radically different from the strategy of centralized encapsulation that had been pursued by previous Afghan regimes. The new program enabled even Afghans who opposed the government to live with it. But most of the country's territory and population remained beyond the reach of the state.

Some officials of the regime, in hopes of assuring their survival, sought links to various social groups in the country, including the militias. This process led to ethnic realignment of political forces. One manifestation of the process was the reemergence of open conflict between Khalq and Parcham, for each group found different allies in the resistance. In March 1990, for example, Khalqi Defense Minister Shahnawaz Tanai, with the support of Hizb-i Islami leader Gulbuddin Hikmatyar and the Pakistani ISI, launched a coup against Najibullah. Ethnic realignment was also manifest in the increasingly open tug-of-war between Najibullah and the non-Pashtun government militias based in northern Afghanistan, which led to the mutiny that toppled him in April 1992.

The withdrawal of Soviet troops and the eventual termination of aid—like the mobilization of troops in the first place—were unilaterally Soviet (later Russian) initiatives. Brezhnev forced Karmal into the role of a puppet; Gorbachev forced Najibullah into the role of a more independent leader; finally, Yeltsin deprived Najibullah of the means to remain in power.

During this period the instruments of Soviet control over the Afghan government, like the instruments of control over the Soviet population itself, gradually became less coercive and more economic and political. Finally Soviet control dissolved altogether. The election of Najibullah took place under Soviet guns. After the last Soviet troops departed in February 1989, the number of Soviet advisers in Afghan government offices decreased significantly, and the staff of the Soviet embassy was reduced as well.

The infrastructural dependence of the Afghan state on the Soviet Union continued to increase for several years, however, despite attempts by Kabul to diversify sources of aid and trade. The Soviet share of official foreign trade approached two-thirds. The increased Afghan state expenditures required to compensate for the Soviet troop withdrawal provoked a severe fiscal crisis after 1986. Najibullah found only one alternative to support from Moscow: printing money. This solution produced hyperinflation that in turn reinforced dependence on Soviet supplies of food and fuel. The Soviets supplied an average of 250,000 tons of wheat per year, slightly more than the estimated consumption of the population of Kabul.[6]

Beginning in March 1989, the Soviets conducted an airlift of weapons and other supplies to Kabul. As one Moscow diplomat said, "Arms, food, fuel, even the money for the army's paychecks comes from here." In 1990 Moscow supplied Najibullah with "54 military airplanes, 380 tanks, 865 armored personnel carriers, 680 antiaircraft guns, 150 R-17 rocket launchers and thousands of tons of fuel." The weapons also included over 500 SCUD missiles, estimated to cost $1 million each. Western sources estimated the value of the aid at $250–300 million per month, or at least $3 billion per year.[7]

Institutions of the Party-State

During the Gorbachev-Najibullah period, Afghan government institutions followed —and sometimes led—those of other Soviet-bloc countries in proclaiming institutional reform. The state was too weak, however, to implement such reforms effectively. Instead, Najibullah manipulated the redistribution of Soviet aid and the disbursement of newly printed money to concentrate power in his own hands. As long as aid flowed from Moscow, his regime endured the factional and ethnic conflict that increasingly permeated state institutions.

The Party

Najibullah became Gorbachev's man in the PDPA, but he remained isolated among the party's leadership. Both Khalqis and the Karmal faction opposed elements of national reconciliation, and this opposition aggravated Najibullah's isolation in the party as the Soviet withdrawal neared an end.[8] Both factions resented Najibullah's attempt to use the support he received from Gorbachev and the KGB to set himself up as absolute dictator within the party and the government. Najibullah appealed to the Khalqis on the basis of Pashtun solidarity while balancing their power in the army with non-Pashtun militias outside the regular chain of command.

Najibullah initially turned to Khalqis for support against the pro-Karmal forces. As he was being elected, teachers and students—evidently organized by Minister of Education Anahita Ratibzad—demonstrated for Karmal in the streets of Kabul; Khalqi-led Interior Ministry troops, meanwhile, helped guard the offices of KhAD, where pro-Karmal sentiment was also strong.[9]

At a Central Committee Plenum on July 10, 1986, Najibullah added forty-four members to the Central Committee, most of them young activists from KhAD, the military, and other organizations who had proven themselves in the war. Over the next few years he gradually purged the Politburo and Central Committee of Karmal's closest supporters. He appointed more non-Pashtuns from Kabul and the North to the Central Committee while increasing the Khalqi contingent on the Politburo from two to four.[10]

On October 13, 1988, Gorbachev appointed Deputy Foreign Minister Yuli Vorontsov as ambassador to Kabul, with a mission to create a coalition government to take power after the Soviet withdrawal. The coalition would include the PDPA, the mujahidin, and representatives of the old regime, but both Khalqis and pro-Karmal Parchamis opposed the plan. Before the convocation on October 19 of a several-times-postponed Central Committee Plenum to discuss the issue, at least seventeen Central Committee members were arrested, including Karmal's top supporters. At the plenum—which was attended by only 93 of 163 members and alternates—Ziari, the senior Khalqi, and Razmjo, the Kabul city party secretary, were expelled from the Politburo. Najibullah denounced "dogmatism and factionalism" and accused unnamed forces of plotting to seize state power. One month later, though never formally dismissed from the Politburo, Khalqi Interior Minister Gulabzoy was bundled onto a plane at night and told of his appointment as ambassador to Moscow.

Still, in January hardliners in the security forces reportedly circulated a petition opposing concessions to the mujahidin or the restructuring of the PDPA.[11]

Vorontsov's efforts failed. As the last Soviet troops left Afghanistan amid fears (and hopes) of an imminent victory of the mujahidin, a besieged Najibullah gave in to the demands of the hardliners. The government declared a state of emergency and announced the distribution of weapons to all party members. On February 19 Najibullah replaced seven nonparty ministers with party members. More important, the state of emergency gave ultimate power not to the Council of Ministers but to a Supreme Military Council for the Defense of the Homeland, which was composed exclusively of party leaders, including twelve of the fifteen full and alternate members of the Politburo. In accordance with the power-sharing arrangement imposed by the Soviets in 1980, about one-third of the PDPA members on both the Defense Council and the Council of Ministers were Khalqis. In June Najibullah also attempted rapprochement with the Karmalites by appointing as first deputy prime minister Karmal's brother Mahmud Baryalai, who had been under house arrest.

The mujahidin offensives immediately after the Soviet withdrawal failed, notably at Jalalabad. As the imminent threat to the regime receded, factional tensions reemerged with, quite literally, a vengeance. The Khalqis had long chafed under their forced submission to the Parchamis. They also resented Najibullah's policy of building up largely non-Pashtun paramilitary forces under his direct command, independent of the Khalqi-led Ministries of Interior and Defense. Najibullah tried to appease the Khalqis, even going to the length of releasing the jailed collaborators of Hafizullah Amin from prison and allowing twenty of them to rejoin the Central Committee in October 1989.[12]

Throughout the summer of 1989 rumors had circulated of a "Pashtun plot" between Khalqis and Gulbuddin Hikmatyar, and in August WAD uncovered evidence of such a network. In December, Najibullah ordered the arrest of 127 Khalqi military officers. Twenty-seven of them fled to Pakistan, where they appeared at a press conference with Hikmatyar. Among those arrested was Pacha Gul Wafadar, who had served Daoud as minister of tribal affairs and Hasan Sharq as minister of civil aviation. After being released at the insistence of Khalqi Defense Minister Shahnawaz Tanai, Wafadar fled to Pakistan, where he claimed to have been working for Hikmatyar since 1980.[13]

On March 6, 1990, Tanai preempted the scheduled start of the trial of the accused plotters by launching a coup. He ordered air strikes against Najibullah's office and other sites, but by then he had virtually no troops in Kabul under his control. The Khalqi forces in the Interior Ministry, most of which were outside of Kabul, remained neutral, and the Parchami-commanded militias, especially the Special Guard, defended Najibullah. Tanai fled to Pakistan, where he established an ISI-brokered alliance with Hikmatyar.

The coup was primarily an intraparty factional battle, not a revolt by the military;

all Khalqi Politburo members except Interior Minister Watanjar supported the coup, but many air force and most army units did not. Even the Khalqi-led Sarandoy failed to come to the aid of Tanai, a clear sign that Khalq, like Parcham, was no longer organizationally coherent, although ethnic bonds remained strong among the Khalqis. In the immediate aftermath of the coup, Najibullah paid a visit to the mountain Pashtun province of Paktia, where he used his Pashto orating skills to soothe resentments among Khalqis and affirm his alliance with those who had remained loyal.[14]

Fear of a Khalqi takeover had long been an obstacle to convening a party congress, but this decisive defeat of the Khalqi leaders enabled Najibullah to call the Second Party Congress, which met on June 26–29, 1990. Despite continuing resistance, the PDPA Politburo and Central Committee were replaced by the Homeland Party's Executive Board and Central Council; party secretaries were now called vice presidents. These executive bodies reflected the increasing power of Parcham: Khalq's share of the positions fell from one-third to one-fourth (the three party secretaries were replaced by four vice presidents to accommodate the new arrangement).[15] The president and first vice president of the party (Najibullah and Sulaiman Laiq) were Parchami Ghilzai Pashtuns; two vice presidents (Najmuddin Kawiani and Farid Mazdak) were Parchami Tajiks, and another (Engineer Nazar Muhammad) was a Khalqi from Paktia.

The struggle over the future of reform in the USSR intensified in 1990 and early 1991, and the various factions in Kabul, as before, looked to their various patrons in Moscow. As the Moscow hardliners prepared for their coup in the summer of 1991, Babrak Karmal returned to Kabul on June 20. His return may have been part of a contingency plan by those who tried to overthrow Gorbachev to restore a more hardline Afghanistan policy after the August coup in Moscow. Najibullah responded by placing both Karmal and his brother Mahmud Baryalai under house arrest and dismissing the latter from his position as deputy prime minister. The failure of the August coup disheartened both the Khalqis and the Karmalites.[16] At this point they may have finally decided that the revolution was over and that they could assure their future only by making ethnic alliances against Najibullah. Najibullah, who had resisted pressure from within the party to congratulate the Soviet junta, publicly restated his support for his patron, Gorbachev, but he must have seen that the arrest of his Moscow patrons in the KGB and the military spelled the end for him. In October, in the aftermath of negotiations held in New York during the U.N. General Assembly, he agreed to resign at the beginning of any transition process.

The prospect of a transition fostered a further ethnic realignment of political forces, as all sides scrambled for allies. Many of the provincial Ghilzai and Paktia Pashtuns in the Khalqi leadership had already joined Hikmatyar. Sultan Ali Kishtmand, the only Hazara in the party leadership, resigned from the party in the summer of 1991. He complained of Pashtun domination and supported the political demands of the Iranian-based Shiʿa parties for regional autonomy and broad representation in the central government. The independence of the Central Asian Republics, as well as the increased discussion of power sharing in a transitional government, also increased tensions, especially between Tajiks and Pashtuns.[17] The changes in the organization of the state, the army, and the economy accentuated the ethnic realignment.

The State

The policy of national reconciliation offered representation to other groups while leaving military power in the hands of the party leadership, especially Najibullah. Leaders of the PDPA-Homeland Party held on to power until the moment Najibullah fell. The president and the ministers of foreign affairs, defense, internal affairs, and state security (KhAD-WAD), as well as all top military officials, were always PDPA Central Committee members and usually members of the Politburo. Except for the minister of foreign affairs (Karmal's second cousin, Abdul Wakil), all were Pashtuns.

The party gradually relinquished its hold over other areas of government, however. This concession was given an institutional framework in the constitution adopted in November 1987 by a Loya Jirga. This constitution was further amended in 1990. The 1987 constitution had given a formal role to the PDPA-dominated National Fatherland Front, but the 1990 version omitted that provision and emphasized that "political pluralism is the basis of the political system of the Republic of Afghanistan." The new constitution provided for a multiparty system; an independent judiciary; an elected national assembly (although part of the upper house was appointed); a council of ministers responsible to the assembly; and a president elected by the Loya Jirga. The constitution made Islam the official religion of Afghanistan and prohibited laws repugnant to sharia.

Both before and after the adoption of the constitution, nonparty members were incorporated into representative-legislative and administrative bodies of the state. The Revolutionary Council was the legislative and representative body until its dissolution in June 1988, when it was replaced by the National Assembly; the main administrative body was the Council of Ministers.

Of the appointed ministers, 54 percent were party members, compared with 92 percent under Karmal. Even more dramatically, party members appointed to the Revolutionary Council decreased from 95 to 35 percent (Table 6.2).[18] According to the government only 21 percent of those elected to the National Assembly in April 1988 were candidates of the PDPA, although at least some of the 44 percent elected as candidates of the National Front and other mass organizations may have been party members.[19]

The non-PDPA members of the representative and administrative bodies came from different segments of the society. The Revolutionary Council included religious figures and qawm leaders who had supported the government, while the members of the Council of Ministers resembled the lower echelons of the old regime. A few Muhammadzais gained prominence in Parcham, including Najibullah's successor as head of KhAD, Ghulam Faruq Yaaqubi, and a number of senior generals.

In ethnic makeup, the Revolutionary Council members reflected the country's population, with significant representation from the northern areas, where the government had the most presence. Only about 40 percent were Pashtun, and both Hazaras (15 percent) and Turki speakers (12 percent) received significant representation.[20] (The former Revolutionary Council, reflecting the composition of the PDPA leadership, had been over 60 percent Pashtun, like the parliaments of New Democracy. It had included few Hazaras or Uzbeks.) Only 12 percent of the new Revolutionary Council members were from Kabul. The nonparty ministers, like the old-regime elite, had a higher proportion of Pashtuns (56 percent) and Kabulis (35 percent). The Revolutionary Council members, since they were largely qawm leaders and a few traditional mullahs, had a much lower level of education than the ministers. Nearly two-thirds of them had no state schooling, whereas over half of the ministers had attended the elite Kabul lycées. Fewer than a quarter of the Revolutionary Council members had higher educations, but more than three-quarters of the ministers did. Furthermore, over 60 percent of the ministers had studied in the West and none in the Soviet bloc.

Through appointments to the Revolutionary Council Najibullah was attempting to co-opt leaders of rural society, especially the northern, non-Pashtun areas, control of which was key to the regime's survival. In the appointments to the Council of Ministers he was making overtures to the Western-educated segment of the educated elite. Under New Democracy as well, parliament had been dominated by landlords and the Council of Ministers by Western-trained technocrats. Now, however, Pashtuns constituted 40 percent rather than 60 percent of the representation of rural society, and Soviet-trained Pashtuns held the top posts in the regime's security forces.

By April 1990, fourteen months after the end of the Soviet withdrawal, Najibullah had survived both mujahidin and Khalqi attacks. He lifted the state of emergency and appointed a new government, fewer than a third of whose members were acknowledged to belong to the PDPA. Virtually the only positions held by party members were those involving security. Nearly half of the cabinet (seventeen of thirty-five) had studied in the West.[21] Both the program of the renamed party and the new constitution renounced the party's previous claim to a "leading role" in the state. In August 1991, on the eve of the Moscow coup, Najibullah approved Decree No. 70 of the Republic of Afghanistan, which struck "the words 'the Sowr revolution, People's Democratic Party of Afghanistan, and primary party organizations' from all legislative documents in force in the country."[22] Less than two months later, Najibullah agreed to resign.

Najibullah lasted this long mainly because he succeeded in using Soviet aid to strengthen the military capabilities of the state. Beyond that, there were two keys to his success: effective mobilization of the regime's supporters and even nonsupporters under his control, and manipulation and promotion of social segmentation. After the withdrawal of Soviet troops, his forces became overextended, and he compensated for the lack of support by increasing the use of "brokerage," the creation of qawm-based militias. The largest such groups were recruited from among non-Pashtuns who lived near the regime's key roads and security and economic installations in northern Afghanistan. The growth of such forces increased tension with the Pashtun- and Khalqi-led forces in the Ministries of Defense and Interior.

Najibullah's ability to mobilize forces under his control increased partly because the party-state apparatus was gradually becoming more effective, at least as long as the Soviet troops were present. Another factor, though, was the increasing size of the population under regime control. The war, especially Soviet bombing raids and food shortages, drove millions of peasants out of their villages. While several million became refugees in Pakistan and Iran, over a million fled to Kabul. The capital's population more than doubled during the war, growing from 870,000 in 1978 to more than two million by the late 1980s.[23] Furthermore, by then a generation of Kabuli children who had spent all or nearly all of their school years receiving PDPA-style instruction began to graduate and enter the military. The youthful human resources available to the government increased in both quantity and quality.

After returning from Moscow in December 1986, Najibullah told a meeting of the primary organizations of the DYOA in the army:

> At the present stage your duty is to enhance the readiness of the Army to a level that will make it possible for the Army to carry out independent armed struggle against the armed counterrevolution and thus ensure the reliable defense of your homeland. . . . History has left us with very little [time?] for bringing about formidable changes in the country.
>
> The fact that all limited contingents of the Soviet Union will return to their homeland is also hidden from no one. The question is just one of time.[24]

Najibullah pursued a two-track strategy. First, he attempted to strengthen the regular armed forces by making conscription more effective, increasing pay, and improving training and preparedness. The second undertaking, which ultimately became more important, was to create forces outside the factionalism-ridden (and Khalqi-dominated) command structures of the Ministries of Defense and Interior. Some of these new forces recruited troops from regime supporters living in government-controlled areas, including militias of armed party members and a new, largely volunteer force attached to WAD called the Special Guard (Gard-i Khas). The qawm-based militias also fit into Najibullah's strategy; some received heavy equipment and were deployed outside their home areas for the first time. Soviet sources claimed that by the end of the Soviet withdrawal, the total armed forces under regime control, including Sarandoy, guards, and militias of various types, approached two hundred thousand, of which the army and air force were a distinct minority.

Najibullah tried various means to manage Khalqi-Parchami conflict in the military. When Babrak Karmal "resigned" as president of the Revolutionary Council in

November 1986, Nazar Muhammad (a Khalqi) had been chief of staff of the armed forces since January 1984 and defense minister since December 1984. Najibullah's first move was to reinstate as defense minister the Parchami Politburo member Gen. Muhammad Rafi, who had just returned from lengthy training in Moscow. Nazar Muhammad was shifted back to his position as air force commander and compensated with a vice presidency. A rising Khalqi officer, Shahnawaz Tanai, was appointed chief of staff. All of these officers were Ghilzai or Paktia Pashtuns.

Rafi, however, was still resented by Khalqis. On June 4, less than three weeks after the Soviet withdrawal had begun, Najibullah promoted Rafi out of the way to vice president. Tanai remained in de facto control for two months as Najibullah left the position of defense minister open, hoping to attract resistance commander Ahmad Shah Massoud to the position.[25] Massoud refused, and Tanai was named defense minister in August. To balance the promotion of a Khalqi minister, Najibullah appointed a Parchami chief of staff, Asif Dilawar, who later served in the same capacity when Massoud finally became defense minister after Najibullah's fall. The political director of the armed forces was a Parchami Pashtun from Paktia, and the head of the armed forces department of the PDPA Central Committee was a Parchami Durrani Pashtun from Qandahar. The first deputy defense minister, who was also commander of the Kabul garrison and reported directly to Najibullah, was a Parchami Muhammadzai (Gen. Muhammad Nabi Azimi), who helped turn the Kabul garrison over to Massoud in 1992.[26] The Khalqi defense minister had no troops in Kabul under his direct command and had to use the air force to launch the March 1990 coup. The Ministry of the Interior forces (Sarandoy) also served under a Khalqi minister and commander, but the political director was a Parchami Pashtun from Paktia, a confidant of Najibullah's (Manokai Mangal, who also joined Hikmatyar in 1992). The command structure of WAD was entirely Parchami, with many Kabuli Tajiks as well as Pashtuns.

In his December 1986 speech to the army youth, Najibullah had emphasized two points: the need to "bring forces up to strength" and to improve the "professional expertise of staff." To bring units up to strength the government had to improve both conscription and morale among conscripts. One of Najibullah's first decrees, in November 1986, called for the conscription of "sons and brothers of leadership cadres" whose evasion of military service through personal influence had been a major source of popular resentment in Kabul.[27]

Another source of resentments had been the March 1984 decree that extended conscript service to four years, followed immediately by indefinite reserve service. Although the government promised lavish benefits to those who completed service, there was virtually no way to predict when service would end. Najibullah both lightened the burden of conscription and created incentives for conscripts to complete their service rather than desert. The new law on military service, adopted on February 23, 1987, reduced the length of conscript service to two years for most, less for those with university or graduate degrees. The new law apparently increased the number of conscripts actually serving. According to Tanai, speaking two years later as defense minister, the shorter service had "a stabilizing effect on [conscripts'] combat spirit."[28]

The regime also took other measures to enlarge the size of the armed forces. As part of national reconciliation, it announced the release of 19,514 prisoners during 1987–90. The decrees releasing prisoners often provided for those in "suitable circumstances" to be "sent to service in the armed forces." Deserters were repeatedly pardoned and urged to return to their units. At the same time, press-ganging continued, according to observations of diplomats in Kabul, although it seems to have been somewhat less indiscriminate.[29]

To increase the expertise of staff, the government laid new emphasis on training and took measures to enforce accountability for performance. In September 1987 a new Military-Political University opened to train "party strugglers" in the armed forces. In February 1988, as the last round of the Geneva talks dragged on, Generals Rafi and Gulabzoy inaugurated a new training center.[30]

As the Soviets departed, they agreed to upgrade the equipment of the Afghan military. In November 1988 the two governments signed a new protocol on military cooperation, under which Kabul received long-range SCUD missiles, as well as short-range missiles. These were supplemented with medium-range missiles in August 1989.[31]

The new weapons did not all go to strengthen the regular armed forces. On the contrary, many were used to equip the new units created outside the Ministries of Defense and Interior. The importance attached to such units was signaled by the upgrading of the organization and leadership of KhAD, the Ministry of Nationalities and Tribes (especially its tribal part), and the youth organization. In January 1986 KhAD, formerly a department of the Office of the Prime Minister, became the Ministry of State Security (WAD, for Wizarat-i Amaniyyat-i Dawlati), a name whose echoes of the KGB (Committee on State Security) were not lost on Afghans. Leaders of WAD, the Ministry of Nationalities and Tribes, and the Youth Organization (Laiq, Yaaqubi, and Mazdak) were promoted to the Politburo.

Just before the signing of the Geneva Accords in April 1988, Najibullah established a new highly paid, mainly volunteer elite unit, the Special Guard, largely recruited from the DYOA and under the command of WAD. Its commander reported to the Kabul garrison, who in turn reported directly to Najibullah, not the defense minister. Special Guard members received twice the salaries of regular soldiers, as well as other privileges. This force played an important role in defeating Tanai's coup. According to official sources, its size was ten thousand by January 1989 and forty thousand by March 1990.[32] The latter figure seems high, but many estimates are in the range of twenty thousand. This largely Tajik force played a role for Najibullah similar to that of Ahmad Shah Durrani's Qizilbash and Kohistani forces, which had served as counterweights to the Pashtun tribal armies.

In the period after the Soviet withdrawal, the party armed and trained all of its members, including women. In June 1988 the president of the provincial party committee in Jalalabad told a Yugoslav reporter, "Even if I had no soldiers, I would succeed in defending the city, because twelve thousand members of the People's Democratic Party of Afghanistan live in it, ready to take arms at any moment." In February 1989, as the Soviet troops left Kabul, thousands of members of the PDPA and DYOA received training. All Kabul primary organizations of the PDPA, DYOA, and trade unions had to send "volunteers" to join "independent units of the Revolution troops . . . to be set up alongside the Special Guards and State Security [WAD] units." These new units received all the privileges of the Special Guards. Najibullah claimed to have armed thirty thousand PDPA members, besides those already in the security forces.[33]

The qawm-based militias (*watanparast,* or operatifi) were also expanded and given new roles. Roy noted as early as 1984 that these militias were more combative and mobile than the regular army. At that time, however, they still operated in their areas of origin. They were under the operational control of the Ministry of the Interior until at least 1985, but at some later date they seem to have been linked more directly to WAD and the Ministry of Nationalities and Tribes.[34]

We can illustrate the variety of such units with four examples: the Andarabi militia led by Juma Khan; the Achakzai militia led by Gen. Ismatullah Muslim; the Ismaili Hazara militia of Sayyid Mansur Nadiri Kayani; and the Jauzjani Uzbek militia of Abdul Rashid Dostum. The first three consisted of armed qawms led by leaders drawn from the established social structure. The fourth was recruited more on an ethnic and regional basis and led by a man of humble social origin who had proven himself militarily.

The Andarabi militia was the least successful. It developed from the search by the government—and by Gulbuddin Hikmatyar—for a force capable of blocking the supply lines of Jamiat commander Ahmad Shah Massoud of the Panjsher Valley, adjacent to Andarab.[35] When this area of northern Afghanistan slipped out of government control in 1979, one of the traditional leaders, Juma Khan, declared his support for the mujahidin. Because Massoud controlled the rival Panjsher Valley, Juma Khan joined Jamiat's main rival in the area, the Hizb-i Islami of Hikmatyar. There was no ideological component to this adhesion. The Andarabis maintained their independence, but they did not fight the government and often blocked Massoud's supplies. In 1983 Massoud took advantage of a truce he negotiated with the Soviets under Andropov to seize control of Andarab in a nearly bloodless commando operation. When the Soviets launched a massive offensive against Panjsher in April 1984, Massoud evacuated the Panjsheri population, sending some of them to Andarab. There were clashes between the two groups, and as the Soviet offensive advanced, Juma Khan declared his support for the government, which recognized him as a militia commander. Juma Khan was assassinated in November 1986, presumably by Massoud's agents, and his militia gradually disintegrated.

Ismatullah Muslim was a Soviet-trained army major at the time of the 1978 coup. He was from a chiefly family of the Achakzai tribe from the area between Qandahar and the Pakistan border. This tribe was known for its raiding and smuggling activities since at least the time of Elphinstone, and Ismat Muslim was no exception. He had engaged in smuggling at least since the days when he was trained in the USSR, where he had the distinction of becoming the first Afghan military officer to be imprisoned there. As early as 1979 he led his tribe into the resistance and was conducting both military and smuggling operations (including heroin trade) in the area between Qandahar and Quetta. A member of the Afghan royal family mentioned Ismat Muslim to a U.S. diplomat in Tehran in 1979 as one of the most important mujahidin leaders around Qandahar, and even after his defection, the military commander of one of the resistance parties spoke with admiration of his combativeness in the resistance.[36]

In 1984, following a dispute with the ISI over his smuggling activities and his refusal to join any of the Islamic parties, Ismat Muslim defected to the regime, which made him a general. His principal role was control of transit points and roads between Pakistani Baluchistan and Qandahar. In January 1986 he was appointed to the Revolutionary Council. He established a large house in Kabul, where he had many parties featuring alcohol, drugs, dancers, and prostitutes. A U.S. diplomat living nearby once observed Ismat Muslim torturing a prisoner in his garden. The general also competed with the interior minister for the affections of a leading singer on Afghan radio. At the November 1987 Loya Jirga that adopted the new constitution, Ismat Muslim tried to enter the hall with his armed bodyguards, setting off a full-scale gun battle in which he was wounded. He later tried to defect back to the other side, but the ISI refused to meet his conditions, one of which was that they return the two Mercedes Benzes they had confiscated from him. Ismat Muslim's militia suffered a bloody defeat at Spin Boldak after the Soviet withdrawal, and he died in a Soviet hospital in 1991, apparently from the effects of drug and alcohol abuse.[37]

The militias of Sayyid Mansur Nadiri of Kayan, Baghlan Province, and of Abdul Rashid Dostum of Jauzjan both developed out of the single most important security problem Najibullah's regime faced after the Soviet withdrawal: how to defend the vital roads and economic facilities (especially the natural gas fields) in northern Afghanistan between Kabul and the Soviet border. This area had been been held by the largest concentration of Soviet troops except for in Kabul city itself, and with the Soviets gone, the regime did not have enough loyal troops or party members to defend it. Instead power was delegated to two main brokers: Nadiri, whose forces dominated the area north of the Salang Tunnel, and Dostum, whose forces guarded the natural gas fields and the roads along the primarily Uzbek steppe around Mazar-i Sharif. Reports also claimed that resistance commander Ahmad Shah Massoud, who led the most powerful mujahidin force in the area, received one-fifth of all goods he allowed to pass to Kabul through the Salang Tunnel. This arrangement, if it existed, may have started when the regime withdrew its remaining forces from Massoud's base area, Panjsher, in May 1988, at the start of the Soviet withdrawal.[38]

Sayyid Mansur Nadiri Kayani is the pir of a qawm of Ismaili Hazaras. (His son and military commander, however, loves fast motorcycles and American rock music.) Because this sect is considered heretical by both Sunnis and Imami Shi'as, it always received even worse treatment from government officials and the dominant ethnic groups than did the other Hazaras.[39] When the war started, most of the Tajiks and Pashtuns in the area around Kayan affiliated themselves to Hizb (Hikmatyar) or to Jamiat. Sayyid Mansur and his community seized the opportunity to arm and defend themselves as a government militia. Sayyid Mansur was eventually made a general, the governor of Baghlan Province, and a member of the Revolutionary Council, a radical reversal in social and political status for this stigmatized group. Originally this militia operated only in its own area, guarding the road. By 1989 Nadiri had thirteen thousand troops and was acting as an important intermediary in distributing Soviet aid. He met large groups of mujahidin, who would deal with him but not directly with Kabul. According to Nadiri, "We tell the opposition groups: we will give you anything you want, from the government funds, as long as you don't interfere with the trucks."[40] By 1991 his forces were deployed south of Kabul together with the Special Guard and the Jauzjanis against a base of Hikmatyar. Especially after Tanai's coup, Najibullah did not trust the Khalqi-dominated Ministry of Defense with such missions.

The largest and most effective militia was the Jauzjanis, commanded by Abdul Rashid Dostum. Unlike most such forces, Dostum's did not strictly correspond to any traditional, local qawm. Most of the members were Uzbeks, but the militia's name designated a region, and Dostum recruited from all local ethnic groups. As Dostum became more powerful, he married the daughter of a Durrani Pashtun (Popalzai) khan, who had served as member of parliament from Jauzjan under New Democracy. Nonetheless, Uzbek ethnic grievances played a role in the militia's recruitment. Uzbeks in Jauzjan Province had long suffered oppression and exploitation by Durrani Pashtun landlords supported by Kabul.[41] They supported Bacha-yi Saqao in 1929, and for similar reasons many came to support the Parcham faction of the PDPA.

This was the only militia large enough to be organized as a full division. By 1991 it claimed over forty thousand armed men. Dostum began his career working for the Afghan state natural gas company, where he organized self-defense units. The Jauzjanis gradually expanded beyond the natural gas fields. In 1988 they gained prominence when they were dispatched to Qandahar to replace the departing Soviet garrison and thwart coup plans involving Durrani mujahidin and army officers. About this time they were formed into the Fifty-third Division, which reported directly to Najibullah, bypassing the Ministry of Defense. When Najibullah addressed the Jauzjanis in September 1989, he praised them for operations that they had undertaken in areas of northern Afghanistan, around Kabul, and in the Pashtun heartland. By then the Jauzjanis "played a decisive role as the regime's only real mobile reserve. It was arguably the only formation capable of aggressive offensive operations."[42]

Like other militias, the Jauzjanis became a virtual law unto themselves, not only in the provinces, but even in Kabul city. On September 1, 1990, all militias were ordered out of Kabul, where they had reportedly engaged in "unruliness and battles in the streets." By then the number of armed men in such militias was estimated at sixty thousand to seventy thousand, or twice the size of the regular army.[43]

Najibullah's efforts to shore up military forces cost immense amounts of money. As we have seen, the Afghan state under the Khalq and then under Karmal compensated for its decreasing ability to collect taxes with Soviet-bloc foreign aid and sales of natural gas to the USSR at ever-increasing prices. By 1982 these two sources of international rentier revenue combined to pay for about 60 percent of expenditure. By the time Najibullah came to power, however, the shift of domestic and international balance of forces pushed the Afghan state into a fiscal crisis (Table 7.1). Growth of government expenditure accelerated, for money and other material incentives had to replace the coercive power of the withdrawing Red Army. At the same time, natural gas exports stagnated, declined, and finally were suspended after the Soviet withdrawal. The difference between increasing expenditure and declining revenue was financed through massive borrowing from the Central Bank, that is, by printing money.

Between 1978 and 1988 government expenditure increased eightfold nominally and doubled in real terms. According to the government, "This large step-up in recurrent expenditure was the result of a major increase in defence expenditure, government employment and wages and salaries. The increase in interest and principal repayment obligations and the growth in subsidies to contain domestic prices also contributed to the increase in recurrent expenditure."[44]

As shown in Figure 7.1, government expenditure increased especially rapidly from 1986. By 1988 defense expenditure amounted to 60 percent of the total, and it could only increase after the departure of the Soviet troops.[45] The salaries of soldiers increased by a factor of five to ten during 1988–89. Special Guards and all militia members received double the pay of regular soldiers.

The government subsidized consumer goods for ever greater sectors of the Afghan population. In his March 1988 budget speech, Prime Minister Kishtmand announced increases in the distribution of commodities to 340,000 state employees and others who held coupons for flour and cooking oil. This number increased to 450,000 in 1990 and 550,000 in 1992. Each coupon holder was said to support about nine people.[46]

The government's effort to buy off resistance commanders and pay militias was also extremely expensive. Reports from the Qandahar area in the spring of 1990 related that money paid to commanders by Kabul was being measured by a new unit: "containers." According to an informant, this English-language term referred to containers of freshly minted banknotes that were delivered unopened to those who supported national reconciliation.

At the same time the government reduced its already minimal efforts at tax collection. As part of the national reconciliation program, the government announced that all debts and back taxes of returning refugees would be canceled.[47] Furthermore,

Table 7.1 Components of the State Fiscal Crisis, 1975–1990
(Millions of Afghanis unless Otherwise Noted)

Year	Total Government Expenditure	Foreign Aid	Exports of Natural Gas (millions of U.S. $)	Exports of Natural Gas	Borrowing from Central Bank	Supply of Currency at Year's End
1975	16,187	4,290	47	2,368	− 129	11,427
1976	19,594	5,758	40	2,004	− 114	14,225
1977	24,326	8,334	39	1,968	1,068	17,784
1978	26,397	8,914	47	2,353	1,029	21,667
1979	30,173	10,746	76	3,851	3,639	26,641
1980	31,692	8,772	216	10,930	−3,374	32,316
1981	40,751	10,491	273	13,794	282	38,750
1982	42,112	11,915	284	14,350	150	46,674
1983	43,193	—	305	15,448	—	48,840
1984	51,177	—	314	15,904	—	58,716
1985	—	—	309	15,656	—	64,390
1986	88,700	25,900	260	13,136	20,600	71,402
1987	—	—	205	10,348	—	112,488
1988	129,900	33,600	143	7,236	56,900	152,330
1989	—	—	0	0	—	222,720
1990	—	—	0	0	—	311,929

Sources: DRA, *Statistical Information of Afghanistan, 1975–1978*; DRA, *SYB, 1358*; DRA, *SYB, 1359*; DRA, *SYB, 1360*; DRA, *SYB, 1361*; R.A., "Afghanistan, 1990"; IMF, *International Financial Statistics.*

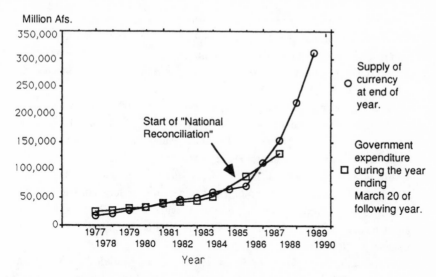

Figure 7.1 Government Expenditure and Supply of Currency, 1977–1990.

Sources: Democratic Repubic of Afghanistan (DRA), *Statistical Information of Afghanistan;* DRA, *Statistical Year Book (SYB), 1359; SYB, 1360;* Republic of Afghanistan, "Afghanistan, 1990"; IMF, *International Financial Statistics,* various issues.

by 1977 three-quarters of all taxes were customs duties, most of which were collected at five locations: Kabul (for trade via air freight); Hairatan (for trade from the Soviet Union, as well as goods transported by rail through the Soviet Union from such points of origin as Europe and the Far East; Islam Qala (for trade with or via Iran); Spin Boldak (for trade with Baluchistan); and Torkham (for trade with or via Pakistan, including goods imported through the port of Karachi). In the fall of 1988, as Soviet troops withdrew, Kabul lost control of Spin Boldak and Torkham.

At least through 1989, foreign aid from the USSR and its allies managed to support a roughly constant proportion of government expenditure. The nature of the assistance changed, however. Before 1982, commodity aid had been about a fifth to a quarter of total aid, and foreign aid as a whole had financed slightly less than two-thirds of development expenditure. In 1982 commodity aid was a third of all aid, and aid financed over 90 percent of development expenditure. By 1988, however, commodity aid was over two-thirds of all aid, and foreign aid actually exceeded development expenditure by nearly 60 percent, indicating that commodity aid was now playing an important role in financing the government's current expenditures.[48]

One of the biggest shocks to the economy was the decline and then suspension of natural gas exports (Table 7.1).[49] The value of the exports in current U.S. dollars peaked in 1984. It remained at about that level in 1985 and then declined in the next years by about a sixth (1986), a fifth (1987), and almost a third (1988). The gas wells were capped by February 1989, at the time of the Soviet withdrawal. The government attributed the decline to "inadequate maintenance of existing equipment, lack of skilled workers, shortage of electricity and diesel fuel and marketing problems." According to the minister of industries and mines, however, the main reason that the wells were shut down was that the Soviet experts who actually ran the gas fields left with the Soviet troops.[50]

Because the government's survival was at stake, an austerity program was out of the question. Instead, the government borrowed from the Central Bank. Economists have treated the strategy of increasing the money supply as a tax—the "inflation tax"—because it transfers wealth from holders of monetary assets to the government. Politically, however, it is radically different from a tax. Like other sources of revenue used by the Afghan government, printing money requires virtually no state capacity either to engage in surveillance or to enforce compliance. It is, in effect, another form of rentier income, derived from the state's internationally recognized monopoly on the issuance of currency.

Whereas in the early 1980s gas exports and Soviet aid had left the government with a nearly balanced budget (and a surplus in 1980, when gas revenues almost tripled), under Najibullah the budget went seriously into the red. In 1986, 23 percent of total expenditures were financed by borrowing from the Central Bank; in 1988, the year of the Soviet withdrawal, such debt financed 43 percent of expenditures. The government that took over from Najibullah in April 1992 found that virtually 100 percent of expenditures had to be financed by distributing banknotes delivered weekly from Russia, where the afghani notes were printed under a commercial contract.

While the data are not adequate to establish causality by the usual statistical methods, it appears that increases in debt-financed expenditure were followed with some lag by proportionate increases in the money supply, as suggested by Figure 7.1 and the data in Table 7.1. When the PDPA took power in 1978, about Af 18 billion of currency was in circulation. By the beginning of the policy of national reconciliation, currency in circulation had increased to about 71 billion, an average growth rate of 17 percent per year from March 1978 to March 1987. In 1987–88, however, the currency supply increased by 58 percent, and for the next three years it grew by 35, 46, and 40 percent, respectively. By March 1991 nearly four-fifths of all the Afghan currency in circulation had been printed since March 1987.

These debt-financed expenditures induced an inflationary cycle. Official data show inflation of consumer prices reaching about 30–40 percent per year in 1987–89, but journalists and others reported that food prices on the open market increased by factors of five or ten. By the summer of 1991 (before the Soviet coup) Najibullah referred to an "ugly economic crisis" in which food prices had increased "in a horrifying manner." The dollar was trading in the Kabul bazaar for about twenty times the official rate, and people changing dollars were reported to have to carry their afghani notes away in sacks.[51]

State-Society Relations

The loss of Soviet military support, along with increased availability of arms for the resistance, led the state to lose autonomy from society in one area after another. Society, however, proved unable to organize itself to provide an alternative form of state.

Islamic Legitimation

In several respects Najibullah went beyond Karmal in articulating support for Islam and in attempting to appropriate the Islamic discourse of the resistance. These measures, together with the Soviet withdrawal, reduced but did not eliminate the stigma of unbelief that besmirched the regime.

Influential if hard to quantify was the difference in speaking style between Karmal and Najibullah. Karmal spoke only in Persian, and his jargon-besmattered speeches always sounded as if they had been written by Soviet advisers, as indeed they may have been. The more Islamic or nationalist their assertions were, the less convincing they sounded. Najibullah, however, whose oratory showed his closeness to his people's roots, was liberated by the departure of the Soviet troops. In Persian and especially in Pashto he deployed a powerful vernacular style, which he used to evoke traditional nationalist or Islamic themes, depending on his audience. He often referred to the defense of the homeland against Pakistanis and Wahhabi Arabs (whose involvement with the resistance became more visible and, to many, more offensive after the Soviet withdrawal).

Najibullah was most effective not when he merely spoke respectfully of Islam but when he spoke Islamically of everything. His speeches to elders, tribesmen, and ulama, broadcast over Kabul Radio, did not just begin with Qur'anic invocations; they referred continually to Qur'an, hadith, the practice of the early caliphate, and Afghan folk traditions. He always justified the policy of national reconciliation by reference to a Qur'anic verse: "If two groups of Muslims are killing each other, reconcile them." By 1990 he was styling himself President Sayyid Muhammad Najibullah, and he even disclaimed credit for national reconciliation, telling a group of ulama, "You initiated the policy of national reconciliation and laid down the cornerstone of peace and prosperity."[52]

Discourse, however, was hardly enough. The government tried to carry out the full range of measures that governments ruling largely Sunni societies have used to legitimate themselves. Under Karmal this approach had largely consisted of expenditures on mosques, ulama, hajj, and religious education; under Najibullah such expenditures continued and were expanded. In the speech to the Central Committee first proclaiming the policy of national reconciliation, Najibullah announced that the salaries of religious leaders would be raised. In 1987 Najibullah claimed that sixteen thousand mullahs were receiving government salaries and coupons for food and commodities; less than a year later this number had risen to twenty thousand. On the eve of the Geneva Accords he announced that the salaries of Islamic officials would again be increased two and a half times.[53]

But Najibullah also introduced measures that went much further than mere economic support. In 1988 a Karmal supporter, in a typical interview, explained in a rather strained way how Islam and Marxism-Leninism were compatible because both strove for the good of humanity.[54] In 1990, however, rather than try to reconcile Marxism-Leninism with Islam, the Homeland Party Congress simply abandoned the former for the latter; "the Party" became an Islamic party, and membership was open only to "believing and practicing Muslims." Similarly, the new constitution stated that Islam was the religion of the state and that sharia, not state law, was the ultimate authority.

Najibullah also expanded the ways in which the state patronized Islam. In his speech to ulama on the eve of the signing of the Geneva Accords, he announced the formation of an Islamic Consultative Council in the office of the president, the establishment of prayer leaders in the armed forces, the expansion of Islamic education, increased religious programming on television, and the registration of a new party, the Islamic Party of the People of Afghanistan. He also reminded his listeners that there were eleven religious figures (loosely speaking) on the Revolutionary Council. The regime made special efforts to win the confidence of Shiʿa clergy, in particular playing up the Saudi and Wahhabi influence among the Sunni mujahidin. Despite all of these efforts, however, no truly influential Sunni or Imami Shiʿa figure supported the government. In March 1989, during the period of great tension right after the Soviet withdrawal, the imam of the main mosque in Kabul was arrested after preaching to Najibullah, "You have done nothing for your Creator, so you cannot do anything for his creatures." Imam Abdul Rauf Logari was jailed for seven months, then released by a presidential decree that declared his arrest a "mistake."[55]

Limited Liberalization

As that arrest suggests, the besieged regime did not transform itself into a tolerant liberal democracy. It did, however, significantly alter the mix of instruments used to control the population it ruled. Under Karmal the regime used pervasive terror and surveillance to forcibly incorporate the people into institutions controlled by the Sovietized party-state. Under Najibullah, the regime gradually moved from this totalitarian model to a more conventionally authoritarian one. The Najibullah regime continued to keep the population under surveillance, but it substituted repression of overt opposition for proactive terror and allowed more social and economic freedom. It also introduced limited measures of political participation.

The regime still had to maintain the external security of Kabul city and other regime strongholds, which required transferring troops from outlying areas after the Soviet withdrawal. Kabul sacrificed control of border regions and parts of the deep interior for control of the capital. These measures succeeded in keeping Kabul almost completely closed to resistance military infiltration, although some commanders around Kabul, largely at the behest of the Pakistani ISI, continued to lob poorly aimed rockets into the city.[56]

The most visible indications of the relaxation of terror were the amnesties for political prisoners. In addition to the 19,514 prisoners the government claimed to have released during 1987–90, about 1,300 releases or pardons—almost all to political prisoners—were announced in the first ten months of 1991. There was no way of verifying these figures, but they were roughly consistent with other evidence. The number of convicted prisoners in November 1991 was 4,432, of whom 2,752 were political, compared with estimated figures of about 20,000 in the early and middle 1980s. The 1990 constitution prohibited torture, which in practical terms meant its use was reduced but hardly eliminated. By 1991 torture in Afghanistan appeared to be similar in type and frequency to torture in other countries of South Asia.[57] Executions also seem to have been reduced, although death sentences were handed down to 97 of those participating in the 1990 coup attempt.

Urban Afghanistan had begun to develop a civil society under New Democracy, but the various newspapers, clubs, circles, and associations organized at that time had been either wiped out or incorporated into the government by the mid-1980s. The government's original approach to free expression and association was similar to Gorbachev's early concept of glasnost: the government encouraged public criticism of policies that it wanted to change, thus facilitating removal of officials who were resisting reform. For instance, in early 1989 state television aired sharp criticisms of the system of higher education by faculty and administrators. Soon thereafter, the Khalqi minister of higher education was replaced by a nonparty educator who oversaw a revamping of the universities.[58]

Later that year the first independent organization to function openly since 1978 announced its existence. The cautiously worded Declaration of Intent of the National Salvation Society (Jam'iyyat-i Rastigari-yi Milli), released on September 20, 1989, called on Afghans to create an atmosphere conducive to negotiation in order to prepare for free elections. This group, led by Muhammad Asghar, a minister of justice under New Democracy, brought together representatives of the old-regime elite who had remained in Kabul. It operated under considerable constraints and was protected by some back-door links to the government. Nonetheless, it provided a voice other than that of the party-state. In May 1990 Asghar suffered no consequences after calling Najibullah a "dictator par excellence" in an interview with the foreign press.[59] Such statements were still not to be found, however, in local media.

The government formalized the new openness in both the new constitution and a series of new laws. In January 1990 Najibullah ratified a law allowing nongovernmental social organizations, and Article 7 of the constitution was amended in May to strike any mention of the role of the party in the formation of such organizations. By the summer of 1990 a number of semi-independent publications published limited criticisms of the government. A year later, the editor of a new paper, *Azadi,* published a favorable article on resistance commander Ahmad Shah Massoud; a letter on the conditions in Pul-i Charkhi prison; and complaints by former Prime Minister Kishtmand of Pashtun domination and lack of democracy in the Watan Party. The editor was finally arrested when he printed a speech by Gulbuddin Hikmatyar in an edition that was seized by the government. He was released after a week as a result of protests from the Journalists Union and the Writers Association, whose new chairman had won an election against the Homeland Party candidate. In October 1991 a group of cultural figures announced the formation of a Movement for Unity, Freedom, and Democracy in Afghanistan, which they compared to the Solidarity movement in Poland. (The group promptly split over whether or not to support the return of Zahir Shah.) In November an Afghan exile naturalized in the United States returned to Kabul, where he organized a pro–Zahir Shah demonstration. The demonstrators, who had received a permit from the Ministry of the Interior, erected banners in a public park reading, "Down with the regime, dissolve the KhAD," but the rally was soon broken up by counterdemonstrators. Later that month the government backtracked and closed down several semi-independent newspapers.[60]

The 1990 constitution abolished the special revolutionary court and provided for an independent judiciary, another essential component of an independent civil society. Nonetheless, the chief justice was still "responsible to the president and . . . duty bound to report to him."[61] In no case did the courts uphold rights of citizens against the government.

The government likewise permitted a limited opening of political society. In 1987 under national reconciliation it had formally recognized the right of alternative parties to form, but the law effectively banned any parties opposed to the PDPA program. In 1988 the government liberalized the law, allowing parties to form so long as they supported the constitution and had their headquarters in Kabul—requirements that still effectively outlawed mujahidin parties. A number of small parties, either front groups or leftist factions enjoying a love-hate relation with the PDPA, participated in the 1988 elections. Liberalization notwithstanding, in 1989 the government arrested members of the newly formed National Unity Party—mostly university professors—on charges, never substantiated, that they had somehow been involved in armed opposition to the government. After international pressure, they were released without being tried. In September 1990 the government further relaxed the law on political parties. The leader of the newly formed Peasants Justice Party still claimed, however, that the Homeland Party had infiltrated and effectively controlled all other parties.[62]

Until the Soviet withdrawal, the regime continued to expand educational links with the socialist bloc. For instance, in March 1988, just before the signing of the Geneva Accords, the government entered into a new protocol on higher education with East Germany. After the 1988–89 upheavals in eastern Europe and the USSR, however, the regime gradually ended the attempt to propagate Marxism-Leninism, Afghan-Soviet friendship, or any other new ideologies. Nonparty figures with links to the old regime took over the Ministries of Education and Higher Education in 1989 and 1990. The statues of Marx, Engels, and Lenin had already been moved out of the Afghan-Soviet Friendship Rooms in the faculties of Kabul University. Instruction in Russian was curtailed, and English and French resumed their place as the foreign languages of choice in both the university and the high schools. Religious instruction was restored, and the classes on Soviet-style political science ended. Because the new textbooks, often based on Soviet examples, were filled with now objectionable material, the schools dug out the ones from before 1978.[63]

The Youth Organization also became less politically active, concentrating instead on promoting good citizenship. There were no more reports of children being sent off en masse to schools in the Soviet Union. By 1991 mujahidin in the Qandahar area were sending their children—at least their sons—to government schools in the city.

The growth of a private sector and the protection of private property also signaled the emergence of civil society. Since 1980, the government had renounced the Khalqis' attempts to nationalize trade, but state efforts at economic development concentrated on the public sector, especially industry. The official economy was increasingly integrated with the official economy of the Soviet Union through state-to-state trade agreements. In April 1986, just before the Gorbachev-imposed change of leadership, the Kabul government noted that Afghan-Soviet cooperative projects accounted for 75 percent of state industry and 60 percent of the country's production of electrical energy; over ninety thousand experts and workers had been trained through work on these joint projects or in the USSR itself. Kabul continued to publicize such statistics for a few years more.[64] Nearly all of these projects were in Kabul or in northern Afghanistan: those parts of the mainly Tajik and Uzbek areas that were under government control attained a high degree of integration into the economies of their co-ethnic republics across the Amu Darya.

One month after Najibullah assumed the office of general secretary, however, Kabul radio publicized a speech that he gave to Hindu and Sikh traders in which he announced "support for private investors and national traders."[65] The declaration that the private sector produced over 80 percent of the national economy became a staple of official propaganda. In April 1987 the government announced a new law governing the private sector and established an Economic Consultative Council of prominent traders and capitalists to advise the president. Immediately after the signing of the Geneva Accords the government announced that forty-seven private-sector projects would be exempted from customs duty for five years—another example of the distributive policies that contributed to the state's financial crisis.[66]

Before the Soviet withdrawal from Afghanistan and the fall of Communist regimes in eastern Europe, these measures, like the halting efforts at reform in the USSR, seemed designed mainly to supplement the public economy and to pacify another group that had resources: the traders. In 1990, however, as the financial situation of the state worsened and parts of the former Soviet empire were heading toward capitalism, the government moved toward much more extensive economic liberalization.

Article 19 of the new constitution proclaimed, "Property is safe from violation." In April a decree announced the restoration to the owners of all property seized by the state and provided for compensation where restitution was not possible. The government also adopted measures allowing private enterprises to be backed 100 percent by foreign investment. In 1991 the government announced plans to privatize some state corporations and to exempt experts working in private companies from conscription. When Prime Minister Khaliqyar presented the budget to parliament in March, he proclaimed privatization of the trade in fuel and proposed creation of a free trade zone in the region and pursuit of joint ventures with Afghanistan's neighbors. Khaliqyar suggested the European Economic Community, the Arab League, the Central American Common Market, and the Association of Southeast Asian Nations as possible models, but not the defunct CMEA. He also proposed the termination of many export and import duties and the abolition of most state monopolies.[67]

In spite of the government's attempts to strengthen and court the private sector, the economy continued to decline, and the population of Kabul continued to depend on the state for most of its employment and vital supplies. Feeding the urban population—as well as avoiding food riots—had been a constant challenge to early modern states in Europe; Najibullah attached such importance to feeding the people that in 1989 he announced the appointment of a commission on the food supply as part of the Homeland High Defense Council. In late 1991 he stated that his first task every morning was to check the supplies in the grain silos; only then would he turn his attention to military matters.[68]

The government supplied most of these goods from wheat and other commodities sent by the USSR. The Soviets shipped an average of 250,000 tons of wheat per year to Afghanistan and also furnished other essential commodities, including kerosene for cooking and heating, tea, sugar, oil, soap, and footwear.

The government distributed these commodities to holders of ration coupons through a network of special stores, three-fourths of which were in Kabul. Government employees and members of the party or of mass organizations were entitled to ration coupons. Over time both the number of ration coupons and the amount of subsidy increased. By 1990 the mayor of Kabul, Gen. Muhammad Hakim, estimated that 80 percent of the population of Kabul was benefiting from coupons.[69] As we have seen, 550,000 citizens were receiving ration coupons by 1992.

The capital's supply of food became particularly critical around the time of the Soviet withdrawal. The Salang Highway to the Soviet Union was closed in the winter of 1989 by resistance attacks and heavy snows. There was fear of famine in the capital, and the U.N. coordinator of humanitarian programs for Afghanistan, Prince Sadruddin Aga Khan, tried to organize an airlift of food for those most in need. Despite emergency purchases at the end of January (10 tons from Mongolia and

160,000 tons from the USSR), by the end of February wheat and flour stocks in Kabul were down to about twelve days' supply.[70] Open-market prices of wheat soared from Af 175 per kilo to Af 1,000. Over 150,000 tons of wheat were piled up at the railhead in Hairatan, north of Mazar-i Sharif, with no available means of transportation over the Hindu Kush.

In mid-March, however, the Soviets began an emergency airlift of flour to Kabul. Furthermore, the Afghan government—partly through the mediation of village elders, but its persuasiveness also enhanced by SCUD missile assaults and brutal attacks by departing Soviet troops—negotiated a truce with mujahidin commanders who had been blocking the road. The United Nations had begun supplying food for children and pregnant and lactating women by the end of March. By May the price of wheat had come down to Af 650 per kilo, and the crisis was over.[71]

The market began to work more effectively in succeeding months. Food from Pakistani Baluchistan was brought to Qandahar by private traders. Much of it went north to Kabul. The mujahidin taxed these shipments but did not stop them. By January 1990 a Western correspondent in Kabul claimed that "the opening of the 'southern route' some two months ago has brought market prices down and eased the government's dependence on the Soviet air bridge." The government increasingly relied on private truckers, who could move freely through resistance-held territory, rather than on the Soviet-aided state transport company. The government also built another road south of the Salang Tunnel, skirting the mujahidin-controlled areas. By January 1990, both the "government road" and the "mujahidin road" were open for business. Government convoys took fuel, weapons, and ammunition down the former. Private truckers freely carried other supplies along the latter, paying taxes to various mujahidin and militias among the way.[72] The state had resolved the crisis at the cost of sharing more power with other social forces.

In the summer of 1991, as food supplies became critical in the Soviet Union itself, Kabul again experienced shortages, and Najibullah observed that the price of food "has gone up in a horrifying manner." This time India and the Central Asian Republics stepped in to try to assure adequate food supplies.[73]

The fuel situation, meanwhile, was becoming critical. The regime was receiving less than 10 percent of the fuel it had contracted for with the USSR. By early 1992 the air force was grounded. The army in the entire western part of the country depended on commercial purchases of fuel from Iran—as did the mujahidin, who had more dollars, thanks to the heroin trade. In the rest of the country the army had at best a few months' supply of diesel and gasoline.

State Retreat from Peasant-Tribal Society

Under Najibullah the state completely abandoned plans for social transformation of the countryside. The regime also retreated from using military force to carry out the

Afghan state's longstanding goal of disarming qawm-based formations in order to encapsulate them; instead, it relied increasingly on patronage and brokerage financed by the USSR. As reporter Ahmed Rashid observed in the summer of 1989:

> In the countryside, Kabul is offering full local autonomy, any weapons up to and including tanks, as well as money and titles to local leaders who can guarantee to keep open communications between the cities. As a result, the country is slipping back towards a pattern of authority from ages past—a pattern reformist kings, Western-influenced technocrats, Islamist theocrats and communist revolutionaries have tried and failed to shift in this century. The state controls the capital and a few other towns, with tenuous negotiated control over the roads between—with a variable ability to collect taxes and conscript soldiers, and a monopoly of the more drastic instruments of violence.[74]

While military operations continued in some areas, these aimed mainly at securing urban centers and breaking up mujahidin offensives, in particular those planned by Pakistan's ISI. The state abandoned for the most part the exertion of constant military pressure on resistance-held areas of the countryside. Instead it offered autonomy, political recognition, and Soviet-supplied goods to commanders and qawm leaders who would abandon their fight against the government. This program was more successful than the defiant rhetoric of some resistance leaders would lead one to believe, but it never succeeded in persuading most of the rural power centers to accept the regime as legitimate.

Even before their withdrawal, the Soviet troops in Afghanistan seem to have ceased most of their proactive counterinsurgency operations. When Najibullah announced national reconciliation, he also proclaimed a unilateral cease-fire beginning January 15, 1987. No mujahidin groups, of course, could formally accept a cease-fire before the USSR had agreed to withdraw its forces, nor did the regime fully honor its commitment, but military activity did decrease, despite the acceleration of weapons deliveries from both sides.[75]

After the Soviet withdrawal the government concentrated its remaining forces around Kabul and a few roads. Within two weeks after the beginning of the implementation of the Geneva Accords, it withdrew its last troops from the Panjsher Valley, where Massoud's control was now uncontested.[76] By the fall of 1988 it had lost or ceded the entire eastern border area to the mujahidin. Whether it was a policy decision or merely a result of the withdrawal of Soviet aircraft, the regime ceased blind bombing of rural areas. It sought not to dislodge or destroy the internal commanders, but to co-opt and incorporate them.

The change in military policy mirrored the new agricultural policy. Whereas Babrak Karmal's regime had used land reform as counterinsurgency, Najibullah's simply ended it. Throughout Karmal's time in office the state-controlled media regularly featured items on the distribution of land to poor peasants and nomads in various regions of the country. The last such item recorded in the *Federal Broadcast Informa-*

tion Service was at Karmal's last Central Committee meeting as general secretary, in April 1986.[77]

In June 1987 the Revolutionary Council passed a new land reform decree that raised the ceiling on land ownership from six to twenty hectares (about fifteen to fifty acres) of first-class land (irrigated orchards or vineyards) or the equivalent. Only about 4 percent of the rural families had properties over the old limit; the number of those over the new limit was minuscule, and in most areas there were no farms of this size and quality. Furthermore, the government decreed, "Those people who play [an] active role in the realization of the process of national reconciliation and ending of bloodshed in the DRA, may hold land areas more than the limit." The decree also explicitly permitted tenancy, sharecropping, the use of wage labor, and the buying and selling of land. Finally, in April 1990 the government decreed restoration of or compensation for all seized property. The 1990 constitution abolished all mention of "democratic changes" in agriculture. Instead it proclaimed the inviolability of property.[78]

Public reports on agriculture now focused on the distribution of free chemical fertilizers and improved seed, often supplied as commodity grants by the USSR. The government continued to urge farmers to produce commercial crops and even held a special conference for cotton growers in February 1988. This conference took place in Kunduz, the market center of an irrigated plain where the government was apparently introducing Central Asian-style cotton monoculture. The Afghan government, however, which had not defeated the local "basmachi" (mujahidin) and had not imposed party-controlled collective farms, lost the battle for social control that the Bolsheviks had won in Soviet Turkestan.[79]

Najibullah observed that cotton production was less than a quarter of what it had been in the 1970s, even though the purchase price had been raised twice and would be doubled in the coming year (1988–89, the year of the Soviet withdrawal). He acknowledged that "the extremists threaten those who grow cotton": the struggle over food versus commercial crops had become a key issue in the battle for social control in the North Afghanistan plains. In the 1970s peasants had been given 65–80 tons of seed and had produced 40,000–50,000 tons of cotton; in 1986 they took 2,000 tons of seed and produced only 14,000 tons of cotton, selling most of the seed for animal feed and planting food crops. The government continued its efforts: in 1991 the purchase price of cotton was again doubled and that of sugar beets raised fourfold.[80]

The government implemented similar measures to win over the more numerous wheat farmers, distributing free Soviet-supplied fertilizer and improved seeds. For the first time the government offered long-term wheat purchasing contracts directly to the peasants instead of buying wheat on the open market from traders. These operations directly competed with resistance commanders in some areas, and the government could offer higher prices: in spite of its pariah status the Kabul regime continued to belong to the IMF and could print money.[81] Nonetheless, the amount of wheat purchased domestically fell after the Soviet withdrawal.

The original national reconciliation program provided a political framework for the co-optation and incorporation of local mujahidin groups. The 1987 and 1990 versions of the new constitution further defined the incipient local power structures. This was the first Afghan constitution to provide for institutionalized representation at the local level and for some devolution of control over administration to these local bodies. These measures would have fallen far short of federalism, however, even if the regime had been able to implement them.

The resolution of the Revolutionary Council on January 3, 1987, provided for commissions of national reconciliation "at the levels of villages, sub-districts, districts, provinces and throughout the country." These commissions hardly got off the ground, for public nomination to one often led to swift execution by the resistance. Nonetheless, some of the functions the commissions were to assume were ultimately carried out by the government, especially by WAD and the Ministry of Nationalities and Tribes. These commissions had authority to distribute medical, food, and agricultural assistance, "including the gratis aid of the Soviet Union . . . to the localities free of charge." They could appoint judges, administer voluntary service in the armed forces or border militia (instead of conscription), remit taxes, and ask the state to "pay monthly salary to the imams and village chiefs." In areas where there were peace agreements, the residents were to have "the right to establish local organs of state power and administration in a democratic manner and to appoint the heads of sub-districts and districts on the basis of the will of the residents." Never before had the Afghan state allowed local choice of administrators. The government also proposed to incorporate armed groups that made peace "to ensure the security of projects and specific establishments by them and the formation of regional [I believe the original was *mahalli*, better translated as "local"] units by them including the granting of the right of transportation and selling of primary goods in the localities." Thus these groups could become not only militias but also profit-making middlemen between government-controlled cities and the countryside. The transformation of local strongmen into dispensers of state-supplied patronage is a classic strategy of states that attempt to transform tribalism into patron-client relations.[82]

The regime preferred to deal with commanders as representatives of local qawms in the national assembly, not as leaders of political parties competing for power. The state had earlier offered representation to qawm leaders who had come over to the government's side by appointing them to the new Revolutionary Council. The constitution adopted in November 1987 provided for the election of local and provincial councils, as well as the national assembly, which was to replace the Revolutionary Council. On the eve of the national assembly elections of April 1988—held just as the Geneva Accords were readied for signing—Najibullah appealed by name to seven major field commanders of the resistance, asking them to participate in elections and take their seats in the senate or parliament. In his speech Najibullah even identified Ahmad Shah Massoud by a qawm name, Dawlatzai, that I have never seen mentioned by anyone else. These commanders, however, were hardly traditional rural leaders:

they included two army officers, two (secular) schoolteachers, an engineering student, a charismatic mountain mullah, and one traditionalist plains mullah–opium warlord. None accepted the offer.[83]

Just before the signing of the Geneva Accords, the government gave special attention to the Tajik and Uzbek areas of northern Afghanistan, including the trip to Kunduz by Najibullah and Prime Minister Kishtmand to promote cotton monoculture. The whole area received a special status, with its own deputy prime minister. The Hazara-majority southern district of Jauzjan Province, Sar-i Pul, was promoted to the status of a province, but this was the only rectification of internal borders in favor the Hazaras.[84]

The impulse behind creation of the Northern Zone was decidedly not to grant autonomy to the non-Pashtun nationalities living there. According to a Soviet source, the strengthening of the administration and infrastructure of northern Afghanistan in 1988 was part of a contingency plan aimed at enabling PDPA leadership to retreat to Mazar-i Sharif if it could not remain in Kabul. Najibullah also created a military command structure for the Northern Zone that placed Pashtun generals in charge of coordinating the activities of the non-Pashtun militias. Najibullah appointed Gen. Juma Atsak as the Northern Zone's military commander, in charge of guarding the aid coming over the border.[85] Atsak, a Durrani (Achakzai) Pashtun from the Southwest (Farah), became known as a Pashtun chauvinist who crudely asserted dominance over the northern militias. Nonetheless, the government's political and economic efforts in the North strengthened the capacity for collective action of that area's inhabitants once the overlay of Pashtun-dominated administration was stripped away.

These institutions and policies constituted the framework for the regime's battle for control of the countryside after the Soviet withdrawal. The regime had given up the revolutionary goal of transforming rural social relations. At least for the foreseeable future, it had also given up the aspiration, held by many postcolonial states, of displacing local power holders as the authoritative setters of rules. Instead, it offered recognition to these power holders on condition that they cease to oppose the regime's continuation in power at the center. To make the offer more palatable, the regime also changed virtually every other aspect of its policy.

State control over rural areas continued to erode. Mujahidin consolidated their hold over some areas, especially the Northeast, and the regime scarcely controlled many of the areas ruled by groups that owed nominal allegiance to it. Both the Jauzjanis and Ismailis seemed to exercise nearly as much independence as Massoud's Council of the North. The Qandahar and Herat garrisons had struck deals with local mujahidin groups that left them poised in a tenuous equilibrium between Kabul and the local population. But Najibullah's fall was due less to the onslaught of the mujahidin than to the loss of Soviet aid, which deprived him of the ability to control factionalism and ethnic conflict in his own ranks. Even while the state's power faltered, the political forces of society remained too fragmented to replace it.

Part Three

The Islamic Resistance:

Mujahidin, Society, and

the International System

Where state authority is too weak to provide structure to civil and political society, the objectives of opposition come to resemble those of competitive state building. Without law or political institutions, the struggle for power becomes as unstructured as the wars among the princes of early modern Europe. Each leader aspires to build an army and a financial apparatus capable of supporting it. Relative success depends upon access to resources and skills in organization and leadership.

The leadership of the state in Afghanistan faced a different structure of opportunities for the mobilization of resources from that available to early modern rulers. So, too, did leaders of revolt. Until the end of the Cold War and the collapse of the USSR, both state and insurgents functioned in an international system where Afghanistan played a strategic role because of its location. International powers that saw their own interests at stake in the conflict distributed resources far beyond those available in Afghanistan itself. Would-be leaders faced problems similar to those of the Kabul regime: obtaining weapons and other material and financial resources; recruiting and training staffs and followers with the appropriate skills and loyalties; combining those resources in organizations capable of carrying out the military and political tasks of struggle; and forging the necessary links to both the society of Afghanistan and the powers in the international system. Besides social structure and ideology, forms of organization would determine the outcome of the conflict.[1]

The resistance to the PDPA government and its Soviet sponsors developed out of the interaction among spontaneous social movements, political elites, and international actors. Most of the uprisings started without any connection to national political organizations. Both the Islamists, who were already established in Pakistani exile, and elements of the old regime who joined them there sought to lead the movement. Foreign powers and organizations tried to aid and influence the mujahidin. These included Pakistan, the United States (plus some European allies), Saudi Arabia, Iran, and China, as well as Islamic and anticommunist movements.

Like the regime, the resistance passed through several stages of development, largely determined by changes in the policies of the international actors, policies shaped both by events in Afghanistan and by the sponsors' shifting relations with one another.

Military aid to the resistance started in the tens of millions of dollars per year. By the late 1980s, combined U.S. and Saudi assistance reached about $1 billion per year. If we add the approximately $5 billion in weapons sent to the mujahidin during 1986–90 and a conservative estimate of $5.7 billion worth sent to Kabul, Afghanistan's total weapons imports during the period eclipsed those of Iraq and were at about the same level as those of Japan and Saudi Arabia—with the difference that personal weapons accounted for a much higher proportion of imports to Afghanistan.[2] The massive number of weapons circulating in the country became a major obstacle to political stability in Afghanistan and the surrounding region.

The first stage of resistance, against the Khalqis before the Soviet invasion, consisted of largely spontaneous uprisings under local leaders. Using local weapons and local resources, insurgents often succeeded in driving the government from their areas. The parallel power networks that had settled local disputes independently of the state under the old regime emerged in the resistance, often under the leadership, symbolic or substantive, of religious figures. The fragmented and apolitical insurgency fittingly expressed the revolt of a fragmented and depoliticized society. Both the Islamist activists and the would-be national leaders in exile played relatively minor roles, and members of political parties participated in only a few of the uprisings.[3] Pakistan supplied some small weapons, but external aid was incidental.

At the same time, political elites were forming parties or organizations—*tanzims*—mainly in exile in Peshawar. The Islamists (Jamiat and the two Hizbs) had already established headquarters and bases there. Various elites of the old regime joined them in 1978 and 1979. Islamic figures issued declarations of jihad. Without substantial international support (only a few million dollars from Saudi Arabia), but under some pressure from both donors and followers to unite, dozens of groups formed fluid alliances that reflected the inchoate political society of Afghanistan. Young Islamists who had received military training in Pakistan since 1974 returned to their native areas in rural Afghanistan to initiate or lead insurgencies.

Uprisings regained for the Hazaras and Nuristanis the autonomy they had lost a century earlier, when Abdul Rahman Khan had conquered them; they threw off the domination of Kabul and did not accept that of Peshawar. The mainly Persian-speaking populations of the West and Northeast also staged important revolts, although, through Jamiat and some other parties, they continued to participate in a common political society with Pashtuns. Tribes joined the movement en masse after Amin killed Taraki and seized complete power in the fall of 1979. Few Uzbeks of the northern steppe participated in the resistance movement, although those living in the mainly Persian-speaking areas joined the Tajiks in revolt.

The next stage of resistance followed the Soviet invasion. In 1980–82 the Soviet troops launched massive, indiscriminate offensives that depopulated certain areas, took back several provincial and district centers, and established posts along major communication arteries. The flow of refugees to Pakistan and Iran reached its height during this period, and the refugee communities took the forms they largely retained until the fall of Najibullah.[4] Increased military pressure forced local insurgent leaders to look to the exiled parties for arms. Seven exiled parties obtained recognition from Pakistan, which controlled an increasing flow of aid from the United States, Saudi Arabia, and China. The parties used the aid they received through Pakistan, along with other resources, to attract potential followers.[5]

The resistance movement began to receive substantial international assistance. The Carter administration allocated $30 million for the program in 1980 and about $50 million in 1981. Under the Reagan administration this amount increased to $120 million by fiscal 1984 (including a $40 million reprogramming of Defense Department funds to purchase the Swiss Oerlikon antiaircraft cannon, which proved useless in Afghanistan). In the fall of 1984 Congress took the initiative of nearly tripling the administration's 1985 request, to $250 million. Saudi Arabia approximately matched U.S. aid. Tens of thousands of fighters received military training in Pakistan.[6] Some Shi'a mujahidin also received aid and training from Iran.

Soviet aid to Kabul, which came from a single source and went to a single organization (the party-state)—or even to a single person (Najibullah)—forced artificial unity upon the PDPA. Aid to the mujahidin, which came from many sources and went to many destinations, reinforced existing disunity and created new conflicts. Pakistan did not want a unified Afghan guerrilla organization on its territory. The Pakistani ISI initially made most decisions about what group would receive how much aid. Even when parties formed alliances or established common headquarters, military aid continued to go to separate military committees. Groups favored by Pakistan, Saudi Arabia, and private Arab donors benefited disproportionately.

During 1983–85 Soviet forces attacked the economic and social base of the insurgents more systematically, targeting agriculture and livestock. Under economic pressure and competition from other elites (Islamists and ulama), more khans emigrated or defected to the government. Many observers—and mujahidin as well— feared that the insurgency might collapse under the heavy military pressure and the destruction of the economy.

In 1985–87, as the Soviet Union prepared to withdraw, external aid to the mujahidin increased significantly, including both higher-quality weapons and cross-border "humanitarian" programs for resistance-held areas. In April 1985, President Reagan signed National Security Directive 166, which authorized a new policy, consistent with the Reagan Doctrine, of driving the Soviets from Afghanistan "by all means available."[7] The U.S. budget for aid to the mujahidin, reportedly still matched by Saudi contributions, climbed to $470 million in 1986 and $630 million in 1987. Starting in September 1986, the United States supplied shoulder-held, laser-guided Stinger antiaircraft missiles to the mujahidin, the first time this ultrasophisticated weapon had been distributed outside NATO.

Cross-border assistance programs provided civilians living in areas controlled by mujahidin with food, cash for food, and support for health care, educational, and agricultural programs. European groups pioneered these operations, but USAID spending soon dwarfed their budgets. During 1986–90 USAID spent $60.6 million on health, $30.2 million on education, and $60 million on agriculture. Additional USAID money financed engineering projects, training programs in various fields, medical care in the United States for the wounded, road building, demining, and direct food supplies.[8]

As aid of all sorts increased, mujahidin became less dependent on the local population. Increasingly they lived in bases (*qarargah*) rather than in their homes and villages. After 1986 the superiority of Massoud's organization emerged more clearly as he moved out of Panjsher, founded the Supervisory Council of the North, and began capturing medium-sized garrisons throughout the Northeast in collaboration with other commanders. Some other mujahidin groups also became more mobile and established more civilian infrastructure.

In 1988–91 the Soviets withdrew their troops but continued to give military and economic aid to the Kabul regime. The eastern and southern frontiers, several important roads, and several provinces fell under mujahidin control in the course of the withdrawal.

After the Soviet withdrawal in February 1989, foreign supporters of the resistance pressured the exiled leaders to form such alliances as the Interim Islamic Government of Afghanistan and to launch offensives planned by Pakistani advisers, at Jalalabad and elsewhere. These offensives failed. To exercise better command and control of larger offensives, the ISI and the CIA increasingly shifted military aid from the exiled parties to specific commanders inside Afghanistan, particularly commanders of small forces who let the ISI control their strategy and tactics. This military policy contradicted the political policy of strengthening the IIGA.

During the first half of 1989, U.S. supplies declined, either in response to intelligence forecasts that the Kabul regime would fall soon after the Soviet withdrawal or because of a devastating fire in a Chinese factory where many of the weapons were made. By mid-1989, however, the United States and Saudi Arabia had agreed to supply $600 million each to the mujahidin by the end of the year; an additional $100 million from the United States brought the total to $1.3 billion. The weapons included Stingers, heavy artillery, and other arms considered appropriate for a shift from guerrilla to conventional warfare.[9] This policy was motivated in part by fear of the increased activity by Iran, which was promoting demands for power sharing by the Shiʻa parties and pursuing a rapprochement with the USSR and Kabul.

By November 1989, the United States and Saudi Arabia came up with another $715 million for fiscal 1990. The U.S. share of the aid was only $280 million, a reduction of the previous outlay by 60 percent. Saudi and Kuwaiti princes also contributed $100 million of their private funds. The weapons would be purchased and delivered with these funds through February 1990, one year after the end of the Soviet withdrawal, by which time, the CIA predicted, the mujahidin would win.[10]

When this prediction was not fulfilled and U.S. funds ran low, Saudi and Kuwaiti government and private sources supplied aid—about $1 billion in 1990 before Saddam Hussein invaded Kuwait on August 2.[11] Most of it went to Hikmatyar and Wahhabi groups, but when these groups opposed the Kuwaiti-Saudi-U.S. alliance in the Gulf War, they lost support from many Kuwaitis and Saudis. Hikmatyar also received tens of millions of dollars from Libya and Iraq.[12]

In March 1990 Hikmatyar, backed by the ISI and the Saudi intelligence agency, supported Tanai's coup, exacerbating dissension among the mujahidin. In May 1990 major commanders inside Afghanistan organized a National Commanders Shura. They claimed that the NCS would simply coordinate military strategy, but in fact they aimed to create an alternative to the ineffectual leadership of the exiled party leaders and the alliance between the ISI and Hikmatyar. After Massoud visited Pakistan as spokesman of the National Commanders Shura in October 1990, more U.S. aid went directly to him and other big commanders.

In Washington the consensus that had existed during the Soviet occupation broke up as a result of the Soviet withdrawal, the end of the Cold War, and the alignment of some resistance leaders with the anti-U.S. forces in the Islamic world during the Gulf War. In the fall of 1990 the Senate-House conference committee on the intelligence appropriations bill for 1991 cut the allocation another $30 million and held half of the $250 million appropriation in reserve—"fenced" it—so that disbursement of the funds would require further congressional approval. In June 1991 the Bush administration approved the off-budget transfer of $30 million worth of captured Iraqi weapons to the mujahidin. The administration's 1992 budget proposal, however, included no allocation for military aid to the Afghan resistance except in a contingency fund, and the program was terminated in fiscal 1992 under an agreement with the dissolving USSR. Private sources in Arab countries of the Gulf continued to provide aid estimated at $400 million per year.[13]

After the Soviet withdrawal, as military pressure on the countryside eased, agriculture and trade revived. Much of this renewed production took the form of opium growing, heroin refining, and smuggling; these enterprises were organized by combines of mujahidin parties, Pakistani military officers, and Pakistani drug syndicates. As the Islamist fighters with foreign funding—and opium revenues—became even more autonomous from the local society, various forms of imported radical fundamentalism also grew, especially among eastern mountain Pashtuns. For the first time, large numbers of Arab radical Islamist "mujahidin" entered the eastern provinces, strengthening nationalist resentments and extremist tendencies. Many other local commanders, regardless of social origin or political affiliation, increasingly behaved like traditional khans.[14]

Despite the continued aid, the spirit of jihad waned after the Soviet troop withdrawal, especially after the alliance between Hikmatyar and Tanai. The government no longer threatened Islam; the only foreign troops present were Arab mujahidin; and resistance leaders increasingly seemed to behave as self-interested power seekers rather than defenders of Islam and Afghanistan.

Those leaders whose efforts were most strongly oriented toward taking state power, notably Hikmatyar and Massoud, continued organization building. Both prepared to move to conventional rather than guerrilla warfare. Hikmatyar enjoyed extensive Pakistani and Arab assistance in this effort, as well as important revenues from the drug trade. In 1991 Massoud used the increased U.S. aid he received to expand his Islamic Army. These turned out to be the only mujahidin units mobile and extensive enough to contest power when the Kabul regime disintegrated.

8

Origins of
the Movement
of Jihad

Before the Soviet invasion in December 1979 and the flow of aid to mujahidin organizations that it provoked, the Afghan resistance's largely spontaneous, decentralized organizational forms reflected the dispersion of social control under the old regime. Modern warfare, aid from foreign powers that wished to reshape Afghan politics, and the participation of Islamist activists—these factors all transformed the movement, but only hindsight magnifies what were then small phenomena.

Soviet intervention and the arrival of foreign aid transformed the structure of the resistance and its relation to Afghan society. The Red Army's adoption of a more aggressive military strategy in 1981 or so, after the consolidation of control over the major cities and roads, escalated military pressures on the resistance. The mujahidin had received some aid and political pressure at least as early as 1979, but the aid began to have decisive political effects in 1981, when the Pakistani military regime officially recognized six parties based in Peshawar as representatives of the refugees and mujahidin.

Origins, Leadership, and Structure of the Uprisings

The resistance in Afghanistan did not begin as a reaction by the state elite of the old regime against the revolutionaries who had ousted them. Nor was it at first an Islamic revolution.

The power of the old regime had rested on a fraying coalition between the royal family's Kabul-based elite, which controlled the state apparatus, and local power holders (mostly khans) whom the state relied on for patronage but had pushed to the margins of national power. Since the time of Amir Abdul Rahman Khan, the Kabul-based state elite had been transformed from a tribal-warrior aristocracy to a rentier stratum dependent on state patronage. By the 1970s it lacked the social and organizational base to lead any popular movement. The weak rentier state on which the elite had depended provided it with no link to society through institutions of civil society, political parties, or the market. As with the elite of the Shah's Iran, individual members of this atomized elite were more likely to flee to the West than to engage in resistance.[1] At the local level the old regime had favored small local power holders, mainly landlords and khans, who acted as brokers for the state with officially recognized segments of the society. These leaders originally played important roles in the movement, especially in tribal areas, but even then they were often subordinate to religious leaders.

The leadership of religious figures, however, did not make the movement an Islamic revolution as the Islamists would define the term. The Islamist activists who later dominated much of the resistance had indeed already begun their struggle against the Afghan state. They had established bases in Pakistan, as well as underground networks of activists inside Afghanistan. But the activists were too few—about three thousand, including those in Pakistan—to set off a national revolt. They were also split by faction and ethnicity and did not have the nationwide cadre structure necessary to organize an uprising. They were thus unable to perform the functions of the communist cadres in the French and Yugoslav resistance movements, whose organizations provided the backbone of larger coalitions.[2]

The uprising against the PDPA started as a mass-based movement of a fragmented society without any unified national leadership. It included established local elites who had been encapsulated by the old regime, as well as various factions of the intelligentsia. It took many forms: local revolts under traditional social leadership; mutinies within the armed forces; revolts organized by Islamist—or in a few cases, Maoist—militants; and urban uprisings, which involved Islamists, Maoists, and many ad hoc leaders without previous political affiliation.[3]

Skocpol argues that a revolution often springs from a weakening of the state, as from defeat in war. The case of Afghanistan supports the theory: the state was weakened internally by the massive purges of the military and the bureaucracy, by military mutinies, and by factional wars in the party (between Khalq and Parcham, then between Khalqi supporters and opponents of Amin). With the state thus enfeebled, isolated revolts coalesced. The intervention of Soviet troops initially caused even further damage to the state apparatus, which was the first target of the Soviets before they turned their attention to the resistance. Several other garrisons mutinied, and desertions accelerated.

The initial purges cost the government ethnic links to such communities as the Nuristanis, some of whom were the first to revolt in July 1978. After the enactment of the reform programs, coercive intervention by the government in local societies provoked violent reactions. Groups revolted in response to the appearance of teams sent for land reform, the literacy campaign, education of women, conscription, and the census.[4] The weakened government's violent but ineffective response encouraged others to revolt.

After the purge of the Parchamis, the government became more Pashtun than any in a century, which further alienated the Shi'a and the Persian-speakers. The Shi'a and the Heratis seem also to have been inspired by the Iranian revolution of February 1979. Starting with the mutiny of the Herat garrison in March 1979, revolt spread throughout the Persian-speaking and Hazara areas. Like Nuristan, the Hazarajat became—and has remained—virtually independent of both Kabul and Peshawar. (These were the last two regions conquered and incorporated into the state of Afghanistan by Amir Abdul Rahman Khan.) Pashtuns reacted more slowly, for the rulers were Pashtun and treated the tribal areas—the ancestral homeland for many of them—with more care. But many of the eastern tribes joined the revolt after the 1979 harvest, and most of the rest did so after the Soviet invasion. Starting in the summer of 1979, a chain of uprisings by students, shopkeepers, and workers challenged the regime on the streets of Kabul itself. The government and Soviets did not bring these outbreaks under control until the summer of 1981.[5]

Whatever the underlying social structures that provided the basis for organization, the discourse that mobilized people was largely the popular tradition of jihad, merged at times with the traditions of self-sacrificing heroism recalled in the Pashto landai or the Persian epic *Shahnamah*. Especially in the immediate aftermath of Soviet intervention, traditional ulama preached, in accordance with Sunni jurisprudence, that when a non-Muslim power attacked the abode of the Muslims, jihad became not just a collective responsibility (*farz-i kifai*) of the community, to be carried out by the ruler, but an individual responsibility (*farz-i 'ain*) of every Muslim. Elders recalled fathers' and grandfathers' tales of the Anglo-Afghan wars. Women listened to tapes praising the role of women in jihad. Imams mobilized their congregations, pirs their murid, ulama and schoolteachers their students, army officers their conscripts, mullahs and khans their tribes, and women their husbands and sons.[6]

Political elites had previously found it difficult to gain followings for their ideological programs in a largely depoliticized society, but now numerous ill-defined, poorly organized, but highly motivated social groups searched for leadership and political direction. A variety of elites competed to meet this demand.

The leaders of most of the original local uprisings were traditional religious figures. Twenty-three of twenty-seven cases sampled from the files of the Cash for Food Program of the Swedish Committee for Afghanistan (SCA) include accounts of the original uprising.[7] Of these twenty-three uprisings, eighteen started with traditional leadership and five with Islamist activists, all in the Persian-speaking Northeast and West. Reports on eleven of the eighteen "spontaneous" revolts explicitly mentioned religious leaders with titles such as mawlawi, mullah, or sayyid. Especially when we consider that the commanders in the sample were more sophisticated than the average (they were interviewed and found reliable by SCA) and that they came disproportionately from Jamiat, the party whose activists were at the forefront in returning to Afghanistan to initiate revolts, the evidence for the traditional religious leadership of most uprisings is strong. Of all types of rural elites, the khans were generally the least active, for jihad was opposed to their economic interest in stability and also tended to strengthen their religious rivals for leadership.

The uprisings, though varied in form, followed a common pattern described by Roy:

> The revolt usually took the form of a mass uprising preceded by preaching and followed by an attack on the government post of the principal town of the district, using small arms (including flintlock guns). The post was usually captured with heavy casualties on both sides. The communist activists were executed, non-communist soldiers and officials allowed to go. Then the revolt would spread to the whole area in which there was tribal solidarity. The people who had taken part in this attack then spread out throughout any neighboring villages of their own ethnic affiliation. [Both *tribal* and *ethnic* are here used as approximations to *qawm*.] When the frontier of the territory of the ethnic or tribal group was reached, the dynamic phase was over. Members of the resistance did not attempt to go beyond their own territory.[8]

Among the tribes, although jihad required religious or nontribal leadership and forms of organization, it used many of the tactics of tribal warfare. In this type of warfare, as in traditional insurgency generally, the armed forces are simply the society in arms.[9] Because the mobilization is based on the society and economy of the social unit, it is vulnerable to interruptions for such economic activities as planting, harvesting, and trading. Insurgents tend to avoid risky actions that might endanger essential economic activities, and they find it difficult to coordinate large offensives because of disputes over the distribution of booty among rivals.

Some of the military uprisings were also spontaneous, organized by army officers with no political affiliation. For instance, in November 1979 Brig. Abdul Rauf and his troops killed the Khalqi officers and Soviet advisers in Asmar garrison, Kunar Province, and joined the resistance.[10] Other uprisings were organized by Islamist officers. Capt. Ismail Khan and Capt. Alauddin Khan, for example, staff officers who were members of Jamiat, led the March 1979 insurrection in Herat.

In areas from which more Islamist intellectuals had been recruited into Jamiat, revolts arose when some who had been exiled infiltrated the country bearing weapons from Peshawar. Unlike in 1975, much of the population rallied to them, for the ulama declared the struggle a jihad.[11] Militants of Hizb seem to have organized underground networks and preached *hijrat* (emigration from an area controlled by unbelievers), but not to have launched attacks until after the Soviet invasion.[12]

Local Organization and Finances

As much of the state apparatus disintegrated, rural society fell back on the parallel power networks that had previously operated within the bounds of state encapsula-

Table 8.1 Distribution of Mujahidin Units by Size within Major Parties

	Number of Units by Size				
Party	20–60 Men	61–100 Men	101–200 Men	Over 200 Men	Total Units
NIFA	140	29	3	1	173
HAR	64	29	21	0	114
HIH	57	36	20	2	115
HIK	19	11	14	4	48
JIA	96	83	42	5	226

Sources: Data from Johnson et al., "Southern Provinces"; Johnson et al., "Nothern Provinces"; Johnson et al., "Eastern Provinces"; and Johnson et al., "Western Hinterland Provinces," with emendations by the author. See Appendix A for further details.

Note: No data were available on Nangarhar or Bamiyan Provinces. The data are extremely approximate and reflect the situation of about 1984–1988. They do not fully account for the military units of the SCN, the Amir Hamza Division of Herat, or the Lashkar-i Isar of HIH. Data are probably less reliable for the traditionalist parties, expecially HAR.

tion. Increased reliance on primary social networks is a typical response to a breakdown of state power; the same pattern emerged in Libya after the Italian conquest led to the collapse of administrative institutions constructed by the Ottomans, and in Tajikistan after independence from Moscow.[13]

A typical group inside Afghanistan consisted of a commander and a small group of men linked to each other by some local social network—usually qawm, but sometimes a religious network, such as a madrasa or tariqa.[14] The men and the commander usually had dyadic patron-client relationships. As late as 1988, after some consolidation had taken place, studies commissioned by the CIA, which undoubtedly missed many small resistance units, found that 56 percent of such units contained twenty to sixty men, about the maximum size for units based on face-to-face interaction (Table 8.1).

A few of the original local uprisings seem to have been led by khans, but khans suffered from several disadvantages compared with the traditional religious figures. During the Khalqi period the state ceased to use the khans as intermediaries and instead treated them as feudal enemies, so many were killed or arrested. What influence the khans retained derived from their success in exploiting the rivalry among qawms. Jihad, however, required Muslim unity. A khan might be able to command a unit of twenty to forty men from his qawm, but for larger operations a leader outside the rivalry of the qawm network was often more effective. Some elders from aristocratic lineages could play such roles, especially in the big landlord–dominated society of Qandahar, but religious leaders whose authority derived from sources outside the tribal, kinship, or property structure were generally better able to lead such alliances.

Most of the original uprisings took place without the participation of political parties. Eleven of the twenty-three cases described in the Swedish Committee files explicitly stated that "no tanzims" were involved in the original uprisings, and in only five were party members involved.

During the spontaneous, traditionalist phase of the revolt, the local fronts supported themselves mainly with local resources. Traditionally organized insurgencies, in which the insurgent organizations are not autonomous or differentiated from the local society, have easy access to the resources of established elites.[15]

The data in the SCA files permit us to divide the resource base of the mujahidin fronts into six categories: Islamic direct taxes (*zakat* and *ushr*); indirect taxes (effective in areas with major trade routes or high-value commodities, such as carpets or, later, opium); donations from wealthy individuals; war booty; aid from the Pakistan-based tanzims; and direct aid from Arab and Western relief organizations.

The Hanafi fiqh requires Muslims to pay ushr (tithe) and zakat to the Islamic ruler. In the absence of a caliph who fulfills the Islamic duties of a ruler, the believers should pay directly to ulama, the poor, and mujahidin. Ushr consists of a yearly tax of one-tenth on production, mainly of grains and fruit. Zakat consists of a levy of 2.5 percent on stocks of wealth, mainly cash and livestock, sometimes including carpets. Modern Islamic economists have proposed ways of modernizing these taxes for a cash economy, but traditionalist ulama in Afghanistan have interpreted them as taxes in kind, which are appropriate to the large noncommercial sector of Afghan agriculture. Modern war finally did require a shift from taxes in kind to cash, a shift that the opium poppy was particularly well suited to accommodate.

Of the twenty-six fronts in the SCA sample, seven reported that in the early years of the war (until 1981 or 1982) ushr and zakat provided the entire year's livelihood for the mujahidin, with some surplus for the poor and ulama. Five fronts reported that these direct taxes covered about half of their needs, and two said they did not need these taxes because of other local sources of income. The files contain no information on how mujahidin collected the taxes. My impression is that no fronts carried out systematic monitoring of income and wealth. In some cases the better-off farmers and flock owners, encouraged by the preaching of ulama, contributed these taxes voluntarily to the mujahidin. In other cases commanders engaged in more forceful requisitions, especially as resources became scarce.[16]

The differences among these areas seemed to be due to the size of the local agricultural surplus (or deficit) and to the social structure. Five commanders of Pashtun tribal groups, mainly from the nang areas of Paktia and Paktika, did not mention any forms of taxation. It would not be surprising if the Islamization of tribal practices in these areas failed to extend to the payment of taxes, even to mujahidin. In these areas, which were fragmented by clan rivalries aggravated by partisan rivalries, any imposition of taxes would have been likely to provoke defections or revolt, as governments had found over the centuries. The main source of income in these areas was not agriculture but smuggling (or trade, as it is known locally).

In a few areas valuable marketed commodities provided easy targets for indirect taxation. A shura of mujahidin in Andkhoy District of Faryab Province in the Northwest levied zakat on the famous carpets of the area; the shura also taxed trucks that transported those carpets, as well as a salt mine that came under its control. Mujahidin continued to collect tax (in cash) on the "famous melons of Kunduz," but at a lower level than before. Mujahidin in Badakhshan and Panjsher mined and exported emeralds and lapis lazuli and levied taxes on merchants transporting the stones to market.

Booty is ultimately a less sophisticated form of indirect taxation. Before the consolidation of the Soviet presence, the Jamiat front of Khan Agha at Shakardara, north of Kabul, comandeered trucks going to Kabul from north Afghanistan or from the Soviet Union, seizing millions of afghanis in cash and tens of thousands of kilograms of food.[17] Most other fronts also reported that during this period they could easily capture food, cash, clothing, and weapons from the posts of the disintegrating Afghan armed forces and administration.

Most fronts also received donations—how voluntary, the files do not reveal—in cash and kind from shopkeepers and other relatively wealthy people. These included tea and sugar (absolute necessities), shoes (a chronic need), and cash, among other items. The original uprisings were in this respect typical peasant revolts, surviving on material contributions and brigandage.

Local military organization was similarly uncomplicated, developing on the basis of the "group": a commander and his men. At the beginning most fighters lived at home, were linked to the commander through a traditional personal network, and fought only to expel communist and government personnel from an ethnically or tribally defined "space of solidarity," to use Roy's term. The base of operations was the commander's guest house (*hojrah* or *mihman khana*), where he reinforced the loyalty of his followers by feeding them (recall that khans "feed the people").[18] The fighters received no systematic training.

These bases were generally localist in their orientation. The Islamic framework of jihad called for the liberation of Islamic territory from unbelievers, but the geography of the nation-state system was not integrated into the Islam of the village. In a qawm-based society with a low level of integration into a national community, both the average believer and the traditional mullah and alim saw that the primary responsibility of each mujahid was to liberate his local space of solidarity. As one of Massoud's coworkers wrote, "To tell a man who has lived in his village for decades 'go out of your district and fight the enemy base in a remote area,' seems not to be very appealing. To him defending the village is more important than [defending] the district or province."[19]

The need for weapons eventually drove even the most spontaneous and local groups of insurgents to seek affiliation with externally based leaders, but at first some traditionalist commanders relied on their own resources to obtain arms. One characteristic of traditionally organized insurgencies is that their "connection with the traditional (or established) elites provides them with easy access to money, goods, and services of various types." For instance, Qari Taj Baba, a traditionalist mawlawi from a prominent religious family of Ghazni Province, initially purchased weapons with his own money in the tribal territories of Pakistan.[20] Even before the influx of massive international aid, however, some fronts sent emissaries to Peshawar to ask for arms from the organizations and leaders who had established themselves there.

The Islamist cadres, on the other hand, did not face this problem: several thousand of them had received Pakistani training and weapons since 1974. After the outbreak of the initial revolts in 1978 and 1979, some Islamists returned to their native regions in rural Afghanistan with small quantities of arms supplied by Pakistan.

Regional Organizations

Throughout the war competing political elites proposed different frameworks for organizing political society in Afghanistan. Foreign powers generally favored exile-led political parties. As in past revolts, however, commanders and local leaders formed coalitions among mobilized social segments within regions. These coalitions often followed the traditional pattern of tribal coalitions led by a sayyid.

One such coalition in eastern Afghanistan was the Alliance of the Tribes (Qawms) of Kunar for Islamic Jihad (in Pashto, Da Islami Jahad da para da Kunar da Qaumuno Ittihad). This alliance, established in early 1980, grew out of a tribal lashkar that formed after the November 1979 revolt of the Asmar garrison under Brig. Abdul Rauf. This tribal unit laid siege to Chaghasarai (Asadabad), the provincial center of Kunar, but left itself vulnerable to aerial bombardment and heavy artillery. It also suffered from conflicts between militants of Hizb and Jamiat, who clashed over possession of the weapons captured from Asmar. The Alliance included the Nuristani fronts that had developed since 1978, together with Pashtun tribes and other ethnic groups of the Kunar Valley. Its leader was Sayyid Shamsuddin Majrooh, a poet and jurist from a leading family of Sufi (Naqshbandi) background who had been the principal author of the constitution of New Democracy.[21]

The Shura of the Hazarajat also followed this model. As the state broke down in the winter of 1979, revolts spread across the Hazarajat; by summer the area was almost free of government presence. For the first time in almost a century, the Hazarajat became independent of Pashtun rule. To reestablish order and some sort of administration, major mirs and sayyids, the traditional ruling strata of the Hazaras, met in Waras, Bamiyan, in September 1979, with some radical young intellectuals (mainly sons of mirs). Together they established the Shura-yi Inqilabi-yi Ittifaq-i Islami-yi Afghanistan (the Revolutionary Council of Islamic Unity of Afghanistan).[22]

The mirs dominated the gathering, but they elected a sayyid and religious leader,

Sayyid Bihishti, as president of the council. Bihishti was a weak rural figure known as a follower of Ayatollah Khui of Najaf, Iraq, rather than of Khomeini. A former army officer (rare among Hazaras), Sayyid Muhammad Jagran became military commander of the shura. Jagran—the name means "major"—was from the same area as Bihishti; rather unusually, he was both a mir and a sayyid. The shura established a government of the Hazarajat, complete with bureaucracy, corruption, and a large but ineffective army.[23]

National Organization

From the beginning of the struggle until the overthrow of Najibullah, the Afghan resistance confronted two major obstacles to forming a national leadership: the political vacuum and social fragmentation left by the old regime, and the necessity of forming that national leadership on foreign soil. Only in Pakistan could leaders be safe from aerial bombing and enjoy easy access to international networks of transportation and communication, neither of which had been a consideration during previous revolts in Afghanistan.

The only national leader recognized throughout the country was the former king, Zahir Shah, who continued to live in Rome. But the royal family had ruled by spending and redistributing foreign aid; ties to its former tribal base had become attenuated. The king himself had been an ineffectual ruler who relied on more strong-willed members of his family and court. His closest adviser, his nephew and son-in-law, Abdul Wali, requested a visa to consult with resistance organizations in Pakistan in 1979, but Pakistan refused.[24] Islamabad would hardly permit a member of the royal family that had demanded self-determination for the Pashtuns in Pakistan to establish a tribal army or an alternative Afghan capital in Peshawar.

Because the old regime had never legalized political parties, no leaders could validate a claim to represent a national constituency through past electoral results or through any other form of activity. Qawm- and religion-based networks had only regional support. No party or even any professional or social group possessed a national organization capable of mobilizing people. The faction-ridden Islamists alone possessed offices, organizational structures, and cadres with political and military training. Originally Hikmatyar's Hizb and Rabbani's Jamiat were the only Islamist organizations. In 1979 Yunus Khalis, a mawlawi from the Ghilzai tribal areas of eastern Afghanistan, split with Hikmatyar to form his own faction of Hizb. Then, after the prisons in Kabul were emptied in the confused amnesty that followed the Soviet invasion, Abd al-Rabb al-Rasul Sayyaf escaped to Peshawar. An Azhar-educated former teacher at the Sharia Faculty, he had been Rabbani's deputy in the Islamic movement at Kabul University. He established his own organization with Saudi support in 1981.

Some leaders who had emerged as loosely acknowledged spokesmen for social groups supportive of the old regime also fled to Peshawar, where they competed for Afghan followers and foreign patronage. Sayyid Ahmad Gailani, the leader of the Qadiri Sufi order in Afghanistan, was closely allied to the royal family by marriage and patronage—he had received the Kabul Peugeot dealership. He arrived in Peshawar in 1978, as did Sibghatullah Mujaddidi, whose father's cousin, killed in Kabul in February 1979, was the last national pir of the Naqshbandi order in Afghanistan. Mujaddidi had a long history of Islamic activism, though he had never joined the Islamists. Another conservative Islamic activist who arrived in 1978 was Mawlawi Muhammad Nabi Muhammadi, an alim who headed a madrasa in Logar Province and had emerged as a spokesman for the traditional ulama in the parliament of New Democracy.

These Islamic leaders succeeded in gaining foreign support or recognition, unlike the various secular or nationalist-oriented politicians who had emerged from the government or parliaments of New Democracy. Before the Soviet invasion, foreigners aligned with the resistance movement were mainly Islamic; the military regime of General Zia and the Islamic parties in Pakistan supported the Islamists, as did both the government and the religious establishment in Saudi Arabia. No foreign power, least of all the regime of General Zia, supported secular or nationalist leaders.[25]

The foreign power most concerned with unity of the resistance during the early stages appears to have been Saudi Arabia. The Saudi government was initially skeptical about the prospects of the resistance, having been disappointed in supporting rebels against leftist regimes in Yemen and elsewhere.[26] Saudi officials repeatedly insisted on unity among Islamic parties as a condition for giving or expanding aid. In practice, the Saudi definition of unity seems to have been the enunciation of a common platform by a group of exiled party leaders. Saudi Arabia funded several such pseudoalliances in 1978 and 1979.

Especially right after the Soviet invasion, leaders of some insurgencies inside Afghanistan, as well as members of the old-regime elite who fled to Pakistan, tried to revive the Pashtun-based traditions of Afghan national identity and resistance, such as the Loya Jirga. For those who identified with aspects of the old regime, the Loya Jirga represented the legitimate and genuine traditions of the Afghan nation, which consisted of a Pashtun tribal core, allied with other ethnic groups living in the country's territory, and acknowledging the important but not dominant role of Islamic figures. For the Islamists and the opponents of Pashtun domination, the Loya Jirga represented political forces they opposed, not a primordial tradition. Recent research in social science, endorsing the arguments of Afghan Islamists, has argued that such national traditions often are political creations, not natural occurrences; their origins can be every bit as artificial as the imposed creations of modernity with which they are sometimes contrasted.[27] Indeed, as we have seen, the institution of the Loya Jirga developed out of the state's attempt to modify Pashtun tribal traditions in order to create a tribal-nationalist legitimation for state power.

Immediately after the Soviet invasion, as increasing numbers of refugees swarmed across the borders, "every day about 1,000 Afghans led by community elders, mujahid commanders and former members of parliament [from the New Democracy period]" met in mosques in Peshawar.[28] Muhammad Umar Babrakzai, a French-educated former Supreme Court justice, became chairman of the Loya Jirga. Babrakzai was typical of the leaders who emerged from the Jirga—educated members of the old-regime elite, nearly all Pashtun with strong tribal backgrounds. Many of the assembled leaders had ties of kinship or patronage to various social networks inside the country, but unlike the tribal leaders who had met in jirgas to elect the Durrani monarchs or summon the tribes to fight the British, they generally did not lead the battle themselves. Babrakzai, for instance, came from the clan recognized by the old regime as leaders of the Jadran tribe in Paktia. He organized a jirga in Peshawar and helped French activists convene a session of the International People's Tribunal in Paris, but in Jadran territory itself the jihad was being led by a charismatic mullah, Mawlawi Jalaluddin Haqqani.

The Peshawar Jirga continued until May 13, 1980, when 916 members proposed setting up an Islamic National Revolutionary Council (in Pashto, Islami Milli Inqilabi Jirga), which would in turn elect an executive committee as a sort of cabinet. The Jirga invited the leaders of Islamic organizations to join as individuals, in accordance with the tradition of the old regime, which honored Islamic figures as a part of the nation and recognized their role in jihad but did not grant them positions as political leaders or representatives of social groups. Only Mujaddidi and Gailani offered any support, however, and their competition weakened the Jirga. The Saudi- and Pakistani-funded alliance of parties, dominated by the Islamists, called the Jirga "another enemy of the sacred Islamic revolution of Afghanistan."[29] Pakistani authorities also withheld support.

The Jirga set up a commission to seek foreign recognition and assistance; the initial reaction from the Saudi royal family was mildly encouraging, but no aid materialized. Generous financial aid to the Jirga might have sustained it, as it later sustained the alliance of the parties, and as foreign aid to the Afghan state had in effect underwritten the Loya Jirgas of past decades. Without external support, however, the Jirga crumbled, undermined by the weakness and fragmentation of Afghanistan's civil and political society. According to Kakar, himself a supporter of the Jirga and a severe critic of Pakistan, "The coup de grace to the Jirga came from within." A member of the Gailani family seized the chair, violating the Jirga's carefully negotiated rules. The resulting boycott by a majority of participants brought the Jirga to an end.[30]

Several other attempts to revive the idea of a Loya Jirga were stymied. Muhammad Yousof, the first prime minister of New Democracy, who had fled to Germany, visited Pakistan in July 1980 to revive the movement. The supporters of the Loya Jirga movement then shifted their center of activities to the Durrani refugee center of Quetta, for the Pakistan refugee administration in Peshawar was openly supporting

Hikmatyar. In September 1981 more than three thousand "influential persons," most from the Durrani tribes of Qandahar, converged on Quetta for a meeting, but Pakistani pressure forced them to reassemble in the smaller town of Pishin. There, too, the police tried to suppress the meeting. Not only did the Islamists denounce it, but the moderate Islamic parties also boycotted it, alleging that Parchamis had infiltrated it.[31] The Jirga proclaimed Zahir Shah national leader—a move some of its members regarded as premature—but the meeting gave rise to no permanent institutional structure.

Proposals for a Loya Jirga continued to emerge, mostly from exiles affiliated with the old regime. In a June 1983 interview with *Le monde,* Zahir Shah called for a Loya Jirga; Afghans, he said, should form a body capable of representing their national interest in international negotiations that were taking place regarding their country. Several of the former king's advisers visited Pakistan and Saudi Arabia in order to canvass support for the move; his cousin and brother-in-law Humayun Assefy visited Pakistan in October 1983, while a number of other former officials gathered in Taif, Saudi Arabia.[32] But this effort also dissolved when the Saudi religious establishment prevailed upon King Fahd to maintain support only for the Islamist groups. The call for a Loya Jirga reemerged periodically as a component of proposals for a political settlement emanating from the former king, his supporters, the United Nations, or Western sources (including this author).

Before Soviet military pressure escalated and massive foreign aid arrived, local resistance fronts, most under the leadership of local elites, had sprung up across Afghanistan. The insurgents carried what weapons they owned or could capture, plus, in some cases, arms from sources in Pakistan. Resistance fronts had few stable organizations that extended beyond the immediate qawm, and few could establish either regional or national political or military leadership. Some mujahidin heard various leaders in Peshawar declare jihad over the BBC or on tape cassettes, but they had few organizational links to these voices. The Islamists introduced their cadres into these struggles, while a variety of leaders in Peshawar joined shifting and shaky coalitions that were encouraged or discouraged by Saudi Arabia and Pakistan. Such structures could not long survive the Soviet invasion and the influx of aid to the mujahidin that it provoked.

9

International Aid, War, and National Organization

The Soviet invasion of Afghanistan violated basic norms of international conduct and law, appeared (if deceptively) to pose a threat to the oil resources of the Persian Gulf, and placed the first Muslim state to join the modern state system under the occupation of an avowedly atheistic power. The Pakistani effort to aid the mujahidin received substantial and growing support from the West, led by the United States; from the Islamic world, led by Saudi Arabia; and from China. Various agencies of the Iranian government also aided Shi'a mujahidin parties who followed the line of Khomeini.

The Pakistani ISI, which administered the distribution of aid, insisted on controlling and directing the military operations of the mujahidin. But because the mujahidin did not form a unified military force under a single political leadership, the ISI relied on a form of brokerage based on the distribution of weapons to parties and to small groups of fighters. This strategy, which exacerbated the social fragmentation of Afghanistan, favored those categories of "strongmen" (commanders) who conformed to Pakistan's military and political goals.

To implement this system of brokerage, the ISI distributed weapons not only for use in operations but also (and in greater quantity) as reward for carrying them out. For each plane confirmed downed by a Stinger, for instance, the commander responsible received two more missiles. Hence the downing of a Soviet plane cost the ISI and its CIA suppliers at least three missiles: one that was fired and two that were delivered as a reward. And Stingers were the most closely held and strictly controlled weapon. This tactic is traditional in governments' pursuit of "tribal" policies; it both corresponded to and stimulated the tribal norm of competing for influence by obtaining resources from external patrons. Together with the even more profligate Soviet aid, this program probably made Afghanistan the world's largest recipient of personal weapons during the late 1980s and left it by 1992 with more such weapons than India and Pakistan combined.[1]

U.S. aid grew from $30 million in 1980 to more than $600 million per year by 1986–89. Saudi and other Arab aid matched or slightly exceeded the American share.[2] The Chinese contributed to the effort mainly by selling Soviet-style weapons to the CIA for transfer to the ISI and then the mujahidin. In addition to the CIA and the ISI, the Saudi General Intelligence Agency (al-Istakhbarah al-'Amah), headed by Prince Turki al-Faisal Saud, helped to manage this immense flow of money and arms. The Afghan operation became the single largest program of each of these agencies.

In Saudi Arabia two major aid sources supplemented the official aid overseen by Istakhbara. The Muslim World League (Rabitat al-'Alam al-Islami, or Rabita), headed by the chief of the Saudi religious establishment, Shaikh Abd al-Aziz bin Baz, funded many schools and madrasas. The support committee led by Prince Salman bin Abd al-Aziz, governor of Riyadh, funded Arab volunteers who wc rked for Sayyaf's party and went to fight alongside the mujahidin in Afghanistan. Arab volunteers, largely recruited by the Muslim Brotherhood and other, more radical organizations, coordinated their humanitarian and military activities through the Islamic Coordination Council. This office, founded by Abdullah Azam, a Palestinian educated at al-Azhar who was assassinated by a car bomb on November 24, 1989, collected money from many Islamist sources in the Middle East.[3]

The arms pipeline consisted of three parts, controlled by the CIA, the ISI, and the resistance parties. The CIA, using Saudi and American funds, bought weapons from China, Egypt, Israel, and elsewhere.[4] To preserve the myth of "deniability," the CIA provided no American weapons until the decision to supply Stingers in 1986. The CIA transported the weapons to Pakistan, mostly by sea to the port of Karachi, but occasionally by air to Islamabad.

Once the weapons had arrived in Pakistan, the ISI took custody. It transported most of the containers to warehouses near Rawalpindi (in Ojhri, the headquarters of the ISI's Afghanistan unit); others went to Quetta, in much smaller amounts. From there the weapons were trucked to depots controlled by mujahidin groups in the border region. The CIA paid for these transport expenses through monthly deposits into special accounts in Pakistan. In addition to weapons, mujahidin needed food, clothing, and other supplies, also paid for from the CIA accounts. When these funds ran short, "Arab money saved the system," but benefited only the Islamists.[5]

It was the responsibility of the parties to distribute the weapons to commanders and to oversee their transport into Afghanistan, although the transport itself was left to the private sector. Attempts to build up a centralized supply network would have interfered with the flourishing businesses of both Afghans and Pakistani Pashtuns from the tribal territories, who had converted smuggling and trucking operations into the far more profitable transport of weapons and drugs. The transport of weapons was extremely expensive; in 1986 it cost $15–20 per kilogram to move supplies from Pakistan to north Afghanistan, amounting to about $1,100 for one mortar or $65 for one bomb. Total delivery costs ran to $1.5 million per month. To pay these costs, the Saudi Red Crescent maintained offices in the border regions. These offices, funded by the Saudi Afghanistan support committee and staffed by Arab volunteers, gave Afghan Islamist parties 100 percent of estimated transport costs plus an extra 5 percent for contingencies; they gave traditionalist-nationalist parties only about 15 percent of total costs.[6] Ironically, this system may have contributed to the greater political consolidation of northern Afghanistan, for fewer parties could actually maintain fronts there, and even traditionalist leaders tended to affiliate themselves with Jamiat or Hizb (or with the government) in order to obtain weapons.

The weapons pipeline provided ample opportunity for corruption. A common scheme through which both ISI officers and their contacts in the Afghan parties could enrich themselves was the false receipt. An official of the party military committee would sign a receipt for more arms that he actually received, and the difference would be sold to private arms dealers by the ISI officer, who would then give a kickback to the Afghans. Commanders could also sell weapons, either to pay for transport of other weapons or for profit (*salah furush,* "weapons seller," became a standard term of abuse). A number of commanders used such proceeds to found profitable businesses, some in legal enterprises and some in the burgeoning drug trade. The logistics system was ideally suited for trade in drugs: it operated under military control and provided a large network of trucks running loaded to the Afghan border and empty coming back.[7]

The mode of distribution of these weapons profoundly transformed political and social relations in Afghanistan, from the national to the local level. The Peshawar Jirga had tried to establish an Afghan national authority in exile modeled on the old regime. The leaders of the Jirga intended to set up a unified military command to receive all foreign aid. If the plan had succeeded in establishing a near monopoly on aid to the resistance, the military command would still have had to rely on brokerage with local commanders, but it could have limited recognition to one or a few in any locality.

Instead, in 1980 the Pakistani military regime officially recognized six mutually hostile Islamic parties as representatives of the refugees and mujahidin. (Pakistan later added a seventh party, that of Sayyaf, because of its Saudi support.) From the ISI's point of view, recognition imposed some organization on a chaotic situation. As Brigadier Yousaf, director of ISI's Afghanistan operations during 1983–87, wrote, "It was then a firm principle that every Commander must belong to one of these seven parties, otherwise he got nothing from ISI."[8] Nor was the ISI alone in playing on interparty rivalries. Anyone seeking power in his locality could offer himself and his followers to one of the parties as a force against its rivals. As a result every locality had up to seven would-be commanders, each with an independent source of supply.

This system served several Pakistani goals. A unified Loya Jirga would threaten Pakistan's control over Afghan refugees and over the military and political conduct of the war. General Zia, the chief martial law administrator, had been a military adviser in Jordan during Black September in 1970, when the PLO nearly overthrew King Hussein. The Arab heads of state who gathered for the First Arab Summit in Cairo in 1964 had established a single, unified Palestine Liberation Organization, with its own treasury, tax system, and diplomatic identity.[9] The main guerrilla organization, Fatah, was then able to wrest control of this internationally constituted apparatus from its sponsors. Iran later created such a united organization for the Shi'a parties, the Hizb-i Wahdat. Pakistan, however, always gave separate checks and separate arms deliveries to each of several recognized parties or commanders.

Furthermore, to guard against Pashtun nationalism, Pakistan insisted that only religiously oriented parties and leaders could operate on its soil. It never recognized Afghan Millat, the Pashtun nationalist party, or permitted members of the Afghan royal family to contact the resistance directly in Pakistan. The Saudis treated Afghanistan as a religious issue and deferred to their own religious establishment, which preferred the Islamists, and particularly the Salafis among them.

In the early days after the invasion, the ISI armed commanders directly, while urging them to join recognized parties. In 1983 Gen. Akhtar Abdul Rahman, director of ISI, discovered that the Achakzai commander Ismat Muslim, who had refused to join any party, had ensnared nearly the entire ISI Quetta operation in a web of bribery, gunrunning and drug smuggling. After the officers involved were jailed, the military regime reorganized the operation. Each party was required to set up a military committee, whose heads would meet jointly with ISI agents every few months, and each commander was required to join a party. (The resulting pressure on Ismat Muslim to join a party was one of the factors that led him to defect to Kabul in 1984.) The ISI set percentage allocations for each party in quarterly meetings. Approximately 80 percent of the weapons were sent to the parties for distribution to the commanders. The rest continued to go directly to commanders for special operations determined by the ISI or as rewards for participating in training, but these weapons still counted towards the party's total allocation. The ISI provided training as well as weapons. Yousaf claims that 80,000 mujahidin passed through courses between 1983, when the program was expanded, and 1987.[10]

Next to withholding aid from nonparty members, the most controversial aspect of ISI operation was the allocation of resources among the parties. The Islamists consistently received more than the traditionalist-nationalists. According to Yousaf, in 1987 the Islamists received over two-thirds of all weapons (Table 9.1), with Hikmatyar's party receiving the most. Sayyaf's party, with virtually no social base in the country, received more than any traditionalist party and almost as much as Jamiat. These parties also received virtually all of the private Arab money.

The ISI claimed that its decisions reflected objective analysis of military effectiveness, not political favoritism toward Hikmatyar and Sayyaf. As dubious as this claim is, there is no doubt whatever that the Arab donors decided on the basis of political preference. Old-regime parties, which received no Arab cash to pay for the transport of weapons or the operation of offices, often sold weapons to pay these expenses. This desperate strategy corroborated the ISI's opinion that the old-regime parties were corrupt.

Apart from its political bias, the ISI advocated a purely military, even tactical view of the war. This approach developed out of the history of the Pakistan military, which considered politics antithetical to government or policy. Pakistani generals had never

Table 9.1 Estimated Distribution of Full-Time Mujahidin by Party within Regions, 1988

	Region							Weapons Allocation, 1987
	Northeast	North	West	Greater Kabul	East	South	Nationwide	
JIA (%)	55	41	65	23	9	19	34	18–19
HIH (%)	25	10	8	15	15	20	16	18–20
HIK (%)	1	3	2	17	28	15	12	13–15
ITT (%)	2	0	4	3	1	1	2	17–18
NIFA (%)	7	12	4	22	30	10	16	10–11
ANLF (%)	0	4	0	2	2	2	1	3–5
HAR (%)	8	27	13	13	11	29	15	13–15
Other (%)	3	4	4	5	4	4	4	—
Total	14,360	6,995	7,450	8,030	16,690	5,970	59,485	
Index of Fragmentation[a]	.62	.73	.55	.83	.79	.81	.79	

Sources: Weapons allocation data from Yousaf and Adkins, *Bear Trap*, 105. Other data from Johnson et al., "Northern Provinces"; Johnson et al., "Southern Provinces"; Johnson et al., "Eastern Provinces"; and Johnson et al., "Western Hinterland Provinces."

Notes: The numbers should be considered rough estimates rather than exact counts. The study undercounts mujahidin with weak party allegiances, members of traditionalist parties, and Shi'a mujahidin. It does not include Massoud's Islamic Army or Hikmatyar's Army of Sacrifice. The numbers for the South may be particularly misleading (see text for details).

The regions are defined as follows:

Northeast: Badakhshan, Kunduz, Takhar, Baghlan, Parwan, Kapisa, Laghman.

North: Samangan, Balkh, Jauzjan, Faryab, Bamiyan.

West: Herat, Badghis, Farah, Ghor.

Greater Kabul: Kabul, Wardak, Logar.

East: Kunar, Nangarhar, Paktia, Paktika, Ghazni.

South: Qandahar, Zabul, Uruzgan, Helmand, Nimruz.

[a]Rae's index of fragmentation of party systems.

accepted orders from political leaders, to whom the military conceded no legitimate role in security issues, let alone war. Hence the Pakistan army's view of the relation of politics to war differed from the views of such strategists as von Clausewitz and Mao Tsetung. The ISI claimed that its strategy during the Soviet occupation was solely to inflict maximum military damage on the Soviet forces in Afghanistan. Many in the Reagan administration and the Congress endorsed this view, adding to it a desire to punish the Soviets for American losses in Vietnam.[11]

The ISI regarded itself as the general staff of the war, planning and commanding the actions of the mujahidin. The ISI would plan operations, pick targets, and promise commanders and parties extra weapons for carrying the operations out. It also sent advisers into Afghanistan to oversee key operations. In the view of the ISI, those fighters who best succeeded in carrying out these operations deserved the most support. Parties with a high level of outside funding, weak links to the local society, educated commanders, and ideological proximity to the ISI were the most effective by these criteria.

The ISI explicitly excluded as criteria for receipt of aid the extent of a party's political support among Afghans or its potential for establishing a stable government. As Yousaf proudly wrote, "My critics were taking into account political consider-ations and biases which, as a soldier, I was fortunately able to ignore." A com-mander's success in mobilizing a large coalition, in setting up a civil administration to replace the state in a region of the country, or in attracting support and defectors from Kabul city or the regime army were all considered irrelevant.[12] Mujahidin with links to local society might hesitate to attack the ISI's designated targets, either to avoid reprisals on the civilian population or to preserve such assets as bridges or oil pipelines that served local communities as well as the regime. An Afghan commander who developed his own political-military organization in Afghanistan might develop strategic priorities different from those of "headquarters" in Rawalpindi. The ISI regarded such upstarts as a general might view a lieutenant who organized his own staff. It would support that commander's rivals or subordinates in order to weaken him or pressure him into accepting ISI directions. Inevitably, no unified Afghan national organization or leadership developed out of this system.

National Organization

Recognition by the ISI gave the parties political resources. Leaders selected by the Pakistanis began with varying levels of support but developed their parties by redis-tributing the money and weapons they obtained through social and political networks. The quantity of outside aid together with the strength and extent of these networks determined the size and structure of each party.

In the relations between society and the parties there were several levels of organization. The local units at the base corresponded to primary social units, such as qawm. The leaders of these units belonged to various elite categories, linked by characteristic social networks. These networks formed the basis for the organization of regional coalitions and national parties. Roy distinguished four networks in the resistance, corresponding to social categories to which commanders belonged: ulama, Sufis, tribal khans, and Islamists.[13] Networks of the first three developed from largely nonpolitical activities unconnected to the Islamic resistance, although they could then be mobilized for political purposes. The Islamists' network belonged to political rather than civil society. The initial Islamists were recruited predominantly from students and a few professors at Kabul University, but their social ties grew out of membership in a political movement, the result of politicization, not a means to it. Another political network, relevant mainly to the exile headquarters of the traditionalist parties, was that of the old-regime elite.

Commanders could belong to several networks at once, and no party corresponded completely to a particular social network. Opportunism and pragmatism played a role in party membership, and each network was also segmented by language and qawm. If a prominent leader of one organization belonged to a particular qawm, members of that qawm tended to join that group. Some organizations, particularly those with superior organization or relations to external donors, were better able than others to provide such practical needs as weapons and food. And a leader might join a different party from that of his local social rivals. For instance, because Panjsher Valley forces were led by Ahmad Shah Massoud of Jamiat, the rival Andarabi Valley forces joined first Hizb-i Islami and then the government, although the commander of Andarab, Juma Khan, was neither an Islamist nor a communist but a traditional khan.[14] This pattern of microsegmentation by qawm, encouraged by the system of distribution of weapons, explained much of the fragmentation of affiliation at the local level.

The political elite of each party consisted of a leader, headquarters staff, and commanders. Commanders usually belonged to parties, but the mass of mujahidin owed loyalty to their commanders on the basis of local social networks. A commander who shifted political allegiance took his followers with him. Only Hizb-i Islami (Hikmatyar) seems to have established party membership for individuals, distributing membership cards inside Afghanistan. The traditionalist parties functioned instead as coalitions of mobilized social segments. Refugees in Pakistan were all required to affiliate themselves with parties, but most refugees joined parties through an intermediary, the refugee malik, just as most mujahidin joined through their commander. At first the malik even received the ration cards for the whole social unit, but the refugee administration eventually distributed cards directly to individuals.[15]

Each party had a characteristic ideology or outlook. The parties also differed in the degree to which they adopted a political or military strategy, the nature of that strategy, and the character of their international links. We can characterize the social base of each party through an analysis of the social and educational background of leaders, headquarters staff, and commanders.

Tables 9.2, 9.3, and 9.4 present the ethnic and educational background of the exiled headquarters staff of the seven Pakistan-based Sunni parties. These tables also include data on commanders of Jamiat, the only group of commanders on whom I had comparable data. Table 9.5 presents the same data on ethnicity and secondary education of exiled leaders in a different format for comparison with data published by Roy on leading resistance commanders.[16] Note that these commanders are those Roy judged to be powerful enough to represent the "new political elite of Afghanistan"; small commanders, especially of the traditionalist parties, are underrepresented. Table 9.6 summarizes these factors, as well as data from Table 9.1 on the geographical distribution of commanders and the share of ISI-distributed weapons each party allegedly received in 1987.

National Islamic Front of Afghanistan (NIFA)

Mahaz-i Milli-yi Islami-yi Afghanistan was the most nationalist party and the closest to the old regime, the structure of which it replicated in the relationships between headquarters staff and commanders. The party leader, Pir Sayyid Ahmad Gailani, the head of the Qadiriyya Sufi order in Afghanistan, is closely aligned with the royal family. The Qadiri tariqa in Afghanistan has been associated with a liberal interpretation of Islam and, like the old regime, has accommodated secular customs of both tribal khans and westernizers.

Gailani married a granddaughter of Amir Habibullah. When the royal family bestowed the Peugeot dealership in Kabul upon Gailani, one of the principal sources of his wealth became royally guaranteed monopoly profits on sales of an imported luxury good to the elite in Kabul, who in turn lived mainly off the circulation of foreign aid and a few export commodities.[17] The Gailani family was thus economically as well as maritally tied to the Kabul elite of the old regime.

The program of NIFA attributes the conflict in Afghanistan not to flaws in the old regime but to "a group of traitors who have sold out their country [and] who have no roots or basis among the Muslim people of Afghanistan." The "traitors," NIFA said, had acted with the "military, political, and economic support of a foreign country." The program repeatedly emphasizes the defense of Afghanistan's national identity, sovereignty, and territorial integrity and says that NIFA supports "nationalism and democracy"—terms that are transliterated from the English.[18] The program is hostile to the Islamists, a hostility reflected in an editorial in the party magazine: "All totalitarians Islamic or non-Islamic, theist or atheist follow the same modus operandi with only different mottos and maxims."[19]

The party was structured patrimonially like the old regime. The core leadership consists of the pir and his sons and daughter. The other headquarters staff consists of the second echelon of the old-regime elite, largely eastern and Ghilzai Pashtuns educated in elite high schools and Western universities (Tables 9.2, 9.3, 9.4).

Table 9.2 Tribal and Ethnic Origin of Exiled Sunni Mujahidin Leaders and JIA Commanders

Party	Number of Leaders from Group							
	Pashtun			Tajik/ Farsiwan	Sayyid	Other	Sample Size	Kabuli
	Durrani	Other	Total					
NIFA	0	13	13	0	3	1	17	4
ANLF	1	8	9	1	4	0	14	5
HAR	0	6	6	1	0	0	7	0
HIH	0	10	10	2	1	1	14	0
HIK	1	5	6	0	0	0	6	0
ITT	0	5	5	1	1	0	7	1
JIA (exiles)	0	4	4	13	1	0	18	0
JIA (commanders)	10	10	20	35	7	9	71	2

Sources: See Appendix A.

Note: No exiled Durrani leaders were Muhammadzais.

Table 9.3 Secondary Education of Exiled Sunni Mujahidin Leaders and JIA Commanders

Party	State Secular School			State Madrasa	Private	Sample Size
	Elite	Military	Other			
NIFA	5	1	2	2	1	11
ANLF	2	0	1	2	1	6
HAR	1	1	0	1	2	5
HIH	0	0	4	3	0	7
HIK	0	0	1	1	3	5
ITT	0	0	1	1	3	5
JIA (exiles)	1	0	3	7	1	12
JIA (commanders)	2	2	26	10	18	58

Sources: See Appendix A.

The commanders had similar ethnic backgrounds but different educations. Eight of ten major NIFA commanders identified by Roy were Pashtun (Table 9.5); almost three-fourths of NIFA commanders in the Orkand surveys were in the tribal East or the southern Pashtun part of Kabul Province. Gailani, or at least the royalist establishment that he in part represented, had a larger following among the tribes of the Qandahar area than the number of his commanders in the survey indicates. The principal commander of the Barakzai tribe, Haji Abdul Latif (assassinated in 1990 and succeeded by his son Gul Agha) was affiliated with NIFA.

Commanders of NIFA included a small number of traditionalist mullahs or ulama, but the largest group, most of whom were khans, had traditional private (but not madrasa) educations. A few NIFA commanders had modern secular educations: these were mainly the sons of khans who remained in NIFA either out of deference to their fathers or because they favored a moderate nationalist government over either Islamism or communism.

Like the leaders of the old regime, Gailani planned not to modernize traditional society but rather to establish—parallel to that society—a modernized apparatus led by Western-trained officials. Most of his commanders led small, traditionally organized insurgent units. There were far more small groups among NIFA commanders than in any other party (Table 8.1). The headquarters used foreign aid to build up a conventional force based in Peshawar, led by U.S.- and Soviet-trained army officers, for cross-border raiding.

NIFA had mixed relations with Pakistan and always resented the failure of the United States to reward its relatively pro-Western orientation with greater assistance. The party did, however, enjoy the patronage of some conservative lobbying groups in

Table 9.4 Higher Education and Training of Exiled Sunni Mujahidin Leaders and JIA Commanders

Party	Sample Size	Leaders, Commanders with Higher Education, by Location					
		Total	Afghanistan	West	Soviet Bloc	Foreign Islamic Institution	Other Asian/Muslim Country
NIFA	17	15	11	11	1	0	6
ANLF	14	9	7	3	0	1	1
HAR	8	5	5	2	2	0	0
HIH	13	13	12	1	0	1	0
HIK	6	2	1	0	0	1	0
ITT	7	4	3	2	0	1	0
JIA (exiles)	18	15	15	2	0	3	0
JIA (commanders)	74	28	27	0	0	0	1

Sources: See Appendix A.

Note: Some individuals studied in more than one location and are counted more than once.

Table 9.5 Ethnicity and Education of Leaders of Major Sunni Mujahidin Parties

Party		Ethnicity					Education				
		Pashtun	Tajik	Sayyid	Other	Sample Size	State Secular	State Religious	Private Religious	Other Private	Sample Size
NIFA	exiles	13	0	3	1	17	8	2	1	0	11
	cmdrs.	8	1	—	1	10	3	0	1	7	11
HAR	exiles	6	1	0	0	7	3	0	2	0	5
	cmdrs.	12	2	—	5	19	0	0	17	2	19
HIH	exiles	10	2	1	1	14	4	3	0	0	7
	cmdrs.	15	4	—	1	20	15	0	1	4	20
HIK	exiles	6	0	0	0	6	1	1	3	0	5
	cmdrs.	9	1	—	0	10	4	1	3	2	10
JIA	exiles	4	13	1	0	18	4	7	1	0	12
	cmdrs. (Roy)	10	26	—	5	41	26	3	9	3	41
	cmdrs. (Rubin)	20	35	7	9	71	30	10	18	3	58

Sources: For exiles and JIA commanders (Rubin), see Appendix A. Other commanders from Roy, "New Political Elite," 77.

Notes: Roy's data on commanders do not distinguish sayyids. Differences in sample size between the two halves of the table are due to missing data.

Table 9.6 Recognized Sunni Mujahidin Parties

Party	Leader	Ideology	Headquarters Staff	Commanders	International Links
NIFA	Sayyid Ahmad Gailani. Spiritual Leader (pir) of Qadiri Sufi order. Arab lineage traced to Prophet. Married into royal clan.	Traditionalist-nationalist (Royalist). Most pro-Western.	Leader's family; Western-educated Pashtuns of old regime.	Tribal khans; some of their educated sons.	Weak; some U.S. conservatives.
ANLF	Hazrat Sibghatullah Mujaddidi. Cousin of executed Pir of Naqshbandi Sufi Order. Long-time conservative Islamic activist. Religious lineage from India.	Traditionalist-nationalist.	Leader's family. Western-educated Pashtuns of old regime.	Too few to analyze; probably khans and some ulama.	Weak.
HAR	Mawlawi Muhammad Nabi Muhammadi. Traditional alim, head of madrasa. Ahmadzai Pashtun of Logar. Member of parliament under New Democracy.	Islamic traditionalist.	Leader's family. Western educated Pashtuns from Logar.	Privately educated ulama, mullahs. Mostly Pashtuns, some Uzbeks. Most Tajiks left for Jamiat.	Weak. Close to one weak Islamic party in Pakistan.
HIH	Gulbuddin Hikmatyar. Former student at Faculty of Engineering,	Radical Islamist. Views Afghan society (not just	State-educated intelligentsia; mainly (not	State-educated intelligentsia; mainly	Favored by Pakistan ISI, Pakistani and Arab

	Kabul U. Kharruti Pashtun from detribalized settlement in North.	communist regime) as un-Islamic. Favors party domination.	only) Pashtuns from outside tribal society.	Pashtuns, but from all Sunni groups.	Islamists.
HIK	Mawlawi Yunis Khalis. Militant alim educated in British India. From Khugiani Pashtun tribe of Nangarhar.	Islamist; no elaborate ideology. Favors rule by ulama. Very anti-Shi'a.	State-trained intelligentsia and ulama from Pashtun tribal families linked to the leader.	Some state-trained intelligentsia, but mostly militant tribal ulama. All Pashtun.	Well supplied by ISI and CIA because of high body counts.
JIA	Professor Burhanuddin Rabbani. Lecturer at Sharia Faculty of Kabul U. Trained at al-Azhar. Tajik from Badakhshan.	Moderate Islamist. Views Afghan society as corrupted but Muslim. Favors alliances.	State-trained ulama, Tajik and some Pashtuns; Tajik secular-trained intelligentsia.	Best and most commanders. State-trained Tajik (and some Uzbek) intelligentsia, including ulama; Tajik Sufis; Alikozai tribal ulama of Qandahar.	Some links to ISI and Arabs; intermittent. Some top commanders favored by U.S.
ITT	Professor Abd al-Rasul Sayyaf. Lecturer at Sharia Faculty of Kabul U. Trained at al-Azhar. Kharruti Pashtun from Paghman.	Radical Islamist, Salafi. Very anti-Shi'a.	A few individuals linked to leader or Saudi Arabia. Mostly Pashtun.	Opportunist, responding to leader's command of Arab funds. Very few, but very well funded and armed. Base in leader's home town, Paghman.	Favored by Saudis, other wealthy Arab donors from the Persian Gulf.

Sources: See text and Appendix A.

the United States, in particular the Committee for a Free Afghanistan (housed in the Heritage Foundation) and Freedom House. Gailani also sent many emissaries to lobby and testify before Congress. The chairman of the NIFA military committee, Col. (later Gen.) Rahim Wardak, was an American-trained professional officer whose good personal relationships with some ISI officers assured NIFA of some supplies. The Arab Islamists, who considered NIFA too "nationalist" (watani) and insufficiently Islamic, refused to provide aid, including payment for transport of weapons.[20]

Afghanistan National Liberation Front (ANLF)

In many respects, Jabha-yi Nijat-i Milli-yi Afghanistan was the Naqshbandi equivalent of NIFA. Its ideology was traditionalist Islamic; the party leader, Sibghatullah Mujaddidi, was a member of a prominent family of pirs, the leaders of much of the Naqshbandi tariqa in Afghanistan; and the party had a patrimonial structure centered on the family of the leader. Perhaps because Mujaddidi is not a pir himself, he was far less successful than Gailani in bringing his family's tribal following into the party. Mujaddidi's mother was a Muhammadzai; he and most of his brothers married women from prominent Ghilzai families, especially of the Sulaimankhel tribe.[21] His family thus had marriage links with the tribal aristocracy of the old regime. He also attended Habibia high school with other members of the elite and is fluent in English, French, and German, as well as Arabic.

In spite of Mujaddidi's links to the westernizing elite and true to the heritage of the Naqshbandi revival, his career was devoted to the teaching and preaching of Islamic orthodoxy. He studied for six years at al-Azhar and taught Islamic studies at virtually all major educational institutions in Kabul during the 1950s and 1960s. When Prime Minister Daoud cracked down on both religious and tribal leaders in the late 1950s, Mujaddidi was among those jailed, probably because he had preached against the country's growing ties with the USSR.[22] Freed under New Democracy, he continued preaching against the threat of communism. He participated in the organization of traditional ulama to protest blasphemy in the newspaper *Parcham* in 1970, and he maintained good relations with the professors who advised the Muslim Youth at Kabul University and later formed the core of Jamiat. He appears to have had no direct relationships with the students themselves, however, and he had a bitterly antagonistic relationship with the main student leader, Gulbuddin Hikmatyar. In 1972 he founded an organization of ulama but fled the country when Daoud once again seized power. Rather than join the Islamist revolutionaries in Pakistan, he went to Europe, where he became the imam of the Islamic Center of Copenhagen, supported by Libya. He came to Peshawar after the April coup in 1978.

Mujaddidi thus represented a link between the most Islamic wing of the old regime and the more moderate Islamists, including Rabbani. He was chosen as the leader of one of the early coalitions of resistance organizations, the ANLF, founded in

June 1978.[23] When the coalition broke up he remained in control of the office and kept the name for his party.

The ANLF program, like that of NIFA, identifies the targets of the jihad as "a handful of deviants of Islam who seized the political power with the force of tanks, heavy artillery, planes and savage killings." The ANLF states its intention "to defend our national traditions," but it identifies the ultimate goal as "the establishment of an Islamic society in which all the political, economic and social affairs [will] be founded on the teachings of Islam," a stance that goes beyond the NIFA program.[24] Unlike the programs of Hizb and Jamiat, the ANLF's tiny pamphlet elaborates no ideology and mentions no organizational structure.

In composition of headquarters staff, ANLF resembled NIFA. The core of leadership consisted of the leader's brothers and sons, who are classified with sayyids in Table 9.2. Nearly all the rest of the staff was Pashtun, reflecting the tribal base of the family's following and the structure of the old regime. Significant numbers attended elite high schools or were educated in the West. The ANLF, however, did not attract as many former high military officials as did NIFA.

Indeed, ANLF hardly existed as a military force, and it had too few commanders to be included in the Roy survey used in Table 9.5. The ANLF lacked both military professionals from the old regime and Pakistan-trained Islamic revolutionaries— either of which might have convinced the ISI that the party could use weapons well— so the party never developed a stable supply relation with Pakistan. The ANLF was so loosely structured, however, that joining it was a viable alternative for commanders and refugees who would have preferred not to join any party at all. This appeal, plus some Naqshbandi allegiances, accounted for the adherence to the party of the Kunar Valley tribal front led by the Majrooh family of sayyids. The Karzai family in Qandahar, leaders of the Popolzai tribe, likewise affiliated themselves with Mujaddidi. (Their Barakzai rivals were affiliated with NIFA.)

Mujaddidi had probably the worst relations with the ISI of any of the seven recognized leaders: because he received the fewest weapons, he had the least to lose. He was the only party leader who publicly denounced ISI's interference in Afghan affairs and its playing favorites among the leaders. In spite of his family's links to the Muslim Brotherhood—his cousin Harun, who lived in Egypt, was arrested by Nasser for his membership in that organization—and in spite of his fluency in Arabic and his good personal relationship with the Saudi royal family, he never received significant assistance from the Arab support groups.

Movement of the Islamic Revolution (HAR)

Harakat-i Inqilab-i Islami-yi Afghanistan was the third traditionalist-nationalist party recognized by Pakistan. Its leader, Mawlawi Muhammad Nabi Muhammadi, is a traditionally educated alim from the Ghilzai Ahmadzai tribe in Logar Province south of Kabul. This party represented the traditional private ulama, including some Naqsh-bandi Sufis and mullahs. The influence of the ulama originally attracted the largest number of mujahidin to this party but also gave rise to the worst organized and most corrupt of the party structures. Harakat seems to have been the party most easily penetrated by KhAD.[25]

Mawlawi Muhammadi directed a large madrasa in Logar and also had extensive landholdings in the Helmand Valley, two areas that would become important strong-holds for his party. During New Democracy he was elected a member of parliament from Logar and emerged as the spokesman for the traditionalist ulama. Like Mujad-didi, he was involved in the 1970 demonstrations against the *Parcham* newspaper.

Muhammadi fled to Pakistan in 1978. Like Mujaddidi, he had a personal reputa-tion as an Islamic leader, but he had no organization. This reputation helped him become the leader of Harakat, the alliance that succeeded the ANLF. When that alliance, too, disintegrated, Muhammadi took its name for his own newly created organization. Despite the name, Harakat-i Inqilab was far from revolutionary. (*In-qilab* can mean "uprising" rather than "revolution" in a Marxist or Islamist sense.)

The party's short program combines traditionalist Islamic appeals (augmented with a few modern references to capitalism, collectivism, and nonalignment) with territorial (not ethnic) nationalism. The program blames Afghanistan's problems on "the destructive and reactionary hands of colonialist powers" and their agents.[26]

The program advocates applying the Holy Qur'an and the Sunna of the Prophet to all areas of social life but provides no specific instructions. Unlike the Islamists, Harakat does not specifically invoke the rightly guided caliphs and does mention the ulama-controlled jurisprudence (fiqh) as a source of law. Politically the program favors a "true and genuine Islamic republic" but does not describe the structure of such a system. There is no explicit criticism of previous governments and no discus-sion of ideology or organization of the Islamic movement.[27]

The headquarters of Harakat was also organized in a patrimonial fashion. The leader and his two sons presided over a staff almost exclusively comprising Pashtuns from Logar. The one prominent Tajik was Yahya Nauroz, a Persian-speaker from Logar, who was a major general and chief of operations in the Defense Ministry under Daoud's Republic.[28] The staff was split between Muhammadi's fellow traditional ulama (who attended private madrasas) and those from the old-regime elite who attended elite secular schools. In spite of the prominence of ulama in Harakat, none of the leadership was educated in a leading international Islamic institution. They thus represent the inward-looking, traditionalist, provincial ulama of Afghanistan.

As in the other two traditionalist parties, the old-regime officials in the leadership are quite socially distant from the commanders, who belong to the same stratum as the leader himself. Of the commanders studied by Roy (Table 9.5) nearly 90 percent were ulama with private madrasa educations, and the rest had less education. The com-manders (during the mid-1980s) were less Pashtun than the leadership; about a quarter were Uzbek, although there were no Uzbeks in the party's leadership.

Because ulama are to some extent outside the ethnic struggles, Harakat (along with Hikmatyar's Hizb) had less regional concentration than the other parties. Its commanders came from all regions and all Sunni ethnic groups in the country. Over time, however, the Tajik members tended to gravitate toward the better organized and better funded Jamiat, and some of the Uzbeks toward the government-funded militias (and to some extent toward Hizb-i Islami); Harakat gradually became more Pashtun as a result, developing particularly important concentrations in Logar and in the Helmand Valley. Harakat commander Mullah Nasim Akhundzada became a powerful warlord in the Helmand Valley based on opium growing. This traditionalist commander sold the raw material to more modernized Islamists and nonpolitical syndicates for processing and export. His power was so extensive that he was the only Sunni traditionalist singled out by Najibullah in his appeal to seven major commanders in April 1988. Akhundzada was assassinated in Peshawar in 1990, and his brother Ghulam Rasul succeeded him. Before his death, Akhundzada greatly reduced opium growing as part of an agreement with the U.S. Ambassador to Pakistan, Robert Oakley, although the State Department later reneged on the agreement, citing laws prohibiting negotiations with drug traffickers.

Because Harakat's staff included some professional military officers and because the party had a large number of commanders—probably more than any other party at the beginning of the war—it received a significant number of weapons from the ISI. But the party never enjoyed the favor of the Arab Islamists who financed the expensive transportation of weapons from Pakistan, a circumstance that may have inspired some commanders of the northern ethnic groups to leave Harakat and turn to the Islamist parties. Many of the weapons that Harakat received were sold, some for profit and some to raise cash to transport the rest. The passive character of Harakat's leader and the social base of its commanders rendered the party politically inconsequential. Mujaddidi, whose forces were numerically dwarfed by Muhammadi's, played a far more prominent role.

Islamic Party of Afghanistan, Hikmatyar (HIH)

Hizb-i Islami-yi Afghanistan (Hikmatyar) was the most revolutionary and most disciplined of the Islamist parties. Whereas Jamiat included the "professors" from the Kabul University leadership, along with most of the Tajik students, Hizb represented the most radical part of the student movement, including most of the Pashtuns. In social and educational background Hizb most resembled Khalq, except that Khalqis came from tribal backgrounds and were often trained in the USSR, whereas Hizb leaders came from less tribal areas and were educated solely in Afghanistan.

The leader of the party, Gulbuddin Hikmatyar, is a Kharruti Pashtun from the settlements of the northern Afghanistan plains (the Imam Sahib District of Kunduz, on the border of Tajikistan). The Kharrutis, once a client tribe of the Hotakis, a leading

Ghilzai tribe, themselves claim to be Ghilzais. Some Pashtuns, however, do not even consider the Kharrutis full Pashtuns by descent, so their status is relatively low in the traditional genealogical tribal hierarchy.

Hikmatyar attended high school in Kunduz and military school in Kabul. He then enrolled in the highly competitive American-sponsored Faculty of Engineering at Kabul University. Hikmatyar joined Parcham while he was a high school student in Kunduz, but at the university he abandoned both that affiliation and his studies, instead embracing activism in the Muslim Youth movement. In the early 1970s he served a prison term for ordering the murder of a Maoist student but was released in time to escape to Pakistan during Daoud's rule.[29] Hikmatyar's radical Islamism (and hence anticommunism) and the superior organization of his party made Hizb the favorite of not only the Pakistani and Arab Islamists—including the ISI officers—but also moderate Pakistani generals and the operations wing of the CIA.

The party included an Islamist core that was well organized on several levels. Members carried cards that reflected at least three degrees of membership: those who joined before the 1975 uprising; those who joined between 1975 and the communist coup in 1978; and those who joined after the coup.[30] Hizb was the only party to hold limited internal elections; the first category of members—the only ones allowed to vote—elected Hikmatyar as leader in 1986. The mujahidin were supposed to follow the party, not their commander, who could be transferred by Hikmatyar. Arms, too, belonged to Hizb, unlike in other parties, where weapons were in effect the property of the commander.

The ideologically committed members of Hizb, including most of those recruited from the refugee camps, generally conformed to this structure. A number of traditionally organized fronts throughout the country affiliated themselves with Hizb, however, to obtain weapons and differentiate themselves from their rivals. Nearly every Pashtun tribe or clan had one branch or faction affiliated with Hikmatyar, however unlikely such an affiliation might appear on social or ideological grounds. The generous weapon supplies and funding for transport available from Hizb made the party attractive to commanders in the North who for whatever reason—often local rivalries—did not want to join Jamiat.

Most headquarters leaders of Hizb, as we have seen, were Pashtuns of provincial origin, and some that are classified as non-Pashtuns are actually Pashto-speaking members of occupational or religious descent groups. They had modern state educations (mostly secular) and university educations in Afghanistan (Tables 9.2–9.4). Unlike in the traditionalist parties, the commanders came from the same social groups as the headquarters staff (Table 9.5). More than other parties, Hizb was an integrated modern organization in which recruitment and promotion were based on individual ideology and skills rather than on social roles.

In no region or Sunni ethnic group of the country was Hizb-i Islami either dominant or absent. The one area where it had a contiguous and strategically important presence was the Dasht-i Shamali (northern plain), just north of Kabul, and the adjacent Kohistan (mountain) region. The one Hizb commander singled out by Na-jibullah in his April 1988 appeal was Ustad Farid, a Tajik schoolteacher with several hundred mujahidin around Charikar, the major town of Shamali. Ustad Farid briefly served as prime minister of the first interim government of the Islamic State of Afghanistan after the fall of Najibullah in April 1992.

Hizb-i Islami (Hikmatyar) was about three-fourths Pashtun. Its strong presence in the Northeast (Table 9.1) included the Shamali and Kohistan fronts, Tajik and Uzbek qawms that joined largely as a result of local rivalries, and Pashtun settler communities (but not, generally, the Pashtun nomads whose tribal structures were intact).

Roy notes that Hizb tended to recruit "in pockets where tribal structures have broken down or which have a mixture of groups originating from different tribes."[31] The largest such pocket of Afghans in the 1980s was not in Afghanistan at all but in the refugee settlements of Pakistan, and it was here that Hizb had its greatest success. With the support of the Pakistani military and administration and with financial aid from Arab supporters, Hizb gained privileged access to the refugee communities. It built an extensive network of schools designed to recruit refugee youth to the party.[32]

The fourteen years between the Khalqi coup and the fall of Najib provided ample time for Hizb to recruit a new generation through these institutions. According to Rastegar, Pakistani favor enabled Hizb "to control more schools than any other Afghan party in Pakistan," a total of 250, with 43,500 students and a staff of 1,500 teachers and administrators.[33] The graduates of these schools formed the core of the new generation in Hizb, including most of the soldiers of Hikmatyar's conventional military force, the Army of Sacrifice (Lashkar-i Isar).

Hikmatyar consistently placed the long-term goal of Islamic revolution above resistance to the Soviets or to the Kabul regime. His militants were commonly engaged in fighting against fronts of all other parties, for his most important strategic goal was securing the dominance of Hizb over all the Islamic forces.[34]

Islamic Party of Afghanistan, Khalis (HIK)

Hizb-i Islami-yi Afghanistan (Khalis) arose from a split within Hizb-i Islami in 1979. Although the rift was ostensibly caused by the desire of Khalis to engage in more active combat against the regime, it also reflected a social cleavage within the Islamist coalition.[35] Khalis represented the charismatic fundamentalist ulama of the eastern tribes. These ulama had opposed aspects of Zahir Shah's government and fought against Daoud, but they differed from the Islamist militants in political orientation, social base, and mode of organization. Although some of the Islamist students from the eastern tribes joined Khalis, the party ultimately came to be dominated by the tribal ulama.

The autobiography of Mawlawi Khalis, which functions as a sort of party program, begins in good Pashtun style with his genealogy.[36] He mentions that both his father and his grandfather were mawlawis and then that he is from the Khugiani tribe, Ibrahimkhel clan, Banikhel lineage. The Khugianis are perhaps the smallest of the seven Durrani tribes, and they settled long ago in the valley of the Kabul River between Kabul and Jalalabad, in the middle of Ghilzai territory.

Mawlawi Khalis, born in Afghan year 1298 (1919–20), was the oldest of the seven leaders, belonging to the same generation as Muhammadi, Mujaddidi, and Gailani and distanced from the youthful leadership of the other Islamist parties. He was educated at home and in private madrasas in eastern Afghanistan and the Northwest Frontier Province of British India before the Afghan government had established a nationwide state school system. He taught and preached for some time in the Friday mosque of the Jabbarkhel clan. This Ahmadzai clan of Nangarhar, neighbors of the Khugiani, had been appointed *khan khel* of the Ghilzai by the Mughal emperor Akbar.

Khalis has been involved in politics, he claims, since 1941, when he was appointed a teacher at the judicial training school in Kabul (Dar al-Quzzat). Like other Islamists, he defines his politics as those of the rightly guided caliphs. He preached over the radio, edited several Islamic publications (one with Mujaddidi), published and translated several books, and taught in several institutions, including Dar-ul-Ulum, the leading government madrasa. He, too, participated in the 1970 protest against the *Parcham* newspaper. He says that he never changed his "color" for the ruler of the day: "I neither assisted the royal regime nor furnished praise for the exactions of the tyrannical rule of Daoud, nor did I stop my tongue from condemnation of the corrupt measures of capitalists and communists."[37]

Khalis, like Mujaddidi and other Islamists, fled the country after Daoud's coup. With his fellow Islamist refugees, Khalis pursued armed struggle from Pakistan, but he found that disputes—which he attributes to corruption in the use of material resources—prevented their work from being effective. He says that he assumed leadership of a separate organization after repeated requests from some of his companions.[38]

At all levels, Khalis's party was almost entirely Ghilzai and eastern Pashtun, although Roy did find one Tajik commander of the party (Table 9.5). The party's fighters, according to Gellner, were largely "tribal puritans," among whom a charismatic mullah or alim assumes leadership of forces that Islamicize tribal practices and fight for an Islamic order.[39] Khalis reverted to his role as the religious leader of a mainly Ghilzai tribal coalition, led by his own family and the Arsala lineage, the leading family of the Jabbarkhel. Besides the leader, the party's most powerful figures were the Arsala brothers: Haji Din Muhammad, the deputy leader who ran the party's internal affairs; Abdul Haq, the Kabul commander; and Haji Abdul Qadir, the Nangarhar commander. Abdul Qadir became the leader of the Jalalabad shura after the fall of Najibullah.

The mujahidin of Khalis were almost all eastern and Ghilzai Pashtun who lived in the area between Pakistan and Kabul. Much of their vigorous military activity was in effect cross-border raiding, for they could hit their targets during brief missions from

Pakistan.[40] Commanders include some Islamist intellectuals of these tribes, but most are fundamentalist ulama.

The Khalis commander with the greatest international reputation was Abdul Haq, who, although he left high school early in order to take to the hills against Daoud, qualifies as an Islamist intellectual because of his state secular education. Like Massoud and Hikmatyar, Abdul Haq tried to overcome the localism and segmentation of Afghan society to build a guerrilla movement that would genuinely threaten the Soviets and the Kabul regime. He had concluded that after 1980 the government was not threatened by rural insurgencies that did not interfere with the operation of the state apparatus.[41] By the mid-1980s he had built up a powerful guerrilla movement around Kabul and an underground network inside the city. This organization controlled at least several hundred fighters, perhaps over a thousand. Abdul Haq tried to enforce the principle that weapons belonged to the organization (the front, not the party as a whole) rather than to the individual fighter, even imprisoning several mujahidin for selling arms.

This organization gradually decayed, however, undermined by KhAD penetration in Kabul and ISI manipulation in Pakistan. The Pakistani officers who wanted to maintain strategic and political control of operations found Abdul Haq too independent. In a system called subcontracting, the ISI supplied Abdul Haq's subcommanders with weapons directly in return for their undertaking ISI-planned actions. Abdul Haq, who communicates effectively in English, traveled frequently to the West with the American journalist and right-wing activist Kurt Lohbeck, who acted as his publicist while simultaneously reporting for CBS Evening News. Abdul Haq met both President Reagan and Prime Minister Thatcher, procuring Stinger and Blowpipe antiaircraft missiles. He also met with Soviet advisers in Kabul, who sought his views on national reconciliation.[42] He traveled to U.N. headquarters in New York in June 1988 to discuss plans for an interim government after the signing of the Geneva Accords, and he cooperated extensively with the U.N. secretary-general's representative for the next four years.

More typical of Khalis's fronts was that of Mawlawi Jalaluddin Haqqani in Paktia, the core of the resistance in that mountainous, tribal province. Haqqani was one of the seven commanders cited by Najibullah in his April 1988 speech. Mawlawi Jalaluddin, like Mawlawi Khalis, was educated in the Northwest Frontier Province, at the Haqqani madrasa in Peshawar. He wrested leadership of the Jadran tribe from the Babrakzai lineage recognized as khans by the old regime.

Mawlawi Jalaluddin both led his own forces and acted as a coordinator of other forces of the Jadrans, including the many small units affiliated with NIFA; for large offensives, he included other tribes as well. He was the main local leader of the offensive that took Khost in March 1991. At the orders of the ISI, Mawlawi Jalaluddin had a huge base built in Zhawar along the Durand Line.[43] The base, which had electric generators, flush toilets, and large storage areas for weapons and other supplies, was built by a Pakistani construction company paid with Saudi money.

Haqqani's front was a traditionally organized, religiously led tribal coalition with many elements of modern infrastructure. Its compact supply lines and excellent relations with both ISI and CIA (which appreciated the high body counts that Haqqani obtained) enabled it to expend ammunition freely in numerous offensives.[44] Haqqani traveled abroad like Abdul Haq, but to Saudi Arabia rather than the West. Other Khalis fronts (like that of Mullah Malang among the Ghilzais of Qandahar) were similar. Because of a Pashtun tribal composition and ready access to weapons supplies, Hizb-Khalis was the party to which dissatisfied Pashto-speaking commanders from NIFA and, less commonly, Harakat, tended to repair.[45]

Islamic Society of Afghanistan (JIA)

I have already described the origins of Jamiat-i Islami-yi Afghanistan as a relatively moderate, predominantly Tajik Islamist party. In the course of the war Jamiat developed into the most powerful party of the resistance, the main voice for non-Pashtuns, especially Persian-speakers. As the party spread beyond its original ideological base, it became a more complex and heterogeneous organization, drawing on Islamist, Sufi, and ulama networks and developing an important presence around Qandahar as well.

The leader of Jamiat, Burhanuddin Rabbani, who became acting president of the Islamic State of Afghanistan in June 1992, is a Tajik from Badakhshan who was educated in the state religious schools and at al-Azhar. He is the senior surviving member of the professors of the Sharia Faculty who led the original council of the Islamist movement. Both a state employee and a relatively young man (he was born in 1940), he did not take a public role in the New Democracy–era Islamic protests in which Mujaddidi, Muhammadi, and Khalis participated.

Rabbani was part of three major networks of the resistance: he was a leader of Islamists at the university, he was respected as an alim, and he had some links to Naqshbandi figures in the North, although he does not seem to practice Sufism himself. These interconnections were reflected in factionalism among the party leadership, which was divided between ideological Islamists and more pragmatic activists linked especially to the party's regional and ethnic base. Some state-trained ulama were Pashtuns and preferred Rabbani to Hikmatyar because of his formal religious training, but the rest of his networks were mainly limited to Persian-speaking areas (including some Uzbeks living in such predominantly Tajik areas as Badakhshan). Just as Hizb-Hikmatyar became identified with the ethnic character of its largely Pashtun base, so Jamiat, despite the ideology of its leader and major commanders, became increasingly (but never exclusively) a vehicle for the aspirations of Tajiks and other Sunni Persian-speakers.

Rabbani allowed his commanders much more autonomy than did Hikmatyar. Commanders retained property rights in the weapons transferred to them and were free to work out their own strategies and organizational models, even when this brought them into conflict with ISI. Jamiat seems to have benefited from more skilled cadres than in Hizb, and the autonomy that the commanders enjoyed—as well as their fortunate distance from the Pashtun areas on the Pakistan border—led to the development of the most sophisticated resistance fronts in Afghanistan. The most sophisticated of all, a veritable protostate, was the front led by Jamiat Commander Ahmad Shah Massoud, including the Supervisory Council of the North and the Islamic Army (Urdu-yi Islami). Three of the seven commanders singled out by Najibullah in his April 1988 speech were Jamiat commanders: Massoud, Capt. Ismail Khan of Herat, and Abdul Basir Khalid, an Uzbek of Faizabad, Badakhshan. Jamiat exercised a measure of independence from the ISI by founding a military academy and running its own three-month training courses for mujahidin.[46]

More than three-quarters of the headquarters leaders of Jamiat on whom I have information are Persian-speaking (including one sayyid), and the rest are Ghilzai Pashtun. There are no native Kabulis among them. Two-thirds of the exiled leaders had religious educations, most in the state system. Nearly all had university educations in Afghanistan, and three had studied at al-Azhar. The Pashtuns in the leadership are state-educated ulama linked to Rabbani.

The commanders' backgrounds are somewhat more varied.[47] Nearly 30 percent are Pashtun, about 60 percent Persian-speaking (including sayyids); most of the rest are Uzbek, with a few Nuristanis (Tables 9.2, 9.5). There are virtually no Kabulis. About half of the commanders, however, studied or worked in Kabul for part of their lives, a proportion similar, for instance, to that of PDPA Central Committee members. This experience introduced them to national politics. A large majority had modern secular educations. Jamiat commanders among both Uzbeks and Durrani Pashtuns, however, are much more traditional leaders, much less likely to have had modern secular educations. The Ghilzai and eastern Pashtuns of Jamiat, often linked to ulama in the leadership, more resembled the commanders of Hizb-Hikmatyar. It is remarkable to note, in view of the generally low level of education in Afghanistan, that thirty of seventy-four Jamiat commanders in the database had attended some institution of higher education, all but one of them in Afghanistan. (One former army officer had been trained in Egypt.)

Jamiat was clearly the dominant party in the mainly Tajik Northeast, where Massoud established the Council of the North, and in the West, around Herat, where the March 1979 uprising developed into the multiprovincial front of Capt. Ismail Khan. Across the North, Jamiat also included a network of ulama, Sufis, and some Tajik and Uzbek khans. In addition, the anti-Pashtun Tajik leftists ("Maoists") split, with some joining the government and others turning to Islamism and joining Jamiat on ethnic grounds. Both Massoud's organization and the headquarters in Peshawar managed to attract some well-educated Kabulis who played important technical roles.

Jamiat also had important commanders north, south, and east of Kabul. Finally, around Qandahar the main commander of the third of the three senior (Zirak) Durrani tribes, the Alikozai, was Mullah Naqibullah, a traditional alim who joined Jamiat after a brief period with Mujaddidi. Whatever his reasons for the shift, one cannot help but notice that among the main tribal groupings around Qandahar, the main Barakzai leader was a member of NIFA, the main Popolzai leader was a member of ANLF, and the main Ghilzai leader was a member of Hizb-Khalis.

Jamiat thus combined the strong Islamist revolutionary background of many of its exiled leaders with the more political and pragmatic approach of some commanders. This was reflected in its complex relations in the international system. Jamiat usually had good relations with the Arab Islamists, but in 1986 the Arabs temporarily cut off supplies to the North because Rabbani met with President Reagan in Washington. Likewise, Jamiat enjoyed ostensibly warm relations with the Pakistani Jama'at-i Islami and the ISI, but party commanders sometimes resisted ISI direction. The arms allocation to Jamiat, though large, was not proportionate to its strength in the country; Hizb-Hikmatyar, for example, received more weapons from ISI.

Massoud's relations with the ISI had ups and downs, for he insisted on planning his own strategy. His distance from Pakistan prevented ISI officers from undermining him through the sort of hands-on subcontracting they had employed against Abdul Haq, but they used Hikmatyar commanders to pressure him. Massoud countered Pakistani pressure with his own links to the West and to the USSR. He negotiated a truce directly with Soviet forces in 1983 without consulting Rabbani, a truce apparently authorized by Andropov in Moscow. On several occasions Massoud sent emissaries independent of Peshawar to the United States, and he maintained his own offices in Peshawar and London (both staffed by his English-speaking brothers), as well as in Paris.[48] Massoud, who had attended Istiqlal Lycée, enjoyed a special relationship with the French government and press, which was the first to publicize him in the West. French intelligence sent its own agents to meet with him. Massoud also enjoyed excellent relations with both the Swedish Committee for Afghanistan (which some Pashtuns referred to as the Swedish Committee for Panjsher) and the British organization Afghan Aid. By the end of the war he was receiving hundreds of thousands of dollars, perhaps millions, in developmental and humanitarian aid from these organizations and from USAID for food, schools, health clinics, and engineering projects.

Jamiat developed good ties to Iran, especially when that nation began emphasizing Persian culture rather than Shi'ism in its dealings with Afghanistan and Central Asia. After the Iran-Iraq war, Rabbani visited Iran frequently and always enjoyed a warm welcome; he also advocated recognizing the Ja'afari school of jurisprudence for Shi'a in Afghanistan. In 1991 Jamiat signed an agreement to promote Persian culture with Iran, Tajikistan, and the Shi'a alliance Hizb-i Wahdat.

Islamic Union for the Freedom of Afghanistan (ITT)

Ittihad-i Islami Bara-yi Azadi-yi Afghanistan, the last of the seven parties to be recognized by Pakistan, was mainly a vehicle by which its leader distributed the funds he collected from Arab sources. The leader, Abd al-Rabb al-Rasul Sayyaf, was a Kharruti Pashtun from Paghman, Kabul Province, like Hafizullah Amin, his mother's second cousin.[49] He studied in the government madrasas and then at al-Azhar, joined the Faculty of Sharia as a junior professor, and was elected deputy leader of the Jamiat shura in 1973. He supported Saudi-style Salafi (Wahhabi) Islam and was an excellent orator in Arabic. He became the mujahidin leader best known in Saudi Arabia.

President Daoud had Sayyaf arrested in his crackdown on the Islamists in 1975. When the Khalqis came to power, Sayyaf's mother asked Amin to release him; Amin refused but had Sayyaf moved out of Pul-i Charkhi prison to a more comfortable detention facility. Hence when the Khalqis killed all the Islamists in Pul-i Charkhi, Sayyaf was not there. He survived until the prisons were opened after the Soviet invasion, when he came to Peshawar.

There he did not join any existing organization but proved adept at raising money from Arab sources. In 1980, when the Pakistanis recognized six parties, Sayyaf was chosen as spokesman for yet another alliance. As Mujaddidi and Muhammadi had done, he made the office he headed into his own party, which took the name of the abortive alliance.[50] In view of Sayyaf's strong financial base and his support from the Saudi religious establishment, the isi eventually recognized his group as the seventh party.

This party was linked to virtually no social networks in Afghanistan. The headquarters staff consisted of a few mainly Ghilzai Pashtun ulama and a collection of individuals linked to Sayyaf (or to Saudi Arabia) in some way (Tables 9.2, 9.3). Arab volunteers played an important role in the operation of the party. Sayyaf had too few commanders for them to figure significantly in any of the available data on commanders from the mid-1980s. They seem to have been a heterogeneous group of individuals who affiliated themselves with Sayyaf because of the money and arms that he could supply.[51] The party did have a strong front in Sayyaf's birthplace, Paghman. The isi had a large base like Haqqani's built for one of Sayyaf's commanders, Mawlawi Arsala Rahmani, near Urgun, Paktika.[52] Hundreds of Arab "mujahidin" trained there for the jihad. As an opponent of nationalism and a supporter of pan-Islamic ideals, Sayyaf strongly supported the enlistment of Arab and other Islamic volunteers, who swelled his ranks and created considerable friction with the Afghan mujahidin.

Major Shi'a Parties

The Iranian regime supported exile-based parties rather than tribal or regional organizations among the Shi'a just as Pakistan did among the Sunnis.

Like their Sunni counterparts, Shi'a (Hazara and Qizilbash) youth in Kabul and other towns had begun organizing radical political groups in the 1960s and 1970s.[53] Some of their leaders were arrested by Daoud in 1974 and 1975, while others fled to

Iran. The number of Shiʿa Islamists was too small to have had significant influence on the initial Shiʿa uprisings in the Hazarajat or the government of the Shura.

Soon, however, various agencies of the Iranian revolutionary regime trained and armed Hazara Islamists. Within two years of its founding, partisan strife tore the Shura's government apart. The Shura had three main political elements: secular, dominated by the mirs and young intellectuals; traditionalist-religious, dominated by sayyids; and Islamist, dominated by clerics and some young men who had returned from revolutionary Iran, where hundreds of thousands of Hazaras had been working since the post-1973 oil boom. The sayyids first allied with the Islamists to oust the mirs, of whom some fled to Quetta and others eventually joined the government. Then the Islamists, mainly those of the Nasr Party, staged a coup against the traditionalist sayyids, who had no power base without the landlords.

The Shura then ceased to be a regional government and became a Hazara traditionalist party with one main front, that of Sayyid Jagran, in Ghazni Province. He was one of the commanders mentioned by Najibullah in April 1988. The Shura, though never officially recognized by Pakistan, developed informal ties to NIFA, which provided it with some facilities in Peshawar. The Shura also maintained an office among the Hazara refugee community in Quetta.

The Shura was the only purely traditionalist and rural-based Shiʿa—really Hazara—party. Three other Shiʿa Islamist parties played significant military and political roles, one primarily Qizilbash and the others primarily Hazara. The Harakat-i Islami (Islamic Movement) was led by Ayatollah Asif Muhsini, a Pashto-speaking religious leader from a Qandahar Shiʿa community known as Khalilis. Muhsini had founded a cultural and political revival movement in the 1960s called Subh-i Danish (Dawn of Knowledge), which attracted some of the Shiʿa youth of Kabul.[54] Roy describes the party as moderate Islamist and claims that it is the Shiʿa analogue of Jamiat, with which it had generally good relations. Its most important commander was Muhammad Anwari, a Kabuli who led a front of several hundred men in Turkmen Valley west of Kabul. Commander Anwari was an Islamist intellectual with a secular education. Besides his rural front, he controlled the most extensive urban underground network of the resistance, according to a number of sources. Muhsini was a religious follower of Ayatollah Khui, with whom he studied in Najaf, rather than a follower of Khomeini; he also seems to have been close to Ayatollah Shariatmadari of Tabriz. Muhsini was imprisoned by the Khomeini government and his party banned in Iran in August 1980, when documents reconstructed from the shredder in the American Embassy in Tehran revealed (or claimed) that the CIA had funneled money to his party through a bank account in Mashhad.[55] Muhsini never regained the confidence of Iranian authorities, but neither did he obtain significant support from Pakistan or the United States. (It was out of the question for a Shiʿa leader to approach Saudi Arabia.)

According to Lorentz, several Hazara or Shiʿa resistance groups first sprang up in

Iran in the fall of 1979. Two of these parties, *Nasr* and *Sipah-i Pasdaran*, became significant forces.[56]

Sazman-i Nasr-i Islami-yi Afghanistan (The Islamic Victory Organization of Afghanistan) was organized by educated Shi'a youth from Afghanistan with the help of the Organization of the Islamic Revolution in Iran. This movement aided Shi'a revolutionaries in foreign countries and was a stronghold of the Iranian hardliners. It operated under the tutelage of Ayatollah Montazeri, whose son Muhammad Montazeri and son-in-law Mehdi Hashemi were successive leaders. The OIR seems to have favored Nasr in the same way that the ISI favored Hizb-i Islami (Hikmatyar). Roy considers Nasr the closest Shi'a equivalent of that party.

Well armed and well organized, at least compared with the Shura, the cadres of Nasr espoused the revolutionary line of Khomeini and militantly opposed the traditionalist elements in the Hazarajat. In 1984 they drove Bihishti out of Waras. They set up an administration modeled on the Iranian revolution, with revolutionary committees led by the militants in charge of administration and with revolutionary *qazis* in charge of judicial affairs.

Some elements in the Iranian government apparently became unhappy with Nasr, which exhibited a certain degree of independence and was also associated with the controversial figure of Montazeri. Sometime in the early 1980s the Iranian Revolutionary Guards (Pasdaran) founded a branch of their own organization among Shi'a from Afghanistan. This organization was called Guruh-i Pasdaran-i Jihad-i Islami (Group of Guardians of the Islamic Jihad), but it is generally known as Sipah-i Pasdaran. Like Nasr, Sipah-i Pasdaran is a party of militant revolutionaries following the line of Khomeini. Sipah-i Pasdaran operates mainly as an Afghan branch of the Iranian organization of the same name, with Iranians playing significant roles. According to Lorentz, the main differences between Nasr and Sipah are apparently in "the degree to which they are committed to the idea of a separate Hazara national identity." Nasr, which became the most powerful Hazara organization, retained a stronger ethnonationalist tinge and moved slightly toward the Peshawar parties in order to balance Iranian influence.[57]

Alliances of Parties

Until 1985, both the CIA and the ISI considered political relations among exiled party leaders to be at most a nuisance obstructing the real task: "killing Russians." The Iranians merged the Shi'a parties into Hizb-i Wahdat (Unity Party) only in response to the Soviet withdrawal in 1988–89. From the start, however, the Saudis exerted pressure on the exiled leaders by making "unity" a condition for funding their offices. In 1981 all parties briefly joined an alliance called the Islamic Union of Mujahidin of Afghanistan (Ittihad-i Islami-yi Mujahidin-i Afghanistan).[58] The Saudi government funded that alliance generously, but by the following February the three traditionalist-nationalist parties withdrew, complaining of rampant corruption and discrimination by Sayyaf, who, as chairman, controlled the Saudi funds. Three splinter groups remained behind, attracted by the money, so that the alliance still had seven members. The three traditionalist-nationalist parties founded what they called the moderate alliance, using the same name as the original alliance. Unlike the alliance of seven, the alliance of three merged its (much smaller) budgets in a number of areas, in particular those dealing with culture and refugees. The bureaucracy of this alliance received no supplemental external support, in contrast to the private Saudi and other Arab money that flowed to the Islamist alliance.

The strategy adopted by the United States in April 1985 under National Security Directive 166 had a political as well as military dimension, although a State Department official charged with implementing it complained that "people in this town don't take political stuff seriously. They think if we just got enough of the right equipment there it would solve the problem. But the experience of the whole twentieth century shows that every guerrilla war is won politically." The first priority was to pressure the resistance into cooperating politically so that it could become a "viable partner for negotiation." Second, the United States would initiate a program of humanitarian assistance for Afghans living in resistance-controlled areas of Afghanistan, so that the resistance would be able to organize genuine base areas. And third, the United States would engage in a campaign of public diplomacy aiming at increasing the diplomatic costs to the Soviets, especially in their bilateral relations with Third World countries.[59]

Both U.S. and Pakistani governments now defined unity of the resistance as an alliance of the seven recognized parties, with the balance of power in the hand of the Islamists.[60] About a month after the signing of NSD 166, General Zia invited all seven leaders to dinner and told them that they had to join a new version of the Islamic Union of Mujahidin of Afghanistan. Prince Turki, head of the Saudi intelligence service, also weighed in. Membership in this alliance was a condition for receiving further aid. The seven leaders rotated in three-month terms as "spokesmen" of the alliance. The alliance sent delegations to New York every fall to the meeting of the U.N. General Assembly. In 1986 the delegation, then led by Rabbani, met President Reagan at the White House; Hikmatyar had refused a similar meeting the previous year despite a long telephone call from ISI chief Gen. Akhtar Abdul Rahman.[61] Similar dissension among alliance parties precluded their opening a single office abroad.

The alliance founded a leadership council of three members from each party and a set of committees—embryonic ministries—for health, education, agriculture, refugee affairs, and other matters. Committees on military and political affairs remained powerless; military assistance continued to go either through the parties or directly to favored commanders.

The United States used the cross-border humanitarian assistance program to build up the Peshawar-based bureaucracy of the alliance. Such European organizations as the Swedish Committee for Afghanistan, which had pioneered the delivery of assistance to Afghans in resistance-controlled areas, had developed a flexible methodology based on direct relations with commanders. Although this method was effective in delivering the aid to those in need, it failed to create a national political center and, indeed, strengthened the autonomy of commanders. The U.S. Agency for International Development, the implementing agency for this part of the program, was accustomed to seeing its aid as nation building: in theory, USAID not only provided a particular service but also built up the local institution charged with implementing that service. The alliance committees, together with a group of American and Afghan nongovernmental organizations, were to become these implementing partners. The foreign aid–funded bureaucracy of Peshawar developed into a caricature of the foreign aid–funded bureaucracy of the old regime in Kabul.

10

International Aid, War,
and Local and
Regional Organization

In much of the colonial and postcolonial world, loss of social control by locally based landholding elites resulted from capitalist penetration and the monetization of tax collection. In such cases those with access to capital and to the market (moneylenders who assumed ownership of land from indebted landlords, for example) became the new strongmen.[1] In Afghanistan coercive rather than capitalist penetration had analogous effects. Those who would reconsolidate control first needed access to political networks (the exile-based parties) that supplied weapons and other resources necessary for insurgency; then they needed the organizational skills to use those resources effectively. Soviet military pressure and increasing foreign arms aid from parties based in Pakistan or Iran strengthened religious leaders against those whose power was based on property and kinship and particularly strengthened Islamists against the traditional elites.

Sale of a cash crop to foreign markets could substitute for access to external political networks. Thus the opium mullahs of the Helmand Valley developed a financial base for despotic warlordism from agricultural exports to developed capitalist countries. A number of relatively modern parties—in particular Hikmatyar's—also tapped these resources by investing in heroin processing and export in collaboration with Pakistani partners, including military and government officials.

Access to these resources enabled some leaders to construct new institutions for the insurgency that were increasingly differentiated and autonomous from the local societies. The precise links between the insurgency and the society varied according to the local social structures and the strategies of commanders. In parts of the country where the political institutions became most differentiated, regional organizations emerged that fostered political mobilization around "macroethnic" identities.[2] These ethnic identities grew in importance not because they expressed preexisting social interests or because of the ideologies of the leaders, most of whom claimed to reject ethnic politics. They emerged, rather, as a result of political and military mobilization over areas larger than the space of solidarity of the qawm.

Local Political Structures of the Insurgency

Like the state, mujahidin organizations had to recruit leaders, organize military and political activities, and find the means to finance them. Perhaps the biggest impact of the international system on local power structures in the early 1980s was the penetration of village and tribal society for the first time by political parties. As we have seen, of twenty-three cases in the SCA files that contain accounts of the original uprising, eleven report that no tanzims were involved, and only five indicate that party members participated. All but one commander agreed, however, that in 1980 or 1981, "because of the lack of weapons, tanzims started work."[3] Weapons from the tanzims enabled leaders to pursue military strategies and to attract followers.

This process weakened the khans, whom the old regime had used as intermediaries in their relations with the rural society. Except for NIFA and ANLF, which received relatively few weapons, the resistance parties distributed most aid from abroad to religious or Islamist leaders rather than to landowners. The few resistance units that were led by khans were of the smallest type, sometimes operating as part of a larger coalition under religious leadership. These revolts resembled that of Mullah-i Lang (the lame mullah) against King Amanullah, or that of Abdul Qadir against the French in Algeria. Such movements developed in parts of eastern and southern Afghanistan, especially in the mountain (nang) areas. Smaller khans joined the jihad at the price of recognizing religious leadership at a higher level. Roy found that NIFA commanders, who were more likely to be khans than were those of any other party, generally led smaller groups.[4] The Orkand data also show that over 80 percent of the NIFA commanders in the survey led groups of no more than sixty men, compared with 40–50 percent of the Islamist commanders (Table 8.1).

Some tribal mujahidin tried to remain independent of the parties, but with little success. The Unity of Jaji Mujahidin in Paktia, the only nonparty resistance unit in the SCA sample, collected money to bribe Pakistani officers to provide weapons and training, but the khan who collected the money stole it and fled to the United States.

After 1980 the wealthy members of rural society were also more likely than the poor to seek refuge in Pakistan, apparently because they could afford the costs of the journey. Furthermore, Soviet counterinsurgency measures that targeted the rural economy destroyed local resources, control of which was a primary source, along with state patronage, of the khans' power. According to an SCA survey, in 1985 substantially more than half of the farmers in Afghanistan reported bombing of their village, more than a quarter reported the destruction of irrigations systems, and more than a quarter reported the shooting of livestock (Table 10.1). Farmers also suffered such indirect effects of the war as the decline in the availability of inputs and services. As a result, from 1978 to 1986 yields decreased by about 50 percent for dry-land wheat and about 33 percent for irrigated wheat, while at least a third of the land was abandoned. The numbers of sheep, goats, and cattle declined by from one-half to two-thirds.[5] Power shifted away from those who controlled the dwindling agricultural

Table 10.1 Direct Effects of War on Agriculture in Resistance-Controlled Areas, Selected Years

Damage Reported by Farmers Remaining in Afghanistan in 1987 ($N = 5,158$)

Percentage reporting:	1978	1980	1985	1986	1987
Destruction of irrigation	0	13	24	20	12
Burning of crop	0	4	11	8	4
Bombing of village	0	23	53	38	22
Destruction of grain store	0	7	13	10	3
Livestock shot	0	9	23	13	6
Livestock killed by mines	0	2	2	1	2

Damage Reported by Farmers Who Left Afghanistan in 1987 ($N = 4,346$)

Percentage reporting:					
Destruction of irrigation	0	12	36	30	0
Burning of crop	0	2	10	9	0
Bombing of village	0	21	65	49	0
Destruction of grain store	0	3	10	6	0
Livestock shot	0	9	31	13	0
Livestock killed by mines	0	2	11	7	0

Source: Data from SCA, *Agricultural Survey of Afghanistan: First Report,* 37.

resources toward those with access to external supplies—away from the khans and toward the Islamists and religious figures.

Pressures of the war also led some commanders who had been traditionalists to defect to the Islamist parties. Amin Wardak, who was the son of a major khan of the Wardak tribe and held a B.A. degree in "documentation française" from Kabul University, established a front in his father's area. His father venerated Pir Gailani, and Amin joined NIFA. He was among the first commanders to attract direct foreign support (from the French), and he established clinics and schools and even printed his own postage stamps in the name of the "Province Libre de Wardak." He attacked Soviet and government targets not only in his own area but as far south as the city of Ghazni. His operations outside the traditional area of his clan, however, created friction with the traditionalist leaders of other clans of the tribe, who appealed to the pir to mediate. Gailani pressured Amin to limit his operations so as not to offend the elders, and he even reduced Amin's arms supplies. In late 1987 or early 1988 Amin switched to Hizb-i Islami (Khalis), the other mainly tribal Pashtun party, because

Khalis was willing and able to provide as many arms as Amin could use. By 1989 he had acquired the Islamic title *Qazi* despite his secular education.[6]

Local leadership thus shifted from khans to religious or Islamist leadership, and among religious leaders from traditional ulama to either Islamist intellectuals or Sufis (mainly in the North) or to fundamentalist mullahs (mainly in the South). Typically the alim who led the initial insurrection might be named amir—nominally a position of leadership, but one with less actual power than that of commander—or he might work in the judicial department; Islamists, by contrast, took command of military and political affairs.[7]

In areas where little fighting occurred, units based on primary social divisions persisted. The commander became or remained a khan, and the fighters became his retainers. Under increased military pressure, however, fighters needed to maintain more permanent mobilization.[8] They built bases (*qarargah* or *markaz*) separate from the villages. Sometimes the mujahidin spent only days there and returned home for the night; in more developed fronts (or where most of the population had fled) they lived at the bases. Except in depopulated border zones and areas where incessant feuding prevented the construction of even rudimentary institutions, commanders responded to increased military pressure by forming at least ad hoc coalitions within localities. They called such coalitions shuras.

Some shuras coordinated activities of commanders within a single party, typically in a more disciplined and differentiated organization, as in Jamiat or Hizb. More commonly, especially in the tribal areas, shuras brought together commanders from different parties. These shuras substituted geographical or tribal bases of political organization for partisan ones—though without ever fully replacing the partisan. In few cases did the shuras become institutionalized with permanent headquarters, fixed membership, departments, or secretariats. More typically, like traditional jirgas or village councils, they met irregularly to solve specific problems.

The adoption of the word *shura* (rather than *jirga,* even in the Pashtun tribal areas) signified the Islamization of political relations. Abu Bakr, the third of the rightly guided caliphs, had appointed a shura to choose his successor ('Uthman), and shura thereafter became a basic principle of Islamic rule. Modernists who seek Islamic arguments in support of Western-style democracy, Islamists who argue that Islam already embodies its own superior form of democracy, and traditionalists who argue that Islam forbids democracy—all refer, with differing interpretations, to the principle of shura. In the social structure of Afghanistan, shuras resembled tribal jirgas in some areas, but the use of the Islamic idiom implied that the council should make decisions according to Islamic rather than tribal principles.

The mujahidin established two basic types of local shuras: councils of commanders and councils of ulama. The ulama functioned sometimes as a judicial committee or department of the commanders' shura, and sometimes as a separate organization. Some shuras appear to have emerged spontaneously, although they may have derived from early examples. Shuras met needs for military and other forms of cooperation and for the settlement of disputes.

Shuras of commanders would make decisions about joint military operations and would address political and economic questions. The degree to which these councils were institutionalized and differentiated from the representatives of local society—the village or tribal elders—varied. Even in a single province, Logar, there was a wide range in the degree of political development. In the Baraki Barak district, where Jamiat had an important presence under Dr. Fazlullah, investigators reported in 1989 that a six-year-old shura had permanent secretaries for military, judicial, social, medical, affairs and four judges working for its judicial committee. In several other districts of Logar commanders had established purely military shuras, which were reportedly resented by some of the local people for excluding elders. In another district there was no shura and the main mujahidin leader was a tribal elder who settled matters by holding jirgas.[9]

Among traditionalist groups the mujahidin remained closely linked to the local elites, though with a greater role for ulama than before the war. For instance, the constitution of the Unity of Jaji Mujahidin established an executive committee of leaders of eight "tribes" (actually clans of the Jaji, a Pashtun tribe from the mountainous province of Paktia on the Pakistan border). These leaders acted on behalf of a council that also included forty-eight "group leaders" (commanders of small segments); this council acted in consultation with the "pious and godfearing people of the tribes." Council members had to swear allegiance to Islam and to the Hanafi fiqh. The constitution called for the suspension of tribal hostilities (*badal*) for the sake of jihad; for trial according to sharia (not Pashtunwali) of any who violated this injunction; and for the breaking of kinship or tribal relations with communists (many of whom were from the area). A committee (*dar al-iftah*) of ulama had to approve all decisions of the council before they became law. Such agreements, reminiscent of Muhammad's first pact with the people of Medina, were widely undertaken—though often violated—in the tribal territories.[10]

The distinction between the legal powers of the ulama and the executive powers of the commanders was recognized at least in theory by many fronts, although the degree to which it was effective varied.[11] Wherever such institutions were established, the political system saw a rough tripartite division among unequal centers of power: commanders (executive); ulama (judicial); and elders (representative, if not legislative).

During the spontaneous, traditionalist phase of the revolt, local fronts supported themselves mainly from local resources. Such insurgencies are vulnerable to counterinsurgency based on the destruction of these resources. Over time commanders increasingly depended on external networks, including both organizations that gave aid (parties and relief organizations) and the international drug market.

Because the number of mujahidin depended on the number of weapons available—the supply of volunteers was endless—more military assistance meant more mujahidin. The increase in military pressure as the Soviets moved against the mujahidin led some commanders to introduce measures of professionalization, in particular the establishment of qarargahs, where mujahidin could live in a state of mobilization apart from their families. These innovations increased the financial demands on the fronts, although only the Arab-funded commanders of Sayyaf and, later, the Salafi organization, Jamaʿat al-Daʿwa, paid wages to mujahidin.[12]

At the same time, destruction of agriculture and pastoralism by Red Army and government forces, as well as a drought in 1982 and 1983, eliminated or reduced the sources of income many fronts had enjoyed, though the effect is difficult to quantify. The SCA files, which include only those commanders who needed food assistance, are a skewed source for the extent of this damage. Commander Qari Taj Baba of Ghazni (Harakat-i Inqilab), whose area was distant from the heaviest military pressure, claimed in an interview that in some years—when the Soviets did not burn the harvest—collection of zakat and ushr actually increased in his area, because organizational improvements enabled him to collect the full amount from more people.[13]

Of the cases in the SCA sample, most commanders had found ushr and zakat sufficient before the Soviet escalation, but none said these taxes could meet more than half of the needs of the front by 1986. Fourteen of twenty-six commanders said they still collected some direct taxes, although these were declining; in some cases revenue was less than 10 percent of its previous level. Five commanders from the hard-fought areas of Kabul Province had collected the taxes before but said they now could not collect any. The representative of Mullah Izzatullah, Jamiat commander of Paghman, Kabul Province, was quoted on April 6, 1986, "Since the Soviet invasion and especially the last one to two years, everything was destroyed. These are the reasons that the people cannot give anything to the mujahedin as ushr and zakat. Instead the mujahedin have to take care of the people."[14] This change had obvious effects on relations between the insurgency and society.

Donations from the wealthy continued in some remote areas. Most fronts, however, reported that individuals who had previously contributed had lost their wealth, emigrated, or been arrested by KhAD.[15] Booty also became more difficult to obtain. Several commanders interviewed by SCA said that Soviet troops had established posts along major roads and had used helicopter gunships either to accompany convoys or to respond quickly to attacks. Even if mujahidin managed to attack and stop a convoy, it had become extremely difficult to obtain the booty.[16]

Most commanders reported that they had received only weapons from the Pakistan-based parties; only those from Islamist parties said that they also received funds for transport of arms from the Saudi Red Crescent. A few major Hizb and Jamiat bases reported that the party had given cash (in Pakistani rupees) for the feeding and maintenance of the full-time fighters in the qarargah. Aid was evolving in those parties from requisitions toward more professional styles of military organization, including cash-based finance.

The international supporters of the mujahidin responded to the problems of the resistance in the mid-1980s by enhancing both the quantity and the quality of military assistance. As the SCA Cash for Food Program exemplified, programs were also developed for the support of civilians living in mujahidin areas and for the nonmilitary needs of the fighters. A few commanders in the file reported that they received support from the Norwegian Committee for Afghanistan, SCA, or other nongovernmental organizations. The Swedish, Danish, and Norwegian Afghanistan support committees, several medical groups, Amitié Franco-Afghane, and Guilde du Raide began cross-border humanitarian assistance to mujahidin fronts, and the USAID effort ultimately dwarfed the others.

Insurgency-Society Relations

Especially as long as Soviet troops fought for the Kabul regime, it labored under a diffuse illegitimacy, for which it could partially compensate by providing benefits to specific groups. Conversely—also especially as long as the Soviet troops were present—the mujahidin (or at least the jihad) enjoyed a diffuse legitimacy, which might or might not be transferable to specific commanders or parties. Afghans, including mujahidin and even commanders, commonly said that they were fighting for Islam and Afghanistan, not for any party, not even the one to which they belonged.

A commander had to ensure that his group of mujahidin would share in the diffuse legitimacy of the jihad. Like leaders of other insurgent groups, he had to provide the community that he intended to mobilize with such benefits as security and a capacity for collective action. An alternative path (chosen by some who had access to sufficient external resources) was simply to bypass local society and to construct parallel institutions for fighters recruited from schools, as the old regime had also done.

A commander's relationship with the elders and ulama was a manifestation of relations between the insurgency and society in that locale. These relations varied a great deal, according to both the local social structure and the access of commanders to external aid. At one extreme, Hizb-i Islami (Hikmatyar), which showed the greatest autonomy from local social structures, followed the totalitarian model of integrating all powers into the party. Hizb did not consult with elders, and according to Roy, recognized only ulama who were members of the party.[17] Traditionalist commanders, in contrast, were themselves members of established social elites; in tribal warfare the military leaders are also the social leaders. Other parties occupied various intermediate positions.

Different approaches to insurgency-society relations could create local conflicts among the parties. For instance, in Char Dehi village near Kabul in 1985, conflicts developed between the mujahidin commanders and the village elders, who met in the mosque after prayers every evening. A frequent cause of such disputes was a request by villagers that mujahidin desist from attacks that would provoke reprisals against the village and its economy. The committees of the seven mujahidin parties in the area called a commanders' shura to decide how to deal with the elders. The four Islamist parties voted to dissolve the council of elders, against the wishes of the three traditionalist-nationalist parties.[18] In parts of Logar, by contrast, Haji Naim, an elder of the Ahmadzai nomads, led the resistance. He received aid from all parties and solved problems through tribal jirgas.[19]

Massoud incorporated representatives of society while maintaining the autonomy of his political and military structures. He institutionalized consultation with councils of both elders and ulama, first in his Panjsheri movement and then in the Supervisory Council of the North.[20]

Because Massoud recruited his fighters from local society and relied for part of his resources on increasingly institutionalized relations with that society, he was repeatedly reminded of the need for consultation. In 1975 he attempted to gain approval for the revolt against Daoud from local ulama and elders. When they refused to recognize the revolt as a jihad, he proceeded without their endorsement and failed. He apparently learned from this experience. After 1978 the support of ulama was key to his success in mobilizing Panjsheris against both the government and a group of Maoist guerrillas in the area. In late 1983, as Massoud's truce with the USSR was about to expire, his intelligence network in Kabul informed him of plans for a large Soviet offensive against Panjsher. When he announced plans to evacuate the civilian population from the lower valley, he faced a near revolt from the ulama and elders. Rather than overpower them, however, he held a conference lasting a day and a half at which he explained his reasoning. He finally won their support, which enabled him to evacuate tens of thousands of people to neighboring valleys before the Soviets attacked.

Regional Resistance

A number of commanders in different regions of the country sought various ways to break out of the localist orientation and to pose a greater military threat to the Soviet forces and Kabul regime. Regional coalitions provided the major forces in the battle for Kabul after the fall of Najibullah.

The successes and failures of these coalitions produced great regional disparities in degrees of fragmentation of the resistance. In particular, some nontribal and hence non-Pashtun areas developed more extensive organizations, whereas tribal areas remained fragmented. Conditions of modern warfare reversed the comparative military advantages of the two social structures from what they had been in the age of the gunpowder empires, when Afghanistan was founded.

Table 9.1 presents some extremely approximate data on one aspect of these differences, namely the pattern of political affiliations. This table shows the distribution of armed mujahidin by party within each region and for the country as a whole. On the basis of these figures I have calculated the value of Rae's index of fragmentation of party systems for each region and for the whole country.[21] Rae originally counted votes rather than Kalashnikovs, but for the period in question the Kalashnikov was the closest analogue to the vote in Afghanistan.

The table clearly shows the differences between the Sunni non-Pashtun areas (top three lines) and the Pashtun areas (next three lines). Jamiat dominates the non-Pashtun areas, which consequently are less fragmented than the Pashtun areas, where no single party dominates. I have reason to believe that the figures for the South, in particular the low numbers for NIFA, are less reliable than those for the other regions. A few Shi'a commanders are included under "other," but by and large the Shi'a are absent from this data set.

The Northeast

In the predominantly Tajik Northeast, the most salient characteristics of the party system were the dominance of Jamiat and the continual conflict between Jamiat and Hizb-Hikmatyar. The Hizb-Jamiat conflict sometimes took the form of ethnic strife between Pashtun colonies (like the community where Hikmatyar was born) and the Tajiks and Uzbeks. More commonly, however, the conflict emerged from either political disputes between the parties or local rivalries not directly linked to any national identities or issues. Harakat was originally the leading party in this area, but most of the Persian-speaking ulama who had joined it switched to Jamiat by 1982.[22] The remaining Harakat commanders were generally Uzbek ulama. Most NIFA commanders were either elders of Pashtun settlements or nomads.

The road from Dushanbe to Kabul and the lower part of the Tashkent-Kabul highway passed through the Northeast, so the government and the Soviets had several large military bases there. During the occupation the government and the Soviets used control over water and subsidies of inputs to force the peasants of Kunduz to grow cotton for government factories, while the resistance, as Najibullah complained, forbade the growing of cotton.[23]

The region's commanders, led by Ahmad Shah Massoud, developed the most extensive protostate in Afghanistan, the Shura-yi Nazar-i Shamali (Supervisory Council of the North, or SCN). The lack of tribal rivalries and the predominance of Jamiat commanders with common ethnic backgrounds and high levels of education (for Afghanistan) facilitated this development. So did the region's distance from Pakistan, which made it difficult for the ISI to exert direct control.[24]

The main strategic task of the resistance, as Massoud saw it, was to overcome segmentation based on qawm and locality in order to build military institutions capable of concentrating forces in space (attacking one target with many forces) and time (attacking many targets at one time).[25] Such military institutions would require the gradual construction of a base of political and economic institutions capable of assuring their supply and recruitment. Unlike General Akhtar, Massoud did not intend to postpone politics until after the success of the jihad. He adopted a grassroots strategy that integrated political and military components. He based his military forces on local institutions that both provided services to the local population and institutionalized consultation with it.[26] He created a welfare system and a variety of economic programs designed to keep the economically productive civilian population in the area. Although it received less publicity, he also developed his own secret police and intelligence service, which made his military forces more effective and frustrated repeated attempts at government infiltration.

Both factions of Hizb-i Islami, in contrast, who relied more heavily on foreign support and cross-border operations, often encouraged the civilian population to emigrate so that the Islamists would have a freer hand militarily. The interrelation of such functions as representation, taxation, provision of services, and recruitment to military forces differentiate SCN not only from other, more fragmented resistance organizations, but also from the previously existing Afghan state, which relied on foreign aid to encapsulate local society rather than integrating that society into the state.

The SCN was the product of years of work. From 1979 to 1983, Massoud worked only in Panjsher. He developed a territorial administration that used the qarargah as the basic unit. Although Massoud was formally accountable to no one, the ulama of Panjsher had on their own organized a shura, which was originally loosely aligned with Harakat. Massoud recognized the shura, consulted it on a variety of issues, and incorporated it into his judicial committee. In addition to judicial and military affairs, he established committees to deal with civil administration, addressing finances and the economy, culture and education (da'wat u tanzim), health, political affairs, intelligence, and Kabul affairs. The committee on Kabul affairs both engaged in intelligence work and collected taxes from Panjsheris in Kabul. The culture and education committee dealt with recruitment and organization building.[27] The committee seems to have concentrated on military and civil institutions, however, not on the party. Unlike Mao or Tito, to whom he is sometimes compared, Massoud devoted little attention to political mass mobilization through the party.

Key to Massoud's ability to carry out these policies was his ability to recruit skilled and motivated cadres. Many Panjsheris, like Massoud, had educational and professional experience in nearby Kabul, and—as Massoud's fame was spread by the BBC, among others—some Kabulis and even people from more distant areas of Afghanistan migrated to Panjsher to work for him.

At the level of the village Massoud organized local (mahalli) forces. At the level of the qarargah (one for each six or seven villages, about twenty in Panjsher) Massoud created a stationary (sabit) militia, known as grup-i zarbati (striking force). Each qarargah also was advised by a local shura and specialized committees. Most important, however, Massoud recruited volunteers to his "mobile group" (grup-i mutaharik): young, highly trained, and highly mobile commandos. The mutaharik units were composed of volunteers who were required to be literate. Their uniforms, unlike the standard Western (or Soviet) army uniforms of the Afghan army, were light blue versions of traditional Afghan clothing, more suitable for the postures of rural Afghan life. These commandos were active not only throughout Panjsher but also in adjacent areas, such as along the Salang Highway, where they continued to ambush Soviet convoys.[28]

Indeed, in 1986 Massoud told a Norwegian reporter that he obtained one-third of his supplies from booty. Another third came from taxes on lapis lazuli and emerald mines, and, he said, 4.5 percent from Jamiat in Pakistan. The remainder apparently came from a 5 percent income tax levied on Panjsheris working for the government and from contributions by businessmen. As a result of heavy fighting, Massoud said, "Most houses and regions in the Panjsher Valley have been destroyed. . . . People are unable to cultivate their land." Hence he collected no zakat or ushr; on the contrary, he ran a welfare system that provided basic foodstuffs.[29]

Massoud began to implement his regional strategy in 1983, after the failure of the Soviets' sixth offensive against Panjsher led to a truce. Massoud rejected offers to negotiate with Kabul, and the Soviets agreed to his demand for direct negotiation. The truce they concluded coincided with efforts by Andropov to seek a negotiated withdrawal on the international scene. The two sets of negotiations may well have been connected in Moscow, but the Soviets do not appear to have discussed broader political issues with Massoud's representatives.[30]

Taking advantage of the truce, Massoud built up his organization in Panjsher; used his commandos in a bloodless takeover of the neighboring valley of Andarab, where Hizb forces had continually blocked his supply lines; and sent emissaries to Jamiat commanders throughout northern Afghanistan to propose a plan of cooperation. In April 1984, after the election of Chernenko as general secretary of the CPSU and the expiration of the truce, the Soviets launched the seventh offensive against Panjsher. Massoud, however, had already evacuated the main valley and left Panjsher himself. From then until late 1988, he made his base in the Worsaj Valley of Takhar Province and continued to work toward regional unity.

In January 1985 Massoud convened a council of Jamiat commanders from five northeastern provinces. They agreed "to coordinate their activities, reorganize and train their forces and help by giving volunteers for the formation of central units." They also "appointed a council of observers who would supervise the implementation of the decisions of the council of the Commanders."[31] This council became the SCN, and Massoud became its amir.

Massoud developed the military forces of SCN by both coordinating existing forces through a commanders' shura and creating new units. He helped create mutaharik units in areas other than Panjsher by forming a military academy and sending advisers to other commanders. These units remained under the authority of major commanders of SCN. Massoud also added a new level, the Central Forces (*qataha-yi markazi*), under his direct command. Volunteers drawn from throughout the areas under SCN control, the Central Forces trained and fought together in mixed units without regard to qawm, locality, or party, although most were Jamiat members. The language of command was Persian, which inevitably if unintentionally gave these units an ethnic character when they were in the field with or against other units commanded in Uzbek or Pashto.

During 1986 to 1988 Massoud carried out a series of meticulously planned military operations with two goals in mind: to eliminate government garrisons from the SCN base areas, and to demonstrate graphically to the people and the mujahidin of the area and elsewhere the benefits of cooperation. In these operations he assembled units from several provinces and parties when possible. He divided the military tasks between commanders from these areas and his Central Forces. Tales of the Central Forces' exploits were then carried back to other areas—and around the world—by the Western and Arab journalists who often accompanied them. Massoud shared booty generously with those who cooperated with him.

During this period he kept the size of the Central Forces relatively small to maintain quality and avoid exciting jealousy. By the summer of 1988 Abolfathi estimated they numbered about two thousand, out of about ten thousand under SCN command.[32]

Although the initial goals of SCN were military, Massoud also began to build up the political and administrative infrastructure to support it. The council included sub-councils of ulama, commanders, and elders and seven functional committees (like ministries): Financial, Education, Military, Law, Cultural, Medical, and Political. Other sources also spoke of a Refugee Committee.[33] Each committee supposedly employed several hundred people.

Some of this organization existed on paper—or in Massoud's mind—more than in reality; most power remained with the local commanders, and local dissension broke out continually. Nonetheless, the SCN succeeded in providing many services to the civilian population of the Northeast.

The North

The northern region of Afghanistan includes the heart of Afghan Turkestan. The amirs of Bukhara continually fomented revolts against the Durrani rulers in this area, and the Uzbek khan, Murad Beg, wrested it from the rule of Kabul during 1817–40. Uzbeks predominate among the ethnically mixed population, which includes all major groups. Unlike in the Northeast, where the mountainous terrain is ideal for guerrilla warfare, most of the population of the North inhabits the largely flat steppe. The urban center of the region, Mazar-i Sharif, occupies a unique strategic position astride the main highway between the Soviet Union (Uzbekistan) and Kabul. As headquarters of the Northern Zone, Mazar became de facto a second capital. The North also includes the natural gas fields and was the site of most of the new economic and industrial projects of the Kabul regime. The area became increasingly integrated with Uzbekistan. The region contained a large concentration of regime forces, including garrisons at the port of Hairatan on the Amu Darya and in Balkh near Mazar itself. By the late 1980s, however, the largest military force in the area was neither the regular army nor any of the mujahidin forces, but the Jauzjani militia.

Among mujahidin Jamiat was the largest party in the North, linked to the Northeast by Naqshbandi networks. Harakat-i Inqilab, Hizb-Hikmatyar, and NIFA all had significant presences as well, and Nasr developed sizable forces among the Hazaras. As was true elsewhere, correspondence between ethnicity and party membership was incomplete, but on the whole Tajiks were more likely to be in Jamiat (represented by Islamists, Sufis, and ulama), Uzbeks in Harakat (mainly ulama), and Pashtun settlers in NIFA (ulama and khans). Hizb-Hikmatyar was found about equally among all Sunni groups.

Until 1984 the Jamiat commander Zabihullah (a former schoolteacher) was building up a shura modeled on Massoud's. He enjoyed considerable success in the mountainous, largely Tajik areas of southern Balkh, and his influence reached up into some of the suburbs of Mazar. His assassination in December 1984 led to a period of turmoil in which many groups joined the government as militias. Zabihullah's successor, Mawlawi Alam, eventually managed to construct a provincial shura but did not extend it over the whole region. In the late 1980s he began cooperating with SCN, and any progress in military development in the area was due to this cooperation rather than to local innovation. By April 1988 Mawlawi Alam headed a military committee and had also established judicial, financial, educational, and logistics committees. He operated forty schools.[34] Nonetheless, three-cornered battles continued among Jamiat, Harakat, and Hizb.

The West

Since ancient times the western area of Afghanistan, consisting of Herat and its hinterland, had been part of the Iranian province of Khorasan. The Safavids ruled it largely through Durrani governors and controlled the hinterland through the uymaq system. This pattern of indirect rule by Sunni tribes may explain why the area never adopted Shi'ism to the same extent as did the heartland of eastern Iran. There is a significant Shi'a Farsiwan population, however, especially along the Iranian border. The area is extremely heterogeneous ethnically.

The two main centers of regime military force in the region were the Seventeenth Division in Herat, where the March 1979 revolt originated, and the air base at Shindand, Farah Province. For a time the government succeeded in recruiting important qawmi militias from this area, but by 1989 these militias were engaged in open warfare against each other, using tanks and other heavy weapons. Ultimately the leader of each militia was assassinated, and the situation became calmer.

This area is economically integrated into Iran; even before the war many families had members working there. Taxes on workers' remittances from Iran provided an important source of funds for the mujahidin. Relations between Iran and the main resistance groups, however, were strained.

Jamiat, under commander Ismail Khan, was by far the predominant group in the area. Next in importance was Harakat-i Inqilab, which was originally more influential than the 13 percent of mujahidin attributed to it in Table 9.1. The major militias in Herat were originally Harakat fronts whose conflict with Jamiat (and, allegedly, infiltration by KhAD and/or Maoists) led them to defect to the government. Besides this conflict, Jamiat forces were also split between those loyal to Ismail Khan and those of Saifullah Afzali (assassinated in Iran in 1988). Like Massoud, Ismail Khan exhibited considerable independence from the ISI and from Jamiat headquarters, where the more ideological Islamists, supported by the ISI, aided Afzali against him.[35]

Ismail Khan and his deputy Alauddin Khan, both former captains in the Seventeenth Division, tried to build a more extensive military and political organization, but not on the same model as Massoud's. This area, much flatter and more densely populated than the mountain valleys of the Northeast, was less suited to guerrilla warfare. Ismail Khan took his military model from his experience as a staff officer in the regular army, from which he adopted Pashto organizational terms. His main fighting force was the Amir Hamza Division, which in 1988 had five regiments (*ghund*), each supposedly including six hundred to nine hundred men. Each regiment was divided into battalions (*kundak*) of about two hundred, which were in turn divided into companies (*tulay*). The companies were composed of "groups" of about twenty-five men.[36] These units were built up directly by Ismail Khan, rather than being recruited from other resistance organizations based in local social groups. In this respect they resembled Hikmatyar's Army of Sacrifice.

The mode of military recruitment may explain why the political institutions of the Herat resistance lagged behind those of the Northeast. In 1988 Ismail Khan directed a regional administration with nine committees: Military, Financial, Medical, Administrative, Judicial, Agricultural, Information, Education, and Investigation. These committees, however, were not as well developed as in Massoud's organization, and the military institutions predominated.[37]

Roy originally found that this system was militarily too heavy and static for the type of guerrilla war required, but that it caused less political disruption than Massoud's. Because the professional mobile forces were volunteers recruited independently of local commanders, they neither made demands on traditional leadership nor required any politicization of it. Later, however, Ismail Khan, like Massoud, attempted to extend his influence beyond his base, in this case central Herat, to the entire region. He did not succeed as Massoud did. The SCA files contain two letters, one from commanders in Farah and another from commanders in Herat and Badghis, which complained that Ismail Khan had proclaimed himself amir of the southern and western provinces without consultation (shura).

In the summer of 1987, Ismail Khan attempted to atone for this omission by calling a conference of commanders from nine provinces. He apparently had hoped for a wider, indeed national, attendance and was reportedly miffed that Massoud did not attend or even send a representative to the conference, which was held in Ghor Province. As the Orkand report states, "While a true regional organization akin to the Supervisory Council of the North did not develop from this, Ismail Khan was able to establish improved regional guidelines for military cooperation throughout the area."[38]

Greater Kabul and the East

Greater Kabul and the East are both largely Ghilzai and eastern Pashtun. Greater Kabul also includes Persian-speaking enclaves that more more closely resemble northern Afghanistan. This accounts for the greater presence of Jamiat in Kabul than in the East.

The East includes the nang Pashtuns in the mountains of Paktia, Paktika, and Kunar. A large number of mujahidin did some of the hardest fighting of the war in this area, which also produced one of the country's largest refugee outflows. Many districts along the border became nearly depopulated. On the other hand, the East borders directly on the main refugee concentrations in Pakistan, and some refugees could "commute" between their land and their refugee residence. Economically, this area became highly integrated into Pakistan. Many cash payments by parties or aid organizations to mujahidin in this area were in rupees, which could be freely used in the region's bazaars.

Despite intense combat activity this area remained politically and militarily fragmented. Establishing extensive guerrilla organizations based on the fractious local tribal social structure would have been difficult; the proximity of Pakistan made it nearly impossible. This area, Kabul, and the North together constituted the Soviets' "strategic Afghanistan."[39] The East and Kabul consequently had an extensive government presence, particularly in Kabul city, Jalalabad, and important bases in Gardez and Khost in Paktia.

Many of the leaders of both Khalq and Parcham came from the eastern Pashtun tribal areas. Several tribes or clans cooperated fully or in part with the government. Local tribal rivalries often gave the government an entrée; once one qawm joined the resistance, its rival might be recruited to either a rival party or the government. For instance, the Alikhel clan of Jaji formed government militias until 1988 mainly to strengthen itself against its Mangal rivals, who otherwise might have seized control of valuable forest resources in the area.

The distribution of mujahidin by political party gives only a rough idea of the degree of fragmentation in this area (Table 9.1). The two main parties with tribal Pashtun support, NIFA and Hizb-Khalis, dominated the resistance in the East, together accounting for nearly 60 percent of the mujahidin in the Orkand estimate. Because of the proximity to Pakistan, the nationalists in this area were affected less than in other regions by the refusal of the "Arabs"—Saudi Red Crescent—to pay for transport of arms. Hizb-Hikmatyar was also well represented here. Indeed, Table 9.1 underestimates the forces Hizb-Hikmatyar had built by the end of the war, since the count does not include the Pakistan-based militias of the party, including the Army of Sacrifice.

DCAR observed that "tribal divisions in Paktia are strong and they have prevented any truly regional administrative body from emerging during the war, aside from the provincial military shura."[40] Similar assessments could be made of most provinces in the area. The proximity of both safe refuge and plentiful supplies negated many of the pressures that led some commanders in other regions to form more extensive organizations.

The proximity of this region to Pakistan and hence to the ISI also hindered commanders from forming more autonomous groups. Abdul Haq, one of the Arsala brothers who played leading roles in Hizb-Khalis, tried to break out of localism by forming a mobile guerrilla army around Kabul and an underground intelligence network in the city. He maintained his operation for several years in the early and mid-1980s, but he never created a civil administration, and his organization was undermined by relentless bombing of his suburban base areas, by KhAD penetration, and by ISI manipulation. The ISI began delivering weapons directly to his subcommanders in order to subvert them from his command.

The main exceptions to the lack of civilian political organization in this region were Amin Wardak and the mainly Persian-speaking commanders of parts of Logar and Kabul Provinces. Most of the latter became integrated into the SCN. Amin Wardak developed a relatively sophisticated administration, including extensive medical, educational, and agricultural programs in the Jaghatu district of Wardak, and as a result his influence spread further, reaching to the city of Ghazni.[41]

Massoud's main partner in the area was Mullah Izzatullah of Paghman, who joined SCN. Dr. Fazlullah, Jamiat's amir of Logar Province, organized an effective local shura. He tried to emulate Massoud by proposing a supervisory council for Jamiat commanders in the East and Logar, but tribal rivalries, in particular opposition from commanders of the Mangal tribe, frustrated his plan.[42]

Fundamentalist mullahs and, to a lesser extent, traditional ulama came to dominate social control at the local level in most of the area. A number of prominent Khalis commanders better fit the profile of the Islamist intellectual, but these men—Abdul Haq and his brothers, for example, and Amin Wardak—generally seem to have come from higher ranking and wealthier backgrounds than did the cadres of Hikmatyar or Jamiat.

The detachment of insurgency from local society, promoted both by extensive emigration and by the relative accessibility of foreign aid, promoted the growth of various types of extremism and sectarian conflict. The Kabul regime had exemplified how excessive foreign dependency can create a debilitating or even pathological degree of autonomy of state from society. A survey of the political, military, and financial situation of the resistance in Kunar, Nangarhar, and Paktia suggests that an insurgency is subject to the same danger.

Kunar, as DCAR noted, "has a history of fundamentalist, Saudi influenced movements."[43] These movements, spread by the Saudi-funded Salafi madrasa in the village of Panjpir, opposed Sufism and other Afghan traditions. In 1980 largely traditionalist mujahidin of Kunar had formed a qawm-based coalition, which soon fell apart as its members joined Pakistan-based organizations to obtain weapons. Thereafter the Nuristani lands in upper Kunar remained politically separate from the Pashtun lowlands. Nuristan saw little warfare, for the government and the Soviets never tried to regain control after 1978. Northern Nuristan came under the control of a Panjpir-educated religious leader, Mawlawi Afzal, who founded the Dawlat-i Inqilabi-yi Islami-yi Nuristan (Islamic Revolutionary State of Nuristan), generally called the Dawlat. The Dawlat received direct financial support from some Salafi religious groups in Kuwait and Saudi Arabia and also enriched itself as a result of its strategic position: it sat astride a road—constructed by Amir Abdul Rahman Khan as part of the conquest of Nuristan—which mujahidin used for the transport of weapons from Chitral in Pakistan to northern Afghanistan. Such convoys had to obtain permits from the Dawlat "consulate" in Chitral and pay heavy tolls along the way.

For several years in the mid-1980s, southern Nuristan came under the influence of Sarwar Nuristani, a former military officer who had become a militia leader. Mawlawi Afzal and other religious leaders of the area at first supported Nuristani but ultimately concluded he was a government (or KGB) agent and expelled him from the area.[44]

In contrast to the relative peace of Nuristan, the Kunar River Valley in the southern part of the province was the scene of many heavy offensives as the Soviets tried to relieve the isolated garrisons along the Pakistan border, which were supplied by air. Only heavily militarized commanders with secure foreign funding could survive. One of them, Jamil al-Rahman, a Panjpir-educated mullah from the Safi tribe, left Hizb-Hikmatyar in 1985 to form a strict Salafi party, the Jama'at al-Da'wa. With extensive support from private Saudi and Kuwaiti sources, Jama'at al-Da'wa grew to be even more powerful in the area than the seven parties. Increasing numbers of Arabs came to fight in its ranks.

Nangarhar was somewhat more organized than Kunar. Here Khalis and NIFA were clearly dominant. The government, however, had a powerful focus of power in Jalalabad city and claimed the allegiance of sections of the Shinwari, Momand, and Afridi tribes. Mujahidin had strong bases in the mountain areas, but much of their military activity consisted of cross-border raiding. Several factors combined to preclude the creation of political or administrative institutions: tribal social structure, the geographical patchwork of government and mujahidin control, large-scale emigration, and the proximity of Pakistan.

Paktia and Paktika are nang tribal provinces par excellence. More PDPA leaders came from these provinces than from anywhere else in Afghanistan (except perhaps Kabul city), and a number of combative militias and army units were stationed in

Khost, Gardez, and Urgun. Here the leadership of the tribes passed to the fighting mullahs. In Paktia, the Hizb-Khalis commander Mawlawi Jalaluddin Haqqani of the Jadran tribe, with aid from Pakistan and the Saudis, constructed an enormous base along the Durand Line and led continual attacks on Khost. In Paktika Mawlawi Arsala Rahmani of Ittihad-Sayyaf also built a large base, where hundreds of Arabs trained. Both commanders had started jihad without party affiliation, and both eventually joined parties that could provide enough ammunition and weapons to support their aggressive style of cross-border raiding.

Although a loose military shura emerged in Paktia, there were no other political or administrative institutions in either province. Most of the population not living under government control had taken the short trip to Pakistan, a traditional temporary home for large numbers of nomads.

Haqqani could at times bring together a powerful tribal coalition of commanders from various parties. His military pressure against Khost helped to keep open important mujahidin supply lines that passed through Paktia. He also enjoyed a certain personal prestige; he headed the committee at the February 1989 Rawalpindi shura that came up with a formula for choosing the interim government.

Nonetheless, even militarily the Paktia shura had no formal organization or headquarters other than Haqqani's base. Sometimes the shura consulted with tribal elders, but these elders were living in Pakistan, not Afghanistan, and there was no formal institutional mechanism for this consultation.

The South

Southern Afghanistan is the Durrani Pashtun heartland, although the region includes Ghilzai territory to the east and part of the Hazarajat in the north. Two rivers that flow through the area water two major centers of population: the Arghandab River of Qandahar Province and the Helmand River of its eponymous province to the southwest. Both are the sites of major dams, the latter built in the late 1940s by the first major American aid project in the country. Irrigated agriculture has formed the basis for the power of large landlords of various sorts. In Qandahar, the Durrani aristocracy retained more power than khans elsewhere. The homeland of the Afghan monarchy, Qandahar was the only area of the country where the leadership of the shuras that emerged after the fall of Najibullah was predominantly traditionalist and included tribal khans of aristocratic lineages in prominent positions. In Helmand, opium cultivation supported despotic warlordism by mullahs. Both Qandahar and Helmand developed some civilian institutions, but of radically different character. Neither one developed an integrated political-military-financial system amounting to an embryonic state like the SCN. The tribal system remained resistant to such grafts.

The tribal system in Qandahar resisted not only protostate structures but also the party system and the ISI. As one commander of Qandahar told SCA, the mujahidin were "not named by tanzims." DCAR found that at least in Qandahar, unlike other areas, "the traditional power structure of the province based on the influence of large landowning khans and their families remains largely intact." This probably overstates the case; khans came to share power with ulama to a much greater extent than before.[45] Still, the tribal system differed from that of the East. Qandahar was the qalang (plains) Pashtun area par excellence. The large khans had extensive networks of patronage and links to both the market and, in some cases, the international system (some were former diplomats or other officials); they were better placed than khans of the East to provide leadership and other collective goods. The growth of politically organized Islamist fronts was limited by the strength of the khans. Furthermore, the relation of the Durranis of Qandahar to the old regime meant that none of the youth of the area had joined the Islamists in the 1960s and 1970s and that none were involved in the leadership of the Islamist movement and the parties that later developed out of it. Hence the shortage of Islamist cadres was far more acute in Qandahar than elsewhere. Most of the fronts nominally adhering to Islamist parties were traditional and tribal in organization.

In Qandahar party and tribal allegiances were as fragmented as in the East, but relations among the fronts were on the whole good.[46] Support of NIFA in this area (more extensive than indicated by the Orkand data in Table 9.1) reflected not only adherence to some local Qadiri pirs, but a general loyalty to the old regime. In the DCAR report on Qandahar, of forty-one "people of influence" listed whose party affiliations are given, fifteen are said to be affiliated to NIFA or working to spread the influence of Pir Gailani. Twenty-eight other "people of influence," however, had no party affiliation; they were simply tribal leaders or ulama, a proportion that indicates where the real power lay in Qandahar.

One can identify the party affiliation of leading commanders in each tribe, but each tribe included commanders affiliated with virtually all of the parties. The leading Barakzai commander, Haji Abdul Latif (assassinated in August 1989), adhered to NIFA, although he sometimes received weapons from Khalis. The leading Popolzai lineage, the Karzais (who were not really commanders), belonged to the ANLF, although in private they often expressed distaste bordering on contempt for all parties and said that they had been forced to join by the ISI in order to obtain weapons.[47] The leading Alikozai commander, Mullah Naqibullah Akhund, at first joined ANLF but then switched to Jamiat, with which he apparently had no previous affiliation.[48] Ismat Muslim, a leader of one of the main Achakzai clans, refused to join any party; the ISI eventually cut off his weapons supply, and he became a major government militia leader. Mullah Lala Malang, a typical fighting mullah, who led a mainly Ghilzai front, affiliated himself to Khalis. Early in the war he had killed many Khalqi prisoners belonging to Durrani tribes, as a result of which his relations with the Durrani mujahidin were strained. This ill-feeling, however, never developed into open warfare.

The main government presence in Qandahar was the garrison stationed at the

U.S.-built airport, which was supplied by air through most of the war. In addition, Ismat Muslim's Achakzai militia controlled the road from Spin Boldak on the Pakistan border to Qandahar city from 1984 to 1988. His influence extended across the border into the Achakzai areas of Pakistani Baluchistan. The Qandahar resistance by and large remained socially closer to the population than were the mujahidin in the East, although the DCAR report found that in several districts military shuras did not include all elements of the population and sometimes did not consult elders. The large commanders of the province—except for Mullah Malang, because of the resentments against him—had united in several organizations. According to the Orkand study, "By 1985 the Resistance in the Qandahar Region was organized into a series of committees, the most authoritative of which was the Judicial Committee of the 'Ulama. Composed of 11 senior 'alims [sic], . . . this committee was independent of any of the Resistance political parties and had the final authority on all political-military-juridical matters. Under the 'Ulama, the Executive Committee . . . of the 'Ulama and the Commanders—has operational responsibility for the Resistance." DCAR described the institutions somewhat differently, but agreed on the influence of the ulama:

> There are two major institutions functioning in Kandahar, the Military Shura and the Islamic Court (*mahkama*). The former is made up of major command-ers and tribal elders from the areas surrounding Kandahar city. The shura has served to coordinate resistance activities around the city and, more recently [September 1989], has attempted to act as an intermediary for relief agencies planning to provide assistance to the province. The Islamic Court has a more widespread basis of legitimacy. Reportedly established at the behest of 300 mujahideen commanders from all over Kandahar to adjudicate civil disputes, the court is composed of Islamic scholars and mullahs from each woleswali and alaqdari in the province.[49]

Military organization remained largely tribal. The mujahidin of Qandahar did not create any new military institutions. Although they did mount large offensives at times, these were organized on an ad hoc basis by the commanders' shura.

Helmand came under the domination of a powerful warlord, Mullah Nasim Akhundzada, a traditional alim affiliated to Harakat-i Inqilab. The population of this area, also Durrani and Baluch, was largely detribalized as a result of the Helmand Valley dam and irrigation scheme, which brought together nomads and others in mixed settlements. Enriched by profits of the opium trade, Mullah Nasim developed a personalistic dictatorship over the detribalized peasantry. He was a semifeudal com-prador engaging in exploitation of the peasantry through an alliance with multina-tional corporations, in this case the heroin cartels. In an interview published in 1987 Mullah Nasim claimed to have established hospitals, clinics, and forty madrasas (but no secular schools).[50]

The Hazarajat

By design, governments of Afghanistan had split the Hazarajat among several provinces; Hazaras were a minority in each. This region includes portions of Bamiyan, Wardak, Ghazni, Uruzgan, Jauzjan, Samangan, and Ghor Provinces. As we have seen, in 1979 the Shura constructed a bureaucratic state in most of the region, although it seems likely that real authority in many localities remained with the mirs. After 1982 the commanders of Nasr, Sipah, and other Islamist organizations seized power. In addition, a few commanders of Harakat-i Islami built powerful fronts west of Kabul and north of Qandahar.

Little detail is available about the precise institutional structures built by the pro-Iranian parties. It appears that the economic situation in the Hazarajat improved, perhaps becoming better than before the war. Pashtun nomads no longer drove their flocks through the area, trampling the fields and extracting usurious interest with the support of the government officials. Some wealthy Hazara merchants returned to their home region from the bazaars of Kabul. Furthermore, since except for some posts on the frontiers of the Hazarajat, this area was free of any Soviet or government presence, many mujahidin supply routes to the North traversed it. Like the Dawlat of Nuristan, local authorities exacted tolls on this transport.

Across the country, the social and political changes created by the war effort and by the influx of aid remained difficult to discern as long as Soviet troops and Soviet aid kept the PDPA in control of the capital, roads, and borders. With the Soviet withdrawal these changes became more visible as the state apparatus that had repressed and encapsulated the new forces contracted.

11

Mujahidin
after Soviet
Withdrawal

The withdrawal of Soviet troops between May 15, 1988, and February 15, 1989, reduced the military pressure on the mujahidin. Resistance fighters captured or occupied all of the frontier with Pakistan, including the customs posts at Torkham (in the Khyber Pass on the Peshawar-Jalalabad road) and Spin Boldak (on the Quetta-Qandahar road). They overran the eastern Afghan provincial center of Kunar, where competing shuras—the seven-party alliance and the Jamaʿat al-Daʿwa—vied for power. A largely Hazara shura took control of Bamiyan, in central Afghanistan. Massoud captured Taliqan, center of Takhar Province, and established a capital for the SCN there near the Soviet (Tajikistan) border. Several other provincial garrisons negotiated truces with local mujahidin.

The fragmentation of the political and military structures of the resistance prevented the mujahidin from turning local victories into a national one. For many of the fighters and commanders, the personal obligation (*farz-i ʿain*) of jihad ended with the Soviet withdrawal. As in more normal times—but with more weapons—they engaged in struggles for local power. Without the unifying impulse of jihad, nationalistic resentments also grew against Pakistan and Saudi Arabia, which had aided the struggle for their own reasons and now tried to control the outcome. Some leaders pursued economic opportunities, especially in opium production and the drug trade, while others elaborated independent political strategies.

The international supporters of the resistance, who still wished to displace Najibullah, tried to reshape the mujahidin into a conventional military force led by a political alliance that would pose a genuine political alternative to Kabul. The evaporation of the Soviet threat, however, brought regional rather than global considerations to the fore, which in turn fomented divisions among the international supporters as well as among the mujahidin themselves. Pakistan's military saw the possibility of gaining "strategic depth" against India by planting a friendly Islamic regime in Kabul, whereas the United States wanted to replace Najibullah with a stable, "moderate" regime. Iran and Saudi Arabia used the various mujahidin forces as proxies for their rivalry. These states developed links to emerging regional-ethnic alliances within Afghanistan. The Soviet Union and the Afghan regime, too, engaged mujahidin leaders in direct or indirect negotiations to incorporate them in some transitional arrangement. Commanders and party leaders played on these rivalries to increase their independence, frustrating the external powers' designs, as local strongmen have often frustrated the policies of the central state.[1]

The withdrawal of the Soviet military thus blurred the differences among local, regional, national, and international organizations. In a largely rural society where the state depends on foreign aid and a few commercial exports (like natural gas), relations between state and society parallel geographical relations between capital and country. Although local power groupings can successfully resist political penetration, state control of roads, combined with reprisals and payoffs to strongmen, makes it difficult for local powers to form larger ethnic or regional coalitions. Under these conditions national politics remains effectively insulated from local and regional forces.

The sudden loss of military power by the Kabul regime as a result of the Soviet withdrawal removed some of the barriers that had insulated the national political arena. Local commanders who headed heavily armed organizations that had developed during the war formed regional coalitions in some areas; major commanders and regional leaders formed a national shura of commanders; and the exiled party leaders increasingly were drawn into international diplomacy. As the political arena widened in which forces mobilized under the banner of jihad could compete, conflict emerged among larger coalitions, which corresponded loosely to ethnic identities.[2] The formerly repressed society in the countryside developed new forms of organization and returned to menace the state and the international system.

International Attempts at Restructuring

When Soviet leaders decided to withdraw troops from Afghanistan, they forced the reshuffled PDPA leadership to propose national reconciliation. At the same time, the Soviets initiated international negotiations over the establishment of a new government in Kabul, which they hoped would take power before the departure of their troops. The Pakistan Foreign Ministry relayed these proposals to the alliance of seven party leaders, who—with the support of the ISI—rejected them. Instead, the leaders announced the formation of a commission to draft statutes for an Islamic interim government.[3]

The Pakistan Foreign Ministry responded more positively to the Soviet position. Foreign Minister Sahibzada Yaqub Khan explored the possibility of an interim government organized around Zahir Shah, to be legitimated by a Loya Jirga. He even traveled to Rome to meet Gen. Abdul Wali. The ISI and the Islamists vetoed the idea, however, and the Soviet attitude remained ambiguous.[4]

Debates over the political future of Afghanistan moved the Iranian government to organize the Shi'a groups they supported so that they, too, would be able to engage in political negotiations. On June 18, 1987, eight groups based in Iran—Nasr, Sipah, and six smaller Shi'a groups—announced the formation of an alliance. The Shura of the Hazarajat joined later, but Harakat-i Islami, still distrusted by the Iranians, never did. At about the same time the Shi'a alliance was formed, commander Ismail Khan of Herat organized his conference of commanders in western Afghanistan, rejecting both Kabul's national reconciliation proposal and any attempt by exiled leaders to impose a solution on the commanders.

At the December 1987 summit in Washington, Gorbachev told Reagan that he was prepared to withdraw Soviet troops from Afghanistan regardless of whether a new government was formed in Kabul. General Zia, however, argued that, with the Soviet commitment to withdraw in hand, the time was right to press for an interim government. As Pakistani government pressure mounted on the seven-party alliance to make a proposal for an interim government, gunmen assassinated Prof. Sayd Bahauddin Majrooh in Peshawar on February 11. Majrooh, a revered poet and philosophy professor from a prominent sayyid family in eastern Afghanistan, was publisher of the widely respected *Afghan Information Centre Monthly Bulletin*. A survey in the *Bulletin* had claimed to show that more than 70 percent of Afghan refugees supported Zahir Shah rather than any of the mujahidin leaders as the future leader of Afghanistan.[5] The assassination of Majrooh was widely interpreted as Gulbuddin Hikmatyar's riposte to the "Zahir Shah option."

Under strong pressure from Zia, the alliance finally presented a proposal for a transitional government in late February. Although the alliance described its proposal as a "broad-based" government, it was too narrow to satisfy even most mujahidin. Under the proposed formula, the seven party leaders would constitute a leadership council, which would appoint a cabinet: two members from each of the seven parties of Peshawar, seven exiles, and seven "Muslims presently serving inside Afghanistan." The party leaders could not agree on even a partial cabinet until June 19, after the start of the Soviet pullout. Reportedly Gen. Hamid Gul, director-general of ISI, drew up the list in exasperation and imposed it upon the leaders after they had repeatedly failed to agree. The list showed considerable deference to Saudi sensitivities, for Saudi princes agreed to pay the "government" $1 million per month. The prime minister was a Wahhabi, a member of Sayyaf's party. The cabinet contained no resistance commanders from inside Afghanistan, no representative of the Shi'a resistance parties, and no independent intellectuals or technocrats. The proposal met with a cold reception from the Afghan refugees and resistance commanders, to say nothing of exiles and the Kabul regime.[6]

During the withdrawal the Soviets again invited resistance leaders to join negotiations. The Soviet ambassador to Kabul, Deputy Foreign Minister Vorontsov, discussed with Sunni and Shi'a mujahidin leaders and with Zahir Shah the formation of a transitional government with the PDPA. Both resistance and ex-king rejected the proposals, as did their foreign supporters.

In one of his first national security decisions after taking office in January 1989, President George Bush committed the United States to continued support of "self-determination" for Afghanistan even after the Soviet withdrawal. Washington and Islamabad concentrated on creating a unified political framework that would enable the mujahidin parties to take over the state after the expected quick military victory by the resistance. At the insistence of their foreign sponsors, the seven Sunni parties chose an "Interim Islamic Government of Afghanistan" (IIGA) at a shura convened in Pakistan as the last Soviet troops were leaving Afghanistan in February 1989. Negotiations with Iran and the Soviets had failed to produce a formula for representation of either the Shiʿa or the "good Muslims" from Kabul, as government delegates were called. The seven party leaders appointed all 519 representatives to the shura, which was composed almost entirely of Peshawar-based party bureaucrats, mostly Ghilzai Pashtuns from eastern Afghanistan. The shura included hardly any commanders, and it excluded all participation by the Kabul regime, the officials of the old regime who had fled to the West, and the Shiʿa parties.

The IIGA chosen by the shura reflected ISI and Saudi manipulation of the electoral process. According to U.S. diplomats, the Saudi intelligence service spent $26 million during the shura; others claimed that each delegate received at least $25,000. ISI Director-General Hamid Gul promised the presidency to Mujaddidi to keep him from walking out in protest. Sayyaf was made prime minister in deference to the Saudis, who had promised to fund a conventional Islamic army for the government if their sect were adequately represented. A plan to make Hikmatyar the defense minister, and hence the commander of the Saudi-funded army, collapsed in the complex deal making that ended the meeting. The shura's domination by one sub-ethnic group intensified ethnic resentments, and the obvious manipulation of the Peshawar-based bureaucrats by the Saudis and the Pakistanis increased nationalist sentiment among commanders. The IIGA never succeeded in establishing itself in Afghanistan or in organizing the elections it promised. Pakistan and Saudi Arabia paid for most of its operations, and the United States shifted some of its "humanitarian" aid to the IIGA's Ministries of Health and Education. Aid was given through these channels in order to build up the IIGA as a credible political alternative, not because this was the most effective way to give humanitarian aid to Afghans.[7]

Having established a new "national" leadership for Afghanistan, the ISI organized a mujahidin military offensive in March that was intended to install the IIGA in the eastern Afghan city of Jalalabad. Resentment of Pakistani manipulation, competition among parties, and unexpectedly stiff government resistance prevented any significant advance.[8] A few months after the failed Jalalabad offensive, Massoud and the SCN tried to present an alternative to the ISI strategy. Massoud's plan to capture the important northern center of Kunduz had to be called off when a commander of Hizb-i Islami (Hikmatyar) captured and killed ten of SCN's senior commanders (and about twenty others) on July 9, 1989. Massoud captured those responsible and hanged four Hizb commanders after a trial by ulama. In the resulting furor, Mujaddidi called

Hikmatyar a criminal and a terrorist, and Hikmatyar suspended his participation in the IIGA. Commanders inside Afghanistan showed increasing resistance to ISI attempts to direct them militarily; some observers said the commanders were "on strike."

In the summer of 1989, however, the shifting global strategic situation altered the place of Afghanistan in the international system. With the advance of the eastern European revolutions of middle to late 1989, the Bush administration gradually acknowledged the end of the Soviet threat. The United States had originally allowed the ISI to distribute aid to Afghanistan with little or no American oversight during a period when exerting military pressure on the Soviets—"killing Russians," in the vernacular—was virtually the only goal. Now the dreaded political considerations came into play.

The United States challenged the large share of aid that went to Hikmatyar and Sayyaf as well as the exclusive use of the Peshawar parties as conduits for assistance. Mujahidin supporters in Congress charged the CIA with incompetence and acquiescence in ISI policies, leading to the dismissal of the head of the CIA Afghan Task Force in September 1989. Under U.S. pressure, the ISI had begun the previous year to distribute more weapons directly to commanders rather than to the parties, but these were still generally either Hikmatyar commanders or small commanders who were charged with carrying out specific acts, such as shelling Kabul city.[9] Large commanders like Massoud or Abdul Haq, whose independent power might threaten ISI control, continued to receive relatively little assistance. Arab aid continued to go directly to favored leaders, mainly Hikmatyar and Sayyaf.

The failure at Jalalabad and the fighting among the parties in the summer of 1989 led Washington to redefine its stance that fall. The new goal of U.S. policy included not only "self-determination" for Afghanistan, but also a negotiated political settlement that would lead to the "sidelining of extremists," including Najibullah, Hikmatyar, and Sayyaf. The United States engaged in a two-track policy, beginning a diplomatic dialogue with the USSR on a U.N.-sponsored political settlement while trying to improve the military performance of the mujahidin.[10] In an attempt to keep the two tracks from conflicting, the United States determined that no weapons paid for by its funds would be given to Hikmatyar or Sayyaf, who opposed such a settlement. Instead, most would go to regional or local military shuras inside Afghanistan.[11] In spite of State Department pleas for cooperation to Pakistan and Saudi Arabia, Saudi and other Arab funds took up the slack in aid to the mujahidin "extremists," so the new U.S. policy made little if any difference on the ground. The operations wing of the CIA, which maintained close links with the ISI and the Saudi Istakhbarah, looked with skepticism if not hostility on the new policy. In practice, U.S. maintenance of the arms pipeline continued to strengthen the Afghan groups that the policy aimed at weakening.

The exit of Soviet troops and the end of the Iran-Iraq war freed the Iranian government to pay more attention to Afghanistan. Although Tehran had opposed the presence of Soviet troops on its Muslim neighbor's soil, it became increasingly concerned about the rise of Pakistani and particularly Saudi influence in Afghanistan through the Sunni Islamists. In the summer of 1989 President Rafsanjani told the Shi'a groups that the jihad was over and that they should seek a political settlement with Kabul. Tehran similarly signaled its support for a political settlement to the Soviet government and the United Nations.[12]

In 1990 Iran induced the Shi'a parties it had organized in an alliance to unite into a single party, the Hizb-i Wahdat (Unity Party). Unlike Pakistan, which still gave aid separately to seven parties and their commanders, Iran now funneled aid to this single center. It also gave some humanitarian and economic aid to Najibullah, whom it preferred to the Saudi-supported IIGA. Iran also took advantage of dissatisfactions with the Saudi-ISI-CIA-Hikmatyar axis to initiate a rapprochement with both its fellow Persian-speakers in Jamiat and the moderate nationalist mujahidin groups. (Ironically, the United States was indirectly aligned with "fundamentalists," while Iran courted the "moderates.") By 1991 Iran had signed a treaty on cultural cooperation with Tajikistan, Hizb-i Wahdat, and Jamiat. Mujaddidi, Gailani, and Rabbani all traveled to Iran and opened offices there.

The Pakistani military and the Saudis began to fear both the rise of Iranian influence and the possibility of a deal between the superpowers to sideline the more militant Islamic forces.[13] Saudi Arabia increased its support for Hikmatyar as the strongest Sunni force. The ISI had made a tremendous investment in Hikmatyar over the years and regarded him as the key guarantor of Pakistani interests in Afghanistan. Both the ISI and the CIA also regarded him as a useful tool for affecting the future of Central Asia. Hikmatyar also received aid from Middle Eastern Sunni Islamists, Muammar al-Qaddhafy, and, later, Saddam Hussein.

In the fall of 1989, as the U.S.-Soviet dialogue began, a Pakistani military mission came to Washington to promote an "action plan" for a new mujahidin political and military offensive. According to this plan, the now discredited IIGA would convene another shura, this time with representation from around the country, and hold elections to provide the council with greater legitimacy. At the same time, Pakistan and the United States would concentrate on turning the mujahidin guerrillas into a conventional military force by improving their command and control capabilities and increasing their supplies of rockets and other heavy weapons. The heart of the military strategy was the creation of a conventional mujahidin army that would consist of eight battalions based in Pakistan, the majority under the command of Hikmatyar.

Hikmatyar's conventional force, known as the Army of Sacrifice (Lashkar-i Isar), developed into the only mujahidin military force other than Massoud's Islamic Army that bypassed local and tribal (though not ethnic) segmentation. Since the soldiers of the army were recruited from the refugee camps, Hikmatyar hardly needed to confront the microsegmentation of Afghan society. The boys who had grown up in the refugee camps were not a part of any social structure in Afghanistan, nor did they live in any locality there. Their education in Hizb schools had taught them loyalty to revolutionary Islam, to the party, and to its leader.

In a strange way, Hikmatyar's army resembled that of the Afghan state. Just as the government army had recruited its officer corps from tribal boarding schools that taught an official ideology (nationalism) different from that of popular culture, so Hikmatyar had recruited his officers and men from the revolutionary Islamic schools. Both armies were funded and supplied by a combination of foreign aid (the USSR on one hand, Islamic sources on the other) and commercialized agricultural exports (karakul, cotton, and raisins for one, opium for the other). The result in each case was an armed force that neither transcended nor suppressed Afghan social structures. The Army of Sacrifice simply bypassed those social structures as it traversed the territories of Paktia and Logar on the way to southern Kabul. In spring 1992 I received estimates that the army could muster between five thousand and six thousand soldiers.

The first attempt to use this force came in March 1990. As part of the covert ethnic realignment of Afghan politics after the Soviet withdrawal, Hikmatyar had begun to negotiate an alliance with his fellow non-Durrani Pashtuns in Khalq. The ISI and the Saudis seem to have supported these efforts, thus becoming closely identified with the "Pashtun plot"—more accurately, a Ghilzai and Eastern Pashtun plot. On March 7, 1990, Shahnawaz Tanai launched his coup. He bombed the presidential palace while trying to open up the security cordon to the south of Kabul to let Hikmatyar's battalions into the city. Hikmatyar announced the formation of a Revolutionary Council with Tanai, and the ISI and Saudi intelligence pressured the other mujahidin leaders to join, reportedly paying commanders as much as $15,000 to support the coup. With U.S. support, the Peshawar leaders resisted.[14] Tanai fled to Pakistan, where Hikmatyar appointed him commander of the Army of Sacrifice.

The force moved again after Pakistani President Ghulam Ishaq Khan, at the behest of the military, dismissed the government of Prime Minister Benazir Bhutto on August 6, 1990, four days after Saddam Hussein's invasion of Kuwait. The military now had a free hand, and the ISI tried to reorganize the IIGA in Peshawar, again backing Hikmatyar for minister of defense. At the same time the ISI tried to coordinate a massive assault on Kabul city by Hikmatyar, to whom they reportedly transferred forty thousand rockets and seven hundred trucks of ammunition.[15] The assault, intended to precipitate chaos that would facilitate a Khalqi coup from within, would have involved an indiscriminate shower of inaccurate rockets on the city, causing thousands of civilian casualties. This effort was finally stopped by forceful intervention by the U.S. State Department.

In late 1990 and early 1991 the conflict in the Islamic world over the approaching Gulf War temporarily weakened the ISI. Hikmatyar and other radical elements of the Afghan mujahidin, as well as their supporters in the Pakistani military and ISI, joined the international Islamist opposition to the U.S.-led coalition operating from Saudi Arabia. The civilian government of Pakistan, along with the nationalists and moderates among the mujahidin, supported the U.S.-Saudi position. The Saudis had arranged to transport two thousand mujahidin to Saudi Arabia to offer symbolic support to the U.S.-led coalition, but the project was repeatedly held up by objections from radical mujahidin groups and Pakistani military officers, including Chief of Army Staff Gen. Mirza Aslam Beg. In February, the Saudi Istakhbarah chief Prince Turki made a special trip to Pakistan to remonstrate with his counterparts; five hundred mujahidin from the most nationalist groups (Gailani and Mujaddidi)—whom the Saudis had hardly assisted—made the journey. The Saudis at least temporarily ceased funding Hikmatyar and some other groups. The United States strengthened its insistence to the ISI that Hikmatyar and Sayyaf be cut off; most U.S. funding for ministries of the IIGA ended in March, but most of the IIGA's funding came from Pakistan.

An alliance then formed between the U.S. government (at least the State Department) and some commanders inside Afghanistan who wished to pursue a military and political strategy independent of the ISI and Hikmatyar. Soon after the Tanai-Hikmatyar coup, a group of mujahidin field commanders convened a National Commanders Shura (NCS). Although organizers claimed that the NCS intended only to coordinate military strategy, most Afghans perceived it as an attempt by internal commanders to seize the initiative from the discredited and foreign-influenced exiled leaders. After holding meetings in May and June 1990 with mostly Pashtun participation from eastern Afghanistan, the NCS called a nationwide meeting of commanders in October. The October meeting was held in Kunar, near the Pakistan border but close to the undefined boundary between the Pashtun South and the non-Pashtun North, so that more northern commanders could attend. At Hikmatyar's orders, his commanders boycotted the NCS. Sayyaf also forbade his commanders to attend, but several did. ISI officers tried to dissuade some commanders from attending by telling them it was an American shura. The ISI's new director-general, Asad Durrani, insisted on traveling to the meeting, where he was forbidden to participate in the sessions.

The October NCS meeting included a broader representation of regions and ethnic groups than had any previous gathering of mujahidin. It passed resolutions against the ISI-sponsored strategy of a direct attack on Kabul by militia units based in Pakistan. Instead it outlined a plan to capture provincial outposts of the regime and set up regional administrations (base areas) in nine zones.

Massoud went to Islamabad on behalf of the NCS to ask that large commanders be given aid directly to carry out plans they formulated themselves without ISI interference. Massoud pressed his complaints that the ISI discriminated against him and other powerful commanders in favor of Hikmatyar. In March 1990 he had sent emissaries with the same message to Washington, where they had received backing from congressional supporters of the mujahidin.[16] U.S. diplomats in Pakistan promised finally to resolve the problem by supplying Massoud and other major commanders directly. The ISI insisted that Massoud first sign a meaningless peace agreement with Hikmatyar. U.S. officials finally took measures to ensure that major commanders in the NCS received supplies, including sophisticated radio equipment that would enable them to communicate in code inside Afghanistan without going through Pakistan. This technology was key to enabling the regional leaders to form a national coalition, for it circumvented the difficulty of mountain transport. The radio sets were delivered after several months of wrangling within the NCS over who would receive them, and a significant quantity of arms and supplies finally began to flow to Massoud and other prominent commanders in the NCS.[17]

U.S.-Soviet dialogue on a settlement, however, had stalled. Soviet Foreign Minister Eduard Shevardnadze had proved unable to sign a projected agreement at a meeting with Secretary of State Baker in December 1990; on his return to Moscow, Shevardnadze resigned, warning against reactionaries. In January 1991 Soviet hardliners, with Gorbachev's apparent support, sent troops into Lithuania and the other Baltic Republics, in what proved to be rehearsals for the August 1991 Moscow coup. The CIA and ISI insisted that with the hardliners in ascendance in Moscow, further military action was necessary in Afghanistan.[18] Immediately after the Gulf War, at the end of March 1991, the CIA and ISI threw their resources, including many Pakistani advisers on the ground, into the battle for the perennially besieged Afghan garrison town of Khost in Paktia.

ISI officers tried to gain influence over the NCS through this campaign, organizing the offensive in a way that seemed consistent with NCS strategy. The ISI convened several tribal shuras or jirgas and reached elaborate agreements before the assault about the distribution of booty.[19] The garrison finally fell to tribal forces led by commander Jalaluddin Haqqani, a prominent figure in the NCS. In the aftermath, however, the coalition broke apart. Although Hikmatyar's forces had played only a minor role in the fighting, Hizb-i Islami managed to seize the radio station and most of the garrison's heavy weapons, in violation of precampaign agreements, and the ISI prevented Haqqani from recovering the loot. Hikmatyar, General Durrani of ISI, and Qazi Hussein Ahmad, leader of the Pakistani Jama'at-i Islami, paid well-publicized visits to Khost, broadcasting the Pakistani role to an increasingly nationalist Afghan public.

The cost in Pakistani effort and the inability of the Pashtun tribal mujahidin to establish a government even in this small town—instead they pillaged it—ultimately exacerbated the loss of credibility of proponents of the military option. The president and prime minister of Pakistan decided that it was time to promote a political settlement. The Saudi government agreed.

Local Organization

The mujahidin commanders themselves, as much as the governments in Kabul and Moscow, frustrated the various foreign plans for a resistance victory. The mujahidin had accepted Pakistani military aid and its accompanying pressures with little complaint as long as Soviet troops remained. After the withdrawal, although postures of intransigence or pretenses of ideological unity were still necessary to gain access to the lucrative flows of cash and guns, many commanders began to make practical deals with their opponents. Mujahidin who still believed in jihad after the Soviet withdrawal confronted with disbelief the alliance of Hikmatyar and Tanai. If Khalq and Hizb could ally, there was no more jihad, just a struggle for power.[20]

Leading commanders sought more autonomy. As early as 1987, whether as a result of a softening of Soviet counterinsurgency or because of the deterrent effects of Stinger missiles, agriculture and trade began to revive, increasing resources available to local commanders.[21] Many commanders seized the opportunity to produce a cash crop for which there was seemingly unlimited demand—opium poppies. In some areas the poppy profits enabled commanders to turn themselves into powerful war-lords, increasingly independent of external donors.

The Soviet withdrawal had another important effect. Recall that the commanders interviewed by the Swedish Committee for Afghanistan unanimously reported that the Soviet intervention had made it nearly impossible for them to seize booty or charge tolls. The Soviet withdrawal enabled the commanders once again to levy tributes on road transport—by traders, smugglers, and government suppliers alike. Commanders engaged in trade themselves, for many of them had developed business relationships with the transport companies that brought their supplies from Pakistan. In spite of repeated pressures from the ISI, commanders generally preferred not to strangle Kabul or major regional centers they surrounded, such as Qandahar and Herat, but to trade with them instead.

Local commanders also received increasing amounts of foreign aid directly rather than through parties. Supply lines from Peshawar became much more secure than during Soviet intervention, and more aid could travel over roads by truck rather than by pack animals on mountain trails. European and U.N. aid programs generally dealt directly with commanders who could implement programs in areas under their control.

No overall figures for the total of such programs are available, but a DCAR report from September 1989 illustrates the level of activity: in Arghandab District of Qan-dahar Province nongovernmental organizations (NGOs) were running or funding three clinics, four other health projects, and cash-for-food programs; rehabilitating farm-land and irrigation systems; establishing schools; and providing improved seeds, insecticides, and water pumps. Twelve separate agencies were involved, including European, American, and Arab NGOs, and the quasiofficial International Committee of the Red Cross. Some of these agencies were operating with funding from USAID or UNHCR. Arghandab had more projects than most districts, but virtually every district of the provinces studied by DCAR was reported to have at least one project.

Just as the states that provided weapons pressured the party leaders to unite politically, aid givers pressured local commanders to form shuras. The aid-giving organizations often insisted that they would provide aid to a locality only if the commanders were united. Otherwise, they said, the aid would be perceived as partisan rather than humanitarian and would result in further fighting rather than in benefits for the civilians. In Afghan villages as in Peshawar, this sometimes led to Potemkin shuras, established only to obtain foreign aid. According to Michael Barry, a scholar who was then acting as field officer for Médécins du Monde, one commander approached him to ask for a clinic in the name of a shura formed by commanders of the seven parties in one area of Wardak. Investigation showed that a number of brothers, cousins, and uncles of one extended family had joined different parties and then called themselves a shura. In some cases foreign humanitarian agencies themselves convened shuras inside Afghanistan.[22] Most of these efforts proved as transitory as the IIGA.

Some commanders used these resources to elaborate independent political strategies, but most emerged as a new stratum of "Islamic khans." The tendency toward politicization of local insurgencies that had grown during the Soviet occupation reversed itself among many groups as a result of decreased military pressure and increased access to local resources. The new local elites, including Islamist intellectuals, were partly reabsorbed into the traditional patterns they had grown up with. Most Islamist activists were village youth who had sojourned in Kabul or regional towns for secondary or higher education. There they had established links to national and international networks that provided the resources through which they had consolidated power as a new generation of local strongmen.

The khans of the old regime, many of whom had fled, continued to lose power, as the new Islamic khans remained antagonistic. Just as the old khans had supported the royal regime but had resisted government interference in local society, the Islamic khans affiliated themselves with Islamic parties while resisting any impositions by the exiled leaders—to say nothing of the ISI. Najibullah recognized this fact in his counterinsurgency strategy. Before the Soviet withdrawal, the National Fatherland Front had tried to recruit traditional khans, members of the "big families" who had served in the parliaments of New Democracy; after the Soviets left, though, Najibullah and his militia intermediaries concentrated their efforts on local commanders of all parties, especially Islamists engaged in local conflicts with rivals.

Most of the revived economic activity was local, under the control of the new strongmen. Hikmatyar was the only leader to exploit opium profits systematically as a basis for a hierarchically organized party and conventional army. In the summer of 1988, expecting that the Soviet withdrawal would lead to decreased foreign support, he seems to have instructed his men to search for precious stones and to cultivate poppy. Unlike the warlord commanders, who were content to sell raw opium at bazaars in Afghanistan and Baluchistan (where paper currency was weighed rather than counted), Hikmatyar seems also to have invested in some processing plants in partnership with Pakistani heroin syndicates.[23]

In the SCN-dominated areas of the Northeast a more differentiated and extensive organization was able to use funds generated by the agricultural revival in a way similar to taxes. In this area only certain parts of Badakhshan seem to have been conducive to opium growing. Foreign aid to the SCN strengthened existing quasistate institutions with a strong local political base. Although I have less information on Herat, it seems that a similar process developed there, with the difference that the regime- and resistance-controlled areas were more integrated into a common economy.

Regional Organization

As communications and travel within the country became easier, broader regional coalitions formed in those areas where social control was not too fragmented. As noted, the enlargement of the political arena promoted ethnic conflict. Soviet control of the axes of communication and of the capital had kept resistance units confined to small localities, where the principal social conflicts were those between local qawms. As some resistance units expanded and the battle for Kabul unfolded, these organizations formed the cores of larger ethnic coalitions regardless of the ideology of the leaders.

As the United States and the USSR disengaged from Afghanistan, regional powers supported different ethnic coalitions there. Rough alliances emerged: Pakistan and Saudi Arabia with eastern and Ghilzai Pashtun Islamists, Iran with the Shiʿa and with Persian-speaking and Turkic groups. The latter groups also enjoyed some sympathy in Central Asia, especially Uzbekistan. Pashtun traditionalists and Durranis negotiated with both of these coalitions, while hoping for more involvement by the United Nations and the United States. All groups found allies within the Kabul regime, largely along ethnic lines: the Pashtun Islamists with Khalqis and the non-Pashtuns with anti-Najibullah Parchamis.

Only a few commanders had developed autonomous bureaucratic and political organizations to provide support for their military efforts. The extent to which such organizations developed was what really marked the differences among regions of the country during this period. Only in the non-Pashtun areas did leaders manage to establish such organizations inside the country. The combination of isi manipulation, tribal segmentation, and a high level of emigration kept the Pashtun areas fragmented. The only large conventional military units of the resistance among Pashtuns were Hikmatyar's battalions organized by the isi among the refugees in Pakistan.

The North

By the time of the Soviet withdrawal, resistance military activity had died down in the North, although Mawlawi Alam, the amir of the Jamiat shura of Balkh, continued to run elements of a civil administration. The vast volume of Soviet aid crossing this territory enhanced its prosperity. The Jauzjani and Ismaili militias brought this area under their influence by distributing Soviet aid to the Islamic khans. They had originally acted as agents of Najibullah, but they increasingly took control of the aid flows themselves, for they got their hands on them before Najibullah did. The Soviets, however, still insisted on recognition of Najibullah's authority as a condition for continuing the aid.

In 1988 Najibullah created the Hazara-majority province of Sar-i Pul in the southern part of Jauzjan Province, and Sar-i Pul apparently became an economic and political base for the northern Hazaras. Under Iranian influence, the Hazara resistance parties worked out a modus vivendi with the regime militias in the area.

The Northeast

Massoud was the commander in Afghanistan who most fully escaped the tendency toward reabsorption in localist patterns of behavior; Hikmatyar, not the local commanders, came to be his main rival. Massoud was strengthened in this rivalry by his lobby in the Jamiat office in Peshawar and by his international influence, thanks mainly to his French publicists. Massoud obtained weapons and other support from Jamiat partly based on his status as amir of the SCN, rather than solely as commander of Panjsher, so he could both build up Central Forces of the SCN and redistribute goods throughout the Northeast. Because Soviet and regime troops had left Panjsher at the very beginning of the Soviet withdrawal, Massoud effectively controlled stretches of the Salang Highway south of the area under control of Sayyid Mansur Nadiri's Ismaili militia. Massoud may have received one-fifth of all goods he allowed to transit to Kabul. Naturally, he resisted pressure from ISI and the CIA to close the road.[24] Western aid organizations also channeled their assistance to resistance-held areas in the Northeast largely through the SCN, which received hundreds of thousands or even millions of dollars from foreign organizations, both Western and Islamic. British Afghanaid opened a year-round office in Taliqan, staffed by an Afghan in the winter and an expatriate in the summer.

After Massoud captured Taliqan, he commanded a capital. He had cleared the Northeast of all regime presence except for a few enclaves. He thus controlled not just a social network, like other commanders, but a substantial contiguous territory. The SCN invested in the infrastructure of this territory, building branch roads neglected during Daoud's construction of a national road network. These roads eased internal communications and marketing within the region, giving it a higher level of internal integration and political cohesion. In 1991, to encourage agriculture and new enterprises, the SCN founded the first mujahidin bank in Taliqan. In spite of its Islamic ideology, the SCN became a de facto political, economic, and geographical base for northeast—and therefore Tajik—power.

Some local commanders in SCN areas sent delegations to both Jamiat and the aid organizations, asking to receive aid directly rather than through Massoud.[25] But they did not match the success of the Afzali front and other dissidents in their appeal against Ismail Khan in Herat. The ISI gave massive aid to Hikmatyar and Sayyaf commanders in the North, who posed a continual but diminishing threat to Massoud.

After the Soviet withdrawal Massoud came under pressure from Pakistan and Jamiat headquarters to increase his forces rapidly for an assault on Kabul, but he refused to substitute quantity for quality of his cadres. He resisted pressure from the ISI to mount what he considered premature assaults on Kabul and other major regime targets. For instance, during Tanai's coup, the ISI ordered him by radio to send troops to relieve Bagram air base, supposedly under rebel control. Massoud's intelligence, more accurate than the ISI's, told him that the government had already recaptured the base, and he refused to throw his forces away in a losing battle. Instead he concentrated on building them for later, more decisive conflicts.

In 1989 Massoud upgraded his Central Forces to a new status, renaming them the Islamic Army (Urdu-yi Islami). The aid he received in 1991 enabled Massoud to equip and expand his Islamic Army to five thousand men, for a total of twelve thousand under his command. Over the summer of 1991 Massoud took control of most of northeast Afghanistan's border with Tajikistan and negotiated an agreement with the Soviet border guards. Najibullah could do nothing but send a few airplanes to bomb Taliqan.[26] Massoud's overpowering force compelled most Hikmatyar commanders and recalcitrant Jamiat commanders to enter into agreements with him.

In a battle on the northern border, Massoud successfully resisted the Jauzjanis. Dostum opened secret discussions with him, possibly brokered by the Iranians, although by this time the ISI had also opened up a back channel with Dostum. Massoud continued to gain credibility with the anti-Najibullah Tajik Parchamis in the party and in the army. The Iranians, who had relations with both the Persian-speaking Parchamis in Kabul and the Persian-speaking mujahidin in the North, seem to have brokered this alliance as they sought to balance the rise of Saudi and Pakistani influence among the Sunni mujahidin, especially Pashtuns.[27] Tehran sought a special relationship with the northern, non-Pashtun part of Afghanistan, which constituted a land bridge between Iran and the Central Asian Republics of Uzbekistan and Tajikistan.

The West

After the Soviet withdrawal, Ismail Khan's organization in the West lost the $500,000 in annual subsidies it had been receiving from the ISI.[28] In view of what happened in other regions, one might speculate that the subsidies stopped because Ismail Khan refused to attack the city of Herat. Some landlords who had previously sold wheat to him now sold it to the government, which was engaged in an expanded program of grain procurement. Ismail Khan retaliated by arresting the khans, who managed to escape and join the government. Nonetheless, except for a few incidents, this area enjoyed relative military calm. Everyone knew the fate of the country would be decided elsewhere. Both the provincial administration and Ismail Khan received aid from U.N. agencies based in Iran. Ismail Khan showed little allegiance to Peshawar, and the Herat garrison owed little to Kabul. As happened more openly in Qandahar, the mujahidin and the garrison worked out an accommodation, and refugees returned.

The East

The East remained fragmented by tribal and partisan divisions. Its commanders, demoralized by repeated ISI manipulations, increasingly devoted themselves to economic activities, including the opium trade. The only modern, mobile military force in the area was Hikmatyar's Army of Sacrifice. In 1991 Hikmatyar, with Pakistani assistance, established a base for this force in Tang-i Wakhjan, south of Kabul, but the Jauzjanis and Ismailis managed to destroy most of this installation. The local mujahidin, who resented the intrusion of Hikmatyar's force, failed to come to its aid.

After the Soviet withdrawal the Afghan government evacuated its garrisons in Kunar. The unorganized and fragmented mujahidin committed a number of atrocities against the civilian population of the government-controlled areas they took over and then engaged in numerous battles with each other.[29] Jamil al-Rahman's Jama'at al-Da'wa and the seven parties of the Peshawar alliance created rival shuras in the provincial capital of Asadabad. Jamil al-Rahman received large Arab donations, and many Arab volunteers joined him. He engaged in a campaign to remove flags and raze monuments erected over tombs, icons that he claimed were un-Islamic, as had that archetypal tribal puritan Muhammad ibn Abdul Wahhab before him. (It is a long-standing Afghan tradition to raise a flag over the tomb of a martyr fallen in jihad and to build a monument [*mazar*] over the tomb of a scholar or pir.)

Hikmatyar's forces emerged as Jamil al-Rahman's main military rival in Kunar. The two leaders took opposing sides in the 1990–91 Gulf War, Jamil al-Rahman supporting his Saudi and Kuwaiti patrons and Hikmatyar the Muslim Brotherhood in its anti-American, anti-monarchy position. This, together with numerous other disputes, led to repeated clashes in the summer of 1991 that ended in August when an Egyptian gunman assassinated Jamil al-Rahman. Kunar seems to have been too unstable even for the opium cartels. By the time Najibullah fell, the valley was so devastated by these conflicts, on the heels of Soviet carpet bombing, that the dispirited mujahidin were continually hungry and thinking of raiding Jalalabad for food.[30]

In Nangarhar the mujahidin drove the army posts and government militias out of an area from Torkham, on the Pakistan border, almost to Jalalabad. In early 1989 the commanders were trying to form a provincial shura to ask for the negotiated surrender of the Jalalabad garrison, but the ISI intervened with its own military plan. Over the next three years there was little military progress by the resistance, but there was a notable economic revival. DCAR reported poppy growing in over half of the districts in 1989. According to one reporter in May 1992, "For miles around Jalalabad, 80 percent of the arable land produces nothing but poppies, U.N. officials say. And the farmers like it that way. Today opium brings the farmer 10 times more money than wheat—and there is plenty of cheap bread for sale in town, thanks to the flow of free flour [from USAID]."[31]

In 1989 and 1990, as part of the ISI's plan to exert pressure on Jalalabad, mujahidin in Nangarhar closed the important trade and smuggling route between that city and the Khyber Pass, arousing protests from the tribes in the area. A settlement reached at a jirga in the spring of 1991 reopened the road and allocated shares of the tolls between tribes and mujahidin fronts.[32]

In Paktia the mujahidin remained combative, but the tribal social structure resisted any statelike authority or a conversion to conventional warfare. A Pyrrhic victory in Khost in March 1991 exemplified the problems of the Paktia mujahidin. After finally overrunning the garrison, they dissipated their military victory in conflicts over booty. The resistance leaders could not establish any stable government in Khost, which they dismantled rather than governed.

The South

After the Soviet withdrawal from Qandahar, in July 1988, the ISI mounted a major effort to oust Ismat Muslim from Spin Boldak. Because Hikmatyar and Sayyaf were weak in the South, the ISI organized a lashkar of all the tribes, who joined in driving the Achakzai militia from the area.[33]

As a result of this defeat, Najibullah feared that the Qandahar garrison might work out an agreement with the nationalist mujahidin. He reinforced the garrison with Jauzjanis. The Uzbeks seemed to take a certain satisfaction in fighting the Durranis, who had long oppressed them in Turkestan. The tensions they caused among the population and even the Pashtun PDPA members led to the removal of the Jauzjanis in 1989. After the Soviet withdrawal the shura and the garrison entered into negotiations, while the ISI tried to force the shura to attack the city, where many mujahidin had relatives.

Despite all ISI efforts, the mujahidin never attacked Qandahar city. During the battle of Jalalabad, commanders were summoned to a meeting at which the ISI offered several truckloads of weapons and "covered the table with money" in an effort to get the mujahidin to attack the city. Later commanders under ISI control blockaded the city's trade with Pakistan, leading to a rise in the price of food and driving much of the population for the first time to ask the government for assistance. Another plan proposed blowing up a large dam and flooding the city, forcing the "Communists" onto the roofs where they could be shot "like birds." The Qandahar shura deputed one commander to guard the government's dam from the ISI.

After several such failures—which the ISI claimed proved the "military inefficiency" of the traditionalist shura—in the summer of 1989 the ISI created a rump shura of Hikmatyar and Sayyaf commanders. Hikmatyar himself was sent to the area, together with a large group of his militia, mostly Ghilzais recognizable from their northern "Pakhto" dialect. Barakzai commander Haji Abdul Latif fired warning artillery shots toward the convoy, and Hikmatyar was forced to leave the province. The next month Haji Abdul Latif was poisoned. Following a common pattern, his son accused WAD publicly and Hikmatyar privately. The Islamic court of Qandahar also issued a fatwa stating that "Wahhabis" were *kafir* (unbelievers), and that Muslims who became Wahhabis could be executed as apostates.[34] The resulting infighting gravely damaged the political structures of the Qandahar mujahidin. The garrison invited the mujahidin into the city without their weapons, and the fighters even started sending their sons to government schools.

In the Helmand Valley Mullah Nasim Akhudzada expanded opium cultivation after the Soviet withdrawal. Opium had traditionally been grown in the mountainous land of North Helmand, but now it spread into South Helmand as well. Farmers who had seen their lands bombed and irrigation systems destroyed desperately needed cash. Under a system called *Salam,* Mullah Nasim paid cash for the crop at the time of sowing, at low prices relative to the yield at harvest. (Some claimed that this system amounted to usury or *riba,* forbidden by the Qur'an.) Mullah Nasim also set production quotas; in 1989, for instance, he decreed that 50 percent of the land had to be sown in poppy. Any landowner who did not fulfill his production quota had to pay the difference, which drove some into debt. Those who failed to meet these provisions were subject to harsh penalties, reportedly including torture and death.

The opium went to a bazaar at Gird-i Jangal, where the representatives of refineries bargained over it. The six main refineries, which belonged to Hizb-i Islami, were in Kuh-i Sultan. The refineries hired smugglers to transport the finished product to Baluchistan via Robat, home of the "smugglers' front." Mullah Nasim had an office in nearby Zahidan, Iran, to handle this trade.

The growth of the opium trade gave rise to various conflicts. In the summer of 1989 Commander Yahya of Sayyaf tried to levy taxes on the opium passing through his area. Mullah Nasim responded by conquering the area.

Mullah Nasim traveled frequently to Pakistan as deputy defense minister of the IIGA. The United States had forced the ISI to cut off his aid because of his drug trafficking, and on one visit to Pakistan in the winter of 1989–90 he popped up unexpectedly at the American Embassy in Islamabad, where he expressed an interest in working out a settlement. U.S. Ambassador Robert Oakley offered him $2 million in return for stopping opium cultivation. Mullah Nasim had expected to receive containers of currency, like the payoffs offered by Kabul, and was somewhat disappointed when he learned that the $2 million would be in the form of development programs funded by USAID. Nonetheless, he agreed, and in the spring of 1990 he ordered a drastic reduction in the amount of opium planted.

In late March (the start of the planting season), however, he and five of his subcommanders were assassinated in Peshawar as they were leaving a meeting with his party leader, Mawlawi Muhammadi. Most observers attribute the killings to the drug cartels, including Hizb-i Islami, which had counted on continued high levels of production of raw opium from Mullah Nasim. This killing led to conflict between Hizb and the other parties in Helmand, and Mullah Nasim's brother Ghulam Rasul assumed control. Finally, the State Department informed Oakley that his agreement with Mullah Nasim violated U.S. policy against negotiating with drug traffickers, and the United States refused to honor those promises.[35] The next year Ghulam Rasul ordered the peasants to go back to full opium production, although in interviews he stated that he was willing to carry out his brother's plan to reduce opium production in return for assistance in finding substitutes.

The Hazarajat

The Soviets had withdrawn from the Hazarajat in 1981, and their withdrawal from the rest of the country had little direct effect there. The main effect of the national withdrawal for the region was that access by Iran became easier as Najibullah's hold on power became weaker, and the Iranians tried to strengthen their position against the Saudi-backed Sunni groups. Kabul and Tehran agreed on a deal in 1991: Iran supplied western Afghanistan, including the armed forces, with petroleum, in return for which Iran was able to supply the Hazarajat directly by flights to Bamiyan. The Hizb-i Wahdat, headed by an Iranian-born leader of Afghan descent, increasingly assumed political and military control under Iranian patronage.

As long as Soviet aid kept Kabul functioning, the structures of power in these regions remained separate. But when the Soviet Union dissolved, so did the Afghan state, and Afghanistan was composed not of national republics but of hyperarmed networks of power.

12

State Collapse after the Cold War: Afghanistan without Foreign Aid

Amir Abdul Rahman Khan created the modern state of Afghanistan with weapons and cash supplied by the British for their own strategic reasons. Foreign powers whose main strategic interests centered on Europe also furnished weapons, cash, and training to Daoud, Taraki, Amin, Karmal, and Najibullah, enabling them to pursue domestic projects that met the strategic goals of the suppliers. When the Soviet Union broke up at the end of 1991, so did the Russian empire in Asia. Bipolar strategic conflict ended, and the European imperialist map of Southwest Asia was redrawn. Foreign aid to Afghanistan from competing, Euro-Atlantic powers ceased, and along with it the century-old project of building a foreign aid–funded, Pashtun-led, centralized buffer state.

Both the United States and the now defunct USSR suspended military aid to their Afghan clients at the end of 1991; Moscow also stopped its shipments of food and fuel. Both announced support for the formation of a U.N.-sponsored interim government that would replace Najibullah. As soon as aid stopped, the northern militias, who no longer needed Najibullah as an intermediary with Soviet aid givers, mutinied against the Pashtun rulers of Kabul and allied with the northern mujahidin.

The armed forces, the principal remaining state institution, dissolved and were absorbed into the country's regional-ethnic power networks. In the North, most units retained their coherence and were reorganized under new commands. In the South, the Khalqi Sarandoy units crossed over to Hikmatyar and became the backbone of his military forces. The army garrisons in the Pashtun areas followed the Khost model: the mujahidin dismantled the installations, demobilized the soldiers, and distributed the equipment among the segments of tribal coalitions.[1]

In the battles for Kabul that followed, alliances formed around the most modernized, hence extensive and mobile, organizations. These coalitions largely followed ethnic patterns in composition if not in ideology. Segments of the population whose organizations remained clientelistic and localistic, especially the tribal Pashtuns, could not participate effectively. The emerging ethnic conflict over control of the central state—and even over the definition of Afghanistan—led some traditionalist forces among Pashtuns to look for leadership to Hikmatyar, who alone among Pashtuns commanded the mobile, conventional forces needed in the struggle for power.

On April 26, 1992, with Kabul torn apart by fighting between non-Pashtun and Pashtun coalitions, the leaders of the seven Pakistan-based parties signed the Peshawar Accords, which provided a framework for an interim government of mujahidin. But this agreement among exiled political party leaders contained no program for integrating the regionally based political-military organizations into a reconstituted state. Conflicts among these groups eventually rendered the Peshawar Accords ineffectual and called the possibility of a united Afghanistan into question. The Afghan regional structure that predated Abdul Rahman Khan reemerged, but with modern weapons and new forms of political and military organization. No great power now supported with guns and money the rule of a Pashtun dynasty over Afghanistan, which was no longer a buffer between contending empires or alliance systems. Billions of dollars worth of modern weapons that had outlasted the strategic interests of their providers circulated in a devastated country with neither national institutions nor national identity.

Plans for a Political Settlement and the End of Aid

In May 1991, the U.N. secretary-general's office, which had conducted multilateral consultations and was encouraged as well by the shift in the Iranian position, the U.S.-Soviet dialogue, and the change in the positions of Pakistan and Saudi Arabia after the Gulf War, issued a statement summarizing an "international consensus" on Afghanistan. According to five very generally worded points, a political settlement would begin with the establishment of a "transition mechanism" in Afghanistan. In conjunction with the beginning of the transition, all external parties would stop supplying weapons to Afghanistan, and all internal parties should cease fire. The interim authority would organize "free and fair elections, in accord with Afghan traditions," to choose a "broad-based government." The invocation of "Afghan traditions" suggested that a Loya Jirga or another form of tribal representation might replace elections in some areas.[2]

As Soviet hardliners gained power in 1991, Washington and Moscow could not reach agreement on the timing of the aid cutoff or on the powers of the transition mechanism; the Soviets insisted that Najibullah remain as president, whereas the United States wanted the transitional mechanism to replace him. When the chiefs of the Soviet security and party apparatus who had insisted on retaining Najibullah were defeated after their August 19 coup attempt, Washington and Moscow quickly reached agreement.

On September 13, 1991, Soviet Foreign Minister Boris Pankin and U.S. Secretary of State Baker agreed to the text that had been prepared for the Baker-Shevardnadze meeting the previous December, but with two additional provisions: a date for the termination of aid by both sides (January 1, 1992) and a statement that the transitional authority should have "independent authority with all powers required to prepare for, conduct and implement" elections. The transition mechanism would be worked out through "intra-Afghan dialogue" sponsored by the United Nations. Both sides would work toward the "withdrawal of major weapons systems," namely the scuds and Stingers.[3] Pakistan and Saudi Arabia quietly indicated that they would comply but declined to announce the decision, which would have been difficult to justify to influential segments of public opinion in both countries.

In early October the Soviet Union told U.N. Secretary-General Javier Pérez de Cuellar that it would not demand that Najibullah be allowed to participate in the transition. In his October 1991 report on the situation in Afghanistan the secretary-general said that he had "been given assurances that some of the controversial personalities concerned would not insist on their personal participation, either in the intra-Afghan dialogue or in the transition mechanism."[4]

In November the USSR and Russia invited representatives of Jamiat, the three Sunni traditionalist parties, and Hizb-i Wahdat to Moscow. These parties had met twice since the spring with the foreign ministries of Pakistan and Iran to discuss implementation of the secretary-general's points. The three Pashtun-led Islamist parties had refused to participate in previous meetings and were not invited to Moscow.

The joint statement issued after the Moscow meeting called for the replacement of the government in Kabul by an "Islamic interim government." This government would hold elections with the aid of the Organization of the Islamic Conference and the United Nations. The Soviet and Russian representatives promised not only to terminate weapons supplies but to withdraw any remaining military advisers and to stop supplying fuel for military operations.[5]

The first U.N. proposal for the transitional mechanism was a coalition government between mujahidin and non-Communists in the Kabul government. Moscow suggested that Zahir Shah or Mujaddidi be installed as president and that Fazl Haq Khaliqyar continue as prime minister. Implicit in this proposal was that government security forces would remain in place during the transition period. The Pashtun radicals (Hikmatyar, Khalis, and Sayyaf) objected, as did Rabbani, so this simple and direct solution had to be abandoned.[6]

Benon Sevan, head of the Office of the U.N. Secretary-General in Afghanistan and Pakistan, then pursued previously discussed plans to use the forum of the United Nations to promote a dialogue among the various Afghan parties. In January the new secretary-general, Boutros Boutros-Ghali, announced a plan under which all Afghan parties would submit to his office lists of candidates for an "Afghan gathering" (*ijlas*). The United Nations would negotiate agreement by all parties on about 150 representatives, and the gathering would elect a committee of about 35. This committee would canvass the entire nation, and on the basis of these consultations would summon a nationwide meeting to establish an interim government and arrange for elections.

This cumbersome procedure was designed to overcome several obstacles. Power-sharing negotiations remained impossible. The resistance leaders still refused to meet or cooperate openly with the existing government, although nearly all parties had met more or less secretly with Najibullah or his representatives. It was still not possible to organize a multiparty council as in Cambodia, where all four parties had signed an agreement. Najibullah had offered to hand over power to Zahir Shah or to a neutral force, but not to a fragmented resistance that had not defeated him and could not govern the country. Any Afghan who tried to convene a gathering would be suspected of promoting his own power; any non-Afghan (including the U.N. secretary-general) would lack legitimacy. The United Nations therefore proposed that the secretary-general's good offices be used to facilitate the creation of Afghan groups that had a realistic chance of gaining the needed authority. The procedure drew on certain Afghan traditions (in particular the "emergency Loya Jirga") described to the United Nations by exiled officials of the old regime, including the former king and his advisers.[7]

The three traditionalist-nationalist parties of the mujahidin submitted a joint list of proposed participants in the gathering, and Hizb-i Wahdat submitted its own list. Zahir Shah and his advisers ultimately refused to propose participants for a gathering that gave such weight to the resistance parties. The Sunni Islamist parties (including Jamiat) also refused, suspecting that the United Nations aimed to exclude them from power or prevent their impending victory. Najibullah postponed giving his list, submission of which would have constituted a more decisive and public signal than had his previous confidential assurance that he was prepared to depart.

By March, Pakistan and the United States were telling Sevan that to pressure the holdouts in the resistance they needed an explicit, public commitment by Najibullah to depart. After several long sessions in Kabul with Sevan, Najibullah presented his list of candidates and agreed to announce his intention to resign. Addressing the nation on television and radio on March 18, 1992, Najibullah read a speech—written by Sevan—saying that he would leave office as soon as a transitional authority was formed.

This statement provoked increased conflict as regional coalitions within Afghanistan crowded into the power vacuum that had been created. As the state threatened to disintegrate before the completion of the lengthy transition process, the United Nations streamlined its plan. On April 10 Boutros-Ghali approved a new version: a "pre-transition council composed of impartial personalities" chosen from the lists submitted to the United Nations would take over "all powers and executive authority" from the current government.[8] This council would then convene a shura in Kabul to choose the interim government.

The United Nations hurriedly canvassed support for the plan, and under pressure from the United States and the Pakistan government, the major leaders in Peshawar and Kabul accepted it. The resistance leaders, Najibullah, and all major figures of the regime signed documents that committed them to the process. Those members of the proposed interim authority who were outside Afghanistan assembled in Pakistan. On the night of April 15–16 a U.N. plane was to fly the members of the interim government into Kabul, where Najibullah would transfer power to them at the airport and leave on the same plane. On April 15 Najibullah handed his resignation to the U.N. office in Kabul and prepared to depart.

The same day, however, at a meeting of more than eight hours at the Islamabad residence of the prime minister of Pakistan, two of the mujahidin parties expressed misgivings about the pretransition council. Rabbani, whose forces, with the support of the northern rebels, seemed on the verge of taking Kabul, wavered. The son of Mujaddidi, who harbored ill-concealed ambitions to serve as president of the country, suggested a mujahidin government. Sevan asked the mujahidin leaders to submit a list of members of such a government. When they were unable to agree on a list, Sevan flew alone to Kabul in the early hours of April 16. He arrived to find that Parchami rebels who resented Najibullah's plan for a safe exit had blocked the former president from reaching the airport. Najibullah had sought refuge in the Kabul U.N. office.

National Struggles among Regional-Ethnic Coalitions

The internationally supported U.N. plan broke down with the disintegration of the state that the interim government was supposed to rule. That state, as we have seen, had become little more than a set of apparatuses headed by mutually antagonistic leaders held together by Najibullah's redistribution of external aid. Only that aid rendered these organizations partly autonomous from the regional societies from which their members were recruited, and only that aid gave them coherence as parts of a single institution. As the government's fiscal crisis became deeper, so did the crisis of state autonomy and coherence.

Absolutely essential to the state's continued existence was its control of the land link to the North, protected by the Jauzjani and Ismaili militias. In January 1992 this link broke. Because Najibullah no longer received Soviet aid and was approaching the limits of sustainable hyperinflation, he had to economize. He warned Dostum, whom he suspected of padding his ranks with phantom recruits, that he would reduce the number of salaries he paid.

Because Najibullah could no longer rule by redistributing externally supplied resources, he turned to the remaining tool of Afghan rulers: manipulation of social segmentation. He tried to assert control over the northern supply lines by using Pashtun solidarity of regular army officers against the militias. The Soviet military had shipped a large stockpile of weapons just before the agreement with the United States went into effect. General Mumin, the Tajik commander of the Hairatan garrison where the weapons were stored, had established ties to both Dostum and Massoud. Mumin had long been diverting aid to Dostum and passing intelligence to Massoud, a classic example of the horizontal linkages that erode state autonomy. In late January,

Najibullah instructed Gen. Juma Atsak, the commander of the Northern Zone, an Achakzai known for his Pashtun chauvinist views, to replace Mumin with General Rasul, a Pashtun Khalqi who was much hated for his service as commander of Pul-i Charkhi Prison under Taraki. Mumin refused to leave, and Dostum not only supported him but raised support for the revolt from Sayyid Mansur Nadiri's Ismaili forces. The revolt also enjoyed the support of the mainly non-Pashtun pro-Karmal forces in Kabul, who saw alliance with the northerners as their insurance policy under a hostile new government and who resented Najibullah's assertion of Pashtun control over the North.[9]

The Parchami and northern rebels allied with commanders of Hizb-i Wahdat, Jamiat (including SCN), and other northern resistance groups. On March 19, the day after Najibullah announced that he would resign, this coalition seized control of Mazar-i Sharif, cutting off Kabul from its main supply lines. Dostum defeated the Khalqi Eighteenth Division in Balkh under General Rasul, and the coalition encountered some resistance from Najibullah loyalists at Mazar's WAD headquarters, taken by SCN, but otherwise the transition took place with little fighting. The regime military forces and the administration were for the most part undisturbed, and the North remained stable. With the collaboration of the militias and Parchamis in Kabul, Massoud's forces took control of the airfields north of Kabul in Bagram and Charikar, where he now set up his base. The northern road to Kabul lay open before him.

Massoud, who commanded legitimacy as a national hero of the resistance, emerged as political spokesman for the alliance, but its most powerful military force consisted of the former regime militias. Dostum had over forty thousand men, more than three times as many as Massoud. He formed a new organization, the Junbish-i Milli-yi Islami (National Islamic Movement), together with Nadiri, Mumin, and other Uzbek and Ismaili commanders.

The northern alliance easily gained control of all military installations between Mazar and Kabul. In an operation coordinated by Karmal's brother, Mahmud Baryalai, Parchami rebels also seized control of the Kabul airport with 750–1,000 troops flown from northern military bases. Baryalai took vengeance on his brother's rival when these forces blocked Najibullah from leaving the country on the night of April 15–16. That same night WAD chief Ghulam Faruq Yaaqubi reportedly committed suicide in the headquarters of the secret police.[10]

Led by Karmal's second cousin, Foreign Minister Abdul Wakil, the Parchami rebels who now controlled Kabul denounced Najibullah as a dictator and secretly asked Massoud to enter the capital as head of state. The Parchamis intended to use Massoud as a figurehead who would continue to depend on them. General Muhammad Nabi Azimi, commander of the Kabul garrison, contacted Massoud in the hope of duplicating in Kabul the "Mazar model" of peaceful turnover of power without fighting or damage to the state apparatus.[11]

Massoud agreed to remain in touch with the Kabul garrison in the hope of managing a peaceful transition, but he refused to enter the capital as head of state. He asked the leaders in Peshawar to accelerate their efforts to form an interim government of mujahidin. In spite of intense Pakistani pressure, however, the leaders in Peshawar argued for ten days over arrangements for a transitional government. In an attempt to avert ethnic conflict, Massoud communicated regularly over his American-supplied radios with Pashtun commanders of the NCS, assuring them that he would not seize power unilaterally.

While the leaders in Pakistan argued, Pashtuns reacted to the northern offensive. In spite of Massoud's assurances, many Pashtuns in both the resistance and government feared an attempt by the northerners to capture power at their expense. Hikmatyar continued to play on Pashtun ethnic fears. In Kabul there had been talk for some time of a "Pashtun solution."[12] As the northern forces closed in on Kabul in April, Pashtuns in the Afghan military—mainly Khalqis, but also some Parchamis close to Najibullah—arranged the infiltration of unarmed fighters of Hizb-i Islami into the city, where they received arms from their co-ethnics in the Interior Ministry.[13] Hikmatyar's conventional military force also crossed over the border from Pakistan and camped south of Kabul, where it was joined by Khalqi units, mostly Sarandoy. Pakistan's official neutrality notwithstanding, Hikmatyar continued to recruit fighters and transfer weapons, oil, and supplies from that country, as well as to use offices and bank accounts there. Jama'at-i Islami continued to support him, as did a sector of the intelligence apparatus.[14]

The threat of an imminent coup by Hizb prompted Massoud to act before the Peshawar leaders had reached agreement. On April 25, the forces of Massoud and Dostum, already in control of the Kabul airport, entered the city. The non-Pashtun Parchamis, assisted by the Iranian embassy, had also armed the Shi'a of Kabul city, and two Shi'a qawmi units of WAD in and near Kabul had joined the northern alliance.[15] After violent battles at the Interior Ministry and the presidential palace, the forces of Dostum, Massoud, and Hizb-i Wahdat expelled the Khalqi-Hizbi Pashtun forces. The defeated Pashtuns, however, had breached the security cordon around the city, and other mujahidin flowed into Kabul, setting up checkpoints and engaging in looting. These guerrillas included Arab Islamists who had flocked to Afghanistan from the Middle East to train for jihad in their homelands or elsewhere.

The Islamic State of Afghanistan

The leaders finally reached agreement on April 26, when they announced the Peshawar Accords. For two months Mujaddidi would be acting president, to be followed by Rabbani for four months. After six months the government would hold a shura to choose an interim government for the next eighteen months, at the end of which time elections would be held. The acting president answered to a "leadership council," composed of the leaders of mujahidin parties, Sunni and Shi'a. Massoud became minister of defense. The interim government arrived in Kabul from Peshawar on April 28 and, amid continuing battles in the capital, proclaimed the establishment of the Islamic State of Afghanistan.

Perhaps this entity was Islamic, but it was hardly a state, and it certainly did not rule Afghanistan. The government had virtually no income. All major customs posts, the government's principal sources of revenue in the absence of foreign aid or natural gas exports, were under the control of regional shuras that kept the revenue for themselves. Tens of thousands of armed men belonging to a variety of forces—or to none—roamed the streets of the capital, looting, fighting, and sometimes raping. With neither tax revenue nor foreign aid, the government paid the disparate groups that constituted its armed forces by distributing freshly printed banknotes that continued to arrive by plane from Russia, where they were printed under commercial contract. (Hikmatyar demanded that Russia stop printing the banknotes, which financed the government that had ousted his forces from Kabul.)

The arrival of the new government intensified competition for power. During the spring and summer of 1992 Shi'a mujahidin armed by Iran controlled about one-fourth of Kabul city and repeatedly clashed with Sayyaf and other Salafi mujahidin, who were aided by Arab volunteers. Hundreds of civilian hostages taken in these clashes in June disappeared.[16]

A more serious threat to peace was Hikmatyar's refusal to accept the agreement, which, by making Massoud defense minister, effectively recognized the northern coalition's military control of Kabul. The long-standing rivalry between Hikmatyar and Massoud, between Hizb and Jamiat, became associated with the feud between Khalq and Parcham and took on the dimensions of a battle for the control of Afghanistan between Pashtuns and non-Pashtuns. Hikmatyar charged that the new government was not a genuine mujahidin government at all but a vehicle for power-sharing with communists. Besides maintaining his alliance with Dostum, which was militarily indispensable, Massoud had kept on Najibullah's commander of the Kabul garrison and his chief of army staff (both Parchami Muhammadzais), as well as the Parchami former defense minister Baba Jan, who now commanded a special forces unit. On the other side, Hikmatyar's main military force now consisted of former Sarandoy troops, he was assisted by several Khalqi former defense ministers and armed forces commanders (all Paktiawal and Ghilzai Pashtuns), and his personal bodyguard consisted of members of a former progovernment Pashtun tribal militia from Helmand. Hikmatyar also enjoyed the support of Jama'at-i Islami of Pakistan, of leftist Pakistani Pashtun nationalists (who were sheltering some of Najibullah's associates), and of former ISI officers. Hikmatyar also received Middle Eastern money, mostly from the Muslim Brotherhood, but also reportedly from Qaddhafy and Saddam Hussein. Most of the rank-and-file mujahidin remained in their regions and villages, where their control was now disputed only by local rivals, not by the state.

From May through August, Hikmatyar periodically bombarded Kabul with rockets. According to the United Nations, by August over 1,800 civilians had been killed. Several thousand more, injured in the shelling, sought treatment in hospitals where damage to the electrical grid and the water system had curtailed services. Food supplies in Kabul were becoming scarce, shops were closed, and over 500,000 people were fleeing the city in all directions.[17] The United Nations and most diplomatic missions withdrew all non-Afghan personnel. By the end of the year over 5,000 people had been killed and perhaps a million had fled the devastated city.

At the end of June, Mujaddidi mounted a campaign to keep his position rather than handing over the presidency to Rabbani. Finally Mujaddidi resigned, however, and went to visit his brother, a professor of obstetrics in Florida, for several months. Newspaper reports called Rabbani's succession the first peaceful transfer of power in Afghanistan since the death of Amir Abdul Rahman Khan, but in fact, Mujaddidi had no power to transfer.[18]

Six months after assuming authority, on October 28, the leadership council reluctantly voted to extend Rabbani's mandate for forty-five days, on the grounds that continued fighting and the destruction of Kabul had made it impossible for him to summon the shura in the time designated. After the extended term, however, the government would summon a nationwide shura-yi ahl-i hall-u-ʿaqd (Council of Resolution and Settlement, an Islamic legal term unfamiliar to most Afghans). The shura would elect a president for the following eighteen months. Somewhat belatedly, Rabbani managed to convene a shura of 1,335 men at the end of December. More than a tenth of the members were drawn from Dostum's organization; Jamiat predominated among the rest. Most areas of the country and ethnic groups had some representation, but most of the parties boycotted the shura, charging that it was manipulated by Rabbani, whom, to no one's surprise, it elected as president on December 29.

During preparations for the shura, Massoud attempted to wrest control of the Kabul University campus (where the shura was supposed to be held) from the Shiʿa militia, and the former allies engaged in bitter street fighting. Dostum's soldiers interposed themselves between the two forces. Hikmatyar took advantage of the conflict within the opposing coalition to isolate Massoud, his principal opponent. He tacitly agreed not to shell Dostum's positions, and in January he signed a formal alliance with Hizb-i Wahdat.

These developments attenuated the sharp division between Pashtun and non-Pashtun, but they reinforced the apparently ethnic character of post-Soviet Afghan national politics. The struggle for power had come to be dominated by four ethnically identified armed forces: Uzbeks under Dostum, supported by Uzbekistan; Shiʿa of Hizb-i Wahdat, supported by Iran; Pashtuns under Hikmatyar, supported by Islamists and intelligence officers in Pakistan; and Tajiks under Massoud, who alone lacked a powerful foreign patron, although they had developed some links to the now defeated opposition forces in Tajikistan. Only Hizb-i Wahdat was truly mono-ethnic, and not all members of the various ethnic groups supported the respective organizations, but ethnicity emerged as a powerful force in practical terms.

As fighting enveloped Kabul once again in January 1993, Saudi King Fahd issued an appeal for peace. This appeal led to another foreign-sponsored accord on March 7, when most of the party leaders signed an agreement in Islamabad with the blessing of Pakistan, Saudi Arabia, and Iran. The leaders then traveled to Mecca, where they swore allegiance to the agreement on the Holy Kaaba.

The Islamabad Accords established an interim government, which was supposed to summon a constituent assembly to draft a constitution within eight months and hold elections within eighteen. The accord reproduced the division of powers between president and prime minister that was then tearing apart the government in Pakistan. Rabbani was to remain as president, and Hikmatyar was to become prime minister. The president (supreme commander of the armed forces) and the prime minister (who formed the cabinet in consultation with the president) immediately argued over the appointment of the minister of defense. Massoud remained in place, although his official role became less clear. Gunmen attempted to assassinate the president while he was on his way to a confidential meeting with the prime minister, who preferred to camp in the suburbs and shell the capital.

With the help of his Shi'a allies, Hikmatyar managed to enter the south and west of the city, where he set up an office and convened cabinet meetings. Dostum met with both sides, offering to act as mediator and demanding a formal government position and recognition of autonomy for the regions. In January 1994 Dostum and Hikmatyar launched a joint offensive against the Jamiat-dominated government. Massoud held on, but the fighting devastated new areas of Kabul, including the money bazaar, and spread to the North as well. New waves of refugees fled toward Jalalabad and Pakistan.

Regional Power Centers

Between the fall of Mazar on March 19, 1992, and the surrender of Jalalabad on April 23, mujahidin had negotiated the surrender of all major government garrisons. The transfer of power in the provinces occurred peacefully except in Mazar, where a Khalqi unit resisted Dostum, and in Faizabad, Badakhshan, where the garrison may not have been fully informed about events elsewhere. Regional councils, some including commanders formerly on opposite sides, formed on the basis of local ethnic and tribal ties.

In the non-Pashtun areas of the North, Northeast, and West, the armed forces and administration (whether government or SCN) remained in place, but under the authority of regional figures rather than of Kabul. The appropriated state apparatus of these areas, where social control was far less fragmented than in the tribal zones, formed a basis for the power of the non-Pashtun groups. The Hazaras also enjoyed an autonomous territorial base in the center of the country. In the South and some other Pashtun enclaves, the state apparatus was divided among tribal segments. Kunar was an extreme case: even school buildings there had been dismantled and the chairs and tables distributed among various mujahidin groups.[19] Army garrisons fared no better. Among Pashtuns, the only modernized military force that survived was Hikmatyar's, precisely because it had no regional or tribal base to fragment it.

The North

By the summer of 1993, Dostum had integrated Uzbek and Ismaili militias, along with regime garrisons from Maimana to Pul-i Khumri, into a northern armed force of 120,000 men. Because he was able to offer salaries and career prospects, he reintegrated even Pashtun army officers, including some Khalqis, who had fled north after their garrisons were dissolved in the South. Mujahidin commanders of various parties also joined Dostum's Junbish. His control of airfields, roads, and fuel depots (replenished by his allies in Central Asia) kept his forces mobile and continued to give him access to and influence in Kabul.

Dostum carved out a political space for himself as the only powerful figure who supported secularism and as an advocate of regional autonomy and the rights of minorities. Many former high party and government leaders, including Babrak Karmal, took up residence in Mazar under his protection.

The United Nations moved its major office in Afghanistan to Mazar from Kabul in August 1992, and seven countries established consulates there: Iran, Pakistan, Turkey, Saudi Arabia, Uzbekistan, Turkmenistan, and Tajikistan. Dostum boasted that he had more functioning diplomatic missions than Kabul. In 1992 he visited Uzbekistan, Turkey, Pakistan, and Saudi Arabia, where he was received by high-ranking government officials.[20] Mazar also became the center of expanding private trade with the newly independent states of Central Asia.

Dostum gave refuge to about half of the sixty thousand refugees from the war in Tajikistan who fled to and remained in Afghanistan between December 1992 and January 1993. The United Nations built a large camp near Mazar and assisted the refugees with Dostum's support. Dostum raised his international profile further by collaborating with UNHCR in a voluntary repatriation of Tajik refugees that began in May 1993.[21]

Under pressure from all regional states, including Uzbekistan, Dostum retreated from his earlier separatist rhetoric and affirmed support for a united, though decentralized, Afghanistan. Nonetheless, while Dostum verbally recognized the "juridical sovereignty" of Afghanistan, the government in Kabul exercised no empirical sovereignty over his area. He collected customs at Hairatan and did not pass them on to Kabul; nor were his military forces subject to any commands from the Ministry of Defense. He controlled about the same territory as had Murad Beg, the Uzbek khan of northern Afghanistan supported by the Amir of Bukhara in the early nineteenth century.

The Northeast

Most of the Northeast remained under the control of the SCN, which was sufficiently institutionalized to continue functioning while Massoud was in Kabul. The SCN furnished about five thousand troops to the interim government. Massoud had some success in integrating the command structure of SCN with the portions of the Afghan army that fell into his hands (mainly the Kabul garrison and the divisions based just north of Kabul in Bagram and Charikar).[22] Massoud lacked any reliable foreign support, however, and his inability to bring security to Kabul or to transcend his regional background tarnished his image as a national leader.

Massoud allowed the exiled leadership of the Islamic Renaissance Party of Tajikistan to establish its office in the SCN capital of Taliqan, and he apparently provided military training to Tajik guerrillas, who wore SCN uniforms.[23] Tajik nationalism played little role in his decision, which seemed dictated more by the desires of Arab and Pakistani funders—the only sources of foreign aid now available—and by rivalries with Hikmatyar and Sayyaf commanders, who were also training Tajik guerrillas.

One major area of the Northeast remained outside of Massoud's control. In central Kunduz, where the irrigated cotton-growing areas have a large population of Pashtun settlers, the Pashtun garrison turned over its weapons to a local Pashtun commander, Amir Chughai of Sayyaf's Ittihad. Dostum controlled Kunduz's major port on the Amu Darya, Sher Khan Bandar. East of Sher Khan Bandar, Uzbek commanders of Hizb-Hikmatyar controlled the town of Imam Sahib, Hikmatyar's birthplace.

Amir Chughai, who had been a minor commander during the war, became the major power in central Kunduz. Most of the thirty thousand refugees from Tajikistan in Kunduz were under his control. With the help of Arab Islamists, who established an office in Kunduz, Chughai supplied weapons and training to the Tajik opposition. Hikmatyar's commanders also provided aid and training to the guerrillas. These activities led to disputes with the United Nations, which finally suspended operations in Kunduz, except for the strip of land controlled by Dostum, through which refugee repatriation also took place.[24] In late 1993 and early 1994 Dostum forces and the shura of Kunduz, dominated by Jamiat and Sayyaf, fought repeatedly over control of Sher Khan Bandar and Kunduz city.

The West

In Herat, Ismail Khan peacefully took control of the garrison and the Seventeenth Division. He integrated the regime military commanders into his shura as military advisers and made his rival, the late commander Afzali's brother, the chief of security in Herat. Militia who joined Hikmatyar took control of Shindand air base, where they found Iranian agents trying to supplement the planes they had gotten from the Iraqi air force during the Gulf War by appropriating Afghan MiGs. Ismail Khan took control of the air base with some air support from Kabul in October 1992, after Hizb units assaulted Herat city. Ismail Khan's shura defeated and disarmed the militias without bloody battles of the sort that rocked Kabul.

Herat turned into a peaceful center of economic revival.[25] Economic growth enabled Ismail Khan to bring more local commanders under his sway. Herat remained stable through 1993 despite pressures from Iran, which demanded more power for the Shi'a in the Herat shura and began pushing Afghan refugees across the border. In early 1994, Ismail Khan's forces clashed with Dostum's in Faryab, where the two zones of control met. Dostum's air force dropped a few bombs on the city in June.

The East

Besides the rival shuras of Kunar established in 1988, the eastern mujahidin established new shuras in the rival Pashtun areas of Nangarhar (Jalalabad) and Paktia (Gardez). The Jalalabad shura mainly included fighters of Hizb-Khalis and NIFA, whose partisan attachments became less important. In 1993 the governor of Jalalabad, Commander Shamali of NIFA, was killed with forty of his men in an attack that NIFA blamed on Haji Abdul Qadir, the shura spokesman from the Arsala family of Hizb-Khalis. Shamali's Ahmadzai tribe demanded badal from the Jalalabad shura and received support from Hikmatyar. They established a base at Sarobi, between Jalalabad and Kabul. Massoud sent SCN forces to dislodge this pro-Hikmatyar group, leading to a monthlong war in November that displaced thousands of members of the Safi tribe.

Many radical Arab Islamists continued to train in Jalalabad. They were widely suspected of responsibility for the assassination of four U.N. personnel, two expatriates and two Afghans, near Jalalabad in February 1993. This attack led the United Nations to terminate programs in the area and to withdraw all expatriates from Afghanistan. In Gardez a tribal shura led by Mawlawi Jalaluddin took over.

Neither of these shuras established mobile military forces or much civil administration. Hikmatyar took over several Sarandoy brigades and WAD units in the region, but the rest of the government's armed forces disbanded, largely without reprisals. The Pashtun tribes of eastern Afghanistan opposed Hikmatyar's attacks on Kabul, but they supported his demand for the removal of communists from the government. Many sympathized with Hikmatyar's attacks against the northern forces, but they did not send troops to help him. They sometimes acted as brokers between Hikmatyar and the government while pledging loyalty to neither. A weak government suited them, for they were occupied with trade in the profitable opium crop, which was planted right up to the roadside around Jalalabad in the spring of 1992.[26]

The South

The Durrani Pashtuns of southwest Afghanistan, although they were represented in the government, opposed its dominance by "fundamentalist" and non-Pashtun elements. They also firmly opposed Hikmatyar. They organized an "Islamic National shura" of mujahidin commanders, ulama, and tribal leaders.[27] Nor did the Qandaharis preserve regime military units or erect any regionwide political or military structures. The stability the South enjoyed in 1992 began to break down in 1993: Hazaras north of Qandahar, encouraged by Iranian aid, became more assertive, and Hizb-Hikmatyar forces in the area attempted to assert themselves against the tribal shura.

Helmand's center, Lashkargah, was taken over by a Khalqi militia that at first joined Hizb and then switched allegiance to Jamiat, but the drug warlords remained the principal powers in the area. In late 1993 Ghulam Rasul Akhundzada dislodged this militia with the help of Ismail Khan.

The Hazarajat

The Shi'a wielded more power in the national political arena of Afghanistan than they ever had before, particularly the Hazaras, both Imami and Ismaili. They were as fully autonomous in the Hazarajat, with their Iranian aid, as Dostum was in the North. They also in effect held the balance of power in Kabul between the two main Sunni forces, Hizb (plus Khalq) and Jamiat (plus Parcham). And they enjoyed the support of important figures of the Watan Party and of powerful former government militias.

Outside analysts, as well as many Pashtuns, interpreted these developments as signs of Iranian attempts to break up Afghanistan, but in reality the assertiveness of the Hazaras and Qizilbash showed their integration, however uncomfortable, into the national political arena. They raised their voice rather than seeking to exit. Shi'a served on the leadership council of the Islamic State (Ayatollah Muhsini of Harakat-i Islami served as spokesman for a time) and built an alliance with Hikmatyar that seemed to endure, as such things are measured in post–Cold War Afghanistan.

The Ruins of Empire

The day the Berlin War fell, in November 1989, I had dinner with other fellows and officers of the United States Institute of Peace at the home of a senior State Department official in the Washington suburbs. Each of us spoke in turn on the heretofore unimaginable events of the day. Among the well justified rejoicing, I remembered a line from the Urdu poet Ghalib, who witnessed the final days of the Mughal empire: "Because of my tears, I was expelled from your feast."

I certainly did not mourn the fall of the Soviet and Russian empires. I had seen

Afghan men and women break down and weep as they relived the tortures of KhAD. I had seen children without arms and legs, paralyzed and burned by Soviet bombs and mines. But I had also seen a photograph of the bloodied corpse of Sayd Bahauddin Majrooh, my teacher and mentor, assassinated with weapons U.S. taxes may have purchased, weapons that were supposed to defend our security.

It is not just, as some now say, that in fighting "communism," the United States strengthened "fundamentalism." As the events in Afghanistan showed, communism and Islamism have much in common, not because they are both extremisms, but because both are radical responses by elites trained for a world they cannot join.

The Cold War integrated these groups into a global order: even a structured bipolar conflict constitutes a kind of order. The great powers showered weapons, cash, and attention on the protagonists of this struggle. The principals in neither Washington nor Moscow could make "their" Afghans into reliable agents, but the resources they supplied shattered much of what the peoples of Afghanistan had preserved from their past. The Afghans had to find new ways to survive and interpret their often devastated environment.

The new leaders are not just old leaders with new weapons, and the new Afghanistan is not just the old Afghanistan with a seat in the United Nations. The boundaries and administrative structure of the Afghan state of 1879 to 1978 represented the balance of power within and around the Afghanistan of that time. Before the nation-state system came to the region, when some (for instance, Pashtuns) lost power and others (for instance, Uzbeks) gained it, the borders of political entities would shift accordingly, as emirates and khanates moved around a map without clear boundaries.

For a hundred years, these processes were frozen as the local and global hegemonic powers strengthened rule by Pashtun dynasties over a buffer state. But the increasing dependence of all Afghan rulers on external aid weakened their local sources of power. After 1978 international developments made the tension between state and society into a part of the struggle between East and West. The effort to topple an illegitimate regime undermined the fragile state itself.

The regional social forces asserted themselves, but the institutions of the nation-state, which constitute the deep structure of our international system, shape and limit them. When Ahmad Shah Durrani created an Afghan empire independent of both Persian and Indian empires in the eighteenth century, he minted coins with the inscription "Commandment came from the peerless Almighty to Ahmad the King: Strike coins of silver and gold from the back of fish to the moon."[28] Sovereignty may still come from God, but today the right to issue currency comes from the IMF. The international system upholds the juridical sovereignty of the Afghanistan defined by the Anglo-Russian agreement of 1907, despite the lack of any organization capable of exercising empirical sovereignty over it.[29] This contradiction virtually forces political leaders into a battle for control of Kabul, a battle to which the regionally segmented social structure of Afghanistan inevitably lends an ethnic character.

These leaders formed themselves in inner struggles with the ideas they learned in the schools built with U.S. and Soviet aid. They armed themselves and mobilized their countrymen for the outer struggles that the superpowers sponsored and paid for. Millions of weapons are the cargo that the Cold Warriors left behind, without delivering the promised gifts of development, socialism, democracy, or, for that matter, a just Islamic order.

Without a global struggle to give strategic value to corners of the world where some of its poorest people live, those people seem to be left to fend for themselves with the legacies of colonialism and superpower competition. But the international impact of domestic conflicts can be as far-reaching as the domestic impact of international conflicts. The continued turmoil in Afghanistan has already contributed to the civil war in Tajikistan, to authoritarianism in Uzbekistan, to growing Russian aggressiveness prompted by fear of Islam along Russia's southern frontier, and to the dissemination of military skills to radical Islamists in South Asia and the Arab world. If the international community does not find a way to rebuild Afghanistan, a floodtide of weapons, cash, and contraband will escape that state's porous boundaries and make the world less secure for all.

Appendix A

Note on Sources

In the course of my research I created or analyzed data sets on the fiscal basis of the Afghan state, on political elites, and on the mujahidin organizations. These data sets were constructed from a variety of sources.

The data on the fiscal basis of the state benefited from the work in Fry, *Afghan Economy,* which covered the entire period from the 1950s (earlier for some variables) through New Democracy. For later years I used data in various published and unpublished Afghan government statistical documents and in scattered press reports; monetary data came from the IMF's *International Financial Statistics.* Although with the breakdown of the state the Afghan government could no longer monitor society, even in a rudimentary way, the state retained the ability to count—roughly, at least—its own incomes and expenditures. The data that I use are internally consistent, they explain outcomes, and they are not by any means flattering to those who assembled them.

In collecting data on political elites of the old regime, the PDPA-Watan Party, and the mujahidin (including prewar Islamists) I consulted Adamec, *Biographical Dictionary.* For the old regime, an interview with the amazingly knowledgeable Hafizullah Karzai filled in the blanks.

On PDPA leadership I also used data published in Arnold, *Afghanistan's Two-Party Communism,* and press reports of appointments. I supplemented these with information taken from vast unpublished databases compiled by Anthony Arnold and David J. Katz, which they kindly permitted me to consult. I also benefited from several lengthy interviews with Miagol, the Kabul government's chargé d'affaires in Washington during 1989–90. I continually queried dozens of people for information on specific individuals for whom I lacked information of one sort or another. This experience drove home the lesson that ethnicity, in particular, is a contested terrain, not an established fact.

Additional published sources on the Islamists and other resistance parties included the memoirs of Sayyed Musa Tawana and Mohammad Es'haq (the deputy leader and a political officer, respectively, of Jamiat), both published in the Jamiat English-language publication, *AfghaNews* (Tawana's was originally written in Arabic, probably to counter successful Hizb propaganda among Islamists, a fact one should take into account in evaluating it); a series entitled "Who's Who in the Mujahideen" published by Es'haq in various issues of AfghaNews; Roy, *Islam and Resistance in Afghanistan* and "The New Political Elite of Afghanistan"; and Edwards, "The Evolution of Shi'i Political Dissent in Afghanistan," which also includes some information on Sunni Islamists. I supplemented the published materials with information collected in interviews with Mohammad Es'haq (who completed a lengthy questionnaire I faxed him in Peshawar), Naim Majrooh (editor of the *Afghan Information Centre Monthly Bulletin* after the assassination of his father), Sultan Mahmud (Voice of America correspondent in Peshawar), and Abdul Jabbar Sabet (VOA Pashto Service in Washington). In addition, the USIA Visitors' Program provided biographical information on leaders who had participated in their programs.

On the distribution of local mujahidin groups by size, region, and party, I have used the database compiled for the CIA by the Orkand Corporation in the four reports by Johnson et al. These reports arrived at my office in the U.S. Institute of Peace in an unmarked brown envelope after I had sent a letter to a post office box whose number Tom Johnson of Orkand had given me. I would like to thank whoever mailed them.

As I have commented in the text, and as their authors would be the first to acknowledge, these reports consist of a mix of fact and guesswork. Nonetheless, there is nothing else like them, except perhaps in the files of the ISI or WAD. The statistical appendixes to these reports include data on 733 resistance commanders. I cleaned the data considerably, eliminating some duplicated names and identifying some individuals from other sources. These data include some commanders who had been killed (or who had switched sides) by the time of publication. The reports do not provide sources for estimates of the size of units. The estimates are said to include only full-time mujahidin, not all those who might be mobilized with a rifle in time of emergency. They undoubtedly undercount small, traditionalist units.

In November and December 1986 I gained access to files in Peshawar belonging to the cross-border Cash-for-Food Program of the Swedish Committee for Afghanistan (SCA), for which I owe a debt of gratitude to Anders Fänge. These files consisted of notes of interviews with field commanders who applied to SCA for food aid. They also included confidential reports collected by Afghan investigators employed by SCA on the character and reliability of the commanders. The interviews dealt with the population and economy of the commander's area, the origins of resistance there, the background of the commander, and the sources of income (material and cash) of the resistance front. As with all such data on the commanders, the answers are at best approximate and include certain biases. The commanders represented in the files were not a random sample but a group that had approached SCA asking for food aid.

Lacking sufficient resources to study all the files, I approximated a stratified sample by studying all files in each of a set of provinces chosen to reflect various

Table A.1 Distribution by Party and Province of Commanders Included in Sample SCA Files

Province	Party							
	NIFA	ANLF	HAR	HIK	HIH	JIA	Tribal	Total
Kunduz	1	0	1	0	0	4	0	6
Bamiyan	0	0	1	0	0	2	0	3
Faryab	0	1	1	0	0	0	0	2
Herat	1	0	0	0	0	1	0	2
Kabul	1	0	0	0	0	4	0	5
Paktia/ Paktika	0	0	1	1	1	0	1	4
Kunar/ Nuristan	0	0	1	0	1	1	0	3
Qandahar	0	0	0	0	0	2	0	2
Total	3	1	5	1	2	14	1	27

regions and ethnic groups of Afghanistan. Within those provinces, I used only those interviews with commanders judged reliable by SCA. I also observed several interviews being conducted (in Persian, not Pashto) in order to obtain an idea of how the information was collected. Some files noted that the commander consulted with colleagues, including in one case a former member of the government's statistical department, in constructing the answers. Table A.1 shows the distribution by province and party of the twenty-seven commanders in my data set. While the files did not always indicate ethnicity, I believe that thirteen of the twenty-seven were Pashtun, nine Tajik or Sunni Farsiwan, two Uzbek, two Nuristani, and one Arab of Kunduz. There were no Shiʻa represented. Jamiat is clearly overrepresented, reflecting the good relations between SCA and that party, as well as the superior level of organization of that party's commanders.

I have also made use of background reports on nine Afghan provinces prepared in 1989 and 1990 by the Data Collection for Afghan Repatriation Project (DCAR), funded by UNHCR. My student Steve Holtzman, a former employee of UNHCR, obtained these reports for me. Each province covered—Laghman, Kunar, Nangarhar, Logar, Paktia, Paktika, Wardak, Ghazni, and Qandahar—was estimated to have had at least 35 percent of its population living as refugees in Pakistan. The following description of the methodology occurs at the beginning of each report:

> Project staff based in Peshawar and Quetta have conducted interviews and
> surveys in refugee camps throughout NWFP [Northwest Frontier Province],
> Baluchistan and Punjab provinces in Pakistan to compile data on refugee ori-

gins, ethnic and tribal affiliation and likely routes of refugee return to Afghanistan. In addition, the project field staff undertake frequent missions into Afghanistan to gather specific information on road conditions, the availability of storage facilities, transportation and fuel, the level of destruction of housing, irrigation systems and farmland, the location of landmines and the political situation at the district (*woleswali*) and subdistrict (*alaqdari*) levels in those provinces of priority concern to UNHCR.

When possible, written sources, including the Afghanistan gazeteers edited by L. Adamec, NGO field reports and bilateral/multilateral agency reports have been consulted to corroborate field data. Project staff also interview Afghan resistance leaders, journalists and other non-Afghan visitors to the region as sources for information and corroboration of information gathered in the field. All survey data and other related information has been stored in the DCAR database.

The reports include information on the many activities of foreign aid organizations inside Afghanistan as of the time of data collection. Each report also bears the following warning:

These provincial reports mainly cover non-government controlled areas and do not claim to be exhaustive. Rather, they are intended as a reference for the targeting of assistance programs, and as guides for those agencies that require general background on target areas, including the major obstacles that may be encountered to the planning and implementing of assistance projects in those areas. Much of the most timely and relevant information is derived from eyewitness accounts, which often defy the most painstaking efforts to render them consistent with existing knowledge. Names of villages, evaluation of road conditions and travel distances, and the identification of influential individuals take on a remarkably subjective character when more than one Afghan source is consulted. These reports, then, cannot substitute for first-hand investigation of local conditions.

Bearing this in mind, I have made use of the reports more to search for general trends than to identify specific facts. I have also used them in conjunction with other sources. *Caveat lector.*

Appendix B

Political Actors
in Afghanistan,
1973-1994

Contemporary political actors in Afghanistan mentioned in the text are briefly identified here to enable a reader to associate names with major organizations or events.
Spelling Afghan names in English is difficult; alphabetizing them satisfactorily is
impossible. Many Afghans do not have personal and family names in the Western (or
east Asian) sense. I have alphabetized by family name, where such can be said to exist,
including cases where a pen-name or nom de guerre (*takhallus*) has become accepted
as a family name (Karmal, Massoud, Majrooh). I do not treat titles like "Khan" or
"Shah" as family names. I do not treat "Muhammad" as a principal name when it is
conjoined with another. All compounds with "'Abdul" (or 'Abd al-) are treated as one
name ('Abdul Rahman, for example, is not presented as Rahman, 'Abdul). If you
cannot find someone under one name, try another. The ayn (') and hamza (') are
included here where appropriate, but in keeping with standard practice in English-
language texts, those diacritics are generally omitted in the text of the book.

'Abdul Basir Khalid. Uzbek schoolteacher, JIA commander in Faizabad, Badakhshan. Joined SCN reluctantly, 1990. Leader of Faizabad shura after April
1992.
'Abdul Haq. Of Arsala family, Jabbarkhel clan of Ahmadzai tribe. Kabul commander of HIK. Brother of Haji 'Abdul Qadir and Haji Din Muhammad. Built
up major organization, undermined by KhAD and ISI. Traveled often to West,
met Reagan, Thatcher, Pérez de Cuellar. Member of NCS.
'Abdul Latif. NIFA commander of Barakzai tribe, Qandahar. Assassinated in 1989.
Father of Gul Agha.
'Abdul Qadir. Of Arsala family, Jabbarkhel clan of Ahmadzai tribe. Nangarhar
commander of HIK. Brother of 'Abdul Haq and Haji Din Muhammad. Became
spokesman of Jalalabad shura after April 1992.

'Abdul Qadir. Soviet-trained Herati Parchami general. Key to coups of 1973 and 1978. Arrested by Taraki, August 1978. Defense minister in 1983. Sent to eastern Europe as ambassador by Najibullah.

'Abdul Rauf. Safi Pashtun of Kapisa. Brigadier, led revolt of Asmar garrison, November 1979. Military adviser to ANLF (Mujaddidi). Named by Massoud as commander of Central Forces (Kabul), summer 1992.

'Abdul Wakil. Kabuli Persian-speaker, second cousin of Babrak Karmal. Foreign minister and PDPA Politburo member, 1986–92. Secretly negotiated with Massoud after Najibullah's resignation.

'Abdul Wali. Cousin, son-in-law, and close adviser of Zahir Shah. General, commander of Central Forces in 1973. Imprisoned by Daoud, 1973–76, then joined Zahir Shah in Rome.

Achakzai, Ismatullah Muslim. Qandahari Achakzai Pashtun. Soviet-trained army officer. Joined mujahidin in Qandahar, 1979. Refused to join any party. Defected to Kabul, 1984, became general and militia commander. Militia defeated in summer 1988. Died in USSR, 1991.

Afzal, Muhammad. Salafi (Wahhabi) mawlawi of Kam tribe in Nuristan. Founder and amir of the Islamic State of Nuristan (the Dawlat).

Afzali, Saifullah. A JIA commander of Herat. Rival of Isma'il Khan supported by ideological faction in JIA headquarters. Assassinated in Iran, 1988.

Ahmad Shah, Mir. Sympathizer of Islamic movement. General, executed after coup attempt in 1974. One source gives family name as Rizwani.

Akhundzada, Ghulam Rasul. Durrani Pashtun (Nurzai?). Brother of Mullah Nasim, whom he succeeded as main HAR commander of Helmand after the latter's assassination in 1990. Major opium warlord.

Akhundzada, Muhammad Nasim. Durrani Pashtun (Nurzai?). Traditionalist mullah. Principal HAR commander and opium warlord of Helmand. Assassinated in Peshawar in March 1990 after making deal with U.S. ambassador to reduce opium production in return for aid.

'Alam Khan. Tajik of Balkh. Graduate of Shari'a Faculty, Kabul. Became JIA Amir of Balkh after assassination of Zabihullah in 1984. Cooperated with SCN.

Ala'uddin Khan. Captain, staff officer of Herat Garrison, JIA member. Led March 1979 Herat mutiny with Capt. Isma'il Khan, whom he served as deputy.

Amin, Hafizullah. Kharruti Pashtun from Paghman, Kabul Province. Attended Columbia University. Headmaster of teachers training school, Kabul. Strongman of Khalq. Deputy prime minister of DRA, April 1978. Prime minister, April 1979. President of DRA and secretary-general of PDPA after he had Taraki assassinated in September 1979. Killed by Soviets, December 27, 1979.

Anwari, Muhammad. Kabul commander of Harakat-i Islami (Muhsini). Shi'a (Qizilbash) from Kabul. Fired rockets at the Polytechnic Institute where Najibullah was holding Loya Jirga in November 1987.

Aqa, ʿAbdul Qadir. Khalqi Pashtun. Soviet-trained air force commander, supported
Tanai's coup, March 1990. Fled to Pakistan.

Asghar, Muhammad. Kabuli. Attended Columbia University. Served old regime as
rector of Kabul University, mayor of Kabul, minister of justice. Founder of
National Salvation Society, Kabul, 1990.

Assefy, Humayun. Muhammadzai. Second cousin and brother-in-law of Zahir
Shah. Active in movement for Loya Jirga, 1983. Lives in Paris.

Atsak, Juma. Achakzai Pashtun from Farah. Parchami general allied with Najibullah. Reportedly the favorite Afghan general of Gen. Valentin Varennikov,
commander of Soviet ground forces. Appointed commander of Northern Zone,
Mazar-i Sharif, 1988. Conflict with ʿAbdul Rashid Dostum contributed to mutiny of northern militias, 1992.

Azimi, Muhammad Nabi. Parchami, Kabuli, reported to be Muhammadzai. Soviet-
trained deputy minister of defense and commander of Central Forces (Kabul)
under Najibullah. After April 1992 stayed on for several months under Defense Minister Ahmad Shah Massoud.

Baba, Qari Taj. Pashtun of Ghazni. Traditional mawlawi of Naqshbandi family.
HAR commander of Ghazni.

Babrakzai, Muhammad ʿUmar. From khan khel of Jadran Pashtuns, Paktia.
French-educated jurist, member of Supreme Court under New Democracy.
Member of NIFA, supporter of Loya Jirga.

Badakhshi, Tahir. Tajik from Badakhshan. Attended teachers training school in
Kabul, became founding member of PDPA and Khalq. Resigned and founded
SAZA (Sitam-i Milli), "Maoist" group opposed to Pashtun domination. Exe-
cuted by Hafizullah Amin, September 1979.

Ba'is, Bahauddin. Tajik from Baghlan. Leader of SZA.

Baryalai, Mahmud. Half-brother of Babrak Karmal, son-in-law of Anahita Ratibzad. Educated in USSR. Parchami, PDPA Central Committee member after
1980, Deputy prime minister, June 1989, fired June 1991 when Karmal returned from Moscow. Sent troops to block Najibullah's exit, April 1992.

Bihishti, Sayyid. Traditionalist Shiʿa religious leader, elected amir of Shura of
Hazarajat in fall 1979. Overthrown by pro-Khomeini groups, 1982.

Chamkani, Muhammad. Also spelled "Tsamkani." Pashtun tribal leader from Paktia. Acting president of DRA Revolutionary Council with no real power,
November 1986–November 1987.

Dilawar, Asif. Parchami Kabuli, either Muhammadzai or Persian-speaking. Soviet-
trained general, chief of army staff, 1988–92. Served Massoud in this position
for several months after April 1992. Injured by car bomb, 1992.

Din Muhammad. Of Arsala family, Jabbarkhel clan of Ahmadzai tribe. Deputy
leader of HIK. Brother of ʿAbdul Haq and Haji ʿAbdul Qadir.

Dost Muhammad. Khalqi Pashtun. Major, political director of the air force, 1990.
Supported Tanai's coup, fled to Pakistan.

Dostum, 'Abdul Rashid. Uzbek from Jauzjan. Organized militia in north Afghanistan that developed into Fifty-third Division. Najibullah's most important militia commander. Mutinied, January 1992, and allied with northern mujahidin. Founded National Islamic Movement of Afghanistan. Principal warlord of North after April 1992, based in Mazar-i Sharif.

Es'haq, Mohammad. Tajik from Panjsher. Attended Engineering Faculty, joined Muslim Youth. Participated in Panjsher uprising (1975) under Ahmad Shah Massoud, and in Panjsheri resistance. After 1983 political officer of JIA, Peshawar, editor of *AfghaNews*. Deputy minister of civil aviation, 1993.

Faiz Muhammad. Parchami from Wazir tribe on Paktia-Pakistan border. Soviet-trained army officer. Minister of interior, 1973, under President Daoud. Minister of frontier affairs, 1980. Assassinated after Jadran jirga, 1980.

Faizani. Islamic scholar and pir from Herat. Supported attempts to overthrow Daoud. Arrested, 1974; probably killed in prison in 1979.

Farid. Tajik schoolteacher ("ustad"). HIH commander of Charikar, Parwan Province. First acting prime minister of ISA, after April 1992.

Fazlullah. Persian-speaking doctor, member of branch of Mujaddidi family. JIA commander in Logar.

Gahiz, Minhajuddin. Pashtun of Kohdaman, north of Kabul. One of founders of Islamic movement. Editor of *Gahiz* (Dawn). Assassinated in Kabul, 1971.

Gailani, Sayyid Ahmad. Member of family of Sayyid 'Abdul Qadir al-Jilani of Baghdad. Pir of Qadiriyya Sufi order in Afghanistan, leader of NIFA. Related by marriage to major Muhammadzai lineages.

Ghulam Rasul. Khalqi Pashtun general. Commander of Pul-i Charkhi prison, 1978–79. Commander of Eighteenth Division, Balkh, 1992. Appointment as commander of Hairatan garrison led to revolt by northern militias.

Gul Agha. Son of Haji 'Abdul Latif and his successor as NIFA commander of Barakzai tribe of Qandahar.

Gulabzoy, Sayyid Muhammad. Khalqi Pashtun general from Paktia. Soviet trained tank officer. Key figure in 1978 coup. Minister of interior, 1980–88. Exiled as ambassador to USSR, November 1988.

Habib al-Rahman. Tajik from north Afghanistan, engineering student, member of Muslim Youth. Responsible for military affairs on shura of Islamic movement, 1973. Arrested, 1974; probably killed in prison in 1979.

Hakim, Muhammad. Muhammadzai Parchami from Kabul. U.S.-trained general. Arrested by Taraki, August 1978. Attributes resulting scar on his forehead to "intraparty debate." Member of PDPA Central Committee after 1986. Mayor of Kabul during 1989 food crisis.

Haqqani, Jalaluddin. Pakistan-educated mawlawi of Jadran tribe, Paktia. HIK commander. Member of NCS. Led forces that took Khost, March 1991. Headed Gardez shura after April 1992. Appointed minister of justice in first government of the ISA, never assumed the post.

Hatif, 'Abdul Rahim. Qandahari Pashtun, trader. Close to Salih Muhammad Ziari, but not a PDPA member. President of NFF, 1986.

Hikmatyar, Gulbuddin. Kharruti Pashtun from Imam Sahib, Kunduz. Attended Engineering Faculty, joined Muslim Youth. Responsible for student affairs on shura of Islamic movement 1973, though then in jail for murder of Maoist student. Released, fled to Pakistan, became leader of HIH. Received largest share of aid distributed by ISI during war. Allied with Tanai and other PDPA Pashtun dissidents in March 1990. Named prime minister of ISA by Islamabad Accords, March 1993.

Isma'il Khan. Born Shindand, Farah. Sunni Persian speaker but has kept his ethnic identity unclear. Fully bilingual in Pashto and Persian. Captain, staff officer of Herat garrison, JIA member. Led March 1979 Herat mutiny with Capt. Ala'uddin Khan. Amir of resistance in Herat, commander of Amir Hamza division. Amir of Herat shura after April 1992.

'Izzatullah, Muhammad. Tajik mawlawi educated in state system. JIA commander of Paghman, Kabul Province. Member of SCN.

Jagran, Sayyid Muhammad. Hazara (sayyid) landowner and army major (*jagran*). Appointed military commander of Shura of the Hazarajat, September 1979. Led front in Ghazni. Member of NCS, 1990.

Juma Khan. Khan of Tajiks of Andarab. Joined HIH, 1979–80. Lost control of Andarab to Massoud in 1983. Defected to government during Soviet offensive against Panjsher in April 1984. Assassinated, November 1986.

Kaihani, Hashmatullah. Parchami Kabuli Persian-speaker. Chief prosecutor of Revolutionary Court. Exiled as ambassador to North Korea in 1988. Sought asylum in Canada.

Kalakani, 'Abdul Majid. Tajik from Kohdaman, north of Kabul. Born in same village, Kalakan, as Bacha-yi Saqao. Founded and led SAMA, a "Maoist" organization. Executed, June 1980.

Karmal, Babrak. Kabuli Persian-speaker. Founder of PDPA, leader of Parcham. Deputy prime minister of DRA, April 1978. Exiled, July 1978; returned with Soviet troops. Secretary-general of PDPA and president of Revolutionary Council, 1980–86. Exiled to USSR until June 1991, when he returned to Kabul. Moved to Mazar-i Sharif after April 1992.

Karwal, Mir Sahib. Khalqi Pashtun, apparatchik. Educated in USSR. PDPA Central Committee member, 1981–90. Supported Tanai coup. Fled to Pakistan.

Karzai, 'Abdul Ahad. Elder of senior lineage (Karzai) of Popolzai tribe of Qandahar. Supported movement for Loya Jirga. Affiliated loosely with ANLF. Spent much of war in Silver Spring, Maryland, but became spokesman of Qandahar shura in April 1992. Appointed minister of frontier affairs in first government of ISA.

Kawiani, Najmuddin. Parchami Tajik from Panjsher. PDPA apparatchik and Politburo member after 1987. Second vice president of Watan Party after June

1990. Supported revolts against Najibullah, 1992. In Tashkent, 1993.

Khaibar (Khyber), Mir Akbar. Pashtun Parchami, married to sister of Sulaiman La'iq. Officer of Royal Afghan Police. PDPA Politburo member responsible for military network, 1977. Assassinated, April 1978, triggering demonstrations, repression, and Sawr Coup.

Khalili, Massoud. Son of poet Ustad Khalilullah Khalili. Political officer of JIA, "pragmatic" faction. Has home in New Jersey.

Khalis, Yunus. Mawlawi from Khugiani tribe (Pashtun), Nangarhar, educated in NWFP, British India. Early leader of Islamic movement. Fled to Pakistan, 1974. Leader of HIK.

Khan Agha. Tajik doctor, JIA-SCN commander, Shakardara, north of Kabul.

Kishtmand, Sultan Ali. Kabuli Hazara, founding member of PDPA and Parcham. Prime minister of DRA, 1981–88, 1989–90. Resigned from Watan Party in summer 1991, protesting Pashtun domination. Badly wounded in assassination attempt soon after.

La'iq, Sulaiman. Son of Naqshbandi pir of Sulaimankhel tribe in north Afghanistan; brother-in-law of both Sibghatullah Mujaddidi and Mir Akbar Khyber. Founding member of PDPA and Parcham, rival of Babrak Karmal. PDPA Politburo member after 1986. First vice president of Watan Party, June 1990. After April 1992 in Pakistan under protection of Pashtun nationalists.

Majrooh, Sayd Bahauddin. Sayyid of Kunar, son of Shamsuddin. Educated in France, Germany. Chair, Department of Philosophy, Kabul University. Author, *Izhda-yi Khudi* (*The Monster of Egoism*), an epic poem in Persian. Fled to Peshawar, 1980, founded *Afghan Information Centre Monthly Bulletin.* Assassinated, February 1988, after publishing results of a survey that purported to show that Afghan refugees in Pakistan overwhelmingly preferred Zahir Shah to any of the mujahidin leaders.

Majrooh, Sayyid Shamsuddin. Sayyid of Kunar, jurist and poet who took the pen name Majrooh, "wounded." Principal author of the Constitution of New Democracy. Fled to Pakistan, 1980. After assassination of his son, came to United States.

Malang, Lala. Ghilzai Pashtun mullah, HIK commander of Qandahar. Responsibility for deaths of many Khalqis, including Durranis, created local tensions. Reported to have sold four Stinger missiles to Iran.

Mangal, Manokai. Soviet-trained Pashtun Parchami military officer close to Najibullah. Political chief of Ministry of interior. Hero of defense of Jalalabad, March 1989. Najibullah's emissary to Hikmatyar, fall 1991. Joined Hikmatyar after April 1992.

Massoud, Ahmad Shah. Persian-speaker of Panjsher, raised in Kabul. Attended Polytechnic Institute, joined Muslim Youth, fled to Pakistan. Led uprising in Panjsher Valley, 1975, returned to Pakistan, joined JIA. Related to Rabbani by marriage. After 1979 led resistance in Panjsher Valley. Negotiated truce directly with Soviets, 1983. Founded SCN, 1985. Established Islamic Army of SCN, 1988. Cooperated with Dostum in capture of Kabul, April 1992. First defense minister of ISA.

Mas'ud, Haidar. Kabuli Tajik, Parchami. PDPA Politburo member after 1987.

Mazdak, Farid. Kabuli Tajik, Parchami. President of DYOA. Promoted to Politburo, 1989. Fourth vice president of Watan Party, May 1990. Established links to Massoud, supported northern rebels in 1992.

Mazduryar, Shair Jan. Soviet-trained Muhammadzai military officer from Uruzgan Province. Khalqi Central Committee member. Cabinet positions in 1979, 1980.

Momand, Niyaz Muhammad. Khalqi Pashtun of Nangarhar. Promoted to Politburo, October 1987. Supported Tanai, March 1990. Fled to Pakistan.

Muhammadi, Muhammad Nabi. Ahmadzai Pashtun of Logar. Traditionalist mawlawi, head of madrasa. Member of Parliament, New Democracy. Leader of HAR.

Muhsini, Sheikh Asif. Pashto-speaking Shi'a from Qandahar. Early Islamist leader. Leader of Harakat-i Islami. Took title *Ayatollah*. Poor relations with Iran.

Mujaddidi, Sibghatullah. Father's first cousin was last member of his family to be main pir of Naqshbandi order in Afghanistan. Leader of ANLF. President of IIGA, 1989. Acting president of ISA, April–June 1992.

Mu'min, Abdul. This linguistically improbable name is given by several sources. Parchami Tajik from north Afghanistan. Soviet-trained general. Commander of Hairatan garrison, 1992. Najibullah's attempt to remove him led to northern revolt. Close links with both Dostum and Massoud. Died under unclear circumstances in January 1994, when Dostum and Massoud went to war.

Nadiri, Mansur. Also called the Sayyid of Kayan. Pir of Isma'ili Hazaras of north Afghanistan. Led large government militia. Allied with Dostum to bring down Najibullah, 1992. Member of council of Dostum's National Islamic Movement.

Naim Khan. Also called Kuchi. Khan of Ahmadzai nomads in Logar. Appointed deputy minister of frontier affairs in first government of ISA. Never assumed his post.

Najibullah. Ahmadzai Pasthun born in Kabul. Student leader of PDPA-Parcham at Kabul University. Exiled by Taraki, July 1978. Director-general of KhAD, January 1980–November 1985. Secretary-general of PDPA and president of Watan Party, May 1986–April 1992. President of R.A., November 1987–April 1992. Resigned or overthrown, April 15, 1992, took refuge in U.N. office in Kabul.

Naqibullah Akhund. Traditionalist mullah, JIA commander of Alikozai tribe in Qandahar. Among the strongest commanders in Qandahar.

Nassery, Khan Zia Khan. Paktia Pashtun, U.S. citizen. Claimed to be mujahidin leader in Pakistan, fall 1979. Arrested in Iran, 1980. Supported national reconciliation, 1987. Organized antigovernment demonstration, Kabul, September 1991. Returned to Afghanistan, spring 1992. Disappeared en route from Mazar-i Sharif to Kabul, spring 1993.

Nauroz, Muhammad Yahya. Tajik of Logar. U.S.- and British-trained general. Director of operations, Ministry of defense, 1976–78. Military adviser to HAR. Minister of defense, IIGA, 1989, then resigned and went to United States.

Nazar Muhammad. Khalqi Pashtun apparatchik. U.S.-trained engineer. Third vice president of Watan Party, June 1990.

Nazar Muhammad. Khalqi Pashtun. Soviet-trained general. Defense minister, 1984. Vice president of Revolutionary Council, 1985. Supported Tanai's coup, March 1990, fled to Pakistan.

Niyazi, Ghulam Muhammad. Pashtun from Paktia. Educated at al-Azhar. Dean of Shari'a Faculty and leader of Islamic movement from 1950s. Arrested, 1974; probably killed in prison, 1979.

Nur, Nur Ahmad. Popolzai (Durrani) Pashtun from Qandahar. Founding member of PDPA and Parcham, son-in-law of Anahita Ratibzad. Exiled, July 1978, Politburo member after January 1980. Diplomatic exile in 1988.

Nuristani, 'Abdul Qadir. Minister of interior under President Daoud, 1974–78. Known as anticommunist. Killed in Sawr Coup.

Nuristani, Sarwar. Soviet-trained military officer from southern Nuristan. Sent to Delhi embassy after Sawr Coup. Went to Pakistan, arrested. Escaped and returned to Nuristan. Established well-supplied militia with Soviet aid. Later expelled from the area by the Dawlat and mujahidin commanders.

'Omar, Muhammad. Tajik doctor from Badakhshan. Joined Muslim Youth at Kabul University. Attempted to lead uprising in Badakhshan, 1974, arrested. Probably killed in prison in 1979.

Paktin, Raz Muhammad. Khalqi Pashtun. Soviet-trained military officer. Member of PDPA Central Committee and Revolutionary Council after January 1980. Did not join Tanai, became minister of the interior after Tanai's coup attempt in March 1990. Joined Hikmatyar, April 1992, then fled to Pakistan.

Panjsheri, Dastagir. Tajik from Panjsher, Khalqi Politburo member. Arrested for supporting Tanai, March 1990.

Rabbani, Burhanuddin. Tajik from Badakhshan. Educated at al-Azhar, lecturer at Shari'a Faculty. Leader of shura of Islamic movement, 1973. Fled to Pakistan, where he became leader of JIA after movement split. Second acting president of ISA under Peshawar Accords from June 1992; acting president of ISA under Islamabad Accords from March 1993.

Rafi', Muhammad. Pashtun from Paghman, Kabul Province. Soviet-trained general. Participated in Sawr Coup as head of Parcham's military network. Member of Politburo from 1981. Minister of defense, 1982–84, 1986–88. After April 1992 reportedly in Paghman with Mullah Izzatullah.

Rahmani, Arsala. Pashtun mawlawi from Paktika. Commander of ITT. Arab money financed his large base, where Arab mujahidin trained. In spite of orders from his party leader (Sayyaf), joined NCS. Head of Urgun shura after April 1992. Appointed minister of Islamic affairs in first government of ISA.

Ratibzad, Anahita. Kabuli of Popolzai descent. Doctor, daughter of royal family physician. Attended Columbia University. Parchami Politburo member. Founded DWOA. Close to Karmal. Daughters married senior Parchamis Mahmud Baryalai and Nur Ahmad Nur. Under house arrest in Kabul after 1988.

Razmjo, 'Abdul Zuhur. Pashtun from Kabul, Parchami. Joined PDPA Central Committee, 1980. Joined Politburo, 1986. Kabul city party secretary. Expelled from PDPA Politburo in October 1988.

Sarwari, Asadullah. Khalqi Pashtun from Ghazni. Soviet-trained military officer. Head of AGSA. Tortured several senior Parchamis. Appointed to Politburo in 1980, but exiled as ambassador to Mongolia after a few months. Tried to return from diplomatic post in Yemen to support Tanai's coup in March 1990. Detained in India, later released.

Sayyaf, 'Abd al-Rabb al-Rasul. Original name Ghulam Rasul. Kharruti Pashtun from Paghman, Kabul province. Educated at al-Azhar, lecturer at Shari'a Faculty. Elected deputy leader of shura of Islamic movement, 1973. Arrested, 1975, while about to board airplane to study law at George Washington University. Survived 1979 prison massacres because of kinship ties to Hafizullah Amin. Released January 1980, came to Peshawar. Established his own organization (ITT), based on his ability to raise funds from Arabs. Known for adherence to Salafi Islam. Prime minister of IIGA, 1989.

Tanai, Shahnawaz. Khalqi Pashtun general from Paktia. Soviet trained, chief of army staff, 1986–88. Minister of defense 1988–90. Central Committee member since 1983, Politburo since 1988. Staged coup against Najibullah in March 1990. Allied with Hikmatyar, fled to Pakistan.

Taraki, Nur Muhammad. Pashtun from Ghazni. Self-educated writer. Founder and general secretary of PDPA, leader of Khalq. President of Revolutionary Council and prime minister of DRA, April 1978. Promised that "those who plot against us in the dark will disappear in the dark." Smothered to death in his bed on orders of Hafizullah Amin, September 17, 1979.

Tawana, Sayyed Musa. Persian-speaking sayyid from Takhar, north Afghanistan. Educated at al-Azhar, professor at Shari'a Faculty. Responsible for cultural affairs on shura of Islamic movement, 1973. Fled to Pakistan. After split of Islamic movement, became Rabbani's deputy in JIA.

Wafadar, Pacha Gul. Khalqi Pashtun Soviet-trained air force officer. Key figure in 1973 and 1978 coups. Minister of frontier affairs, 1973. Minister of civil aviation, 1988. PDPA Central Committee member since 1977. Fled to Pakistan, December 1989. Claimed to have been secretly working for Hikmatyar since Soviet invasion.

Wardak, Qazi Muhammad Amin. Son of important khan of Wardak tribe. B.A. in French from Kabul University. Independent commander in Jaghatu district, then joined NIFA. Received much aid from French organizations, printed his own postage stamps. Joined HIK in 1988 to get more weapons. Close to 'Abdul Haq. Prominent leader of NCS.

Wardak, 'Abdul Rahim. Pashtun from Wardak. General, trained at Sandhurst and
in United States. Left post in New Delhi, April 1978, came to Pakistan. Became chief of military affairs, NIFA. Appointed by Massoud as chief of army
staff, summer 1992.

Watanjar, Muhammad Aslam. Khalqi Pashtun from Paktia. Soviet-trained tank officer, key to coups of 1973 and 1978; his tank led assault on Daoud's palace.
Member of Politburo of PDPA after 1981. Minister of interior, 1988. Did not
join Tanai's coup, became minister of defense afterward, March 1990. Helped
HIH forces enter Kabul, April 1992. Reportedly escaped to Pakistan under protection of Pashtun nationalists.

Ya'aqubi, Ghulam Faruq. Muhammadzai from Kabul, Parchami. Trained as police-
man in West Germany. Succeeded Najibullah as director general of KhAD and
joined PDPA Central Committee, November 1985. Minister of state security
(WAD) from January 1986. Joined Politburo, November 1986. Reportedly committed suicide in his office, April 15–16, 1992.

Yousof, Muhammad. Kabuli Persian-speaker. Engineer, educated in Germany. First
prime minister of New Democracy. Deposed after demonstrations led by
Babrak Karmal and supported by Daoud. After April 1978 moved to Germany.
Adviser to Zahir Shah, supporter of Loya Jirga.

Zabihullah. Tajik from Balkh, schoolteacher. Became JIA commander of Balkh.
Was developing organization modeled on Massoud's when he was assassinated
in December 1984. Resistance in Mazar area never fully recovered.

Zahir Shah, Muhammad. Son of Muhammad Nadir Shah. King of Afghanistan,
1933–73. Educated in France. Called for Loya Jirga, 1983 and several times
since. Met with diplomats from United Nations, United States, Soviet Union,
Pakistan, India, in effort to find political solution. Offered to take any role desired by Afghan nation, but ruled out restoring monarchy. Lives in Rome.

Ziari, Salih Muhammad. Qandahari Ghilzai Pashtun, Khalqi. In charge of Khalqi
land reform. Joined Politburo, January 1980. Karmal's favorite Khalqi. Expelled from Politburo, October 1988. Arrested for supporting Tanai coup,
March 1990.

Appendix C

Financing of
Government Expenditure,
1952-1988

	Expenditure			Sources of Financing				
Year	Total (millions of afghanis)	Ordinary (%)	Development (%)	Domestic Revenue, Excluding Gas (%)	Sales of Natural Gas (%)	Foreign Aid (%)	(Rentier Income) (%)	Domestic Borrowing (%)
1952	830	80	21	74	0	18	18	8
1953	838	80	21	93	0	7	7	0
1954	1,030	80	20	94	0	6	6	1
1955	1,260	74	26	102	0	9	9	−11
1956	1,291	71	30	89	0	8	8	3
1957[a]	740	71	29	113	0	30	30	−43
1958[b]	2,627	38	62	51	0	52	52	− 4
1959[b]	3,228	39	61	48	0	53	53	0
1960[b]	4,177	33	67	38	0	53	53	9
1961[b]	5,805	27	73	36	0	50	50	14
1962[c]	3,221	27	73	22	0	60	60	18
1962	6,440	29	71	33	0	51	51	17
1963	7,079	34	66	38	0	49	49	14
1964	7,348	35	65	42	0	49	49	10
1965	8,107	36	64	49	0	52	52	− 1
1966	8,504	40	60	50	0	50	50	− 1
1967	8,109	45	55	51	1	41	42	7

1968	8,333	51	49	49	5	39	45	7
1969	8,642	55	45	54	5	29	34	13
1970	8,130	63	37	61	9	23	32	7
1971	8,964	61	39	59	7	28	34	8
1972	10,298	55	45	53	7	37	44	4
1973d	11,318	58	42	55	8	31	38	7
1975	16,187	60	40	63	12	31	42	4
1976	19,594	57	43	62	10	29	39	− 1
1977	24,326	49	51	53	8	34	42	4
1978	26,397	47	53	54	9	34	43	4
1979	30,173	56	44	40	13	36	48	12
1980	31,692	62	38	50	33	28	61	−11
1981	40,751	66	34	40	34	26	59	1
1982	42,112	69	31	37	34	28	62	0
1986	88,700	74	26	31	17	29	46	23
1988	129,900	84	16	24	6	26	32	44

Sources: Data from Fry, *Afghan Economy*, 158–59, 170–71; Democratic Republic of Afghanistan (DRA), *Statistical Information of Afghanistan (1975–1978)*; DRA, *Statistical Year Book (SYB) 1358 (March 1979–March 1980)*; DRA, *SYB 1359 (March 1980–March 1981)*; DRA, *SYB 1360 (March 1981–March 1982)*; DRA, *SYB 1361 (March 1982–March 1983)*; Republic of Afghanistan, "Afghanistan 1990."

Note: Government expenditure equals ordinary plus development expenditure. Foreign aid includes both commodity assistance and project aid, loans, and grants. Rentier income is the sum of foreign aid and sales of natural gas. Domestic borrowing is a residual which does not correspond to figures in monetary surveys. Except as noted, years are Afghan (Islamic solar) years beginning in the given Common Era year. No data available for some years.

aFirst half of 1336.

bCommon Era years.

cSecond half of 1340.

dEstimate; final figures not available.

Notes

Chapter 1 / Afghanistan, Mirror of the World

1. For an estimate of 1.24 million deaths between 1978 and 1987, based on a demographic survey, see Sliwinski, "Decimation of Afghanistan." For a somewhat lower estimate (876,825 deaths), see Khalidi, "Demographic Consequences of War."

2. *New York Times,* March 19, 1992.

3. On opposing plans for arms exports see *New York Times,* February 24, 1992; on pension see Reuters, Moscow, April 14, 1994.

4. Kipling, "The Ballad of East and West," *Complete Verse,* 233.

5. "The Young British Soldier," ibid., 416.

6. For critiques of these concepts and their use in Afghanistan, see Roy, "'Révolution' par le vide"; Roy, *Islam and Resistance.*

7. On modernity and the state see Giddens, *Nation-State and Violence.* See Fukuyama, *End of History,* for a treatment of that theme.

8. On elections in general see Kimmitt, Speech to the Asia Society. On their application to Afghanistan see U.N. Department of Public Information, "Statement by Secretary-General Javier Pérez de Cuellar."

9. Dahl, *Polyarchy.*

10. On drug smuggling see *New York Times,* February 8, 1993. I owe the quotation from the poem to Nejat Khalili.

11. Tilly, *Coercion, Capital, and European States,* 1.

12. Giddens, *Nation-State and Violence;* Eisenstadt, *Political Systems of Empires;* on the variety of premodern state forms see Tilly, *Coercion, Capital, and European States,* 19–28.

13. Tilly, *Coercion, Capital, and European States,* 2. Max Weber focused on legal-rational legitimacy as the essence of the "modern state." Giddens, *Nation-State and Violence,* refers to the "nation-state" or "modern" state.

14. Weber, *Theory of Social and Economic Organization,* 156.

15. Smith, *Ethnic Roots of Nations;* Smith, *State and Nation;* Smith, "State-Making and Nation-Building."

16. Giddens, in *Nation-State and Violence,* deals at length with surveillance. Mann, in "Autonomous Power of the State," distinguishes between "infrastructural" and "despotic" power.

17. Gellner, *Nations and Nationalism;* B. Anderson, *Imagined Communities.*

18. In contrast, the rulers of the Chinese empire, whose hegemony was subject to no effective

challenge from competing states, saw in merchants mainly rivals for power. Hence they tended to keep them under strict control. An incipient industrial revolution under the Sung Dynasty (thirteenth century) was halted by state policies. See McNeill, *Pursuit of Power*, 24–62. On the importance of war for state formation and capitalist development, see also Tilly, "History of European State-Making," 3–54; Skocpol, *States and Social Revolutions*, 21; and Giddens, *Nation-State and Violence*, 112.

19. Tilly, "History of European State-Making," 46.

20. Quotation from Delacroix, "Distributive State in the World System," 8. Skocpol, in *States and Social Revolutions*, argued that revolutionaries are above all would-be state builders. Among works not previously cited that deal with this issue are Alavi, "State in Post-Colonial Societies"; L. Anderson, *State and Social Transformation;* L. Anderson, "State in the Middle East and North Africa"; Badie and Birnbaum, *Sociology of the State;* Barkey and Parikh, "Comparative Perspectives on the State"; Beblawi and Luciani, *Rentier State;* Callaghy, *State-Society Struggle;* Chaudhry, "Price of Wealth"; Delacroix, "Distributive State"; Jackson and Rosberg, "Why Africa's Weak States Persist"; Karl, "Petroleum and Political Pacts"; Mahdavi, "Pattern and Problems"; Migdal, *Strong Societies and Weak States;* Rubin, "Lineages of the State"; Stallings, "International Lending"; Stepan, *State and Society.*

21. Chaudhry, "Price of Wealth," 105–9, distinguishes among international capital flows by several criteria, including the presence or absence of an identifiable transnational actor who is the source of the flow and is therefore capable of exerting pressure.

22. Tilly, *Formation of National States*, 28–29; quotation from Badie and Birnbaum, *Sociology of the State*, 100. The relevant work of Ibn Khaldun is most accessible to nonreaders of Arabic (including this author) in Ibn Khaldûn, *Muqaddimah*. An influential development of some of Ibn Khaldun's ideas is Gellner, *Muslim Society*, especially chapter 1, "Flux and Reflux in the Faith of Men," 1–85. Collections dealing with these issues are R. Tapper, *Conflict of Tribe and State;* Khoury and Kostiner, *Tribes and State Formation;* and Luciani, *Arab State*, especially Salamé, "'Strong' and 'Weak' States." See also the works by Lisa Anderson cited above.

23. R. Tapper, "Anthropologists, Historians, and Tribespeople," 68.

24. L. Anderson, in *State and Social Transformation*, 203–22, argues this point in the case of Libya.

25. Hager, in "State, Tribe, and Empire," 84, defines the tribe as a polity with jurisdiction over persons rather than territory. Ibn Khaldun argued that tribes occurred naturally (*Muqaddimah*, 91–93). He recognized, however, that the kinship bonds among them are often fictive, (100–1). Recent research has shown that tribes can even be created by states as means of indirect rule (R. Tapper, "Anthropologists, Historians, and Tribespeople," 55; Migdal, *Strong Societies and Weak States*, 116; Albert Hourani, "Tribes and States in Islamic History").

26. Gellner, "Tribalism and the State,"109.

27. Ibid.

28. Barfield, "Tribe and State Relations."

29. *Muqaddimah*, 120–22.

30. Gellner, "Tribalism and the State," 113–14.

31. Gellner, "Flux and Reflux," 73–77.

32. On the "overdeveloped state" see Alavi, "State in Post-Colonial Societies."

33. Chaudhry, "Price of Wealth"; Callaghy, "External Actors," 61–83.

34. Evans, "Predatory, Developmental, and Other Apparatuses"; Kohli, *State and Poverty in India;* Skocpol, "Bringing the State Back In"; Trimberger, *Revolution from Above.*

35. See Stepan, "State Power and the Strength of Civil Society," for a typology of state-society relations; quotation from Migdal, *Strong Societies and Weak States*, 29. The paradigmatic case of autonomy as the pursuit of self-interest by state officials is Mobutu's Zaire, as described in Cal-

laghy, *State-Society Struggle.* For variants of the economic role of the state stratum, see Azarya, "Reordering State-Society Relations"; Bardhan, *Political Economy of Development;* Fatton, "Bringing the Ruling Class Back In"; Marenin, "Nigerian State as Process and Manager"; Rubin, "Economic Liberalisation and the Indian State"; Rudolph and Rudolph, *In Pursuit of Lakshmi;* Waterbury, "Twilight of the State Bourgeoisie?"

36. Quotations from Mann, "Autonomous Power of the State," 113; on monitoring see Giddens, *Nation-State and Violence,* 172–97.

37. See Beblawi and Luciani, *Rentier State;* Chaudhry, "Price of Wealth"; L. Anderson, *State and Social Transformation,* the section on Libya; Badie and Birnbaum, *Sociology of the State;* Rueschemeyer and Evans, "State and Economic Transformation."

38. Stepan, *State and Society,* 302.

39. Roy, "'Révolution' par le vide," 78.

40. Badie and Birnbaum, *Sociology of the State,* 97; O'Donnell, *Modernization and Bureaucratic-Authoritarianism,* 77–84.

41. Migdal, *Strong Societies and Weak States,* 33.

42. Definition of strategies of survival from ibid., 27.

43. Ibn Khaldûn, *Muqaddimah,* 130; Migdal, *Strong Societies and Weak States,* 28–29.

44. Ghassan Salamé, *Al-Mujtama' wa al-Dawla fi al-Mashriq al-'Arabi* [*Society and the State in the Arab East*] (Beirut, 1987), 23–24, quoted in Tibi, "Simultaneity of the Unsimultaneous," 129.

45. L. Anderson, *State and Social Transformation,* 27–35.

Part I / The Old Regime

1. Skocpol, *States and Social Revolutions,* 54–57.

2. Bradsher, *Afghanistan and the Soviet Union,* 24–25. Figures for military aid include 1979.

3. Callaghy, in *The State-Society Struggle,* calls this a "cover-over" strategy; R. Tapper, in Introduction to *Conflict of Tribe and State,* uses the anthropological term *encapsulation.*

4. On the Neo-Destour, see L. Anderson, *State and Social Transformation,* 158–78.

Chapter 2 / Social Structure under the Old Regime

1. Gregorian, *Emergence of Modern Afghanistan,* 21–24; Dupree, *Afghanistan,* 316.

2. G. Etienne, *Aléas de la coopération,* 160–61.

3. Nyrop and Seekins, *Country Study,* 177.

4. According to the Islamic law (*sharia*) an inheritance is first divided among the surviving children, with sons receiving equal full shares and daughters equal half-shares. Each widow (for there may be several) receives one-third of the divisible property of her sons. Among most ethnic groups in Afghanistan, the requirements of female inheritance are ignored or evaded, for fear of losing the family inheritance to the families into which the women marry. Some groups, however, have attempted in recent times to Islamicize their customs by protecting female inheritance; see ibid., 120.

On agnatic rivalry see Dupree, "Tribal Warfare"; and Ahmed, *Pukhtun Economy and Society.*

On marriage politics see J. Anderson, "Cousin Marriage in Context." In the following example Anderson describes marriage patterns in one lineage of Ghilzai Pashtun: "Three . . . brothers established a colony on land granted in the territory of a neighboring tribe by a former king about a generation ago. . . . The elder of the brothers was the *khan* [leader] of that settlement and married a total of four women over a long life: one from a tribe opposed to his own and to the one in which the settlement was located, one from the same leading family of an allied tribe from which his youngest brother also took a wife, one from his own tribe (but a different lineage), and one from the tribe whose territory surrounded the new settlement. A second brother, who married a 'kerib' [agnatic kinswoman] died without issue. The third brother married a woman from another family in the opposed tribe from which his older brother took a wife, plus another woman from a family in the allied tribe. The effect of these marriages is, pointedly, to cover both sides of every alignment which obtains locally."

5. Uberoi, in "Men, Women, and Property," 400, found that 15 percent of the men in a Tajik village in the Andarab Valley had more than one wife. Most studies report somewhat lower incidences of polygyny. N. Tapper, in "Matrons and Mistresses," 65, for instance, found that about 10 percent of the men were polygynous at any one time among Durrani Pashtun nomads in Sar-i Pul District of Jauzjan Province.

6. N. Tapper, in "Abolition of Brideprice," 298, finds marriage so important among Ishaqzai Durrani nomads that, she says, "production is for the sake of reproduction." See also Uberoi, "Men, Women, and Property," 405.

7. Note that this system is in a sense the reverse of the dowry system of India and Pakistan, in which the flow of property at marriage is from the bride's family to the bridegroom's. Daughters can be a considerable financial burden to a family in a dowry system, which gives rise to such abuses as "dowry death" or "bride burning," in which the husband's family kills the new wife if the dowry was insufficient. Such murders are rare under the brideprice system, in which brides are highly valued in a purely economic sense; the bride represents a needed resource for which a family has paid dearly. On brideprice, *mahr*, debt, and attempts at reform, also see Barfield, *Central Asian Arabs*, 78–89; Barth, *Political Leadership Among Swat Pathans*, 36–37; G. Etienne, *Aléas de la coopération*, 95–99; J. Anderson, "Cousin Marriage in Context"; N. Tapper, "Abolition of Brideprice," 299; Schuyler Jones, *Men of Influence*, 151.

8. Nancy Tapper has done a variety of analyses of her data on Durrani Pashtuns, which can be found in "Matrons and Mistresses"; "Abolition of Brideprice"; "Pashtun Nomad Women"; and "Direct Exchange and Brideprice." Jon Anderson has found similar results among Ghilzai Pashtun, as related in "Cousin Marriage in Context." Uberoi presents a model of sexual and economic relations among Tajiks of Andarab in "Men, Women, and Property."

9. J. Anderson, "Cousin Marriage in Context," 8; Taniwal, "Impact of Pashtunwali."

10. Elphinstone, *Kingdom of Caubul*, 1:239. Veiling is less prevalent among nomads. See R. Tapper, "Holier Than Thou," 258; and N. Tapper, "Matrons and Mistresses," 77. Uberoi, "Men, Women, and Property," reports strict pardah among Andarabi Tajiks.

11. On women and namus, see Ahmed, *Pukhtun Economy and Society,* 250 ff. Malalai's couplet, quoted in Dupree, *Afghanistan,* 411. A similar event was reported during the First Anglo-Afghan War: "In May [1842], Nott's forces had sallied forth to engage the Durrani tribesmen led by Aktur Khan, and witnessed a scene not uncommon in Afghan history: a woman (widow of Akram Khan, executed earlier by the British) riding her husband's horse, waving his standard, and exhorting the men to fight on to victory—in vain." Ibid., 396–97. Nahid's name was used for the main girls' high school for Afghan refugees in Peshawar, "Lycée Nahid Shahid" (The Martyr Nahid High School). She is also the subject of a poem by the late Khalilullah Khalili, *Nahid va Dukhtaran-i Qahraman-i Kabul (Nahid and the Heroic Girls of Kabul)* (Haqq-i Chap Mahfuz: n.p., 1404 Q.H.). Also see Mehrabodin Masstan, " 'Nous, les femmes afghanes,' entretien avec T. Kakar," *Défis Afghans* 14 (May–June–July 1987): 12.

12. Roy, *Islam and Resistance,* 10–29. Roy tends to overlook the role of the state in determining the identity of qawms. See also R. Tapper, Introduction to *Conflict of Tribe and State;* Beattie, "Kinship and Ethnicity," 41–42; and J. Anderson, "Tribe and Community," 596–97.

13. Anderson and Strand, *Ethnic Processes and Intergroup Relations.* For an analytic compari-

son and critique of various ethnic maps of Afghanistan see Centlivres and Centlivres-Demont, *Et si on parlait de l'Afghanistan?* 54–63.

14. The Persian spoken in Afghanistan is officially known as Dari. Its degree of difference from Iranian Persian seems to this nonlinguist to be about the same as that of American from British English.

15. Non-Muslims, including tiny groups of Hindus, Sikhs, and Jews, played roles more akin to consulting firms in trade and finance than of citizens. A small group of urban Shi'a (Qizilbash) played a similar role in the bazaar and bureaucracy.

16. Roy, "Ethnies et politique."

17. Some Pashtuns call themselves Pakhtuns, in the northern dialect of Pashto (Pakhto). In India and Pakistan they are known as Pathans. The term Afghan seems to be of Persian origin. There is an extensive literature on Pashtuns, especially those in Pakistan. The classic account is in Elphinstone, *Kingdom of Caubul*. Two major works by scholars who were also political agents in tribal areas of British India and Pakistan, respectively, are Caroe, *The Pathans;* and Ahmed, *Pukhtun Economy and Society.*

The various segments of Pashtun tribes are generally known by names formed from that of the common male ancestor followed by the suffix *zai* (born of, or sons) or *khel* (branch), such as Yusufzai (sons of Yusuf) or Sulaimankhel (branch of Sulaiman). My labels for the various levels of affiliation follow R. Tapper, Introduction to *Conflict of Tribe and State,* 10.

18. J. Anderson, "Tribe and Community," 587–88.

19. Ahmed, *Millennium and Charisma,* 69–83, presents an ideal type of the nang-qalang distinction. On Pashtunwali see Elphinstone, *Kingdom of Caubul,* 1:210–35, 295–301; Ahmed, *Pukhtun Economy and Society,* 90 ff.; Willi Steul, *Paschtunwali;* Dupree, *Afghanistan,* 125–28; J. Anderson, "Khan and Khel"; J. Anderson, "How Afghans Define Themselves."

The description of Pashtunwali here is an ideal type that operates in various social contexts. The degree to which Pashtuns live up to this cultural ideal varies. According to Ahmed, *Pukhtun Economy and Society,* 3, the ideal model of Pashtunwali becomes more operational in poorer economic zones and when interaction with the state is minimal.

20. Elphinstone, *Kingdom of Caubul,* 1:295.

21. Shahrani, "State Building and Social Fragmentation"; Caroe, *The Pathans,* 252; Reisner, "Feudalism among the Afghans," 50; Barfield, "Tribe and State Relations"; Elphinstone, *Kingdom of Caubul,* 2:105, 151; Ghani, "Administration," 1:559.

22. For a description of a Pashtun-dominated society where qawm is more akin to caste, see Barth, *Political Leadership among Swat Pathans.*

23. Beattie, in "Kinship and Ethnicity," describes a village in Balkh Province where Pashtuns are one of several qawms who settled the area in the 1920s. They keep track of descent for only three or four generations.

24. Elphinstone, *Kingdom of Caubul,* 1:404; Centlivres, in *Bazaar d'Asie centrale,* 158, reports that in Tashqurghan Tajik means anyone integrated into urban, Persian-speaking culture, including some of Uzbek descent. Barfield, in "Tribe and State Relations," 174, quotes the Mongol Ghazan Khan, ruler of Iran (1195–1204), contrasting his tribesmen to the "Tazik ra'iyyat [Persian peasant]."

On qawms among Tajiks see Beattie, "Kinship and Ethnicity," 47; and Uberoi, "Men, Women, and Property," 398. Davydov, in "Rural Commune," describes communal institutions among Tajiks in several regions of northern Afghanistan.

25. According to Lapidus, in "Tribes and State Formation," 42: "Iran [from 1501 to 1722] was essentially a Safavid suzerainty over a society organized into regional *uymaq* states." For a summary of debates about the uymaqs see R. Tapper, "Anthropologists, Historians, and Tribespeople," 57–58.

26. Barfield, "Tribe and State Relations," 175.

27. On these *muhajirin* (refugees or emigrants) from the Soviet Union, see Shalinsky, "Central Asian Emigres."

28. Canfield, *Faction and Conversion.*

29. Elphinstone, *Kingdom of Caubul,* 1:211.

30. Qizilbash means "red heads." Among Turkic tribes, colors denote directions of the compass, and different tribes claimed rights to pasture in different regions, which led to their identification by the colors of those regions. Red is associated with south, as in the Red Sea, an Ottoman name for what the Bible calls the Sea of Reeds.

31. On the conversion of Nuristan and social life among Nuristanis of the Waigal Valley, see Jones, *Men of Influence.* The practice of hospitality is even more codified among Nuristanis than among Pashtuns. Nuristani men achieve strictly codified ranks only by offering particular sequences of feasts. At one time, killing Muslims was also a way of achieving status; this was later replaced by killing "Afghans" or by cattle rustling and, in the recent war, by killing Soviets or Communists. On Nuristani conflict with neighbors and the role of the state, see Strand, "Ethnic Competition and Tribal Schism."

On the Arabs see Barfield, *Central Asian Arabs.* The Arabs are descended from the Central Asian Arabs of Bukhara, who apparently migrated to Afghanistan in the 1870s after the Russian conquest of Bukhara. They are divided into clans but do not keep track of extensive genealogies and no longer have a tribal social organization. Barfield traces this weakened social structure to their encapsulation by states. They have (or had before the war) a pastoral economy. Similar groups still live near Bukhara and in southern Tajikistan.

32. Shahrani, *Kirghiz and Wakhi.*

33. Data on production and labor force from Democratic Republic of Afghanistan (DRA), *Statistical Year Book of Afghanistan (SYB) (1979–1980),* 41. Agriculture and forestry accounted for 58 percent of gross domestic product. According to Nyrop and Seekins, in *Country Study,* 174, these figures are too low because they omit the production of goods for the cultivator's own subsistence. Figures are for 1356 Sh.H. The official calendar of Afghanistan uses solar (Shamsi) years beginning on the Persian New Year (Nawruz), March 21, and dating from Muhammad's emigration (Hijra) to Mecca. The year starting each March 21 is 621 years behind the concurrent year A.D.

Among the settled population, about 60 percent were employed in agriculture. Using the estimate of 2.5 million for the nomads (DRA, *SYB (1979–1980),* 37), I assumed (1) that the proportion of labor to total population was the same for nomads as for the settled population; (2) that there was no unemployment among nomads; and (3) that all working nomads worked in pastoralism. I then added the number of working nomads to the total labor and to the labor in agriculture and pastoralism. This gave an estimate of 67 percent of the population engaged in agriculture and pastoralism.

Mathonnat, "Economie impulsée de l'extérieur," provides the estimate of 85 percent living from agriculture. The government of Afghanistan estimated that 72 percent of the labor force was "directly or indirectly engaged in agriculture" in 1975–76 (DRA, *Afghan Agriculture in Figures,* 1. Nyrop and Seekins, in *Country Study,* 174, note that the share of agriculture in the labor force decreased sharply after the mid-1960s. The share of agriculture in the labor force is likely to be an underestimate because women's participation is undercounted.

Estimates derived from the incomplete 1979 census of settled and nomad populations, as well as of labor, are given in DRA, *SYB, 1979–1980,* 37. For earlier estimates and discussions of the difficulty of defining nomads, see Ferdinand, "Nomad Expansion and Commerce," 123; Dupree, *Afghanistan,* 164; R. Tapper, "Nomadism in Modern Afghanistan: Asset or Anachronism?" 127–28; and Barfield, *Central Asian Arabs,* xvii.

34. DRA, *Afghan Agriculture in Figures,* 1, 37, 169. According to U.N. estimates, only 20 percent of the wheat reached the bazaar (United Nations, "Afghanistan," *Economic Bulletin for Asia and the Far East* 22 [1971]: 24–53, cited in Barfield, *Central Asian Arabs,* 96). Afghanistan in the 1970s tied with Greece as the world's third-largest producer of raisins, after the United States and Turkey. According to one Muscovite, the initial sign of the Soviet invasion was the sudden appearance of raisins in all of Moscow's food stores in the winter of 1980.

On water and irrigation see J. Anderson, "Tribe and Community," 583–84. On water in Afghan agriculture see Dupree, *Afghanistan,* 33–42. On effects of the Green Revolution see G. Etienne, *Aléas de la coopération,* and J. Anderson, "There Are No Khans Anymore."

35. DRA, *Afghan Agriculture in Figures,* 21, 34–35, 127. R. Tapper, in "Nomadism in Modern Afghanistan," 132, discusses complementarities between nomadism and agriculture in Afghanistan. Livestock ownership fluctuates because peasants and nomads sell or slaughter more head for meat during poor agricultural years or other times of distress. The number of head declined by about one-third during the drought of the early 1970s.

36. See the map in Dupree, *Afghanistan,* 165, for major migration routes. Shahrani, in *Kirghiz and Wakhi,* focuses on the effects of political change on nomadism for one group. On nomad trading see Ferdinand, "Nomad Expansion and Commerce." Kakar, in *Government and Society,* 126–27, reports the spread of these traders as far as Assam.

37. G. Etienne, *Aléas de la coopération,* passim; Barry, *Royaume de l'insolence,* 103; Centlivres and Centlivres-Demont, "Société afghane"; Centlivres, *Bazaar d'Asie centrale,* 139; Tabibi, "Afghanische Landreform," 53–56. Kakar, in *Government and Society,* 188–89, provides a survey of sharecropping systems in late nineteenth-century Afghanistan. The types of farm given in the text are abstract categories; in actual cases the types are more complex.

38. Barfield, *Central Asian Arabs,* 33–42, 110–11.

39. G. Etienne, *Aléas de la coopération,* has many observations on rural debt. The best general discussion is Tabibi, "Afghanische Landreform," 57–60. Ferdinand, in "Nomad Expansion and Commerce," discusses geraw, especially as a form of loan from nomads to peasants. A survey in 1963–64 found that in four districts of Nangarhar Province the average debt per family was Af 6,204 (about $140) at an average interest rate of 33 percent (DRA, *Afghan Agriculture in Figures,* 105). All indications are that both indebtedness and interest rates increased significantly in the fifteen years after that survey. There seems to be no information of even modest accuracy on the indebtedness of the peasantry in Afghanistan before 1978.

40. Twenty-six to 36 percent of the agricultural households were landless according to Glukhoded, "Economy of Independent Afghanistan," 242. Mukherjee, in *From Tragedy to Triumph,* 177, claims that "over 30 percent" were landless. Both authors apparently use figures supplied by the Soviet-installed Kabul government, although neither cites sources. The 1972–73 survey results are in DRA, *Afghan Agriculture in Figures,* 154.

41. Mukherjee, *From Tragedy to Triumph,* 177. On size distribution of holdings in Afghanistan, see the table in Shahrani, "Marxist 'Revolution' and Islamic Resistance," 19. Data on India are for 1970–72, *National Sample Survey (Twenty-sixth round),* cited in Kohli, *State and Poverty in India,* 81. Data for Iran are from Iran Ministry of Interior (Vizarat-i Kishvar), *First National Census of Agriculture: Mahr 1339* (October 1960), 15:32.

42. Dupree, *Afghanistan,* 147. No source given.

43. Elphinstone, *Kingdom of Caubul,* 1:389.

44. In Paktia Province, closest to the nang Pashtun ideal, 94 percent of the cultivated land was tilled by the owner in 1963. The same seems to have been true of other tribal highland areas. In a village in the Waigal Valley of Nuristan, 300 of 337 families belonged to the landowning class. Data on Paktia are from government statistics cited in Dupree, *Afghanistan,* 147. Data on Nuristan are from an anthropological study—Schuyler, *Men of Influence,* 95. See also the data on the high-

land Pashai in Keiser, "Rebellion in Darra-i Nur." On Qandahar and the North see G. Etienne, *Aléas de la coopération,* 162; Centlivres, *Bazaar d'Asie centrale,* 23. Etienne also found more big landlords in the plains between Kunduz and Baghlan (p. 133). Reisner, in "Feudalism among the Afghans," 52, attributes the development of greater inequality of landownership around Qandahar to the penetration of the countryside by an urban-based division of labor. Like all the Soviet and pro-Soviet authors, Reisner calls this system feudalism, despite the separation of landownership from political power, which Marx considered characteristic of the capitalist mode of production. The early period of the Durrani monarchy (1747–1818) could properly be called feudal, for Durrani tribal chiefs received grants of land in return for military service. The accumulation of land through participation in a market economy, however, is capitalist, not feudal.

On the ethnic dimension of landlord-tenant relations in the North, see R. Tapper, "Ethnicity and Class"; R. Tapper, Introduction to *Conflict of Tribe and State,* 40; and Centlivres, *Bazaar d'Asie centrale.* On Logar and Maidan (the former name of Wardak Province) see G. Etienne, *Aléas de la coopération,* 175, 181.

45. Data of food availability from DRA, *Afghan Agriculture in Figures,* 163. Quotations from G. Etienne, *Aléas de la coopération,* 102; Elphinstone, *Kingdom of Caubul,* 1:391.

46. Elphinstone, *Kingdom of Caubul,* 1:276; Barry, *Royaume de l'insolence,* 58–59. (My translation.)

47. Canfield, *Faction and Conversion;* Shahrani, *Kirghiz and Wakhi.*

48. Roy, *Islam and Resistance,* 33–34. Specialists disagree about the degree to which the Islam of the village in Afghanistan (the Little Tradition) is part of that high civilization (the Great Tradition). Dupree, in *Afghanistan,* 104, claims that "the Islam practiced in Afghan villages, nomad camps, and most urban areas (the ninety to ninety-five percent non-literates) would be almost unrecognizable to a sophisticated Muslim scholar." Scholars who have partly based their conclusions on popular behavior during the war have argued that this distinction is exaggerated. Roy, in *Islam and Resistance,* 30–53, argues that the basic beliefs of popular Islam do not contradict more elaborate versions of the religion but are instead the common basis on which more elaborate versions are constructed. According to Shahrani, in "Local Knowledge of Islam," the behavior of the peasants in the resistance shows that Islam is not just a set of superstitious beliefs but a comprehensive worldview that accords with that of the Islamic political forces (as represented by ulama and Islamic intellectuals) that they have chosen to follow. The basic beliefs and worldview of Islam are disseminated among a largely nonliterate audience through recitation (now often on tape cassettes) of popular Islamic texts based on the writings of the great poets of medieval Persian culture, such as Saadi and Jalaluddin Rumi.

49. On mullahs in Afghanistan see Shahrani, "Local Knowledge of Islam." On Iran see Arjomand, *Shadow of God.*

50. Roy, in *Islam and Resistance,* 35, describes an anticlerical reaction in tribal areas as "the mullahs to the mosque." Shahrani, in "Local Knowledge of Islam," draws on his experience growing up in a Tajik and Uzbek village of Badakhshan Province to challenge the image of the ignorant mullah of low status. Clearly there are regional variations in villages and mullahs, as well as individual differences. On mullahs see also Shahrani, "Responses to the Saur Revolution," 150 ff.; J. Anderson, "How Afghans Define Themselves," 270; Barth, *Political Leadership among Swat Pathans,* 46–47; Kakar, *Government and Society,* 152; Elphinstone, *Kingdom of Caubul,* 1:249–50, 282–86.

51. Alim means "scholar," literally "one who knows." Mawlawi, originally a term of address, means "my master." It is related to mawlana (our master), often used in India and Pakistan.

52. Gellner, *Muslim Society;* Gellner, "Tribalism and the State"; Barth, *Political Leadership among Swat Pathans,* 58–61; Ahmed, *Millennium and Charisma,* 53–55; Ahmed, *Pukhtun Economy and Society,* 103.

53. On heterodox Sufi practices in Afghanistan see Dupree, *Afghanistan*, 104–8. On Sufism, ulama, and other major aspects of Islam in Afghanistan see Roy, *Islam and Resistance*, 30–68. For further background on South Asian Islam, especially the Naqshbandiyya order, see Ahmad, *Studies in Islamic Culture*. On Sufism among various Pashtun groups see R. Tapper, "Holier Than Thou"; Tavakolian, "Religiosity, Values, and Economic Change"; and J. Anderson, "How Afghans Define Themselves."

54. On resistance see Scott, *Weapons of the Weak;* on landai see Dupree, *Afghanistan*, 90; on sexual liaisons as protest see Shalinsky, "Reason, Desire, and Sexuality."

The notion that Pashtun women view themselves as warlike has some basis in the behavior of those few women who were able to act out such fantasies. Here is the historian Hasan Kakar's description of the senior wife of Amir Abdul Rahman Khan: "In the past the principal wives of the Afghan rulers had been active in politics behind the scenes, but Bibi Halima was the most active of all. She was the first queen to appear in public in European dress without a veil and to ride horses with armed guards accompanying her. She held military exercises in the harem and trained her maids in the military art. In 1888, while on the way to Turkestan with the amir her own 'guard consisted not only of a body of the amir's soldiers, but of a regiment of mounted Amazons, some two hundred, the female slaves and servants of the Harem. These rode on men's saddles, were veiled, and wore on the head, over the veil, solar hamlets [*sic*], or felt hats. Each was armed with a sabre and a carbine'" (*Government and Society*, 18). The internal quotation is from the memoirs of John Gray, an Englishman who advised the amir. For a more recent account of the views of a Pakistani Pashtun woman, see Keegan, "Amazon of Peshawar."

55. Barth, *Political Leadership among Swat Pathans*, 74; R. Tapper, "Holier Than Thou," 259.

56. On the political process among khans see the classic, though disputed, study by Barth, *Political Leadership among Swat Pathans*. A partial critique of Barth is found in Ahmed, *Millennium and Charisma*. See also Barry, *Royaume de l'insolence*, 96–116; Roy, *Islam and Resistance*, 25–29; J. Anderson, "Khan and Khel."

57. Fazelly, "Loya Djirga."

58. On tribal war in Afghanistan see Dupree, "Tribal Warfare"; and Roy, *Islam and Resistance*, 59–62. For a broader view of tribal war see Gellner, "Tribalism and the State," 113–14.

59. Shahrani, "Kirghiz Khans." For some Marxists the khan is simply the landlord, and his patronage or tribal relationships with other villagers, including his tenants and hired laborers, are mechanisms of domination creating a hegemonic ideology of "tribalism," which "divides the oppressed from each other," as Halliday writes, in "Revolution in Afghanistan," 35. This was the conception of khans that underlay the land reform program of the Khalqi government in 1978 and 1979. Halliday fails to note that tribalism also divides the oppressors from each other and prevents them from forming a coherent political class in relation to the state. Indeed, it is such divisions that lead the khans to recruit followers.

60. Tabibi, "Afghanische Landreform," 53–66; J. Anderson, "Khan and Khel," 137–38; Glatzer, "Pashtun Nomads and the State," 224; Elphinstone, *Kingdom of Caubul*, 1:217. See also J. Anderson, "There Are No Khans Anymore," 170–71. Barfield, in *Central Asian Arabs*, 63–64, describes leaders called *bai* who play a similar role. See also Shahrani, "Kirghiz Khans."

61. Salih Ziari, quoted in Gille, "L'accession au pouvoir des communistes," 195–96. Dupree, in *Afghanistan*, 249–50, notes that villagers do not cooperate voluntarily for projects of mutual benefit, but have to be paid or forced to work on them. This self-interest is a common characteristic of real, as opposed to romanticized, peasants, as is also confirmed by the Chinese revelations about bogus stories of voluntary labor during the Cultural Revolution and the Great Leap Forward. Dupree notes that the villagers try to isolate themselves behind a "mud curtain," because "sustained relations with the outside world have seldom been pleasant, for outsiders usually come to *extract* from, not bring anything *into*, the village."

62. Canfield, *Faction and Conversion.*

63. On Islamic coalitions see Canfield, *Faction and Conversion;* Canfield, "Islamic Coalitions in Bamyan"; and Canfield, "Ethnic, Regional, and Sectarian Alignments."

64. On tribal puritans see Gellner, *Muslim Society,* 51–53. For an example among the Pashtuns of Pakistan see Ahmed, *Religion and Politics in Muslim Society.*

Chapter 3 / State, Tribe, and the International System

1. Ahmad Shah modeled his institutions on those of Persia, with which he was familiar. See Elphinstone, *Kingdom of Caubul,* 2:258.

2. For an account of this foundation myth, see Dupree, *Afghanistan,* 333.

3. Gankovsky, in "Durrani Empire," 90, states that 76.5 percent of the revenue was from India.

4. Elphinstone, *Kingdom of Caubul,* 1:258.

5. Ghani, "Administration," 558.

6. Elphinstone, *Kingdom of Caubul,* 1:245–46.

7. Muhammadzai rulers of Afghanistan from Dost Muhammad to Amanullah (during the early part of his reign) called themselves by the Arab-Islamic title amir, rather than the Persian-secular titles shah or padishah. Amir al-muminin (commander of the believers) was one of the titles of the caliph. Dost Muhammad took this title in 1836, when he undertook jihad against the Sikhs to re-cover Peshawar, and its continued use evoked an Islamic, rather than tribal, legitimation of the ruler's power.

8. Recall from Chapter 1 Delacroix's suggestion in "Distributive State," 8, that we direct our attention to the structure of opportunities available to state builders.

9. According to Ghani, "Administration," 559, "peasantization" started immediately after the fall of the Saddozais in 1818. Before that date, he writes, "inhabitants of Afghanistan proper [as opposed to the Indian provinces of the empire] were either exempted [from taxes] or assessed lightly, while large tracts of land were also held as grants (*toyul*) by khans or Pashtun clans. All this changed fundamentally after 1235/1818. In the absence of tribute from abroad, the new states had to secure their financial needs from resources at home. The most dramatic illustration was the case of the Dorrani clans of Qandahar, who had been the military backbone of the Dorrani expansion. Until the end of the empire, their lands had been exempted from taxation. Between 1235/1818 and 1255/1839 with the advent of the Mohammadzay brothers, they were turned into a subjugated tax-paying peasantry. According to Henry Rawlinson, the British political agent for Qandahar during the first Anglo-Afghan war (1839–42), the Dorrani clans were subdued by the systematic use of violence against their leaders, the appointment of hostile Persian-speaking tax agents, and the raising of a military force composed of non-Dorranis."

10. On this theme see Rubin, "Political Exiles."

11. Ghani, "Administration," 559.

12. Ibid., 559–60.

13. According to Ghani, in "Administration," 560, "The impact of the second British invasion on Afghan institutions was summarized by the viceroy of India in a communication to the secretary of state for India: The British military operations and occupation 'have left the Civil government and the military resources of the Afghans in a state of dilapidation which will require a long time to repair.'"

14. The Durand Line, which today separates the tribal areas of the Northwest Frontier Province of Pakistan from Afghanistan, has not been recognized as an international border by any Afghan government. It is not demarcated or monitored at most points.

15. Dupree, *Afghanistan;* Adamec, *Afghanistan,* 37–38; and Gankovsky et al., *History of Afghanistan,* 163–65, 175–76.

16. Ghani, "Administration," 560.

17. Luciani, "Allocation vs. Production States," 69. On the subsidy, see Adamec, *Afghanistan,* 17–18. According to a statement the amir furnished to the British in 1885, the yearly expenditure on all military and police was 8.6 million rupees, but Kakar, in *Government and Society,* 90, considers the figure exaggerated. The latter work is the major source on this period, together with Kakar's earlier *Internal Political Developments.* According to Ghani, in "Administration," 560, the pay of the troops alone amounted to 7.26 million rupees, or 58.6 percent of state expenditures.

18. According to Kakar: "By 1891 the yearly revenue in the reign of Amir ʻAbd al-Rahman had increased by slightly less that four times the revenue of the last year of the reign of Amir Sher ʻAli Khan." (*Government and Society,* 90).

19. Migdal, *Strong Societies and Weak States,* 52–96.

20. The amir's measures to isolate Afghanistan were extreme. He did not even allow the British to send an English officer to represent them at Kabul, but insisted that their ambassador had to be an Indian Muslim. The only foreigners he allowed into the country were those employed by him, generally for the manufacture of weapons or for other military purposes. The amir refused to allow foreign military advisers—which Dost Muhammad and Sher Ali had both employed— fearing that "a neighboring power, by offering military officers from its own army, under the pretense of teaching the Afghan soldiers British military tactics might also teach them to attend to foreign interests." (Mir Munshi Sultan Mahomed Khan, ed., *The Life of Abdur Rahman, Amir of Afghanistan* [London: Murray, 1900], quoted by Gregorian, *Emergence of Modern Afghanistan,* 141.) This and similar statements gave some of the amir's words a prophetic ring after April 1978 and especially after December 1979. The main route used by Soviet forces entering Afghanistan was the Salang Highway, which the Soviets had blasted through the Hindu Kush north of Kabul in the 1960s, ostensibly for the sake of trade. Furthermore, the introduction of modern education, including sending Afghans abroad and inviting foreign experts to Afghanistan, was instrumental in the introduction of new ideologies into the country, including both Marxism and Islamism.

21. On the forms of internal consolidation under absolutism, see Giddens, *Nation-State and Violence,* 85. These overlap considerably with the tripartite categorization of rebellions against Abdul Rahman given in the text, which derives from Kakar, *Afghanistan.*

22. On the amir as imam see, e.g., the agreement with the Muhammadzais reproduced in Kakar, *Afghanistan,* 291–97. On courts see Ghani, "Islam and State Building"; Ghani, "Disputes in a Court of Sharia."

23. Dupree, *Afghanistan,* 421.

24. Gellner, *Muslim Society,* 73–74.

25. Kakar, *Government and Society,* 24. See also ibid., 16; Kakar, "Fall of the Afghan Monarchy," 196.

26. Kakar, *Government and Society,* 19–20. Kakar argues that "the amir was probably inspired by the *devshirme* system of the Ottomans under which children of the Christian subjects were recruited for training to fill the ranks of the Janissaries (Ottoman regular infantry) and to occupy posts in the palace service and in the administration." For a discussion of bureaucratic lineages in a different type of tribally based state (a Rajput state under British suzerainty in India), see Rudolph and Rudolph with Singh, "Bureaucratic Lineage."

27. Ghani, "Administration," 561. On Habibullah's reign also see Adamec, *Afghanistan's Foreign Affairs;* and Gregorian, *Emergence of Modern Afghanistan,* 181–205.

28. Gellner, *Muslim Society,* 74; Centlivres, *Bazaar d'Asie centrale,* 60–61; Majrooh, "Past and Present Education."

29. Kakar, *Government and Society,* 163; Majrooh, "Past and Present Education."

30. Gregorian, *Emergence of Modern Afghanistan,* 184, 192. According to Ghani, in "Administration," 561, both were founded in 1907.

31. Dupree, *Afghanistan,* 438. Musahiban means something like "aides-de-camp" or "ad-

visers." The family received this title from Amir Habibullah. Hasan Kakar, personal communication, 1990; see also Caroe, *The Pathans*, 307.

32. Kakar, *Government and Society*, 20.

33. Janissaries played an important role for the Young Turks, just as the ghulam bachas did for the Young Afghans.

34. Gregorian, *Emergence of Modern Afghanistan*, 220–28. Although an orderly was later executed for dereliction of duty, no clear responsibility for the assassination of Habibullah was ever established. Some believe that either Amanullah himself contrived it or that it was a joint action of both his forces and the conservatives.

35. On this period see Poullada, *Reform and Rebellion;* Gregorian, *Emergence of Modern Afghanistan*, 227–92; Dupree, *Afghanistan*, 441–57; Gankovsky et al., *History of Afghanistan*, 212–25; Adamec, *Afghanistan's Foreign Affairs*, 77–172; Roy, *Islam et modernité politique*, 62–68; and Shahrani, "State Building and Social Fragmentation," 45–50.

36. Giddens, *Nation-State and Violence*, 148–71; Migdal, *Strong Societies and Weak States*, 52–96.

37. The figure is from Gurevich, *Afghanistan*, 39, cited in Guha, "Economy of Afghanistan," 173.

38. On the various forms of tenure that had existed previously see Guha, "Economy of Afghanistan," 167.

39. Dupree, *Afghanistan*, 447; Gregorian, *Emergence of Modern Afghanistan*, 240. According to Ghani, in "Administration," 561, "The budget for the ministry of education had been six thousand rupees under Habibullah, but it was raised to more than five million rupees by 1928. . . . Between 1924 and 1928, 322 primary schools—at least one in every administrative district— were established. During the same period, 4,823 students finished primary school, 158 graduated from high-school, and 151 were sent for training abroad. . . . These students provided the staff of the bureaucracy in subsequent decades."

40. Poullada, *Reform and Rebellion*, 111–19.

41. Pre-1978 accounts of the Bacha were usually derived from Afghan state or elite sources and were generally hostile. Events since then have led to a reevaluation of his movement in works such as Roy, *Islam and Resistance;* and Shahrani, "State Building and Social Fragmentation." Shahrani's account uses certain Persian sources for events that have largely been ignored by Western scholarship.

42. On continuity with Amanullah see Ghani, "Administration," 561. An interesting analysis of this period, from which I have greatly benefited, is Ghani, "State, Economy, and Ideology." On Nadir Shah and the "avuncular" period see Gregorian, *Emergence of Modern Afghanistan*, 293–400; Dupree, *Afghanistan*, 458–98; and Gankovsky et al., *History of Afghanistan*, 226–36.

43. Gregorian, *Emergence of Modern Afghanistan*, 297–99, 335; Adamec, *Afghanistan's Foreign Affairs*, 221–22.

44. Gregorian, *Emergence of Modern Afghanistan*, 316–17.

45. For views of this period see Akhramovich, *Outline History of Afghanistan;* Gankovsky et al., *History of Afghanistan*, 236–62; Dupree, *Afghanistan*, 499–558; Poullada, "Afghanistan and the United States"; Poullada, "Road to Crisis"; Ghani, "State, Economy, and Ideology"; and Shahrani, "State Building and Social Fragmentation," 58–63.

46. Fry, *Afghan Economy*, 158.

47. Land and livestock tax amounted to 0.6 percent of GNP in 1952–53 and 0.08 percent of GNP in 1973–74, in an economy where "the agricultural sector is thought to contribute about 50 percent of the total value of Gross Domestic Product" (ibid., 49). In the 1920s the land tax alone had often amounted to 20 percent of the crop (Barfield, *Central Asian Arabs*, 163).

Fry, in *Afghan Economy*, 181–89, calculates Afghanistan's tax effort using the same method used in the study of forty-nine countries in Bahl, "Regression Approach to Tax Effort." The tax effort scores ranged from 1.63 (Ivory Coast) to 0.32 (Nepal), with a median of 0.995. Afghanistan scored 0.44. Iran ranked twenty-eighth of fifty (Bahl's forty-nine plus Afghanistan), with a tax effort of 0.97, and Pakistan ranked forty-third with an effort of 0.72.

48. Luciani, "Allocation vs. Production States," 72. Luciani suggests that we define "allocation states as all those states whose revenue derives predominantly (more than 40 per cent) from oil or other foreign sources and whose expenditure is a substantial share of GDP." Afghanistan meets the first part of the definition but not the second. Luciani does not offer a definition of *revenue*.

49. Military aid is notoriously hard to find in government statistics and does not appear clearly in the data presented here. On conscription see Khalilzad, "Politics of Ethnicity," 667.

50. Ghani, "State, Economy, and Ideology," 30; Fry, *Afghan Economy*, 48.

51. Chaudhry, "Price of Wealth," 101–45.

52. Williams et al., "U.S. Assistance to Afghanistan."

53. Arnold, *Afghanistan's Two-Party Communism*, 29–30.

54. Dupree, *Afghanistan*, 598.

55. Weinbaum, "Legal Elites in Afghan Society," 46, 48.

56. Eberhard, "Afghanistan's Young Elite," 10t; G. Etienne, *Aléas de la coopération*, 37.

57. Ibid., 39. It is not clear whether this number includes those sent for military training. A reviewer of an article containing the figures considers this number too high.

58. Bradsher, *Afghanistan and the Soviet Union*, 29. Kakar, in "Fall of the Afghan Monarchy," 212, estimates that seven thousand were trained in the USSR and Czechoslovakia, compared with six hundred trained in the United States.

59. Dupree, "Political Uses of Religion," 203–4; Dupree, *Afghanistan*, 530–33. Shafiq later became the last prime minister of the New Democracy period. He was among the first people executed by the PDPA after the April 1978 coup. Bazgar, *Résistance au coeur*, 29–36, includes a memoir of the author's childhood spent confined to a house in Kabul after his father, a khan of the Momand tribe, was arrested by the army in 1959. The arrest seems to have been ordered by Daoud, and the family was released by Zahir Shah in 1963.

60. As described by J. Anderson in "There Are No Khans Anymore."

61. Barfield, *Central Asian Arabs*, 140 ff.; Centlivres, *Bazaar d'Asie centrale*.

62. Ghani, "State, Economy, and Ideology," 12–14.

63. For a description, see Dupree, *Afghanistan*, 563–90.

64. According to Johnson et al., in "Northern Provinces," the two parliaments elected were 64.4 and 60.6 percent Pashtun.

65. See the study of Tunisia in L. Anderson, *State and Social Transformation*.

66. The parliament refused all tax increases and abolished a small tax on livestock that had persisted until 1965. Fry, in *Afghan Economy*, 177, argued that the parliament resisted taxes because the government provided no services. On New Democracy see Dupree, *Afghanistan*, 559–658; and Kakar, "Fall of the Afghan Monarchy." On the effects of the decline in foreign aid, see Poullada, "Road to Crisis," 53.

67. Halliday seems to have been the first in print on the effect of the shah's initiative, in "Revolution in Afghanistan," 29. Harrison's first publication on this appeared as "Shah, Not Kremlin, Touched Off Afghan Coup"; he elaborated his assessment in "Dateline Afghanistan." Fukuyama took issue with this view, emphasizing Soviet aggressiveness, in "New Soviet Strategy." Harrison and Fukuyama subsequently debated in the letters column of *Commentary* 68 (December 1979): 4–6. I owe Selig Harrison thanks for supplying me with a complete set of both his writings on Afghanistan and many of the attacks on them, together with his replies.

68. Harrison, "Shah, Not Kremlin, Touched Off Afghan Coup."

69. Bradsher, *Afghanistan and the Soviet Union*, 61–62; Ispahani, *Roads and Rivals*, 120–21.

70. Democratic Republic of Afghanistan, *Statistical Information of Afghanistan, 1975–1978.*

71. Dupree, "Red Flag over Hindu Kush," part 2. Dupree's subtitle, "The Accidental Coup," refers to the random timing of the coup and the bumbling—though bloody—way it was carried out.

72. Majrooh, "Past and Present Education," 82; Centlivres, *Bazaar d'Asie centrale,* 61.

73. Fröhlich, *Nationalismus und Nationalstaat,* 196. Some tribal leaders welcomed education. Shahrani, in *Kirghiz and Wakhi,* 212, reports that the chief and elders of the Kirghiz in the Wakhan corridor repeatedly asked the government to establish schools there. The perception that state training led to benefits to the kin group from which the students were recruited also existed among the Balkan Christians who furnished the Ottoman Janissaries (Gellner, *Muslim Society,* 75).

74. Sawitzki, *Elitegruppe der Akademiker,* 52.

75. In a survey of Kabul University students in 1967, 93 percent reported attending lectures by foreign professors (ibid., 77). Quotation from ibid., 71.

76. Williams et al., "U.S. Assistance to Afghanistan"; Glaubitt at al., *System der Staatseinnahmen,* 57, 174; Fry, *Afghan Economy,* 159; G. Etienne, *Aléas de la coopération,* 239n.

77. Sawitzki, *Elitegruppe der Akademiker,* 107; Glaubitt et al., *System der Staatseinnahmen,* 59; Fry, *Afghan Economy,* 164. Shahrani, in "State Building and Social Fragmentation," 63, speaks of "ideological and generational class struggles in all Afghan government institutions."

78. Shahrani, "State Building and Social Fragmentation," 38.

79. On the importance of roads in general see Ispahani, *Roads and Rivals.* On their effects in Afghanistan see Fry, *Afghan Economy,* 48, 55–56, 59; Ghani, "State, Economy, and Ideology," 30; Barfield, *Central Asian Arabs,* 110–112; Barry, *Royaume de l'insolence,* 39.

80. Ghani, "State, Economy, and Ideology," 43. J. Anderson, "Tribe and Community," 584, observed in Ghazni during the early 1970s that every family had someone abroad working in the subcontinent or the Gulf region.

81. An interesting traveler's account of the effect that labor migration to Iran had, especially on western Afghanistan, is in Chaffetz, *Journey through Afghanistan.* One particularly interesting observation in this book is the converging influence of the Shah's Iran and the Soviet Union as conveyers of westernized modernity to Afghanistan. Chaffetz (222–25) describes how Soviet-educated Parchami Kabuli employees of a government dam project shocked some Pashtun nomads by showing them the models in an Iranian women's magazine called *Zan-i Imruz (Today's Woman).*

82. Centlivres and Centlivres-Demont, "Société afghane," 60–62; G. Etienne, *Aléas de la coopération,* 57; Mathonnat, "Economie impulsée de l'extérieur," 158.

83. Centlivres-Demont, "Types d'occupations," 275; Dupree, *Afghanistan,* 661; Ghani, "State, Economy, and Ideology," 31.

84. G. Etienne, *Aléas de la coopération,* 95, 101; Shahrani, *Kirghiz and Wakhi,* 79.

85. G. Etienne, *Aléas de la coopération,* 84, 92; J. Anderson, "There Are No Khans Anymore," 178; Barfield, *Central Asian Arabs,* 117–21.

86. Migdal, *Strong Societies and Weak States,* 91–93.

87. Knabe, *Frauenemanzipation in Afghanistan,* 142, 267; Dupree, *Afghanistan,* 532–33.

88. Knabe, *Frauenemanzipation in Afghanistan,* 280, 255; Sawitzki, *Elitegruppe der Akademiker,* 44; Knabe, "Women in the Social Stratification of Afghanistan," 329–30.

89. Centlivres and Centlivres-Demont, *Et si on parlait de l'Afghanistan?* 281; Centlivres and Centlivres-Demont, "Société afghane," 78–79; quotation from Sawitzki, *Elitegruppe der Akademiker,* 95 (translated by Konrad Stenzel).

Chapter 4 / Rentier State and Rentier Revolutionaries

1. Stepan, *Rethinking Military Politics,* 3–4.

2. Skocpol, *States and Social Revolutions,* 165. For a review of a variety of studies of revolutionary counterelites, see Putnam, *Political Elites,* 170–72.

3. *Khalq* (The Masses) and *Parcham* (The Flag) were the names of the factions' newspapers. On factionalism in the PDPA, see Arnold, *Afghanistan's Two-Party Communism;* Roy, "Double code afghan"; and Anwar, *Tragedy of Afghanistan.*

4. Maoist groups had access to neither state power nor foreign aid. Some later fought against the Soviets, whereas others ultimately joined the PDPA government. The main Maoist group was called Shu'la-yi Javid (Eternal Flame). A recent work analyzing Afghanistan from a point of view sympathetic to this group's ideology is Emadi, *State, Revolution, and Superpowers.* The main separatist group was known as Sitam-i Milli (Against National Oppression), although it was formally called SZA (Sazman-i Zahmatkishanan-i Afghanistan, Organization of the Toilers of Afghanistan). It was led by Tahir Badakhshi, a Tajik from Badakhshan, who left the Khalq faction of the PDPA after quarreling with Hafizullah Amin. This organization later split; the offshoot, led by Bahauddin Bais, was called SAZA (Sazman-i Inqilabi Zahmatkishanan-i Afghanistan, Revolutionary Organization of the Toilers of Afghanistan). Another important organization, perhaps affiliated with Shu'la-yi Javid, was SAMA (Sazman-i Azadbakhsh-i Mardum-i Afghanistan, Liberation Organization of the People of Afghanistan), led by Abdul Majid Kalakani, who came from the native village of Bacha-yi Saqao.

5. Arnold, *Afghanistan's Two-Party Communism,* 18–19, 55–56.

6. Es'haq, "Islamists Felt Need"; Tawana, "Historical Background of the Islamic Movement," part 1. The articles by Tawana and Es'haq give the Jamiat view of the early years of the Islamic movement. For a brief summary of the Hizb view, see Rastegar, "Education and Revolutionary Political Mobilization," 112.

7. Es'haq, "Islamists Felt Need," 8; Tawana, "Historical Background of the Islamic Movement," part 4. Tawana's article contains a detailed account of the meeting and describes the choice of name for the organization.

Sayyaf, in line with more purist teachings, later changed his given name, Ghulam Rasul— slave or worshiper of the Prophet—to Abd al-Rabb al-Rasul, or worshiper of the Master of the Prophet.

8. Es'haq, "Life in Exile"; Roy, *Islam and Resistance,* 76–77. Roy does not indicate whether the support came from the Saudi government or (more likely) from the Muslim World League (Rabitat al-'Alam al-Islami, commonly known as Rabita).

9. Tawana, "Historical Background of the Islamic Movement," part 8. For a summary of Hizb's rather different view of the split, see Rastegar, "Education and Revolutionary Political Mobilization," 112.

10. Many Afghans—and others in the Third World—have been radicalized or convinced of the need for reforms by travel to more developed areas. Even the rather undynamic Amir Habibullah was apparently convinced of the need for reforms in Afghanistan after a visit to India in 1907, according to Adamec, *Afghanistan,* 66. Amanullah returned from Europe in 1929 impatient with how far "behind" Afghanistan was and convinced of the need for repression of the mullahs (Poullada, *Reform and Rebellion,* 125). The experience of Amanullah was cited by McLuhan, in *Understanding Media,* as an example of the cultural effect of the encounter with technology. On Islamic modernism more generally see Rahman, *Islam and Modernity;* Hourani, *Arab Thought in the Liberal Age.*

11. On the contrast of "mentalities" with ideologies see Linz, "Totalitarian and Authoritarian Regimes," 266–70.

12. Majrooh, "Past and Present Education," 83. See also Arjomand, *Turban for the Crown*, 103–5.

13. According to Aleksandr Morozov, a KGB agent who worked with Hafizullah Amin, e.g., the only "Marxist" work that Amin had read was Stalin's biography of Lenin ("KGB et le conflit Khalq-Partcham," 16.) As Roy put it in "'Révolution' par le vide," 85, Soviet-supported socialism was simply "la seule modernité à portée de leur bourse"—the only modernity that they could afford.

14. Platform published in *Khalq* on April 11, 1966. Reproduced in a translation obtained by the U.S. Embassy in Kabul in Arnold, *Afghanistan's Two-Party Communism*, 137–48.

15. Reproduced in Arnold, *Afghanistan's Two-Party Communism*, 149–59.

16. According to Tawana, they chose the name Jam'iyyat for the movement "because it resembled the word 'Jamaat' in the name of 'Jamaat Ikhwan Muslemeen' of Egypt and 'Jamaat Islami' of Pakistan but was also distinct from both" ("Historical Background of the Islamic Movement," part 4, p. 5). On links to Qutb see Roy, *Islam and Resistance*, 70.

17. On Islamic reformers and "tribal puritans," see Gellner, *Muslim Society*. On Sunni Islamic revolutionaries in the Arab World see Sivan, *Radical Islam;* and B. Etienne, *Islamisme radical*. On Islamism in Afghanistan see Roy, *Islam and Resistance*. For an analogous discussion of revolutionary Shi'a Islam, see Arjomand, *Turban for the Crown*.

18. On Sunni political quietism see Von Grunebaum, *Medieval Islam*, especially pp. 142–70. My sometime student Khalid Abou El Fadle taught me a great deal on this subject. Quotation from al-Turtushi, *Siraj al-muluk wa nazm al-suluk*, quoted by Charnay, *Islam et la guerre*, 58.

19. Es'haq, "Islamists Felt Need," 8.

20. *Maram-i Hizb*. All translations from party programs are mine.

21. Ansari, "Islamic Militants in Egyptian Politics," 140. See also Roy, *Islam and Resistance*, 77–78.

22. For this use of the term jahiliyya see *Fishurdah-yi hadaf va maram-i Jam'iyyat*, 8; *Maram-i Hizb*, vav [vi], and elsewhere.

23. *Maram-i Hizb*, ha [v], 38

24. Ibid., 51, 69.

25. The fullest analysis in English of the ideological dimensions of the split is in Rastegar, "Education and Revolutionary Political Mobilization," 115–127. On Tilimasani see "Ustad Umer al-Talmesani."

26. The name means "group for the call to the Qur'an and people of the Hadith." The Hadith are the authenticated sayings of the Prophet Muhammad, which together with the Qur'an and the practice (*sunna*) of Muhammad, constitute one of the three valid sources of Islamic law, according to Sunni tradition. The People of the Hadith is a movement—perhaps deserving of the abused term *fundamentalism*—that rejects all traditions of jurisprudence (*fiqh*) in favor of direct reliance on these three sources.

27. Hikmatyar has taken this position verbally at times, but in view of the massive aid that he received from the United States, Afghans do not take his statements on this subject seriously.

28. *Fishurdah-yi hadaf va maram-i Jam'iyyat*, 10–11, says, "Jamiat has no inherent opposition to any individual or group" and states its willingness to cooperate with any that share its general goals. On p. 12 it calls for a union of "all believing and valiant compatriots, courageous youth, . . . ulama, . . . brave and valiant [military] officers, . . . those educated in modern sciences, . . . honorable and faithful peasants, . . . workers, . . . and . . . the whole believing nation" without insisting on a leading role for itself.

29. On sources of data see Appendix A.

30. For a fuller treatment, see Rubin, "Old Regime in Afghanistan."

31. I have also included some prominent individuals like Mawlana Faizani and Minhajuddin Gahiz, who were part of a broader Islamic movement but did not join the formal organization. I have not included Sibghatullah Mujaddidi, of the famous family of Naqshbandi pirs. Mujaddidi, whose family represented the most Islamic wing of the old regime, was a prominent activist who was arrested by Daoud in 1959. His brother Harun was active enough in the Ikhwan in Egypt to have been imprisoned by Nasser, and he was also connected to the Brotherhood himself. Mujaddidi long had a good relationship with Rabbani (with whom he shares a Naqshbandi connection) and a bitterly antagonistic one with Hikmatyar, but after being displaced by Rabbani as acting president of the Islamic State of Afghanistan in June 1992, Mujaddidi allied with Hikmatyar. In Pakistani exile, whenever the resistance parties split between Islamists and traditionalist-nationalists, Mujaddidi joined the latter. Hence I have not included him among the Islamic revolutionaries. His case illustrates, however, that the distinction between the Islamic revolutionaries and the Islamic establishment is not so absolute in Afghanistan as in some other Sunni countries.

32. Roy, "Double code afghan."

33. The ethnic identity of several Parchamis was difficult to determine. Many were Kabulis of mixed ancestry. Babrak Karmal, for instance, who is here counted as a Kabuli Persian-speaker—his father's family seems to have been of Kashmiri origin—at times claimed to be of Ghilzai background.

34. This is consistent with findings about the social background of Islamic militants and leftist activists in Egypt and Iran. See Ibrahim, "Egypt's Militant Islamic Groups"; Abrahamian, "Guerrilla Movement in Iran," especially tables 1 and 2, p. 5.

35. The varying ethnic composition of the graduates of different schools demonstrates this point; see Rubin, "Old Regime in Afghanistan," 88.

36. The lone Khalqi from the elite schools was Muhammad Ismail Danish, a Qizilbash Shi'a from the Chindawul District of Kabul, who is triply unusual among Khalqis: by birthplace, ethnicity, and education.

37. The former deputy leader of Hizb, Qazi Muhammad Amin, who formed his own splinter party after a dispute with Hikmatyar, also attended a government madrasa. After March 1993 he became one of Hikmatyar's deputy prime ministers.

38. See Ibrahim, "Egypt's Militant Islamic Groups"; and Abrahamian, "Guerrilla Movement in Iran."

39. Stalin quoted in Carrère d'Encausse and Schram, *Marxisme et l'Asie*, 252, as cited in Roy, "Double code afghan," 846–47n. My translation. Chicherin quoted in Umnov, "What Price the Dogma?" 21. Arnold, *Afghanistan's Two-Party Communism*, 6, lists founding dates of Communist parties in other countries on the Soviet border: Korea, 1925; China, 1921; Mongolia, 1921; Iran, 1920; Turkey, 1920; Romania, 1921; Czechoslovakia, 1921; Poland, 1918; Finland, 1918; and Norway, 1923.

40. Hough, *Struggle for the Third World;* Bradsher, *Afghanistan and the Soviet Union,* 126–48.

41. According to Selig Harrison (personal communication), the KGB had invested in Parcham, especially Babrak Karmal, and the GRU in Khalq, especially the military officers. See also "KGB et le conflit Khalq-Partcham."

42. Bradsher, *Afghanistan and the Soviet Union,* 64–66.

43. Harrison, in "Shah, Not Kremlin, Touched Off Afghan Coup," describes the articles. According to post-Soviet revelations, these articles were orchestrated by the KGB ("KGB et le conflit Khalq-Partcham"). The Indian one, the most important, was N. K. Krishnan, "Prospects of Democratic Advance in Afghanistan," *Party Life* (May 22, 1976), cited in Bradsher, *Afghanistan and the Soviet Union,* 93. Bradsher provides details (68–71), including a written statement by a senior CPI official that mediation between the Afghan factions occurred "with the knowledge and con-

sent of [the] Communist Party of [the] Soviet Union; otherwise [the] CPI would not have undertaken it. Possibly, the suggestion for such an initiative on the part of [the] CPI also came from Moscow."

44. According to Yuri Gankovsky, some officials in the Ministry of Foreign Affairs dealing with Afghanistan called him after the April 1978 coup to find out who Taraki was. They later learned it from other organs of the Soviet government. Quotation from Bradsher, *Afghanistan and the Soviet Union*, 71.

45. Harrison, *In Afghanistan's Shadow*, described these maneuvers. According to Edwards, in "Shi'i Political Dissent," 219, the Pakistanis, in response to Daoud's actions on Baluchistan, also supported a Hazara separatist group, called Tanzim-i Nasl-i Naw-i Mughul (Organization of the New Mongol Generation).

46. Caroe, *The Pathans*, 530.

47. *New York Times*, April 24, 1989; Roy, *Islam and Resistance*, 76–77.

48. Tawana's account of the most important events in the history of the Islamic movement during 1964–71 consists of a list of public demonstrations. ("Historical Background of the Islamic Movement," part 3.) See Abolfathi, "Reassessment of the Afghan Conflict," 2-5–14; Abolfathi refers to this as the "cadre phase" of an insurgency.

49. Es'haq, "Islamists Felt Need," 5, 8.

50. For similar ethnic reasons the Shi'a Islamist party, Harakat-i Islami, led by Sheikh Asif Muhsini, was the most successful resistance organization in building underground networks among the Kabuli working class during the anti-Soviet war. On Khalqi recruitment strategy see Arnold, *Afghanistan's Two-Party Communism*.

51. See, e.g., the Khalqi document entitled "The Establishment of the Marxist-Leninist Party in Afghanistan," written in 1976, published in Arnold, *Afghanistan's Two-Party Communism*, 160–77; the document underlines the establishment ties of Parcham, including ties to the military.

52. Es'haq, "Daud's Hostile Attitude," 6.

53. *A Short Biography of Noor Mohammad Taraki* (Kabul? 1978), 17, quoted in Arnold, *Afghanistan's Two-Party Communism*, 48.

54. Es'haq, "Daud's Hostile Attitude," 6.

55. Tawana, "Historical Background of the Islamic Movement," part 5.

56. Edwards, "Shi'i Dissent," 220. According to Edwards, this coup was organized not by Jamiat-i Islami but by three other partly allied groups who were inspired by Mawlana Faizani, a revered Sufi pir from Herat. Engineer Habib al-Rahman of the Polytechnic Institute, who was in charge of military affairs for Jamiat, also was arrested at this time.

Es'haq, in "Daud's Hostile Attitude," 6, recalls that he participated in this attempt but evaded arrest. He claims that the uprising was not part of the coup but was inspired by the coup's failure. Tawana, in "Historical Background of the Islamic Movement," part 5, claims that Omar was one of a group of activists who "were arrested when they had gone to the provinces to warn the people about advent of communism." Jamiat encouraged a combined uprising by the army and the population in Herat in March 1979.

57. See Es'haq, "Daud's Hostile Attitude," 6, for an account of this incident and a description of the arrests of Islamist leaders in 1974.

58. For a participant's account, see Es'haq, "Panjshir Uprising," 6–7.

59. Quotation from Abolfathi, "Reassessment of the Afghan Conflict," 3. As Roy puts it, in *Islam and Resistance*, 76, the Islamists "were still hooked on the myth of left-wing guerrilla warfare so central to the thinking of the sixties generation: Guevara's idea of revolutionary cells that infiltrated the peasantry with groups of intellectuals whom the peasants were supposed to follow." On the failure in Panjsher see Es'haq, "Panjshir Uprising," 7.

60. Edwards, "Shi'i Political Dissent," 220, gives Mir Ahmad Shah's family name as Rizwani.

61. Halliday, "Revolution in Afghanistan," 27.

62. Harrison, "Shah, Not Kremlin, Touched Off Afghan Coup." Evidence that has since emerged indicates that Khaibar was assassinated on the orders of Hafizullah Amin. One result of the imposed unity of Parcham and Khalq was that, although they had agreed to merge their underground networks in the armed forces, neither was in fact willing to do so. This may have led to conflict between Amin, the Khalqi Politburo member in charge of military recruitment, and Khaibar. In a speech to the Second Congress of the PDPA (where the party renamed itself the Watan, or Homeland Party), Najibullah alluded to this problem. In his review of the party's history, he mentioned some "negative phenomena" that persisted after the July 1977 Unity Conference, first of all "the absence of unification of military organizations" ("Report of the Central Committee"; I owe the possession of this document to Jochem Hippler and Steve Galster).

63. According to a story circulated by Hafizullah Amin and believed by most who have reported on the event, Amin was held under house arrest for several hours before being taken away. During this time he supposedly scribbled instructions to Khalqi officers in the military to carry out a coup according to plans they had rehearsed. Amin said that he sent the instructions out with his sons, who, being children, were allowed out of the house by the guards. Amin later claimed that there were 2,000 Khalqi officers (from an officer corps of 8,000) who were prepared to follow these instructions.

Soviet Afghanistan expert Yuri Gankovsky has characterized this story as "fairy tales for children" (personal communication, April 10, 1990). According to Gankovsky, Amin was arrested along with all the other civilian leaders of the PDPA. Daoud and his police did not know of the secret PDPA networks in the armed forces and did not arrest their leaders. Nonetheless, the Khalqi and Parchami military leaders were afraid that the civilians might crack under torture and reveal their names, in which case the military officers would certainly be executed. These leaders held a meeting attended by four people: Abdul Qadir, whose Afghan Revolutionary Organization was sympathetic to Parcham but separate from the PDPA; Muhammad Rafi, head of the Parchami organization; and Sayyid Muhammad Gulabzoy and Muhammad Aslam Watanjar, who led the Khalqi organization. According to Gankovsky, Abdul Qadir had 1,000 loyal followers, Rafi 500, and the Khalqis 600. Most but not all were officers; some were noncommissioned officers. The total roughly matches Amin's 2,000. Even if the numbers are exaggerated, they might give an accurate reading of the balance of forces among the factions. These figures and Gankovsky's account would explain why the first announcement of the coup made no mention of the PDPA but instead announced that power had been taken by a Revolutionary Council of military officers headed by Abdul Qadir.

Part II / The PDPA in Power

1. This estimate was given by Soviet Premier Nikolai Ryzhkov in 1989 (*Far Eastern Economic Review,* July 13, 1989, pp. 16-17); an identical estimate in the archives of the CPSU Central Committee Politburo was quoted in *Washington Post,* November 15, 1992.

2. Anthony et al., "Trade in Major Conventional Weapons," 199, 208.

Chapter 5 / Failure of Revolution from Above

1. Anwar, *Tragedy of Afghanistan,* 186-93. This same KGB special forces unit (Group Alpha) assaulted the Lithuanian government in January 1991 and refused to attack the parliament of the Russian Republic, led by President Boris Yeltsin, during the abortive Soviet coup in August 1991 (*New York Times,* August 26, 1991). In October 1993, at Boris Yeltsin's order, Group Alpha attacked the Russian parliament.

2. Bradsher, *Afghanistan and the Soviet Union,* 90, 96–98.

3. The Soviet share of imports did not continue to increase in the mid-1980s, mainly because of an increase of imports from Japan: These Japanese imports supplied not a burgeoning market in Afghanistan but smugglers' markets in Pakistan's tribal territories. See chapter 10 for a discussion of the importance of smuggling to the wartime political economy of Afghanistan.

Specifics of the assassination of Dubs have never been fully clarified. It appears that Dubs was kidnapped by members of a Maoist group demanding the release of their arrested leader. Dubs and his captors were killed when Afghan police, apparently aided by Soviet advisers, fired into the hotel room where he was held. On numbers of Soviet advisers see Bradsher, *Afghanistan and the Soviet Union,* 90; cable of May 12, 1979, from U.S. Secretary of State [Cyrus Vance], in Danishjuyan-i Musulman-i Piru[-yi] Khat-i Imam, *Asnad-i lanah-yi jasusi,* 29:97; undated document (probably June 1979) "Section One—Soviet Activities in Afghanistan," in ibid., 29:136. These cables estimated that of the 3,000 advisers 1,000 were military. The British government estimated there were 1,500 military advisers, and the West Germans estimated 3,000, according to a cable from U.S. Mission to NATO, August 23, 1979, in ibid., 30:43.)

4. Arnold, in "Ephemeral Elite," cites a "Western estimate" that the Parcham-Khalq membership ratio in 1980 was 15:85, increasing to 40:60, the ratio in the 1978 government, by 1984.

5. Bradsher, *Afghanistan and the Soviet Union,* 77–81; Ahady, "Afghanistan: State Breakdown," 177.

6. Before 1978 the Afghan police had been aided by West Germany. KhAD was organized and assisted by the KGB and, apparently, the East German Stasi. The GRU may have been more closely involved with AGSA and KAM.

7. Hyman, *Afghanistan under Soviet Domination,* 172–73.

8. On the Mujaddidis see Naby, "Afghan Resistance Movement," 66. The only imprisoned Islamist spared was Sayyaf. Sayyaf's mother, a cousin of Hafizullah Amin, had asked Amin to release her son. Amin refused, but he did move Sayyaf from Pul-i Charkhi prison, where the Islamists were held, to a more comfortable accommodation used by the old regime for high-status prisoners. When the order was given to kill the Islamists, those held in Pul-i Charkhi were taken to the execution ground. Sayyaf was not harmed—whether by oversight or by intent is unknown. I owe this account to Abdul Jabbar Sabet. On Kerala see Girardet, *Soviet War,* 107–10. On repression during the Khalqi period also see Barry, "Repression et guerre soviétiques"; Girardet, *Soviet War,* 107–34; Dupree, "Red Flag over the Hindu Kush," parts 5 and 6; Amnesty International, *Annual Report 1980,* 177–79; Rubin, "Human Rights in Afghanistan."

9. These decrees were published in English in the *Kabul Times.* The only publication of the complete texts in the West appears to be the Italian translation in Vercellin, *Afghanistan, 1973–1978,* 99–132. The most detailed and careful analysis of their contents and implementation is in Tabibi, "Afghanische Landreform," 150–95. Critical analyses that have shaped my thinking on these matters are Roy, "'Revolution' par le vide"; Roy, *Islam and Resistance,* 84–97; and Shahrani, "Marxist 'Revolution' and Islamic Resistance." For a defense of the reforms—and the would-be reformers, especially Hafizullah Amin—see Male, *Revolutionary Afghanistan.*

10. Tabibi, *Afghanische Landreform,* 167–68, and Halliday, "War and Revolution in Afghanistan," 24, both claim that loans from bazaar merchants were not included, although, according to Tabibi, "the bazaar generally represented the most important source of indebtedness." Halliday also claims that moneylenders were not included, which appears to be a mistake (Male, *Revolutionary Afghanistan,* 123n9).

11. Vercellin, *Afghanistan, 1973–1978,* 106–7; Anwar, *Tragedy of Afghanistan,* 142.

12. Amir Abdul Rahman Khan had allowed women to repudiate certain types of forced marriages, e.g., and had prohibited the payment of any brideprice greater than thirty rupees (Kakar,

Government and Society, 170). A 1950 law outlawed ostentatious displays at ceremonies such as weddings (Dupree, *Afghanistan,* 209). All such measures were ignored.

13. Tabibi, "Afghanische Landreform," 177–84, gives a chronology of government claims about the progress of the land reform. Regime claims and Kishtmand's comments are from Kabul Domestic Service (KDS), October 26, 1987, in *Federal Broadcast Information Service/Near East and South Asia (FBIS/NES),* October 28, 1987, 39; KDS, April 28, 1986, in *FBIS/South Asia (SA),* April 29, 1986, p. C4. Soviet estimates are from "Afghanistan: Preliminary Results— *Ogonyok* correspondent Artem Borovik Interviews Maj. Gen. Kim Tsagolov, Doctor of Philosophy and Chairman of the Department of Marxism-Leninism at the M. V. Frunze Military Academy," *Ogonyok,* July 23–30, 1988, pp. 25–27. Condensed text translated as "Will Kabul Fall after Soviet Withdrawal?" *The Current Digest of the Soviet Press* 40, no. 33 (September 14, 1988): 1–5.

During a visit to the area around the Ghaziabad State Farm in Momand Dara District, Nangrahar Province, in February 1989, I saw plots of land that had formerly been cultivated by what the mujahidin referred to as five-jarib communists—people who had supported the government because they received land. These plots had all been part of the Ghaziabad State Farm, a project developed in the 1960s on desert land brought under cultivation by a Soviet-funded water project. Even in this area, right by the main highway between Jalalabad and the border post at Torkham, there appeared to have been little actual penetration of the villages by land reform. Interviews in Peshawar with refugees who had fled the area in late 1988 confirmed this impression.

14. There was debate over whether the main cause of opposition was the content of the reforms or the behavior of the implementing cadres. In my view this argument is pointless, for the reforms aimed at asserting Khalqi control over rural society, and the behavior of the Khalqis made this aim clear.

In surveying the various explanations of state breakdown in 1978–79, I have referred to the following: Abolfathi, "Reassessment of the Afghan Conflict"; Amstutz, *First Five Years of Soviet Occupation;* Barfield, "Links on a Rusty Chain"; Barry, *Royaume de l'insolence;* Beattie, "Effects of the Saur Revolution"; Bradsher, *Afghanistan and the Soviet Union;* Centlivres and Centlivres-Demont, *Et si on parlait de l'Afghanistan?;* Dupree, "Marxist Regimes"; Gankovsky et al., *History of Afghanistan;* Gerber, *Islam, Guerrilla War and Revolution;* Halliday, "War and Revolution in Afghanistan"; Hyman, *Afghanistan under Soviet Domination;* Katz, "Responses to Central Authority in Nuristan"; Keiser, "Rebellion in Darra-i Nur"; Metge, *URSS en Afghanistan;* "Report of the Central Committee"; Roy, *Islam and Resistance;* Shahrani, "Marxist 'Revolution' and Islamic Resistance"; Shahrani, "Responses to the Saur Revolution"; and Zolberg, Suhrke, and Aguayo, *Escape from Violence.*

15. Ølesen, "The Musallis."

16. On views of khans see Shahrani, "Kirghiz Khans." The major exceptions to the rejection of land reform were tribal areas in which the Khalqis in effect allocated land from a senior to a junior clan. In these cases, the reform actually strengthened the qawm, (namely, the junior clan), which generally became a government militia. Taking advantage of the reform to seize land from a rival clan accorded with the tribal code (Pashtunwali) although it contradicted the Islamic respect for private property (Roy, *Islam and Resistance,* 92).

17. Migdal, *Strong Societies and Weak States,* 206–37; Gankovsky et al., *History of Afghanistan,* 315; "Report of the Central Committee," unpaginated.

18. The former figure is a summary of the discussion in Arnold, *Afghanistan's Two-Party Communism,* 115–19; the latter is from *World Marxist Review* (January 1988), p. 4, cited in Arnold, "Ephemeral Elite." Hafizullah Amin reportedly told the American chargé d'affaires J. Bruce Amstutz in September 1979 that the regime was "desperately short of qualified people." (Cable from

U.S. Embassy Kabul, September 27, 1979, in Danishjuyan-i Musulman-i Piru[-yi] Khat-i Imam, *Asnad-i lanah-yi jasusi,* 30:91).

19. Bradsher (*Afghanistan and the Soviet Union,* 91), from the coffee-drinking United States, refers to the PDPA members as teashop revolutionaries; Abolfathi, ("Reassessment of the Afghan Conflict," 2-31), born in tea-drinking Iran, prefers the term coffeehouse revolutionaries, perhaps because he adopts a comparative perspective.

20. Recall Stepan's observation in *State and Society,* 302, that state autonomy can be helpful in the installation phase of a regime determined to carry out social transformation from above, but can become a liability during the consolidation phase.

21. The first argument is associated with Tilly, *From Mobilization to Revolution,* and the latter with Skocpol, *States and Social Revolutions.* Shahrani made a similar point in a paper written in 1980, "Marxist 'Revolution' and Islamic Resistance," when he noted that peasant mobilization must be explained by the relationship of the peasantry to the "field of power," in particular to urban-based, ideological leadership.

22. See, e.g., Callaghy's description of the army in Zaire (*State-Society Struggle,* 44).

23. Trimberger, in *Revolution from Above,* 42, emphasizes that political cohesion among "military bureaucrats" is an essential condition for revolution from above. She also argues (43) that in "relatively decentralized states . . . dissident military bureaucrats must have a provincial base of power separate from the central government to stage a revolution from above." Contrary to the common assumption that legitimacy is in some sense a democratic notion, Weber emphasizes that its principal function is to enable the ruler to maintain effective control over "the personal executive staff and the implements of administration" (Max Weber, "Politics as a Vocation," in *From Max Weber,* 80).

Chapter 6 / Under Soviet Occupation

1. For U.S. diplomatic views see J. Bruce Amstutz, "Afghanistan's Khalqi Regime at 18 Months: Still in Power, but Facing Long-Term Instability," cable, Department of State, November 20, 1979, cited in National Security Archive, *Making of U.S. Policy,* 1:91. Effect of losing control of roads from interview with a former official of the Interior Ministry who was in charge of municipal governments in 1981, Washington, D.C., October 1986.

2. A former Soviet adviser to the Afghan Ministry of Defense reported that Gen. Muhammad Hakim, a Parchami who was tortured at the time, attributed the scar on his forehead to "intraparty debate" (interview, Washington, D.C., November 11, 1989). The Khalqis who fled were Sayyid Muhammad Gulabzoy, Muhammad Aslam Watanjar, Shair Jan Mazduryar, and Asadullah Sarwari.

3. For the postinvasion Soviet view of human rights under the Khalq, as well as the official depiction of the "complete amnesty for political prisoners" declared on December 28, 1979, see *Truth about Afghanistan,* 176 ff. See also Rubin, "Human Rights in Afghanistan," 353–54.

4. See the depiction of this process in Kundera, *Unbearable Lightness of Being.*

5. Interview with a former Soviet adviser, Washington, D.C., November 11, 1989. According to this source, "Sometimes Babrak would insist on something, but when his Soviet advisers said no, he would prefer to drink himself to death."

6. On advisers see Roy, "Politique de pacification." Several Afghan defectors from the Ministry of Justice mentioned Rajabov. According to the Soviet source cited above, "For gold bars he freed many mujahidin commanders."

7. A confirming anecdote: One of my undergraduate students at Yale, a Soviet immigrant to the United States, led a student tourist group to the Soviet Union in the summer of 1988. At the desk of her hotel on the outskirts of Moscow, a man asked for a room but was told that the hotel

was full. He then pulled out some documents and told the woman behind the desk in fluent but accented Russian that he was a member of the Bulgarian KGB and a veteran of Afghanistan. The desk clerk advised him to take his complaint to the KGB.

8. Interview, Washington, D.C., November 11, 1989.

9. Anwar, *Tragedy of Afghanistan*, 196–97, 203, 208–14.

10. Anwar, *Tragedy of Afghanistan*, 213–24. The three Khalqi Politburo members appointed in 1980 were Dastagir Panjsheri, Salih Muhammad Ziari, and Asadullah Sarwari. Sarwari—who as the head of AGSA under Taraki had supervised and possibly participated in the torture of prominent Parchamis (including Sultan Ali Kishtmand)—was removed from the Politburo and exiled as ambassador to Mongolia in 1981. All three original appointees later supported the March 1990 coup by Defense Minister Gen. Shahnawaz Tanai. Panjsheri and Ziari were then jailed; Sarwari, who had meanwhile become ambassador to Yemen, tried to return to Afghanistan via India, where he was arrested for overstaying a visa.

11. Arnold, "Ephemeral Elite," 51; Anwar, *Tragedy of Afghanistan*, 214.

12. National Security Archive, *Making of U.S. Policy*, 1:151.

13. Arnold, "Ephemeral Elite," 57–58.

14. On taxes see Bakhtar (Afghan government news agency), April 11, 1983, in *Federal Broadcast Information Service/South Asia (FBIS/SA)*, April 12, 1983, pp. C1–4. According to *Afghanistan Forum* 11 (1983), no. 4, *Kabul New Times* of the same date estimated agricultural taxes in 1981–82 as Af 13 million. For one example of tax cancellation see Kabul Domestic Service (KDS), March 20, 1986, in *FBIS/SA*, March 21, 1986, p. C1. The same source deals with public enterprise, as does Bakhtar, March 16, 1988, cited in *Afghanistan Forum* 16 (1988), no. 3, p. 35. At times the government stated that 50 percent of state domestic revenues came from government enterprises (Bakhtar, January 1, 1986, in *Afghanistan Forum* 16 [1986], no. 2, p. 3). These revenues derived almost entirely from export of natural gas to the Soviet Union.

15. By 1988, the share of Afghanistan's foreign aid that came from CMEA countries was 97 percent, 81 percent from the USSR alone. (Bakhtar March 16, 1988, in *Afghanistan Forum* 16 [1988], no. 3, p. 35.)

16. Afghanistan exported about 2.2 billion cubic meters of gas per year to the USSR in 1978–79, 1979–80, and 1980–81, for which it received $34.3 million, $97.6 million, and $253.8 million. (*Statistical Information of Afghanistan 1358*, 66; *Statistical Information of Afghanistan 1359*, 62.) In 1988, a former minister of mines stated that Afghanistan sold 2 billion cubic meters of gas per year to the Soviet Union, so the quantity remained unchanged until then. (*Washington Post*, April 24, 1988.) The wells were capped after the Soviet withdrawal. For other statements see Bakhtar, January 25, 1984, in *Afghanistan Forum* 12 (1984), no. 2, p. 37; KDS, February 26, 1985, in *FBIS/SA*, February 27, 1985, p. C2.

17. There were some reports of Soviet KGB personnel participating directly in such KhAD activities as interrogation—and hence torture—of prisoners. See Laber and Rubin, *"Nation Is Dying,"* 92–94; Amnesty International, *Torture of Political Prisoners*, 17–19. On army advisers see Roy, "Politique de pacification."

18. This was how he described his job on Budapest Domestic Service, February 20, 1980, in *FBIS, Middle East and North Africa: South Asia (MENA:SA)*, February 22, 1980, pp. S1–2.

19. At the same time Abdul Qadir was promoted out of the way by being renamed vice chairman of the Revolutionary Council (KDS, December 3, 1984, in *FBIS/SA*, December 4, 1984, p. C3). He was later appointed ambassador to Poland and was said by a Soviet source in 1988 to be living in Bulgaria.

20. On supplies and the officer ratio see the interview with a supply officer who had defected, Brig.-Gen. Muhammad Nawaz (Agence France Press [AFP], January 11, 1983, in *FBIS/SA*, January 12, 1983, pp. C1–2). On training see the interview with First Deputy Minister of Defense

Muhammad Nabi Azimi with Budapest Domestic Service, February 18, 1985, in *FBIS/SA*, February 22, 1985, pp. C1–2, in which he mentions that he has just returned from training in the USSR.

21. In 1987 Najibullah reportedly said that 92 percent of the conscripts were from Kabul. (Arnold, "Ephemeral Elite," 58.)

22. KDS, October 24, 1980, in *FBIS/SA*, October 28, 1980, pp. C2–4; AFP, January 14, 1981, in *FBIS/SA*, January 15, 1981, p. C3; KDS, January 25, 1981, in *FBIS/SA*, January 26, 1981, pp. C1–3; KDS, January 30, 1981, in *FBIS/SA*, February 2, 1981, pp. C2–4; KDS, February 7, 1981, in *FBIS/SA*, February 9, 1981, pp. C2–3; *Anis* (Kabul), January 22, 23, 24, and 25, 1981, in *FBIS/SA*, February 18, 1981, pp. C5–9; KDS, April 10, 1981, in *FBIS/SA*, April 13, 1981, pp. C3–4; KDS, September 7, 1981, in *FBIS/SA*, September 8, 1981, pp. C1–3; AFP, January 19, 1982, in *FBIS/SA*, January 21, 1982, p. C1; KDS, April 5, 1982, in *FBIS/SA*, April 6, 1982, p. C2; KDS, August 2, 1982, in *FBIS/SA*, August 3, 1982, pp. C2–4; AFP, August 3, 1982, in *FBIS/SA*, August 4, 1982, pp. C4–5; KDS, September 28, 1982, in *FBIS/SA*, October 1, 1982, p. C1; AFP, November 10, 1982, in *FBIS/SA*, November 12, 1982, p. C3; AFP, February 1, 1983, in *FBIS/SA*, February 2, 1983, pp. C2–3; AFP, March 25, 1983, in *FBIS/SA*, March 29, 1983, p. C2; AFP, May 11, 1983, in *FBIS/SA*, May 12, 1983, pp. C1–2; KDS, August 3, 1983, in *FBIS/SA*, August 5, 1983, pp. C1–2; KDS, January 1, 1984, in *FBIS/SA*, January 4, 1984, p. C2; KDS, March 8, 1984, in *FBIS/SA*, March 9, 1984, p. C1; KDS, October 25, 1984, in *FBIS/SA*, October 26, 1984, p. C2; KDS, January 5, 1985, in *FBIS/SA*, January 7, 1985, p. C2.

23. KDS, January 11, 1980, in *FBIS/MENA:SA*, January 14, 1980, p. S2; Fullerton, *Soviet Occupation*, 133.

24. Amnesty International, *Reports of Torture*.

25. Johnson et al., "Southern Provinces," 72. These were similar to numbers given by various KhAD officials themselves, including both defectors and officers interviewed by journalists. A KhAD defector in late 1982 said that the agency had 25,000 employees (AFP, December 17, 1982, in *FBIS/SA*, December 17, 1982, p. C2). Both KhAD and its enemies might have had an interest in exaggerating its strength.

26. Democratic Republic of Afghanistan (DRA), *Statistical Year Book (SYB) 1980–1981*, 40; DRA, *SYB 1981–1982*, 63. These publications do not indicate at what point in the year the number of government employees was counted.

27. Amnesty International, *Unfair Trials;* Laber and Rubin, *"Nation Is Dying,"* 99–103. Karmal's statements in KDS, November 1, 1984, in *FBIS/SA*, November 7, 1984, p. C1. On regular courts see the interview with the chief justice of the Civil Court, Sayed Gharib Nawaz, who defected (Karachi Domestic Service [KDS], May 15, 1984, in *FBIS/SA*, May 15, 1984, p. C1); Ashrati, "Soviet Influence on the Afghan Judiciary." On socialist legality see Babrak Karmal's long speech to the September 21, 1984, session of the Revolutionary Council (KDS, September 2, 1984, in *FBIS/SA*, October 4, 1984, pp. C1–8).

28. The assassination of Faiz Muhammad, a violation of the Pashtunwali code of hospitality, set off a feud between the Jadrans and their neighbors and rivals, the Wazirs, to whom Faiz Muhammad had belonged. On renaming the ministry see KDS, May 28, 1981, in *FBIS/SA*, May 29, 1981, p. C1. As noted in Roy, "Modèles anthropologiques," the more usual term for "nationality" is *milliyat*, as in the ministry's publication *Milliyatha-yi baradar (Fraternal Nationalities)*. As noted in Chapter 2, the referent of qawm is fluid and depends on the context. On splitting the ministry see Johnson et al., "Southern Provinces," 76.

29. Roy, "Modèles anthropologiques."

30. Laber and Rubin, *"Nation Is Dying,"* 121–22; KDS, March 28, 1985, in *FBIS/SA*, April 1, 1985, p. C1; Johnson et al., "Southern Provinces," 73–74.

31. Polska Agencja Prasowa (PAP) English Service (Warsaw), January 3, 1980, in *FBIS/*

MENA:SA, January 4, 1980, pp. S1–3. (This document contains an English translation of Karmal's broadcast of December 29, 1979.)

32. Bradsher, *Afghanistan and the Soviet Union,* 234–37; Bakhtar, June 18, 1981, in *FBIS/SA,* June 19, 1981, pp. C16–19; AFP, January 18, 1983, in *FBIS/SA,* January 19, 1983, pp. C1–3; Bakhtar, March 24, 1983, in *FBIS/SA,* March 24, 1983, p. C1; KDS, May 6, 1985, in *FBIS/SA,* May 7, 1985, p. C1.

33. Laber and Rubin, *"Nation Is Dying,"* 112–14.

34. KDS, September 10, 1986, in *FBIS/SA,* September 11, 1986, p. C1; KDS, June 21, 1987, in *FBIS/SA,* June 24, 1987, p. P1.

35. Amnesty International, *Unfair Trials,* 5–6. The figure for executions omits those killed without trials.

36. Giddens, *Nation-State and Violence,* 172–80; U.N. Commission on Human Rights, "Human Rights in Afghanistan," 19–20; Laber and Rubin, *"Nation Is Dying,"* 81–94; Dadfar, "Victims of Torture."

37. Nyrop and Seekins, *Country Study,* 152–53; Kabul English South Asian Service, April 20, 1982, in *FBIS/SA,* April 26, 1982, p. C1; ADN International Service (East Berlin), January 22, 1980, in *FBIS/MENA:SA,* January 23, 1980, pp. S11–12; KDS, February 9, 1980, in *FBIS/MENA:SA,* February 11, 1980, p. S2; Kabul English South Asian Service, February 17, 1980, in *FBIS/MENA:SA,* February 19, 1980, pp. S3–4; KDS, November 16, 1980, in *FBIS/SA,* November 21, 1980, p. C2; KDS, January 20, 1981, in *FBIS/SA,* January 30, 1981, p. C1; KDS, April 26, 1982, in *FBIS/SA,* April 27, 1982, p. C3; Bakhtar, May 25, 1983, in *FBIS/SA,* May 27, 1983, pp. C2–3; KDS, June 2, 1983, in *FBIS/SA,* June 3, 1983, p. C1; KDS, May 21, 1984, in *FBIS/SA,* May 23, 1984, p. C3; Bakhtar, July 10, 1984, in *FBIS/SA,* July 12, 1984, p. C1; Bakhtar, September 22, 1984, in September 27, 1984, p. C3; KDS, May 14, 1985, in *FBIS/SA,* May 15, 1985, p. C1; KDS, January 14, 1980, in *FBIS/MENA:SA,* January 15, 1980, p. S1; KDS, February 1, 1982, in *FBIS/SA,* February 2, 1982, p. C1; Shroder, "Afghanistan Resources," 101; Shroder and Assifi, "Afghan Mineral Resources."

38. On early supplies of consumer goods see KDS, February 13, 1980, in *FBIS/MENA:SA,* February 14, 1980, p. S3. This announcement valued one hundred thousand tons of wheat at Af 1.3 billion, or Af 13 per kilogram. It was to be sold at Af 70 per sair (about seven kilos), or Af 8.75 per kilo. On wheat see also KDS, December 22, 1982, in *FBIS/SA,* December 27, 1982, p. C2.

The estimated total produced in Afghan year 1356 (spanning 1977–78) was 2.7 million tons (DRA, *Statistical Information of Afghanistan [1975–1978]* 46). On fuel see Bakhtar, June 7, 1984, in *FBIS/SA,* June 8, 1984, p. C1.

39. A woman living in Kabul who left the country temporarily to receive medical treatment in 1986 stated that those who joined mass organizations such as the Committee for the Defense of the Revolution in her neighborhood received special food coupons valid in government stores. In 1988 the government said that it had established stores "where the personnel of the armed forces and their families can buy foodstuffs and industrial products at low price." (*Kabul New Times,* March 16, 1988, in *Afghanistan Forum* 16 (1988), no. 3, p. 35.)

40. Amin, "Sovietization of Afghanistan," 316. Several refugees whom I interviewed told of being summoned to the offices of the headmaster or other official and being pressured to inform on other students. See Laber and Rubin, *"Nation Is Dying,"* 113–14.

41. On curriculum see Amin, "Sovietization of Afghanistan," 319–21. On repression of faculty see Elmi, "Impact of Sovietization," 80–81, 96–125. On foreign faculty see *Kabul New Times,* May 22, 1983.

42. Amin, "Sovietization of Afghanistan," 321.

43. Trottier, "Soviet Influence on Afghan Youth," 47. The numerous announcements of train-

ing programs indicate that this was a fair estimate, not just Cold War propaganda. See, e.g., KDS, April 16, 1984, in *FBIS/SA*, April 17, 1984, p. C1, and Bakhtar, March 25, 1985, in *FBIS/SA*, March 26, 1985, p. C2, which describe programs under which between 1,500 and 1,700 Afghan students were to be sent to the USSR for training and another program under which 2,000 students were trained for three years in Afghanistan in new schools and training courses set up by Soviet advisers.

44. Laber and Rubin, *"Nation Is Dying,"* 126-37; Amin, "Sovietization of Afghanistan," 317-18, 323-24.

45. KDS, November 5, 1984, in *FBIS/SA*, November 6, 1984, p. C1.

46. Interview in Peshawar, August 1985. While on a visit to Kabul in 1985 Jan Goodwin interviewed Marzia Jahish, secretary of the Social Commission, who claimed that 53,000 children had been sent abroad for training, 47,000 to the USSR, and 6,000 to Bulgaria, East Germany, and Cuba; 10,000 more were to be sent in the next twelve months. These figures seem exaggerated but may indicate the scope of the regime's ambitions (Goodwin, *Caught in the Crossfire*, 125-31).

47. Goodwin (*Caught in the Crossfire*, 127) was introduced in Kabul to a girl who had been sent to the USSR after being orphaned by bombing in Panjsher. For other accounts by refugees see Laber and Rubin, *"Nation Is Dying,"* 129-32.

48. Allan and Stahel, "Tribal Guerrilla Warfare."

49. "Supplement No. 1 to DRA Revolutionary Council Decree No. 8," issued as a decree of the Presidium of the DRA Revolutionary Council on August 9, 1981, KDS, August 15, 1981, in *FBIS/SA*, August 20, 1981, pp. C1-2.

50. Land belonging to mosques, madrasas, and shrines was also exempted.

51. Interview with Rudy Seynaeve, Peshawar, August 1985; Laber and Rubin, *"Nation Is Dying,"* 17-22.

52. Sliwinski, "Decimation of Afghanistan."

53. Roy, *Islam and Resistance*, 196.

54. For one example among many, see the speech by Prime Minister Kishtmand in KDS, May 21, 1983, in *FBIS/SA*, May 23, 1983, pp. C2-3.

55. Kabul International Arabic Service, February 2, 1980, in *FBIS/MENA:SA*, February 4, 1980, p. S5. In 1983 the procurement price of cotton was again raised by 60 percent and that of sugar beets by 40 percent. (*Kabul New Times*, December 28, 1983, cited in Gupta, *Afghanistan Politics, Economics, and Society*, 124.)

56. Interview with mujahid from Baghlan Province, Peshawar, September 1984; interview with refugee in the United States, January 1986.

57. Bakhtar, March 21 1984, in *Afghanistan Forum* 12 (1984), no. 3, p. 33; Bakhtar, March 5, 1985, in *FBIS/SA*, March 5, 1985, p. C2; Bakhtar, March 21, 1986, in *Afghanistan Forum* 14 (1986), no. 3, p. 38. Karmal quotation from KDS, January 12, 1984, in *FBIS/SA*, January 13, 1984, p. C1. On farm power generally see Swedish Committee for Afghanistan, *Agricultural Survey of Afghanistan, Second Report*, 1:13-40.

58. On local government see KDS, January 17, 1984, in *FBIS/SA*, January 18, 1984, p. C1; Bakhtar, February 12, 1984, in *FBIS/SA*, February 14, 1984, p. C2; KDS, June 24, 1984, in *FBIS/SA*, June 27, 1984, pp. C2-3. On the elections see Arnold, "Ephemeral Elite."

Chapter 7 / Soviet Withdrawal, Political Retreat

1. *Washington Post*, April 17, 1988; minutes of Politburo meeting quoted in *Washington Post*, November 16, 1992.

2. After Karmal's resignation from the presidency, Haji Muhammad Chamkani, a nonparty

tribal leader who had been close to Daoud, served as figurehead acting president for a few months, after which Najibullah took the post.

3. *National Reconciliation,* 6; Kabul Domestic Service (KDS), July 24, 1990, in *Federal Broadcast Information Service/Near East and South Asia (FBIS/NES),* July 26, 1990, p. 39.

4. Interview with Yuri Gankovsky, Villanova, Pa., October 30, 1992.

5. Tilly, *Coercion, Capital, and European States,* 29, 53.

6. Republic of Afghanistan (R.A.), "Afghanistan, 1990," 5, gives the average amount supplied. The mayor of Kabul estimated in January 1989 that the city consumed 630 tons of flour per day, or about 230,000 tons per year (KDS, January 27, 1989, in BBC, *Summary of World Broadcasts, Far East (SWB/FE),* January 28, 1989, p. C1). Soviet Politburo documents from 1990 give a slightly lower figure: 15,000 tons per month, or 180,000 tons per year (*Washington Post,* November 16, 1992).

7. Quotations from *New York Times,* June 24, 1989; *Washington Post,* November 16, 1992, citing Politburo documents. See also *Washington Post,* July 16, 1989. *New York Times,* June 5, 1990, gave an estimate of $4 billion in military and $1 billion in other aid; *The Independent,* January 24, 1991, reported that Najibullah had been assured of 400 million rubles in 1991 (the ruble was then exchanged for about $1.60), including 280 million in grants, up from 120 million in 1990. The latter figures may exclude weapons.

8. According to a former ambassador to Washington, Anatoly Dobrynin, who was secretary for international relations of the CPSU Central Committee during national reconciliation, "As far as national reconciliation is concerned, not a single member of the Afghan politburo supports Najibullah" (Minutes of CPSU Politburo meeting of November 13, 1986, quoted in *Washington Post,* November 16, 1986). Najibullah later complained that the Khalqis who supported the March 1990 coup "said about me: He is abandoning the party. He is going to the Ikhwanis [Muslim Brotherhood, i.e., the Islamists]. He is asking Zaher Shah to come back—the one against whom we brought revolution and so many were killed. He sold the revolution, he sold our ideology" (KDS, March 11, 1990, *FBIS/NES,* March 13, 1990, p. 47). My impression, for which there is inadequate evidence at present, is that Parchamis opposed any coalition with "extremists" like Hikmatyar (see statement by Hashmatullah Kaihani, Tiskovna Agencja Naroda Jugoslavije [TANJUG], June 23, 1988, in *FBIS/NES,* June 24, 1988, p. 44), whereas the Khalqis opposed ties to the old royalist elites in Kabul. This difference would explain why Tanai and his allies, said to be hardline opponents of national reconciliation, formed an alliance with Hikmatyar. Tanai claimed that the conflict arose because his group wanted Najibullah to resign for the sake of peace, which would have placed the Khalqis in a more advantageous position (*Pakistan Times* [Islamabad], in *FBIS/NES,* March 12, 1990, p. 43).

9. Interview with diplomat and PDPA member, Washington, D.C., March 1990.

10. At the July 1986 meeting Najibullah's partner in tribal policy, Sulaiman Laiq, the minister of nationalities and tribes, replaced him on the Politburo. Karmal "resigned" from both the Central Committee and the Politburo on November 20, 1986. Ghulam Faruq Yaaqubi, Najibullah's former deputy at KhAD and then minister of state security, took Karmal's place on the Politburo. When Najibullah announced the policy of national reconciliation, on December 31, 1986, he appointed two more Parchamis, Babrak's cousin and rival Abdul Wakil and the party secretary of Kabul city, Abdul Zuhur Razmjo. At a Central Committee Plenum on October 17, 1987, Anahita Ratibzad and Karmal's brother Mahmud Baryalai were dismissed from both the Central Committee and the Politburo, where Baryalai was an alternate member. Three new members were elected: Najmuddin Kawiani and Haidar Masud, both Parchamis and Kabuli Tajiks, and Niyaz Muhammad Momand, a Khalqi apparatchik and a Pashtun from the tribal areas of Pakistan. A pro-Karmalite Politburo member, Nur Ahmad Nur, was sent as a diplomatic exile to Warsaw as ambassador in March 1988, and in July 1989 he was assigned to the United Nations. In October

1989 two new full Politburo members were elected: Farid Mazdak, a Parchami Tajik and leader of the DYOA, and Mir Sahib Karwal, another Khalqi apparatchik.

Of the three Khalqis appointed in 1980, Asadullah Sarwari had been replaced by Watanjar in 1981 and Dashtagir Panjsheri dismissed in November 1985, when Najibullah was made a secretary of the Central Committee. Muhammad Salih Ziari and Muhammad Aslam Watanjar remained, and they were joined by Gulabzoy in June 1987 and Niyaz Muhammad Momand in October 1987. As noted, after Gulabzoy was sent to Moscow, Karwal replaced him.

11. Karmal himself was not arrested because he had already been exiled to Moscow. Information on the arrests from KDS, October 19, 1988, in *FBIS/NES*, October 20, 1988, p. 50; *New York Times*, October 19, pp. 26, 29, 31, 1988; *Guardian*, October 20, 1988. According to a former Soviet adviser to the Afghanistan Ministry of Defense, (interview, Washington, D.C., November 1989), Gulabzoy had told Eduard Shevardnadze that he would never accept Najibullah's leadership. On the hardliners' petition see AFP, January 10, 1989, in *FBIS/NES*, January 11, 1989, p. 52.

12. According to a defecting brigadier general, "Armed clash between Afghan army and Guard-i Khas [Special Guard] can take place any time" (IRNA [Islamic Republic News Agency, Tehran], January 9, 1990, in *FBIS/NES*, January 10, 1990, p. 39). The Special Guard was a largely Kabuli unit attached to WAD, as KhAD was then called.

Amin's foreign minister, Shah Wali, had been released in February 1989 and made a minister-counsellor in the hardline government appointed at that time. The public announcement of the October Central Committee changes (Bakhtar, October 25, 1989, in *FBIS/NES*, October 26, 1989, pp. 58–59) did not identify the nineteen full and one alternate members elected, for the reappointment of the much reviled Amin faction would have been a propaganda victory for the resistance. Najibullah admitted in an interview with a Turkish journalist that the new members were in fact Amin's collaborators (Bakhtar, December 1, 1989, in *FBIS/NES*, December 7, 1989, p. 59).

13. *Financial Times*, August 7, 1989; *The Independent*, August 12, 1989; AFP, December 30, 1989, in *FBIS/NES*, January 2, 1990, pp. 47–48; IRNA (Tehran), January 9, 1990, in *FBIS/NES*, January 10, 1990, p. 39; Attaul Haq and Tookhi, "Interview with an Ex-Minister."

14. Among Khalqi Politburo members, Ziari and Panjsheri were arrested in Kabul. Gulabzoy was apparently put under house arrest in Moscow and replaced as ambassador, and Asadullah Sarwari made his way from his diplomatic post in South Yemen to India, from where he attempted to return to Kabul. He was arrested by the Indian authorities in July for overstaying his visa but released in November 1991. Niyaz Muhammad Momand, Mir Sahib Karwal, and Gen. Nazar Muhammad supported the coup and accompanied Tanai to Pakistan. The coup was also supported by the main Khalqi leaders of the air force, including Nazar Muhammad's successor as commander, Abdul Qadir Aqa, and the political director, Dost Muhammad. For the list of "traitors" expelled from the Politburo and Central Committee, see KDS, March 8, 1990, in *FBIS/NES*, March 9, 1990, p. 37; KDS, March 18, 1990, in *FBIS/NES*, March 19, 1990, p. 39. For Najibullah's speech in Paktia see KDS, March 12, 1990, in *FBIS/NES*, March 13, 1990, pp. 41–47.

15. Hamid Rogh, editor of the party newspaper *Payam*, claimed in May 1990 that the "elitist section" of the party that had benefited from the war was resisting reform (AFP, May 8, 1990, in *FBIS/NES*, May 9, 1991, p. 23). For the list of appointees see KDS, June 28, 1990, in *FBIS/NES*, July 2, 1990, p. 35. Of the nine Parchamis on the executive board (formerly the Politburo), two were old-line Karmal supporters: Nur Ahmad Nur and Mahmud Baryalai. Karmal himself was elected to the Central Council.

16. Interview with a former member of the Indian Embassy in Kabul, New York, October 1992.

17. *AfghaNews* 7, no. 15 (August 1, 1991): 3; *Washington Post*, October 20, 1991.

18. Although the new Revolutionary Council was appointed in January 1986, while Karmal

was still general secretary, it belonged to the Gorbachev-Najibullah period, both because it included many nonparty members and because of the makeup of the party members it included. Not one close ally of Karmal was on the council, and only one Khalqi, the apparatchik Mir Sahib Karwal. Among the party members were four factory workers (identifiable by the surname Kargar, or worker) and two militia leaders from Kabul province. PDPA sources claim that these party members had no ideological commitment or factional loyalty.

19. KDS, April 21, 1998, in *FBIS/NES*, April 22, 1988, p. 81. The rest of the seats went to four other parties: SAZA, SZA, the Peasants Justice Party, and the Islamic Party of the People of Afghanistan, representing progovernment mullahs and ulama.

20. Names of government officials came from official announcements. Data on these individuals came from the same sources as data on PDPA elites (see Appendix A).

21. Reuters, Kabul, June 12, 1990. Following the new power-sharing formula, three of twelve party members were Khalqis, including the ministers of defense and interior.

22. Kabul Radio Afghanistan Network (KRAN), August 17, 1991, in *FBIS/NES*, August 20, 1991, p. 40.

23. Democratic Republic of Afghanistan, *Statistical Information of Afghanistan, 1975–1978*, 139. According to Muhammad Hakim, mayor of Kabul, the population of the city grew to 1.3 million in 1986 and surpassed 2 million in 1989 (*Daily Telegraph*, May 17, 1989, in *FBIS/NES*, May 18, 1989, p. 48).

24. KDS, December 21, 1986, in *FBIS/South Asia* (*SA*), December 22, 1986, p. C1.

25. There were widespread rumors of the offer to Massoud at the time. A Soviet Afghanistan specialist who was at that time working in Kabul confirmed that the offer had been extended and claimed to have seen Massoud's reply, which he summarized: "This train has already left the station" (not an Afghan expression). The Soviets may have pressured Najibullah into making the offer. Another Soviet Afghanistan specialist claimed that despite his rhetoric, Najibullah actually wanted to rule as a dictator without any opposition and had sabotaged repeated Soviet attempts to work out arrangements with resistance leaders, including Massoud.

26. AFP, August 2, 1990, in *FBIS/NES*, August 2, 1990, p. 35; interview with Muhammad Nabi Azimi, Tashkent, May 1993.

27. KDS, November 11, 1986, in *FBIS/SA*, November 19 1986, p. C2; KDS, April 2, 1988, in *FBIS/NES*, April 5, 1988, p. 40. For similar exhortations see KDS, February 13, 1989, in *FBIS/NES*, February 14, 1989, p. 39.

28. KDS, February 25, 1987, in BBC, *SWB/FE*, February 26, 1987, pp. C1–2; quotation from Danas (Zagreb), December 20, 1988, in *FBIS/NES*, January 4, 1989, p. 43.

29. Amnesty International, "Unfair Trials," 6; quotation from KDS, June 1, 1990, in *SWB/FE*, June 4, 1990, p. C1; KDS, May 29, 1986, in *FBIS/SA*, May 30, 1986, p. C3; KDS, January 31, 1990, in *FBIS/NES*, February 1, 1990, p. 51.

30. KDS, September 24, 1987, in *FBIS/NES*, September 29, 1987, pp. 33–35; KDS, February 24, 1988, in *FBIS/NES*, February 25, 1988, p. 44.

31. KDS, November 12, 1988, in *FBIS/NES*, November 14, 1988, p. 47; AFP, August 11, 1989, in *FBIS/NES*, August 14, 1989, p. 36; AFP, September 7, 1989, in *FBIS/NES*, September 8, 1989, pp. 40–41.

32. *Xinhua*, April 29, 1990; AFP, January 10, 1989, in *FBIS/NES*, January 11, 1989, p. 52; *Pakistan Times* (Islamabad), March 21, 1990, in *FBIS/NES*, March 23, 1990, p. 41.

33. Quotation on Jalalabad from TANJUG, June 23, 1988, in *FBIS/NES*, June 24, 1988, p. 44. Quotation on other party military units from KDS, February 6, 1989, in *FBIS/NES*, February 7, 1989, p. 46. See also KDS, February 13, 1989, in *FBIS/NES*, February 14, 1989, p. 39; and AFP, February 21, 1989, in *FBIS/NES*, February 22, 1989, pp. 50–51. For interviews with women militia members, see *The Times* (London), February 28, 1989. The actual strength of the women's

militias seems questionable. The leader interviewed in the *Times* article appears from her name to have been the wife of a high official of WAD (Razminda), a possibility that escaped her interviewer.

34. On operatifi see Roy, "Politique de pacification," 22. In Peshawar in August 1985, I interviewed a recent defector who stated that he had worked in the section of the Ministry of the Interior responsible for command and control of the operatifi. Under Najibullah, however, descriptions of meetings between officials and the militias do not mention the Ministry of the Interior.

35. For an anthropologist's description of Andarab, see Uberoi, "Men, Women, and Property."

36. Elphinstone observed, in *Kingdom of Caubul,* 1:299, "The tribes most addicted to rapine in the West, are the Atchukzye branch of the Dooraunees, and those of the Noorzyes." He also claimed that the Achakzais were utterly impious as Muslims. Information on Ismat Muslim from Katz, "Biographic Database"; Danishjuyan-i Musulman-i Piru[-yi] Khat-i Imam, *Asnad-i lanah-yi jasusi,* 30:132; and interview with Rahim Wardak, chief of military committee, National Islamic Front of Afghanistan, Peshawar, November 22, 1986.

37. James M. Ealum (U.S. Embassy, Kabul), "Afghanistan Situation Report July 13–19, 1987," document no. 2018, in National Security Archive, *Making of U.S. Policy;* interview with Indian diplomat, New York, October 1992; interview with Pakistani diplomat at the United Nations, July 1988. For a slightly different account, see Johnson et al., "Southern Provinces," 158–59.

38. *The Independent,* August 19, 1989 (report by Ahmed Rashid); AFP, May 30, 1988, in *FBIS/NES,* May 31, 1988, p. 51.

39. Canfield, *Faction and Conversion.*

40. Olivier Roy, personal communication, December 1988, based on his trip to the area; *Philadelphia Inquirer,* September 3, 1989; quotation from *Far Eastern Economic Review,* July 13, 1989, pp. 16–17.

41. R. Tapper, "Ethnicity and Class."

42. Katz, "Biographic Database"; interview with U.N. officials, New York, April 1992; Johnson et al., "Southern Provinces," 158; Rubin, "Author Responds," 278. Najibullah's speech in KDS September 13, 1989, in *FBIS/NES,* September 15, 1989, pp. 41–42; quotation from Davis, "Afghan Army."

43. KDS, August 22, 1990, in *FBIS/NES,* August 23, 1990, pp. 42–43; AFP, September 5, 1990, in *FBIS/NES,* September 5, 1990, p. 51; International Institute of Strategic Studies, *Military Balance,* 45.

44. R.A., "Afghanistan, 1990," 4.

45. The actual change shown on Figure 7.1 is from 1984 to 1986, as the data for 1985 are missing. The monetary data also shown in Figure 7.1 suggest that the change in the rate of growth occurred in 1986, not before. On defense spending see Reuters, Kabul, August 9, 1988.

46. Bakhtar, March 16, 1988, and *Kabul New Times,* March 16, 1988, in *Afghanistan Forum* 16 (1988), no. 3, p. 35; KDS, February 4, 1990, in *FBIS/NES,* February 8, 1990, p. 45; Ashraf Ghani, personal communication, New York, March 1992.

47. KDS, May 5, 1987, in *FBIS/SA,* May 7, 1987, p. C1.

48. On the sources of these data see Appendix A.

49. It is somewhat difficult to determine exactly how these exports contributed to the budget. At least on paper, they were paid for by the USSR in dollars, although proresistance sources claim that this was simply an accounting device, and that the sales were used to offset the cost of the Soviet contingent and other aid. Values of natural gas exports are given in official documents either in U.S. dollars or in afghanis converted at the official exchange rate of Af 50.6 per dollar, which overstates the real value of the afghani by at least a factor of ten in the late 1980s and a

factor of twenty in the summer of 1991. The tables reflect the official conversion. At some point the countertrade rate was raised to Af 81 (AFP, November 8, 1991, in *FBIS/NES*, November 8, 1991, pp. 42–43).

50. Quotation from R.A., "Afghanistan, 1990," 6; AFP, August 18, 1990, in *FBIS/NES*, August 21, 1990, p. 43.

51. Quotation from KRAN, June 11, 1991, in *FBIS/NES*, June 14, 1991, p. 31. See also *AfghaNews*, July 15, 1991.

52. Qur'anic quotation in *National Reconciliation*, 19, or the speech to ulama broadcast on KDS, February 28, 1988, in *FBIS/NES*, March 1, 1988, pp. 46–54. Other quotations from KDS, July 24, 1990, in *FBIS/NES*, July 26, 1990, pp. 39–40.

53. Bakhtar, January 1, 1980, in *FBIS/SA*, January 5, 1987, pp. C1–5; KDS, June 21, 1987, in *FBIS/SA*, June 24, 1987, p. P1; KDS, February 28, 1988, in *FBIS/NES*, March 1, 1988, p. 50. In October 1987, Politburo member Mir Sahib Karwal claimed that the state was paying thirteen thousand imams of mosques (KDS, October 19, 1987, in *FBIS/NES*, October 30, 1987, p. 29).

54. Interview with Hashmatullah Kaihani, TANJUG, June 23, 1988, in *FBIS/NES*, June 24, 1988, p. 44.

55. Speech to ulama in KDS, February 28, 1988, in *FBIS/NES*, March 1, 1988, pp. 46–54; speech to Shiʿa commanders in KDS, March 16, 1990, in *FBIS/NES*, March 19, 1990, pp. 30–39. The Shiʿa resistance parties later denied that this meeting had occurred, but a commander of the Nasr party from Ghazni confirmed to me that it had taken place and that he had attended. On Logari's arrest see Amnesty International, *Report, 1990*, 27; U.N. Commission on Human Rights, "Human Rights in Afghanistan," 11; Asia Watch, *Forgotten War*, 76–77. The sermon probably made use of a play on the Arabic root for "create," KhLQ, from the which the word khalq (people) in the name of the PDPA derives.

56. Asia Watch, *Forgotten War*, 43–51. Asia Watch researchers saw documents according to which the ISI actually paid commanders per rocket fired.

57. Amnesty International, *Unfair Trials*, 6; U.N. Commission on Human Rights, "Human Rights in Afghanistan," 17–21; Asia Watch, *Forgotten War*, 93–95.

58. KDS, February 20, 1989, in *FBIS/NES*, February 21, 1989, p. 34. The sacked minister was Muhammad Ismail Danish, who had been brought home from exile as ambassador to Libya as part of Najibullah's reconciliation with the Khalqis in late 1987.

59. The wife of Najibullah's brother Siddiqullah, who had defected to the mujahidin, wrote in an article for an Afghan publication in California that Asghar Khan was related to Najibullah's wife. In 1990 one of the members of the NSS, Muhammad Anwar Arghandiwal, a professor at the Faculty of Law and Political Science of Kabul University, agreed to become a deputy prime minister, apparently without first informing the NSS, which caused the latter some embarrassment. Quotation from AFP, May 13, 1990, in *FBIS/NES*, May 17, 1990, p. 34.

60. Bakhtar, January 28, 1990, in *FBIS/NES*, January 31, 1990, p. 53; KDS, May 19, 1990, in *FBIS/NES*, May 25, 1990, p. 43; Asia Watch, *Forgotten War*, 71–73; AFP, August 12, 1991, in *FBIS/NES*, August 13, 1991, p. 35; AFP, August 19, 1991, in *FBIS/NES*, August 19, 1991, p. 51–52; AFP, October 7, 1991, in *FBIS/NES*, October 7, 1991, p. 47; AFP, November 13, 1991, in *FBIS/NES*, November 14, 1991, p. 44; *AfghaNews*, December 1, 1991, pp. 1 ff.; Reuters, Kabul, November 28, 1991. Khan Zia Khan Nassery, who organized the demonstration, announced publicly that there was no real freedom in the country, but he left behind a representative with instructions to open an office. In early 1993, after returning to Afghanistan, he disappeared en route from Mazar-i Sharif to Kabul.

61. Article 110. KDS, May 19, 1990, in *FBIS/NES*, May 25, 1990, p. 45; U.N. Commission on Human Rights, "Human Rights in Afghanistan," 36–39.

62. AFP, September 14, 1990, in *FBIS/NES*, September 14, 1990, p. 39.

63. KDS, March 27, 1988, in *FBIS/NES*, March 30, 1988, p. 45; *New York Times*, December 12, 1988; *New York Times*, October 2, 1991.

64. Bakhtar, March 31, 1986, in *FBIS/SA*, April 1, 1986, p. C1; KDS, October 19, 1987, in *FBIS/NES*, October 28, 1987, p. 39.

65. KDS, June 1, 1986, in *FBIS/SA*, June 3, 1986, p. C1.

66. Bakhtar, July 9, 1986, in *FBIS/SA*, July 9, 1986, p. C2; KDS, February 4, 1990, in *FBIS/NES*, February 8, 1990, p. 45; KDS, April 19, 1987, in *FBIS/SA*, April 22, 1987, pp. C1–5; Bakhtar, May 1, 1988, in *FBIS/NES*, May 3, 1988, p. 54.

67. KDS, February 4, 1990, in *FBIS/NES*, February 8, 1990, p. 45, 48; KDS, May 19, 1990, in *FBIS/NES*, May 25, 1990, p. 43; KDS, March 31, 1990, in *FBIS/NES*, April 2, 1990, p. 31; AFP, August 8, 1990 in *FBIS/NES*, August 8, 1990, p. 151; KDS, September 26, 1990, in *FBIS/NES*, September 28, 1990, p. 53; KDS, December 30, 1990, in *FBIS/NES*, January 1, 1991, p. 46; KDS, March 24, 1991, in *FBIS/NES*, March 27, 1991, p. 57; KDS, April 1, 1991, in *FBIS/NES*, April 2, 1991, p. 34; KRAN, August 12, 1991, in *FBIS/NES*, August 13, 1991, p. 35; AFP, November 8, 1991, in *FBIS/NES*, November 8, 1991, pp. 42–43.

68. KDS, November 21, 1989, in *FBIS/NES*, November 22, 1989, p. 35; Ashraf Ghani, personal communication, New York, March 1992.

69. In May 1986 the government stated that there were fifty-four special stores in the capital, seventeen in the provinces, and two in factories (Bakhtar, May 25, 1986, in *FBIS/SA*, May 29, 1986, p. C2). Some of the figures given by the government (as reported by *FBIS*) are not fully consistent. In May 1987 the government claimed that it paid about Af 1.5 billion per year for subsidies on coupons, and that each coupon was worth about Af 20,000 per year (KDS, May 16, 1987, in *FBIS/SA*, May 19, 1987, p. C1). This would work out to 75,000 coupons. Only ten months later, in March 1988, while presenting the budget to the Council of Ministers, Prime Minister Kishtmand said that there were 340,000 coupon holders and four million beneficiaries, or nearly twelve beneficiaries per coupon, which seems high even for Afghanistan. Two years later, in February 1990, the government said there were 450,000 coupon holders, and that 15 percent of the country's population were beneficiaries. At twelve beneficiaries per coupon, that estimate would have meant Afghanistan had a population of thirty-six million, more than twice the actual number. A year later (KDS, March 26, 1991, in *FBIS/NES*, March 27, 1991, p. 56) the total cost of the coupon subsidies was said to be Af 2 billion per year. If the number of coupons had increased slightly to 500,000, the total value of a coupon would have been Af 40,000 per year, or double what it had been four years earlier—a plausible increase. See also KDS, February 4, 1990, in *FBIS/NES*, February 8, 1990, p. 45.

70. KDS, January 27, 1989, in *SWB/FE*, January 28, 1989, p. C1; AFP, February 24, 1989, in *FBIS/NES*, February 24, 1989, p. 52. Kabul was said to consume 630 tons of wheat per day, and stocks went down to 7,700 tons.

71. AFP, March 12, 1989, in *FBIS/NES*, March 13, 1989, p. 55; AFP, March 26, 1989, in *FBIS/NES*, March 27, 1989, p. 41; *Daily Telegraph*, May 17, 1989, in *FBIS/NES*, May 18, 1989, p. 48–49.

72. Quotation from AFP, January 24, 1990, in *FBIS/NES*, January 26, 1990, p. 25. See also AFP, March 12, 1989, in *FBIS/NES*, March 13, 1989, p. 52.

73. Quotation from KRAN, June 11, 1991, in *FBIS/NES*, June 14, 1991, p. 31. See also KRAN, August 22, 1991, in *FBIS/NES*, August 27, 1991, p. 40; *India Today*, January 15, 1992.

74. Ahmed Rashid, "Back to Feudalism," *Far Eastern Economic Review*, July 13, 1989, pp. 16–17.

75. Demographic data show a marked decline in casualties beginning in 1987. Sliwinski, "Decimation of Afghanistan," attributes the decrease to the delivery, beginning in September 1986, of Stinger antiaircraft missiles to the mujahidin. At the time U.S. official sources discounted all

claims by Moscow or Kabul that any genuine political transformations were under way. Sliwinski also took this view at the time and did not consider alternative explanations.

76. AFP, May 30, 1988, in *FBIS/NES*, May 31, 1988, p. 44.

77. Bakhtar, April 29, 1986, in *FBIS/SA*, April 29, 1986, p. C4.

78. KDS, June 7, 1987, in *FBIS/SA*, June 11, 1987, p. P2; KDS, March 31, 1990, in *FBIS/NES*, April 2, 1990, p. 31; KDS, May 19, 1990, in *FBIS/NES*, May 25, 1990, pp. 43-44.

79. Rumer, *Soviet Central Asia*, 62-75.

80. KDS, February 6, 1988, in *FBIS/NES*, February 8, 1988, pp. 51-52; KDS February 6, 1988, in February 10, 1988, pp. 45-47; KDS, March 24, 1991, in *FBIS/NES*, March 27, 1991, p. 58.

81. KDS, April 2, 1986, in *FBIS/SA*, April 7, 1986, p. C1. According to Olivier Roy (personal communication, Washington, D.C. November 1985), after the Soviet withdrawal from Herat the government offered the landowners much higher prices for their wheat than did the dominant resistance commander, Ismail Khan, who had lost some of the financial support he had been receiving from Western aid organizations. Ismail Khan responded by jailing the landowners, who escaped and joined the government as militia leaders.

82. Quotations from *National Reconciliation*, 20-23. On the general process see L. Anderson, *State and Social Transformation;* Migdal, *Strong Societies and Weak States.*

83. Olivier Roy (personal communication, Princeton, N.J., December 1990) says that Massoud's qawm is Nawruzkhel, but that no one knows this or cares about it. For the offer see KDS, March 29, 1988, in *FBIS/NES*, March 31, 1988, p. 43. The commanders, in the order mentioned, were Ahmad Shah Massoud (Jamiat, Tajik, former Polytechnic student, northeast); Mullah Nasim Akhundzada (Harakat-i Inqilab, Durrani Pashtun, mullah and opium warlord, Helmand Valley); Ismail Khan (Jamiat, Persian-speaking Durrani, former army captain, Herat); Sayyid Jagran (Shura, Hazara, former army major, Hazara part of Ghazni); Farid (Hizb [Hikmatyar], Tajik, schoolteacher, Charikar-Kapisa); Mawlawi Jalaluddin Haqqani (Hizb [Khalis], Jadran Pashtun, alim, Paktia); and Abdul Basir Khalid (Jamiat, Uzbek, schoolteacher, Faizabad-Badakhshan). Farid briefly became prime minister in July 1992.

84. Kyodo (Tokyo), March 29, 1988, in *FBIS/NES*, March 29, 1988, p. 53.

85. According to the same Soviet source, Juma Atsak's appointment mainly resulted from the favor he found in the eyes of Gen. Valentin Varennikov, commander of Soviet ground forces. Varennikov wanted Atsak to be made a Hero of the DRA, but the Khalqis on the Politburo blocked him.

Part III / The Islamic Resistance

1. Abolfathi, in "Reassessment of the Afghan Conflict," has insisted the most on this point.

2. Anthony et al., "Trade in Major Conventional Weapons," 199.

3. Shahrani, in "Responses to the Saur Revolution," disputes the contention that the revolt was a spontaneous reaction by traditional elites. His study pointed out the prominence of Islamist elites and of conscious political action in the resistance before many observers recognized their importance. Surveys of the entire country, however, partial and inconclusive though they are, suggest that the majority of the original uprisings were traditional in nature.

4. On refugee communities in general and on Afghanistan in particular see Zolberg, Suhrke, and Aguayo, *Escape from Violence.*

5. Roy, in *Islam et modernité politique*, 296, presented what is still the only map of these patterns. The map, which reflects the situation in the early 1980s, does not appear in later English editions of the book.

6. Harrison, "Inside the Afghan Talks," 50. For slightly different figures on aid see Khan, *Un-*

tying the Afghan Knot, 351–52. On training see Yousaf and Adkin, *Bear Trap*. On the 1985 increase see the article by Bob Woodward and Charles Babcock in the *Washington Post*, January 13, 1985.

7. Harrison, "Inside the Afghan Talks," 50.

8. "US AID Humanitarian Assistance to Afghanistan." I owe thanks to Ambassador Robert Oakley for supplying me with this document.

9. *The Independent*, June 20, 1989; *Far Eastern Economic Review*, July 13, 1989.

10. *Los Angeles Times*, November 19, 1989; *Far Eastern Economic Review*, December 7, 1989; interviews with U.S. and congressional officials.

11. *The Independent*, August 1, 1990. The sources do not make clear whether the $1 billion figure includes the $535 million ($435 million from the Saudi government, plus $100 million from private Saudi and Kuwaiti sources) allocated the previous fall; my guess is that it does. Some of the aid may have been promised before the invasion of Kuwait (which occurred the day after the *Independent* article appeared) but not delivered.

12. Interviews with U.S. officials, March 1993; *The Independent*, May 28, 1990.

13. *Wall Street Journal*, September 27, 1990; *Washington Post*, October 23, 1990; *Time*, June 24, 1991; *Washington Post*, October 1, 1991; *Far Eastern Economic Review*, October 3, 1991; *New York Times*, May 11, 1991; interviews with U.S. officials, March 1993. *Daily Telegraph*, October 30, 1991, gave the amount of private Arab aid as £250 million.

14. Roy, "Guerre comme facteur."

Chapter 8 / Origins of the Movement of Jihad

1. On the depoliticization of the elites of rentier states see Najmabadi, "Depoliticisation of a Rentier State." The market can provide networks for political organizing. In French-ruled Tunisia, for instance, the penetration of rural areas by the cooperative bank provided a ready-made network for mobilization once the bank's chairman switched his support to the Neo-Destour (L. Anderson, *State and Social Transformation*, 167–77).

2. In 1986 Hizb-i Islami claimed to have had fifteen hundred members who had joined before the coup in 1978 (Rastegar, "Education and Revolutionary Political Mobilization," 151). This number may be exaggerated, and Jamiat probably had about the same number as Hizb. For comparisons with other insurgencies see Abolfathi, "Reassessment of the Afghan Conflict."

3. Roy, in *Islam and Resistance*, 98–109, classifies revolts by whether they were spontaneous or organized. Hence he places the March 1979 mutiny of the Herat garrison, led by Capt. (Turan) Ismail Khan, a member of Jamiat, in the same category as the attack on government posts in Badakhshan by Jamiat militants who had returned from Peshawar with light weapons. (On the latter see Shahrani, "Responses to the Saur Revolution.")

4. Roy, *Islam and Resistance*, 99–100; Schneiter, "Guerre de libération"; Strand, "Anti-Communist Resistance." The Nuristanis reacted to the killing of Abdul Qadir Nuristani and some of his associates. Nuristani, Daoud's minister of the interior, was known for his strong anticommunism. According to Hasan Kakar (personal communication, March 1990), there was a localized tribal revolt in Paktia even earlier. On causes of revolt see Roy, *Islam and Resistance*, 90–97; Keiser, "Rebellion in Darra-i Nur."

5. Roy, *Islam and Resistance*, 102–104; Abolfathi, "Reassessment of the Afghan Conflict," 2-34–43, contains a chronology.

6. For a sampling of the popular culture of jihad from northern Afghanistan, see *Sima-yi jihad dar farhang-i 'amiyyanah*. This pamphlet contains a collection of popular poetry in the vernacular Persian of Afghanistan, often in traditional *do-baiti* (couplet) or *chhar-baiti* (quatrain) form, on the war. Themes include grief at the destruction of Afghanistan, defiant assertions that Soviet

power will fail, and, above all, praise for the figure of the mujahid as a model for humanity, compared to such heroes of the Shahnamah as Rustam. Although this pamphlet was published by Jamiat and contains references by name to foes (all the Soviet and PDPA leaders), it does not mention by name any leader of the jihad.

On the laws of the jihad and their use in anti-imperialist struggle see Peters, *Islam and Colonialism*. For an explication of this law by an Afghan alim engaged in the war, see al-Qandahari, *Sarf al-ijtihad fi ahkam al-jihad*. On the mechanisms by which popular knowledge of Islam is transmitted see Shahrani, "Local Knowledge of Islam." On women see Shalinsky, "Models of Women's Roles." For a depiction of the latter, see Hyman, *Propaganda Posters*, fig. 18 (no pagination).

7. See Appendix A for a description of these files and my sample. Each case consisted of data on one commander and his organization. In some cases I was able to supplement the files where information was lacking with inferences or other information. For one file about Herat, e.g., I assumed that the uprising was started by Islamist activists in view of the well-known origin of the Herat resistance. Similarly, I counted central Kunduz as an Islamist-led uprising. In cases where the commander himself was a traditional leader rather than an educated activist, I presumed that the uprising had traditional leadership. In most cases, however, the information was explicit.

8. Roy, *Islam and Resistance*, 106; I have slightly amended the translation to match the original better.

9. Gellner, "Tribalism and the State"; Louis Dupree, "Tribal Warfare"; Ahmed, *Pukhtun Economy and Society;* Roy, *Islam and Resistance*, 176–80; on traditionally organized insurgency, see Abolfathi, "Reassessment of the Afghan Conflict," 3-10.

10. They were then surrounded by a detachment of mujahidin from Hizb-i Islami commanded by Mawlawi Husain, who confiscated their weapons. Mawlawi Husain later adopted the name Jamil-ur-Rahman, left Hizb-i Islami, and established the Salafi organization Jama'at al-Da'wa.

11. Accounts are available of these uprisings in Herat (a combined military and popular uprising), Panjsher, and Badakhshan (Roy, *Islam and Resistance*, 107–8; Abolfathi, "Reassessment of the Afghan Conflict," 2-38–43; Shahrani, "Responses to the Saur Revolution"). Maoist militants in Badakhshan also staged an uprising, but the support of the ulama for the Islamists left them isolated and easily defeated.

12. Roy, *Islam and Resistance*, 110.

13. Barfield, "Links on a Rusty Chain"; L. Anderson, *State and Social Transformation*, 203–33; Rubin, "Fragmentation of Tajikistan."

14. Roy, *Islam and Resistance*, 112–18.

15. Abolfathi, "Reassessment of the Afghan Conflict," 3-10.

16. One Jamiat commander from Bamiyan, a very poor area, told SCA that at the beginning of the war the people paid ushr voluntarily and that there was no need for requisition. The implication is that requisition became necessary later.

17. SCA files. According to the file, this front captured "thousands of seers" of food. One seer equals about seven kilograms. Another commander of northern Kabul Province also said that "for mujahidin near the highway, [booty] is the best income."

18. Roy, *Islam and Resistance*, 106. Quotation from Anderson, "Khan and Khel," 134. Barry, in *Royaume de l'insolence*, analyzes the role of the guest house in the resistance.

19. Es'haq, *From Theory to Practice*, 2.

20. Interview with Qari Taj Baba, Peshawar, December 8, 1986. Quotation from Abolfathi, "Reassessment of the Afghan Conflict," 3-11.

21. Interview with Abdul Rauf, Washington, D.C., March 1990; interview with Naim Majrooh, Washington, D.C., July 1990; Strand, "Anti-Communist Resistance."

22. Edwards, in "Shi'i Political Dissent," 223, says that those who formed the shura began as-

sembling in Waras in June 1979. Lorentz, in "Anatomy of an Entanglement," says the shura was formed at the end of the summer, and Roy gives a September date (*Islam and Resistance*, 141).

23. Roy, *Islam and Resistance*, 142–43.

24. George G. B. Griffin, "Memorandum of Conversation," Department of State, September 20, 1979, in Danishjuyan-i Musulman-i Piru[-yi] Khat-i Imam, *Asnad-i lanah-yi jasusi*, 30:61.

25. Khan, *Untying the Afghan Knot*, 73.

26. Intsum [Intelligence Summary] 914—October 11, 1979, Secret Cable #266505, item no. 694 in National Security Archive, *Making of U.S. Policy*.

27. See, e.g., Hobsbawm and Ranger, *Invention of Tradition*.

28. Kakar, "Soviet Invasion," 100. Kakar's account of the Jirga seems to be largely drawn from Wajdi, *Pah Afghanistan ke da unanawi jirgo nan aw parun*. Wajdi served as chief of the publications department of the Islamic and National Revolutionary Council chosen by the Jirga.

29. Kakar, "Soviet Invasion," 103.

30. Ibid., 104, citing Wajdi, *Pah Afghanistan ke da unanawi jirgo nan aw parun*, 264–67.

31. Kakar, "Soviet Invasion," 105.

32. *Le monde*, June 22, 1983; Khan, *Untying the Afghan Knot*, 76; interview with Mohammad Yousof (who was one of those who went to Saudi Arabia), Rockville, Maryland, October 24, 1986. Assefy's visa to Pakistan allowed him to visit Islamabad, but not Peshawar, where the refugees and jihad leaders were concentrated.

Chapter 9 / International Aid, War, and National Organization

1. On Stingers see Yousaf and Adkin, *Bear Trap*, 177. See Introduction to Part III for the comparative data on weapons imports; on the comparison with India and Pakistan see Piquard, "Pourquoi le chaos afghan peut faire exploser l'Asie centrale," 7.

2. According to Yousaf and Adkin, *Bear Trap*, 77.

3. "Sheikh Abdullah Azzam Is Martyred."

4. Yousaf and Adkin, *Bear Trap*, 97–112. Both China and Egypt manufactured versions of the Kalashnikov rifle and the SAKR ground-to-ground missile. Israel had captured many Soviet-manufactured weapons in Lebanon in 1982.

5. Yousaf and Adkin, *Bear Trap*, 106. Many of these bank accounts were reputed to be in the Bank of Credit and Commerce International.

6. Roy, in *Islam and Resistance*, 163–64, first drew attention to the role of the private sector in transport. Cost data from Yousaf and Adkin, *Bear Trap*, 106. Data on political discrimination from interview with logistics officer of a traditionalist-nationalist party, Khyber Agency, Pakistan, February 1989. According to a NIFA commander of Pashtuns in Kunduz, as quoted in the SCA files, "In NIFA party there is no transportation cost for mujahedin. . . . Usually weapons of NIFA and Professor Mojaddedi are sold because of this transportation cost."

7. Lifschultz, "Empire of Heroin." According to one report, these unofficial corruptions pale beside a major official one; Lifschultz also writes that until November 1986 the Afghan arms pipeline was "the back door to Iran-Contra." He claims that Pakistani, Israeli, and American intelligence sources confirmed that hundreds of millions of dollars of weapons purchased with money allocated by Congress for the mujahidin were diverted from Peshawar to Iran. (Lifschultz, "Iran-Contra's Secret Back Door.") Brigadier Yousaf maintains (*Bear Trap*, 102) that during his watch (1983–87) the ISI Afghan operation was free of corruption.

8. Yousaf and Adkin, *Bear Trap*, 40.

9. Khan, *Untying the Afghan Knot*, 73; Cobban, *Palestinian Liberation Organisation*, 28–29.

10. Yousaf and Adkin, *Bear Trap*, 102, 117.

11. According to Yousaf, in *Bear Trap*, 209, "General Akhtar [director of ISI] was conscious

that if political activities were initiated before the capture of Kabul it would so weaken the Jehad that a military victory might prove unattainable." I have heard the wish for revenge for Vietnam expressed by U.S. government officials myself. For quotations from Director of Central Intelligence William Casey and U.S. Congressman Charles Wilson (Democrat, Texas) see Yousaf and Adkin, *Bear Trap*, 63, 79.

12. Quotation from Yousaf and Adkin, *Bear Trap*, 105. Apparently the same views existed among "American observers," presumably the CIA (Abolfathi, "Reassessment of the Afghan Conflict," 3-43).

13. Roy, *Islam and Resistance*, 112–18.

14. Ibid., 182.

15. Edwards, "Marginality and Migration."

16. Roy, "New Political Elite," 77. On data sources see Appendix A.

17. Adamec, *Biographical Dictionary*, 61–62. Recall the French exile background of the royal family and the favor they showed to Lycée Istiqlal. Control of the French auto dealership was a sign of particular royal favor. Control over patrimonially distributed automobile dealerships is an important source of wealth for royal or presidential favorites in many rentier states. See Beblawi, "Rentier State in the Arab World," 92.

18. Quotations from *Mahaz-i Milli-yi Islami-yi Afghanistan*, 21, 22, 23.

19. "Fundamentalism in Islam," 4.

20. Interview with an NIFA official, Peshawar, November 30, 1986.

21. Mujaddidi's wife, who died in the early 1970s, was the daughter of a prominent Naqshbandi pir of the Sulaimankhel tribe and the sister of the Parchami leader Sulaiman Laiq. Sulaiman Laiq was originally named Ghulam Mujaddidi (slave of the Mujaddidis) and lived for a time in the house of Sibghatullah's father.

22. The government spread the charge that Mujaddidi had plotted to assassinate Khrushchev and Bulganin during their visit to the country in 1955, but it never produced any evidence. Nonetheless, many foreigners and Afghans have accepted these probably false charges as true.

23. Roy, *Islam and Resistance*, 120–21.

24. "Objectives of the Afghan National Liberation Front," 2.

25. Roy, *Islam and Resistance*, 129–30.

26. *Fishurdah-yi az maram-i Harakat*, 10. I am grateful to Farshad Rastegar for making this available to me.

27. Ibid., 11–13; Rastegar, "Education and Revolutionary Political Mobilization," 158–67.

28. Adamec, *Biographical Dictionary*, 133–34.

29. According to Rastegar ("Education and Revolutionary Political Mobilization," 109n), his associates do not dispute the charge.

30. Rastegar, "Education and Revolutionary Political Mobilization," 151. By some accounts there are six levels of membership.

31. Roy, *Islam and Resistance*, 111–12.

32. This process of recruitment is the main subject of Rastegar, "Education and Revolutionary Political Mobilization."

33. Ibid., 189–90.

34. Roy, *Islam and Resistance*, 133.

35. Ibid., 128–29.

36. Khalis, *Man kistam va bara-yi chih mubarizah mikunam?*

37. Ibid., 9.

38. Ibid., 11–12.

39. Gellner, *Muslim Society*, 72.

40. Abolfathi in ("Reassessment of the Afghan Conflict," 4-19–23) notes that they could even

return to comfortable bases in Pakistan in the event of severe storms, not a common luxury in the history of guerrilla warfare.

41. Interviews with Abdul Haq, Peshawar, September 1984, and Washington, D.C., January 1985.

42. Interview with former Soviet adviser to Afghan Ministry of Defense, Washington, D.C., November 1989.

43. Yousaf and Adkin, *Bear Trap*, 182.

44. Abolfathi, "Reassessment of the Afghan Conflict," 4-20n.

45. Mullah Malang is reported to have boasted at the 1989 shura in Rawalpindi that he had sold four Stinger antiaircraft missiles to Iran for a million dollars each. On changes in party affiliation see Roy, "Ethnies et politique," 22–23; Roy notes that language, not ethnogenesis as defined by descent, seems to have been the determining factor in party allegiance.

46. Rastegar, "Education and Revolutionary Political Mobilization," 191.

47. On sources of data see Appendix A.

48. These emissaries came to see me on several occasions in order to complain about interference in Afghanistan by "regional powers" (Pakistan) and to pursue direct relations with the United States. In the spring of 1990 they met with National Security Adviser Brent Skowcroft and his deputy Robert Gates, later director of Central Intelligence.

49. Reports differ on the precise relationship between Sayyaf and Amin.

50. Roy, *Islam and Resistance*, 122–23.

51. In February 1989 in Nangarhar, I stayed one day with an Ahmadzai nomad commander of NIFA, who recounted how "Arabs" from Sayyaf's party had offered him huge amounts of money to join. "I spit on their shoes," he said. "They think jihad is a business." Later I heard that the commander had indeed taken their money and joined Sayyaf for a while. He later went back to Gailani.

52. Yousaf and Adkin, *Bear Trap*, 182.

53. Edwards, "Shi'i Political Dissent"; Lorentz, "Anatomy of an Entanglement"; and Roy, *Islam and Resistance*, 141–47.

54. Roy, *Islam and Resistance*, 146–48; Edwards, "Shi'i Political Dissent," 226.

55. Cable from CIA, Los Angeles, August 15, 1979, in Danishjuyan-i Musulman-i Piru[-yi] Khat-i Imam, *Asnad-i lanah-yi jasusi*, 30:133.

56. Lorentz, "Anatomy of an Entanglement," 30.

57. Ibid., 35. In May 1990 I met a Nasr commander who had been invited to Washington, D.C., along with commanders from the Sunni parties as part of a USIA program for promoting "democratic pluralism." He advocated stronger American involvement in choosing an interim government in order to overcome excessive influence by Pakistan and Saudi Arabia.

58. The conventional translation of this alliance has been Islamic Unity of Afghan Mujahidin (IUAM). The Arabic loan word *ittihad* is better translated here as "union." More important, the Persian title refers to Afghanistan, the territory, not Afghan, an ambiguous term with ethnic connotations.

59. Interviews, Department of State, Washington, D.C., May 14, 1985, and May 17, 1985.

60. One State Department official cited above said that Sayyaf, Hikmatyar, Rabbani, and Khalis mattered politically.

61. Khan, *Untying the Afghan Knot*, 80, 159; Yousaf and Adkin, *Bear Trap*, 41.

Chapter 10 / International Aid, War, and Local and Regional Organization

1. Migdal, *Strong Societies and Weak States*, 28–33.

2. On "macro-ethnie" and its relation to qawm see Roy, "Ethnies et politique."

3. This quotation comes from the file of a Qandahar Jamiat commander, and similar expressions occur frequently.

4. On Algeria see Peters, *Islam and Colonialism,* 53–62. On NIFA commanders see Roy, "New Political Elite," 78.

5. Swedish Committee for Afghanistan, *Agricultural Survey of Afghanistan: First Report,* 17, 24–30, 19.

6. Data Collection for Afghan Repatriation Project (DCAR), *UNHCR Background Report (UBR):* Wardak, 20. On this series see Appendix A.

7. Roy, *Islam and Resistance,* 150–53. According to SCA files these two patterns occurred in Bagrami and Mir Bacha Kot, respectively, two districts of Kabul Province.

8. Roy, in "Guerre comme facteur," describes in greater detail the effect of Soviet-style total war on the structure of fronts. Es'haq, in *From Theory to Practice,* 3, says that commanders in areas with no fighting became known as local kings.

9. DCAR, *UBR: Logar,* 12 and passim.

10. Jaji documents from SCA files. Notes based on unverified English translation in the files of Pashto original. Text of the Medina agreement in Watt, *Islamic Political Thought,* 130–34. The elevation of loyalty to Islam and umma over tribe is common to the two documents; the role given to the ulama, who did not exist in the early days of Islam, had no equivalent in the Medina document.

11. Roy, *Islam and Resistance,* 153–56.

12. In the summer of 1989, the ISI brought two commanders from Wardak, a Ghilzai area, to attack Qandahar after the commanders' shura of that city had refused. According to one Qandahari, "They paid each of their mujahidin Rs 500 per day, plus Rs 50,000 in case of death and Rs 20,000 in case of injury [twenty rupees were the equivalent of one dollar]. This created a terrible reaction. It was not jihad but a mercenary war. People began to ask themselves, is this still jihad?" (Interview, Arlington, Va., May 1990.)

13. Interview, Peshawar, December 8, 1986.

14. SCA files.

15. I have noticed that many asylum applicants from Afghanistan on whose behalf I have written affidavits claimed that they were sought or arrested by KhAD for feeding or making donations to mujahidin groups.

16. In a 1986 interview, however, Massoud claimed that he still obtained about a third of his supplies from booty (*Arbeiderbladet* [Oslo], March 11, 1986, in Federal Broadcast Information Service/South Asia [FBIS/SA], March 21, 1986, p. C3).

17. Roy, *Islam and Resistance,* 153–56.

18. Interview with a mujahid of Harakat from Char Dehi, Peshawar, December 5, 1986. Hikmatyar (interview, Peshawar, December 6, 1986) attributed this conflict to the fact that Char Dehi, only six kilometers from Kabul city, was not "completely liberated": because it was not possible to establish a stable mujahidin administration, military considerations had to prevail. The reasons they *could* prevail over the demands of local society were described by the Harakat informant: "We were young men with beards on our faces and Kalashnikovs on our shoulders." The beards symbolized the legitimation of jihad, and the Kalashnikovs came from foreign aid. Similarly DCAR reported that Qarghai district in the south of Laghman was controlled by mujahidin commanders who did not consult elders (DCAR, *UBR: Laghman,* 26).

19. DCAR, *UBR: Logar,* 3. Haji M. Naim Khalin Kuchi (as his name was announced on Kabul Radio on May 5, 1992) later became deputy minister of frontier affairs (i.e., of tribes) in the first Council of Ministers of the Islamic State of Afghanistan.

20. Johnson, et al., "Northern Provinces," 231–35.

21. Rae, *Political Consequences of Electoral Laws,* 46–64; Sartori, *Parties and Party Systems,* 302–15.

22. Local rivalries also divided Jamiat commanders. See Dorronsoro, "Situation politique." On change from Harakat to Jamiat see Roy, *Islam and Resistance,* 129–30; Johnson et al., "Northern Provinces," 230.

23. SCA files, interviews with both NIFA and Jamiat commanders of Kunduz; interview with Baghlan mujahid, Peshawar, September 30, 1984.

24. In 1983, Brigadier Yousaf, head of ISI Afghan operations, decided that the strategic northern provinces were not getting enough assistance and launched a crash program to remedy the problem. In what may have been a blessing in disguise for the northern mujahidin, General Akhtar soon put a stop to it. (Yousaf and Adkin, *Bear Trap,* 137.)

25. See Es'haq, *From Theory to Practice;* and Es'haq, *Situation in the North of Afghanistan 1987,* which includes an interview with Massoud.

26. Abolfathi, "Reassessment of the Afghan Conflict," 3-47.

27. Gall, *Behind Russian Lines,* 156; Abolfathi, "Reassessment of the Afghan Conflict," 3-38.

28. Roy, *Islam and Resistance,* 181–82; Abolfathi, "Reassessment of the Afghan Conflict," 3-29–36.

29. *Arbeiderbladet,* March 11, 1986, in FBIS/SA, March 21, 1986, p. C3.

30. Interview with Mohammad Es'haq (a participant in the negotiations), Peshawar, December 2, 1986.

31. Es'haq, *From Theory to Practice,* 7–8.

32. Abolfathi, "Reassessment of the Afghan Conflict," table opp. 3-52.

33. Johnson et al., "Northern Provinces," 231, 234; Abolfathi, "Reassessment of the Afghan Conflict," 3-4–48; Es'haq, *Situation in the North,* 39–40.

34. Johnson et al., "Northern Provinces," 244.

35. Roy, *Islam and Resistance,* 2d ed., 222.

36. Roy, *Islam and Resistance,* 180–81; Johnson et al., "Western Hinterland Provinces," 88–89. The former observed three regiments per battalion, the latter, writing several years later, five.

37. Johnson et al., "Western Hinterland Provinces," 88. In November–December 1986 in Peshawar I saw unedited raw videotapes taken in Herat by Massoud Khalili, a political officer of Jamiat. These films showed various education, health, and economic programs run by Ismail Khan's organization.

38. Johnson et al., "Western Hinterland Provinces," 89; "A Meeting of Resistance Commanders inside Afghanistan," *Afghan Information Centre Monthly Bulletin* 7, no. 7 (August 1987), 9–10.

39. Roy, *Islam and Resistance,* 189–90.

40. DCAR, *UBR: Paktia,* 4.

41. DCAR, *UBR: Wardak,* 20–21; in addition I have interviewed many journalists and relief workers who visited or worked in the area, and I have seen a film on the agricultural program.

42. DCAR, *UBR: Logar,* 3–4.

43. DCAR, *UBR: Kunar,* 3.

44. DCAR, *UBR: Kunar,* passim.; interviews with emissary of Dawlat, Peshawar, November 21, 1986; interview with Rahim Wardak, Peshawar, November 22, 1986.

45. DCAR, *UBR: Kandahar,* 2. Johnson et al., in "Southern Provinces," 6, claimed that "the orthodox clergy—the 'ulama—have moved into the vacuum left by the departing tribal khans."

46. Olivier Roy, personal communication, Bonn, June 1988; DCAR, *UBR: Kandahar,* passim.

47. Many members of the Karzai family lived in Silver Spring, Md., throughout the war. I have interviewed them both in the Washington area and in Quetta.

48. SCA files.

49. Johnson et al., "Southern Provinces," 6; DCAR, *UBR: Kandahar,* 3.

50. "Situation in Helmand."

Chapter 11 / Mujahidin after Soviet Withdrawal

1. This is the central theme of Migdal, *Strong Societies and Weak States.*

2. One of the hypotheses of the "ethnic competition" model is that expansion of the political arena encourages ethnic mobilization. See Nagel and Olzak, "Ethnic Mobilization"; Olzak, "Contemporary Ethnic Mobilization."

3. Rubin, "The Next Round"; Khan, *Untying the Afghan Knot,* 190–201.

4. Khan, *Untying the Afghan Knot,* 191–201.

5. "What Do the Afghan Refugees Think?" In my view the survey methodology was flawed, for Majrooh's field workers did not have the resources to carry out a genuine random survey of the entire refugee population. The survey did, I believe, accurately reflect the views of elders living in refugee camps. The younger generation, who would not have contradicted the elders in front of visitors, probably was less favorable to the old regime.

6. Khan, *Untying the Afghan Knot,* 258; *The Independent,* September 13, 1988; "Gouvernement introuvable."

7. Interview with U.S. diplomat in Riyadh, March 20, 1989; Cronin, "Afghanistan after the Soviet Withdrawal," 7; *The Independent,* February 2, 1989; Rubin, "Political Exiles"; interview with USAID official, Peshawar, January 1989.

8. Rubin, "Fragmentation of Afghanistan," 157–59; Yousaf and Adkin, *Bear Trap,* 226–32.

9. *Washington Post,* September 2, 1989; *International Herald Tribune,* August 31, 1988.

10. For details, see Rubin, "Post–Cold War State Disintegration," 478–83.

11. *Washington Post,* September 9, 1989; *New York Times,* November 19, 1989.

12. *The Times,* June 21, 1989; *Washington Post,* July 9, 1989; *The Independent,* July 31, 1989; Olivier Roy, personal communication, Washington, D.C., November 1989.

13. Yousaf and Adkin, *Bear Trap,* 6–7.

14. *Financial Times,* August 7, 1989; *Independent,* August 12, 1989; *Washington Post,* March 17, 1990; *Insight,* April 9, 1990, 8–18. U.S. State Department sources state that the ISI was involved in this coup attempt "up to their necks." Pakistani diplomatic sources have denied this to me.

15. While in Pakistan in October 1990 to observe the elections, I heard reports of CIA involvement with this effort. See *Independent,* October 2, 1990; *New York Times,* January 3, 1991.

16. I met with them during their visit. See also *Washington Times,* May 8, 1990.

17. *Washington Post,* April 1, 1991.

18. *New York Times,* February 17, 1991; Reuters, March 5, 1991.

19. Interview with State Department officials, April 4, 1991.

20. I heard this often from mujahidin interlocutors in 1990, though not from party officials.

21. Swedish Committee for Afghanistan, *Agricultural Survey of Afghanistan, First Report,* 38, written before the Geneva Accords went into effect, attributes the revival to the missiles.

22. According to DCAR, *UNHCR Background Report (UBR): Kandahar Province,* 12, dated September 1989, a shura in Arghistan district was set up specifically to facilitate NGO assistance. The same source reported (24) that Mercy Corps International, an American NGO; Volunteers in Technical Assistance, an American NGO funded by USAID; and the Austrian Relief Committee each convened a shura in Qandahar Province.

In December 1986 I observed the interview of a Harakat-i Inqilab commander from the Maidan area of Wardak by an Afghan employee of SCA. Maidan had witnessed endemic factional battles, largely between Hizb-i Islami and Harakat commanders. The interviewer told the Harakat commander, a former schoolteacher, that SCA could not offer any help to the region unless they settled their conflicts.

Michael Barry information from personal communication, London, December 1988.

23. *Washington Post,* May 13, 1990. I have also conducted interviews on these subjects with a number of informants who are in a position to know the truth of what they claim.

24. *The Independent,* August 19, 1989.

25. In a December 6, 1986, interview in Peshawar, Hikmatyar claimed that most of the Jamiat commanders of northeast Afghanistan had come to Pakistan to ask Rabbani to press Massoud to leave Takhar and return to Panjsher.

26. Roy, "Facteur Massoud"; *Le Monde,* September 4, 1991.

27. Hussain, "Road to Central Asia," 57; interview with Afghan diplomat, New York, December 8, 1992.

28. Roy, personal communication, Washington, D.C., November 1989.

29. Asia Watch, "Actions of the Pakistan Military"; this account was based on my own reporting from Peshawar and Nangarhar.

30. *Philadelphia Inquirer,* May 24, 1992.

31. DCAR, *UBR: Nangarhar,* passim. Quotation from *Philadelphia Inquirer,* May 24, 1992.

32. *Far Eastern Economic Review,* June 6, 1991, 44.

33. Johnson et al., "Southern Provinces," 162.

34. Interview with Qandahari source, Arlington, Virginia, March 28, 1990.

35. Oakley claimed in an interview that he had kept Washington fully informed of every step of the negotiations and had asked USAID to brief Congress on them. The relevant officials at US-AID, Oakley said, had hesitated to support the plan and had finally pulled back for fear of the political consequences. Probably there is at least one other side to this story.

Chapter 12 / State Collapse after the Cold War

1. Davis, "Afghan Army."

2. U.N. Department of Public Information, "Statement by Secretary-General Javier Pérez de Cuellar."

3. *Washington Post,* September 14, 1991.

4. "Situation in Afghanistan," 12.

5. "Joint Statement on the Negotiations in Moscow."

6. Interviews with mujahidin leaders and Pakistani diplomats, New York, October 1992; Reuters (Islamabad), October 11, 1991.

7. Interview with Zahir Shah, Rome, August 2, 1991.

8. U.N. Department of Public Information, "Statement by the Secretary-General."

9. Interviews with Parchami Central Committee members in Almaty (October 1992), Tashkent (May 1993), and New York (April 1992); interviews with journalist Richard Mackenzie in Washington (August 1993), several U.N. officials (September 1992), and U.S. diplomats (February 1993); Davis, "Afghan Army."

10. Interviews with U.N. and Afghan diplomats, September–October 1992. A Western diplomat interviewed in early 1993 claimed that Yaaqubi had been "shot in the back of his head by someone he knew." Journalist Richard Mackenzie, who accompanied Massoud into Kabul, said he had seen the body, and the wounds indicated suicide.

11. Interviews with Parchami former Central Committee members, New York, April 1992, and Almaty, October 1992. Interview with Muhammad Nabi Azimi, Tashkent, May 22, 1993.

12. *Washington Post,* October 20, 1991.

13. Leading figures of the regime who supported Hikmatyar included Defense Minister Watan-

jar and Interior Minister Paktin, both Khalqis, and Political Director of the Armed Forces Manokai Mangal, a Parchami, whom Najibullah had sent to Peshawar several months earlier to negotiate with Hikmatyar.

14. In January the Pakistani Islamists had demonstrated their power when former ISI director Gen. Hamid Gul, now the corps commander of Multan with no official connection to Afghan policy, had prevailed on Hikmatyar to renege on an agreement that he had made to release a prisoner of war to Russian Vice President Alexander Rutskoy in Islamabad. Pakistan Chief of Army Staff Gen. Asif Nawaz then forced Gul to resign from the armed forces, but Gul appears to have kept access to both Middle Eastern money on the one hand and cadres of the ISI on the other.

15. Interview with exiled Parchami Central Committee member in Almaty, October 1992; Davis, "Afghan Army"; interview with U.S. diplomat.

16. *Guardian,* October 14, 1992.

17. U.N. Office for the Co-ordination of Humanitarian and Economic Assistance Programmes, "Immediate Humanitarian Needs"; U.N. Department of Humanitarian Affairs, "Note on Winter Emergency Needs," 2.

18. I owe this perceptive witticism to Mary Ann Siegfried.

19. Interview with A. Rasul Amin, Peshawar, January 1989.

20. Davis, "Afghan Army"; interviews with Pakistan diplomats, Villanova, Pa., September 1992, and U.N. officials in Tajikistan, June 1993.

21. Rubin, "Fragmentation of Tajikistan," 82–83.

22. Davis, "Afghan Army."

23. *Washington Post,* April 27, 1993.

24. Rubin, "Fragmentation of Tajikistan," 83–86.

25. Interview with Ashraf Ghani, New York, March 1993; *New York Times,* July 27, 1993.

26. Interview, New York, May 1992, with journalist who traveled from Peshawar to Kabul by road with Mujaddidi.

27. "Da Qandahar da aqwamo aw jihad[i] shura gadah a'lamiyyah"; interview with Abdul Qayyum Karzai, Maryland, April 1992.

28. Shahrani, "State Building and Social Fragmentation," 67n16.

29. Jackson and Rosberg, "Why Africa's Weak States Persist."

Glossary

Specialized terms are listed here; many are Arabic (A.) loan words commonly used in Persian/Farsi/Dari (F.), Pashto (P.), or Turkic (T.) languages. In such cases I use the Persian transliteration, but I note the Arabic origin and, if useful, the etymology. When Afghans use an Islamic Arabic term in its Arabic sense, I note only the Arabic origin. Muslims use these words in the same way in virtually all languages they speak, including English. In cases where a loan word has developed a somewhat particular local meaning, I note both the Arabic origin and the use in another language. I omit some terms that appear only once, as well as proper names. The ayn (') and hamza (') are included here where appropriate, but in keeping with standard practice in English-language texts, those diacritics are omitted in the text of the book.

'*alaqdari* (P., partly from A.). Subdistrict; administrative unit smaller than an *uluswali* (q.v.), but not a subdivision of an uluswali. An 'alaqdari is administered by an '*alaqdar.*

'*alim* (A., pl. '*ulama*). Islamic scholar.

arbab (F. from A., pl. of *rabb,* "master"). Despite plural form, used in the singular to denote a village headman, usually appointed by the state. Same Semitic root as for "rabbi."

'*asabiyya* (A.). Solidarity of a group, from an Arabic root meaning "to bind." A key term in Ibn Khaldun's theory of history.

atraf (F., from A., pl. of *taraf,* "direction"; *atrap* in P.). Used in Afghanistan to mean "the provinces" or "the countryside," as opposed to Kabul or the city.

awqaf (A., sing. *waqf* [q.v.]).

badal (P., from A.). Revenge or feud. Literally, "exchange" or "reciprocity."

barakat (F. and P., from A.). Power to confer blessings.

basmachi (T.). The Islamic and traditionalist fighters who resisted Soviet rule in

Central Asia; literally, "bandits." Originated as a term of Soviet propaganda that gradually evolved into a proper noun; some prefer *mujahidin* (q.v.).

bazgar (F.). Sharecropper. Literally, "one who has to return something."

chadri (F.). Also *chador.* Garment worn by women in accord with Islamic law or local custom to cover required parts of the body.

da'wa (A.). The call to Islam; spreading Islam through preaching.

fatwa (A.). Legal ruling issued by *'ulama* (see *'alim*).

fiqh (A.). Jurisprudence or school of jurisprudence of Islamic law (*shari'a*). Because there is no code of shari'a, Islamic judges refer to works of fiqh for precedents and arguments for cases.

geraw (P.). Mortgage.

ghulam bacha (F., partly from A.). Slave bureaucrats, like *mamluks.*

hadith (A.). Precept attributed to the Prophet Muhammad; source of Islamic law.

hajj (A.). Islamic pilgrimage to Mecca.

hamsaya (F., partly from A.). Client; literally, "co-shadow," or one who sits under the same tree.

hasht nafari (F., partly from A.). A form of conscription in which one of eight young men is drafted; literally, "eight person."

hijab (A.). Garment worn by women in accord with Islamic law to cover required parts of the body; also the requirement of veiling. From a root meaning "to hide" or "to separate."

hojra (P.). Guest house.

imam (A.). Leader of any Islamic community, from the entire *umma* to a group at prayer (the imam of a mosque is the prayer leader). In Shi'ism, imams are the descendants of Muhammad through 'Ali, who constituted the legitimate rulers of the Islamic community.

jahiliyya (A.). The pre-Islamic state of "ignorance"—the literal meaning—or barbarism; used by modern Islamists to refer to societies not under Islamic rule.

jarib (F., from A.). Unit of area traditionally equal to 1,952 square meters; defined by modern legislation as 2,000 square meters or one-fifth of a hectare.

jihad (A.). Effort or struggle in defense of Islam or aimed at spreading Islam; in some contexts, refers specifically to armed struggle.

jirga (P., from T.). A tribal or clan council; literally, "circle," denoting the equality of participants.

kafir (A.). Non-Muslim, unbeliever; literally, "denier."

karez (P.). Underground gravity-fed irrigation canal.

khan (P. and F., from T.). A socially recognized leader of a *qawm.*

khan khel (P., from T. and A.). Lineage of chiefs.

landai (P.). Genre of Pashto poetry, composed mainly by women.

lashkar (P.). Army, especially a tribal army.

Loya Jirga (P.). Great Council; highest representative institution in the Afghan state.

madrasa (A.). School for secondary or advanced Islamic studies.

mahalli (F., from A.). Local; a type of military or paramilitary unit developed by both the DRA/R.A. and Massoud.

mahr (A.). Gift of precious metal given to a bride as security. Required by Islamic law.

maktab (A.). Elementary school.

malik (F. and P., from A.). Chief of a tribe or clan, usually one appointed by the state, as opposed to a *khan*. Literally, "ruler." In some contexts can mean "owner" or "boss."

mamluk (A.). Military and bureaucratic slaves, usually of Turkish origin, who became rulers of several dynasties in the Middle East. The mamluk model of ruling through a slave bureaucracy was a premodern alternative to ruling through the ruler's cotribesmen.

markaz (P. and F., from A.). *Mujahidin* base, Pashto equivalent of *qarargah;* literally, "center."

mawlawi (F. and P., from A., literally, "my master"). *'Alim;* originally a term of address.

mazar (F. and P., from A.). Monument built over the tomb of an important figure; literally, "place of pilgrimage," but distinct from *hajj.*

melmastia (P.). Hospitality, especially feeding guests.

mihman khana (F., partly from A.). Guest house.

mir (F., from A.). Lord or ruler, especially of Hazaras, derived from the Arabic *amir.*

mirab (F., partly from A.). Village official responsible for distribution of irrigation water (literally, "water master").

mujahidin (A., sing. *mujahid*). A mujahid is one engaged in *jihad* (q.v.); armed fighters of the Islamic resistance parties in Afghanistan were termed mujahidin.

mullah (F. and P., from A.). In Afghanistan, a village-level religious leader; in Iran, can denote higher clergy as well.

murid (F. and P., from A.). Follower of a *pir.*

mutaharik (F., from A.). Mobile; used to describe a type of military unit developed by Massoud.

namus (F. and P., from A.). Law, principle, honor; those things a man must defend to preserve his honor. May derive from the Greek *nomos,* "law."

nanawati (P.). Offer of refuge, especially from *badal.*

nang (P.). Honor; an egalitarian type of Pashtun or other tribal society where disputes are regulated by *badal*. According to a Pashtun proverb, "Honor [nang] ate up the mountains; taxes [*qalang* (q.v.)] ate up the plains."

operatifi (Russian). Paramilitary groups; same as *watanparast.*

pardah (F.). Seclusion or separation of women from men; literally, "curtain."

Pashtunwali (P.). The Pashtun tribal code.

pir (F. and P.). Sufi master; literally, "elder."

Pishahangan (F.). Pioneers; children's organization modeled on Soviet Pioneers.

pishkhidmat (F., partly from A.). A type of state employee under Amir Abdul Rahman Khan; literally, "attendant."

qaba'il (F., from A., sing. *qabila*). Tribes; in Afghanistan, refers to small tribes on either side of the Durand Line.

qalang (P.). Tribute, taxes, or rent. A hierarchical type of Pashtun or other tribal society where leaders (*khans*) create patronage networks by redistributing tribute. Compare *nang*.

qanat (F., from A.). Irrigation canal.

qarargah (F., partly A.). Military base of *mujahidin;* literally, "resting place."

qawm (F. and P., from A., pl. *aqwam*). A group united by a norm of solidarity within the group and by competition with parallel groups. Depending on context, can refer to tribe, clan, ethnic group, regional group, or professional caste. Afghan equivalent of *'asabiyya*.

qazi (A.). Islamic judge.

riyasat (F., from A.). Directorate, as in KhAD.

ruhani (F., partly from A.). In Afghanistan, denotes a leader of a large Sufi order; in Iran, denotes any of the higher clergy; literally, "spiritual leader."

sardar (F.). Chief or military commander; in Afghanistan, used especially for Muhammadzais.

sayyid (P. and F., from A., pl. *sadat*). Member of a group claiming descent from the Prophet Muhammad by his daughter Fatima and his cousin and son-in-law 'Ali. Literally, "lord" or "master."

shari'a (A.). Islamic law; literally, the "way."

shura (A.). Consultation, or a council; a principle or institution of Islamic government.

sunna (A.). Practice of the Prophet Muhammad; source of Islamic law.

takfir (A.). Excommunication; declaring a nominal Muslim to be an unbeliever (*kafir*); used against political enemies by the most radical Islamists, in accord with teachings of Sayyid Qutb.

tanzim (F. and P., from A.). Organization; refers to *mujahidin* parties in Peshawar.

tarbur (P.). Cousin, especially agnatic first cousin.

tariqa (A., pl. *turuq*). Sufi order or brotherhood; literally, "path."

'ulama (A., sing. *'alim*).

uluswali (P.). Administrative district; administered by an *uluswal*.

umma (A.). The community of all Muslims.

'ushr (A.). Islamic tithe, levied on certain types of income.

uymaq (T.). A type of Turkish chieftancy used for indirect rule by the Safavids.

wali (P., from A.). Governor of a province (*wilayat*).

waqf (A., pl. *awqaf*). Religious endowment or foundation.

watan (F. and P., from A.). Homeland; national or tribal. The object of patriotism.

watanparast (F., partly from A.). Literally, "patriot"; paramilitary forces of
DRA/R.A., same as *operatifi*.

zakat (A.). Islamic tax, equal to 2.5 percent of wealth.

zan, zar, zamin (F.). Woman, gold, land; central elements of *namus* and the source
of disputes.

Bibliography

Books and Articles

Abrahamian, Ervand. "The Guerrilla Movement in Iran, 1963–1977." *MERIP Reports,* no. 86 (March–April 1980):3–15.

Adamec, Ludwig W. *Afghanistan, 1900–1923: A Diplomatic History.* Berkeley: University of California Press, 1967.

———. *Afghanistan's Foreign Affairs to the Mid-Twentieth Century: Relations with the USSR, Germany and Britain.* Tucson: University of Arizona Press, 1974.

———. *A Biographical Dictionary of Contemporary Afghanistan.* Graz, Austria: Akademische Druck- und Verlagsanstalt, 1987.

Ahady, Anwar-ul-Haq. "Afghanistan: State Breakdown." In *Revolutions of the Late Twentieth Century,* edited by Jack A. Goldstone, Ted Robert Gurr, and Farrokh Moshiri, 162–93. Boulder: Westview, 1991.

Ahmad, Aziz. *Studies in Islamic Culture in the Indian Environment.* Oxford: Oxford University Press, 1964.

Ahmed, Akbar S. *Millennium and Charisma among Pathans: A Critical Essay in Social Anthropology.* London: Routledge and Kegan Paul, 1976.

———. *Pukhtun Economy and Society: Traditional Structure and Economic Development in a Tribal Society.* London: Routledge and Kegan Paul, 1980.

———. *Religion and Politics in Muslim Society: Order and Conflict in Pakistan.* Cambridge: Cambridge University Press, 1983.

Ahmed, Akbar S., and David M. Hart, eds. *Islam in Tribal Societies: From the Atlas to the Indus.* London: Routlege and Kegan Paul, 1984.

Akhramovich, Roman T. *Outline History of Afghanistan after the Second World War.* Moscow: USSR Academy of Sciences, 1966.

Alavi, Hamza. "The State in Post-Colonial Societies: Pakistan and Bangladesh." In *Imperialism and Revolution in South Asia,* edited by Kathleen Gough and Hari P. Sharma, 145–73. New York: Monthly Review, 1973. [Originally published in *New Left Review,* no. 74 (July–August 1972):59–81.

Allan, Pierre, and Albert A. Stahel. "Tribal Guerrilla Warfare Against a Colonial Power." *Journal of Conflict Resolution* 27 (December 1983):590–617.

Amin, A. Rasul. "The Sovietization of Afghanistan." In *Great Game Revisited,* edited by Klass, 301–34.

Amstutz, J. Bruce. *Afghanistan: The First Five Years of Soviet Occupation.* Washington, D.C.: National Defense University Press, 1986.

Anderson, Benedict. *Imagined Communities: Reflections on the Origin and Spread of Nationalism.* Rev. ed. London: Verso, 1991.

Anderson, Jon W. "Tribe and Community among the Ghilzai Pashtun: Preliminary Notes on Ethnographic Distribution and Variation in Eastern Afghanistan." *Anthropos* 70 (1975):575–601.

———. "There Are No Khans Anymore: Economic Development and Social Change in Tribal Afghanistan." *Middle East Journal* 3 (1978):167–83.

———. "Cousin Marriage in Context: The Construction of Social Religion in Afghanistan." *Folk* 24 (1982):7–28.

———. "Khan and Khel: Dialectics of Pashtun Tribalism." In *Conflict of Tribe and State,* edited by R. Tapper, 119–49.

———. "How Afghans Define Themselves in Relation to Islam." In *Revolutions and Rebellions,* edited by Shahrani and Canfield, 266–88.

Anderson, Jon W., and Richard F. Strand, eds. *Ethnic Processes and Intergroup Relations in Contemporary Afghanistan.* Asia Society Afghanistan Council Occasional Paper, no. 15. New York: Asia Society, 1978.

Anderson, Lisa. *The State and Social Transformation in Tunisia and Libya, 1830–1980.* Princeton: Princeton University Press, 1986.

———. "The State in the Middle East and North Africa." *Comparative Politics* 20 (1987):1–18.

Ansari, Hamied N. "The Islamic Militants in Egyptian Politics." *International Journal of Middle Eastern Studies* 16 (1984):123–44.

Anthony, Ian, Agnès Courades Allebeck, Gerd Hagmeyer-Gaverns, Paolo Miggiano, and Herbert Wulf. "The Trade in Major Conventional Weapons." In *SIPRI Yearbook 1991: World Armaments and Disarmament,* 197–279. Oxford: Oxford University Press, 1991.

Anwar, Raja. *The Tragedy of Afghanistan: A First-Hand Account.* Translated from the Urdu by Khalid Hasan. London: Verso, 1988.

Arjomand, Said. *The Shadow of God and the Hidden Imam: Religion, Political Order, and Societal Change in Shi'ite Iran from the Beginning to 1890.* Chicago: University of Chicago Press, 1984.

———. *The Turban for the Crown: The Islamic Revolution in Iran.* New York: Oxford University Press, 1988.

Arnold, Anthony. *Afghanistan's Two-Party Communism: Parcham and Khalq.* Stanford, Calif.: Hoover Institution, 1983.

———. "The Ephemeral Elite: The Failure of Socialist Afghanistan." In *State and Social Transformation,* edited by Banuazizi and Weiner, 35–71.

Ashrati, Abdul Ahad. "Soviet Influence on the Afghan Judiciary." In *Decade of Sovietisation,* edited by Elmi, 22–55.

Attaul Haq and Zalmay Tookhi. "Interview with an Ex-Minister." *Mujahideen Monthly* 4, no. 1 (January 1990):25.

Azarya, Victor. "Reordering State-Society Relations: Incorporation and Disengagement." In *Precarious Balance,* edited by Rothchild and Chazan, 3–21.

Azarya, Victor, and Naomi Chazan. "Disengagement from the State in Africa: Reflections on the Experience of Ghana and Guinea." *Comparative Studies in Society and History* 29 (1987):106–31.

Badie, Bertrand, and Pierre Birnbaum. *The Sociology of the State.* Translated by Arthur Goldhammer. Chicago: University of Chicago Press, 1983.

Bahl, R. W. "A Regresssion Approach to Tax Effort and Tax Ratio Analysis." *International Monetary Fund Staff Papers,* no. 18 (November 1971):570–612.

Banuazizi, Ali, and Myron Weiner, eds. *The State, Religion and Ethnic Politics: Afghanistan, Iran and Pakistan.* Syracuse: Syracuse University Press, 1986.

———. *The State and Social Transformation in Afghanistan, Iran and Pakistan.* Syracuse: Syracuse University Press, 1994.

Bardhan, Pranab. *The Political Economy of Development in India.* Oxford: Basil Blackwell, 1984.

Barfield, Thomas J. *The Central Asian Arabs of Afghanistan: Pastoral Nomadism in Transition.* Austin: University of Texas Press, 1981.

———. "Links on a Rusty Chain: Structural Weaknesses in Afghanistan's Provincial Government Administration." In *Revolutions and Rebellions,* edited by Shahrani and Canfield, 170–83.

———. "Tribe and State Relations: The Inner Asian Perspective." In *Tribes and State Formation,* edited by Khoury and Kostiner, 153–84.

Barkey, Karen, and Sunita Parikh. "Comparative Perspectives on the State." *Annual Review of Sociology* 17 (1991):523–49.

Barry, Michael. "Repression et guerre soviétiques." *Les temps modernes* 36 (July–August 1980):171–234.

———. *Le royaume de l'insolence: La résistance afghane du Grand Moghol à l'invasion soviétique.* Paris: Flammarion, 1984.

Barth, Fredrik. *Political Leadership among Swat Pathans.* London School of Economics Monographs on Social Anthropology, no. 19. London: Athlone, 1959.

Bazgar, Shah, with Régis Guyotat. *Afghanistan: La résistance au coeur.* Paris: Denoël, 1987.

Beattie, Hugh. "Kinship and Ethnicity in the Nahrin Area of Northern Afghanistan." *Afghan Studies* 3–4 (1982):39–51.

———. "Effects of the Saur Revolution in the Nahrin Area of Northern Afghanistan." In *Revolutions and Rebellions,* edited by Shahrani and Canfield, 184–208.

Beblawi, Hazem. "The Rentier State in the Arab World." In *Arab State,* edited by Luciani, 85–98.

Beblawi, Hazem, and Giacomo Luciani, eds. *Nation, State, and Integration in the Arab World.* Vol. 2, *The Rentier State.* London: Croom Helm, 1987.

Borovik, Artem. "Afghanistan: Preliminary Results—Ogonyok Correspondent Artem Borovik Interviews Maj. Gen. Kim Tsagolov, Doctor of Philosophy and Chairman of the Department of Marxism-Leninism at the M. V. Frunze Military Academy." *Ogonyok* (July 23–30, 1988):25–27.

Bradsher, Henry S. *Afghanistan and the Soviet Union.* Durham: Duke University Press, 1983.

Callaghy, Thomas M. *The State-Society Struggle: Zaire in Comparative Perspective.* New York: Columbia University Press, 1984.

———. "External Actors and the Relative Autonomy of the Political Aristocracy in Zaire." In *State and Class,* edited by Kasfir, 61–83.

———. "The State and the Development of Capitalism in Africa: Theoretical, Historical, and Comparative Reflections." In *Precarious Balance,* edited by Rothchild and Chazan, 67–99.

Canfield, Robert Leroy. *Faction and Conversion: Religious Alignments in the Hindu Kush.* Anthropological Papers, no. 50. Ann Arbor: University of Michigan Museum of Anthropology, 1973.

———. "Islamic Coalitions in Bamyan: A Problem in Translating Afghan Political Culture." In *Revolutions and Rebellions,* edited by Shahrani and Canfield, 211–29.

———. "Ethnic, Regional and Sectarian Alignments in Afghanistan." In *State, Religion and Ethnic Politics,* edited by Banuazizi and Weiner, 75–103.

———. "Afghanistan: The Trajectory of Internal Alignments." *Middle East Journal* 43 (Autumn 1989):635–48.

———, ed. *Turko-Persia in Historical Perspective.* Cambridge: Cambridge University Press, 1991.

Caroe, Olaf. *The Pathans*. Oxford: Oxford University Press, 1958.

Carrère d'Encausse, Hélène, and Stuart Schram. *Le marxisme et l'Asie*. Paris: A. Colin, 1965.

Centlivres, Pierre. *Un bazaar d'Asie centrale: Forme et organisation du bazaar de Tashqurghan (Afghanistan)*. Wiesbaden: Dr. Ludwig Reichert, 1972.

Centlivres, Pierre, and Micheline Centlivres-Demont. "La société afghane, structures et valeurs." In *Colonisation impossible*, edited by Centlivres-Demont et al., 57–80.

———. *Et si on parlait de l'Afghanistan? Terrains et textes 1964–1980*. Neuchâtel: Editions de l'Institut d'Ethnologie; Paris: Editions de la Maison des Sciences de l'Homme, 1988.

Centlivres-Demont, Micheline. "Types d'occupations et relations interethiques dans le nord-est de l'Afghanistan." *Studia Iranica* 5 (1976):269–77.

Centlivres-Demont, Micheline, Pierre Centlivres, Bernard Dupaigne, Etienne Gille, Alain Marigo, Jacky Mathonnat, Jean-José Puig, Gilles Rossignol, and Olivier Roy, eds. *Afghanistan: La colonisation impossible*. Paris: Cerf, 1984.

Chaffetz, David. *A Journey through Afghanistan: A Memorial*. Chicago: University of Chicago Press, 1981.

Charnay, Jean-Paul. *L'islam et la guerre: De la guerre juste à la révolution sainte*. Paris: Fayard, 1986.

Chaudhry, Kirin Aziz. "The Price of Wealth: Business and State in Labor Remittance and Oil Economies." *International Organization* 43 (1989):101–45.

Cobban, Helena. *The Palestine Liberation Organisation: People, Power and Politics*. Cambridge: Cambridge University Press, 1984.

Cole, Juan R. I., and Nikki R. Keddie, eds. *Shiʿism and Social Protest*. New Haven: Yale University Press, 1986.

Cronin, Richard. "Afghanistan After the Soviet Withdrawal: Contenders for Power." Washington, D.C.: Congressional Research Service, May 1989.

Dadfar, Muhammad Azam. "Victims of Torture in Afghanistan." In *Decade of Sovietisation*, edited by Elmi, 141–58.

Dahl, Robert A. *Polyarchy: Participation and Opposition*. New Haven: Yale University Press, 1971.

Davis, Anthony. "The Afghan Army." *Jane's Intelligence Review* 5, no. 3 (March 1993):134–39. Reproduced in *Afghanistan Forum* 21, no. 3 (May–June 1993):25–29.

Davydov, A. D. "The Rural Commune in the Tadzhik Areas of Afghanistan." *Central Asian Review* 8 (1965):121–30.

Delacroix, Jacques. "The Distributive State in the World System." *Studies in Comparative International Development* 15 (1980):3–21.

Dorronsoro, Gilles. "La situation politique au Badakhchân." *Les Nouvelles d'Afghanistan*, no. 56 (April–June 1992):6–8.

Dupree, Louis. "The Political Uses of Religion: Afghanistan." In *Churches and States: The Religious Institutions and Modernization*, edited by Kalman H. Silvert, 195–214. New York: American University Field Service, 1967.

———. "Red Flag over the Hindu Kush." Part 2, "The Accidental Coup or Taraki in Blunderland." *American Universities Field Services Reports, Asia*, no. 23. New York: American Universities Field Services, 1979.

———. "Red Flag over the Hindu Kush." Part 5, "Repressions, or Security through Terror Purges I–IV." *American Universities Field Services Reports, Asia*, no. 28. New York: American Universities Field Services, 1980.

———. "Red Flag over the Hindu Kush." Part 6, "Repressions, or Security through Terror." *American Universities Field Services Reports, Asia*, no. 29. New York: American Universities Field Services, 1980.

———. *Afghanistan*. Princeton: Princeton University Press, 1980. [First edition 1973.]

———. "The Marxist Regimes and the Soviet Presence in Afghanistan: An Ages-Old Culture Responds to Late Twentieth-Century Aggression." In *Revolutions and Rebellions*, edited by Shahrani and Canfield, 58–74.

———. "Tribal Warfare in Afghanistan and Pakistan: A Reflection of the Segmentary Lineage System." In *Islam in Tribal Societies*, edited by Ahmed and Hart, 266–86.

Dupree, Louis, and Linette Albert, eds. *Afghanistan in the 1970s*. New York: Praeger, 1974.

Eberhard, Wolfram. "Afghanistan's Young Elite." *Asian Survey* 1, no. 2 (February 1962):3–22.

Edwards, David Busby. "Marginality and Migration: Cultural Dimensions of the Afghan Refugee Problem." *International Migration Review* 20, no. 2 (1986):313–25.

———. "The Evolution of Shi'i Political Dissent in Afghanistan." In *Shi'ism and Social Protest*, edited by Cole and Keddie, 201–29.

Eisenstadt, S. N. *The Political Systems of Empires*. New York: Free Press, 1969. [First edition 1963.]

Elmi, Sayed Muhammad Yusuf. "The Impact of Sovietization on Afghan Education and Culture." In *Sovietization of Afghanistan*, edited by Majrooh and Elmi, 71–125.

Elmi, Sayed Muhammad Yusuf, ed. *Afghanistan: A Decade of Sovietisation*. Peshawar: Aghan Jehad Works Translation Centre, 1988.

Elphinstone, Montstuart. *An Account of the Kingdom of Caubul and Its Dependencies in Persia, Tartary, and India. . . .* Karachi: Oxford University Press, 1972. [First edition, 1815.]

Emadi, Hafizullah. *State, Revolution, and Superpowers in Afghanistan*. New York: Praeger, 1990.

Es'haq, Mohammad. *From Theory to Practice*. Peshawar: Political Office of Jamiat Islami Afghanistan, September 1986.

———. *Situation in the North of Afghanistan, 1987*. Peshawar: Political Office of Jamiat Islami Afghanistan, 1987.

———. "Evolution of the Islamic Movement in Afghanistan." Part 1, "Islamists Felt Need for a Party to Defend Islam." *AfghaNews* 5 (January 1, 1989):5, 8.

———. "Evolution of the Islamic Movement in Afghanistan." Part 2, "Daud's Hostile Attitude towards Islamists Led to Confrontation." *AfghaNews* 5 (January 15, 1989):5–6.

———. "Evolution of the Islamic Movement in Afghanistan." Part 3, "Panjshir Uprising of 1975." *AfghaNews* 5 (February 1, 1989):6–7.

———. "Evolution of the Islamic Movement in Afghanistan." Part 4, "Life in Exile from 1975 to 1978." *AfghaNews* 5 (February 15, 1989):6.

Etienne, Bruno. *L'islamisme radical*. Paris: Hachette, 1987.

Etienne, Gilbert. *L'Afghanistan, ou les aléas de la coopération*. Paris: Presses Universitaires de France, 1972.

Evans, Peter. "Predatory, Developmental, and Other Apparatuses: A Comparative Political Economy Perspective on the Third World State." *Sociological Forum* 4 (1989):561–87.

Evans, Peter B., Dietrich Rueschemeyer, and Theda Skocpol, eds. *Bringing the State Back In*. Cambridge: Cambridge University Press, 1985.

Fatton, Robert Jr. "Bringing the Ruling Class Back In." *Comparative Politics* 20 (1988):253–65.

Fazelly, Mohammad Kacem. "La Loya Djirga." Paris: Centre de recherches et d'etudes documentaires sur l'Afghanistan, [1988?].

Ferdinand, Klaus. "Nomad Expansion and Commerce in Central Afghanistan: A Sketch of Some Trends." *Folk* 4 (1962):123–59.

Fröhlich, Dieter. *Nationalismus und Nationalstaat in Entiwicklungsländer: Probleme des Integration ethnisches Gruppen in Afghanistan*. Meisenheim am Glam: Anton Hain, 1970.

Fry, Maxwell J. *The Afghan Economy: Money, Finance, and the Critical Constraints to Economic Development*. Leiden: E. J. Brill, 1974.

Fukuyama, Francis. "A New Soviet Strategy." *Commentary* 68 (October 1979):52–58.

———. "Patterns of Soviet Third World Policy." *Problems of Communism* 36 (September–October 1987):1–13.

———. *The End of History and the Last Man.* New York: Basic Books, 1990.

Fullerton, John. *The Soviet Occupation of Afghanistan.* Hong Kong: Far Eastern Economic Review, 1983.

"Fundamentalism in Islam." *The Front* 1, no. 6 (March–April 1988):4–5.

Gall, Sandy. *Behind Russian Lines: An Afghan Journal.* London: Sidgwick and Jackson, 1983.

Gankovsky, Yuri. "The Durrani Empire: Taxes and Tax System, State Incomes and Expenditures." In *Afghanistan Past and Present,* edited by Social Sciences Today Editorial Board, 76–98.

Gankovsky, Yuri V., M. R. Arunova, V. G. Korgun, V. M. Masson, G. A. Muradov, G. A. Polyakov, and V. A. Romodin. *A History of Afghanistan.* Translated by Vitaly Basakov. Moscow: Progress Publishers, 1985. [Russian edition, 1982.]

Gellner, Ernest. *Muslim Society.* Cambridge Studies in Social Anthropology, no. 32. Cambridge: Cambridge University Press, 1981.

———. *Nations and Nationalism.* Ithaca: Cornell University Press, 1983.

———. "Tribalism and the State in the Middle East." In *Tribes and State Formation,* edited by Khoury and Kostiner, 109–26.

Gerber, Haim. *Islam, Guerrilla War and Revolution: A Study in Comparative Social History.* Boulder: Lynne Rienner, 1988.

Ghani, Ashraf. "Islam and State-Building in a Tribal Society: Afghanistan 1880–1901." *Modern Asian Studies* 12 (1978):269–84.

———. "Conjunctures of State, Economy, and Ideology in Afghanistan, 1950–1978." Paper presented at the Conference on Social Movements in the Contemporary Near and Middle East, Columbia University, New York, 1980.

———. "Afghanistan." Part 11, "Administration." In *Encylopaedia Iranica,* edited by Ehsan Yarshater, 1:558–64. London: Routledge and Kegan Paul, 1981.

———. "Disputes in a Court of Sharia, Kunar Valley, Afghanistan, 1885–1890." *International Journal of Middle East Studies* 15 (1983):353–67.

Giddens, Anthony. *The Nation-State and Violence: Volume Two of a Contemporary Critique of Historical Materialism.* Berkeley: University of California Press, 1987.

Gille, Etienne. "L'accession au pouvoir des communistes prosoviétiques." In *Colonisation impossible,* edited by Centlivres-Demont et al., 179–212.

Girardet, Edward. *Afghanistan: The Soviet War.* New York: St. Martin's, 1985.

Glatzer, Bernt. "Political Organization of Pashtun Nomads and the State." In *Conflict of Tribe and State,* edited by R. Tapper, 212–32.

Glaubitt, Klaus, Fawzi Saadeddin, Bernd Schäfer, and Jürgen Kaune. *Das System der Staatseinnahmen und seine Bedeutung für die Wirtschaftsentwicklung Afghanistans.* Afghanische Studien, no. 10. Meisenheim am Glan: Anton Hain, 1975.

Glukhoded, Vladimir. "Economy of Independent Afghanistan." In *Afghanistan Past and Present,* edited by Social Sciences Today Editorial Board, 222–45.

Goodwin, Jan. *Caught in the Crossfire.* New York: Dutton, 1987.

Goody, Jack, and S. J. Tambiah. *Bridewealth and Dowry.* Cambridge: Cambridge University Press, 1973.

"Un gouvernement introuvable." *Défis Afghans* (February–June 1988):14–15.

Greenstein, Fred, and Nelson Polsby, eds. *The Handbook of Political Science.* Reading, Mass.: Addison-Wesley, 1975.

Gregorian, Vartan. *The Emergence of Modern Afghanistan: Politics of Reform and Modernization, 1880–1946.* Stanford: Stanford University Press, 1969.

Guha, Amalendhu. "The Economy of Afghanistan during Amanullah's Reign, 1919–1929." *International Studies* 9 (1967–68):161–82.

Gupta, Bhabani Sen. *Afghanistan Politics, Economics and Society: Revolution, Resistance, Intervention.* London: Francis Pinter, 1986.

Gurevich, A. *Afghanistan.* Second edition. Moscow: USSR Academy of Sciences, 1930.

Hager, Rob. "State, Tribe and Empire in Afghan Inter-Polity Relations." In *Conflict of Tribe and State,* edited by R. Tapper, 83–118.

Hall, John A., ed. *States in History.* Oxford: Basil Blackwell, 1986.

Halliday, Fred. "Revolution in Afghanistan." *New Left Review,* no. 112 (November–December 1978):3–44.

———. "War and Revolution in Afghanistan." *New Left Review,* no. 119 (January–February 1980):20–41.

Harrison, Selig S. "The Shah, Not Kremlin, Touched Off Afghan Coup." *Washington Post,* May 13, 1979, p. C1.

———. "Dateline Afghanistan: Exit Through Finland?" *Foreign Policy,* no. 41 (Winter 1980–81):163–87.

———. *In Afghanistan's Shadow: Baluch Nationalism and Soviet Temptations.* New York: Carnegie Endowment for International Peace, 1981.

———. "Inside the Afghan Talks." *Foreign Policy,* no. 72 (Fall 1988):31–60.

Hobsbawm, Eric, and Terence Ranger, eds. *The Invention of Tradition.* Cambridge: Cambridge University Press, 1983.

Hough, Jerry. *The Struggle for the Third World: Soviet Debates and American Options.* Washington, D.C.: Brookings, 1986.

Hourani, Albert. *Arabic Thought in the Liberal Age, 1798–1939.* Oxford: Oxford University Press, 1970.

———. "Conclusion: Tribes and States in Islamic History." In *Tribes and State Formation,* edited by Khoury and Kostiner, 303–11.

Huldt, Bo, and Erland Jansson, eds. *The Tragedy of Afghanistan: The Social, Cultural and Political Impact of the Soviet Invasion.* London: Croom Helm, 1988.

Hussain, Mushahid. "The Road to Central Asia." *Newsline* (November 1992):56–58.

Hyman, Anthony. *Afghanistan under Soviet Domination, 1964–83.* London: Macmillan, 1984. [First edition, 1982.]

———, ed., *Propaganda Posters of the Afghan Resistance.* Incidental Papers Series, no. 3. *Central Asian Survey* (January 1985).

Ibn Khaldûn, Abdul Rahman. *The Muqaddimah: An Introduction to History.* Translated by Franz Rosenthal; abridged and edited by N. J. Dawood. Princeton: Princeton University Press, 1967.

Ibrahim, Saad Eddin. "Anatomy of Egypt's Militant Islamic Groups: Methodological Note and Preliminary Findings." *International Journal of Middle East Studies* 12 (1980):423–53.

International Institute of Strategic Studies. *The Military Balance, 1991–1992.* London: Brassey's, 1991.

Ispahani, Mahnaz Z. *Roads and Rivals: The Struggle for Access in the Borderlands of Southwest Asia.* Ithaca: Cornell University Press, 1989.

Jackson, Robert H., and Carl G. Rosberg. "Why Africa's Weak States Persist: The Empirical and Juridical in Statehood." *World Politics* 35 (October 1982):1–24.

Jones, Schuyler. *Men of Influence in Nuristan: A Study of Social Control and Dispute Settlement in Waigal Valley, Afghanistan.* London: Seminar, 1974.

Kakar, Hasan Kawun. *Afghanistan: A Study in Internal Political Developments, 1880–1896.* Lahore: Punjab Educational Press, 1971.

————. "The Fall of the Afghan Monarchy in 1973." *International Journal of Middle East Studies* 9 (1978):195–214.

————. *Government and Society in Afghanistan: The Reign of Amir Abd al-Rahman Khan.* Austin: University of Texas Press, 1981.

————. "Afghanistan: The Soviet Invasion and the Afghan Response." San Diego, 1992.

Karl, Terry Lynn. "Petroleum and Political Pacts: The Transition to Democracy in Venezuela." In *Transitions from Authoritarian Rule: Latin America,* edited by Guillermo O'Donnell, Philippe C. Schmitter, and Laurence Whitehead, 196–220. Baltimore: Johns Hopkins University Press, 1986.

Kasfir, Nelson, ed. *State and Class in Africa.* London: Frank Cass, 1984.

Katz, David J. "Responses to Central Authority in Nuristan: The Case of the Väygal Valley Kalasha." In *Revolutions and Rebellions,* edited by Shahrani and Canfield, 94–118.

Keegan, John. "The Amazon of Peshawar." *Atlantic Monthly* 257 (April 1986):18.

Keiser, R. Lincoln. "The Rebellion in Darra-i Nur." In *Revolutions and Rebellions,* edited by Shahrani and Canfield, 119–35.

"Le KGB et le conflit Khalq-Partcham: Le témoignage d'Alexandre Morozov." *Les nouvelles d'Afghanistan* 13 (January–March 1992):16–18.

Khalidi, Noor Ahmad. "Afghanistan: Demographic Consequences of War, 1978–1987." *Central Asian Survey* 10 (1991):101–26.

Khalili, Khalilullah. *Nahid va Dukhtaran-i Qahraman-i Kabul [Nahid and the Heroic Girls of Kabul].* N.p.: Haqq-i Chap Mahfuz, 1983.

Khalilzad, Zalmay. "The Politics of Ethnicity in Southwest Asia: Political Development or Political Decay?" *Political Science Quarterly* 99 (Winter 1984–85):657–79.

Khan, Riaz Mohammad. *Untying the Afghan Knot: Negotiating Soviet Withdrawal.* Durham: Duke University Press, 1991.

Khoury, Philip S., and Joseph Kostiner, eds. *Tribes and State Formation in the Middle East.* Berkeley: University of California Press, 1990.

Kipling, Rudyard. *Complete Verse: Definitive Edition.* New York: Doubleday, 1989.

Klass, Rosanne, ed. *Afghanistan: The Great Game Revisited.* New York: Freedom House, 1987.

Knabe, Erika. *Frauenemanzipation in Afghanistan.* Afghanische Studien, no. 16. Meisenheim am Glan: Anton Hain, 1977.

————. "Women in the Social Stratification of Afghanistan." In *Commoners, Climbers and Notables,* edited by van Nieuwenhuijze, 329–43.

Kohli, Atul. *The State and Poverty in India: The Politics of Reform.* Cambridge: Cambridge University Press, 1987.

Kundera, Milan. *The Unbearable Lightness of Being.* Translated by Michael Henry Heim. New York: Harper and Row, 1984.

Laber, Jeri, and Barnett Rubin. *"A Nation Is Dying": Afghanistan Under the Soviets, 1979–1987.* Evanston: Northwestern University Press, 1988.

Lapidus, Ira, M. "Tribes and State Formation in Islamic History." In *Tribes and State Formation,* edited by Khoury and Kostiner, 25–47.

Lifschultz, Lawrence. "Pakistan: The Empire of Heroin." In *War on Drugs: Studies in the Failure of U.S. Narcotics Policy,* edited by Alfred W. McCoy and Alan A. Block, 319–58. Boulder: Westview, 1992.

————. "Pakistan Was Iran-Contra's Secret Back Door." *Sunday Times of India,* November 24, 1991.

Linz, Juan J. "Totalitarian and Authoritarian Regimes." In *Handbook of Political Science,* edited by Greenstein and Polsby, 3:175–411.

Lorentz, John. "Anatomy of an Entanglement: Afghanistan and Iran." Paper presented to the Conference on the Afghanistan Legacy, University of Texas, Austin, October 19–20, 1989.

Luciani, Giacomo. "Allocation vs. Production States: A Theoretical Framework." In *Rentier State,* edited by Beblawi and Luciani, 49–82.

———, ed. *The Arab State.* Berkeley: University of California Press, 1990.

Magnus, Ralph H., ed. *Afghan Alternatives: Issues, Options, and Policies.* New Brunswick, N.J.: Transaction Books, 1985.

Mahdavi, Hossein T. "The Pattern and Problems of Economic Development in Rentier States: The Case of Iran." In *Studies in the Economic History of the Middle East,* edited by Michael Cook, 428–67. Oxford: Oxford University Press, 1970.

Majrooh, Sayd Bahauddin. "Past and Present Education in Afghanistan: A Problem for the Future." In *Tragedy of Afghanistan,* edited by Huldt and Jansson, 75–92.

Majrooh, Sayed Bahauddin, and Sayed Muhammad Yusuf Elmi, eds. *The Sovietization of Afghanistan.* Peshawar: n.p., 1986.

Male, Beverly. *Revolutionary Afghanistan: A Reappraisal.* London: Croom Helm, 1982.

Mann, Michael. "The Autonomous Power of the State: Its Origins, Mechanisms and Results." In *States in History,* edited by Hall, 109–36.

Marenin, Otwin. "The Nigerian State as Process and Manager: A Conceptualization." *Comparative Politics* 20 (1988):215–32.

Masstan, Mehrabodin. " 'Nous, les femmes afghanes,' entretien avec T. Kakar." *Défis Afghans* 14 (May–July 1987):12.

Mathonnat, Jacky. "Une économie impulsée de l'extérieur." In *Colonisation impossible,* edited by Centlivres-Demont et al., 143–78.

McLuhan, Marshall. *Understanding Media: The Extensions of Man.* New York: New American Library, 1964.

McNeill, William H. *The Pursuit of Power: Technology, Armed Force and Society since A.D. 1000.* Chicago: University of Chicago Press, 1982.

Metge, Pierre. *L'URSS en Afghanistan: De la coopération à l'occupation, 1947–1984.* Cahiers d'Etudes Stratégiques 7. Paris: Centre Interdisciplinaire de Recherches sur la Paix et d'Etudes Stratégiques. 1984.

Migdal, Joel S. *Strong Societies and Weak States: State-Society Relations and State Capabilities in the Third World.* Princeton: Princeton University Press, 1988.

Mukherjee, Sadhan. *Afghanistan: From Tragedy to Triumph.* New Delhi: Sterling, 1984.

Naby, Eden. "The Afghan Resistance Movement." In *Afghan Alternatives,* edited by Magnus, 59–81.

Nagel, J., and S. Olzak. "Ethnic Mobilization in New and Old States: An Extension of the Competition Model." *Social Problems* 30 (1982):127–43.

Najmabadi, Afsaneh. "Depoliticisation of a Rentier State: The Case of Pahlavi Iran." In *Rentier State,* edited by Beblawi and Luciani, 211–27.

Nyrop, Richard F., and Donald M. Seekins, eds. *Afghanistan: A Country Study.* Washington, D.C.: U.S. Government Printing Office, 1986.

O'Donnell, Guillermo. *Modernization and Bureaucratic-Authoritarianism: Studies in South American Politics.* Berkeley: University of California Institute of International Studies, 1973.

Ølesen, Asta. "The Musallis: The Graincleaners of East Afghanistan." *Afghanistan Journal* 9 (1982):13–19.

Olzak, S. "Contemporary Ethnic Mobilization." *Annual Review of Sociology* 9 (1983):355–74.

Peters, Rudolph. *Islam and Colonialism: The Doctrine of Jihad in Modern History.* Religion and Society, no. 20. The Hague: Mouton, 1979.

Piquard, Patrice. "Pourquoi le chaos afghan peut faire exploser l'Asie centrale." *L'événement du jeudi*, January 13, 1993.

Poullada, Leon B. *Reform and Rebellion in Afghanistan, 1919–1929*. Ithaca: Cornell University Press, 1973.

———. "Afghanistan and the United States: The Crucial Years." *Middle East Journal* 35 (Spring 1981):178–90.

———. "The Road to Crisis, 1919–1980." In *Great Game Revisited*, edited by Klass, 37–70.

Putnam, Robert D. *The Comparative Study of Political Elites*. Englewood Cliffs, N.J.: Prentice Hall, 1976.

Rae, Douglas W. *The Political Consequences of Electoral Laws*. New Haven: Yale University Press, 1971.

Rahman, Fazlur. *Islam and Modernity: Transformation of an Intellectual Tradition*. Chicago: University of Chicago Press, 1982.

Rastegar, Farshad. "Education and Revolutionary Political Mobilization: Schooling versus Uprootedness as Determinants of Islamic Political Activism among Afghan Refugee Students in Pakistan." Ph.D. thesis, University of California, Los Angeles, 1991.

Reisner, Igor. "Special Features of the Development of Feudalism among the Afghans." In *Afghanistan Past and Present*, edited by Social Sciences Today Editorial Board, 45–59.

Rothchild, D. and Naomi Chazan, eds. *The Precarious Balance: State and Society in Africa*. Boulder: Westview, 1988.

Roy, Olivier. "La 'révolution' par le vide." *Esprit* 4 (1980):78–88.

———. "La politique de pacification sur le terrain." In *La guerre d'Afghanistan*, edited by Olivier Roy and André Brigot, 65–76. Paris: Documentation française, 1984.

———. *L'Afghanistan: Islam et modernité politique*. Paris: Seuil, 1985. Translated as *Islam and Resistance in Afghanistan*. Cambridge: Cambridge University Press, 1986.

———. "Le double code afghan: Marxisme et tribalisme." *Revue française de science politique* 36 (December 1986):846–61.

———. "La guerre comme facteur du passage au politique." Paper presented at the Congrès National de l'Association Française de Science Politique, Bordeaux, October 5–8, 1988.

———. "Afghanistan: Modèles anthropologiques et pacification." *Cahiers du monde russe et soviétique* 31 (April–September 1990):405–512.

———. "Ethnies et politique en Asie centrale." In *Des ethnies aux nations en Asie centrale*. Special edition of *Revue du monde Musulman et de la méditerranée*, edited by Olivier Roy (1991), 17–36.

———. "Le facteur Massoud." *Afghanistan Info* (March 1992):7.

———. "The New Political Elite of Afghanistan." In *State and Social Transformation*, edited by Banuazizi and Weiner, 72–100.

Rubin, Barnett R. "Economic Liberalisation and the Indian State." *Third World Quarterly* 7 (1985):942–57.

———. "Human Rights in Afghanistan." In *Great Game Revisited*, edited by Klass, 335–58.

———. "Lineages of the State in Afghanistan." *Asian Survey* 28 (1988):1188–209.

———. "Afghanistan: The Next Round." *Orbis* 33 (Winter 1989):57–72.

———. "The Author Responds." *Orbis* 33 (Spring 1989):275–81.

———. "The Fragmentation of Afghanistan." *Foreign Affairs* 68 (Winter 1989–90):150–68.

———. "Afghanistan: Political Exiles in Search of a State." *Journal of Political Science* 18 (Spring 1990):63–93. Reprinted in *Governments-in-Exile*, edited by Yossi Shain, 69–91. New York: Routledge, 1991.

———. "The Old Regime in Afghanistan: Recruitment and Training of a State Elite." *Central Asian Survey* 10 (1991):73–100.

————. "Political Elites in Afghanistan: Rentier State Building, Rentier State Wrecking." *International Journal of Middle East Studies* 24 (1992):77–99.

————. "Post–Cold War State Disintegration: The Failure of International Conflict Resolution in Afghanistan." *Journal of International Affairs* 46 (Winter 1993):469–92.

————. "The Fragmentation of Tajikistan." *Survival* (Winter 1993–94):71–91.

Rudolph, Lloyd I., and Susanne Hoeber Rudolph. *In Pursuit of Lakshmi: The Political Economy of the Indian State*. Chicago: University of Chicago Press, 1987.

Rudolph, Lloyd I., and Susanne Hoeber Rudolph with Mohan Singh. "A Bureaucratic Lineage in Princely India: Elite Formation and Conflict in a Patrimonial System." *Journal of Asian Studies* 34 (May 1975):717–53.

Rueschemeyer, Dietrich, and Peter B. Evans. "The State and Economic Transformation: Toward an Analysis of the Conditions Underlying Effective Intervention." In *Bringing the State Back In*, edited by Evans, Rueschemeyer, and Skocpol, 44–77.

Rumer, Boris. *Soviet Central Asia: A Tragic Experiment*. Boston: Unwin Hyman, 1989.

Salamé, Ghassan. "'Strong' and 'Weak' States: A Qualified Return to the Muqaddimah." In *Arab State*, edited by Luciani, 29–64.

Sartori, Giovanni. *Parties and Party Systems: A Framework for Analysis*. Cambridge: Cambridge University Press, 1976.

Sawitzki, Henning. *Die Elitegruppe der Akademiker in einem Entwicklungsland Dargestellt am Beispiel Afghanistans*. Afghanische Studien, no 5. Meisenheim: Anton Hain, 1972.

Schneiter, Vincent. "La guerre de libération nationale au Nouristan." *Temps modernes* 36 (July–August 1980):237–44.

Scott, James C. *Weapons of the Weak: Everyday Forms of Peasant Resistance*. New Haven: Yale University Press, 1985.

Shahrani, M. Nazif Mohib. *The Kirghiz and Wakhi of Afghanistan: Adaptation to Closed Frontiers*. Seattle: University of Washington Press, 1979.

————. "Causes and Context of Responses to the Saur Revolution in Badakhshan." In *Revolutions and Rebellions*, edited by Shahrani and Canfield, 139–69.

————. "Introduction: Marxist 'Revolution' and Islamic Resistance in Afghanistan." In *Revolutions and Rebellions*, edited by Shahrani and Canfield, 3–57.

————. "State Building and Social Fragmentation in Afghanistan: An Historical Perspective." In *State, Religion and Ethnic Politics*, edited by Banuazizi and Weiner, 23–74.

————. "The Kirghiz Khans: Styles and Substance of Traditional Local Leadership in Central Asia." *Central Asian Survey* 5 (1986):255–71.

————. "Local Knowledge of Islam and Social Discourse in Afghanistan and Turkistan in the Modern Period." In *Turko-Persia in Historical Perspective*, edited by Canfield, 161–88.

Shahrani, M. Nazif, and Robert L. Canfield, eds. *Revolutions and Rebellions in Afghanistan: Anthropological Perspectives*. Berkeley: University of California Institute for International Studies, 1984.

Shalinsky, Audrey C. "Central Asian Emigres in Afghanistan: Problems of Religious and Ethnic Identity." Afghanistan Council Occasional Paper, no. 19. New York: Asia Society, 1979.

————. "Reason, Desire and Sexuality: The Meaning of Gender in Northern Afghanistan." *Ethos* 14 (1986):323–43.

————. "Models of Women's Roles in Jihad: Tabligh-i Jihad Tapes and Popular Discourse among Ferghanachi Uzbeks as Afghan Refugees in Pakistan." Paper presented at a meeting of the Middle East Studies Association, November 1991.

"Sheikh Abdullah Azzam Is Martyred." *Mujahideen Monthly* 4 (January 1990):10–11.

Shroder, John F., Jr. "Afghanistan Resources and Soviet Policy in Central and South Asia." In *Af-*

ghanistan and the Soviet Union: Collision and Transformation, edited by Milan Hauner and Robert L. Canfield, 101–19. Boulder: Westview, 1989.

Shroder, John F., Jr., and Abdul Tawab Assifi. "Afghan Mineral Resources and Soviet Exploitation." In Great Game Revisited, edited by Klass, 97–134.

SIPRI Yearbook 1991: World Armaments and Disarmament. Oxford: Oxford University Press, 1991.

"Situation in Helmand: Interview with Maulawi Nasim Akhundzada." Afghan Information Centre Monthly Bulletin 6 (September 1986):9–11.

Sivan, Emmanuel. Radical Islam: Medieval Theology and Modern Politics. New Haven: Yale University Press, 1985.

Skocpol, Theda. States and Social Revolutions: A Comparative Analysis of France, Russia and China. Cambridge: Cambridge University Press, 1979.

———. "Bringing the State Back In: Strategies of Analysis in Current Research." In Bringing the State Back In, edited by Evans, Rueschemeyer, and Skocpol, 3–43.

Sliwinski, Marek. "The Decimation of Afghanistan." Orbis 33 (Winter 1988–89):39–56.

Smith, Anthony D. State and Nation in the Third World. Brighton: Harvester, 1983.

———. The Ethnic Roots of Nations. Oxford: Basil Blackwell, 1986.

———. "State-Making and Nation-Building." In States in History, edited by Hall.

Social Sciences Today Editorial Board, eds. Afghanistan Past and Present. Moscow: USSR Academy of Sciences, 1981.

Stallings, Barbara. "International Lending and the Relative Autonomy of the State." Politics and Society 14 (1985):257–88.

Stepan, Alfred. The State and Society: Peru in Comparative Perspective. Princeton: Princeton University Press, 1978.

———. "State Power and the Strength of Civil Society in the Southern Cone of Latin America." In Bringing the State Back In, edited by Evans, Rueschemeyer, and Skocpol, 317–46.

———. Rethinking Military Politics: Brazil and the Southern Cone. Princeton: Princeton University Press, 1988.

Steul, Willi. Paschtunwali: Ein Ehrenkodex und seine rechtliche Relevanz. Wiesbaden: Steiner, 1981.

Strand, Richard F. "Ethnic Competition and Tribal Schism in East Nuristan." In Ethnic Processes and Intergroup Relations, edited by J. Anderson and Strand, 9–14.

———. "The Evolution of Anti-Communist Resistance in Eastern Nuristan." In Revolutions and Rebellions, edited by Shahrani and Canfield, 77–93.

Tabibi, Latif. "Die afghanische Landreform von 1979: Ihre Vorgeschichte und Konsequenzen." Ph.D. dissertation, Free University of Berlin, 1981.

Tai, H. C. Land Reforms and Politics. Berkeley: University of California Press, 1974.

Taniwal, Hakim. "The Impact of Pashtunwali on Afghan Jehad." Quarterly Journal of the Writers Union of Free Afghanistan 2 (January–March 1987):1–24.

Tapper, Nancy. "Pashtun Nomad Women in Afghanistan." Asian Affairs 8 (1977):163–70.

———. "Matrons and Mistresses: Women and Boundaries in Two Middle Eastern Tribal Societies." Archives européenes de sociologie 21 (1980):59–79.

———. "Direct Exchange and Brideprice: Alternative Forms in a Complex Marriage System." Man 16 (1981):387–407.

———. "Causes and Consequences of the Abolition of Brideprice in Afghanistan." In Revolutions and Rebellions, edited by Shahrani and Canfield, 291–305.

Tapper, Richard. "Nomadism in Modern Afghanistan: Asset or Anachronism?" In Afghanistan in the 1970s, edited by Dupree and Albert.

———. "Introduction." In Conflict of Tribe and State, edited by R. Tapper, 1–82.

――――. "Ethnicity and Class: Dimensions of Intergroup Conflict in North-Central Afghanistan." In *Revolutions and Rebellions*, edited by Shahrani and Canfield, 230–46.

――――. "Holier Than Thou: Islam in Three Tribal Societies." In *Islam in Tribal Societies*, edited by Ahmed and Hart, 244–65.

――――. Anthropologists, Historians, and Tribespeople on Tribe and State Formation in the Middle East." In *Tribes and State Formation*, edited by Khoury and Kostiner, 48–73.

――――, ed. *The Conflict of Tribe and State in Iran and Afghanistan*. New York: St. Martin's, 1984.

Tavakolian, Bahram. "Religiosity, Values and Economic Change among Sheikhanzai Nomads." In *Islam in Tribal Societies*, edited by Ahmed and Hart, 287–301.

Tawana, Sayyed Musa. "Glimpses into the Historical Background of the Islamic Movement in Afghanistan: Memoirs of Dr. Tawana." Part 1. *AfghaNews* 5 (April 1, 1989):6–7.

――――. "Glimpses into the Historical Background of the Islamic Movement in Afghanistan." Part 3. *AfghaNews* 5 (May 1, 1989):6.

――――. "Glimpses into the Historical Background of the Islamic Movement in Afghanistan." Part 4. *AfghaNews* 5 (May 15, 1989):5 ff.

――――. "Glimpses into the Historical Background of the Islamic Movement in Afghanistan: Memoirs of Dr. Tawana." Part 5. *AfghaNews* 5 (June 1, 1989):6.

――――. "Glimpses into the Historical Background of the Islamic Movement in Afghanistan." Part 8. *AfghaNews* 5 (July 15, 1989):6.

Tibi, Bassam. "The Simultaneity of the Unsimultaneous: Old Tribes and Imposed Nation-States in the Modern Middle East." In *Tribes and State Formation*, edited by Khoury and Kostiner, 127–52.

Tilly, Charles. "Reflections on the History of European State-Making." In *The Formation of National States in Europe*, edited by Charles Tilly, 3–83. Princeton: Princeton University Press, 1975.

――――. *From Mobilization to Revolution*. Reading, Mass.: Addison Wesley, 1978.

――――. *Coercion, Capital, and European States, A.D. 990–1990*. Oxford: Basil Blackwell, 1990.

Trimberger, Ellen Kay. *Revolution from Above: Military Bureaucrats and Development in Japan, Turkey, Egypt and Peru*. New Brunswick, N.J.: Transaction Books, 1978.

Trottier, Paul. "Soviet Influence on Afghan Youth." *Department of State Bulletin* 86 (March 1986):46–51.

Uberoi, J. P. Singh. "Men, Women and Property in Northern Afghanistan." In *India and Contemporary Islam: Proceedings of a Seminar*, edited by S. T. Lokhandwalla, 398–417. Simla: Indian Institute of Advanced Study, 1971.

Umnov, Alexander. "Afghanistan: What Price the Dogma?" *New Times*, no. 19 (May 9–15, 1989):21–23.

"Ustad Umer al-Talmesani." *Mujahideen Monthly* (May 1986):15 ff.

Van Nieuwenhuijze, C. A. O., ed. *Commoners, Climbers and Notables: A Sampler of Studies on Social Ranking in the Middle East*. Leiden: E. J. Brill, 1977.

Vercellin, Giorgio. *Afghanistan 1973–1978: Dalla repubblica presidenziale alla repubblica democratica*. Venice: Quaderni del Seminario di Iranistica, Uralo-Altaistica e Caucasologia dell' Universita degli Studi de Venezia, 1979.

Von Grunebaum, Gustave E. *Medieval Islam: A Study in Cultural Orientation*. Chicago: University of Chicago Press, 1953. [First edition 1946.]

Wajdi, Abdul Jalil. *Pah Afghanistan ke da unanawi jirgo nan aw parun* [*The Present and Future of Traditional Jirgas of Afghanistan*]. Peshawar: Aman Kitab, 1986.

Waterbury, John. "Twilight of the State Bourgeoisie?" *International Journal of Middle East Studies* 23 (1991):1–17.

Watt, W. Montgomery. *Islamic Political Thought: The Basic Concepts.* Edinburgh: Edinburgh University Press, 1968.

Weber, Max. *The Theory of Social and Economic Organization,* edited by Talcott Parsons. New York: Free Press, 1947.

———. *From Max Weber: Essays in Sociology,* edited by H. H. Gerth and C. Wright Mills. London: Routledge and Kegan Paul, 1948.

Weinbaum, Marvin G. "Legal Elites in Afghan Society." *International Journal of Middle East Studies* 12 (1980):39–57.

"What Do the Afghan Refugees Think? An Opinion Survey in the Camps." *Afghan Information Centre Monthly Bulletin* 7 (July 1987):2–8.

Yousaf, Mohammad, and Mark Adkin. *The Bear Trap: Afghanistan's Untold Story.* London: Mark Cooper, 1992.

Zolberg, Aristide R., Astri Suhrke, and Sergio Aguayo. *Escape from Violence: Conflict and the Refugee Crisis in the Developing World.* New York: Oxford University Press, 1989.

Official Publications, Government Reports, Documents, and Document Collections

Abolfathi, Farid. "A Reassessment of the Afghan Conflict, 1978–1988." Prepared under contract for the U.S. Government. Fairfax, Va., March 1989.

Afghanistan, Democratic Republic of. *Afghan Agriculture in Figures.* Kabul: Central Statistics Office, Ministry of Planning, 1978.

———. *Statistical Information of Afghanistan (1975–1978).* Kabul: Central Statistics Office, 1979.

———. *Statistical Year Book 1358 (March 1979–March 1980).* Kabul: Central Statistics Office, 1981.

———. *Statistical Year Book 1359 (March 1980–March 1981).* Kabul: Central Statistics Office, 1982.

———. *Statistical Year Book 1360 (March 1981–March 1982).* Kabul: Central Statistics Office, 1983.

———. *Statistical Year Book 1361 (March 1982–March 1983).* Kabul: Central Statistics Office, 1986.

Afghanistan, Republic of. "Afghanistan 1990." Country Presentation at the Second United Nations Conference on the Least Developed Countries. Geneva, April 1990. Mimeo.

Amnesty International. *Report 1980.* London: Amnesty International, 1981.

———. *Afghanistan: Torture of Political Prisoners.* London: Amnesty International, 1986.

———. *Report 1990.* London: Amnesty International, 1991.

———. *Afghanistan: Reports of Torture and Long-Term Detention Without Trial.* London: Amnesty International, 1991.

———. *Afghanistan: Unfair Trials by Special Tribunal.* London: Amnesty International, 1991.

Asia Watch. "Actions of the Pakistan Military with Respect to Afghanistan: Human Rights Concerns." *News from Asia Watch,* February 27, 1989.

———. *The Forgotten War: Human Rights Abuses and Violations of the Laws of War since the Soviet Withdrawal.* Washington, D.C.: Human Rights Watch, 1991.

"Communique of Meeting between Foreign Minister Boris Pankin and Secretary of State James Baker." Moscow, September 13, 1991.

Constitution of Republic of Afghanistan. Kabul: Alberuni Publishing House, 1990.

Danishjuyan-i Musulman-i Piru[-yi] Khat-i Imam [Muslim Students Following the Imam's Line], eds. *Asnad-i lanah-yi jasusi [Documents from the Espionage Nest],* vol. 29, *Afghanistan (1),* and vol. 30, *Afghanistan (2).* Tehran, 1980.

Data Collection for Afghan Repatriation Project. *UNHCR Background Report: Paktika Province.* Peshawar, 1989.

————. *UNHCR Background Report: Nangarhar Province.* Peshawar, 1989.

————. *UNHCR Background Report: Paktia Province.* Peshawar, 1989.

————. *UNHCR Background Report: Kunar Province.* Peshawar, 1989.

————. *UNHCR Background Report: Kandahar Province.* Peshawar, 1989.

————. *UNHCR Background Report: Logar Province.* Peshawar, 1989.

————. *UNHCR Background Report: Laghman Province.* Peshawar, 1989.

————. *UNHCR Background Report: Wardak Province.* Peshawar, 1990.

————. *UNHCR Background Report: Ghazni Province.* Peshawar, 1990.

Fishurdah-yi az maram-i Harakat-i Inqilab-i Islami-yi Afghanistan [A Summary of the Program of the Movement of the Islamic Revolution/Uprising of Afghanistan]. [Peshawar?: 1979?]

Fishurdah-yi hadaf va maram-i Jam'iyyat-i Islami-yi Afghanistan [*Summary of the Aims and Program of the Islamic Society of Afghanistan*]. [Peshawar?: 1978 or 1979?]

Iran Ministry of Interior. *First National Census of Agriculture: Mehr 1339* [Tehran: October 1960].

Johnson, Thomas H., Philip E. Jones, John Hill, Margo Grim, and Joseph Newman. "Afghanistan: The Northern Provinces." Produced under U.S. Government Contract no. 85-N104800-00. Silver Spring, Md.: Orkand Corp., 1988.

————. "Afghanistan: The Eastern Provinces." Produced under U.S. Government Contract no. 85-N104800-00. Silver Spring, Md.: Orkand Corp., 1988.

Johnson, Thomas H., Philip E. Jones, Margo Grim, John Hill, Joseph Newman, and John Mariz. "Afghanistan: The Southern Provinces." Produced under U.S. Government Contract no. 88-404300-000. Silver Spring, Md.: Orkand Corp., 1989.

Johnson, Thomas H., Philip E. Jones, John Mariz, Margo Grim, and John Hill. "Afghanistan: The Western Hinterland Provinces." Produced under U.S. Government Contract no. 88-404300-000. Silver Spring, Md.: Orkand Corp., 1989.

"Joint Statement on the Negotiations in Moscow between the Delegations of Afghan Mujahideen and the Soviet Side." Moscow: [November 1991].

Katz, David J. "Afghanistan Biographic Database Comprehensive List." Washington, D.C., 1989.

Khalis, Mawlawi Yunus. *Man kistam va bara-yi chih mubarizah mikunam?* [*Who Am I and What Am I Fighting For?*]. Peshawar: Publications of Hizb-i Islami-yi Afghanistan, [1981].

Kimmitt, Robert. Speech to the Asia Society. Washington, D.C., April 18, 1990.

Mahaz-i Milli-yi Islami-yi Afghanistan: Maramnamah [*National Islamic Front of Afghanistan: Program*]. [Peshawar?: 1979?]

Maram-i Hizb-i Islami-yi Afghanistan [*Program of the Islamic Party of Afghanistan*]. [Peshawar?: 1986–87]. [First Edition, 1979?]

National Reconciliation: Documents. Kabul, 1987.

National Security Archive, ed. *Afghanistan: The Making of U.S. Policy, 1973–1990.* Alexandria, Va.: Chadwyck-Healy, 1991.

"The Objectives of the Afghan National Liberation Front." [Peshawar?: 1979?]

Da Qandahar da aqwamo aw jihad[i] shura gadah a'lamiyyah [Declaration of the United Council of Tribes and Jihad Forces of Qandahar]. Qandahar, [April 20, 1992]. Fax.

al-Qandahari, Akhtar Muhammad. *Sarf al-ijtihad fi ahkam al-jihad* [Analysis of Jurisprudence on the Laws of Jihad]. Quetta: Joint Court of the Southwest in the State of Baluchistan for Afghan Refugees and Mujahidin, n.d.

"Report of the Central Committee of the People's Democratic Party of Afghanistan to the Second Congress of the Party." Kabul, [June 1990]. Mimeo.

Sima-yi jihad dar farhang-i 'amiyyanah [Manifestation of Jihad in Popular Culture]. Peshawar: Jamiat-i Islami, n.d.

"The Situation in Afghanistan and Its Implications for International Peace and Security: Report of the Secretary-General, U.N. General Assembly and Security Council." U.N. document A/46/577, S/23146. New York: United Nations, 1992.

Swedish Committee for Afghanistan Agricultural Committee. *The Agricultural Survey of Afghanistan: First Report.* Peshawar: Swedish Committee for Afghanistan, 1988.

———. *The Agricultural Survey of Afghanistan: Second Report.* Vol. 1, *Farm Power.* Peshawar: Swedish Committee for Afghanistan, 1989.

The Truth about Afghanistan: Documents, Facts, Eyewitness Reports. Moscow: Novosti Press Agency, 1980.

United Nations. "Afghanistan." *Economic Bulletin for Asia and the Far East* 22 (1971):24–53.

United Nations Commission on Human Rights. "Report on the Situation of Human Rights in Afghanistan, Prepared by the Special Rapporteur of the Commission on Human Rights [Felix Ermacora] in Accordance with Commission Resolution 1985/38." United Nations General Assembly document A/40/843: November 5, 1985.

———. "Situation of Human Rights in Afghanistan." United Nations General Assembly document A/44/669: October 30, 1989.

———. "Situation of Human Rights in Afghanistan: Interim Report by the Special Rapporteur." United Nations General Assembly, document A/46/606: November 5, 1991.

United Nations Department of Humanitarian Affairs. "Note on Winter Emergency Needs in Afghanistan." New York, November 1, 1992

United Nations Department of Public Information. "Statement by Secretary-General Javier Pérez de Cuellar." New York, May 21, 1991.

———. "Statement by the Secretary-General on Afghanistan." Geneva, April 10, 1992.

United Nations Educational, Scientific, and Cultural Organization. *Statistical Yearbook.* Paris: UNESCO, various years.

United Nations Office for the Co-Ordination of Humanitarian and Economic Assistance Programmes Relating to Afghanistan. "Immediate Humanitarian Needs in Afghanistan Resulting from the Current Hostilities." Press Release, August 23, 1992.

"US AID Humanitarian Assistance to Afghanistan." USAID, July 1990.

Williams, Maurice, John Kean, Charles Jenkins, Joann Feldman, and Patricia Fisher-Harris. "Retrospective Review of U.S. Assistance to Afghanistan 1950–1979". Bethesda, Md.: Devres, Inc., for USAID, contract no. PDC-0085-I-00–6095, October 31, 1988.

News Sources

Afghan Information Centre Monthly Bulletin (Peshawar).

AfghaNews (Peshawar; after April 1992, Kabul).

Afghanistan Forum.

British Broadcasting Company, *Summary of World Broadcasts.*

Christian Science Monitor.

Current Digest of the Soviet Press.

Daily Telegraph (London).

Far Eastern Economic Review (Hong Kong).

Financial Times (London).

Foreign Broadcast Information Service.

The Guardian (London).

The Independent (London).

India Today (New Delhi).
Insight (Washington, D.C.).
Los Angeles Times.
Le Monde (Paris).
The Nation (Lahore).
New York Times.
Philadelphia Inquirer.
The Times (London).
Wall Street Journal.
Washington Post.
Washington Times.

Index